Get Off the Interstate!

By
Valerie Evans Goddard

Best Wishes
Valerie Evans
Goddard

For more information please contact:
Valerie Evans Goddard
Verita Publishing
PO Box 498
St. Marys, Georgia 31558
www.veritapublishing.com
1st edition, First printing

Dedicated to

Rusty & Jason

With all the love in my heart,
Mom

TABLE OF CONTENTS

ACKNOWLEDGMENTS

The True Stories behind Florida's East Coast Historical Markers is finally complete. To thank each and every person who have had a hand in seeing this project to completion would be impossible. So many individuals and groups have provided me with leads, blessed me with their dear family stories, wills, land deeds, historic records and helped me track down elusive out of print books for my research; I am grateful to each and every one. I am thankful for being forgiven when my library materials were returned late as research consumed me and I lost all track of time and day.

I wish to thank the Florida Historical Society and each of the county historical societies that have been so generous with information, sources and contacts to help me along this journey to complete this edition of *Get Off the Interstate*. The city Chambers of Commerce, Welcome Centers, Tourism Departments, County Libraries, museums, State Parks, historic sites, lighthouse associations, the William Bartram Conference, historic churches, local garden clubs, historic colleges, the many businesses occupying historic buildings and homes including the wonderful Bed and Breakfast Inns along the Atlantic coast have been absolutely wonderful and I thank each from the bottom of my heart; I can't thank you all enough for the cooperation and welcome I have received during the writing of this book.

A special thanks to Linda McDonald, my wonderful publicist without whom I could never bring my work to the public; she has stood beside me through thick and thin. Thank you to Rachel Hunt who took the time to read the manuscript, edit and make suggestions so that the product we produce is as professional as we can make it. A special thanks goes to Johnny Barlow, who is the best graphics design person in the business, without his help this book would never have been so beautiful or well done. Thanks also to a wonderful friend, fellow writer and mentor Caryn Suarez who understands the effort it has taken me to get the book out. Foremost, Bill, my husband of twenty-five years and the love of my life, is simply the reason that this labor of love is possible. He gives unselfishly of his time, provides me with input when I need it and another point of view when I am stumped. I am so thankful that he enjoys this work with as much passion as I do, it makes the work fun for us; a research trip becomes a vacation and we are both happy in the pursuit of historical markers.

Our boys, Rusty and Jason have done their parts in helping out Mom. (They're cheap labor!) I know they get tired of listening to the stories over and over but bless their hearts they never say so. Jason often travels with me; sits with me at festivals, fetching drinks and food while I sign books and tell stories; and he is very talented in designing publicity materials for me. Maybe one day someone will pay him more than homemade chicken pot pie or chicken and dumplings, his favorite foods. Rusty works with the technical GPS coordinates, entering information and working with our mapping programs. His assistance has been invaluable. Rusty gets paid in lasagna.

Thanks are certainly due my extended family who support me whole-heartedly. To my Daddy, my wonderful sister and friend, Cindy and her family, my father in law who has been extremely supportive, my sisters-in-law and their families, aunts and uncles, cousins; Everyone has been so great with their encouragement and belief in me ~ I love you all. A special note to my sister, Thank you for being there for me always! To Mary Lynne and Jeff with love, incredible friends that share our love for tropical breezes and blue waters. Mary Lynne is my bestest buddy and I don't go through a day without hearing her voice. Thank you to wonderful neighbors Joe, Caroline and Susan Wirth who always take the time to check in with me and keep up with a hermit author on a deadline. And last but certainly not least Rodney, a great guy whose friendship is cherished.

INTRODUCTION

This project began in early 2003 with much enthusiasm, fear and wonder about the daunting task ahead for the second book in the "Get off the Interstate!" series. The Georgia book has sold well over two thousand copies at our one-year anniversary of release and the preliminary response to the Florida book has been very exciting. I knew from the beginning that the Florida book would more than double the materials and territory we had covered in the past considering Georgia has some ninety miles along six coastal counties whereas Florida has nearly six hundred miles of coast line and thirteen counties to cover. Still I've approached these tasks with fascination and interest in anticipation of all there is to learn about Florida and her history.

I fell in love with Florida as a child when my parents would bring the family down for vacation once or twice each year. We spent a good deal of time in a little suburb of Daytona called Holly Hill where my father's uncle and aunt lived. Their cute little mint green cracker box house with windows lining each room. They had an enormous fig tree in the back yard that became a secret hide-away for a six year old little girl and her toys. I remember catching sand fleas on the beach, picking figs and discovering that the cute little plant lining the driveway with pretty multicolored pods were in fact hot peppers that severely burned my mouth. My aunt taught me that eating white bread and drinking milk would soothe the fire. My uncle was the retired fire chief for Holly Hill and riding the shiny red truck with gleaming chrome was the highlight of my trip.

Years later after I had married, my husband's grandparents had retired to Jupiter and he had uncles in West Palm Beach. So visiting the in-laws who kindly took in a young couple on their first vacation on a tight budget that we had saved all year for was so wonderful, thanks again. Visiting with Grandma, Grandpa and Aunt Phyllis who introduced us to the American German Club in Jupiter and the families' heritage was incredible. All of these experiences allowed us to become acquainted with southeast Florida. The magnificence of Henry Flagler's mansion Whitehall and the celebrity homes were exciting. The Metro Zoo, Monkey Jungle, Parrot Jungle and Lion Country Safari were so much fun our young children; we had an absolutely glorious time. Our very first vacation without the children as a married couple was spent in the Florida Keys and we were smitten from the beginning. The exotic tropical feel of the Keys won us over from the moment we saw the clear blue water. Then we discovered scuba diving, the slow easy lifestyle of Key Largo, party atmosphere of Key West and the Sunset Festival. We thought that this was heaven on earth and we never wanted to go home. Unfortunately you soon wake from the dream and within moments our ten days in paradise was over. But we have returned many times over the years.

In 1992 I transferred with my government job to the marshes of St. Marys, Georgia. Only forty minutes to the north of Jacksonville, we loved living in the tiny fishing community with the culture, art, theater, museums, music, shopping and adventures that the large city had to offer just forty-five minutes down the road. Fernandina Beach was the closest beach and we spent countless weekends lounging there in the Florida sun, getting fresh shrimp as the boats would come in and soaking up the ambiance of Amelia Island. Then we feel in love with St. Augustine; the history that surrounded us was incredible, the lighthouse became a favored spot and the kids loved the Alligator Farm and Marineland. We would often wander through the countryside and discover the beauty of Florida inland away from the beach as well. The children were enamored with the Cape Canaveral and their dreams were fulfilled to see an actual launch in the early morning hours watching the rockets light up the darkened sky and trace its course across the horizon.

Still we had only seen a small part of Florida as we began research for "Get off the Interstate," we discovered so much more. We were aware of the proud Spanish influence; the valiant struggle of the Seminole to remain in their home; though the most surprising aspect of Florida's history was the freedoms enjoyed by African Americans in the safety of the Florida haven while the south fought to maintain a way of life that kept the downtrodden people in bonds. Florida was the first wilderness dominion explored before the expansion into the American west.

The Spanish fleets left an indelible mark still prevalent today as treasures continue to be discovered in the warm Atlantic waters. The proud Seminole persevere in spite of the decimation of the Europeans; through slavery, disease and theft of their land while slowly food sources shrank until they could no longer support the great people. Three Seminole Wars were fought before the tribe was finally vanquished to the western territory. Still many brave souls escaped into the depths of the Everglades where ghost warriors continued to haunt land so harsh that few white people dared to venture into its heart.

Once again we enjoyed discovering the wealth of history and celebrated not only the common themes of history from the state of Georgia but reveled in the diversity of Florida. South east Florida's history though sparse in the years of a fledgling United States, the state comes alive during the last century packing an abundance of wonderful stories within a span of just over one hundred years.

Lists of historical markers received from the state, though they are taking great strides to correct this, are certainly wanting. So after gathering as much information on historical accounts we set out to discover historical markers. Did we get them all? I'm sure the answer to that question is no, but hopefully we were able to collect the majority. The terrible tragedy of the hurricanes of 2004 have certainly taken its toll on the historical markers along their paths and others taken for repair have probably been replaced but that is very common in this business, we call it the case of disappearing and reappearing markers. Know that no marker is ever intentionally left out. We also had to determine what did and did not constitute a marker. There are many plaques placed by families whose members were responsible for improving the city in which they lived and that is certainly important and should be passed from generation to generation but does not qualify as a state historical marker.

Recently we have developed a new companion CD to go along with the book that can be plugged into most any map program and shows the location of each of the markers. The CD is available for purchase on our website at www.veritapublishing.com and at all of my personal appearances. You will notice a letter and number designation alongside the GPS Coordinate listing, that designation is used on the CD to represent the specific historical marker on the program.

Several instances have been quite eerie when writing this book, which has taken more than two years to put together. I was writing a certain article concerning a battle and discovered that the day was the anniversary of that event, in fact it was Christmas when I wrote an article of the murder of civil rights leaders Mr. and Mrs. Moore in Mims and found the explosion that cost the couple their lives actually happened on Christmas. The occurrence happened so many times that it was as if a spirit was guiding me through the process, maybe ~ I don't really know if I believe that but so many coincidences really made me wonder. I'll leave the final verdict up to you.

I have also done my best to be as accurate as possible when reporting the stories behind the markers. Unfortunately, as I have said over and over again, through the ages history like times change and evolves and I've investigated until I felt the story was most plausible but it may still vary from the exact truth. This was not intentional and if for any reason you find any errors I will be glad to correct them in a subsequent printing if you will simply notify me at valerie@veritapublishing.com .

It is my hope that you enjoy and gather the nuances of "Get off the Interstate" as much as I have in the writing of it. As in the Georgia book it was simply a dream come true and I will continue the series with the third edition "The True Stories Behind Eastern South Carolina's Historical Markers" that I began research just over a year ago. I plan to release it 2006. So now open the book, pick a county, "Get off the Interstate" and discover the real Florida.

Nassau County

FAIRBANKS HOME

Built in 1885 by George Rainsford Fairbanks, lawyer, historian, and editor. Born in 1820 at Watertown, New York, Fairbanks moved to Florida in 1842 and became a major in the Confederate Army.

He edited the Fernandina Florida Mirror, presided over the Board of Trade, pioneered in developing the citrus industry, and helped establish the University of the South at Sewanee, Tennessee. Thousands of school children used his "History of Florida" as a textbook. He was one of the founders of the Florida Historical Society in 1856.

227 South 7th Street, Fernandina Beach
N1 ~ GPS Coordinates: 30.667267, -81.460183

George Rainsford Fairbanks has often been described as "a dogged, determined, relentless humble follower of ideals, which is not quite the same as, though it may be rarer than, an idealist." Born in Watertown, New York, he moved with his brother to St. Augustine in 1842. The two northern born brothers quickly adapted to the southern slave-owning culture finding success as mill and plantation owners.

Classically educated, George became immersed in the political climate of the fledgling state of Florida. He was appointed senator serving terms from 1846 until 1848. His avid interest in Florida's history led to the creation of the Florida Historical Society. Though his aptitude for history was vast, it was but a small aspect of this great man. George was a pioneer in the citrus industry becoming President of the Fruit Growers of Florida. Times were good and George prospered until war loomed heavily on the southern horizon. During the Civil War, he chose to side with the Confederacy and accepted the position of Quartermaster for the Confederate States of America, stationed in Georgia. Letters from this period voiced his views of political and social concern. The Fairbanks Brothers shared concerns of their adopted home.

Shortly after the south's surrender at Appomattox Courthouse, George built a cottage on land that would eventually become the campus of the University of the South at Sewanee, Tennessee. The cottage, called Rebel's Rest, was used six months each year while George established the university and actively promoted the school during reconstruction.

The original University of the South campus was donated by the Sewanee Coal Company and selected chiefly for its location near the center of an area reaching from Virginia to New Mexico and from Missouri to Florida. Accessibility was a major concern as was the many springs on the property providing fresh water. The location was far enough inland to be free of prevalent coastal diseases such as malaria and yellow fever.

The founders realized that tuition and fees or endowments from the sponsoring Episcopal Church would completely support the institution. They began leasing tracts to parents of students, the Episcopalian diocese, priests, alumni and friends of the university. These leases provided the necessary operating expenditures. The university, built to model then modern Germanic institutions, offered studies in medicine, nursing, law and theology. The University of the South far exceeded all expectations of her founders and would easily compare to universities of today.

Although maintaining Rebel's Rest in Sewanee, he continued to call Florida home. He described Fernandina citizenry in his "History of Florida," as follows:

"All these families were old Confederate people - rather hidebound. If a newcomer came to Fernandina, there was great quizzing around to get his pedigree, and ascertain what designs he might have on the town. If he wished to buy property, the price on the plot desired was immediately raised sky-high, and the discouraged would-be purchaser went elsewhere. This spirit was a detriment to the city's progress, and is the reason the development dropped behind. We came to Jacksonville, a progressive and forward-moving community, and lots of others did the same. If among the early settlers, the former residents of Fernandina and their descendant sent back to Nassau County, there would not be anybody left in Jacksonville."

A renaissance man, George added to his accomplishments three noted publications. One of the three, "History of Florida" published in Jacksonville in 1842, was used for many years as a textbook for school children. Other volumes include:

"History and Antiquities of St. Augustine, Florida," published by Horace Drew at Jacksonville, Florida in 1881.

"The Spaniards in Florida, Comprising the Notable Settlement of the Huguenots in 1564, and the History and Antiquities of St. Augustine, Founded a.d. 1565." C. Drew at Jacksonville published the work in 1868.

"History of Florida from its Discovery by Ponce de Leon, in 1512, to the Close of the Florida War, in 1842." Published by J. B. Lippincott & Company at Philadelphia in 1871.

In 1879, David L. Yulee, Fernandina businessman, Florida entrepreneur and statesman, hired George as editor of Fernandina's well-known newspaper the "Florida Mirror." Known as the oldest newspaper in Florida, the operation was located in the Duryee Building, which is widely known today as the Marina Restaurant. The "Florida Mirror" was later renamed the "Fernandina Beach News-Leader" and continues to report local news today.

The Fairbanks home at 227 South 7th Street was designed and built in 1885 by New York architect Robert Schuyler. Like the man who commissioned its construction, the home was filled with the most modern innovations such as indoor running water, telephone and concrete sidewalks. The Italiante structure boasts four stories including twenty rooms with a fifteen-foot tower. The magnificent tower was embellished with arched windows on all sides, creating quite a stir among the local town folk. It was said that in 1901, George's granddaughter watched the great Jacksonville fire, which was approximately fifty miles away, from this very tower. Featuring twelve-foot ceilings, floors of heart pine and an extraordinary staircase of Honduras mahogany, the impressive dwelling remains a showplace of exceptional quality today. The library held impressive display bookcases constructed of orange wood taken from George's own groves in central Florida.

Ten fireplaces warmed the Fairbanks home; two of them constructed of English tiles illustrating scenes from Shakespearean plays and Aesop's fables. Six other fireplaces were intricately carved of soapstone while the remaining two were constructed of brick. Another first in the home was the lift or elevator. Used chiefly as a dumb waiter, the lift supplied wood to the various fireplaces throughout the house.

A cistern located in the basement collected pure rainwater for use in the kitchen via a novelty of the era, an indoor pump. The water used in the two bathtubs was supplied by Fernandina's sulfur artesian well. The kitchen was separate from the main house by means of a long hallway, common in houses of this era of cooking with open flames. Most of the food prepared in the Fairbanks kitchen was exported with the exception of fish and seafood. A steamer shipped ice from New England and was stored in a chest, which contained fresh pails of butter and eggs from Tennessee. Barrels of flour came from New York.

The first floor featured an entrance hall, parlor, dining room, library and guest room, while the second floor had four bedrooms and a playroom over the kitchen. The exterior coloring of the home was Victorian mustard yellow with windows accented in deep green; the window sashes and arches were painted a bright red. To this day the home still has the original color scheme, although somewhat toned down. Original architectural details, such as moldings, fireplaces, floors, wainscoting, staircase and the elegant columns in the foyer remain though only one or two original light fixtures remain today.

George Rainsford Fairbanks died at his Rebel's Rest retreat at the age of 87. Through the years he left an indelible mark on the state of Florida. Interestingly enough, though a land developer, his thinking was very advanced. One of his greatest concerns was the loss of so many trees due to careless cutting. Members of the Fairbanks family continued to live in the family home until the early 1920s, when the Bussel family leased the house and later a private school held classes there.

In 1930, W. T. Haile purchased the property. Relocating from Farmington, Missouri with his wife and four daughters. Haile passed away in 1941. Members of his family resided in the home until 1981.

Buff Gordon and Sally Dickinson acquired the home in 1982. The ladies renovated the aging mansion and transformed the abode into stylish apartments. It is said that they were not the first ladies to take on needed repairs of the home. The Haile family recalled, to their horror, finding elderly grandmother Haile perched with a bucket of tar atop the roof mending a leak.

In 1993, Nelson and Mary Smelker converted the mansion into a bed and breakfast inn. In 1997, Bill and Theresa Hamilton purchased the inn and continue to host guests today. Known in its day as Fairbanks' Folly due to the innovative ideas of its original owner, the mansion continues to present a beautiful picture today. The graceful Inn has an ambiance of old world charm and sense of affluence that was George Rainsford Fairbanks.

FAIRBANKS HOUSE

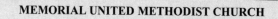

MEMORIAL UNITED METHODIST CHURCH

Methodism first came to Amelia Island in 1822 when the South Carolina Conference of the Methodist Episcopal Church appointed the Reverend Elijah Sinclair as the first minister to East Florida. Sinclair arrived within months of Florida being ceded to the United States by Spain in 1821 and was welcomed by Protestant Scotch and English settlers who opened their homes to him for services. The congregation continued to worship in homes and the Pioneer Hotel after the town was relocated in the 1850s from Old Town, about a mile north of the present site of Fernandina Beach. In the mid-1800s a wood frame church was built on the northwest corner of Broome and Sixth Streets. The old church was torn down after it was replaced by the building on Centre Street. Construction of the brick Classical Revival style building began in 1926 on property donated by E. W. Bailey and John W. Simmons. The sanctuary was complete by 1930 and the first services were held on the second Sunday in February. Fund raising to complete work on the church was difficult during the Great Depression of the 1930s, and the three-story classroom section at the rear of the building was still unfinished when Bishop Paul Kern dedicated the church in 1940. The work was finally completed in 1951. It is the oldest United Methodist congregation in the Florida conference.

Northeast corner of Centre and Sixth Streets, Fernandina Beach
N2 ~ GPS Coordinates: 30.671350, -81.465067

When Reverend Elijah Sinclair was appointed leader of the Amelia Island and St. Marys Methodist circuit, there was no established congregation in the area. He arrived in a township of approximately one hundred fifty residents. Reverend Sinclair traveled from home to home conducting services for the Scottish and English settlers. Services were later centralized in the Pioneer Hotel, which was located in the newer section of Fernandina.

By the mid 1800s the need for a sanctuary was realized and a large wooden structure was built. Called the Amelia Mission Church, the congregation consisted of twenty white and ten black members. The structure managed to remain through the Civil War and into the south's reconstruction only to be torn down during the 1920s when a new sanctuary was proposed.

Construction of the present edifice began in 1926 only to be struck down by a new obstacle, the Great Depression. The church was heavily in debt and the congregation began to dwindle. Handicapped by its meager membership the congregation raised funds to return the church to solvency. Within three years the church was flourishing in both membership and funding.

The Memorial United Methodist Church opened its doors later that same year. The impressive Neo-Classical Revival design is encased in redbrick with three stories rising above Centre and Sixth Streets. Eighteen wide steps lead to the entrance with two Grecian platforms serving as resting places along the way. A broad porch or portico aligns the front, a gabled roof held in place with Ionic columns top the triangular structure.

The church was designated as a historical site, established as the first Methodist Church in Florida. Memory Chapel was dedicated in 1938 and is in place to remind parishioners of their rich Methodist heritage.

THE LESESNE HOUSE

This Classical Revival style residence, built by Dr. John F. Lesesne circa 1860, is one of the oldest homes in Fernandina Beach. Lesesne left Fernandina during the Civil War and did not return. In 1868 the house became the property of the family of Judge John Friend, who had been appointed district tax commissioner after the war by President Andrew Johnson. Friend was a lawyer and served as a county commissioner and judge. At the time of his death in 1878 he was state senator - elect from Nassau County. The descendants of the Friend family still occupy the home. This double galleried home, constructed of hand - hewn lumber fastened with wooden pegs, is one of the major points of interest in the Fernandina Historic District which was listed in the National Register of Historic Places in 1973.

415 Centre Street, Fernandina Beach
N3 ~ GPS Coordinates: 30.671100, -81.461467

Dr. John F. Lesesne moved from Charleston to Fernandina during the summer of 1860 and it was in August that he purchased this property for the construction of his home. The lots were attained from the Florida Railroad Company for one thousand dollars. The transaction was recorded on the deed dated August 19, 1860. Construction began on the home shortly after the deed changed hands.

The original house was a typical ante-bellum design common of homes built during the 1860s in Florida and Georgia. The dwelling was a two-storied frame structure having a central hallway and four rooms. A porch embraced the southern and western sides of the home on both the first and second floor, though it is believed the second story porch was added at a later date. Constructed of heart pine, the wood is said to be so hard that nails can not be driven into it. The home was constructed using wooden pegs.

Unfortunately, Dr. Lesesne did not have the opportunity to enjoy his new home for long. Florida seceded from the Union on January 10, 1861 Civil War was imminent. When Confederate forces fired on Fort Sumter on April 12, 1861, the war officially began and it was then that Dr. John F. Lesesne left his Fernandina home to join the Confederacy. Dr. Lesesne treated the wounded, diseased and dying of the war but tragically paid the ultimate price for his service. He would never return to his Fernandina home.

The Lesesne home was left to Josephine, Dr. Lesesne's thirteen-year-old daughter. Because of her youth the estate was left in trust under the guardianship of Anthony T. Porter. The home and property was sold on May 2, 1868 for thirty-six hundred dollars to Mrs. John Friend.

John Friend arrived in the United States from Germany in 1846 and began the practice of law in Cleveland, Ohio in 1855. When President Andrew Jackson appointed him Tax Commissioner for the state of Florida, Friend moved south to attend his duties. In 1865, Friend moved to Fernandina and in 1868 the deed to the Lesesne house was transferred to his wife. Eventually Friend served as a county judge and was elected a state senator. Unfortunately John Friend passed away on November 29, 1878, never assuming his elected senatorial seat.

THE LESESNE HOUSE

The Lesesne House remains in the Friend Family today after five generations of ownership. Though the dwelling has experienced some modest changes and modernization over the years the home continues to be much the same as the day Dr. John F. Lesesne first crossed the threshold

Atlantic Avenue & Front Street at Welcome Center, Fernandina Beach
N4 ~ GPS Coordinates: 30.671333, -81.464567

Until the 1850s development in Florida were clustered coastal communities accessible only by boat. Due to the Internal Improvement Act the Florida Railroad Company was founded in 1853. The railroad company's intent was to establish a route from Fernandina across the state to Cedar Key on the Gulf coast.

Railroad construction began in 1855, one hundred and fifty-five miles of track was required to extend the line to Cedar Key. In 1861, the Florida Railroad Company purchased an old timber locomotive named for its first engineer, the "Abner McGee." As the railroad progressed, small towns developed every twenty to thirty miles along its route, civilization followed transportation. The lumber industry followed the railroad and there was plenty of work for everyone. Near the tracks would be placed a lock box where railroad employees collected their compensation each month.

Connecting the Atlantic coast with the Gulf had long been the dream of David L. Yulee, Florida Railroad pioneer and president. Eight years before, he organized the Florida Railroad Company with stock totaling one million dollars and began to build the railroad. During the years following the track, imported from England, pushed to Gainesville then on to Archer. It was slow going, the forest was all but impenetrable. Trestles had to be built to bridge marsh areas.

People living in the undeveloped areas objected to the railroad construction, farmers' wives claimed that traveling over the tracks broke their eggs while driving their produce to market. Backwoodsmen objected to the turpentine operators who followed the railroad into the forest, saying that they ruined the land for hog ranges.

In 1857, the company purchased its first new locomotive; an eight-wheeler named the "Governor Broome". Just as the line reached completion, about 1860, the company purchased two new engines, the "Alachua" and "Marion", both eight-wheelers. Two passenger and fourteen freight cars made up the rest of the line. However, despite objections the track from Fernandina to Cedar Key was finished in March 1861, narrowly meeting the timetable set by the railroad months before.

Financially, the company suffered. By 1872, the railroad was unable to pay the one-percent interest on its bonds. That year the company entered into receivership and was reorganized under the exotic name of Atlantic Gulf and West Indies Transit Company. However, conditions in Cedar Key improved and by 1880 it was a bustling place. The population grew larger than Tampa and three sawmills began turning out wood for pencils.

Travel reached a new high in 1881 and the railroad company began running two trains per day. The tracks ran out to a large loading dock where goods could be moved directly from ocean-going ships, which docked at Cedar Key. On Thursdays, the railroad ran special excursion trains from Jacksonville. The beaches were soon crowded with people.

General Grant toured the line in his special car, upon arriving at Cedar Key, he presented the engineer, J. A. Ferlara, giving him a box of his special big black cigars. Sadly, Ferlara left the box in the engine cab where an Indian found them and began passing them out to the crowd. The cigars must have been terribly strong or the people unaccustomed to smoking them, for as General Grant gazed down at the crowd he noticed that a good number in the crowd were holding their stomachs and heaving their dinner.

The railroad was thriving, in December 1881 the editor of the "Gainesville Bee" wrote:

"The company while possessing more rolling stock than any other road in the state is still slightly deficient in this respect. We are informed by an official of the Transit as the line was then popularly known, that a night train with sleeping cars attached will be added to the service. Passengers will then be able to make the trip to Cedar Key from Fernandina without changing cars. The Transit is on a big 'boom' and we predict the day is not far distant when it will eclipse all other roads in the state."

In 1902, the railroad was over taken by the Seaboard Airline Railroad. Timber destined for the sawmills of Cedar Key began to give out and boats began docking in other ports. Later a road was built to Cedar Key and that finished the railroad. In 1931, Seaboard filed for permission to end rail service from Archer to Cedar Key and in 1932, the Interstate Commerce Commission granted the request. The last trip out was made by a work train, which took up the rails as it went along. The railroad had come and gone from Cedar Key, leaving nothing but memories.

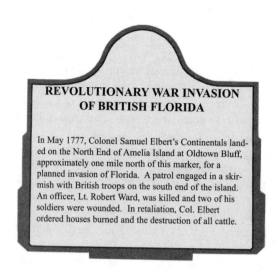

REVOLUTIONARY WAR INVASION OF BRITISH FLORIDA

In May 1777, Colonel Samuel Elbert's Continentals land-ed on the North End of Amelia Island at Oldtown Bluff, approximately one mile north of this marker, for a planned invasion of Florida. A patrol engaged in a skir-mish with British troops on the south end of the island. An officer, Lt. Robert Ward, was killed and two of his soldiers were wounded. In retaliation, Col. Elbert ordered houses burned and the destruction of all cattle.

Centre Street at the Welcome Center, Fernandina Beach
N4 ~ GPS Coordinates: 30.671333, -81.464567

Florida was, during the Revolutionary period, a haven for British loyalists. Patrick Tonyn, governor of East Florida, issued invitations in the Savannah and Charleston newspapers for Loyalists to gather in Florida. Stephen Egan's flourishing indigo plantation attracted many other planters to Amelia Island, which was widely known for its accommodating port. Though the population of loyalists grew in numbers they had no strength because the plantations were widely dispersed on the island. Revolutionary patriots across the St. Marys River in Georgia were constantly raiding Amelia Island settlers.

Governor Tonyn begged for the help of British forces and in the end was forced to form a protective force of his own called the "Rangers." Daniel McGirt, well known for his dastardly acts in favor of the British during the Revolutionary War, was said to have begun stealing cattle and slaves while serving as a Ranger under the direc-tion of Governor Tonyn. The Rangers eventually numbered approximately three hundred men with license to com-mit whatever acts they deemed necessary to police the area.

Stephen Egan with his wife and children escaped the escalating ravages of the patriot raiders by moving inland accompanied by served other planter families in 1776. The abandonment left Amelia Island with only a widely placed miniscule population. On May 18, 1777 Colonel Samuel Elbert led his Continental forces on an assault of British held Amelia Island. The detachment silently rowed their skiff ashore on the north end of the island at Oldtown Bluff. Lieutenant Robert Ward was ordered to lead a patrol to the south end of Amelia Island. The contingent was ambushed by British troops just short of their destination. Lieutenant Ward was killed and two of his troops were wounded. News of the attack was immediately reported back to Colonel Elbert along with a scouting report that local resident William Pryce had been dispatched to solicit additional British troops.

Colonel Elbert was incensed. He immediately ordered Lieutenant Winface to select twenty of his men to set the torch to every home on the island and destroy all livestock. Colonel Elbert stationed his troops at the Egmont Plantation while Lieutenant Winface's detachment carried out their gruesome mandates. The devastation lasted for four days after which Colonel Elbert and his Continental forces boarded their ships at anchor in the Amelia harbor and set sail. Amelia Island was left a smoldering ruin, a cloud of thick black smoke hung in air, bringing another era of life on the island to an end.

Stephen Egan eventually returned to rebuild. He had lost everything except a herd of one hundred horses, which were running wild in the meadows of Amelia Island. With the assistance of twenty-two slaves, Egan began to rebuild and gradually established a successful naval stores business on the St. John's River. Unfortunately the enterprise was short lived. Egan was forced to close down his business in 1784 when the Spanish returned to the Island. Another era was coming to a close with Spain's second procession and Amelia Island would begin again.

Fernandina Harbor Marina at the foot of Centre Street, Fernandina Beach
N5 ~ GPS Coordinates: 30.671350, -81.465067

William Bartram, son of the noted Botanist for King George III, John Bartram, was born on February 9, 1738 at his family home located along the Schuylkill River near the city of Philadelphia. Young William had the benefit of a formal education due the offspring of John Bartram's social stature. By all accounts, William's youth was a happy one though his father was seldom present in the family home. As a young man William was sent to Ashwood, North Carolina to live with his Uncle William. In 1765, John enlisted William to assist in a botanical collecting expedition financed by King George III.

The expedition was undertaken to augment knowledge of the Florida territory, which had been recently acquired by England through the Treaty of Paris as a result of the French and Indian War of 1763. The purpose of the expedition was to collect plants and maintain a journal detailing the flora and fauna of the area, sending the information back to England. The expedition lasted for three years when John was forced to return to Philadelphia due to ill health, William followed a year later.

In 1773, Dr. John Fothergill agreed to finance an exploration of the southeastern United States for William alone. Fothergill was a noted British physician, Quaker philanthropist and respected botanist in his own right. It was Dr. Fothergill who was first to note the symptoms of diphtheria in England and held the distinction of the first accurate descriptions of migraine headaches.

Dr. Fothergill would patron William Bartram in exchange for specimens, drawings and written recordings of his observations of the southeastern United States natural resources. The exploration began in March of 1773. Sailing from Philadelphia to Charleston, William was to meet with Dr. Lionel Chalmers upon his arrival. Dr. Chalmers acted as Dr. Fothergill's agent, supervising the travels and issuing fifty pounds per year to William for payment of his efforts.

It wasn't until 1774 that William Bartram progressed into the Florida territory. As he traveled the St. John's River, William's ship landed at Cumberland Island[1], there he met a trading schooner. Passengers on the schooner spoke of Indian raids on nearby settlements and the captain of Bartram's ship decided to return to Fort Frederica to await orders. William Bartram was determined to continue his travels and instructed the captain to let him ashore at Cumberland.

Cumberland Island, off the Georgia coast, was largely uninhabited. A military outpost called Fort William made up most of the population and was located at the southern tip of the island. Bartram described Cumberland as having "harsh treatment from thorny thickets and prickly vines." It was the captain of Fort William who was to see to the transport of Bartram to Amelia Island.

Bartram was put ashore on the north end of Amelia Island and traveled from there across Clark's Creek which was then known as Egan's Creek named for the plantation manager Stephen Egan of Lord Perceval Egmont's indigo plantation. The plantation comprised of eight to nine thousand acres was also the location of Egmont Town, which was to the northeast of present Fernandina Beach. Bartram was highly impressed with the indigo growing there and of Stephen Egan, noting "the gentleman is a very intelligent and able planter, having already greatly improved the estate, particularly in the cultivation of indigo."

While exploring Amelia Island, William Bartram noted several large Indian burial mounds. The mounds were located at the site of Public School Number 1, today known as 12th Street on the north side of Atlantic Avenue. Large portions of the sand mounds had been removed during the building of the school so it is impossible to estimate the original size, what remained was about ten feet in height. Daniel Brinton's published work in 1859, detailed that the mounds as approximately twenty to thirty-five feet tall and additionally reported human bones and crude utensils were dug from the site.

Bartram departed Egmont Plantation by sailing across Nassau Sound traveling to Cow Ford which is today known as Jacksonville. By January 1777, he would return to Philadelphia. Having accomplished much during his exploration, William Bartram was left bewildered as to what had become of his research and precious samplings, all traces of his work it seemed had disappeared in London.

By 1788, still unable to locate his work, Bartram penned a correspondence to Robert Barclay. The missive read[2]:

> "I collected these specimens amongst many hundreds others about 20 years ago when on Botanical researches in Carolina, Georgia and Florida [,] duplicates of which I sent to Doctor Fothergill; very few of which I find have entered the *Systema Vegetabilium*, not even in the last Edition.
>
> The number of specimens that I sent were submitted to the examination of Doctor Solander which by returns I received from the Doctor (the nos. corresponding with those of my duplicates) appear'd most of them to be either New Genera or Species; soon after Doctor Solander deceas'd & Doctor Fothergill soon after followed him. I have never learn'd what became of the speci mens.
>
> These remains with some more than I have kept by me to this time, which I cheerfully offer for the inspection and amusement of the curious, expecting or desiring no other gratuity than the bare mention of my being the discoverer, a reward due for traveling several thousand miles most ly amongst't Indian Nations which is not only difficult but dangerous, besides suffering sickness, cold & hunger. But with a perfect Sense of gratitude I with pleasure acknowledge that Noble Fothergill liberally supporting me whilst in his employ with ample pecuniary assistance."
>
> —Wm. Bartram, Nov. 1788.

Today the British Museum of Natural History houses two hundred and forty seven Bartram plant samplings including thirty eight which were sent to Robert Barclay with the quoted communication. Sir Joseph Banks had purchased Bartram research and samplings from Fothergill's estate and it was he who subsequently donated the property to the British Museum.

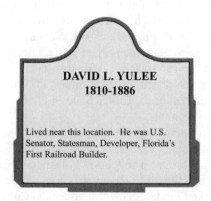

DAVID L. YULEE
1810-1886

Lived near this location. He was U.S. Senator, Statesman, Developer, Florida's First Railroad Builder.

Corner of Alachua & N 3rd Streets, Fernandina Beach
N6 ~ GPS Coordinates: 30.672517, -81.462517

David Levy was born to Jewish parents at St. Thomas, West Indies in 1810. When he was but ten years old, his parents immigrated to Norfolk, Virginia and it was there that young David received the basics of a classical education common to the upper class of that time. By the age of seventeen, David and his father suffered a difference of temperament forcing the younger Levy to depart from the family home. He took his leave of Virginia after his father's decision to withdraw financial support. David was taken in by one of the overseers of the family plantation in Florida and trained to manage its operation. Upon reaching the age of twenty-three young Levy moved to St. Augustine where he would read law under the tutelage of Judge Robert R. Reid and learn the planter's trade. Levy gained admittance to the Florida Bar in 1836.

David Levy was a 5'7", explosive man of constant motion. His ability to remain adept on most any given subject was limitless. Levy's enthusiasm easily drew people to follow his lead and because of his family's social position, he was exposed to most of early Florida's more prominent citizens. He was elected Congressional Delegate from the Florida territory. His main lobby during this period time was statehood for Florida, which was gained after six years of heated debate on March 3, 1845.

David Levy became a Delegate to the State Constitutional Convention and was then elected United States Senator from Florida as a Democrat, serving one term. He was the first "known" person of the Jewish faith to ever serve in the senatorial body. In the early days of December in 1845, Levy shocked Washington by emerging with a new name, David Levy Yulee. The reason is unknown. Though it was speculated that the name change was used to downplay his ancestral heritage for political reasons. In John Quincy Adams' diary, reviewed and quoted by historian Leon Hubner, the entry dated June 21, 1841 read: "Levy is said to be a Jew, and what will be, if true, a far more formidable disqualification, that he has a dash of African blood in him."

Adams' notation was a likely reference to Yulee's grandmother Rachael and her dubious past. Rachael was sailing to the British West Indies accompanied by her Jewish physician father when pirates overtook their vessel and Rachael was kidnapped. She was taken as a slave and auctioned into the vizier's[3] harem. Rachael eventually became pregnant and gave birth to Yulee's father Moses. Yulee's grandfather was Muhammadan Jacoub ben Youli, Grand Vizier to the Sultan of Morocco. When the Sultan and his vizier were overthrown, Rachel managed to escape with Moses and his unborn sister to Gibraltar. It was there that she left her past. After her escape, she renamed her children for her Jewish family, Levy.

Shortly after changing his name, David Yulee wed the beautiful and well-connected Nannie Wickliffe whose father was a former Kentucky governor and Postmaster General. The union was said to be near perfect, both politically and personally. The Yulee's were devoted to one another throughout their lives.

Yulee was Chairman of the Senate Naval Affairs Committee from 1847 until 1851. He returned to the Senate in 1855 for six years until his Confederate leanings forced his retirement. Throughout the Civil War Yulee remained a member of the Confederate Congress. At the conclusion of the war Yulee was reportedly imprisoned at

Fort Pulaski for aiding in the escape of former Confederate President Jefferson Davis. However, other sources reveal that Yulee spent a year in a prison as a result of a treasonous letter written while serving in the Senate.

Yulee, who had fought doggedly for Florida's statehood, announced her secession from the union saying, "The people of Florida will ever preserve a grateful memory of past connection with this Government and just pride in the continued development of American society." With this statement Yulee resigned his seat in the Senate and returned to Fernandina. He was later pardoned for his crimes against the United States. It was Nannie who led the campaign, going as far as the President of the United States, to fight and gain her husband's release from prison. Her devotion to her husband had no limits.

It was David L. Yulee's accomplishments in Washington that led to his most noted achievement fostering the Federal Swamp Land Act. The Act granted twenty-nine million acres to the Florida Internal Improvement Commission to promote transportation in Florida. The Florida, Atlantic and Gulf Central Railroad connected Jacksonville with Lake City. The Florida Railroad Company was born with Yulee as its President. Three million dollars were guaranteed in bonds from the Florida Internal Improvement Commission, however, Yulee only required three hundred forty-five thousand dollars to complete his railroad. The railroad was completed only to be destroyed during the Civil War.

David L. Yulee died in New York, New York on October 10, 1886, leaving Florida a grand legacy for all of his works on her behalf. Today the small Nassau County town to the west of Amelia Island was named in his honor.

PHELAN~VEROT HOUSE
BUILT PRIOR TO 1866

On February 5, 1875, Jean-Pierre Augustin Verot, Bishop of Saint Augustine, purchased this cottage from Sara Phelan. The Sisters of Saint Joseph lived here in the year 1877, when a devastating epidemic of yellow fever swept over the Amelia Island community. From this place, for three weeks as the epidemic raged, the small coterie of sisters risked their lives, night and day, as they nursed the stricken of every race, Catholic, non-Catholic, rich and poor. They offered comfort and prayers for the sick and dying, and even helped bury the dead. Grateful citizens thereafter called them "Angels of Mercy." Mother Celenie and Sister de Sales, young French nuns far from their motherhouse in LePuy, France, died of the fever. They rest in Bosque Bello Cemetery, their graves marked with simple stone crosses bearing the date 1877.

North 4th Street, between Alachua and Broome Streets, Fernandina Beach
N7 ~ GPS Coordinates: 30.672917, -81.461783

The pretty Victorian cottage that stands at 116 North 4th Street holds within its walls a remarkable history. Once the home of William and Sarah Phelan, the home was sold on February 5, 1875 upon the death of William. Florida's Bishop Jean-Pierre Augustin Verot purchased the dwelling to be used as a temporary convent for the Sisters of Saint Joseph.

The Sisters of St. Joseph have a long and distinguished chronicle. Founded in LePuy, France in 1650 by Henry de Maupas, the order has long served the Holy Family with great devotion. St. Joseph's LePuy congregation suffered a tragic disruption during the French Revolution, when five Sisters of the order met a heartbreaking demise as they were solemnly led, hands bound, to the French guillotine. The convent was reorganized in 1807, guided by Mother St. John Fontbonne. In 1836, at the request of the Bishop of St. Louis Rosati, the first Sisters of St. Joseph prepared to travel to America.

As the Civil War drew to a close, Verot realized the need for increased spiritual guidance in the vast diocese for which he was responsible. Slaves newly released from their bonds required attention to their spiritual as well as physical needs. Keenly aware of the complications of the South's reconstruction, Bishop Verot knew extra hands were essential if the needs of the people were to be met. The Bishop addressed the only source he knew the Motherhouse of the Sisters of St. Joseph at LePuy, seeking aid.

Eight Sisters were selected to serve the American frontier at Florida. The land was considered wilderness as opposed to France in the 1870s. After a treacherous ocean voyage lasting five weeks, the Sisters arrived in Florida. Bishop Verot selected several of the sisters to serve at Fernandina and purchased the Phelan House as temporary housing.

The home was soon to be known as the "Nuns House." The Sisters offered selfless, loving aid to the community. In 1877, their devotion was put to the test with the onslaught of a deadly yellow fever epidemic. The first victims appeared to the Sisters with complaints of high fever, muscle aches, convulsions and nausea. The Sisters were not readily aware of the dangers of the disease, which often doesn't reveal itself for up to a week after exposure. However as others began to exhibit more advanced symptoms of yellowed jaundiced skin, severe abdominal pains and profuse bleeding, the Sisters quickly realized the impact of the deadly epidemic.

The Sisters lovingly cared for all patients regardless of race, financial or community status. The less severe cases often recovered within four days while those more acutely affected often agonizingly lingered for ten to fourteen days before death brought them peace. Four of the Nuns contracted yellow fever while battling the epidemic, two failed to recover. The fallen Sisters of St. Joseph were laid to rest at Bosque Bello Cemetery in old town Fernandina. The simple crosses of stone mark their graves bearing only the date, 1877.

The "Nuns House" will forever be known as the Phelan-Verot House where the Angels of Mercy physically and spiritually ministered to a community ravaged by yellow fever. A historical marker stands as a reminder of the heroism and devotion of the Sisters of St. Joseph.

THE PHELAN-VEROT HOUSE

FERNANDEZ GRANT

During the Spanish and English periods of Florida history, many
large tracts of land were granted primarily to induce settlement.
All that remains of the Don Domingo Fernandez Spanish Grant is
the family cemetery and this park. Royal title to this property was
granted August 9, 1807. This land was once a part of the Earl of
Egmont property on Amelia Island, which included the present
site of the City of Fernandina Beach.
On January 1, 1825, the Legislative Council of the Territory of
Florida passed "an act to incorporate the city of Fernandina."
Little development resulted until 1852 when the Florida Railroad
Company announced that Fernandina would form the eastern terminus for the first cross state railroad in Florida. This stimulated
the growth of Florida by making a portion of the interior more
accessible for further development and population growth.

North 4th Street between Broome & Calhoun Streets, Fernandina Beach
N8 ~ GPS Coordinates: 30.674200, -81.461583

Amelia Island was an English settlement in 1763, having passed first to the French then becoming
Spanish dominion. General James Edward Oglethorpe, Georgia's founder named the island, for King George II's
daughter Amelia. The young Amelia was reported as being a most lovely damsel. Amelia Island was then granted
to the Second Earl of Egmont, John Perceval. The grant was originated by Florida's then governor, James Grant,
and remained part of the Perceval family estate for twenty years under the name "Egmont."

It is said that Egmont never visited his Florida holdings. Though at one time he owned as much as seven-
ty-five thousand acres on Amelia Island and property along the St. John's River. The settlement was known as
"Mount Royal". The Earl of Egmont remained in England as a high-ranking politician. He loaned ten Mount
Royal slaves to establish Egmont Town, which in 1770 was Amelia Island. However, by the end of that year the
Second Earl of Egmont was dead.

Heirs of Egmont decided to establish an indigo plantation to produce and import dye from the Egmont
Town location. The deep harbor made an excellent berth for ships laden with goods bound for Europe. The indigo
plantation flourished in the humid, semi-tropical climate and the Earl of Egmont's widow hired Stephen Egan to
oversee her operations there. Records of 1774 indicate that over two thousand pounds of indigo were stored at
Egmont Town.

Unfortunately, while indigo exportation thrived, the colonies prepared for war. Continentals from Georgia
just across the St. Marys River made regular raids on Egmont Town and the British holdings there. Egan begged
for assistance from British Governor Patrick Tonyn for protection. Continental troops landed on the British held
island in May of 1777. The ensuing skirmish resulted in the death of one man and wounding two others by the
British militia. The Continentals, in retaliation, burned every house and business on the Island. The indigo stored
in Egmont Town warehouses choked out large black clouds from the flames soon reducing the entire stored crop to
ash; Egmont Town and the Egmont Plantation were completely destroyed and never to be resurrected.

Stephen Egan survived the American Revolution to build a profitable naval stores business along the St.

John's River. Unfortunately he, along with thousands of British settlers, would soon find themselves displaced when Florida was returned to Spain in 1783. Once under Spanish control, the ten thousand acres that was Egmont Town now became Amelia Island again. The acreage was then granted to Spaniard, Domingo Fernandez, thus the "Fernandez Grant". Fernandez was a ship's captain and planter. The new settlement was named "Fernandina".

The town overflowed with people of all nations; Russians, Swedes, French and Germans. The harbor teemed with ships flying all colors of the rainbow. The streets, warehouses and businesses flourished with domestic and foreign goods. A criminal undercurrent of corruption, smuggling and piracy was boldly practiced.

It was said that Fernandez's Commandant, Captain Pangua, was allowed to host *fiestas* on fine Sunday afternoons. The parties were well attended by all the principal families on the island. These *fiestas* always included an afternoon banquet and a starlight ball. However the real excitement was during the afternoon crowd-pleasing bullfight.

After a picnic style banquet the invited patrons would be led to the arena where seats were tiered surrounding a great open field. The matador, an elegantly dressed Spaniard, ceremoniously marched in waving bright red flags attached to stilettos. While the matador paraded, dogs were released into the arena, which the young Spaniard proceeded to taunt into a barking frenzy. During the playful exchange, a hush stilled the crowd as murmurs of "the bull is coming," rippled through the excited congregation.

A half-grown white bull tore into the field and was immediately set upon by the dogs. Further incited by the flag waving matador, the bull would charge to cries ringing in the air, "*Bravo el torete*!" and "*Bravo el Matador*!" when the valiant matador gained the advantage, piercing the bull's tough leather hide with the needle sharp stilettos. At last the weakened animal was led from the site, tamed by the matador's spear.

The crowd was escorted once again to the ball where luscious fruits of watermelon, peaches and figs were served. Dancing commenced with a band playing lilting tunes until the wee hours of morning. Then the tired and sated guests were serenaded to their awaiting buggies or boats to deliver them home.

Amelia Island would exist under numerous flags during her vast history, until finally the United States flag proudly waved in 1821. In the 1850s, the Fernandez property was sold by his heirs to David L. Yulee, Florida Senator and President of the Florida Railroad Company. The only condition of the sale was that the Fernandez family would retain rights in perpetuity of the private family burial site. The condition was granted and the property changed hands.

The burial site contains gravestones bearing the names Fernandez, Villalonga and Stewart. The cemetery remains today. Stunning imported white marble memorials are located in the park between St. Michael's Church and St. Michael's Academy on North 4th Street, Fernandina Beach. It is said that when the full moon lights the sky, the white marble stones seem to glow against the backdrop of the dark night.

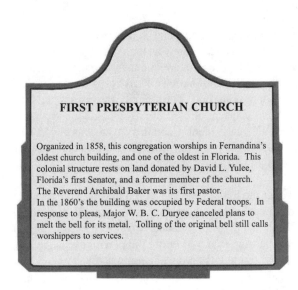

FIRST PRESBYTERIAN CHURCH

Organized in 1858, this congregation worships in Fernandina's oldest church building, and one of the oldest in Florida. This colonial structure rests on land donated by David L. Yulee, Florida's first Senator, and a former member of the church. The Reverend Archibald Baker was its first pastor.
In the 1860's the building was occupied by Federal troops. In response to pleas, Major W. B. C. Duryee canceled plans to melt the bell for its metal. Tolling of the original bell still calls worshippers to services.

911 6th Street, Fernandina Beach
N9 ~ GPS Coordinates: 30.671850, -81.460350

The First Presbyterian Church was built at 14 North 6th Street in 1860 as the pet project of the wife of David L. Yulee, one of Fernandina's most noted citizens. Built in the New England meeting house style, the church is noted as one of Florida's oldest continually used sanctuaries. Thus the church was still in its infancy at the dawning of the Civil War and by 1862, the war found its way to the First Presbyterian Church.

When parishioners arrived for worship one glorious spring Sunday in March of 1862, the Reverend Archibald Baker failed to greet them at the welcoming doorway. The lighthearted parishioners were soon dashed when instead of their faithful minister meeting them at the door, a crudely scrawled sign proclaimed: "HEADQUARTERS, Battery A Sixth Artillery." The Union Army had appropriated their beloved sanctuary, now serving as an infirmary for the diseased and wounded Union soldiers. Most of the congregation, including Reverend Baker and his family, were forced from their homes escaping to central Florida where the effects of war were not so pronounced.

Remarkably, the First Presbyterian Church suffered little ill use during the Union occupation. The only threat coming when Union officers decided that the church bell would be melted for use as ammunition. The remaining stalwart parishioners beseeched a young Union officer, Major William B. C. Duryee to save the church's lyrical call to worship. Major Duryee used what leverage he had and the bell was spared the melting pot. The small Presbyterian congregation heralded him, a hero.

During the south's reconstruction, the First Presbyterian Church resumed worship services, never to be interrupted again. Major Duryee returned to Fernandina in 1880 purchasing property on what is today Centre Street. He began by constructing a unique two-story masonry structure, unique in that it was built atop pilings buried deep in the ground for support in the sandy soil. The building was completed in 1882 and housed Major Duryee's grain business.

The Duryee building was eventually utilized as the first Customs House in the United States with Major Duryee serving as the Collector of Customs. The United States Treasury leased the structure for one hundred eighty dollars per year, housing the Customs offices until the early 1900s. Soon it would be home to the oldest newspaper in Florida, the "Florida Mirror," which continues to this day as the "Fernandina Beach News-Ledger." The First Bank of Fernandina was located in the building at one time. The bank was later sold and the site became the First National Bank of Florida. Today the old Duryee building is home to the popular Marina Restaurant.

In 1866, Major Duryee built a modest home at 414 Broome Street and lived in the residence until his death. Major William B. C. Duryee is buried in the cemetery of St. Peter's Church. The First Presbyterian Church forever reveres his memory.

THE FIRST PRESBYTERIAN CHURCH

ST. PETER'S CHURCH

ST. PETER'S CHURCH (EPISCOPAL)

The church was organized as a mission in 1858 and was consecrated the following year by the Rt. Rev. Francis Huger Rutledge, first Bishop of Florida. During the War it was used by Federal forces occupying Fernandina and many of its interior possessions were lost. The building was restored to sacred use during the Reconstruction Period, but was destroyed by fire in 1892. The present neo-Gothic church was completed in 1893.

Atlantic Avenue & 8th Street, next to church, Fernandina Beach
N10 ~ GPS Coordinates: 30.670717, -81.458417

The year 1850 found the Episcopal Diocese all but defunct in Florida. The annual convention recorded only two clergy to represent the state that year and only four clergymen the following year, 1851. State contributions amounted to little more than three thousand dollars and the convention realized that prompt action must be taken to save the declining diocese. A resident Bishop was chosen to breathe new life into Episcopal Florida.

The Reverend Francis Huger Rutledge, rector of St. John's Church, Tallahassee, was appointed the first Bishop of Florida. He was consecrated at St. Paul's Church, Augusta, Georgia. Rutledge realized his mission from the onset, enlisting mission priests to serve as traveling evangelists or circuit riders. It was in 1858 that a mission was established at Fernandina under the leadership of Reverend Owen P. Thackara. Reverend Rutledge consecrated St. Peter's Episcopal Church the following year and a permanent wooden church structure was built.

Florida seceded from the Union in 1861 and the Florida Episcopalian Diocese followed. The Protestant Episcopal Church of the Confederate States of America was born. St. Peter's was ill used by Union forces during the Civil War and most of the original church interior was gutted. After the defeat of the Confederacy, the Church renamed the Protestant Episcopal Church in the Southern Diocese of the United States. The Diocese managed to reunite in February 1866 and St. Peter's congregation returned to worship after repairing the sanctuary.

In 1881, construction began on a new edifice under the direction of Robert Shuyler, a well-known New York architect. The Gothic Revival building was constructed of tabby made from sand, lime, oyster shells and water then overlaid with stucco. The building took three years to complete. The first services were held on Good Friday, 1884. The new structure boasted magnificent windows of stained glass. The Rose window was designed by Schuyler and adorned the west wall with little angel faces glowing through amber cherub glass in the tower vestry window. The interior is supported by arched beams meant to remind parishioners of the hull of a ship, meaning worshippers are but voyagers on a journey through time.

During the twilight of February 24, 1892, disaster struck in the form of fire. The blaze reportedly began beneath the flooring and in the bell tower, destroying the interior furnishings and the roof. Robert M. Henderson, a woodworker of extraordinary skill, built the original lectern, baptismal font and prayer desk. Henderson risked his life to rescue the treasured furnishings to no avail. Robert Schuyler returned to rebuild St. Peter, but tragically a fall from the scaffolding of the church tower brought about his untimely death in July 1895. Schuyler's remains rest, forever honored, in the cemetery of St. Peter's Church.

The focal point of St. Peter's sanctuary is the more than one hundred years old Harrison Gothic-style Pipe Organ. The instrument is recognized by the Organ Historical Society of Richmond, Virginia as the largest and perhaps the only intact example of its kind. The massive musical piece dominates the room with gold and green painted scrollwork and eight hundred fifty pipes ranging from fourteen feet in length to a miniscule over two inches.

Today St. Peter's Parish Episcopal Church enjoys a very busy congregation. Offering three Sunday services to accommodate parishioners, each hosting more than one hundred twenty members and guests.

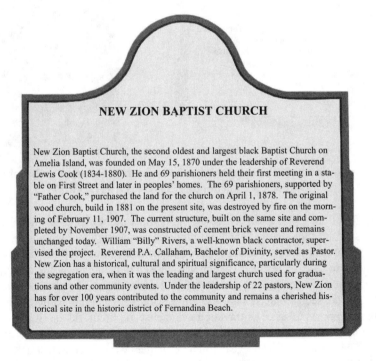

NEW ZION BAPTIST CHURCH

New Zion Baptist Church, the second oldest and largest black Baptist Church on Amelia Island, was founded on May 15, 1870 under the leadership of Reverend Lewis Cook (1834-1880). He and 69 parishioners held their first meeting in a stable on First Street and later in peoples' homes. The 69 parishioners, supported by "Father Cook," purchased the land for the church on April 1, 1878. The original wood church, build in 1881 on the present site, was destroyed by fire on the morning of February 11, 1907. The current structure, built on the same site and completed by November 1907, was constructed of cement brick veneer and remains unchanged today. William "Billy" Rivers, a well-known black contractor, supervised the project. Reverend P.A. Callaham, Bachelor of Divinity, served as Pastor. New Zion has a historical, cultural and spiritual significance, particularly during the segregation era, when it was the leading and largest church used for graduations and other community events. Under the leadership of 22 pastors, New Zion has for over 100 years contributed to the community and remains a cherished historical site in the historic district of Fernandina Beach.

10 South 10th Street, Fernandina Beach
N11 ~ GPS Coordinates: 30.670467, -81.457167

Today known as the New Zion Missionary Baptist Church, the original congregation was founded in 1870. It was during that year that a wooden structure was erected serving sixty-nine parishioners. Fire claimed the sanctuary in 1904 and it was replaced with a gray fireproof cement edifice having a corner belfry, which continues to house services today. The building's small exterior is deceptive, once the threshold is crossed the interior is revealed as a spacious house of worship. The effect is achieved by a hard pine cathedral ceiling, fir rafters and supporting trusses. Steel rods and bolts anchor the ceiling assembly. Shining hardwood floors slant slightly toward the lectern while stained glass windows illuminate the heart of the sanctuary with radiant color.

Mrs. Willie Mae Ashley penned a history of the church beginning with the story of William Rivers, a local black contractor, responsible for the construction of the sanctuary. Ashley described how members of the congregation would bring wicker clothes hampers filled with lunches and lemonade to the workers during construction of the sanctuary in 1904.

The local African American school, Peck High, held graduation ceremonies and baccalaureate services at New Zion Baptist Church until the construction of the school gymnasium in 1956. Today, the New Zion Missionary Baptist Church continues to serve its congregation and community with the same proud tradition held for over one hundred and thirty years.

NEW ZION BAPTIST CHURCH

MCCLURE'S HILL

Site of the Battle of Amelia, September 13, 1817. On this hill, Spaniards erected a battery of four brass cannon. With about 300 men, supported by two gunboats, they shelled Fernandina, held by Jared Irwin, adventurer and former Pennsylvania Congressman. His "Republic of Florida" forces numbered 94, the privateer's Morgiana and St. Joseph, and the armed schooner Jupiter. Spanish gunboats commenced firing at 3:00 p.m. and the battery on this hill joined the cannonade. Guns of Fort San Carlos, on the river bluff northwest of here, and those of the St. Joseph defended Amelia Island. Cannon balls killed two and wounded other Spanish troops concentrated below this hill. Firing continued until dark. The Spanish commander, convinced he could not capture the island, withdrew his forces.

East on Centre Street, Atlantic Avenue to 14th Street 0.8, turn left, Fernandina Beach
N12 ~ GPS Coordinates: 30.682217, -81.449517

George Clark, appointed Surveyor-General by Florida Governor White in 1811, established the town of Fernandina. Clark's plan entailed the establishment of home sites in a gridiron pattern. Unfortunately residents had already established ownership of some of these sites and Clark's rezoning would nullify those titles. Governor White, in an attempt to compensate those affected, granted that each titleholder could claim another tract of land equal in value. Most residents did not dispute the Governor's order; however, John McClure was extremely dissatisfied.

McClure complained directly to the Governor who refused to meet with him. The Governor's only response to McClure's concerns was to order Clark to begin staking out the property as designed on the grid. McClure retaliated by pulling up the stakes each time they were driven into the sandy soil. The resulting hostility was likely the cause of John McClure's untimely death, which occurred shortly thereafter. A cousin, also named John McClure, inherited the entire estate as well as the dilemma over the property. Cousin John McClure issued a threat to Clark stating that he would shoot the surveyor if he so much as stepped foot on McClure property. The Governor stepped in and issued a warning to McClure that he would cease and desist. The veiled threat must have solved the problem, Clark continued with his grid plan and the design of Fernandina. The name John McClure faded into history with only a vague recollection of either cousin ever having lived. Though from that time forward the site would be known as McClure's Hill. Fernandina played a major role during the battle of Amelia Island just six years later.

The battle began with the arrival of a Spanish contingent on a hot September day in 1817. The Spanish assumed a position on McClure's hill armed with four brass cannon ready to lay siege on Fernandina. The bombardment erupted with shots fired from two gunboats at anchor in the Fernandina harbor. The Spanish cannon responded immediately. Jared Irwin, stationed at Fort San Carlos, realized he faced overwhelming odds but stood his ground and returned fire. The volleys continued through the day though neither side suffered any losses.

Irwin finally turned his guns on McClure's Hill but overshot his target. The round shot exploded into the Spanish encampment just beyond the hill, killing two men and wounding several more. The Cuban officer leading the Spanish troops retreated in panic, believing he was outnumbered and could not take Fernandina. The Spanish troops returned to St. Augustine their heads hung low in defeat. When the Spanish contingent arrived the officer was charged with cowardice. His actions were later downgraded incompetence and he was relieved of command. Jared Irwin was overjoyed with his victory but celebration was short lived. Taking stock of his situation, Irwin quickly realized that they were severely lacking in supplies and had no money. Irwin's dilemma would be short lived. Four days later on September 17, 1817, Frenchman and Privateer Luis Aury sailed into Amelia's harbor and within days claimed the island for the Republic of Mexico with these words:

> "Fernandina, East Florida, September 20: The inhabitants of the Island of Amelia are informed that tomorrow the Mexican flag will be hoisted on the fort.... All persons are invited to return to their homes.... or if desirous of recovering their property are invited to send written orders, with out which nothing will be allowed to be embarked. Proclamations for the organization of this place will immediately be issued."

Eventually Aury's piracy based on Amelia Island would come to an end at the hands of the American Navy. President Monroe issued orders to seize the island. Jared Irwin sailed away with Aury to South America. On September 20, 1818, Jared Irwin died of typhoid following a fantastic hurricane, which resulted in an epidemic.

The United States ensign[4] waved in the brisk sea breeze of Amelia Island for more than forty years until the Civil War again brought conflict to her harbor.

FORT SAN CARLOS

On this bluff overlooking the Amelia River, Fort San Carlos was completed by the Spanish in 1816. The fort was made of wood and earthworks and was armed with eight or ten guns. As the Spanish Empire disintegrated, Fort San Carlos became increasingly vulnerable to foreign intervention. Commissioned by representatives of revolting South American countries to liberate Florida from Spanish control, Sir Gregor MacGregor seized the fort in June, 1817. After his withdrawal in September, the Spanish attempt to reassert their authority was repelled by forces led by MacGregor's lieutenants, Jared Irwin and Ruggles Hubbard. Somewhat later, the pirate Luis Aury gained control of the fort. Because Aury's privateering threatened negotiations concerning the cession of Florida, United States troops occupied Fort San Carlos in December 1817. Although upset by U.S. interference at Fort San Carlos, Spain did cede Florida in 1821, and the U.S. abandoned the fort shortly after the transferal. Archaeologists estimate that two-thirds of the area has disappeared through erosion.

Estrada Street, Fernandina Beach
N13 ~ GPS Coordinates: 30.689000, -81.456217

Spanish forces built Fort San Carlos in 1816 to protect their holdings in Northern Florida. However, by mid year 1816 Scotsman Gregor MacGregor seized the fort with his American troops financed by United States businessmen. MacGregor soon abandoned his men when it became clear that his supporters would no longer supply additional money or weaponry. He relinquished control to Ruggles Hubbard, former High Sheriff of New York and Jared Irwin, former United States Congressman from Pennsylvania.

The Spanish attacked on September 13, 1817, the Battle of Amelia ensued. By a simple twist of fate Hubbard and Irwin mounted a feeble defense but managed to win the day. Their men went unpaid and loyalty began to waver, though Hubbard and Irwin maintained morale as best they could. Less than a week later, French pirate Luis Aury boldly sailed into the port of Fernandina with two privateers sailing alongside. Hubbard welcomed the pirate and begged for financial support, Aury agreed upon the condition that he be recognized as Supreme Commander of Fernandina. Hubbard and Irwin complained vigorously until a compromise was struck. The agreement enabled Hubbard to be the civilian governor and Aury would control the military and naval forces with Irwin as his general. The Mexican flag was flown because the South American country supported Aury. He agreed to pay Hubbard and Irwin's troops their past due compensation and the deal was set. The local citizenry fled in the face of pirating and plunder.

The population was very diverse including Americans, English, Irish, Scotsmen, French and one hundred thirty mulattos known as "Aury's Blacks." Racism was a huge bone of contention early on when Aury expected his mulattos to be housed alongside Hubbard and Irwin's white troops. All out war began as the men fought among themselves. Hubbard became ill with fever and Aury seized the opportunity to overtake him and force his concession. Hubbard died soon afterward.

Less than a week after Hubbard's death, thirty British officers arrived. Aury welcomed the group but told them they would be forced to serve amidst the ranks of his pirates and mulattos should they wish to stay. Most of the officers quickly departed, however, a few mounted an attempt to overtake Aury. On November 5, 1817, Aury laid siege on Fernandina, he retained control of the island and imposed martial law for ten days. By mid November, the United States War and Naval Department on behalf of President Monroe finally expelled Aury.

Though Luis Aury's reign over Fernandina was a short one, his time there was extremely profitable. It is said that an agent representing Lloyd's of Savannah reported over a half million dollars of prized goods had been sold at Fernandina.

Fernandina never became a thriving metropolis. The construction of Fort Clinch in 1847 forced the abandonment of Fort San Carlos. By 1853, Fernandina proper had moved south with the railroad and tourism of the beach community boomed. Though the town site was moved, the original plans and street grid developed by the Spanish remain in old town Fernandina today.

PLAZA SAN CARLOS

This land high above the Amelia River was a campsite for Indians in pre-historic times, as early as 2,000-1,000 B.C. In the early history of the state, it assumed military importance because of the fine protected harbor on the northern boundary of Spanish Florida. In the first Spanish period, a village of Franciscans and Indians was established here by 1675, and a Spanish sentinel's house was documented in 1696. From 1736 to 1742, James Oglethorpe stationed Highlanders on this site. After the withdrawal of Oglethorpe's troops in 1742, the area served as a buffer zone between the English and the Spanish until 1762 when Florida became a British possession. When Spain regained possession of Florida in 1783, this harbor was an embarkation point for British Loyalists leaving Florida. The U.S. Embargo Act of 1807, which closed all U.S. ports to European trade, made the border town of Fernandina a center for smuggling. On March 17, 1812, a group of Americans known as the Patriots overthrew the Spanish battery, but the U.S. flag replaced the Patriots' standard after one day. Spain regained control in May, 1813, and completed Fort San Carlos in 1816. As the fort's parade ground, this site was named Plaza San Carlos.

Estrada Street, Fernandina Beach
N13 ~ GPS Coordinates: 30.689000, -81.456217

Imagine this picturesque site on the banks of the Amelia River in the mid 1600s teeming at the time with thousands of Timuquan Indians. The population of Indian inhabitants during the period dwarfed that of today's census. By the early 1700s, Oglethorpe had the established the Scottish Highlanders here to serve as a buffer between the English in Georgia and Spanish held St. Augustine. Eventually Oglethorpe withdrew his forces and the location fell into Spanish hands once again.

President Monroe secretly passed the United States Embargo Act restricting all trade with European ports. The United States Congress issued the Act in December of 1807. The shipping industry suffered from the restriction of both British and French trade. Thomas Jefferson, then ambassador to France, assumed the issue and sought to prove the importance of European trade to the United States government.

Jefferson's first attempt was the Nonimportation Act of 1806. The act was an attempt to force Britain to relax its strenuous embargo against American cargoes and sailors. It was of little value and eventually America passed the Embargo Act in retaliation. In January 1808, the act was extended to curtail inland trade with ever expanding Canadian markets. Merchants, sea captains and sailors were devastated without income and watched helplessly as ships rotted away in port. Every means necessary to circumvent the vigorous restriction was attempted, though all of them failed.

One year later, the United States Congress passed another act to relieve some of the economic hardships on merchants and traders who were reaching rebellious times. The Nonintercourse Act, passed in January 1809, restricted trade with all of Europe except Britain and France.

During the economic shipping restrictions with European ports, Fernandina became a pirating stronghold. With no other means of income, accepting piracy was easy. The unsavory element forced law-abiding citizens to leave the harbor town. The city's population plummeted; it was not until the organization of Florida's first East Coast railway system, that an increase in populace was noted. With the onset of the Civil War the railway declined and the population suffered. The shrimping industry and tourism became Fernandina and Amelia Island's saving grace. The site of Plaza San Carlos is today a wide expanse of open meadow with only a sea breeze and historic marker remnant of days long past.

HISTORIC AMERICAN BEACH

American Beach was established in 1935 under the leadership of Abraham Lincoln Lewis, one of seven co-founders of the Afro-American Life Insurance Company, and one of Florida's first black millionaires. His vision was to create a beach resort as a benefit for company executives and as an incentive for employees to exceed in sales. Florida's beaches were racially segregated until the passage of the 1964 Civil Rights Act. Because of this, American Beach became regionally popular since it was one of the few beaches in the Southeast open to African Americans. Other sites in American Beach trace their history to the Civil War era. Amelia Island was home to several Sea Island cotton plantations, including the Harrison Plantation. In 1862 Union Forces captured Amelia Island and the freed slaves founded Franklin Town at the south end of this island. The Franklin Town cemetery, which had been given by the Harrison family to their slaves as a burial place for their families, still exists today on the west side of Highway A1A. In 1972, encroaching development forced Franklin Town residents to move north to American Beach. Their Methodist Church, built in 1949, was also moved here where it now serves as the church's fellowship hall.

1830 Lewis Street, Amelia Island
N14 ~ GPS Coordinates: 30.573800, -81.445200

The history of American Beach began with a Spanish land grant issued to Captain Samuel Harrison in 1781 on Amelia Island. Captain Harrison arrived from Belize, Honduras with his wife Elizabeth and two children establishing Harrison Plantation producing cotton. Like other plantations of its day, the operation depended on the use of slave labor to exist.

When the Civil War brought Union Troops to Amelia Island and emancipation freed the enslaved; a community called Franklintown was born. The community centered on an African American burial plot donated to Harrison Plantation slaves by Captain Harrison. Special Field Order Number 15 granted ownership of many Confederate holdings to the former slaves, Harrison Plantation being one such property.

Moving forward a number of decades American Beach was established in 1935. The property was the concept of Abraham Lincoln Lewis, known to his acquaintances as A. L., one of seven founders of Florida's

African American Life Insurance Company in 1919. The insurance company was the first of its kind in Florida owned by anyone, black or white. A. L. Lewis held the distinction as one of Florida's first African American millionaires. Further information on the life and times of A. L. Lewis are addressed in the Duval County section under Abraham Lincoln Lewis Mausoleum and Florida's First African American Insurance Company

Lewis' fortune as well as the success the life insurance company, of which he was the President, allowed him to initiate the purchase and development American Beach. The transaction involved two hundred acres extending along thirteen miles of coastline. The resort he was to establish there would provide "relaxation without humiliation" for the employees of the insurance company as an incentive toward increased sales. But further than that, the haven created a resort for African Americans when segregation laws prevented the use of existing facilities.

Black families often traveled for days to visit the resort, which grew to be a bustling center of activity. Famous faces like those of Cab Calloway and Joe Louis were not uncommon. African American children could play unrestricted in the sand and surf; the restaurants welcomed their business, bathrooms and water fountains did not display the insulting "whites only" signs.

The 1970s brought many changes to Amelia Island. Desegregation opened the doors of establishments previously slammed in the faces of Black Americans; American Beach began seeing a few white faces among the usual crowd and the Amelia Island Plantation Company initiated construction of a billion-dollar resort next door. Soon Amelia Island became a mecca for summer beach resorts and American Beach residents began to feel crowded by the conglomerates.

MaVynee Oshun Betsch, the great granddaughter of A. L. Lewis, has made it her life's mission to advocate for and protect American Beach. Betsch, who is known to locals as the "Beach Lady," is surely noticeable with six-foot dreadlocks styled to emulate West Africa's Niger River. The Beach Lady discarded a career as a Grand Opera Diva who performed works such as Madame Butterfly and Carmen before European audiences to become the unofficial mayor of American Beach.

During the last several years Amelia Island Plantation has desperately tried to purchase eighty-three acres of American Beach for the establishment of an assisted living facility, golf course and seventy houses. The beach residents have struggled to stop the erosion that threatens to obliterate the historical beach by having many of the homes there listed on the National Registry of Historic Places. The story has become the focal point of the media. Though it might seem futile to some, trying to restrict the tide of progressive Amelia Island Plantation, that is essentially what the Beach Lady intends to do. Her zeal for life and motto for living are surely an inspiration and there is no doubt MaVynee Oshun Betsch, the Beach Lady, will be successful. In her own words, "getting the most from the least and living peacefully in harmony with nature is the most rewarding lifestyle." American Beach lives on.

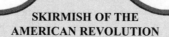

**SKIRMISH OF THE
AMERICAN REVOLUTION**

June 30, 1778, a force of 300 American Cavalry commanded
by Colonel Elijah Clarke, participating in General Robert
Howe's invasion of Florida, attacked a column of British at
this place (Alligator Creek Bridge), but were unable to pene-
trate the nearby entrenchments of 450 British Regulars and
South Carolina Royalists under the command of Major James
Marc Prevost. In this skirmish, Colonel Clarke was wounded
and the Americans withdrew. The next day, the British retired
in the direction of the St. John's River.

**On U.S. 1 at the SE side of Alligator Creek bridge, Callahan
N15 ~ GPS Coordinates: 30.566526, -81.833082**

THE ACTUAL MARKER

During the American Revolution Florida was a British stronghold. Loyalists to the British Crown sought a safe haven here. British sympathizers were likely incarcerated if apprehended by Americans just across the border in Georgia. The Rebels[5] fought relentlessly to claim Florida as the 14th state in the newly form-ing Confederation, however the territory remained steadfastly British anchored at St. Augustine.

Twice Rebel forces attacked British Regulars in Florida but the debilitating heat and rampant disease thwarted their attempts. Quite possibly the largest Revolutionary skirmish in Florida was the battle at Alligator Creek. Many minor raids and marauding expeditions erupted before the battle as well as after, even so Florida steadfastly maintained its British allegiance to the end.

In 1778 as the mild days of spring became sweltering summer; Rebel forces led by General Robert Howe prepared to invade British Florida. Accompanying Howe was Patriot officer, Colonel Elijah Clarke and three hundred cavalrymen. Four hundred fifty British Regulars were firmly entrenched at Alligator Creek under the command of Lieutenant Colonel James Marcus Prevost and Colonel Thomas Browne of Savannah.

Several difficulties involving both sides of the battle were evident, including a power struggle between commanding factions of the British Regulars. The Patriots had no idea that the British were amassed directly in their path, however, the British were unprepared for the assault. The power struggle was resolved by Lieutenant Colonel Prevost's brother General Augustine Prevost by appointing his younger sibling commander of all British Regulars, Loyalists and militia in East Florida; a prime example of nepotism at its best.

The American militia crossed the St. Marys River into Florida on June 30, 1778. They were six hundred men strong with nine hundred militia and infantry following closely behind. As they approached Alligator Creek, Colonel Browne and the British Rangers circled behind and attacked the American flanks. The attacking Rangers were grossly unprepared for assault. In fact, the British Regulars and Loyalists at Alligator Creek were enjoying an afternoon respite; a number were actually bathing in the creek. Colonel Browne's forces delayed the advancing Rebels long enough for the British encampment to gather themselves and as the Patriots reached Alligator Creek they were met with a volley of musket fire.

The first volley resulted in fourteen Patriot causalities and many wounded. The Rebels, at the quick step, retreated. Browne and the Rangers, assisted by Indians, continued to assault the withdrawing Rebels, finishing off the wounded and continuing to inflict casualties.

Over the next few weeks the forces met in several smaller skirmishes, neither side suffering a complete rout. The heat, malaria and lack of supplies took their toll on the American forces whom finally conceded the fight and returned to Georgia. The skirmish at Alligator Creek was the last Rebel attempt to take British East Florida.

Colonel Clarke, who led the Americans at Alligator Creek, was wounded during the battle. He recovered and led seven additional engagements, where he suffered serious wounds in two subsequent battles. Clarke emerged from the Revolution a hero and was granted a substantial estate in his native Georgia.

After the Revolution, Clarke found himself in one predicament after another. He was brought before a government tribunal on more than one occasion. Due to his popularity in Georgia he was never convicted of any crime. He was finally charged with land fraud for his involvement with the Yazoo Land Company. When Clarke and his associates conspired to sell all of the property between the Atlantic Ocean to the Mississippi River. There were two problems with the plan: (1) the men sold more acreage than actually existed and (2) they did not own the property sold. Still Clarke managed to escape this latest scheme as well. When he passed away in 1799, the militia issued a general order of mourning. Clarke County, Georgia was named in his honor and in Athens a monument was erected in recognition of his patriotism during the American Revolution.

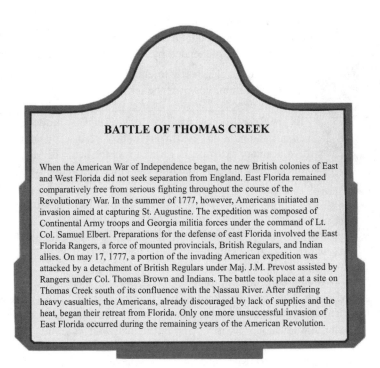

In median of U.S. 1 on the Nassau-Duval County lines & Thomas Creek,
South of Callahan
N16 ~ GPS Coordinates: 30.505967, -81.791750

The era was spring 1777, Button Gwinnett was Georgia's acting governor and General Lachlan McIntosh of Georgia was in command of the state's militia forces. The two men were at odds for various political and personal reasons. Gwinnett conceived a plan to take British-held Florida but refused to allow McIntosh to lead the ill-fated campaign, which he vehemently opposed. Instead Samuel Elbert led the Georgia troops for the invasion of Thomas Creek and was soundly defeated. Elbert and his contingent quickly retreated back to Georgia. Gwinnett managed to dodge the blame, for the doomed attack. Unfortunately McIntosh was officially the General of Georgia's state militia; he was not as lucky.

The Battle of Thomas Creek's was initiated to silently attack the British held settlement of Cow Ford, now known as Jacksonville. The American forces, led by Colonel Samuel Elbert of Savannah, drove the British south until their eventual target at St. Augustine was taken. Meanwhile Cow Ford remained in the hands of Colonel John Baker and his Georgia militia.

Colonel Baker and the militia crossed the St. Marys River toward Sawpit Bluff. It was there that they were to rendezvous with Elbert and the Continentals. Baker and his men spent several days waiting for Elbert's arrival and conducting raids between the Nassau and Trout Rivers.

British Loyalist forces arrived on May 10, 1777. Lieutenant Colonel Thomas Brown, in command of the East Florida Rangers, sailed north to Cow Ford searching for raiding parties. Scouts found the Georgians camped nine miles from Trout creek, but before the Loyalists could attack they were spotted by a Rebel and forced to retreat. Colonel Brown ordered his Indian scouts to steal the Georgians' horses. The Indians were tracked to Brown's ships at Trout Creek and a brief skirmish ensued. Colonel Brown ordered a southern retreat.

British regulars, under the command of Major Mark Prevost, marched from Cow Ford to Frederick Rolfe's sawmill on Trout Creek on May 16. The Rangers, who searched the King's Road to the St. Marys River for Baker, followed them. When the Georgians' camp was found south of Thomas Creek, Brown sent word for reinforcement. At dawn on May 17, the British attacked an unsuspecting Colonel John Baker with his one hundred nine gallant mounted militia. They were brutally ambushed by four hundred British Regulars, Tory Florida Rangers, and Creek Indians at Thomas Creek. Daniel McGirth's loyalists mutilated Colonel Baker's brave American patriots. Eight men killed, nine wounded and thirty-one captured. Fifteen of the captured souls were brutally executed, their scalps taken as trophies by the Indians. Two days after the Battle of Thomas Creek, Elbert arrived at Sawpit Bluff and rescued the few remaining survivors. This battle was the only Revolutionary War battle fought on what is today, Duval County.

Button Gwinnett's plan to capture northern Florida had fail dismally but rather than take the brunt of accusation, Gwinnett laid all responsibility at General Lachlan McIntosh's feet. To add fuel to the already growing fire, Continental Congress President John Hancock ordered Gwinnett to arrest McIntosh's brother, George, for treason. George McIntosh was accused of selling rice to support British forces in Florida. The accusation was untrue, however, George had knowledge of others conducting the treasonous acts but refused to named them. George McIntosh was arrested and refused bail. Enraged, Lachlan McIntosh vilified Gwinnett as ''a scoundrel and lying rascal'' before the state assembly and the infamous duel resulted.

The date was set for May 16, 1777, to the south of what is known today as Colonial Park Cemetery in Savannah, sunrise was the appointed time when one man would meet his demise. The two marksmen were placed at ten paces; they turned and fired simultaneously. Both men fell to the ground wounded, however, it is said that McIntosh managed to struggle to his feet and go to Gwinnett who was unable to rise due to a broken thigh. The men shook hands noting that satisfaction had been found and Gwinnett was taken away only to die of his injury three days later.

General Lachlan McIntosh was tried for murder and acquitted, however his reputation in Savannah was severely questioned. General George Washington called McIntosh north where he served under the General's command. Lachlan lived to see seventy-ninth year and was revered as a great statesman. Ironically, when he was buried at Colonial Park Cemetery in February 1806, Lachlan McIntosh was but a pistol shot away from his old nemesis, Button Gwinnett.

End Notes

[1] Erroneously identified by Bartram as Little St. Simons Island

[2] Bartram states, Dr. Solander preceded Dr. Fothergill in death this is erroneous.

[3] A high executive officer of Muslim countries and especially of the Ottoman Empire

[4] flag

[5] American Patriots known as simply Patriots, Rebels or Continentals.

Duval County

THE HUGUENOT MEMORIAL SITE

In 1562, when France was being torn by religious strife, Gaspard de Coligny, Admiral of France, sent two vessels to the New World in search of a refuge for the oppressed Huguenots. Leading the expedition was the Huguenot explorer, Jean Ribault, who charted a new course across the Atlantic and arrived off the coast of Florida. On Friday, May 1, 1562, Ribault party first landed in the New World here on the east shore of Xalvis Island. In the presence of friendly Indians, the Frenchmen fell to the ground and gave thanks to God in the first Protestant worship service held in the New World. Ribault sailed on up the coast where he founded the colonial settlement of Charlesfort - named in honor of his king. Charlesfort did not last and in 1562 a new Huguenot settlement - Fort Caroline - was established on the St. Johns. There, sometime before 1565, the first Protestant white child was born in what is now the United States. On his second voyage to the Americas in 1565, Ribault and his men were shipwrecked near St. Augustine. The bold explorer and most of his followers were cold-bloodedly murdered at Matanzas Inlet, near St. Augustine, by Spanish Governor Pedro Menendez, who feared the encroachment of France on Spain's Florida empire.

Huguenot Park, A1A, past the State Cultural Site, Fort George Island
D1 ~ GPS Coordinates: 30.411074, -81.420520

Jean Ribault[1] was born near Dieppe, France in the year 1520. He was known to be an explorer and navigator. It was in this capacity that Admiral Gaspard de Coligny, head of the Protestant party in France, commissioned him to lead an expedition to the New World. Ribault was instructed to establish an asylum for persecuted French Huguenots seeking religious freedom.

Captain Ribault set sail in February 1562. He commanded a flotilla of five vessels transporting one hundred fifty would-be colonists. After two rigorous months at sea, favorable winds brought the beleaguered crew and immigrants by way of the Rivere de Mai[2] to the Florida shore. It was from this vantage-point that Ribault, along with his second in command Renéé Goulaine de Laudonnièère, explored the coast from the mouth of the river to Port Royal Sound in Carolina[3].

After sailing north, Ribault choose to settle a contingent of colonists at what is today known as Parris Island, South Carolina. He christened the settlement Charlesfort. Ribault then returned to France in July of 1562. Twenty-eight men were left behind at Charlesfort to maintain the settlement. A disastrous fire destroyed most of their provisions, leaving the men starving and without hope. Eventually the settlers mutinied and killed the French officer left in charge by Ribault. The remaining men managed to forage enough wood to build a hastily constructed ship. Then abandoned Charlesfort and set sail for home. The sea tossed adventurers were eventually plucked from the briny sea by an English vessel.

The Spanish at St. Augustine began hearing rumors of the Charlesfort settlement. A warship was dispatched to annihilate the fledgling village and all inhabitants. Though by the time the Spanish arrived, Charlesfort had been deserted.

Ribault arrived in France only to discover the Roman Catholics and Huguenots in the midst of a brutal civil war. He escaped to England where he wrote and published *The Whole and True Discouerye of Terra Florida* in 1563. The text was Ribault report on his voyage to the New World promised to Admiral Coligny. The greatest asset derived from Ribault trip to the New World came at the hand of his pilot, Nicolas Barré. The pilot recorded every inlet, river and harbor discovered by the French explorer giving each a French name. Eventually the information was used as a basis of maps published in Amsterdam, Paris and Frankfurt.

At the insistence of Queen Elizabeth I of England, Ribault agreed to join Thomas Stucley in a second venture to the New World charged with the establishment of an English colony in Florida. Stucley, who was said to be the illegitimate son of Henry VIII, was somewhat of a shady character. He and Ribault were accused of planning an escape to France in the process stealing English ships. The Queen imprisoned both men in the Tower of London though they later issued a pardon after a short incarceration.

Renéé de Laudonnièère, a relative of Admiral Coligny, was chosen to lead a second colonization attempt in 1564. The result was the establishment of Fort Caroline, named for Charles IX of France, situated on the southern bank near the mouth of the St. Johns River. The settlers quickly felt the wrath of the Native American tribes through repeated raids on their unsuspecting camps. Soon the colonists refused to work toward the establishment of the fledgling community, some opted for piracy, eventually the majority abandoned the settlement in rebellion. Fort Caroline was in desperate straits until English privateer Sir John Hawkins sailed into the waning port in August 1565. Hawkins sold Laudonnièère provisions and one of his ships so that the remaining colonists could escape the failing settlement.

In 1565, Ribault again sailed for the New World as commander of seven ships with a cargo of supplies and reinforcements meant for Fort Caroline. Laudonnièère had made preparations to sail for France when Ribault arrived with the much-needed essentials. Ribault also carried with him a message for Laudonnièère to return to his homeland and answer charges of mismanagement of Fort Caroline.

Phillip the Second of Spain was acutely aware of the French settlement and even though France and Spain were on peaceful terms he ordered Governor General Pedro Menendez de Aviles from Hispaniola[4] to overtake the settlement. Menendez led a flotilla of thirty-four ships with a total crew of two thousand six hundred forty-six men to annihilate the French presence. Ribault spotted the Spanish fleet on September 4, 1565 but chose to avoid the fight. Menendez appeared to set sail toward St. Augustine enticing Ribault, who intended to attack from rear, to follow. Fort Caroline was virtually defenseless. Don Pedro Menendez de Aviles marched his contingent overland attacking Fort Caroline on September 21. Fort Caroline's remaining colonists were virtually massacred, very few escaped the blood bath. According to the priest, Mendoza, one hundred forty-two Huguenots were butchered not even the defenseless women and children were spared. Many of the men were hung in the trees beneath an inscription that read: "Not as Frenchmen, But as Lutherans." Laudonnièère was one of the fortunate few; he eventually reached France in January 1566. His accounting of the events at Fort Caroline was detailed in his *Histoire notable de la Floride* in 1586.

Ribault set sail in retaliation against the Spanish fleet, but alas his vessels were torn asunder by a violent hurricane near Matanzas Inlet. His only hope was the settlement at Fort Caroline by land. Ribault was unaware that the fort was now in the bloody hands of the Spaniards who had slaughtered all but sixteen of the three hundred fifty surrendering settlers, two hundred Frenchmen had escaped into the Florida wilderness. Only a few managed to escape in two ships captained by Ribault son.

During the trek overland, Ribault and his men were accosted by a Spanish detachment. The men were induced to surrender by false assurances of safety. Ribault and his men were put to the sword in October 1565. A little more than two years later, in 1568, Dominique de Gourgues would avenge the slaughter at Fort Caroline as well as the butchery of Ribault and his men.

ABRAHAM LINCOLN LEWIS
MAUSOLEUM

Pioneer Abraham Lincoln Lewis (1865-1947) and others founded Florida's oldest African-American Insurance Company. Afro-American Life in 1901 which spread throughout the south as far as Texas. In 1926, A. L. Lewis opened Lincoln Golf and Country Club where the famous played such as heavyweight boxing champion Joe Lewis (1914-1981). Later Lewis founded American Beach, which in 1935 was a recreational haven for blacks during segregation. Although most noted for the Afro, A. L. Lewis started Florida's first black owned and operated bottling company and assisted Booker T. Washington the National Negro Business Leaders, throughout his life A. L. Lewis continued to serve as a leader in countless organizations such as the 33rd degree of the Masons and the African Methodist Episcopal Church where he was a principle financial supporter. He also provided financial support to Edwards Waters College and Bethune Cookman College. Interred in this nationally historic mausoleum, which was registered in 1997, are his immediate family and his first wife Mary Sammis Lewis (1865-1923), who was the granddaughter of Anna and Zephaniah Kingsley of Kingsley Plantation, today a national park on Fort George Island.

Edgewood Avenue & Moncrief Road, Jacksonville
D2 ~ GPS Coordinates: 30.381344, -81.696165

Abraham Lincoln Lewis was born to a poverty stricken family at Madison, Florida in 1865. Finances forced the family move to Jacksonville though the change in geography made little difference. Monetarily the Lewis family didn't have much, however, in love, moral values and religious commitment the relations were wealthy.

After arriving in Jacksonville Lewis attempted to attend Oakland Public School, unfortunately the family's financial situation forced him to work as a water boy at the local lumber mill. He was eager, reliant and dedicated qualities which brought Lewis to the attention of his employer. He was destined to succeed and his employer steadily advanced him through the ranks until he became the highest paid Black employee at the mill. Lewis remained in the employee of the lumber mill for twenty-two years.

Realizing the importance of savings, Lewis continually set aside a portion of his earnings each week. By the age of twenty-three, in 1888, he managed to put away enough money to invest in the first shoe store owned and operated by a black man in Jacksonville. The business proved successful and Lewis was rewarded with the dividends.

Lewis believed strongly in fraternal solidarity and actively supported this principle throughout his life. He directed the Sons and Daughters of Jacob5 for many years and acted as treasurer for the Masonic Order. His management skills, leadership abilities and business sense were supreme assets. Abraham Lincoln Lewis was a born community leader.

Beginning with an initial investment of one hundred dollars each, Lewis and six of his contemporaries united to form the Afro-American Life Insurance Association. The company was the first of its kind, black or white, to be chartered in the state of Florida. The insurance company began operations in March of 1901 with Lewis as its treasurer. The accounting ledger showed a profit during the first year. The Afro-American Life Insurance Association was A. L. Lewis' crowning achievement but the laundry list of successes continued.

Abraham Lincoln Lewis believed in black business. He invested in black businesses and mentored black owners to improve their various endeavors. Lewis assisted in the organization of the Negro Business League and the National Negro Insurance Association. Though he was known as the wealthiest black man in the United States, Lewis never lost his sense of community or faltered in his commitment to lending a hand to others in need. Wilberforce University in Ohio rewarded his outstanding accomplishments when they conferred upon him a degree of Doctor of Laws and Letters. Lewis made a number of very generous contributions to all of Florida's black colleges and served as trustee and treasurer of Edward Waters College. Quietly and without fanfare, Lewis provided financial support to many young men and women seeking higher education.

A. L. Lewis was not finished yet. The Lincoln Golf and Country Club, founded under the guidance of A. L. Lewis, was a major effort in elevating the recreational opportunities available in Jacksonville for its black citizens. His next great achievement came in the 1930s when he purchased a span of shoreline property on Amelia Island, which he called American Beach. Essentially due to segregation, blacks were not allowed the use of public beaches. Lewis provided a place where his black employees, eventually opened to the entire black community, could come with their families and enjoy a day at the beach. American Beach continues to this day. Unfortunately over the last several years encroaching large resort facilities have been eroding the historic area. American Beach and the surrounding community have a continually growing number to champion the cause, which will surely be preserved as a priceless historical asset.

From 1884 until his death at eighty-one years of age, Lewis was an active member of the Mount Olive AME Church where he served as Sunday School Superintendent for fifty-four years. At the time of his death, Lewis was worth an approximate one and a half million dollars. He was a true leader in the black community and an exceptional man without regard to race. Abraham Lincoln Lewis' life long belief as stated in his words:

ABRAHAM LINCOLN LEWIS
MAUSOLEUM

"I managed to get where I am without education. But mine was the unusual case. Prayer, hard work and a strong determination to excel are indispensable keys for unlocking the doors to great opportunity, and with a good education added to these qualities, more and more Negro young people will enter business, be successful, and improve race relations by their industrial competence and economic sufficiency."

"MOTHER" MIDWAY A.M.E. CHURCH

Midway A.M.E. Church was organized on Sunday, June 10, 1865, a few weeks after the Confederate Army in Florida surrendered to the Union Army. It was thus the first black independent church organized in Florida. William G. Steward was sent to Florida by the African Methodist Episcopal Church, and founded a church at Midway, a settlement east of Jacksonville, on his second day in the state. Mr. Steward appointed Brother G. B. Hill as the pastor of Midway Church before going on to organize congregations in middle Florida and in the panhandle section of the state. In later years Mr. Steward became involved in politics in Leon and Gadsden Counties and served a term in the Florida Legislature. Midway Church is recognized as the "mother" of both the Florida Conference of the A.M.E. Church, organized in 1867 in Tallahassee, and of the East Florida Conference organized in Palatka in 1877. While the original church building is no longer standing, the congregation of "Mother" Midway has been in continuous existence since its founding.

1462 Van Buren Street in Springfield, Jacksonville
D3 ~ GPS Coordinates: 30.341212, -81.641416

The Civil War brought many changes throughout America. Though African American parishioners had long felt alienated from southern Methodist Church, secession increased the tension in these congregations. More than forty percent of the Methodist membership in Florida were African Americans in 1860. Once Civil War ended over half of the Black parishioners had founded churches of their own.

Peace initiated the start of African Methodism in Florida. By May 1865, the African Methodist Episcopal[6] Church had organized the first South Carolina Conference in Charleston. The Conference included representatives from South Carolina, North Carolina, Georgia and Florida. At the time Florida had only one district, known as the Tallahassee District. Reverend Branch, pastor of the Methodist Church of Jacksonville granted Deacon William G. Steward[7] permission to preach and organize an African American church in Jacksonville on February 19, 1865. Bishop Daniel A. Payne appointed Deacon Steward, Pastor of Florida on May 22, 1865.

Reverend Steward arrived in Jacksonville on June 8, 1865 and began organizing African Methodist Episcopal churches for the newly freed slaves in Florida. Steward, known as the one-armed preacher, formed the "Mother" Midway AME Church near Jacksonville on June 10, 1865. The church holds the distinction as the oldest church in Florida to be organized by an official of the AME denomination. The name "Mother" refers to the notability as the "Mother Church of African Methodism" in the state.

Bishop Payne replaced Steward as Florida's Pastor in February 1866. Elder Charles H. Pearce arrived in Jacksonville from Canada and became the state's first Presiding Elder. Pearce, like his predecessor Steward, believed strongly in higher

MOTHER MIDWAY AME CHURCH

education, both religious as well as public.

Reverend William G. Steward went on to serve as a Delegate for the Republican National Convention of 1884 along side another notable Florida African American, Joseph E. Lee. Six years later Reverend Steward would be one of three Presiding Elders of the Florida AME Conference.

The original edifice of "Mother" Midway AME Church no longer stands yet in its place is a red brick sanctuary that graces 1462 Van Buren Street. The present sanctum's construction began in 1969 and was completed in 1973 under the direction of the Right Reverend H. N. Robinson, Bishop. The Midway AME Annex was dedicated on September 20, 1964 with Bishop E. C. Hatcher at the helm. In 1997, the church underwent renovations and was rededicated on February 23, 1997. The church still after more than one hundred thirty years continues to support its conference, congregation and community.

FLORIDA'S FIRST AFRICAN-AMERICAN INSURANCE COMPANY~~1901-2001

(Side One)

The Afro-American Insurance Company, formerly the Afro-American Industrial and Benefits Association, was founded in 1901 to provide affordable health insurance and death benefits to the state's African-Americans. Founded by the Reverend E. J. Gregg, E. W. Latson, Abraham Lincoln Lewis, A. W. Price, Dr. Arthur W. Smith, J. F. Valentine, and the Reverend J. Melton Waldron, the Afro's first office at 14 Ocean Street was destroyed by the great Jacksonville Fire two months after it opened on May 3, 1901. It then moved to 621 Florida Avenue, the home of treasurer and future president, Abraham Lincoln

FLORIDA'S FIRST AFRICAN-AMERICAN INSURANCE COMPANY~~1901-2001

(Side Two)

Lewis (1865-1947). From their next home office at 105 E. Union Street, the company wrote millions of dollars of insurance policies and started district offices in Georgia, Alabama, Louisiana and Texas. Lewis formed the African-American Pension Bureau and in 1935, land was purchased on Amelia Island for the black resort called American Beach. On April 22, 1956, the company dedicated its new million-dollar building at Ocean and Union Street. After over 80 years of serving black southerners, the company closed on July 17, 1987. The 11th Episcopal District of the African Methodist Episcopal Church owns the Building.

101 East Union Street, Jacksonville
D4 ~ GPS Coordinates: 30.332162, -81.654935

"Times they were a changing." It had been thirty-five years since the end of the Civil War and generally southern black Americans struggled to find their niche in a traditionally white business world. Insurance was unknown to black Americans. In the case of a loved ones death, more times than not a simple slat board box and Sunday dress were the only burial essentials. Then along came a new process called embalming. By the turn of the century, the law required that all deceased persons must be embalmed before burial. The process involved replacing bodily fluids with chemicals to preserve the corpse. Embalming was an expensive process. The new legislation forced church congregations to assist bereaved families financially, often "passing the hat" to collect donations to pay for burial costs.

Jacksonville's entrepreneur and financial wizard, A. L. Lewis, devised a plan along with six of his contemporaries including: Reverend E. J. Gregg, E. W. Latson, A. W. Price, Dr. Arthur W. Smith, J. F. Valentine and the Reverend J. Melton Waldron. The group was associated by virtue of their membership in Bethel Baptist Institutional Church. Each man invested one hundred dollars toward the establishment of the African American Insurance Company, founded in March 1901. Business began in an office located at 140 Ocean Street, Jacksonville. The "Afro" as the company was lovingly called, offered both health and life insurance at a rate of ten cents per week.

Disaster struck on May 3, 1901 when the great Jacksonville fire decimated one hundred and forty-six blocks of the city. The blistering inferno ravaged the city as it transformed everything in its path to ash and molten mass. As the flames threatened 140 Ocean Street, Afro clerk Eartha M. M. White risked her life as she bravely plunged into the building to retrieve the two-month-old business' vital records. The company temporarily conducted business as usual at 621 Florida Avenue, home of treasurer and future president, A. L. Lewis. The company moved to Main Street and remained there for ten years.

Within the first year, Afro began showing an unprecedented profit. The company books revealed a fifty dollars per week earning. During the next ten years business was good and a new one million-dollar facility was built at 101 East Union Street. The Afro moved into its new building in 1911. By 1918, the Afro's capital stock increased to ten thousand dollars and the Miami Mutual Insurance Company was purchased. A. L. Lewis became company president in 1919 and the Afro continued to flourish under his leadership.

Much of the Afro's success resulted from its employment policies. Employees developed a family relationship. The company offered free annual medical exams for the employee's children, hosted a once a week office devotional and in 1935, A. L. Lewis founded American Beach for the recreational use of the employees during a time when black Americans were restricted from public beaches. Leota Davis, the oldest living retired Afro employee at one hundred years of age, stated in 2001, "I liked it because they were helping somebody that couldn't help themselves. That was the best job you could get back then. It was a wonderful thing."

The Afro subsequently opened offices in Georgia, Alabama and Texas. By 1937 the companies' net worth had grown to nine hundred twenty seven thousand dollars. This was an exorbitant sum compared to the initial seven hundred-dollar investments of its founders. The East Union Street location was refurbished in 1955 with the addition of a "sunset coral" granite facade. As the company grew, its operations expanded business into mortgages and lending. A great number of loans were issued for the development of black businesses and various homes, churches and schools were built with the assistance of the African American Insurance Company.

The Afro reported eleven million dollars in assets in 1975. The company handled a quarter of a billion dollars in insurance. Integration had a decisive impact when white insurance companies began offering black citizens reasonable benefits at affordable rates. Many of the investments made meager, if any financial returns. By the late 1970s, the Afro accounting ledgers showed lost revenues. Debts began to mount and eventually the multi-million dollar company was in the red. In 1987, the African American Insurance Company was ordered to liquidate its assets by a Leon County Circuit Court Judge.

Though the Afro eventually was forced to close its doors, the benefits it brought to the community, state and country went well beyond material worth. The company flourished to become Florida's only million-dollar, black owned business during the Depression era. The Afro was a cornerstone of Jacksonville's black society and many owe their livelihood to the foundation built by A. L. Lewis, Reverend E. J. Gregg, E. W. Latson, A. W. Price, Dr. Arthur W. Smith, J. F. Valentine and the Reverend J. Melton Waldron.

1960 CIVIL RIGHTS DEMONSTRATION

On Saturday, August 27, 1960, 40 Youth Council demonstrators from the Jacksonville Branch of the National Association for the Advancement of Colored People (NAACP) advised by local civil rights leader Rutledge H. Pearson (1929-1967), sat in at the W. T. Grant Department Store, then located at the corner of West Adams and North Main Streets, and at Woolworth's Five and Ten Cent Store on Hogan Street across from Hemming Park. Seeking access to the whites-only lunch counters, the youths were met by 150 whites males wielding axe handles and baseball bats. Many of the youths were injured while others sought safety at the adjacent Snyder Memorial Methodist Church. Although not the beginning of the Jacksonville civil rights movement, this conflict was a turning point, it awakened many to the seriousness of the African-American community's demand for equal rights, equal opportunity, human dignity and respect, and inspired further resolve in supporters to accomplish these goals. Within the decade, lunch counters were integrated. Duval County public schools began to desegregate, four African-Americans were elected to City Council, and segregation of public accommodations, including parks, restrooms, and water fountains ended.

Duval and Hogan Streets at Hemming Plaza, Jacksonville
D5 ~ GPS Coordinates: 30.329406, -81.659351

The beginnings of the civil right movement can be traced to many different events. Maybe the 1954 Supreme Court ruling desegregating public schools or perhaps the Montgomery bus boycott in 1955 with Rosa Parks and possibly the leadership of Martin Luther King could be sited as the Civil Rights genesis. In Jacksonville, earlier court cases corrected the injustice of unequal pay for white and black teachers and eliminated all white Democratic-voting primaries. However most would say the definitive beginning of the civil rights movement in Jacksonville was a steamy day in August 1960.

Members of the NAACP8 Youth Council gathered at the Laura Street Presbyterian Church in anticipation of a demonstration about to take place at two downtown department stores' all-white lunch counters. Adults had amassed at the church along with the young men and women to offer support and prayer for the young people's safety. Rutledge Pearson was the charismatic advisor to the NAACP Youth Council. Rodney Hurst, youth council president at the tender age of sixteen, stated, "At the time, we did not measure whether or not what we were going to do or what we did would cost us." He further added that the students were on a mission and would have disobeyed their elders if directed to remain in the church.

Sit-in demonstrations began on August 13 and it was there that protesters were kicked, spit upon and subjected to racial slurs. By the morning of Augustine 27, Jacksonville sensed trouble looming on the horizon and nervous anticipation electrified the air. In groups of twos and threes, the members of the youth council stepped outside the protective embrace of the Laura Street Church into the uncertainty of downtown Jacksonville.

Approximately thirty of the youth defiantly walked toward the W. T. Grant department store on Main Street while the remainder of the group headed toward Woolworth's on Hogan Street. Hurst and several others bought various items at Grant's to show that the business was not hesitant about taking their money at the register. However, once the members of the group sat at the lunch counter reserved for white clients, the waitress quickly placed a closed sign on the counter refusing them service. The room went dim as the overhead lights were turned out and condiments were cleared from the tables. The protesters remained for a strained ten minutes until they were satisfied that the Grant's lunch counter would not reopen for lunch that day.

One hundred fifty white men congregated at Hemming Park, some representing the Klu Klux Klan. The raucous mob menacingly wielded baseball bats and axe handles. It was obvious that violence would soon erupt. Hurst said a crush of white men lunged toward the black youth as they exited the store. The youth dispersed and Hurst ran until an adult member of the NAACP eventually picked him up.

Meanwhile, only a few blocks away at Woolworth's the group accompanying twenty-four year-old Alton Yates, vice president of the youth council, sat down at the white lunch counter there. Yates said, "We got the usual runaround from the waitresses. Some of them taunted the kids to get them to do something foolish." Woolworth's lunch counter was also closed, but Yates and the others remained, until a commotion outside alerted them. As Yates attempted to hurry the group outside, while hordes of zealot white men attacked. Yates was pushing a path to the doorway when he received a vicious blow to head. Much to the youth's amazement, members of a black gang the "Boomerangs" came to their rescue by offering themselves as a buffer between the fleeing group and the stalking mob.

The NAACP youth sought the safe haven of the white Memorial Church located only one block away at Monroe and Laura streets. Though the shortest route to the church was through Hemming Park, now called Hemming Plaza, it was the scene of the most fighting, cutting off that avenue of escape. Observers spoke of the 'idyllic peaceful, green square' of Hemming Park on August 27th as a battleground of racial prejudice.

The warring mob obstructed the intersection at Laura and Adams streets, bringing traffic to a halt. The confrontation between the white masses and Boomerangs escalated. The Boomerangs were forced toward the black neighborhood where gang members enlisted supporters from a pool hall. Members of the Jacksonville police observed but did not get involved in the altercation until the tide began to turn in favor of the black protesters and supporters. Several reports noted that fourteen whites and forty-eight blacks were arrested as result of the brawl, as many as fifty people sought medical attention for various injuries.

August 27, 1960 became known as "Axe Handle Saturday," a date recognized as the beginning of integration in Jacksonville. The event brought glaringly to Jacksonville's attention that the civil rights movement had arrived and would not be silenced. Photographs taken during the worst of the conflict blazed across the pages of both Life and Time magazines, stories filled the front pages of the New York Times, the Los Angeles Times and the London Times. Across the state of Florida television screens and radio airwaves buzzed with horrifying reports of the bloody events. The Jacksonville Times Union carried the story without pictures.

Within weeks, committees representing both blacks and whites were formed to discuss integration in Jacksonville's public and private establishments. The youth's efforts were certainly heroic, though only a limited amount of success was achieved. Lunch counters were forced to integrate, though restaurants were allowed to continue to choose their patrons. In April 1961, Rodney Hurst and the NAACP's youth council secretary Marjorie Meeks had lunch every day for a week at Woolworth's white counter to prepare segregationists for the evolution of integration.

Demonstrations in 1964 to desegregate restaurants led to more rioting. Passage of the 1964 Civil Rights Act by Congress, however, brought the long awaited legal integration. When Congress passed the Civil Rights Act, the laws concerning separate water fountains, bathrooms and stores were amended to allow all races use of the facilities.

Within three years blacks in Jacksonville began to experience change. In 1967, Sallye Mathis and Mary Singleton became the first two blacks elected to city council in sixty years. Following consolidation, a predominantly white population elected Earl Johnson at-large. In 1968, Wendell Holmes became the first black elected to the Duval County School Board, eventually its first black chairman. Two decades later, Nat Glover became Jacksonville's first black sheriff elected by a predominately white population. Nat Glover has entered the 2004 mayoral election in Jacksonville but this attempt was unsuccessful.

African Americans have been appointed to management and professional positions in Jacksonville, for the school system and with independent authorities. Dr. Adam Herbert became the first African American State University president of a predominantly white institution. Subsequently the Chamber of Commerce chose Herbert as the first black to lead that body.

The list continues endlessly of outstanding black youngsters succeeding at magnet schools, having successful businesses and as professional men and women buying homes in an increasingly residentially integrated city. Jacksonville's forced evolution brought about the inevitable change and the city continues to flourish as a result.

HEMMING PLAZA

JACKSONVILLE'S 1901 FIRE
"The Great Fire"

On May 3, 1901 at 12:30 p.m., a fire began at the Cleaveland Fibre Factory, ten blocks northwest of this site. Chimney embers ignited sun-dried moss to be used as mattress stuffing. Fueled by wind and dry weather, the fire roared east destroying most structures in its path. By 3:30 p.m., the fire reached this site, then called Hemming Park. The park and its renowned live oaks were devoured by the flames and only the Confederate Monument survived, its base glowing red from heat. The fire continued an eastward march to Hogan's Creek, where a citizens' bucket brigade stayed the flames. Then, turning south, the inferno roared to Bay Street's riverfront docks. Extreme heat caused a waterspout in the river where rescue boats trolled for survivors. The fire was so intense, black smoke clouds could be seen as far away as South Carolina. As flames moved west on Bay Street, the firefighters' gallant stand and dying winds brought the fire under control by 8:30 p.m. In just eight hours nearly 10,000 people were homeless, 2,368 buildings were lost, 146 city blocks were destroyed, but miraculously only seven people perished. Jacksonville's 1901 Fire remains the most destructive burning of a Southern city in U.S. history.

Duval and Hogan Streets at Hemming Plaza, Jacksonville
D5 ~ GPS Coordinates: 30.329406, -81.659351

Jacksonville was a boomtown in the 1890s. Northern tourists arrived in droves during the mild winter months bringing the normal population of thirty thousand to well over the one hundred twenty thousand mark. The attraction of Florida's sunny shores augmented by the ever-expanding amusements brought steamships filled with northerners escaping the chilled landscape of ice and snow.

43

Grand hotels appeared on the Jacksonville skyline. Hotel guest books bore the signatures of European royalty as well as names like Astor and Vanderbilt began to appear. Outlying areas were now connected to the city proper by a trolley system making transportation in and around the city an easier endeavor. Jacksonville heard the whistle of one hundred trains per day bringing in human as well as supply cargo. By the mid 1890s more than one million dollars worth of new construction took place in just one year.

Little did anyone realize life in Jacksonville was about to change. The most dramatic and devastating event in the cities' history was on the horizon and soon the entire country would take notice of the determined spirit of Jacksonville.

Spring filled the air with promise on the morning of May 3, 1901. Jacksonville residents awoke to a sultry, dry heat that had become common of late. There had been little rain during the spring and summer was making herself known early this year. The noon hour approached and Jacksonville streets would soon be filled with businessmen hurrying to lunch then returning to work.

Meanwhile, in a small house on Lavilla a woman fired up her wood burning stove to prepare lunch for her hungry brood. The stove fire sprang to life and the wood shifted as it began to burn; embers drew up the flue escaping into the warm stirring breeze.

The glowing orb floated lazily to land softly on a spread of drying moss. The Cleveland Fiber Factory produced mattresses filled with dried Spanish moss and was just across the way from the Lavilla home. The factory's loading platform was carpeted with drying moss, it never occurred to anyone that the soft filler could bring the city of Jacksonville to her knees.

The dried moss ignited immediately and soon flames flickered higher, then higher still. Factory workers noticed the blaze and set to work putting out the relatively small fire. A blast of wind fanned the flames and noxious black smoke began to fill the air. Sixteen-year-old, George Hodan had the presence of mind to sound the fire alarm summoning the horse drawn fire brigade who arrived within minutes. By the time the fire department arrived the fire had spread to the interior of factory. Workers formed a bucket brigade in an attempt to save the building.

Within thirty minutes of the first floating ember the fire had spread to nearby Hansontown, an African American neighborhood. Folks gathered whatever belongings within their grasp flinging precious cargo into hastily loaded wagons to flee the raging inferno. Pine wood cabins erupted in flames immediately, sizzling sap and acrid tar. Black smoke stung the eyes and burned the lungs. Hungry flames consumed the three blocks of Hansontown within a half-hour.

Telegraph lines buzzed with messages summoning support from Fernandina, St. Augustine and Savannah. Runners sped through the streets yelling a warning of "Fire! Fire!" The thirty-two inch copper steam whistle called "Big Jim"9 warned residents with its one hundred ten-decibel voice. Trees burst into flames and people scattered. Various men opened corrals of anxious livestock to free the pinned herds of cattle and horses saving them from the roasting blaze.

The first out of town fire department to arrive was Fernandina Beach. By this time the fire had been raging for two hours, it was now 2:20 p.m. The rolling fire line had widened its path to devastate Julia and Church Streets. Homes on Ashley, Cedar and Hogan Streets burst into infernal flame like tendered cigar boxes. People hustled toward the safety of the St. Johns with frightened children held close to their breast. Faces covered in soot and ash, streaked with tears.

The First Baptist Church, the Methodist Church, the Presbyterian Church all burned to the ground taking with them the birth, baptismal and death records of entire congregations. The grand Windsor Hotel was brought to her knees next with a thunderous groan of agony. Beautiful fixtures, personal belongings and exquisite furnishings reduced to molten ruins. The St. James Hotel, though it had been closed for almost a month, was tragically lost with all of its historical significance. Few buildings could be saved from the devastating inferno. Brittan's Furniture was standing alone amidst the rubble.

The Savannah Fire Department arrived at 3:30 p.m. but all hope of saving homes or business east of the St. James Hotel had been abandoned. Jacksonville's Fire Chief Thomas Haney directed the men to Duval and Adams Streets when suddenly the wind changed. The blaze reached the County Courthouse known to have sturdy thick walls. Many people had placed belongings there, believing the Courthouse would keep them safe within. The red bricks of the structure turned white as ash then as the temperature increase blazed red like hot coals. Even with the intense heat, the walls held firm and refused to fall; the roof gave way in a deafening crash. The rolling volcanic flames reached to Duval County Armory and the report read:

> "The flames were hottest as they attacked the public buildings and the armory. The latter had the reputation of being fireproof...It crumbled like an egg shell, its walls went down together, and here would have been the climax of the day in great loss of life had not the previous heat driven out all the refugees."

The fire showed no mercy taking City Hall, the new Furchgott building, the Gardner building and the St. Johns Emery Auditorium. The St. John's Episcopal Church, the Catholic Church and St. Joseph's Orphanage and Convent were all reduced to heaping piles of ash.

Fire Chief Haney declared the fire under control at 8:00 p.m. Eight full hours of fighting the blaze that resulted in the loss of one hundred forty-eight city blocks and two thousand three hundred sixty-eight buildings. Ten thousand residents were left homeless. Miraculously only seven people were killed in the devastation. The disaster left over fifteen million dollars in damages.

Jacksonville citizens awoke to a bleak scene Saturday, May 4, 1901. City officials met immediately to devised a plan. Tent city was erected to offer shelter to the homeless and through donations, the government fed over ten thousand persons the first day. The government arranged to bring in architects and plans to rebuild the city began.

Like a phoenix risen from the pyre, Jacksonville recovered. The first building permit was issued to Mr. Gunthal on Monday, May 6, 1901.

At Post Office, corner of Monroe and Julia Streets, Jacksonville
D6 ~ GPS Coordinates: 30.329461, -81.661255

The grand village of Ossachite was located at what is today downtown Jacksonville. Bordered on one side by Hogan's Creek, which is the dividing line separating mid-town Jacksonville from Springfield and the east-side. The other side was bounded by McCoy's Creek flowing west to east near the southern perimeter of LaVilla, near the Prime Osborn Convention Center. During its heyday approximately one thousand years ago these streams were pure crystal clear rivulets, today that is not the case. The higher-ranking Timucua selected the riverbanks as their home sites, obviously a taste for prime real estate remains much the same over the centuries.

It is said that there were as many as twenty Timucua villages in what is Duval County today. All settlements were located along the banks of the St. Johns or "Welaka", as the Indians would have known it. The villages were set about two miles apart. The villages were surrounded by maritime hammocks, which were small wooded areas situated on sand dunes or shell middens[10]. The only middens that were selected for home sites were those that supported the growth of trees and teeming with wildlife. The hammocks provided good drainage and were largely protected from wildfires. Few of these picturesque knolls exist today due to extensive lumbering and urban sprawl.

Ossachite village was larger than most in the area. Though the days of plenty for the community was more than one thousand years ago, the village survived until about 1700. The site was selected because of inland protection from tropical storms, good drainage and accessibility to the river. The "Welaka" not only provided an outstanding source of food but since the Timucua had no horses, the river was their major means of transportation. Besides walking, the canoe was their only vessel capable of leaving the village to hunt or trade. Ironically the same reasoning was used by white settlers in 1822 for founding Jacksonville on the very site that Ossachite was located.

Ossachite was home to approximately three hundred natives. Their homes were small round structures made of tree trunks driven into the ground and covered with woven palm fronds to protect the inhabitants from the elements. The only openings in the claustrophobic chamber were tiny doors with a hole in the roof to allow for rising smoke. The inner walls were lined with wooden benches, which were covered with furs or hide for sleeping comfort and warmth against the chill of the evening. Small smoking fires would be lit at night to ward away buzzing and biting insects. There would also be room for a cook fire and a place to store food and belongings.

The village consisted of a religious building, food storehouses and isolated huts for women recovering from the rigors of childbirth. Though the most impressive building in the village would be the Council House. The large round building would be lined with benches that had the capacity to seat the entire village. Assemblies, ceremonies, celebrations and tribal government all were hosted under this one roof. Each morning the chief would meet with his counselors and like business meetings of today, they sipped their hot, black caffeine.

The "Black Drink" was steeped from the leaves of the Yaupon Holly, the only native North American plant to contain caffeine. The drink was only served to Timucua men providing energy because these warriors only ate one meal per day in the evening. The Black Drink was thought to be medicinal as well, inducing sweating which the Timucua believed purified the system physically and spiritually. The thinking was that the drink would cleanse the dirt from the skin, overcoming fear and laziness.

Ossachite was a bustling village. The Native Americans were craftsmen producing pottery, paintings, woodcarvings, shell work and copper art. The Timucua traded goods with tribes as far away as the Great Lakes.

By the end of the 17th century, the Spanish were feeling the threat of the British Empire and ordered the Timucua to help them build a fort of stone and coquina11 at St. Augustine. That fort was the Castillo de San Marcos. Construction began in 1672 and was completed in 1695. The Timucua were virtually enslaved by the Spanish and forced to fight the British. The fort held strong during the British attack. Most of the Timucua were either killed or taken as slaves to be sold in the largely British Carolinas.

When a treaty was signed between Spain and Britain, the Spanish took the remaining eighty-nine Native Americans to Cuba in order to guarantee their safety. Only twelve were Timucua. In 1767, Juan Alonso Cabale, the last remaining Timucua died. A great culture died with him.

"THE GREAT ENDURANCE RUN"

In November 24, 1909 the "Autoists" participating in "The Great Endurance Run" reached the "Turn Around Checkpoint" at the Jacksonville City Hall which was located at this exact site. The location marked the halfway point for the "Drivers and Observers" of the eighteen automobiles that took part in the grueling four day "Endurance Run" from Tampa to Jacksonville to Tampa to promote good roads for Florida. The event did, indeed foster bond issues and highway construction throughout Florida. The original "Run" was sponsored by The Tampa Daily Times under the auspices of The Tampa Automobile Club with Coca Cola being advertising sponsors.

Hogan and East Forsyth Streets, Jacksonville
D7 ~ GPS Coordinates: 30.327540, -81.660558

Prior to the time of Spanish occupied Florida, "roads" were in fact abundant though they were little more than Indian trails for trading game. The Spaniards, in order to move military detachments, enlarged these trails and the beginnings of more permanent roads emerged. These roads were sometimes "paved" with logs or loads of sandy clay in spots where soldiers bogged down in the swampy goo.

By colonial times, leading to the time when Florida was made the 27th state, bridges and ferries began to be built and roads were expanded to accommodate wagons.
Seaports received first priority for pavement, very rarely were inland town streets paved in this manner. Paving usually consisted of the most available material, ships ballast stones. Ships carried these stones when sailing without cargo as a way to maintain upright as they sailed. Unfortunately when discarded for cargo the heavy stones would often sink into Florida's sandy soil. An alternative to these great heaps of stone had to be found.

"Corduroy" roads were simply logs laid across the path to provide a hard surface, although a very bumpy one, for wagon traffic. This indeed worked for wagons but horses had great difficulty walking on the logs. Plank roads smoothed the corduroy roads by laying planks across the roadbed and placing planks lengthwise along the wagon ruts making a comparatively smooth road. Using sawed-faced logs instead of the round variety gave the horses a smoother-walking surface. These roads were terribly expensive to build and required constant maintenance. During the mid-1800s, a plank road was built inland so that cotton plantation could deliver their crops to port. Tollgates were placed at each end of the plank road to help pay for its construction and maintenance. By the time a road was paid for it had deteriorated so badly it could no longer be used.

By the early 1900s, fundamental changes in transportation needs were evident. People had previously lived on farms or in small rural communities close to their food supply. Larger cities were being built and inhabited, meaning now food and other needs must be transported to a centralized market. The advent of the automobile made this a much easier process.

"The Great Endurance Run" was sponsored to encourage bond issues for highway construction throughout the state. In 1909 Jacksonville was selected as the half way-point for the torturous four-day event which involved driving from Tampa to Jacksonville and return to Tampa. The "Endurance Run" became an annual event and in fact, was reenacted as late as 1984.

The influx of tourists into Florida during the early 1900s necessitated the increase of roadways. It was determined that in order to develop new roads the state was in dire need of cheap labor. This need spurred the use of Florida inmates, chain gangs were put to use. The gangs were comprised of criminals ranging from murderers to the mentally ill. The only segregation was race and those inmates having tuberculosis. Prisoners wore heavy shackles riveted permanently to their legs, which cut deep gashes into their flesh. Correctional officers guarded their charges with shotguns aimed to kill should a prisoner attempt escape. The expense of keeping the prisoners was nominal. They were fed only beans with molasses and slept on the ground protected from the elements with thin, lice infested blankets.

By the 1930s Florida's roads received a much-needed boost with the advent of a six-cent per gallon gas tax. Half of the proceeds went toward road construction and the remainder went to each county to repay existing debts. Of course most roads were still unpaved, the hard packed clay turned to a slick furrow of mud when it rained. Travelers often had to wander into nearby forests to cut pine saplings to pry their automobiles out of the muck or to fill in deep ruts along their route.

Speed was not the danger on the roadways of the 1930s that we experience today on modern interstates. Most vehicles could only achieve a top speed of 50 miles per hour. The major hazard on Florida roads were the result of an unusual source ~ livestock. Florida was a major cattle-producing state during this era and there were no laws requiring livestock to be corralled. Herds of cows were allowed to roam free across the countryside.

Imagine, if you will, tooling along in your automobile at a bustling thirty-five miles per hour when you suddenly encounter cows lounging in the road. Many wrecks resulted from these unexpected collisions. Blood, guts and cow pies would be splattered on every surface from roadway to automobile. Fortunately Florida's Thirtieth Governor had the foresight to introduce legislation known as the "fence law." Thanks to Governor Fuller Warren who enacted this law requiring cattle to be contained. Thus removing the common cow hazard from Florida's roadways. Even though the 1949 legislation kept cows off the roads, chickens were not included. Feathers continued to fly.

Modern highways began to become a reality in the 1940s. Federal funds were made available, the evolution of modern transportation and the beginnings of paved highways made travel easier. Florida's tourism flourished and the now cattle free roadways were crowded with a newly discovered species, "snowbirds".

LINE OF INTRENCHMENTS
1862-1865
Just East of here began
The Line of Intrenchments
Eighth Maine and
Sixth Connecticut Infantry
Federal Army of Occupation

**Southwest corner of Union Railroad Station,
at Prime F. Osborne III Convention Center entrance, 1000 Waters Avenue, Jacksonville
D8 ~ GPS Coordinates: 30.327439, -81.669965**

Although Florida was not the site of numerous battles during the Civil War, it did play an integral part for both the Confederacy and the Union. Jacksonville, by all accounts, was a city divided. Union sympathizers believed the institution of slavery wrong and felt the need to keep the nation whole. Confederate supporters clung to the right to own slaves and thought individual states should have the option to decide their own slavery issues. Florida voted by majority to join the Confederacy in 1861.

Florida dispatched as many a militia of fifteen thousand troops to fight for the Confederacy, however approximately twelve hundred white men and as many former slaves opted to stand for the Union. The ability to use Florida's rivers and harbors as shipping routes for supplies to the Confederacy and the abundance of beef cattle, hogs and other food made the state a great asset to the southern cause.

Jacksonville was repeatedly taken and lost by both sides of the war. Few buildings were left untouched by the retreating armies who always set the torch to any structure left standing. The Union regarded Jacksonville as an important occupation to interrupt the line of supplies to the Confederacy.

The Fourth Georgia Cavalry comprised of two hundred seventy-seven men and three artillery guns faced the Eighth Maine and the Sixth Connecticut Infantry Regiments at Jacksonville on March 27, 1863. Some fifteen hundred African Americans of the First and Second South Carolina Volunteers joined the Union forces. The northern troops were firmly entrenched at Jacksonville and the Forth Georgia Cavalry was determined to break the blockade. The following are the orders that guided the South Carolina Volunteers:

HEADQUARTERS, BEAUFORT, S. C.,
March 5, 1863

COLONEL, —You will please proceed with your command, the First and Second Regiments South Carolina Volunteers, which are now embarked upon the steamers *John Adams*, *Boston*, and *Burnside*, to Fernandina, Florida.

Relying upon your military skill and judgment. I shall give you no special directions as to your procedure after you leave Fernandina. I expect, however, that you will occupy Jacksonville, Florida, and intrench yourselves there.

The main objects of your expedition are to carry the proclamation of freedom to the enslaved; to call all loyal men into the service of the United States; to occupy as much of theState of Florida as possible with the forces under your command; and to neglect no means consistent with the usages of civilized warfare to weaken, harass, and annoy those who are in rebellion against the Government of the United States.

Trusting that the blessing of our Heavenly Father will rest upon your noble enterprise,

I am yours, sincerely,

R. SAXTON,
Brig.-Gen., Mil. Gov. Dept. of the South.

By February 1864, Union General Truman Seymore marched out of Jacksonville toward Lake City with the intent to disrupt the main railroad depot located there. He was met by Rebel troops of Georgia and Florida volunteers in the little railway depot at Olustee. The Battle of Olustee was Florida largest battle during the entire Civil War. The Confederacy soundly defeated Federal troops sending them scurrying again back to Jacksonville and the railroad remained open. Angered by their defeat at Olustee, Union troops retaliated by destroying farms and slaughtering entire herds of cattle along their trek to Jacksonville.

Rumors of the south's imminent defeat began to filter into Florida by early spring 1865. Though every Union offensive in Florida had been deflected, Florida's Governor John Milton was keenly aware of the dire straits of the Confederacy. Florida troops were rapidly declining due to the death toll, battle wounds and disease. Milton was inconsolable when Confederate President Jefferson Davis requested more of Florida's sons be offered up to the defeated southern cause.

Governor Milton, his wife and son traveled to Marianna to inspect the destruction of area farms when he received word that several Confederate soldiers had raided Tallahassee in an attempt to kidnap the Governor. The men had left the army to plant crops for their families suffering at home and had escaped after being charged with desertion. They hoped by getting the attention of the Governor, that he might be sympathetic to their plight. They were executed before Milton's arrived to intervene.

So grief-stricken over the losing Confederate cause and its effect on Florida's citizenry, Governor John Milton retreated to his Sylvania mansion, firmly closed the door of his study and committed suicide. Eight days following Milton's death, Confederate General Robert E. Lee surrendered his sword at Appomattox Courthouse. Small Rebel divisions refused to accept the south's defeat and hid for a time in the dense forests, marshes and inland swamps of Florida.

Confederate President Jefferson Davis and Secretary of the Confederate Navy, Stephen Mallory were captured en route to Florida. Secretary of the Confederate Treasury Judah Benjamin managed to escape by sailboat out of Sarasota Bay. It is said that the entire Confederate Treasury was buried near Newberry, though no one has ever discovered its whereabouts.

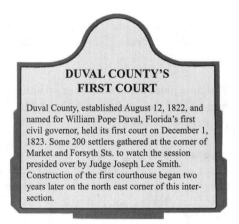

Northwest corner of Forsyth and Market Streets, Jacksonville
D9 ~ GPS Coordinates: 30.327367, -81.656479

The first council under Governor William Pope Duval's administration created Duval County on August 12, 1822. Formerly a part of St. Johns County, Duval boundaries reached from Suwanee River in the west toward the St. Johns River as it flowed to the Atlantic Ocean to the southeast then to the St. Marys River and Georgia state line in the north. Nassau County was eventually created from a part of Duval County. Jacksonville was listed as the Duval County seat.

The 30th of November 1823 saw Jacksonville filled to the rafters. Every available bed and nook was filled from Mrs. Sarah Waterman's Inn to Abraham Bellamy's law office. W. G. Dawson spread blankets on the floor of his store for people to sleep, private residences threw open their doors and invited travelers in. Darkness fell on the city packed with spectators. The event was a first in Duval County history – Court Day.

The Monday morning sun rose on December 1, 1823, and by 10:00 a.m. over two hundred people gathered near Market and Forsyth Streets to witness the first session of court in Duval County. Standing beneath the trees, the crowd listened intently to hear the call of "Here ye, Here ye" that signified the opening of court and appearance of Judge Joseph L. Smith.

From the assembled crowd a Grand Jury of men was chosen. They were required to reappear the following day to hear the first case. The first civil case was that of Ephraim Harrison versus John D. Vaughan. Unfortunately documentation does not reveal the nature of the case but Judge Smith conveyed enough importance on the issue that he continued the action to the next court session.

Court Days were exciting for the town folk. Settlers from the rural areas would make a special trek into town for the event, whether they had business with the court or not. The people gathered to trade in the local stores hear the "news" of town or horse trade with one another. When the town crier sounded the call to order, the people amassed for court. Their attention was riveted on the business of the court out of little more than shear curiosity.

Court continued to be held under the trees until 1825 when John Warren constructed a two-story building at the corner of Bay and Newnan Streets. The lower floor was used as a residence and later the space was divided adding a store to the location. The upper floor, consisting of only one room housed Superior Court. Unfortunately, Warren's second floor "courthouse" was little better than standing bareheaded underneath the trees. There were no sash[12] windows in the space, therefore the room was open to the elements of wind and rain.

John Brady donated property at the northwest corner of Market and Forsyth Street, which was valued at the considerable sum of fifteen dollars, for the construction of a proper courthouse. Construction did not begin until 1825, though the citizenry volunteered and had a frame for the structure erected in just two days. The courthouse remained at this stage for three years. Though in 1826 and court was held in the basement for a time. By 1829, the structure was nearing completion when the city realized they were out of funding. They petitioned the United States government for assistance and an agreement was struck where the government paid rent to use the facility for federal cases. The government was not a very good tenant, often failing to pay rent in a timely manner. Jacksonville continued to feel the pinch of a tight budget and the courthouse was left uncompleted.

Townsmen Joseph B. Lancaster, Isaiah Hart and William Mills approached the Territorial Legislature for permission to run a lottery to raise the additional six thousand dollars required to finish the courthouse construction. The scheme was approved. It is understood that these men were all church members in good standing, one was even a church deacon and therefore the inference is that the lottery was not considered gambling during this time. Though it does seem odd that during a time of prosperity when planning was in motion for the construction of a seventy five thousand dollar bank building and a million-dollar railway system for Jacksonville, the local government opposed a special tax levy to raise a mere six thousand dollars for the completion of the courthouse. The courthouse was finally completed in the early 1840s. Funds were appropriated through a scrip issue[13].

Federal troops burned the Duval County Courthouse on March 29, 1863.

SITE OF BLOCKHOUSE
Here stood the Blockhouse
erected for the defense of the
settlers
against the indians
during the Seminole War
1835-1842

On northeast corner of Monroe and Ocean Streets, Jacksonville
D10 ~ GPS Coordinates: 30.328225, -81.655959

Isaiah David Hart, founder of Jacksonville, feared for the city's settlers during the Second Seminole War. He felt the need for a fortification where citizens could retreat in the event that Native American's led an attack on Jacksonville. Obviously Hart's campaign was successful; the small building was completed in 1836.

Today when one hears the word blockhouse, we would assume a structure of concrete block was built. However, there was no concrete during this period and the fortification hardly looked like anything we would imagine. The building appeared more like a log cabin situated on pylons raising it well off the ground. The upper room extended well over the base. This feature made it possible for gunmen to shoot down on raiders through holes in the floor if they attempted to sneak into the structure from below. Portholes on every side allowed for the armed settlers to fire on approaching attackers.

The entrance was a door placed in the floor of the building with a ladder extending to the ground. After all of the residents were safely inside the ladder could be drawn up and the entrance sealed with shutters. The blockhouse was located at the very edge of Jacksonville. Little else was beyond the structure other than vast wilderness. Today the blockhouse, if it still existed, would be only five blocks from "Jacksonville Landing," the city's shopping mecca, on the northeast corner of Ocean and Monroe Streets.

Every rumor of Native American presence sent the settlers scurrying to the blockhouse. Sentries would be posted and the citizens would huddle together until they felt the threat had passed. The Seminole raided the Mandarin settlement and various homesteads to the west of the city, though they never attacked Jacksonville. The blockhouse was never fired upon in anger throughout its entire history.

When the Second Seminole War came to an end in 1842, the blockhouse was used for other purposes. The First Baptist Church held services there during its early days in 1838. For fifteen years the blockhouse remained intact.

The building was burned in the Great Fire of Jacksonville in 1901 and rebuilt in 1902. Through the years the structure has been remodeled and enlarged several times. At one point a Winn Dixie grocery store occupied the original blockhouse site which is today home to the Duval County Supervisor of Elections Office.

THE BEGINNING

Here at the foot of Market St. stood a bay tree, which served as the starting point for the original survey of Jacksonville in June 1822. Market was the first street laid off and named. A total of 20 squares were platted, bounded by Ocean, Duval, Catherine and Bay Sts. One of the first lots sold for $12 and was in the center of the present courthouse block.

Bay Street on City Hall grounds, Jacksonville
D11 ~ GPS Coordinates: 30.325350, -81.654527

Isaiah David Hart set up camp near a little community called Cow Ford in January of 1821. His meager homestead consisted of a cotton cloth tent near the shore of the murky St. Johns River. The site would be located at what is today the end of Liberty Street. If you can imagine, the total population at this time was two settlers then with the addition of Isaiah, the popular soared to three. The only other establishment was a mercantile. Isaiah continued to live in his humble abode until a small cabin could be completed. Once the cabin was in place, he moved his family from St. Marys, Georgia.

Isaiah Hart was determined to build a townsite and approached his neighbor, John Brady with the idea. Though Brady was unenthusiastic about the plan, he finally acquiesced and agreed to donate property essential for the street design. The plan nearly came to an untimely demise when Brady and Isaiah could not agree where exactly the borders of their properties began and ended. Lewis Hogans, another early Cow Ford settler, managed to serve as a mediator and helped to resolve the issue. It was decided that a large bay tree standing at the foot of present day Market Street, on the banks of the St. Johns River would be the starting point for the town survey.

The survey began in June 1822, conducted by David Solomon Hill Miller who was Captain of the St. Johns River Rural Militia. The names of the streets today remain as they were christened in 1822. Market Street was the first to be situated; though the rationale for the moniker has been lost, no market was located at this site. It was reported, with skepticism, that Bay Street was named for a picturesque tree on the riverbank. Liberty and Washington Streets were patriotic symbols of the original settlers. Newnan was named for Colonel Daniel

Newnan, who gained fame for his battle with Indian King Payne in central Florida and later was appointed Inspector General of Georgia. General John Forsyth, United States Minister to Spain, led negotiations for the acquisition of Florida was memorialized with Forsyth Street. Adams for then Secretary of State (and later United States President), John Quincy Adams. Adams played a significant role during the fight for Florida's statehood. Monroe was named for President James Monroe and Duval Street got its name from Governor William P. Duval, first civil governor of Florida.

Miller's survey divided each town square into six lots, however, a problem with the original plan was suddenly evident. According to the plan John Brady's house on Square One would be located in the middle of the street. To save Brady's dwelling another tier of lots was added to Square Number One. Thus Liberty and Market Streets are the only blocks in Jacksonville with eight lots versus the standard six.

John Warren dubbed the town, "Jacksonville." Warren, though not actually a resident of the city, greatly admired his former commander General Andrew Jackson and the town was named in his honor. General, later President, Jackson gained a great deal of notoriety as an Indian fighter and victor against the British during the Battle of New Orleans. He was at one time named Governor of Florida when Florida was first acquired from Spain. The title was in name only and lasted for a very short period of time until a proper governing system could be put into place. Records show that Jackson only visited the state three times and it is doubtful that he ever visited Jacksonville.

Miller's survey detailed the city plan with Catherine Street to the east, Duval to the north, Ocean to the west and at the St. Johns River on the southern perimeter. Laura Street, named for one of Isaiah Hart's daughters, was a hammock[14], which no one ever crossed. Main Street was then a muddy ooze of swamp; Liberty and Catherine Streets were bordered by a towering scenic bluff; to the east was marsh grass waving in the breeze and northward were fresh scented pine leading to flush of Hogans' Creek. The only passable land transportation was by way of Kings Road, the St. Johns River provided access to inland settlements as well as a direct link to the sea.

The first real estate transaction was a deal between John Brady and Stephen Eubanks. Brady sold Eubanks Lot 2, Square 1 including access to the river. The deed was transferred on July 1, 1822. Eubanks paid $12.00 for the property. The deed was registered, as all deeds were initially, in St. Johns County. Duval County was not created until August 12, 1822 and all deeds were edited to reflect the change.

Jacksonville's founder Isaiah Hart lived to see the population grow to two thousand inhabitants. He owned most of the property now known as the old city and most of what is today Springfield. His wife Nancy, who was an invalid, tragically burned to death in 1861 and Isaiah followed her shortly thereafter. The couple, along with their six children and a favored niece, was buried in a family crypt. The Hart burial site was vandalized in 1896 and everything of value was removed including the silver nameplates affixed to the coffins. The Great Jacksonville fire of 1901 severely damaged the crypt and rather than rebuild the charred ruins, the families' remains were moved to a lot in Evergreen cemetery. The original Hart family crypt was demolished. Isaiah left a prophetic inscription engraved on his original tomb, reading:

> When I am dead and in my grave,
> And these bones are all rotten;
> When this you see, remember me,
> That I may not be forgotten.

> May Isaiah Hart be long remembered.

SITE OF COW FORD

This narrow part of the St. Johns River, near a clear freshwater spring was a crossing point for Indians and early travelers. The Indian name Wacca Pilatka, meaning "Cow's Crossing", was shortened by the English to Cow Ford, and Jacksonville was known by this name for many years. This crossing was used by the English when they made an old Timucuan Indian Trail into King's Road.

Bay Street on grounds of the old Courthouse, Jacksonville
D12 ~ GPS Coordinates: 30.324916, -81.652799

There was a moment of silence in the action between the warring factions of France and Spain over control of Florida. It was 1764 and the English were beginning a short period of occupation. Florida was experiencing an infrequent peaceful period. British soldiers would occasionally camp on the high bluffs that sloped downward stretching toward the St. Johns River. The Spanish often described the area as daunting and heavily timbered with expansive live oaks, willowy palms swaying in breeze and fragrant wild orange trees.

At the base of what is today Liberty Street, a robust clear water spring gushed pure drinking water. The aquifer still to this day lies beneath the city of Jacksonville. A short distance from the river was home of a fading Native American village, the Timucua village of Ossachite.

The Timucua called the area "Wacca Pilatka" or place where the cows cross over. The English simplified the name to "Cow Ford". The ford was one of the most popular sites along the river located near the origin of Liberty Street across the river divide to its southern banks. Cow Ford was the settlement predecessor to Jacksonville, to be established in 1822.

From inland Cow Ford trailing southerly through St. Augustine and continuing to New Smyrna was a Timucuan footpath. Over the expanse of time the narrow trail became a well-trodden passage through the dense vegetation of the forest. Later mules bearing the packs of traders followed suit and the course became wider; ox carts altered the topography establishing a more passable road, eventually wagon trains then automobiles would traverse the Native American trail. The trail became King's Road.

England placed great pride in St. Johns County, though two months after Jacksonville's founding the county would be divided and Duval County established. The Marquis of Waterford was extended a King's grant of twenty thousand acres along the river between Pottsburg and Julington Creek. The tract of land was cultivated and became a profitable indigo plantation. Other plantations began to appear along this stretch of river near the ford.

In 1774, famed naturalist William Bartram visited Cow Ford and noted his observations during his time there. The river ferry was in operation hauling travelers across the expanse of ebony tinged river. Indigo plantations dotted the rivers edge and the population of white settlers near the ford, continued to expand choking out the Timucua.

Cow Ford gave way to Jacksonville, which became the county seat of Duval County in 1822. Though long after Jacksonville came to be, the name Cow Ford still hung on lips of her citizens.

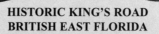

**HISTORIC KING'S ROAD
BRITISH EAST FLORIDA**

The King's Road, built by the British prior to the American Revolution began at the St. Mary's River, passed through Cow Ford (Jacksonville), crossed the St. John's River, it is believed, at present day Liberty Street, approximately one mile east of this marker, and continued south to New Smyrna.

During the Revolution, American troops used this route to make attacks on British forces. The most notable of these engagements was at Alligator Creek Bridge, 30 June 1778. Following this battle the invasion of Florida by American troops ceased.

1025 Museum Circle, Jacksonville
D13 ~ GPS Coordinates: 30.319970, -81.659991

Britain gained control of Florida in an exchange with Spain for Havana in 1763. The British gained control of Havana during the Seven Years' War with Spain. When Spain evacuated the Florida peninsula it was virtually deserted. The garrison at St. Augustine had fewer than five hundred houses.

The British had great plans for the territory. First Florida was split into two sections, east and west. St. Augustine would be the capital eastern and Pensacola, west. The Apalachicola River was the boundary line. The next order of business was to encourage settlers to establish homesteads in the wilderness territory.

The only way to encourage civilization was to establish means of transportation. The British planned to build a modern roadway. Previously roads were established using routes of Indian trails or game runs. This road would be the exception.

The Spanish originally began road construction in 1632, developing a road from today's New Smyrna north to St. Augustine. In 1763, the British began improving the road and extended it more than one hundred fifty miles north to Savannah, Georgia. The road was to be called, King's Road in honor of the King of England.

Agriculture and trade shipments were responsible for the development of most Florida towns. Jacksonville came to be due to accessibility of the King's Road crossing near Cow Ford, which had a ferry for transport across the St. Johns River. The British surveyed most of the land and coastline then attempted to begin trade with a group of Georgia Native Americans migrating into the area. The Seminoles or "wild ones" were of Creek descent.

During the same period, the British encouraged white settlers with offers of land and farming assistance. The British had little time to work with, their occupation only lasted for twenty years not enough time to develop the struggling colony. The American Revolution began in 1776, both east and west Florida remained loyal to the Britain Crown. Their alliance made little difference in the outcome of the war.

The only significant skirmish to take place along King's Road during the American Revolution was the battle at Alligator Creek Bridge. On June 30, 1778, a regiment of American Cavalry led by Colonel Elijah Clarke ambushed a column of British at Alligator Creek. The Americans were unable to break the line of four hundred fifty British Regulars combined with a detachment of South Carolina Royalists. Major James Marc Prevost led the British. Colonel Clarke was wounded and the Americans were forced to withdraw. The following day the British marched toward the St. Johns River. General Robert Howe, who was in command of the American forces' invasion into Florida, never attempted another attack.

Spain entered the Revolution on the side of the Americans and as allies to France in June 1779. The largest battle fought in Florida came in May 1781, the battle for Pensacola. Spain regained control of Florida with the peace treaty that ended the American Revolution in 1783. The King's Road remains today, following the very same path as it did in 1771 when the road was completed.

THE ST. JOHNS
A River of Many Names

Discovered by Juan Bono Quexos, 1520 - First named Rio de Corrientes by Spain - Explored by Pedro Menendez - Called Rivere de Mai by France, 1562-4 - San Mateo, Salamatoto and Picolata were among its other Spanish names - Its Indian name, Welaka, meant River of Lakes - San Juan, then St. Johns, its English version, replaced all other names by 1821 when Florida was ceded to the U.S. by Spain. The mighty river is famed in verse and story by Bartram, Wordsworth and Coleridge. Essential to the ecology of peninsula Florida - Rises just south of Lake Helen Blazes - Flows northward for most of its 276 mile length.

1025 Museum Circle, Jacksonville
D13 ~ GPS Coordinates: 30.319970, -81.659991

The St. Johns River has a distinctive and precise timeline outlined vividly by the evolution of its proper name. Before any white man of European descent placed a foot on the soil of Florida, the Timucuan Indians were there. The Timucuan held dear the river, which they called "Welaka" or in the English translation, the "River of Lakes."

When Spanish explorers, Francisco Gordillo and Pedro de Quexos, arrived in June of 1521 they named the tea like waters for St. John the Baptist. The explorers laid claim to the land at the mouth of the waterway for Spain and contrary to the orders of their superior, Lucas Vasquez Ayllon, the captains captured and enslaved one hundred and fifty Native Americans. Gordillo and Quexos attempted to return home with their human cargo to Santo Domingo, however, only Quexos arrived safely. Gordillo, his crew and the slaves packed in their bilge were lost at sea. Upon arrival, Diego Columbus headed an investigation concerning Quexos and Gordillo's slavery trade, ordering that the surviving Native Americans be returned to their home and freed.

Later, other Spanish seaman would travel the St. Johns, calling it the "Rio de Corrientes," meaning "River of Current." Though, like the others, this name was not destined to stand the test of time. In 1562, famed French mariner, Jean Ribault sailed the St. Johns. He chose the name "Riviere de Mai" or River of May, reportedly because he arrived on May 1st. When the Spanish marched inland from St. Augustine and slaughtered the French at Fort Caroline they again changed the watercourses' name, this time "San Mateo" was selected. San Mateo, Spanish for Saint Matthew, was used because the Feast of St. Matthew[15] was the day following their arrival, September 20.

The river was later renamed for a mission, San Juan de Puerto located near its mouth. The English translation simply means St. Johns River. And so it's been and remains today, the St. Johns River, through English, Confederate and American occupation.

Infamous botanist, traveler and explorer, William Bartram recorded the nuisances of the river in 1765 with his father and again on his own in 1774. His recollections, published in 1791 as "Travels," appear to be the definitive resource for information on the river lasting for more than two hundred years. By the 1800s, steamboats traveled the St. Johns creating a tourist mecca of north Florida. White clouds of smoke could be seen on the horizon from Charleston and Savannah as the steamers traveled weekly to Jacksonville and points south along the St. Johns.

The 1900s saw miles of the river floodplain16 drained for the cultivation of indigo, sugar cane, citrus and other cash crops. More than seventy percent of the marshland was lost due to agriculture and urban expansion. The trend prompted a commentary in "Parade of Diversities" published in 1943 to say of the St. Johns, "the 'Nile of the Americas' had lost its luster, its artistic legacies unseen to all but an enterprising few willing to re-learn just how impressive – and influential—this Florida river had once been."

The St. Johns begins its meandering trail out of the saw grass shallows of Lake Okeechobee and travels to greet the Atlantic Ocean just east of Jacksonville some three hundred ten miles away. Along the river's course are more than a dozen lakes are connected like a string of pearls over the miles of slowly moving black water. Lake Helen Blazes is one of the first lakes among the inland chain. The name for this lake is often written as Lake Hell 'n Blazes as in, "Where in hell 'n blazes am I?"

The river is unique in the fact that it runs northerly though strangely enough in times of drought has been known to reverse its flow. Salt water ebbs into the river from the Atlantic making the water brackish[17] for approximately one hundred sixty miles of its total length. The St. Johns is said to be salubrious[18], its waters capable of curing aliments varying from tuberculosis to insomnia.

A large number of wildlife species call the St. Johns River home; alligators, large mouth bass and various other fish species, blue heron, bald eagles, the list could go on and on. An interesting fact relates that the typically salt water dwelling Atlantic stingray has managed to inhabit the river. Stingrays have been found to be quite abundant in the St. Johns River, living, reproducing and completing their lifecycle in fresh water.

John James Audubon, noted illustrator, came to the river in 1832. The admired painter sketched magnificent portraits of the glossy ibis and great blue heron along the banks of the St. Johns. Audubon was only one of many authors, poets, artists and composers who lamented the beauty of the noted waterway. Poets William Cullen Bryant and Sidney Lanier; composer Frederick Delius; landscape painter Winslow Homer; and authors Harriet Beecher Stowe and Marjorie Kinnan Rawlings to name but a few. But perhaps Rawlings, author of "The Yearling" and "Cross Creek" said it best:

**The
ST. JOHN'S
RIVER
TODAY**

**LOCAL
MANATEE ART
PROJECT
AT RIVER
FRONT PARK**

"If I could have, to hold forever,
one brief place and time of beauty,
I think I might choose the night
on that high lonely bank above the St. Johns River."

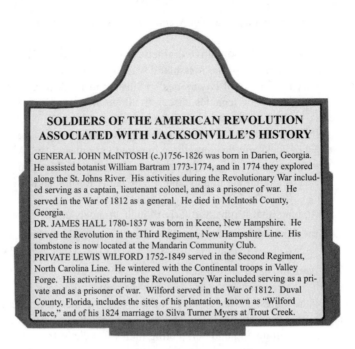

SOLDIERS OF THE AMERICAN REVOLUTION ASSOCIATED WITH JACKSONVILLE'S HISTORY

GENERAL JOHN McINTOSH (c.)1756-1826 was born in Darien, Georgia. He assisted botanist William Bartram 1773-1774, and in 1774 they explored along the St. Johns River. His activities during the Revolutionary War included serving as a captain, lieutenant colonel, and as a prisoner of war. He served in the War of 1812 as a general. He died in McIntosh County, Georgia.

DR. JAMES HALL 1780-1837 was born in Keene, New Hampshire. He served the Revolution in the Third Regiment, New Hampshire Line. His tombstone is now located at the Mandarin Community Club.

PRIVATE LEWIS WILFORD 1752-1849 served in the Second Regiment, North Carolina Line. He wintered with the Continental troops in Valley Forge. His activities during the Revolutionary War included serving as a private and as a prisoner of war. Wilford served in the War of 1812. Duval County, Florida, includes the sites of his plantation, known as "Wilford Place," and of his 1824 marriage to Silva Turner Myers at Trout Creek.

Behind Jacksonville Hilton, 1201 Riverplace Boulevard, Jacksonville
D14 ~ GPS Coordinates: 30.320067, -81.656650

East Florida was under British rule throughout the Revolutionary War. Spain had surrendered Florida in exchange of Hispaniola at the end of the Seven Years War in 1763 and the British maintained a strong hold here for just over twenty years. Florida was not exactly a hot bed of action during the Revolution; a total of three engagements were recorded.

The only significant battle fought in east Florida was perhaps the Battle at Thomas Creek. A historical marker dedicated to this altercation is located on the Duval ~ Nassau County line at the bridge crossing Thomas Creek. The article entitled appropriately Battle at Thomas Creek (Nassau County) recounts the battle as it occurred. But suffice it to say the Americans were soundly thrashed and several days later Colonel Samuel Elbert managed to rescue the survivors. About six months later, a lesser skirmish was fought at Alligator Creek. Today the area is known as Callahan, again the American rebels took a beating.

John McIntosh, before he attained the title General, accompanied William Bartram during his trek through north Florida. McIntosh was then a very young man of seventeen and the trip was an entertaining experience for him. Still a young man when the Revolutionary War began, McIntosh quickly ascended the officer ranks. Perhaps his significant family influence gave him a little shove up the ladder; his uncle Lachlan had once been leader of the entire military force in Georgia. Lachlan also had some staunch political opposition ending in a duel with Button Gwinnett who died several days later as a result. Because of the controversy concerning this altercation Lachlan was sent to serve with General George Washington at Valley Forge.

McIntosh was eventually given command of his own contingent. Fort Morris, near Midway, Georgia, was his garrison and it was here that the young man proved his metal. Against tremendous odds he defended his fort against the British. When ordered to surrender his command, he responded:

"We would rather perish in a vigorous defense than accept your proposal sir. We sir, are fighting
the battle of America and therefore disdain to remain neutral til its fate is determined. As to surrendering the Fort receive this reply, Come and take it!"

From that time on the garrison was known as "Fort Defiance!"

Teenager James Hall joined the Continental forces late into the war but managed to see action at Yorktown in 1781. Following the Revolution, Hall completed his training as a physician and returned to north Florida. He was the first known physician to practice medicine in Duval County. A historical marker detailing his life was placed in the Mandarin area. Dr. Hall was given a land grant in 1790 near Cow Ford, today known as Jacksonville. He was active in medical and civic affairs in the area and managed to amass a substantial amount of property through grants and as a result of his marriage to Eleanor Pritchard.

Unfortunately in 1810, Dr. Hall was banished from Florida by the Spanish as a result of his participation in Florida-Georgia Rebellion. Dr. James Hall returned to Florida three years later and continued to practice medicine until December 25, 1837 when he passed away. He is buried in Mandarin near what is today the Mandarin Community Center.

Private Lewis Wilford was noted during the Revolutionary War as having served with Captain Coleman's Company, Second Regiment North Carolina. The detachment wintered at Valley Forge alongside General Washington's men.

After the war, Wilford returned to his Bertie County, North Carolina home where he married Cloe Holley in 1781, nothing further is known of this union and no children are listed. Reportedly Lewis Wilford served with Captain Jackson's Company of Florida Volunteers during the War of 1812. Wilford must have been quite a man for during the war he would have been approximately sixty-one years old. His second wife, Silva Turner hailed from Trout Creek (Jacksonville, Florida). According to the state census, at the time of their marriage Lewis Wilford was seventy-three years old. Mrs. Wilford was twenty-six. Over the next three years the happy couple had three children. One would think that the Wilford marriage was doomed to be a short one, mainly due to the advanced age of the groom. However, the couple were wed for twenty-five years when Lewis Wilford died in Duval County at the age of ninety-eight. Life begins at...

The British deeded Florida back to Spain after twenty-five years, with the Peace Treaty of 1783. Florida became a United States territory thirty-six years later and on March 3, 1845 was named the 27th state in the Union.

BLUE STAR MEMORIAL HIGHWAY

A tribute to the Armed Forces that have defended the United States of America.

Holmesdale & Ridgewood, Jacksonville
D15 ~ GPS Coordinates: 30.305900, -81.637217

The Garden Club of Jacksonville was founded in 1922. The first meeting was held at the Riverside home of Mrs. Ninah May Holden Cummer. Although the first meeting attracted only twenty members, the Garden Club of Jacksonville has grown to a hefty membership of over fifteen hundred today. Membership is divided into fifty-seven local clubs called circles.

The original Club was founded in order to pursue interests in gardening research and civic planting. Meetings were held on a rotation basis at various members' homes because they had no permanent clubhouse, therefore the enrollment was restricted to twenty members. In a very short time word of the club spread and within months over one hundred women had requested membership, it was at that time the idea of garden circles was formulated.

Each circle consists of approximately twenty members and gathers monthly from October until May. From the original seven circles, the Garden Club has grown to include more than fifty-seven circles to encompass neighborhoods all over the greater Jacksonville area. The Garden Club of Jacksonville was one of four Clubs uniting to establish the Florida Federation of Garden Clubs. The Florida Federation was, at one time, the largest Associations of Garden Clubs in the world having more than three thousand members and one hundred forty five circles.

The early years were geared toward community projects. The formation and revitalization of Jacksonville parks was an ambitious endeavor. The Jacksonville Garden Club was instrumental in an effort to preserve many of the city's ancient oaks and adhere to the motto, "Save the Trees and Make Jacksonville an Evergreen City."

As the Jacksonville Garden Club continued to blossom, it became quite apparent that a clubhouse was the next order of business. Much planning and fundraising went into the project when finally the clubhouse located on Riverside Avenue became a reality. The first building was temporary housing known as the Exhibition Building until the official Clubhouse was dedicated on January 3, 1948. With the continued growth of the organization, a Ballroom was added ten years later. Their works are evident in the alluring city parks, along her streets and in private gardens. After more than eighty years, the Garden Club of Jacksonville continues to bring beauty to the city.

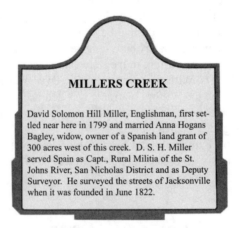

MILLERS CREEK

David Solomon Hill Miller, Englishman, first settled near here in 1799 and married Anna Hogans Bagley, widow, owner of a Spanish land grant of 300 acres west of this creek. D. S. H. Miller served Spain as Capt., Rural Militia of the St. Johns River, San Nicholas District and as Deputy Surveyor. He surveyed the streets of Jacksonville when it was founded in June 1822.

Atlantic Boulevard at Mayfair Road, east of Miller's Creek Bridge, Jacksonville
D16 ~ GPS Coordinates: 30.305983, -81.627717

Isaiah D. Hart is unilaterally considered the father of Jacksonville, of course with the help of John Brady and Lewis Zachariah Hogans. Hart was a native Georgia patriot and a dreamer. He imagined Cow Ford could evolve into a thriving city on the picturesque banks of the St. Johns River. Brady owned the only ferry service crossing the St. Johns River in these parts and Hogans' wife, the widow Maria Taylor, owned the city. Brady and Hogans did not quite share Hart's vision, at first.

Hogans and Hart conducted the first high dollar real estate deal in the area. Hart traded $72 worth of cattle for an eighteen-acre plot of land. He built a log cabin for his family on the south side of what was to be Forsyth Street between Market and Newnan. Hundreds of real estate transactions have transpired over the years but undoubtedly Isaiah Hart made the best deal.

By 1822, the three men had come to terms but the question remained; where to begin? Hogans suggested a well-known landmark, a big shady bay tree near the market hence resulting in the names Bay and Market Streets. Surveyor David Solomon Hill Miller was assigned the task of gridding the city blocks and streets.

Miller, Captain of the St. Johns Militia unit from San Nicholas across the river, was husband of Spanish land-grant owner Anna Hogans Bagley. Notice the reoccurring family names, obviously a certain amount of nepotism came to play. Francis Ross, Benjamin Chaires and John Bellamy completed the survey company. Chaires was the first judge for Jacksonville and also conducted the survey of Georgia's first capital at Milledgeville.

The eventual plat covered a span of twenty blocks and was titled "Hart's Map of Jacksonville." Isaiah Hart's dreams for the future and ideas for a budding fortune were taking shape. John Warren suggested a more dignified name for the city known as Cow Ford, Jacksonville for General Andrew Jackson was selected. Jackson was the first governor of Florida, though he only served for a very short time after the Spanish relinquished control of the territory. He agreed to serve until a government could be established, which he did. General Jackson never visited the city bearing his name.

David Solomon Hill Miller was paid for his survey work with several Jacksonville lots consisting of the property between Liberty and Washington, Forsyth and Bay streets, extending across the St. Johns River to his militia headquarters at San Nicholas. Miller wasn't given the honor of naming any of the streets. His daughters eventually married lumbermen partners, David L. Palmer and Darius Ferris. Many of the St. Nicholas area streets bear the names of Miller descendants today including Palmer Terrace, Holmesdale, Call and Nicholson streets.

John Brady left Jacksonville for Alabama; Lewis Hogans remained but died penniless. Of the trio only Isaiah Hart, with his dreams of grandeur, prospered. He named numerous streets of downtown Jacksonville after his children including Laura, Julia and Ocean for his son Ossian. Hart died in Jacksonville an old man in 1861 and was buried at the intersection of State and Laura streets. Vandals desecrated Hart's final resting-place and the tragic fire of 1901 finished the job. The founding father's remains were removed to Evergreen Cemetery. Isaiah Hart's true monument, laying very much the way David Solomon Hill Miller planned it, remains at the heart of Jacksonville.

BLUE STAR
MEMORIAL HIGHWAY

A tribute to the
Armed Forces
that have defended the
United States of America.

San Pablo Park, Jacksonville Beach
D17 ~ GPS Coordinates: 30.288416, -81.393328

The National Garden Clubs, Inc. have had a program in place to honor service men and women since 1945. It's the Blue Star Memorial Program, and it began with the planting of 8,000 Dogwood trees by the New Jersey Council of Garden Clubs in 1944 as a living memorial to veterans of World War 11. The following year the National Council of State Garden Clubs, as it was called at the time, adopted the program and began a Blue Star Highway system, which covers thousands of miles across the Continental United States, Alaska and Hawaii. A large metal Blue Star Memorial Highway Marker was placed at appropriate locations along the way.

The program was expanded to include all men and women who had served, were serving or would serve in the armed services of the United States. Memorial Markers and By-Way markers were added to the Highway Markers, to be used at locations such as National cemeteries, parks, veteran's facilities and gardens.

The Blue Star became an icon in World War 11 and was seen on flags and banners in homes for sons and daughters away at war, as well as in churches and businesses. This program has been active all through the years to the present, a fitting tribute always and especially now. Many states and regions have been very dedicated, but there is room for growth in some areas. A "Guidelines" booklet can be ordered from Member Services for $5.00, which explains all procedures, including awards available to clubs. I would be happy to be of assistance at any time.

ALL TO SEE, LEST WE FORGET,
THOSE WHO HELP TO KEEP US FREE

Maria Nahom,
National Garden Clubs, Inc.,
Blue Star Memorial Chairman

DOOLITTLE'S 1922 RECORD FLIGHT

Florida's mild climate made it attractive to aviation pioneers. This area, known until 1925 as Pablo Beach, served as takeoff or terminal point for several early coast-to-coast flights, the first of which occurred in 1912 and required 115 days to reach Pablo Beach from Pasadena, California. On September 4, 1922, Army Lieutenant James H. ("Jimmy") Doolittle piloted a DeHavilland DH-4 biplane from Pablo Beach to San Diego in an elapsed time of 22 hours and 35 minutes. He made one stop during his flight for fuel, at Kelly Field in San Antonio, Texas. Doolittle's feat established a new speed record and helped demonstrate the practicality of transcontinental flight. Jimmy Doolittle remained active in aviation. During World War II, he led the first American bombing raid against the Japanese home islands, a daring stroke which provided a psychological lift to the nation's war effort.

San Pablo Park, Jacksonville Beach
D18 ~ GPS Coordinates: 30.288422, -81.393247

Born James Harold Doolittle, the son of Frank H. and Rosa C. Shephard Doolittle, on December 14, 1896 in Alameda, California. Jimmy, as he was called, grew up in Los Angeles. Known as a fast punching boy in his teen years, Jimmy never ran from a street fight. After a subsequent arrest for brawling, he decided to try his hand at amateur boxing. Jimmy became the amateur flyweight champion of the West Coast. He attended Los Angeles Junior College for a short time until turning his attention to the University of California School of Mines.

After a year at the university, Jimmy again dropped out of school to enlist as a flying cadet in the Aviation Section of the Signal Corps Reserve in October 1917. He trained at the School of Military Aeronautics, University of California and Rockwell Field California. While there he met and married the love of his life, Josephine Daniels, on December 24, 1917.

During World War I, Jimmy served as a flight instructor in the Air Corps. When the war ended, he was faced with the decision to return to college or stay in the military. The choice was easily made, he decided to continue flying. Jimmy honed his skills in air aerobatics, performing the first outside loop, and became a regular on the air service show circuit. In 1921, Jimmy flew with the First Provisional Air Brigade under the direction of General Billy Mitchell. The brigade performed bombing demonstrations to show the effectiveness of air power against battleships.

On September 4, 1922, Lieutenant James H. "Jimmy" Doolittle piloted a U. S. Army Air Service de Havilland DH-4B on the first coast-to-coast flight in less than twenty-four hours. The DH-4, originally a British combat plane, was redesigned in the United States in 1917 for the Liberty engine. It carried the nickname "The Flaming Coffin" due to the reported ease with which it burst into flames. In reality, only eight of the thirty-three

DH-4s manufactured in the United States lost in combat burned as they fell. Jimmy often flew at speeds exceeding one hundred miles per hour on his coast-to-coast adventures, traveling a distance of two thousand one hundred sixty-three miles from Pablo Beach, Florida to San Diego, California, in twenty-one hours and twenty minutes. The only brief stop was a required refueling at Kelly Field, Texas. He received the Distinguished Flying Cross for this feat; the citation credited Doolittle with demonstrating "the possibility of moving Air Corps units to any portion of the United States in less than 24 hours."

Jimmy was determined to pursue an engineering degree and in 1922, he achieved his goal. In 1925, Jimmy received one of the first doctorates in aeronautics ever awarded from the Massachusetts Institute of Technology, writing his final dissertation on the effects of the wind velocity gradient on flying. His education provided the credentials to serve as an engineering test pilot at McCook Field in Dayton, Ohio, the army's aviation test facility, and later the Navy's facility at Mitchell Field, New York. He was one of the first scientific test pilots, working on aircraft acceleration tests and the development of instruments that would enable pilots to fly when they were unable to see the ground called "blind flying."

In 1925, he won the Schneider Marine Trophy while flying a Curtiss seaplane and the next day he set a world speed record of two hundred forty-five miles per hour using the same plane. He received the Mackay Trophy for these feats in 1929. On September 24, 1929, Jimmy made the first "blind" flight, taking off, flying a set course, and landing while blindfolded beneath a fabric hood. He received the Harmon Trophy for the feat.

The demands of family life compelled Jimmy to accept an offer from the Shell Oil Company managing their Aviation Department at a salary of three times his military pay. In 1930, he resigned his active commission and became a major in the Air Corps Reserve. Jimmy frequently returned to active duty for test flights and to serve on special committees. At Shell, he campaigned for the development of one hundred-octane aviation fuel.

Jimmy won the Bendix Trophy Race in 1931 and became the only pilot, with the exception of Wiley Post, to win both the Bendix and the Thompson trophies within the same year. He won the latter while flying the Granville Gee Bee, a strangely shaped airplane that was known as a flying death trap. Jimmy could fly anything with wings, but was happy to walk away from the *Gee Bee*, reportedly he called it the most dangerous plane he had ever flown.

As the United States mobilized for World War II in 1940, Air Corps Chief of Staff Hap Arnold recalled Jimmy to active duty, assigning him to work with auto manufacturers on the conversion of their plants to airplane production. After the bombing of Pearl Harbor, he requested to be moved to flight duty. His request was denied, Jimmy was transferred to Army Air Force Headquarters in Washington with a promotion to lieutenant colonel. He worked on special assignments until he was called into Arnold's office one day in late January to be briefed on a proposed raid of Tokyo. Arnold asked Lieutenant Colonel Doolittle to investigate aircraft to be used in the raid, he agreed to do the research with the stipulation that he lead the mission. The offer was accepted.

On April 18, 1942, sixteen Mitchell B-25 medium bombers took off from the aircraft carrier *USS Hornet* positioned seven hundred fifty miles off the coast of Japan. The men knew upon take off that the chances of returning from the flight were not in their favor. The squadron dropped their bombs on Tokyo, then flew on to China, where most of the crews had to bail out. The raid caused little damage to Tokyo, but the boost to American war morale was great. Jimmy received the Medal of Honor, presented to him by President Roosevelt at the White House, for planning and leading this successful operation. His citation read:

> "For conspicuous leadership above and beyond the call of duty, involving personal valor and intrepidity at an extreme hazard to life. With the apparent certainty of being forced to land in enemy territory or to perish at sea, Lt. Col. Doolittle personally led a squadron of Army bombers, manned by volunteer crews, in a highly destructive raid on the Japanese mainland."

Jimmy spent the remainder of the war as commander of various air force units. He led the 12th Air Force during the invasion of North Africa, the Strategic Air Force during the invasion of Italy and in late 1944 he was promoted to lieutenant general, assigned to the 8th Air Force in England and the Pacific. He was known as a good commander of bombing groups, frequently inspiring his men by flying with them. Always a proponent of daytime, precision bombing and whose philosophy it was as a "basic American principle" to harm as few civilians during war as possible.

While with the 8th Air Force, stationed in England, Jimmy was excited about the opportunity to be the first commander to lead air raids on the capital cities of all three of the enemies. He had led the first bombing raids on both Tokyo and Rome and when the 8th began to organize the first raid on Berlin, Jimmy was confident that he would lead this raid as well. Unfortunately because Jimmy had been briefed on several top-secret operations, his superiors decided that his capture was too great a risk and he would not be allowed to fly over enemy territory. Jimmy understood the reasoning yet he was very disappointed.

After the war, Jimmy retired from the air force and returned to Shell Oil as a vice president. He continued to serve the air force on special committees concerning space and ballistic missiles issues, chaired the board of Space Technology Laboratories and served as the first president of the Air Force Association. During the late 1950s, as the last chairman of the National Advisory Committee for Aeronautics, he laid the foundation for its successful transformation into the new National Aeronautics and Space Administration.

During a ceremony at the White House on April 4, 1985, Jimmy was promoted to the position of general and given his fourth star. Eight years later, General James Harold Doolittle died at the age of ninety-seven. He was buried in Section 7-A of Arlington National Cemetery beside his loving wife of seventy-one years, Josephine Daniels Doolittle.

Pioneers of flight rarely saw old age often dying in fiery accidents, but Jimmy Doolittle survived to live a full and illustrious life. When asked the secret of his longevity in such a high-risk profession, he replied that he never took an uncalculated risk. After contemplating a moment, Jimmy added, he wouldn't want to live his life over because "I could never be so lucky again."

SAN PABLO PARK

U.S. 90 (Beach Boulevard), San Pablo Park, Jacksonville Beach
D18 ~ GPS Coordinates: 30.288422, -81.393247

The details surrounding the establishment of Ruby, Florida were meticulously preserved during a 1939 interview with Eleanor Kennedy Scull. Eleanor was 78 years old at the time and was described as a tall, thin woman with sparkling brown eyes, graying hair with a hint of its natural red and clear porcelain skin. True to her red haired nature, Eleanor was spunky and full of life. She was ready to pass on her story of the early days at the beach.

The story began in 1872 when William Edward Scull arrived in Florida from Ohio seeking his fortune. Seven years later William married a local girl, Eleanor Kennedy, and the couple built their home in the Lackawanna Springs area, today known as Edison Avenue.

By 1883, an enterprising group of Jacksonville businessmen decided to construct a railway to the beaches east of the city. F. F. L'Engle was commissioned to survey the railroad right of way to the coast. L'Engle hired William Scull who was a civil engineer and surveyor. The Jacksonville and Atlantic Railway Company were chartered in 1883. Sixteen and a half miles of narrow gauge railway would run from south Jacksonville to the beach.

The Scull family, which now included a daughter named Ruby, moved to the beach where William could be near his work. The family moved into a tent on the beach in October 1884. When the Scull family arrived the settlement had been laid out but there were no other residents. They promptly named the settlement "Ruby" for their young daughter and proceeded to erect another tent for use as a general supply store. The store was a necessity for workers at the beach, the trip from there to Jacksonville, before the railway, consisted of a two-hour buggy ride to Mayport then an additional three hours traveling up the St. Johns River by boat. A steamboat called *Katy Spencer*, captained by future Florida governor Napoleon Broward, delivered supplies and mail once a week from Jacksonville.

Eleanor Scull tells many amusing stories of life at the beach. She stated that early settlers at the beach lived mostly on fish, while that fact isn't surprising, she went on to say that the demand for canned salmon and sardines was so great, the store could hardly keep it in stock. Another anecdote centers on a dinner guest, F. F. L'Engle. It happened that the very evening L'Engle was invited for dinner, there came a torrential rain. Unfortunately the Scull's kitchen/dining room had a palmetto frond thatched roof, which leaked profusely. L'Engle asked William Scull why he didn't put a solid roof on the kitchen, Scull replied, "Well, when it's raining, I can't; and when it's dry we don't need it."

The Jacksonville and Atlantic Railway Company offered the Scull family a home site on the beach to build a permanent dwelling in 1884. By spring the home was well under construction. One spring afternoon a German barque[19] sprang a leak and was forced to beach itself at the mouth of the St. Johns. The ship was loaded with mahogany lumber and when the ship struck the shore, the timber washed overboard. William Scull quickly gathered as much of the wood as possible and tethered it to two rafts to haul it to their beach lot. The remainder of the lumber was washed out in the river and lost. Thus it was that the Scull home had underpinning and windowsills of solid mahogany. Years later the house became known locally as the "Dixie House."

On November 12, 1884, the railroad offered lots along the beach for sale. Seventy-four men took advantage of the sale and thirty-four lots were sold. A total of seven thousand five hundred fourteen dollars was collected that day, meaning the lots sold at a cost of two hundred twenty-one dollars each. Can you imagine beachfront property at that price; today that would only equal a fraction of the monthly payment.

Eleanor Scull served as Postmistress for Ruby in 1884. When the mail arrived at Mayport the long trip had to be made by horse and buggy over the route returning the post to Ruby Beach. In the spring of 1885, the first train chugged its way to beach and a weekly mail service was established. As the population began to grow, the Railroad Company now known as the Jacksonville and Beach Railway began a daily mail service. The Post Office and settlement became known San Pablo after the San Pablo River to the west. Later the name was shortened to Pablo Beach.

Mr. John Christopher built Pablo Beach's first resort, which was completed by mid 1886. It was an impressive multi-story wooden structure and called the Murray Hall Hotel. The hotel had an occupancy of three hundred fifty guests and the estimated cost of construction was a whopping one hundred fifty thousand dollars. The hotel advertised such modern amenities as an elevator, electric bells, hot, cold and sulfur baths, a tavern, bowling and billiards.

Murray Hall it was beautifully furnished and was rumored to be the finest hotel on the Atlantic coast. Tragedy struck during the midnight hour of August 7, 1890 when a fire in the boiler room of the hotel erupted and the exquisite Murray Hall Hotel was completely destroyed. Mrs. Christopher was noted as saying that the hotel had seen a loss in profits over its four years of existence and quite possibly the fire was a blessing in disguise. Strangely enough for a considerable time after the fire, an artesian well on the site sprang to life from which water would spout three hundred feet into the air and rain down like a fountain. Eventually Murray Hall was succeeded by various other resorts such as, the Adams House, the Perkins House, the Continental, the Ocean View and the Palmetto Lodge. All of these hotels were destined to be devastated by fire. By 1890, the only surviving hotel was ironically called the Burnside.

By the mid 1890s the government completed construction of the jetties at mouth of the St. Johns River. Unfortunately the widening and deepening of the channel resulted in the water rushing in with great force behind the jetties. The Burnside Hotel was swept into the ocean by a strong tidal surge. The Atlantic House was moved away from the shore twice but finally it, too, was washed away.

PABLO HISTORICAL PARK

The Jacksonville and Beach Railway began experiencing financial setbacks in early 1900. Millionaire developer Henry M. Flagler stepped in and took over the terminus making the railway part of the Florida East Coast System. The rails were improved to standard gauge and extended to Mayport. Transportation became easier in 1910 when a winding oyster shell road was laid in the area that is today known as Atlantic Boulevard.

Pablo Beach was incorporated on May 22, 1907 and the name was changed again in 1925 to its current, Jacksonville Beach. A settlement that began life humbly as a simple tent city has blossomed into an impressive business, resort and residential community. Today the population numbers over twenty-one thousand residents.

MAPLE LEAF

Since this book was started the historical marker concerning the Maple Leaf has been removed due to inaccuracies. However, I had already written the article and felt it was ashamed to disregard the wonderful piece of history. I was treated to the display of the Maple Leaf at the Mandarin Museum, which is absolutely incredible. For additional information and to view some of the artifacts making this wonderful piece of history come alive visit the museum.

MANDARIN MUSEUM

Mandarin Museum, 11964 Mandarin Road, Mandarin
D19 ~ GPS Coordinates: 30.166305, -81.645688

The *Maple Leaf* was built around 1850 in Kingston, Ontario to serve the needs of Lake Ontario carrying passengers, freight and livestock. She later became a very popular vessel as a luxury excursion steamer. She was sold to Boston merchant traders in August of 1862. The owners in turn leased her to the United States Army Quartermaster Department for use as an Army transport.

On the evening of March 31, 1864, the *Maple Leaf* was slowly meandering her way along the St. Johns River. The only sound was of her paddle wheels rhythmic swat of the coffee colored water and the steady hum of her engine. She had a manifest of forty persons including passengers and crew, three of which were ladies. Her hold contained four hundred tons of military equipment, sutlers goods, tents, garrison equipment and Union soldiers' personal belongings all of which had been loaded at Hilton Head, South Carolina. The cargo was to be delivered to Jacksonville, however, no sooner had the *Maple Leaf* reached the port when she was dispatched on urgent business to Palatka.

Romeo Murray, a black man born at nearby Fort George Island, was a sixteen-year veteran pilot on the St. Johns River and knew it well. He and his wheelman, Sam Jones were intently watching the river ahead, their faces dimly lit by the shaded light of the binnacle20. They were about twelve miles south of Jacksonville; it was now the early morning hours of Friday, April 1, 1864.

Suddenly a staggering concussion rocked the ship with a tremendous roar. The force of the great explosion catapulted Murray and Jones, both men struck hard against the pilothouse roof and crumpled to the deck. The planking beneath them gave way as the upper portion of the *Maple Leaf* sagged. The blast had targeted about thirty feet from her bow, breaking the back21 of the once luxurious ship.

The shrill scream of the ship's steam whistle broke the revelry of her sleeping crew and passengers. Though five of her crew would never awaken again. Two firemen and three deck hands, sleeping near the forecastle, were instantly killed. The remaining passengers and crew immediately boarded two small lifeboats and watched as the *Maple Leaf* slid beneath the ebony water. There was no time to gather personal baggage, only the clothes on their backs and their lives would be saved. The entire cargo was lost.

The *Maple Leaf* had struck a mine22 made from floating beer barrels filled with gunpowder having three percussion prongs, which detonated upon impact. Records indicate that Confederate Lieutenant Joshua O'Hern, who served as sheriff of Clay County between 1863 and 1865, set the mine. The mine was one of twelve placed near Mandarin Point under a cover of darkness on March 30. The concussion must have been quite large for when it exploded the bow of the steamer was thrown completely out of the water and the forecastle flew into the air. The pilothouse was detached and fell to pieces. Murray was fortunate to come away with only a bump on the head.

When word of the explosion reached Jacksonville, three companies of the Seventh Connecticut Regiment under the command of General Hatch were dispatched to search for additional mines. Confederate deserters supplied information concerning the additional mines and within twenty-four hours another one was found about two miles up the river. During the next week the remaining ten mines were also found.

St. Johns Archaeological Expeditions, a group of history buffs led by Jacksonville dentist Keith Holland and the late Lee Manley, a commercial diver, discovered the *Maple Leaf* in 1984. With the assistance of the Program in Maritime History and Nautical Archaeology at East Carolina University, the group spent ten years researching and excavating one and one half tons of cargo from the site. The *Maple Leaf* served as a classroom for students of underwater archaeology, provided text for a number of master's theses as well as material for a book written by Larry Babits of East Carolina University, released by Plenum Press.

Thousands of artifacts such as plates, smoking pipes, cups, flutes, bottles, a sewing kit, swords and even soap were recovered between 1988 and 1994. In the summer of 1996, a follow-up dive found that the *Maple Leaf* and her remaining three hundred ninety-eight tons of cargo were once again safely entombed in the mire of the St. Johns River.

The Mandarin Museum houses a magnificent display of *Maple Leaf* artifacts and replicas dedicated to this most important representation of the Civil War. A scale model of the ship is on display revealing amazing detail of the ship before she met her explosive end on the St. Johns River. The interesting and informative display at Mandarin Museum is not to be missed. The wreck is listed on the National Register of Historic places, the state historical marker has been removed presumably because of errors in the verbiage.

Walter Jones Historical Park, which hosts the Mandarin Museum also features an 1875 farmhouse and 1876 barn owned by Mandarin notable Major William Webb. Nature walkways, an 1800s sawmill, whose remains were actually found in the river, and collected antique farming implements are impressively placed throughout the property. The wonderful wooden walkway along the river provides a scenic view and very pleasant way to spend an afternoon at one of several seating areas available or the picnic area complete with representative antique facilities.

Permanent exhibits consist of author Harriet Beecher Stowe's winter home furnishings and memorabilia, an amazing replica of the Tiffany stained glass window donated to the Church of Our Savior, which was donated by the Stowe family. Hurricane Dora in 1964 completely destroyed the window. Original works of art ranging from noted artist Charlie Brown to current local artist talent are displayed throughout the museum. Rounding out the displays are various artifacts representing the original inhabitants of Mandarin, that of the Timucua Indians. The museum is lovingly cared for by the Mandarin Historical Society, their work there is truly a fantastic preservation project. The Mandarin Museum is open daily.

OLD MANDARIN POST OFFICE & GENERAL MERCANTILE

**CHURCH OF OUR SAVIOR
(EPISCOPAL)**

Situated on the St. Johns on a portion of the
Fairbanks Grant, this congregation was organized
in 1867. The church was completed in 1883 under
the Rev. C.M. Strugess, a mission priest assigned
to the St. Johns Valley. The church was regularly
attended by Harriet Beecher Stowe, author of
"Uncle Tom's Cabin", and the west window is a
memorial to the Stowe family who were winter
residents of Mandarin for many years.

**12223 Mandarin Road, Mandarin
D20 ~ GPS Coordinates: 30.162663, -81.652220**

The Church of Our Savior might have been first conceived in 1867 but it was 1880 before a sundry group of parishioners representing Episcopalians and other denominations left the Church of England to form the congregation. It is understood that the group had often met in the home of Professor Calvin E. Stowe and his author/wife, Harriet Beecher Stowe.

Under the direction of mission priest, Reverend C. M. Strugess the congregation built a small, plain sanctuary completed in November 1883. The edifice was designed to model the Church of the Good Shepherd located at Recquette Lake, New York. The Church of Good Shepherd still conducts services to this day.

Most interesting in the construction of the church were perhaps its various memorial windows, many of which were installed when the edifice was first constructed. The amazing stories behind each window are as follows:

The Huntington windows are dedicated to the Huntington family who were founding members of the church. The windows are adorned with daisies representing purity. Though they appear to be stained glass, the windows are actually painted or stamped with the design and color. This process is a rarer and a much more fragile technique than that of stained glass. These windows are dated 1883.

The Maynard family memorial was dedicated to Caleb Crane, the first senior warden[23] of the church. Caleb Crane was the grandfather of the Maynard family. The window features the passionflower and lily, characterizing the Crucifixion and Resurrection.

The choir loft features a memorial window of biblical musical instruments dedicated to Mr. Hoge and his wife who were the choirmaster and organist. Trumpets and cymbals are cleverly depicted.

The altar window represents the Bible verse "Suffer the little children to come unto me." The window is illustrated with a young girl offering her little brother to Jesus. This window signifies with a single gesture the terrible loss of small children to the rampant epidemics during this era. The date reads 1883.

The Mead family, also founding members, memorialized their young son Charles who died on a voyage to England. A severed rope represents a life cut short, a weathered wooden cross entwined with ivy is a symbol of eternity and the lily of the valley symbolizes the Virgin Mary.

The Stowe window honors Harriet and Calvin Stowe. Designed in 1884 by Margaret Huntington Hooker, the piece was constructed by Louis Comfort Tiffany. The window portrays the St. Johns River against a setting sun. This window met with much undue criticism due to its lack of reli -gious significance. Though the work is likely the most admired in the church. The window was not actually installed until 1916.

- The Schulting window was the last to be placed. Set in the 1920s, the piece is very detailed. The work is derived from religious literature and art rather than that of the Bible. The symbol ism is that of the authors of the four gospels: Matthew – man; Mark – lion; Luke – ox; and John – eagle. The window is dedicated to the mother of Mandarin resident Victor Bird.

The Trimble window is of unknown history. Opalescent glass defines two types of lilies repre -senting the Resurrection.

Other original furnishings include pews made with wooden pegs; the altar carved at St. Augustine and delivered via train, boat and finally horse and wagon; the lectern and prayer desk designed by noted architect Robert S. Schuler; a pine wood cross inlayed with curly pine, which is an oddity because this wood is only avail- able in the second growth of felled trees. The font was carefully brought from England in the early 1800s by the Winton family and later gifted to the church. Its hexagonal shape with flat cover is truly unusual. Hanging gaslights were designed and made by Bruno Alberts famous for his stained glass work. Though Alberts is more widely known in Mandarin for his talent for growing orchids. The exterior of the Church of Our Savior is of clas- sic board and batten siding featuring a fern motif on the doors and bell tower. The theme is carried out within the confines of the interior as well.

On September 9, 1964, disaster struck the church. Hurricane Dora roared through the Mandarin area and even though parishioners had taken care to protect the edifice, the Church of Our Savior sustained major damage. A large oak was snapped by the punishing hurricane winds crushing the roof of the church.

The Stowe window was completely unsalvageable. The entire community grieved the loss of the church when it became evident that there was too much damage to restore the 1883 edifice. The congregation desperately wanted to cling to the charm of the original structure and preparations were made to construct a sanctuary having much the same feel of the old edifice while bringing modernization to the building. The effect is disarming. While the sanctuary has all of the modern conveyances a sense of history remains.

A new window was added in memory of Reverend Davis, who served as priest in charge around 1900. The window portrays four religious symbols: the Alpha and Omega; the open Bible; the star and the cross.

**THE
BEAUTIUL
CHURCH OF
OUR SAVIOR**

HARRIET BEECHER STOWE HOME

In 1867, Mrs. Harriet Beecher Stowe and her husband Calvin bought thirty acres of the Fairbanks Grant in Mandarin, which served as their winter home until the winter of 1883-1884. The move to Florida was due to plans for philanthropy among the Negroes and a desire to benefit her son's health. While in Florida, Mrs. Stowe, author of "Uncle Tom's Cabin", wrote sketches called "Palmetto Leaves". The Stowes were active in local charitable and religious activities.

**Mandarin Road 1.6 miles west of SR 13, Mandarin
D21 ~ GPS Coordinates: 30.162030, -81.659033**

Harriet Beecher Stowe came into the world on June 14, 1811, born to Reverend Lyman Beecher and his wife, Roxanna. Harriet was one of eleven children born to the couple, though Roxanna died when Harriet was only five years old. The Beecher children were all raised in a strictly religious household and encouraged to seek intellectual pursuits. It was uncommon during the 1800s for a female child to be educated, however by all accounts each of the Beecher children with no regard to sex received exceptional schooling. In fact Harriet's sister, Catharine, founded Hartford Female Seminary where Harriet was first a student and later a teacher. Hartford Female Seminary and Catharine Beecher were integral in changing the country's thinking, which allowed young women to be educated similar to their male counterparts.

In 1832, Harriet met and married Calvin Stowe, a professor at Lane Theological Seminary where her father was President. The couple had seven children, only three were destined to out live their parents. Harriet was very fortunate in her choice of a husband who supported and encouraged her career as an author at a time when it was unacceptable for a woman to work outside the home. Calvin wrote the following to his wife in 1840:

"my dear, you must be a literary woman. It is so written in the book of fate...Make all your calculations accordingly."

Harriet's most famous work, *Uncle Toms Cabin* was published in 1852. The volume describes the desperate flight of a slave, Eliza, as she attempts to escape with her son who is about to be sold. Harriet's anguish over the loss of her eighteen-month-old son to a cholera epidemic was used as a basis for understanding the slave woman's feelings over the loss of her child.

Uncle Toms Cabin was a tremendous success, selling more than ten thousand copies during its first week of publication. Harriet became an immediate celebrity, she was sought after to speak against slavery in America and throughout Europe. Upon meeting President Lincoln after the start of the Civil War, legend has it he said to her, "So you're the little woman who wrote the book that started this Great War!"

In the 1860s, Calvin and Harriet purchased property in Mandarin on the St. Johns River. The couple built a house there and began to winter there every year from their Andover, Massachusetts home. Harriet came to love the Mandarin area and wrote about it a number of times. The following is an excerpt of "Our Florida Plantation" an article written by Harriet and published by Atlantic Monthly magazine in 1879:

"It was a hazy, dreamy, sultry February day, such as comes down from the skies of Florida in the opening of spring. A faint scent of orange blossoms was in the air, though as yet there seemed to be only white buds on the trees. The deciduous forests along the banks of the broad St. John's were just showing that misty dimness which announces the opening of young buds. The river lay calm as a mirror, streaked here and there with broad bands of intenser blue which melted dreamily into purplish mists in the distance..."

Harriet described their Florida Plantation home as a "rambling, one-story cottage, with a veranda twelve feet wide in front." The yard was encircled by a picket fence and the property heavily shaded by magnificent oaks. It was said that the nine thousand-acre plantation once employed five hundred slaves raising cotton, sugarcane and, until the great frost of 1835, had a productive orange grove (no longer viable at the time of the Stowe's purchase).

In 1872, Harriet published the much-lauded *Palmetto Leaves*. The work is a compilation of stories written while in residence at their Mandarin home. The work is filled with drawings and stories of area citizens and wildlife. Magnificent views of the St. Johns River as well as a "stately orange tree, thirty feet high with a spreading, graceful top and varnished green leaves" that stood outside her Mandarin window. The work is serene and relaxing until the end when the work turns serious and Harriet concludes with a discourse in support of human rights. Though the work has long since been out of print, *Palmetto Leaves* has recently been reissued and is available at your local bookstore.

The Stowe's made use of their Florida property for close to twenty-five years. While there Harriet helped to establish schools for African American children and the Stowe's were active members of the Church of Our Savior congregation, which was open to members of all faiths. Today the school founded by Harriet Beecher Stowe is the Mandarin Community Club. A portrait of Harriet, commissioned by the organization, hangs as a memorial to her selfless works and community service.

After fifty-one years as an author and a long life, lived to its fullest, Harriet Beecher Stowe passed away at noon on July 1, 1896, she was 85. It was in her Hartford, Connecticut home that she peacefully slipped away of what was termed congestion of the brain. The New York Times said the following about an amazing woman, wife, mother, author, activist:

"The death of Harriet Beecher Stowe is more than the ending of a woman's life of whatever degree of fame. It marks the extinction of genius in a family, and is one of the closing leaves in an era of our century."

JAMES HALL
SOLDIER OF THE REVOLUTION

(Side One)

James Hall was born on October 8, 1760, in Keene, New Hampshire. Records of the Continental Army indicate that James Hall of Keene was mustered into service about August 20, 1776. Hall served throughout the Revolutionary War as an infantry soldier of the Continental Army line. New Hampshire units participated in the important campaign of the fall of 1777 which culminated in the surrender of Burgoyne at Saratoga on October 17, 1777. Hall continued to serve with the Continental Army as it endured the winter of 1777-78 at Valley Forge. On June 28, 1778, he was in the ranks of Poor's Brigade at the battle of Monmouth where he participated in the final advance of the day in that "hottest day of battle". James Hall was promoted to sergeant on April 1, 1780. He served on through the war and was present at Yorktown in October, 1781, in Col. Alexander Scammell's Third New Hampshire Regiment. When the war ended, twenty-one year old James Hall was a full-time fighting patriot.

JAMES HALL
DOCTOR OF MEDICINE

(Side Two)

During the next two decades, James Hall became a doctor. At length, he decided to move to the Spanish territory of Florida. In 1790, Dr. James Hall, then aged thirty, settled near Cow Ford (now Jacksonville). He was the first known American physician to sustain the practice of medicine in Florida. In 1803, the first settler of Cow Ford, Robert Pritchard, died. Since his arrival in 1783, Pritchard had acquired considerable land holdings. These included seven hundred acres in the Goodby's Lake region and sixteen thousand acres on Julington Creek. Within the year of Robert Pritchard's death, his thirty-six year old widow, Eleanor (nee Plummer) married the forty-four year old Doctor James Hall. The Halls made their home in what is now called Plummer's Cove. Here Dr. Hall sustained his practice until 1810, at the age of fifty, he was banished from East Florida by the Spanish for having participated in the "Florida-Georgia Rebellion." On February 22, 1819, Spain ceded Florida to the United States, and in 1822 Doctor Hall returned to what had become Jacksonville. He continued his medical practice and was active in many community matters, such as testifying at Spanish Land Grant hearings. James Hall died at LaGrange, Florida (on Plummer's Cove) on December 25, 1837.

Mandarin Road, Mandarin
D22 ~ GPS Coordinates: 30.160850, -81.659383

Life was tough for a young boy such as James Hall entering the Continental Army at the age of fifteen. Living conditions were deplorable, if he were fortunate enough to sleep beneath the cover of a tent; he shared the space with six to eight other men. Further, if a soldier had a tent, he was not entitled to a blanket. To claim a blanket the soldier must sleep in the open air.

Everyone in a Revolutionary encampment was assigned specific duties and to shirk an assignment meant immediate dismissal. Pay was often promised but rarely forthcoming. Repeatedly the men were told that after the war the Patriots would be compensated for their work. The Continental forces accepted General Washington's word and fought for virtually nothing.

Disease was a common occurrence around camp due to lack of food, sleep and sanitary conditions. Soldiers resorted to eating sheep heads or other animal parts which were not commonly eaten to fill their growling bellies. It is said that in times of casualties, strange-tasting meat would become plentiful, the author will allow you to draw your own conclusion there. When there was no food at all young James simply went hungry. When real beef or other meet was available, the camps rarely had cooking utensils. It was not uncommon for the raw meat to be consumed. Raw meat was preferred over no meat at all.

Exposure to these conditions likely influenced young James to pursue his future vocation as a physician. A recommendation from his Lieutenant was to never visit the camp hospital and especially avoid the surgeon. The soldiers looked after each other rather than go to the hospital where it was likely that the injury would result in the loss of a limb or life.

James Hall was present at the Battle of Saratoga, which was a decisive victory against the British. After three weeks of skirmishing, where the advantage often swayed from British to American and back again, the British suffered over one thousand casualties while the Continentals had lost approximately five hundred men. Burgoyne, the British commander, waited patiently for supplies that never appeared and was forced to either retreat or advance. With a starving and miserable British Army, Burgoyne led his troops through the mud and rain taking refuge in a fortified camp near Saratoga. It was there that American forces of nearly twenty thousand strong surrounded the exhausted British Army. Faced with overwhelming odds, Burgoyne was forced to surrender on October 17, 1777.

The winter was spent among General George Washington's troops at Valley Forge. Conditions were even more desperate than normal and the weather constantly punished the unprepared American troops. Many lost their lives to influenza and congestive conditions during this encampment. Young James managed to survive the winter and join Poor's[24] Brigade for the Battle of Monmouth.

Monmouth was the last major battle fought between the two main armies of the American Revolution. James Hall fought alongside John Hayes, who was wounded during the battle. Hayes' wife, known as the legendary Molly Pitcher, often followed the camp and brought water to the troops during battle. When Hayes was wounded, Molly stepped up and volunteered to assume his position at the canon. Though the Americans did not have a decisive victory at Monmouth, they inflicted heavy damages on the British. The British were in fact only there to defend their baggage train and were not prepared for an all out battle. However, since the Americans held the field, they claimed the battle as won. Most believe Monmouth was at least a draw or perhaps a British victory. Both sides lost approximately three hundred fifty men killed, wounded or captured. Heat exhaustion claimed lives on each side of the battle lines.

The war was coming to end in the summer of 1781, when young James found himself marching toward Yorktown, Virginia. General Cornwallis led his British army of seven thousand troops to the tiny village of Yorktown in hopes of being met there by General Sir Henry Clinton delivering supplies. General Clinton was slow to respond. Meanwhile, General Washington and Rochambeau heard rumors of Cornwallis predicament and began a hasty march from Rhode Island down the Atlantic Coast to surround Cornwallis at Yorktown. As the siege wore on the British began to exhaust all of its food and ammunition. General Cornwallis was forced to sue for peace. Cornwallis surrendered his army to the American and French allies on October 19, 1781. The British soon appealed for peace. The United States of America was now an independent nation. James Hall, now a grown man of twenty-one, mustered out of the Continental Army as a Sergeant under Colonel Alexander Scammell's Third New Hampshire Regiment.

The circumstances surrounding James Hall's medical training is unknown. However, it is certain that he did formally study medicine. Whatever the case, James became a physician after the Revolutionary War. By the age of thirty, he had established himself as the first physician in Florida. James came to live in the settlement of Cow Ford and began the practice of medicine under Spanish rule for twenty years.

Medicine in these early days was crude at best. Many self-proclaimed backwoods physicians treated settlers administering castor oil, calomel, blue mass, rhubarb and opium as well as remedies garnered from roots, herbs and berries found in the forest. Turpentine, sulfur, spirits of niter and paregoric were as essential as clothing, cornmeal and bacon on any plantation. When home remedies failed, the physician was summoned. The most common malady was the "fever." In reality most of the fever illnesses were malaria. Unfortunately the treatment for malaria was quinine which was virtually unknown in Florida during this time. The lancet was used freely for bleeding and that became the most popular cure-all. Other prevalent diseases were measles, diarrhea, and epidemics of yellow fever. However, it appears that Duval County was relatively healthy until the turn of the century.

Over the years, Dr. Hall was not only engaged in the practice of medicine but was active in community affairs as well. He testified on the behalf on many local settlers before the Board of Commissioners concerning Spanish land grants in Florida. He assisted at least one Revolutionary War veteran in obtaining his government pension.

Dr. Hall met and married the widow of Robert Pritchard, one of the first settlers of Jacksonville. Eleanor Pritchard Hall inherited a vast amount of property upon her husband's death and after marrying Hall the couple settled at Plummer's Cove.

In 1810, James Hall was banished from Florida by the Spanish due to his involvement in the Florida-Georgia Rebellion again Spain. On February 22, 1819, Spain relinquished control of Florida to the United States and Dr. James Hall returned to Jacksonville. He continued to serve the area as a physician and active citizen for the next eighteen years. Dr. James Hall patriot, physician and civic leader passed away on Christmas Day, December 25, 1837. Over time Dr. Hall's burial site was lost.

However, in 1924 Annie Locke, Chairman of the Historic Spots Committee, Jacksonville Chapter of the Daughters of the American Revolution managed to relocate his grave. The chapter hired a caretaker to tend the plot unfortunately the man became ill, undergrowth hid the location from view once again. Mrs. Jessie Fritot found the gravesite for a second time on August 3, 1944. The marker was restored and photographed.

MULBERRY GROVE PLANTATION

Although East Florida was under Spanish control from 1783 to 1821, English speaking settlers lived along the St. Johns River in the late eighteenth century. In 1787, the Spanish crown granted a large parcel of land to Timothy Hollingsworth, who named his plantation Mulberry Grove after trees native to the area. In 1805, Mulberry Grove was purchased by a Georgia planter named John H. McIntosh. In 1812, he became a leader in the so-called Patriot War, an attempt by U.S. citizens to seize East Florida from the Spanish. After these efforts failed, McIntosh returned to Georgia. During the next decades, cotton was grown on the plantation, which came to be owned by Joshua Hickman. Prior to the beginning of the Civil War, Arthur M. Reed, a Jacksonville businessman, purchased Mulberry Grove, and in 1862 took his family there to live when Union forces occupied the town. Oranges, cattle and many varieties of fruits and vegetables were produced on the plantation in the decades after the Civil War. The main house with an oak shaded avenue leading to the river was an attraction for excursionists travelling on the St. Johns. In 1939, the U.S. government acquired a portion of Mulberry Grove Plantation for the Jacksonville Naval Air Station.

Jacksonville Naval Air Station, Mustin Road, Jacksonville
D23 ~ GPS Coordinates: 30.202817, -81.681967

Though the trail of ownership concerning Mulberry Grove Plantation is quite clear little is written of its early history prior to the Civil War. What we do know is that Timothy Hollingsworth, most probably the first to receive a Spanish land grant for the property, acquired the vast parcel in 1787 and formally named the plantation Mulberry Grove. Mulberry trees supporting the silk industry at St. Augustine were planted in numerous quantities through out the region and it is through those trees that Mulberry Grove Plantation derived its name.

John Houstoun McIntosh settled in East Florida as a young man and became a noted planter in the region. In 1804, McIntosh purchased what is now known as Kingsley Plantation at Fort George Island. It was there that he managed to successfully revive the Sea Island cotton industry and become one of the wealthiest men in the province. The next year, McIntosh expanded his Florida holdings to include Mulberry Grove.

McIntosh eventually rose to the esteemed position of Governor of the Republic of Florida in 1812. Unfortunately, politics brought about his downfall. He led the Patriot Rebellion against Spain in an effort by Americans living in East Florida to take the colony from Spain. The uprising was met with unexpected resistance from the Spaniards, who were aided by the Seminole. When the United States withdrew military support, the Patriot Rebellion crumbled. Fearing retaliation from the Spaniards, McIntosh fled back to Georgia. Mulberry Grove was abandoned.

It was then that Joshua Hickman gained ownership of the plantation. It is noted that Hickman continued to produce Sea Island Cotton and little else is known concerning him. Some years prior to the Civil War, Jacksonville businessman Arthur M. Reed purchased the plantation. A wealth of edification is available pertaining to Arthur M. Reed and Mulberry Grove courtesy of his granddaughter, Margaret Pearson Hall, based on an interview given in March 1939. Mrs. Hall, born at Mulberry Grove in 1883, was the granddaughter of Arthur M. Reed. She lived at the plantation until the age of eight.

Reed moved to the plantation from downtown Jacksonville fearing the bombardment of Federal gunboats ported at the Jacksonville harbor in 1862. Reed felt it safer for his family at Mulberry Grove. He was a noted businessman, founder of the Bank of Jacksonville and owned a mercantile company in the city.

His wife, Harriet Douglas Reed was the daughter of Judge Thomas Douglas, a native of Connecticut. Judge Douglas settled in St. Augustine in 1826 and was appointed as Judge of the Supreme Court of Florida that year by President John Quincy Adams. He served in the position for nineteen years, being reappointed by three successive Presidents.

The plantation then consisted of more than fourteen hundred acres. Mrs. Hall remembered it as being "a grand old place." The substantial house had a panoramic view of the St. Johns River, which ran almost due south to north. The wood-framed dwelling was two-stories painted gleaming white with a red tin roof. A long wide porch ran the full length of the front and around to the south providing a pleasant place to while away the evening hours watching the St. Johns.

The interior of the home had a wide hallway running through the middle. To one side was a large living room, a dining room and a smaller room used as a sitting room. The other side featured two large bedrooms and a bathroom. A wide staircase ran up in the center of the hall leading to two lovely bedrooms on the second floor, with the back section being used for storage and attic space. An artesian well provided running water in the interior bathroom, built in the late 1800s.

A door in the dining room lead to a wide hallway, off of which was a food locker or pantry, where kitchen supplies and linens were stored. The hall continued to the back of the house where Reed's considerable library and office could be found. From the office was a porch with steps leading down to a brick walk that lead to the little brick kitchen where the family cooking was done. It was common during this time for kitchens to be separate from the main house due to the hazards of cooking with fire.

The brick walk routed around the house from the front door to the back yard, dividing with one walk leading to the greenhouse, the other to the kitchen. There was a stone smokehouse in the back yard, where a kind of commissary was kept having a room upstairs where dry goods were stored. A two-room frame laundry featured wash tubs and scrub boards. One of the rooms contained a stove where the staff heated water and boiled the clothes. Mrs. Hall remembered that men's shirts were snowy white; the bosoms, attached collars and cuffs starched stiff and highly polished with searing irons that were heated on top of the wood stove. A kitchen garden provided seasonal vegetables year round for the plantation table.

To the south of the house was a large flower garden, where roses, geraniums and the usual perennials of spring brought color to the yard. The greenhouse, with its glass top, contained bins for fall flower bulbs, shelves of geraniums and more tender plants. An old cotton house, alive with scurrying rats, provided a distraction for the plantation children who would wage afternoon battles chasing them about. Entertainment on the plantation was obviously in short supply.

Chickens were raised in great numbers, as well as turkeys, ducks, geese and guineas. The fowl provided meat for the table as well as down picked from the breasts of geese and made into eider-down quilts. The voice of songbirds filled the air with their incessant chatter — mockingbirds, redbirds, blue jays and sparrows. Enormous trees were all around live oaks, water oaks, tall pines and palms, and all were massive. A long avenue of large oaks flanked the front porch. The oaks provided an intertwining canopy overhead and beneath was carpeted with St. Augustine grass, which led to the river about three hundred feet away. According to a University of Florida study, "the world's first known record of planting St. Augustine grass was November 11, 1880, as turf alongside an avenue at Mulberry Grove plantation. Reed recorded day to day activities on the farm, such as, "George planting St. Augustine grass in avenue in afternoon." By this time only a few of the old mulberry trees remained scattered about the property.

Orange trees surrounded the house, though they required much attention. In the late 1880s a freeze killed the citrus trees and they were never replanted. In the early days quantities of oranges were gathered, packed and shipped from Mulberry Grove. Other fruit trees, including pears, peaches, plums, as well as strawberries and blackberries provided sweet treats for the family larder. A large cellar contained surplus fruits and vegetables, which had been canned, dried or made preserves and jellies. The cellar was kept locked at all times to ward off the temptation of sweet seeking children.

At the end of the oak avenue to the river was a long dock. St Johns river traffic was heavy then and ships would land at the deep water dock when the Reed family flew a flag signaling a need for shipping freight into Jacksonville and often the ships delivered orders of food and supplies. The riverboats seen most often were the *Crescent City, Mary Draper, Manatee* and sometimes the *Three Friends* would tie up at the dock. In the boathouse under the docks Arthur Reed kept his two boats, *John Perry* and *Fanny Perry*. Both were four-oared rowboats, which he used to ferry to Jacksonville. In later years, when telephones came into use, there was a telephone in the house and also in the boathouse. The children would often play with the telephones calling each other from the house and boathouse.

Beyond where the mulberry trees once stood was a large Indian camp and ancient burial mound. The mound was noted as being quite large and high, overlooking the river. In the early 1900s, a representative of the Smithsonian Institution excavated the mound and found the remains of twenty-four native Americans buried there. The remnants of an old fireplace was found as well with the remains placed in a circle about it, their heads positioned toward the hearth.

After the death of Arthur M. Reed, Mulberry Grove Plantation was left to his grandson, Reed Pearson. Eventually the "Pearson tract", as Mulberry Grove came to be known to locals was sold to the United States government for the construction of Naval Air Station Jacksonville.

NAS[25] Jacksonville was officially commissioned on October 15, 1940 with Captain Charles P. Mason as its first commanding officer. Commander Jimmy Grant was the first pilot to land on the still unfinished runway in his N3N-3 biplane and more than ten thousand pilots and eleven thousand air crewmen earned their wings of gold at the station during World War II. Today NAS Jacksonville is a multi-missioned base hosting more than one hundred tenant commands. The facility is the third largest naval installation in the entire United States.

Roosevelt, near Naval Air Station Jacksonville, Jacksonville Beach
D24 ~ GPS Coordinates: 30.294000, -81.720050

NAS Jax[26] was first commissioned on October 15, 1940. The first commanding officer was Captain Charles P. Mason. The command included Naval Air Station Cecil Field and Naval Station Mayport.

During the initial days more than seven hundred buildings were constructed including an eighty-acre hospital and a prisoner of war compound housing more than fifteen hundred World War II Germans prisoners. The jet age came to Jacksonville in the late 1940s and brought the first Navy jet carrier air groups and squadrons to the base. In fact as the 1940s came to a close there were more aircraft stationed at NAS Jax than any base from Nova Scotia to the Caribbean.

The 1950s found the Navy base bustling in support of the Korean Conflict. Glad arrivals and sad departures including newcomers Fleet Air Wing Eleven and the departure of the Blue Angels. The Blue Angels performed for the last time on April 29, 1950 it would be two years before they returned to entertain an enthusiastic crowd at the base once again.

The Overhaul and Repair Department was assigned the tremendous task of reworking the R4D transport airplane and H04S-3 helicopter in order to accompany Byrd on his exploration to the South Pole. The Navy's impact on the Jacksonville area was indeed a positive one, providing more than five thousand civilian positions and bringing over eleven thousand military members into the area. The payroll amounted to more than thirty-five million dollars, more than any other employer in Duval County.

As the fifties came to a close America entered the space age. The first satellite was launched and the first "astronauts" were blasted into space. NAS Jacksonville did their part when VP-18 spotted and tracked the astronaut's craft. After dispatching two destroyers and a seagoing tug to the landing site, the astronauts were successfully recovered. Alpha and Baker, chimpanzee astronaughts were safely back home.

The 1960s began with the presidential election of a former Naval Officer who spent a short period during World War II at the Naval Hospital in Jacksonville, John F. Kennedy.

When Kennedy ordered the naval blockade of Guantanamo Bay, NAS Jacksonville supplied an attack squadron to monitor Soviet shipping and processed daily spy plane films.

NAS Jax celebrated twenty-five years of duty in 1965, but the festivities were hampered by the order of more than one hundred thousand young men and women to the jungles of Vietnam. Two years later the war hit very close to home when a pilot from Cecil Field was brought down over North Vietnam while flying a combat mission. His name was John McCain, he was held as a prisoner of war for five and a half years.

Jacksonville felt the pain of loss when native and Hospital Corpsman Second Class E. Scott Hancock was killed eleven days after arriving in Vietnam. Hancock paid the ultimate price in the service of his country. Several wounded Marines owed a supreme debt of gratitude to Scott Hancock, for he gave his life in an effort to save theirs. For his bravery and valor in the face of certain death he was awarded the nation's second highest award, the Navy Cross.

Into the 1970s the conflict in Vietnam continued to rage. As the first prisoners of war were released, the naval hospital was used for examination and debriefing of returning soldiers. Opportunities at NAS Jax were great and the duty station became the most requested throughout the Navy.

During the early eighties Kings Bay Naval Submarine Base was established some fifty miles to the north and NAS Jax established an antisubmarine force to be reckoned with. About the same time, a new helicopter training facility was dedicated and named the Paul Nelson Helicopter Training Facility after the former commanding officer of HS-3 who had died the year before while flying from the aircraft carrier, *USS Nimitz*.

The community supported Armed Forces Day in conjunction with Scout World27 in 1981. The first year had a recorded attendance of six thousand, last year the crowd soared to more than fifteen thousand participants.

The 1980s were a challenging decade for NAS Jax Naval Investigative Service. A fire destroyed the Naval Investigative Service building early in the decade. Unfortunately it was discovered that the fire was the result of arson and the culprits, were two NAS Jax sailors. Obviously the men were attempting to destroy evidence in an on-going investigation. Their troubles were not over. The Naval Investigative Service was burned out again but this time the Navy Absentee Collection Unit, the Naval Rework Facility and some Naval Regional Data Automation computer equipment were all lost. This time a faulty boiler was to blame.

The Blue Angels returned to celebrate NAS Jax golden anniversary with a dramatic air show. Additionally, a luncheon was given honoring the first class of naval aviators who earned their wings at Naval Air Station Jacksonville. The festivities were shadowed by impending doom of military downsizing and trouble brewing in the Middle East. Funding was reduced, government realignments and tensions continued to increased in Iraq and Kuwait. Several squadrons flew off of carriers supporting Operation Desert Storm.

NAS Jacksonville was awarded the Commander in Chief's Installation Excellence Award as the best station in the Navy for 1991. Eighty Medal of Honor recipients from World War II to the present were paid well-deserved homage with the dedication of Patriots Grove in 1996. Three years later the base name was changed to Commander, Navy Region Southeast as a part of the regionalization program. In support of the community NAS Jax hosted its first Special Olympics Spring Games.

Regardless of the funding constraints, base closures, realignments and on going problems in the Middle East throughout the 1990s, NAS Jax continues to grow and expand. Many men and women have been deployed from NAS Jax in support of Operation Enduring Freedom, there is not a man, woman or child that has not been affected in some way. More than sixty years have passed with many changes along the way.

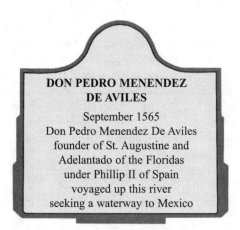

**DON PEDRO MENENDEZ
DE AVILES**

September 1565
Don Pedro Menendez De Aviles
founder of St. Augustine and
Adelantado of the Floridas
under Phillip II of Spain
voyaged up this river
seeking a waterway to Mexico

**Memorial Park, Riverside Avenue and Memorial Park Drive, Jacksonville
D25 ~ GPS Coordinates: 30.311472, -81.678747**

Pedro Menendez de Aviles was born at Avila, Spain28 on February 15, 1519. Menendez rose to prominence in the Spanish Navy, gaining the title of General and amassing a modest fortune. He had managed to gain the favor of his king, Phillip II, even commanding the vessel that bore Phillip to England for his marriage to Queen

Mary in 1554. Menendez later captained a fleet of treasure galleons on a voyage from Mexico to Spain. Unfortunately the journey was an ill-fated one; the vessels transporting his son, several relatives and numerous friends was lost at sea. Menendez requested permission from King Phillip to return in search of the lost ship but was refused for several years until the king had need of his services once again.

King Phillip proposed that Menendez could conduct a search for his lost vessel on the condition that he do so on a mission to explore and colonize Florida. The expedition was to be funded solely by Menendez. As he made preparations to set sail a mandate from the king was received; Menendez was ordered to annihilate any Protestant he should discover, on land or at sea.

Phillip received news that French Huguenots had taken refuge in the New World and in order to cease the spread of their heresy, as he saw it, the Huguenot Protestants had to be eliminated. Menendez had no choice but to obey the king's edict, the alternative was the dungeons of the Spanish Inquisition. The king now regarded the venture as a holy mission and gave Menendez additional ships and treasure.

Spanish soldiers and sailors alike were all anxious to join the venture. Menendez set sail with eleven ships, one of which was a galleon of nine hundred tons and twenty-six hundred men. Along with the standard crew of military men and seamen were explorers and priests. Menendez was a devout Catholic and hoped to spread the religion to natives of the New World.

The fleet's arrival on the coast of Florida was a ceremonious occasion. As the regal ceremony concluded, Menendez held his sword aloft and proclaimed possession of the entire country for Spain. It was then that St. Augustine was founded, forty years prior to any other city in America. In order to tell the full story without repeating information a complete accounting of the events is detailed under the historical marker denoting the Mission Nombre de Dios in St. Johns County, where the arrival spectacle took place.

Menendez soon prepared to carry out the grizzly duties assigned by King Phillip. He would march overland to Fort Caroline and slaughter the Huguenots settled there. The stories of these brutal massacres that followed are recounted in the historical marker entitled The Huguenot Memorial in Duval County. The aftermath of the atrocities are related in Massacre of the French-Matanzas Inlet, St. Johns County.

Don Pedro Menendez de Aviles established a firm Spanish foothold at St. Augustine and continued his exploration as far as Chesapeake Bay. He continued to charter settlements along the Atlantic seaboard, his favorite being Santa Elena today known as Parris Island, South Carolina. It was there that he established his wife, Dona Maria de Solis.

Achieving the rank of High Admiral of the Spanish navy and Adelantado[29] of the Floridas, Don Pedro Menendez de Aviles died in battle with the British at Santander, Spain. Strangely enough this was not an end to his travels. For several years his body remained at Santander until finally it was removed to a family parish at Aviles. After two centuries Menendez' tomb was remodeled and his remains were moved. During the 1920's, he was on the move again this time to a handsome marble tomb located at an Avila church. The body was taken from its original wooden coffin and placed into a new lead casket. Representatives from St. Augustine witnessed the re-interment. The wooden coffin was gifted to the City of St. Augustine and it lies in state at the Shrine of Our Lady of la Leche at the Mission Nombre de Dios.

It would be another thirty years before Menendez would reach his presumed final resting-place. During the Spanish Civil War in the 1950's, the body was once again moved to another church in Avila when the church that had housed Menendez was bombed. Possibly now the explorer is home for good.

SITE OF THE MISSION OF
SAN JUAN DEL PUERTO

The establishment of missions chiefly for the purpose of Christianizing the Indian population was one of the methods used by Spain in attempting to colonize Florida in the sixteenth century. The Mission of San Juan del Puerto was founded late in the 1500's by the Franciscan Order of friars to serve the Timucuan Indians living in the area. While working at this mission around 1600 Father Francisco Pareja prepared a Timucuan dictionary, grammar and several religious books in that language for use by the Indians. The Mission of San Juan del Puerto continued to exist throughout the seventeenth century in spite of the growing conflict between Florida's Spanish inhabitants and English, and French invaders. In 1696, Jonathan Dickinson, a Philadelphia Quaker who had been shipwrecked off the coast of Florida, passed this way and recorded a visit to "the town St. Wan's, a large town and many people." In 1702, Governor James Moore of the British Colony of South Carolina attempted to take St. Augustine from the Spanish. His effort failed, but in the process of the raid into Spanish territory, Moore destroyed the Spanish missions from St. Augustine northward, including the Mission of San Juan del Puerto.

Fort George Island
(marker has been taken down and is in storage at Little Talbot Island State Park)
Jacksonville

History tells us that the Mission of San Juan del Puerto existed before 1587. Initial reports of the mission reveal it to be quite successful in bringing the Native American Timucua to Christianity. The mission's close proximity to St. Augustine leads us to believe that religious leaders traveled northward to establish relations with the native tribe.

The Timucua were described as tall and hardy. The Spanish observed at their first meeting with a Timucua Chief, that the man was seven feet tall. This seems highly unlikely, but due to the small stature of Spanish the man must have appeared to be quite tall and imposing.

Spanish friars were dispatched to La Florida using the rationale that they could bring a better life to the Native Americans. The intent appeared to be good but appearances can be deceiving. Spain's major motivation was driven by their need for manual labor to establish Spanish strongholds. In fact, it was the European influence of disease and war that brought about the eventual extinction of the Timucuan.

The San Juan del Puerto mission was located to the north of St. Augustine, less than a half days walk from the Timucuan village of Ossachite. Today the area is known as Fort George Island. Father Francisco Pareja, prominent leader of the Spanish mission, began his work there in 1595. By 1602, Father Pareja recorded the Christian population of San Juan and its nine visitas[30] as five hundred strong.

Father Pareja believed that the Timucua understood and accepted Christianity with even greater zeal than did the Spanish. He noted in his writing that native superstitions had been banished so far that the Native Americans —

"do not even remember them...so much so that the younger generation which has been nourished by the milk of the Gospel derides and laughs at some old men and women..."

History is greatly indebted to Father Pareja for his contribution toward our understanding of the Timucuan nation. His knowledge of the language and customs of the tribe is without equal. The Franciscan Friar recorded his observations in a volume entitled, "Confessionario," which was published in 1612. He translated the Lord's Prayer and a bilingual catechism book for the Timucua to aid in his teachings. The words appear, in part, as follows:

> "Heca, Yrimile Numa, hibuantema, Visamilenema, aboquano, letahauema nahi abomohaue, bahunu namemima, mine hibuantema atichicolonica Su..."

Translation:

> "Our Father, which art in Heaven, hallowed be thy name, thy kingdom come, thy will be done as it is in heaven. Give us this day..."

Father Pareja was transferred to a mission in the Mexican province in 1610. His various books concerning the Timucua were published there. Father Francisco Pareja died while in Mexico in 1628. Spain used the Native Americans for all types of manual labor from cultivating crops to building roads and from trading goods to construction of massive fortifications. By the end of the 17th century the Timucua nation had virtually ceased to exist. Those not killed during various battles defending Spain against the British were taken as slaves and eventually worked to death; disease and harsh conditions took care of the remainder.

In November of 1702, English Governor James Moore of South Carolina marched southward with a force of more than five hundred men. Moore's goal was the capture of Spanish St. Augustine and gaining Florida as an English territory. As the contingent march toward its destination, Moore ordered the destruction of every Catholic mission the troops passed. San Juan del Puerto, the longest standing Spanish mission, was decimated.

FORT GEORGE ISLAND

Ft. George Island presents a cross-section of the Florida story. This island was called Alicamani by the Timucuan Indians who were living here when French explorer Jean Ribault landed nearby at the mouth of the St. Johns River in 1562. The French were soon driven from the area by the Spanish who established an Indian mission called "San Juan del Puerto" before 1600. Later the island became known as "San Juan." The mission was destroyed by the British during South Carolina Governor James Moore's 1702 raid into Spanish Florida. In 1736, another invading Britisher, Georgia founder and governor James Oglethorpe, built a fort on this island. He named both island and fort "St. George." From 1763 to 1783, when Florida was a British possession, plantations began to flourish on Ft. George Island. During the 2nd Spanish Period (1783-1821), three American planters in succession owned this island: Don Juan McQueen, John Houstoun McIntosh, and Zephaniah Kingsley. Two tabby and wood plantation houses dating from that period are still standing on Ft. George Island, along with the ruins of several tabby slave dwellings. These buildings are listed on the National Register of Historic Places. Shortly after the Civil War, Ft. George Island was acquired by John F. Rollins of New Hampshire. He remodelled the Kingsley Plantation main house and called his new Florida residence the "Homestead." As postmaster, Rollins had the area's post office removed to nearby Batten Island to take advantage of river traffic on the St. Johns. Although Ft. George Island could be reached only by boat, it became a popular tourist resort during the 1880's. There were new year round residents as well. The construction in 1881 of St. George's Episcopal Church signified the growth of the island's population. But by about 1890, the extension of the railroad along Florida's east coast combined with a yellow fever epidemic and destructive fire to end the tourist era on Ft. George Island. Later, during the Florida "Boom" of the 1920's, the island experienced new prosperity. Two fashionable clubs opened there, and a road – Hecksher Drive – built by New York millionaire August Hecksher brought the automobile to the island. After World War II, part of Ft. George Island became a state park, and tourists once again were attracted to this historic island.

Fort George Island
(marker has been taken down and is in storage at Little Talbot Island State Park)
Jacksonville

John McQueen (some say Don Juan McQueen) obtained Fort George Island in 1791 as terms of a Spanish land grant. He built a sawmill and most of the island was completely cleared of timber. McQueen built his two-story home, the first story of tabby and wood frame for the second, on the island. The home still stands today and is quite possibly the oldest house in the state of Florida. It was in that home that McQueen hid with his family and friends as Indians threatened their safety. McQueen complained to the Spanish government and begged for an armed militia to protect his home and loved ones. McQueen's pleas fell on deaf ears no assistance was forthcoming. By 1804, John McQueen was destitute. A flood had taken his sawmill and he was heavily in debt. McQueen had no other alternative but to sell Fort George Island. John Houstoun McIntosh bought the property.

Shortly after moving into his Fort George home, John Houstoun was treated to an unexpected guest. Vice President Aaron Burr had been traveling to St. Augustine when a storm forced his craft ashore. Unable to continue on his voyage, Burr sought shelter at Fort George Island. You see, Aaron Burr had fought a duel with Alexander Hamilton in New York, in which Hamilton was killed. Burr was accused of murder and his loyalty to the United States was questioned. Aaron Burr was forced to escape New York and chose to hide in Spanish Florida. It was from Fort George Island that Burr wrote to East Florida's Spanish Governor Enrique White to remind him of a planned meeting. The question was, did Aaron Burr plan to betray his country to Spain? We will never know, eventually the storm blew through and Burr returned to New York.

The War of 1812 was quickly approaching and President Madison decided that Florida should become a part of the United States. Madison realized that if the Americans did not take Florida, the British would and he was forced to act. He approached John Houstoun McIntosh, as the wealthiest north Florida resident for assistance, McIntosh agreed. John Houstoun McIntosh was made Governor of the Independent Republic of East Florida and war was declared.

McIntosh realized that to control East Florida, one must control the capital at St. Augustine. Reinforcements from the Georgia militia arrived and the military action began, it was called the Patriot's Rebellion. John Houstoun McIntosh was now a traitor to Spain and retreated to Georgia. He left Fort George Island in 1814 and established New Canaan Plantation in St. Marys, Georgia. The Florida property was rented to Zephaniah Kingsley.

Kingsley was born in Scotland in 1765 and remained there until his family immigrated to Charleston, South Carolina in 1773. He had gained wealth through coffee and slave trading. Kingsley arrived in St. Augustine in 1803 and eventually built a plantation called Laurel Grove at what is today Orange Park. He also had a rice plantation called White Oak and a town house in St. Augustine where he ported several ocean going vessels.

Zephaniah Kingsley wed a slave he had purchased from Senegal, West Africa. Her name was Anta Majigeen Njaay or Anna as she was called. He brought Anna to Laurel Grove but the couple, even though they had three children together, was unable to live as man and wife due to the complications of race. Anna actively managed the plantation, even owning slaves of her own. Kingsley presented his wife with her freedom and that of her children in 1811.

Anna managed to amass five acres of her own across from Laurel Grove and was attempting to establish a poultry farm when disaster struck. In 1812, Laurel Grove was overrun with United States troops and the Seminoles attacked the plantation. Forty-one slaves were killed or carried off. To keep the plantation from falling into American hands, Anna burned Laurel Grove to the ground and then set the torch to her own home.

The Spanish commander rewarded Anna with three hundred fifty acres, however she and her children were still homeless. Anna moved to Fort George Island in 1814, still living separately from her husband though now they lived on the same property. In 1817, Zephaniah Kingsley purchased the Fort George Island property from John Houstoun McIntosh for the sum of seven thousand dollars. The property was called Kingsley Plantation. The Kingsley's fourth child, a son, was born on the plantation. John Maxwell Kingsley was the only child Anna was to give birth to as a free woman.

Kingsley Plantation consisted of the main house, twenty-five slave cabins and a large brick and tabby barn. The plantation slaves, now numbering more than two hundred grew Sea Island cotton, citrus, sugar and corn much of which was exported to Charleston. Eventually Kingsley would own thirty-two thousand acres in north Florida including four additional plantations.

The United States acquired Florida in 1821 and President Monroe appointed Zephaniah Kingsley to the State Legislature. Throughout his time there, Kingsley's thoughts on slavery kept him at odds with the remainder of the constituency. The government became more and more rigid on the subject of slavery and Florida sought to re-enslave the free men of color it had once harbored. Finally, Kingsley resigned.

Florida passed strict laws governing slavery, which greatly affected Anna and the Kingsley children. To protect his family Zephaniah moved them to Haiti, which would eventually become the Dominican Republic. Fifty of their slaves opted to sail with the family and since slavery did not exist in Haiti, the slaves became contracted laborers obligated to nine years of service at which time they would be freed in accordance with Haitian law.

Two of the Kingsley daughters stayed in the United States and married white men. Kingsley Plantation was sold to a nephew, Kingsley Beatty Gibbs in 1839. Zephaniah Kingsley died on a business trip to New York on September 30, 1843. He was buried there beside white relatives. Anna moved to Jacksonville, her will was probated there in 1870.

Martha Kingsley, Zephaniah and Anna's daughter, married Charles J. McNeill and the couple owned Kingsley Plantation in the late 1850s. Charles' sister, Anna McNeill Whistler would often come to the plantation for extended visits. Her son James Abbott McNeill Whistler painted the famous portrait of her entitled, "Whistler's Mother," in 1873. John F. Rollins of Dover, New Hampshire purchased Fort George Island in 1868.

In the 1960s, Kingsley Plantation was taken over by the state of Florida and twenty years later the National Park Service assumed management. As one travels north on Florida's A1A the turn for Fort George Island State Cultural Site is clearly marked. Kingsley Plantation is now part of the Timucuan Ecological and Historic Preserve administered by the National Park Service. The restored plantation house features furnishing appropriate for the time when the Kingsley's resided there. One of the slave cabins has been restored and the rest stand as a reminder of what once was. The grounds are open daily, at no charge. Tours are available.

One is welcomed to Kingsley Plantation down a shady lane called the Avenue of Palms. Upon arrival the strikingly beautiful white plantation house waits to greet her guests. Beyond the house is a sublime vista of sparkling water and a cool salty sea breeze keep temperatures moderate. As you depart, take one last glance of the Kingsley Plantation House, perhaps you'll see Anna standing by the door and waving good bye. Some say she still remains in her Fort George Island home.

**KINGSLEY PLANTATION,
FORT GEORGE ISLAND**

End Notes

[1] Spelling Ribault is found is various references, both appear to be accepted.

[2] Translated as River of May, today known as the St. Johns River.

[3] At this time Carolina had not been divided into North and South colonies.

[4] Today known as Havana.

5 Religious organization.

[6] Known as AME Churches

[7] Other references record the name as "Stewart"

8 National Association for the Advancement of Colored People

9 "Big Jim" began marking the key times of the workday in 1895 with few interruptions since. He continues to this day to signal important historic events as well as the arrival of electricity and ringing in each New Year's Day since 1896.

10 Large Native American mounds made of shells, broken pottery and refuse. An ancient land fill.

11 A soft whitish limestone formed of broken shells and corals cemented together with sand and water then dried used for building.

12 Opening and closing

13 A free issue of shares to shareholders when a business transfers money from its reserves to its permanent capital.

[14] A low mound or ridge of earth.

15 Saint Matthew is the patron saint of tax collectors.

16 Level land that may be submerged by floodwaters due to tidal surges.

17 A mixture of salt and fresh water.

18 Favorable to promoting health or wellbeing.

19 A sailing vessel having three to five masts.

20 A lamp and housing for the ship's compass.

21 keel

22 Called a torpedo

23 Also called "The Rector's Warden, is responsible for the personal well being of the Rector and family, acting as an advocate for the Rector and providing the same with assistance in ministerial functions.
   * Acts as an advisor to the Rector.
   * Chairs the Vestry Meetings when Rector cannot attend.

24 General Enoch Poor

[25] Naval Air Station

26 Naval Air Station Jacksonville

27 now called Scout Blast

[28] de Aviles meaning of Aviles

29 leader

30 Outlying mission posts.

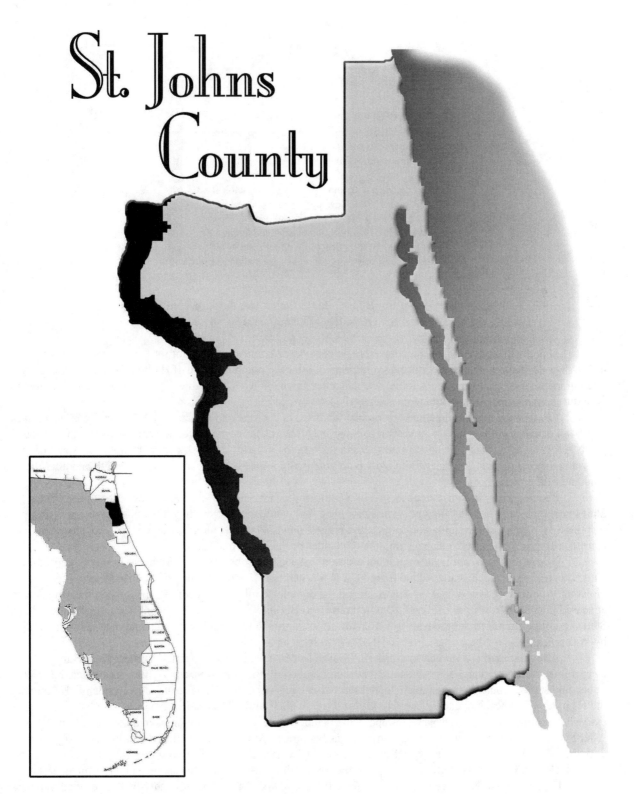

St. Johns County

WORLD WAR II
OPERATION PASTORIUS

On the night of June 16, 1942, German U-boat U-584 landed four trained Nazi agents here dressed as American civilians. After burying four boxes containing explosives and incendiaries in the sand, they boarded a bus en route to New York to rendezvous with another team of saboteurs. Two members of the New York team betrayed the operation to the FBI. All were apprehended, tried and convicted. The informers went to prison and the others were electrocuted on August 8, 1942.

200 Ponte Vedra Boulevard, Ponte Vedra Inn & Club, Ponte Vedra
SJ1 ~ GPS COORDINATES: 30.242150, -81.378683

This group of would-be saboteurs could be considered comical were it not for the seriousness of their intent. The entire operation began during World War II, after the bombing of Pearl Harbor. Walter Kappe, a high-ranking member of Nazi Germany's military intelligence force known as the Abwehr, was given the task to identify and train operatives for a sabotage mission against America.

The mission was code-named Operation Pastorius, in deference to Franz Daniel Pastorius the leader of the first band of Germans to settle on American soil in 1683. The intent was to target key American manufacturing plants responsible for constructing airplanes, create disruptions in railroad travel, communication lines and cripple the water supply of New York City. The plot could potentially impede American military strength and alter the outcome of the war.

Requirements for enlistees consisted of a command of the English language, knowledge of the United States geographically and that they be skilled in a trade that would aid in their disguise while in America. Kappe's ineptitude as a judge of character was perhaps the biggest downfall in this plot. It was Kappe who chose the first recruit, who was then tasked with selecting the remainder of the eight-man team.

Kappe's choice for this all-important mission was George John Dasch. Dasch had in fact lived in the United States for nineteen years. While there he was arrested twice, once for operating a brothel and the other for violating Prohibition laws. While on American soil, he completed all requirements for citizenship though he never appeared in court to be sworn. In 1941, Dasch returned to Berlin where he was eventually hired to monitor United States radio transmissions for the Nazi government. It was through this employment that he met and was recruited by Walter Kappe.

After eliminating a number of "nitwits," Dasch selected for his first operative, Ernest Peter Burger. Burger joined the Nazi Party at seventeen but later immigrated to the United States. While in America, he elected to become a citizen but when the Great Depression left Burger without work he returned to Germany. He rejoined the Nazi Party and became aide-de-camp to Ernest Roehm, chief of the Nazi Storm Troopers. He later wrote an extensive diatribe critical of the Nazi Gestapo, which landed Burger seventeen months in a concentration camp. After his release he entered the German army. It was his time in America that qualified him for the assignment with the sabotage team, however, given Burger's history why he was chosen is a mystery.

Herbert Haupt was the third member of the team to be conscripted. He was the youngest member, but had lived in the United States for sixteen years from the age of six. At the age of twenty-two, he elected to return to Germany. It seemed as if he were running away but the reason was not evident. From Mexico City he hoped a freighter bound for Yokohama, Japan in 1941; there he boarded a German steamer headed for Bordeaux. While serving as midnight watch on the steamer Haupt spotted an enemy ship and was awarded the Iron Cross for his diligence.

Heinrich Heinck was the final member of this team to be selected. Heinck had entered the United States illegally in 1926 and remained here for thirteen years. However, at the onset of World War II, Germany offered any German citizen a one way ticket home, called the repatriation program, Heinck leapt at the opportunity. Although he could speak English, Heinck accent was so pronounced that he was ordered not to speak unless the situation was completely unavoidable. He would complete the New York Team.

The second group would be lead by Edward Kerling. He was described as having puffy cheeks, a heavy jaw and dimpled chin; making Kerling a "decidedly Irish type." Kerling had spent approximately twelve years in the New York area and upon his return to Germany, he was assigned to run propaganda shows in movie theaters. His group would land in Florida at Ponte Vedra near St. Augustine, why this location was favored is unknown.

Herman Neubauer traveled to America in 1931. After nine years and various jobs, he returned to his native Germany and was drafted into the Army. While stationed at the Russian front Neubauer was wounded in the face and leg, then sent to an army medical center. As he recuperated, Neubauer was recruited for a "special assignment."

After only twelve years in the United States, Richard Quirin had found only limited success. Though while in New York he was employed by General Electric. When he returned to Germany through the repatriation program, his former employment made Quirin a prime candidate for the sabotage mission.

The final member of the Florida sabotage team was Werner Thiel. He was the only one of the entire team who had ever stepped foot on Florida soil. In fact, Thiel had only worked in Florida for a short time. But in the eyes of Dasch, he was a qualified recruit and all eight members of the two teams were now in place.

The entire group was sent to a farm confiscated from a wealthy Jewish shoe manufacturer near Brandenburg for training. Heavily guarded, the training areas consisted of sections of railroad track, various bridges, pistol and rifle ranges, a hand-grenade practice field and a gymnasium for boxing and judo instruction. Classrooms and laboratories for explosive manufacturing were situated over the garage. Even a nearby greenhouse supplied the group fresh vegetables, fruit and ironically, flowers. The men were also taught to sing "The Star Spangled Banner" and "Oh, Susanna," they were required to read American newspapers and magazines; all in an attempt to Americanize them as much as possible.

Each man was given an alias with the exception of Haupt and Burger, because both men held American citizenship. All saboteurs were required to sign contracts guaranteeing their silence on penalty of death. The contracts stated that if they died during their service to the Third Reich, their wives would receive compensation to be determined by the German government. If the mission were to be successful all would be given lucrative jobs after the war.

The teams were set to travel across the Atlantic by U-boat[1] and land under a cover of darkness in two separate locations, Ponte Vedra, Florida and Long Island, New York. Each team would be supplied with crates of explosives and tools. Each leader was given fifty thousand dollars in American currency the money was to be used for bribes and expenses. Each of the other members was given nine thousand dollars each. Dasch and Kerling received white handkerchiefs inscribed with messages written in disappearing ink. When exposed to ammonia fumes their contact information would appear.

A short time was allotted to spend with their families. Then teams met at Lorient, France. It was here that the Germans based the U-boat transporting each team. The Florida group departed on May 26, the New York group two days later. Planning and training took nearly a year, the trip across the Atlantic would last fifteen days. However, within a matter of minutes upon arrival, the entire scheme would fall apart.

The Florida team landed encountering no problems. They made their way north and waited for further instructions. The New York team was doomed from the start. Once they landed on the beach, Burger immediately decided to betray the sabotage mission. Away from the others he dropped an empty German cigarette tin, further along the beach Burger left a schnapps bottle, socks, a vest and a bathing suit; like Hansel and Grettle leaving bread crumbs in the old fairy tale. Little did the team know they were being observed from a distance.

**PONTRA VEDRA INN & CLUB
SITE OF THE FLORIDA SABOTOURES LANDING**

Coast Guardsman John Cullen was on midnight patrol duty, when he saw dark figures in the distance. Later he was quoted as saying, "I thought they were fishermen, local residents until I saw one of the guys dragging a sea bag into the dunes and speaking German." When Cullen approached to question the men, Dasch immediately took charge leading the young man away, aware that he had heard the German conversation. Dasch threatened Cullen with his life then offered a small bribe, which Cullen at first refused. Dasch upped the ante, Cullen by this time was very afraid, accepted the money and walked away.

Burger dragged the sea bag through the sand leaving an obvious trail, Cullen rushed back to the Coast Guard Station to sound the alarm. The Germans buried their uniforms and began making their way to the train station and New York City. The Coast Guard formed a search party of the beach. The search team could immediately smell diesel of the submarine, which was stuck on a sandbar off the coast. The ground beneath them trembled as the submarine finally broke free and headed out to open water. In the dawning hours of daylight the explosive crates were uncovered, along with Burger's obvious clues and the German army uniforms. The FBI was alerted at 11:00 a.m. and within one hour they had impounded the entire stash.

The Germans found themselves free in New York and loaded with money. They took full advantage of the opportunity shopping, partying in clubs and soliciting prostitutes. The men separated into two groups staying in different hotels. The Florida group was still making their way toward New York. Dasch and Burger were paired in one hotel. They immediately confided that neither wanted to fulfill the sabotage mission. Burger admitted leaving clues at their landing site. Dasch realized he must contact authorities to lessen his involvement. Little did they know that the plot had already been discovered.

Dasch called the FBI and Agent Dean McWhorter made a note of his call but did nothing with the information. After abandoning Burger, Dasch made a second call to the FBI. Agent Duane Traynor acted immediately on the call, having Dasch picked up. Within two days the entire New York team was in custody. Several days later the Florida team was arrested as well.

The FBI officially arrested Dasch on July 3. He was advised to plead guilty and not to mention his duplicity; if he followed these instructions he was promised that the President would issue a pardon after only a short jail sentence. After a year of planning and training, all of the Germans were incarcerated and only two weeks in the United States without ever committing a single act sabotage. A news black out was issued and President Roosevelt was briefed on the situation. The President declared that the two American citizens were guilty of high treason. The remaining Germans were considered spies and all deserved the death penalty. Roosevelt was determined that no civil court would release these men, something had to done.

J. Edgar Hoover broke the news to the country on June 27. The public, still smarting from Pearl Harbor, was incensed. Headlines read, "The Eight Nazi Saboteurs Should Be Put To Death." When the South Bend, Indiana Tribune polled its readership, the count was 1,097 to 1 in favor of the death penalty. In fact one reader suggested that the men be fed to Gargantua, a giant circus gorilla. Of course the reader feared that "surely," as a result of the German meal, "Gargantua would die of such poisonous eating."

Attorney General Biddle informed the President that a military tribunal would be fitting for just such an occasion. It would be quick, secret and the death penalty could be imposed with only a two-thirds-majority vote.

Roosevelt unearthed cases used in both Revolutionary and Civil War eras that justified his reasoning to invoke a military tribunal. Eventually, after sentencing had already been imposed, the Supreme Court upheld Roosevelt's decision.

The tribunal was selected: Major General Frank R. McCoy, presiding; three generals and three brigadier generals completed the panel: Attorney General Biddle lead the prosecution and Brigadier General Albert L. Cox was selected provost marshal. Colonel Cassius M. Dowell and Colonel Kenneth C. Royall were ordered to serve as defense counsel. Only Dasch received separate representation. Five of seven members of the panel were required for conviction and sentencing. The President was to make the final decision. There were no appeals allowed.

The prisoners were moved to the District of Columbia Jail under heavy guard. Each man was isolated, clad only in pajamas and paper slippers. No media contact was allowed, including newspapers or magazines and all meals were served with paper spoons and plates. There were no opportunities for suicide. No requests for family, friends or clergy were ever made by the prisoners.

Each man was allowed to speak in his own defense. Other witnesses were called including Cullen who was the first to make contact with the defendants. After sixteen days the tribunal went into deliberation. Royall appealed to the Supreme Court on the grounds that a military tribunal was unconstitutional, he was denied. The panel was out for two days. When the verdict was in, it was immediately delivered by Army plane to President Roosevelt at Hyde Park for final sentencing.

Four days later on August 7th General Cox received instructions from the President: The saboteurs were to be electrocuted at noon on August 8th, except Dasch and Burger. Dasch was sentenced to thirty years of hard labor and Burger received life in prison. After a breakfast of eggs, bacon and toast, the condemned men were informed of their fate; within hours they would die. The process began precisely at noon and went in alphabetical order. Each execution took approximately fourteen minutes including time to enact the sentence, record the time of death, remove the body and ventilate the room for the next man. By 1:30, the sentences had been imposed. It was fifty-six days from the time the saboteurs landed on American soil until their penalties were carried out.

The bodies of the saboteurs were interred in a pauper's cemetery at Blue Plains, Washington D.C. Six wooden markers bore the simple inscriptions 276, 277, 278, 279, 280 and 281. All records were sealed until the end of World War II. Dasch and Burger spent six years in American prison and were then deported to Germany in 1948. Burger simply disappeared into history. Dasch, seeking publicity, published "Eight Spies Against America" in 1959. The book never found an audience. He spent the remainder of his life working as a travel agent and tour guide in Germany, often under great harassment due to his betrayal. Strangely enough he later befriended Charlie Chaplin, who was in exile in Switzerland, each commiserating on how J. Edgar Hoover destroyed their lives. Dasch continued to hope for the presidential pardon promised by the FBI for the remainder of his life. It never happened. Dasch died in 1992.

Note: Among the many attorneys working on this case was Lloyd Cutler who went on to become the White House counsel for Presidents Jimmy Carter and Bill Clinton. President Bush consulted Cutler in an attempt to set up military tribunals in the aftermath of the terrorist attacks of September 11, 2001.

FORT SAN DIEGO
(DIEGO PLAINS)

In 1736 Diego de Espinosa owned a cattle ranch on Diego Plains, a flat, open area east of here. For protection against Indians, his house was surrounded by a 15-foot high palisade with two bastions at opposite corners. Manned later by Spanish soldiers, this post was known at Fort San Diego. On May 23, 1740, during the British expedition against St. Augustine, General James Oglethorpe's 400 man army captured the fort and its 50 defenders. The British added a ditch and breastwork, and used the fort to protect the St. Johns River-St. Augustine supply line. They evacuated the fort on July 25. By 1743 it lay in ruins.

Landrum Middle School, Landrum Lane, Ponte Vedra Beach
SJ2 ~ GPS Coordinates: 30.163283, -81.389833

Before the arrival of the first Spanish explorer, Don Juan Ponce de Leon on Easter, March 27, 1513, the native Timucua Indians occupied what would later be dubbed "Diego Plains". Burial mounds uncovered in this area revealed Timucua arrowheads, pottery and bones. Six attempts to establish Spanish settlements in *La Florida*[2] all failed, though the Timucua village continued to flourish. The French managed to establish a fort and settlement on the St. Johns River in 1564. When news of the colony reached King Phillip II of Spain, Don Pedro Menendez de Aviles was dispatched to remove the threat to Spanish territory. Menendez was ordered to drive out any settler or pirate that might threaten Spain's treasure fleet that navigated the waters of the Florida coast.

Diego de Espinosa[3] received a Spanish land grant prior to 1703 and settled in the area. The area was ideal for cattle ranching having both flat and open grasslands. Diego's massive ranch and the surrounding property became known as Diego Plains. The Timucua resented the invasion of the Spanish. The Spaniards realized the need fortify the Diego property against Indian attack. A fifteen-foot palisade having two bastions at opposite corners was installed in the 1730s

Trouble began brewing on a different front for Diego Plains by 1739. The British, who had settled to the north in Georgia, were threatening to invade Spanish territory. Britain and Spain were at war and General James Oglethorpe, Governor of the Georgia colony, was determined to take St. Augustine. Fort San Diego was garrisoned with fifty Spanish soldiers. General Oglethorpe sailed south with fifteen ships and on January 1, 1740, he entered the St. John's River. Fort Picolata was burned. Fort St. Francis de Papa, only twenty miles from St. Augustine, was captured. Oglethorpe was very nearly killed during the capture of Fort St. Francis de Papa and he determined that additional forces would be necessary to stage an invasion of the great Castillo.

By May 1740, Oglethorpe was filled with confidence and moved on Fort San Diego. The fortification's fifty Spanish soldiers were easily overwhelmed and General Oglethorpe garrisoned the fort with British troops and their Indian allies. Oglethorpe's ranks were reinforced with the arrival of Captain McIntosh, a company of Scottish Highlander Soldiers of the Foot and a contingent of Carolina troops by mid May. General Oglethorpe, commanding an army of nearly sixteen hundred men, prepared to capture the Castillo.

Oglethorpe laid siege to the impervious Castillo de San Marcos for twenty-seven days and the fort continued to hold firm. In defeat, General Oglethorpe retreated to the Georgia coast. Fort San Diego was abandoned. Through lack of attention and maintenance, Fort San Diego lay in ruins by 1743.

The area was virtually ignored for the next one hundred years. Though constantly occupied, the settlement did not grow due to access difficulties. In 1908 a canal was dug connecting Diego Plains by means of the San Pablo River to the north with the Tolomato River near St. Augustine. The intracoastal Canal improved access to the valley and the population began to increase. Residents settled in Diego Plains and began to establish farms, logging operations and selling palm fronds to religious groups. The abundant palm trees inspired the name "Palm Valley". After petitioning Washington D.C., the name was officially changed from Diego Plains to Palm Valley in May 1908.

The Volstead Act implemented on October 28, 1919 brought new opportunity to Palm Valley. The Act forbade the manufacture, transportation and sale of intoxicating beverages. Prohibition, as the era was called, gave some valley residents another source of income - moonshine. The abundant water supply and remoteness of the valley made it an ideal site to conceal illegal whiskey distilling. The moonshine industry continued to thrive even after the Volstead Act was repealed in 1933. The rising price of sugar finally brought an end to the illegal whiskey operations.

Today Palm Valley is a quiet area of Ponte Vedra Beach, between highways A1A and US 1. The suburban community is home to many small farms raising produce and livestock, as well as numerous residences lining both scenic banks of the intracoastal waterway. The St. Johns County Historical Commission recognized Fort San Diego with a historical marker just west of its original site. Today the marker is located near the grounds of Landrum Middle School, Landrum Lane at Ponte Vedra Beach.

NEW SWITZERLAND PLANTATION

Francis Philip Fatio, Sr. (1724-1811) a Swiss native, brought his family, slaves and personal possessions here shortly after Spain ceded Florida to Great Britain in 1763. After obtaining a crown grant of 10,000 acres in this area, Fatio imported materials from England and built a country estate where he lived the life of a frontier baron. The plantation buildings were destroyed during the East Florida Patriot revolt in 1812.

2159 Mandarin Road (SR 13) at Volunteer Fire Department, Mandarin
SJ3 ~ GPS Coordinates: 30.075483, -81.648000

Francis Philip Fatio[4], Sr. was born in Switzerland on August 6, 1724. He studied law at the University of Geneva to please his family but failed to complete his education electing instead to join the Swiss Guards. As an officer, Fatio was in France during the War of the Austrian Succession.

While living in England, the virtues of British Florida came to his attention. At the age of forty-seven, Fatio sailed for Florida with his family in tow. The family purchased a large coquina house on the St. Johns River near St. Augustine. From there he acquired three plantations raising indigo, oranges and sheep. Fatio was excited about the prospects for naval stores[5] in the New World. The tall white pines provided excellent wood for building ships, fine long timber for masts and flooring as well as turpentine for making tar was utilized as a water sealant.

Fatio, with the help of his eldest son, bought a ship for continual shipments between Florida, England and Spain. The exports financed comforts and luxury items that insured his family's happiness in remote Florida. He provided pinewood and shingles for much needed repairs to the Governor's house in St. Augustine on credit. Thus the Governor found himself in Francis Philip Fatio's debt. The high profile business deals elevated the Fatio family's status in the community.

Fatio enjoyed the wealth but preferred the life of a country gentleman. In 1772 he garnered a considerable land grant away from the bustle of St. Augustine extending twelve miles along the St. Johns River. Like a great baron ruling from his estate, Fatio conducted his business through his sons and all the while he enjoyed the view from a chair on the wide porch of his home. The boys traveled extensively and sometimes lived abroad; Sardinia, England, Cuba, Charleston and New York were frequent stops on the Fatio sons' agenda. Often they served the community in government posts or wheeling and dealing for the family business.

The grand plantation along the St. Johns was called "New Switzerland" in deference to Fatio's homeland. The doors there were always open to entertain. Guests were given a soft bed, abundant food as well as access to horses and boats, whatever means of transportation they preferred. Spanish soldiers were welcomed and often spent days of rest and recreation on the estate. No one was turned away even the Seminole were given a haven of rest and nourishment after they had crossed the St. Johns on Fatio's river ferry.

Regardless of the comforts Fatio offered the Seminole, it did not ensure him any special consideration. In the early evening hours of August 31, 1801, a band of Seminole raided New Switzerland and made off with thirty-eight slaves. As the moon rose above the horizon the full face illuminated their path to the St. Johns and on to Miccosukee[6]. Many of the slaves were delivered to William Augustus Bowles, an adventurer of Scottish and Creek Indian parentage. Bowles kept areas of Spanish Florida and American, Alabama and Georgia, in turmoil for fifteen years with his schemes and daring raids. Fatio contacted Benjamin Hawkins, an Indian Agent, to assist in the return of the stolen slaves. Bowles refused to release them.

Francis Philip Fatio, Sr. died on the eve of the War of 1812 and was buried alongside the St. Johns River on the grounds of his beloved estate. Fortunately he did not live to see the Seminole, that he had opened his home to, burn the grand plantation. Fatio, Jr. barely escaped with his life during the attack. He and ten others were forced to take refuge at the Fort Stallings blockhouse[7] on Davis Creek. During the attack, according to Dr. James Cusick of the University of Florida, Fatio's decayed remains were scattered about the family cemetery.

Francis Philip Fatio, Jr. died in 1831, his son passed away only six months later. New Switzerland was willed to Fatio's sister. Miller Hallowes, after he resigned from a long army career in Simon Bolivar's Irish Legion, arrived at New Switzerland in 1832 to oversee his mother's property. In short order he married Catherine Nichol and for a number of years the couple resided at New Switzerland.

In 1836, during the Seminole War, New Switzerland was assaulted once again. While trying to defend the manor Hallowes took a bullet to the neck. Medical aid was given at the United States Army post but the surgeon was unable to remove the lead. The injury caused Hallowes severe anguish for the remainder of his life.

During the Civil War, Hallowes established Bolingbroke a plantation located at St. Marys in South Georgia. He grew cotton, corn, potatoes, sugar cane and produced arrowroot starch. His son joined the Confederacy but as the Federal army approached his Georgia home Hallowes strung up the Union Jack ensign and Bolingbroke was left uninjured. Hallowes never relinquished his British citizenship.

At the conclusion of the Civil War, Bolingbroke was sold. Hallowes returned to New Switzerland where he built a plantation called Claremont. He spent the waning years of his life and was buried there in 1877. Portions of Bolingbroke became what is known today as Kings Bay Naval Submarine Base. New Switzerland became a small Northeast Florida town, which still exists today.

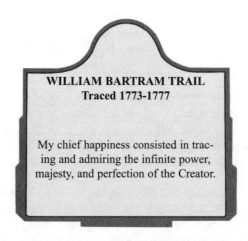

WILLIAM BARTRAM TRAIL
Traced 1773-1777

My chief happiness consisted in tracing and admiring the infinite power, majesty, and perfection of the Creator.

SR 13 at Kentucky Branch Bridge, St. Johns County
SJ4 ~ GPS Coordinates: 30.055467, -81.667783

William Bartram recorded his observations throughout the south in a book entitled "Travels." Obviously having the heart of a poet, his words were lyrical and romantic as Bartram described the people, places, flora and fauna along paths of unexplored terrain. It is said that Bartram's works contained some inaccuracies, though his offering was then and still remains the most complete accounting of the areas he traversed for the time.

Actually "Travels" is a collection of four books combined into one text. The editions included his experiences in Florida, Georgia, Alabama, Mississippi and Louisiana; the final work examined the Native Americans of those regions. Bartram detailed the cycles of life and nature based on his experiences.

William Bartram resisted a common tendency to offer a wordy scientific diatribe more informative than entertaining. He took great pains to arrange the manuscript into an easy to read narrative. Often he resorts to the arrangement of his travels seriatim or chronologically though he uses a topical format as well. One brief subject would lead to an account of the entire species, for example: encountering a single wild turkey in the evening under the vast shade of a towering oak draped with the hanging lace of Spanish oak led to a meticulously detailed version of the entire turkey genus.

A great deal of Bartram's travels involved very mundane treks through the wilderness. Days upon days of nothing more exciting than the morning dew clinging to the leaves or white tailed deer grazing on an especially enticing meadow of tender spring grass. Occasionally Bartram did stumble upon some excitement, for example: he wrote of a chance meeting with a Native American, who glared menacingly at him, yet softens to calm by Bartram's hardy greeting. William Bartram stated that he had later learned that this particular Indian had been "extremely ill-treated the day before" and had vowed to take the life of the first white man he encountered. His story was said to have been slightly embellished for effect, though entirely plausible.

To suggest that Bartram's renderings were nothing more than a scientific manifest would be completely inaccurate. In fact, Bartram was very literary. His attention to present and past tense when describing his surroundings was an attempt to bring the reader into the forest. "Travels" allowed a glimpse into Bartram's world, a chance to transport the reader back in time and see through his eyes the beauty of Florida surroundings. His vivid descriptions made it possible to figuratively walk by his side, when he spoke of Florida springs one could envision the crystal clear water as "the blue ether of another world " or "almost as transparent as the air we breathe!"

William Bartram's writing revealed reverence to the diversity of the forest, open plain, saw grass marshes and salt kissed ocean shores of Florida. Describing each realm of natures landscaped bounty as decorated in it's own unique scheme and inhabited with a vast variety of wildlife as diverse as the land itself. From the throwbacks to ancient times with the mighty marsh alligator to the sleek predator panther; diminutive key deer to the abundance of the oceans gifts; every aspect of Florida's fauna had a place in the circle of life.

Bartram's personality was suitably represented in his work. Unlike his father John, Botanist to the England's King George, who was said to be very blunt often to the point of rudeness; William exuded the passion of an artist. His realistic expectations of his travels were revealed with a thoughtful countenance and a lilting, melodic voice that lent an air of poetry to his scientific presentation. Bartram described himself and his work as:

> "Continually impelled by a restless spirit of curiosity, in pursuit of new productions of nature, my chief happiness consisted in tracing and admiring the infinite power, majesty, and perfection of the great Almighty Creator. And in the contemplation, that through divine aid and permission, I might be instrumental in discovering, and introducing into my native country, some original pro ductions of nature, which might become useful to society."

Recorded in "Travels" are observations of the migratory patterns of North American birds. Bartram's work is the first complete and accurate listing of birds published is America. Yet he downplayed his accomplish-ments saying humbly that other naturalists of the era had much greater abilities and knowledge of the subject.

The only departure from his preset outline was Book IV detailing the customs, character and image of native tribes that he encountered. Bartram's stance is one of complete fairness. He neither takes a sympathetic nor adversarial view of the people; merely describing them, their every day life and the customs he observed, both the good and bad being noted. Bartram seemed to have had a very cordial relationship with the native people; he was called, "Puc Puggy" or Flower Hunter, the name identified him as a trusted equal who had come in peace.

William Bartram led an exceptional life; his travels, observations and knowledge of nature's gifts setting him apart from the average man. That said, Bartram was also no more than any ordinary man. In fact when faced with the temptations of the flesh he described the experience provocatively as having been introduced to "young, innocent Cherokee virgins very difficult to resist." Above all, Bartram remained a man filled with wanderlust and a thirst for greater knowledge. He carefully prepared for his missions and meticulously recorded his observations for posterity. Bartram never sought fame or fortune, yet occasionally they managed to find him. Once when detained by local dignitaries anxious to hear tales of his travels, he artfully escaped pleading a blinding headache when all he really desired was the solitude of the forest and the sound of a gurgling creek.

THE ACTUAL MARKER

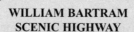

**WILLIAM BARTRAM
SCENIC HIGHWAY**

Within a mile and a half of this marker are numerous prehistoric sites, several of which date from 2000 BC. Native Americans occupied the northern river section from about 4000 BC until the arrival of Europeans after 1500 AD.

Riverbank settlements, permanent villages, and small seasonal campsites were common prehistoric site types. Abundant natural resources provided inhabitants with opportunities to hunt, fish, and collect shellfish and plants.

By the 1770's when William Bartram explored this area and Francis Fatio establish his homestead, few native peoples remained in the region.

Today, shell refuse deposits, pieces of pottery, stone and bone tools, and soil stains provide archaeological evidence reflecting the lifeways of those early Florida residents.

**SR 13 about .5 mile S of Kentucky Branch Bridge, St. Johns County
SJ5 ~ GPS Coordinates: 30.045650, -81.666233**

Humans have lived, worked and died in this area for more than twelve thousand years, their stories are told in the amazing archaeological sites uncovered continually about the region. Just as our ancestors left clues to their identity and lifestyles, we continue to do so today. As we build, preserve, bury our dead and dispose of our refuse, we leave the same identifying evidence to future generations.

Habitation in this region has been divided into five distinct periods, which can be identified through the social interaction, political structure and the use of tools in their daily lives. The periods are:

The Paleo-Indian Period[8] in the Southeast was believed to be the first emergence of man in this region, however resent discoveries seem to point to perhaps an even earlier date. Humans lived from hunting megafauna, all of which are now extinct. This megafauna included such oddities as Wilmington's Giant Ground Sloth weighing anywhere from three to five tons, its fossilized bones have been found in Florida; Giant Beavers weighing up to four hundred fifty pounds, which would have fed a small village for a day or so. Villages were sparse, very small and short term. The people seemed to be nomadic and move with their food sources. Sea level was approximately two hundred and thirty feet lower during the Paleo-Indian period, therefore any remains of this period would be found deeply entrenched and well off the coast.

Archaic Period[9] brought an environment very much like that of today. People congregated in more centralized locations with smaller camps on the outskirts. By the end of this period populations began establishing a long-term settlements especially long the coast. Shellfish and the bounty of the sea became preferred food sources. During this time soapstone and ceramic came into use. Most vessels were thick and crude using moss and plant fibers combined with mud then fired to harden.

Woodland Period[10] was easier to identify based on more permanent settlements. People began experimenting with farming; very distinctive social structures developed and distinguished individuals were now buried beneath rock mounds with trinkets common in their lives.

Mississippian Period[11] is identified through the use of large structures, usually rectangular and flat topped. The mounds were used as homes and religious structures. Populations grew in droves and permanent towns and farms resulted. Agricultural cultivation of corn, beans and squash supplemented hunted meats including deer, small game, fowl and fish. Nuts, berries, fruits and seeds were harvested from the forests.

Historic Period[12] Europeans arrived and brought with them their customs, language, religion and disease. The Europeans taught Native Americans to hold dear material things known as trade goods never needed in the past; such as beads and guns. Europeans brought the slave trade, introduced livestock breeding and the Native American populations began to suffer.

By the time of William Bartram's travels throughout the region in the 1770s, very few Native Americans actually remained. Most had been forced into the deep south of the everglades or to the southwest just beyond the grasp of European settlers. Over the next several decades the Native American would continue to make a valiant stand but ultimately in the end entire tribes were erased from the earth.

During Bartram's 1774 visit, around the middle of April, he visited the Marshall Plantation near Goodby's Creek across the St. Johns River from Cow Ford. Today we know the area as Ortega. Bartram traveled to the New Switzerland Plantation of Francis Philip Fatio formerly of Berne, Switzerland. It is said that Fatio assured Bartram that travel was safe and he could proceed up the St. Johns without fear.

William Bartram had learned his craft at the foot of a master, his father John, Botanist to the King of England. He grew to become an accomplished naturalist, a poetic writer and talented illustrator. Though he traveled extensively throughout the southeast, Florida held a special place in his heart. He spent approximately twelve years exploring the peninsula.

His subjects included a vast array of topics from roaring alligators to delicate tropical blossoms. His work was considered the last word in natural studies for the time. William Bartram's writing style influenced such poets as Wordsworth, Shelley and Coleridge. He traded American plant specimens and seeds with European botanists, introducing numerous American plant species in Europe and establishing some European species into the New World.

Bartram offered a fair accounting of the Seminole, Creek and Cherokee Indians. Seminole leader, Cowkeeper invited William to join their band as an honored member and in response noted, "the women and children saluted us with cheerfulness." He found the Seminole to be a happy people living in the remote Florida interior. Unfortunately time would change the Seminole. The tribe could no longer survive in Florida and only a few would survive hidden deeply in the Everglades. William Bartram became the age-old seer of natural science. His travels educated a generation of naturalists but his work continues to influence both science and literature today.

**CAN YOU FIND THE HIDDEN MARKER
IN THIS PICTURE?**

WILLIAM BARTRAM TRAIL
Traced 1773-1777

At Fort Picolata, Nov. 18, 1765,
William Bartram and his father,
John saw Creek Indian Treaty
signed and began their Florida
plants survey.

SR 13 near River Forest Road, Picolata
SJ6 ~ GPS Coordinates: 29.921317, -81.594083

During the first days of November 1765, John and William Bartram journeyed to Fort Picolata, located on the banks of the St. Juan[13] River. They arrived to observe a momentous occasion, the signing of a treaty between the Creek Indians and British government. The treaty would result in the annexation of Creek Territory for the British. British representatives arrived from St. Augustine while the Creek set up an encampment just outside the fort. Several days elapsed while the British awaited a vessel bringing token gifts for the Creek to arrive. During this time, John Bartram led several botanical excursions into the nearby forest.

Due to boredom around the fort, William decided to accompany his father on one of these tours through the swamp. After hiking over a quarter mile from the camp, William was startled by a warning from his father. He had walked a few paces ahead and the ever-watchful John noticed that his son was about to step flat footed into a very dangerous situation. Looking down William was alarmed to find a rattlesnake coiled menacingly at his feet.

Obviously the snake had taken a defensive position because he was tightly coiled and ready to strike. William Bartram described the serpent as about six feet in length and "as thick as an ordinary man's leg." Without giving the situation a second thought, William snapped off a nearby branch and killed the snake immediately. The encounter ended the tour for that day.

William tied a vine about the great snake and dragged his scaly body back to camp. Once he arrived with his trophy, he was at once the center of attention. The Indians and soldiers all strained to catch a glimpse of the rattlesnake. Once the news of the kill reached the ears of the fort commander, he sent an officer to request that the snake be delivered to the mess tent. Governor Grant was in residence for the treaty signing and it seemed that rattlesnake meat was a favored meal to him. William gratefully turned over the kill.

That night around the table the story was told again and again. William Bartram tasted the snake but alas could not swallow it. You see conscience had come in to play and he deeply regretted the killing. All though the rattlesnake certainly was capable of ending Bartram's life with one injection of his venomous fluid, he had not. The serpent had only defended himself from injury and in one felled stroke, William Bartram had easily slain him. Bartram vowed from that day forward, that "I should never again be accessory to the death of a rattle snake." He never killed another.

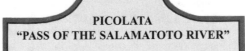

PICOLATA
"PASS OF THE SALAMATOTO RIVER"

Here where the St. Johns River narrows, was a
natural crossing used by Indians, and later by
the Spaniards, in pushing west. A Spanish fort,
built in 1700, protected the crossing and trail
that led to Apalache, near Tallahassee. From
1836 to 1870, a stage line, connecting with
river steamers, ran from this point to St.
Augustine.

SR 13 & SR 208, Picolata
SJ7 ~ GPS Coordinates: 29.914950, -81.592883

The Spanish established a garrison some eighteen miles west of St. Augustine in the late 1600s on the
banks of the St. John's River. The outpost was later called Fort Picolata. Across the river on the opposite bank
was situated a sister fort called San Francisco de Pupo. Around 1735, these garrisons were enlarged and fortified
to protect travelers and guard St. Augustine against Native American attack from the west. The location was ideal
with a make shift Indian trail road leading to Apalache and having an easy ford across the St. Johns river.

A small, light palisade[14] surrounded each fort, which consisting only of a small wooden sentry box.
Eight soldiers having two swivel guns or cannon manned the fortification. Strangely enough by 1737 the two simple wooden fortifications were already in a state of disrepair. The following year Spain granted permission to rebuild the forts with more permanent materials[15] but the construction never took place.

Two years later the English General from Georgia, Oglethorpe, ordered Lieutenant Dunbar on a reconnoitering mission, to scout the defenses of St. Augustine. Dunbar, with forty British soldiers and ten Native
Americans attacked Fort Picolata. Seven brave Spanish soldiers valiantly defended their post against seven hours
of mortar shelling, eventually driving away the English intruders. Unfortunately the deteriorated Fort Picolata
structures were demolished and the Spanish soldiers' efforts were for naught. Fort Picolata was evacuated, a week
later when the English returned and burned what remained to the ground.

The British Redcoats, led this time by General Oglethorpe himself, attacked Fort Francisco de Pupo. A
single return volley from the fort grazed Oglethorpe's face nearly costing the General his life. After this one shot,
Fort Francisco de Pupo surrendered. Oglethorpe, having taken both forts, opened the St. Johns River to British
navigation. The Spaniards at St. Augustine were cut off from their friendly Native American allies. Oglethorpe
then left a garrison to man the forts and returned to Georgia once again.

At the end of the war, Spain again assumed control of forts Picolata and Francisco de Pupo. Fort Picolata
was rebuilt in 1755. The fort was constructed much more durably this time of coquina block taken from Anastasia
Island. By the time of Florida's British occupation[16] (1763- 1783), Fort Picolata was again deserted and left to
ruin. The most accurate details concerning the fortification come from writings of British botanist and explorer
William Bartram. He observed and recorded the following:

"[The fort is] "dismantled and deserted . . . very ancient, and . . . built by the Spaniards. It is a
square tower, thirty feet high, invested with a high wall, without bastions, about breast high,

pierced with peepholes and surrounded with a deep ditch. The upper story is open on each side, with battlements supporting a cupola or roof: these battlements were formerly mounted with eight four-pounders, two on each side. The work was constructed with hewn stone, cemented with lime. The stone was cut out of the quarries on St. Anastasius Island, opposite St. Augustine; it is of a pale reddish colour, and a testaceous composition, consisting of small fragments of sea-shell and fine sand . . ."

Both forts faded into the mist of history. Over time the St. Johns River shifted course slightly and by the mid-19th century had completely claimed both fortifications. It is believed that as the riverbanks eroded, both forts disappeared beneath the murky waters of the river.

The Florida Bureau of Historic Sites and Properties began a project to relocate the forts in the early 1980s. The search utilized historical documents and maps at the request of the Bartram Trail Conference. It was believed that what remained of Fort Picolata was beneath five to fifteen feet of water approximately six hundred, fifty feet off the eastern bank of the St. John's River near the present day town of Picolata.

Florida State University's Scientific Diving Techniques class conducted an underwater survey in 1981 to find remains of the sunken fort. Using modern technology, for that time, the student reconstructed how the riverbank would have appeared during the time the forts stood on dry land. Divers braved very limited visibility, ranging from two to zero feet, in the murky water of the St. Johns to find some evidence of the forts. Tree stumps were found to indicate that the site was once dry land, however, the search resulted in little else. One diver felt what he described as a structure, possibly the remains of a wall; unfortunately the site could not be relocated.

The remains of Fort Picolata remain a mystery. No further research has been done, though with modern technology perhaps another attempt will be made. Until that time Fort Picolata will be but a footnote in history beneath a watery tomb.

THE ACTUAL MARKER

NINE MILE ROAD

Nine Mile Road was so named because its early eastern terminus at the Kings Road, built in 1775, near U.S. Highway Number 1, is nine miles north of St. Augustine.

Between the terminus of Nine Mile road at the Kings Road and State Road Number 16. Nine Mile Road passes through portions of Twelve-Mile Swamp and crosses land originally granted to the Indian trading firm of Panton Leslie and Co. by the British Crown some time after 1763. In 1813, the same tract of 10,000 acres passed to the St. Augustinian, Antonio Huertas, through a grant from the Spanish governor, Sebastian Kindelan. From the early 1800s the pine flatwoods bordering the road were noted for grazing cattle and for producing turpentine. From its early inception to the present. Nine Mile Road has provided a mean of transportation for residents of St. Johns County and remains an integral part of our heritage.

International Golf Parkway, 1/2 mile east of Interstate 95, St. Johns
SJ8 ~ GPS Coordinates: 29.988100, -81.450950

Nine Mile Road was named in reference to the nine miles of scenic roadway leading to St. Augustine. In 1998, the St. Johns County Board of Commissioners recognized the historical significance of the throughway with two plaques promoting the scenic land and water panoramas revealed to the motoring public. The road meanders through an area known as Twelve Mile Swamp nettled between Kings Road and State Road Number 16. History of the area expanded to some two thousand to five thousand years, when in 1996 archaeologist uncovered two spear points along the road proving the presence of Native Americans during that time.

Panton, Leslie and Company was established in 1783 and headquartered in Pensacola from 1785-1830. William Panton and John Leslie were merchants from Scotland who immigrated to Georgia. When the American Revolution heated up, the men moved to St. Augustine in British held East Florida due to their Loyalist stance. Experienced in the Indian trade, the company became the Sears and Roebuck of their time. Forced out of Florida when Spain again assumed control of Florida, Panton and Leslie retreated to the Bahamas only to return two years later in 1785.

By 1795 the company had a monopoly on the Indian trade from present day Memphis to St. Augustine, possibly due to the fact that one of their primary stockholders[17] was Alexander McGillivray, chief of the Creeks. As a result, by the late 1700s, the Company had annual business dealing that exceeded to the exorbitant sum of two hundred thousand dollars. In 1795, the northern boundary of Florida expanded to the 31st parallel, Natchez and St. Stephens in Alabama became part of the United States. The shear land mass made it difficult for the company to collect money owed to it by those residing in that area, especially the Indians. Through intense negotiations between the Panton-Leslie Company and the United States Government, a deal was struck which made it possible for such debts to be paid through the transfer of property rights. This deal resulted in the Panton-Leslie Company acquiring over three million acres of land, including the land encompassing Nine Mile Road.

Governor Vicente[18] Manuel de Zespedes wished to maintain good relations with the increasing number of Creeks and realized the Native Americans provided a buffer zone between St. Augustine and the American settlements. In order to maintain the strong alliance with the Creeks, the Spanish allowed Panton and Leslie to establish the fur trade business. Though the fur trade was only a small portion of their endeavor, the firm sold the Native Americans every conceivable product with the exception of rifles, which were disallowed by Spanish law.

Florida Governor Sebastian Kindelan issued a Spanish land grant of ten thousand acres to St Augustine resident Antonio Huertas in 1813. The area included the property surrounding Nine Mile Road. In December 1838, Jno. Fontane filed an application with the Judge of the County Court of St. Johns for the probate of Antonio Huertas' estate. We can only naturally assume that Huertas had died at this point. However, strangely enough the name appears in history again though he appears to have no relation to the first Antonio Huertas.

Confederate soldier Anthony T. Welters used the names Anthony Wetters, Tony Fontane and that of, Antonio Huertas. The names Fontane and Huertas are linked at the probate of Huertas' estate in 1838 and here again. The coincidence is striking, though it is unlikely that the two are connected.

Anthony T. Welters was born in 1810 and enlisted in the Confederate Army as a fifer in 1861, he was fifty-one years old. He participated in the battles of Perryville, Murfreesboro, Vicksburg, Chattanooga, Chickamauga, Atlanta, Franklin and Nashville. Welter returned home to St. Augustine after the war and is recorded as having lived at 79 Bridge Street. He became active in politics and with the E. Kirby Smith Camp, who was a noted Confederate General. Anthony T. Welters died in 1902; he was ninety-two years old.

Though his life was certainly remarkable, what made Welters so different from other Confederate veterans? Anthony T. Welters, sometimes using the name Antonio Huertas, was a former slave fighting for the Confederacy. Colonel John Masters of St. Augustine, retired United States Army, stated in an article expertly done by Peter Guinta for the St. Augustine Record, "Nobody wanted to be a slave, but this was their home and the North was an aggressor nation." All six recorded St. Augustine African American Confederates survived the war.

Masters has documented nine thousand Confederate graves in Florida. Only six of them are black, he said, because most records of the time did not list race. Civil War histories virtually ignore the fact that more than seventy thousand African-Americans served with the Confederate Army. Anthony T. Welters is one of at least two African American Confederate veterans buried at San Lorenzo Cemetery on US 1 in St. Augustine.

Today, Nine Mile Road is recognized by a different name – that of International Golf Parkway. The moniker was derived when World Golf Village was built on the western end of Nine Mile Road near Interstate 95. When a golfer goes to heaven he or she prays that it be just like World Golf Village.

World Golf Village is home to the World Golf Hall of Fame, an interactive golf museum, which not only honors the most notable participants who ever swung a club, but also is filled with exhibits and displays that exemplify the sport. An IMAX theater, a wide variety of shops and a number of outstanding restaurants await the arrival of golf enthusiasts daily. Golf merchandise is featured in the many shops, but there is also a bookstore, toy store and various other retailers from the St. Augustine and Jacksonville areas. Great restaurants abound. For a quick lunch at the World Golf Hall of Fame Café, Legends Grill & Tap Room, comedian Bill Murray and his five brothers present their lighthearted Caddyshack™ restaurant, Sam Snead's Tavern tees up with much memorabilia and a hardy meal or treat yourself to an elegant sit-down dinner at Cypress Point Restaurant and Lounge. World Golf Village has something for the dining pleasure of everyone. PGA Tour Stop is a first of its kind retail and sport experience. An amusement park for golfers as well as a retail mecca complete with sand bunkers and water hazards where customers can try out new putters.

For vacationers and devotees who want to stay awhile, World Golf Village offers first rate resorts including the Sheraton Vistana and The World Golf Village Renaissance. Both hotels offer superb luxury accommodations and world-class service and style.

Of course, the featured attraction of World Golf Village is golf. The challenging and pristine courses include: The Slammer & The Squire, named after player consultants "Slammin'" Sam Snead and Gene "The Squire" Sarazen. Golf Hall of Famer's, Arnold Palmer and Jack Nicklaus designed the King & The Bear. Nine Mile Road has covered the miles of history from its founding days in 1775 over the course of more than two hundred twenty-five years.

**CR 208 West from I-95 on the north side of the road just east of Pellicer Road,
St. Augustine
SJ9 ~ GPS Coordinates: 29.921594, -81.434120**

When General Thomas S. Jesup failed to capture the Seminole Chiefs in the summer of 1837, he changed course. He relied on lies and subterfuge to seize the Native Americans. In September, Jesup enlisted the aid of Coacoochee, known by his Americanized named Wild Cat to help bring in Osceola. General Jesup set a trap using Coacoochee to take a message to Osceola requesting a meeting under a flag of truce to negotiate peace. The location of this conference was to be about one mile south of Fort Peyton.

Coacoochee's father, a Miccosukee chief known as King Philip, was captured and it was Coacoochee's intention to deal for his release. General Jesup did not intend to even initiate peace talks. He first demanded Osceola give up all escaped slaves and that the Indians surrender, allowing them to be removed from Florida. When Osceola declared his purpose, under the white flag, to only stop the fighting and have peace General Hernandez was signaled. The trap was sprung, Hernandez with two hundred dragoons surrounded the small band of Seminole. The shocked captives were comprised of less than one hundred chiefs, warriors, women and children were taken without a shot fired.

By October of 1837, the prisoners arrived at the Castillo de San Marco in St. Augustine where they would be incarcerated. The captives were crowded into small quarters. Among them were Chiefs King Philip, Coacoochee, Coa-Hadjo, Yuchi Billy, Yuchi Jack and of course, the most prized prisoner, Osceola. Disease was rampant under the horrendous conditions. During the night in the fall of 1837 a stomp dance was held, terrifying the St. Augustine citizens into believing the Seminole were about to revolt.

Coacoochee and nineteen others began to starve themselves. Under a cover of darkness on November 29, 1837, Coacoochee and his followers escaped their confines. So emaciated the group slipped through an eight-inch opening, fifteen feet from the floor of their prison. Coacoochee utilized a knife to climb the wall and blankets to pull the remaining prisoners to the window ledge. They ran for cover in the forest. These brave warriors managed to breakout of an escape proof cell. Osceola was ill and refused to go, fearing he would slow them down. The stubborn Chief also believed that he had done nothing wrong and right would prevail. Osceola never knew freedom again and would die in captivity. Yuchi Billy died only days after the escape, either by the excessive starvation or disease.

The able leader, Coacoochee went on to orchestrate, with Sam Jones, the Battle at Lake Okeechobee in December 1837 where Colonel Zachary Taylor, who eventually ascended to the highest office in the land,[19] men outnumbered the Seminole by two to one but suffered the greater loss of men.

Coacoochee abandoned peaceful intentions and attacked. On May 23, 1840, he and a group of warriors ambushed the stage bound for St. Augustine. The stage was transporting a traveling Shakespearean Theater Troupe and several other passengers. One of the actors was murdered along with five other travelers. The massacre incited fear throughout the area, this was amplified when the Seminole braves were dressed in the distinctive pieces of the troupe's costumes easily identified. This incident initiated a mass manhunt for Coacoochee who was captured alive in 1841.

The famed Seminole was taken by force to Oklahoma soon after his apprehension. Coacoochee, it is said, stated that the white man had lied and that all the Seminole had asked for was enough land to plant, live upon and inter their dead but this was denied to them. Conditions on the reservation in Oklahoma proved to be little better than the prison Coacoochee had escaped from. He, along with a black Seminole called John Horse, fled to Mexico with some eight hundred followers. Coacoochee, known as Wild Cat, succumbed to smallpox in 1857.

The cell at the Castillo de San Carlos in St. Augustine, which once held Coacoochee and other prisoners, is now sealed. This section of the long-lived fortification is unsafe for entrance.

ST. JOHNS RAILWAY

This highway follows closely the route of the old St. Johns Railway between Tocoi Landing on the St. Johns River and St. Augustine. Chartered in 1858, it was the first railroad to serve the city. Steam power was temporarily used on the line in the late 1860's but later abandoned for mule teams. In 1878 steam engines were permanently installed. The Florida East Coast Railway acquired the road in 1888, and continued its operation until 1894.

Calvin Pete Park, Kings Street, St. Augustine
SJ10 ~ GPS Coordinates: 29.887650, -81.354017

The St. Johns Railroad was first chartered in 1856 at the hands of Democratic National Convention Delegate Dr. Westcott. Two years later the good doctor moved to St. Augustine and in 1874 the railway became a reality. Wooden rails extended from the San Sebastian River to Tocoi Landing. Mule teams actually pulled the cars along the route. Dr. Westcott's commitment to Florida transportation involved his active participation in the development of the Intracoastal Waterway linking the St. Johns River to Miami.

Dr. Westcott sold the railway to William Astor, son of John Jacob Astor. Richard McLaughlin was named president and John Stockton, treasurer of the St. Johns Railroad. Under Astor's management the railway prospered and became a financial success. When William passed away in 1884, John Jacob Astor IV inherited the business.

The St. Johns Railway was a short wooden line of fifteen miles. Six miles of the tracks from St. Augustine combined the St. Johns and Palatka railroads until they divided toward their separate destination. Two steam locomotives with little "coffee mill" engines replaced mule teams. When Henry and Mary Flagler took the St. Johns Railway on their first trip to St. Augustine the fare was two dollars per person and the trip took several hours.

In 1886, John Jacob Astor IV suggested that he and Flagler work together to develop Florida's railway system. Flagler countered with a proposal to buy the St. Johns from Astor, which was respectfully declined. Henry Flagler purchased the railway two years later. John Jacob Astor IV died on April 15, 1912, aboard the Titanic.

Once Flagler owned the railway he immediately began replacing the wooden tracks with standard gauge iron rails. While the work was in progress, based on Flagler's instructions, no train schedule was interrupted. With the purchase of the Palatka line Flagler now had a direct link south to Daytona. These transactions resulted in his realization that bridges at Jacksonville, Tocoi Landing and Palatka were priorities. Unfortunately Tocoi's development was halted in 1894 because of the nature of the river there and the construction at Jacksonville and Palatka had claimed Flagler's complete attention.

Along the railway near Tocoi Landing, a Minorcan settler John Rogero raised his family with his wife, Mary Ann Goff and grew sugar cane. He cooked down the cane juice for molasses to be sold at nearby St. Augustine. The barrels of molasses were delivered aboard the train. The little train depot was located at the intersection of Tocoi Road and County Road 13A today.

A story is often told of John Astor standing by the tracks as the train squealed to a steamy halt and began to load the barrels of sticky, black molasses. As Astor hoisted the heavy oak barrels onto the railway car, one began to slip and like dominoes the rest followed. The barrels came crashing down splattering John from head to toe in dark, thick gunk. Mary Ann refused to let John in the house that evening until he had scrubbed clean. From that day forward that particular intersection has been known fittingly Molasses Junction.

The Rogero Farm currently houses the fifth generation of Minorcan descendents. They no longer produce the molasses that Grandpa John did, Donald and Marianne Rogero have introduced a wonderful line of products made from the hot Spanish Datil peppers grown on the family farm.

ZORA NEALE HURSTON

Noted author Zora Neale Hurston (1891-1960) rented a room in this house in 1942. One of the few surviving buildings closely linked with Hurston's life, it is an example of frame Vernacular construction, with cool, north-facing porches on both floors. The owners frequently rented to female students at nearby Florida Normal and Industrial Institute (now Florida Memorial College in Miami). While living here Hurston taught part time at the Institute and completed her autobiography, Dust Tracks on a Road. Also, she met novelist Marjorie Kinnan Rawlings, a St. Augustine resident and author of The Yearling. Earlier in 1927 Hurston married Herbert Sheen, a Chicago medical student, at the St. Johns County Courthouse. Hurston was one of the first to appreciate the significance of Fort Mose north of St. Augustine, the first town settled by free black people in the United States. Her article on Fort Mose appeared in the October 1927 issue of the Journal of Negro History. During her lifetime Hurston traveled the back roads of Florida collecting folk stories and songs that she used to write musical plays, short stories, and novels.

791 West King St., St. Augustine
SJ11 ~ GPS Coordinates: 29.889627, -81.339551

Zora Neale Hurston was born, of this we are sure, yet the day and year are questionable. While most sources agree that she was born in January the date varies between the seventh and the fifteenth with the year being named from 1891 through 1903. Hurston recorded her birth year as 1903, however the United States census of 1900 records her birth as 1891 in Notasulga, Alabama. Regardless of the year, her parents were Lucy Ann Potts, a teacher and John Hurston, a carpenter and Baptist minister. As a child, Zora moved with her parents and seven siblings to a sleepy little hamlet north of Orlando called Eatonville. Her father was elected mayor for three terms in Eatonville, the first all-black community to be incorporated in the United States.

Hurston said in her autobiography, that as a child:

"I used to climb to the top of one of the huge chinaberry trees which guarded our front gate and look out over the world. The most interesting thing that I saw was the horizon.... It grew upon me that I ought to walk out to the horizon and see what the end of the world was like."

The statement reveals the depth of her ambition and drive, which propelled her, the remainder of her life. Unfortunately dreamy childhood was not in young Zora's future, in 1904 her mother died. Unfortunately her father and stepmother cast the young girl out to live first with one relative then another, by the time she was fourteen Zora was on her own.

Zora was determined to be educated and make something of herself. Never one to bend to the will of others, work as a maid came to a screeching halt when she refused the advances of male employers. She later traveled about the south as a wardrobe girl with Gilbert and Sullivan's repertory company. Zora was finally able to achieve her high school diploma in Baltimore and enrolled in Morgan Academy[20] working her way through life as a governess. By January 1925, Zora moved to New York City with a buck fifty in her pocket, no job, no friends but a lot of hope. Education remained to be an important endeavor throughout her life; Zora attended Howard University, received her Bachelor of Arts degree from Barnard College in 1928 and did graduate studies at

Columbia in 1934-35.

She married Herbert Sheen on May 19 1927, though he later said their union was doomed from the start. Sheen observed that Zora's ambition was first in her life and that the idealistic youthful dreams they shared were not enough to bind them together. An amicable divorce quickly followed in July 1931. Zora's view of writing illustrates the commitment, which led to ruination of her marriage:

"...the force from somewhere in Space, which commands you to write in the first place, gives you no choice. You take up the pen when you are told, and write what is commanded. There is no agony like bearing an untold story inside you."

For more than thirty years, Zora Neale Hurston was the most prolific female author in American literature. She published seven books, numerous short stories, periodical pieces, plays and musicals. Generally Zora's plot lines revolved around strong black women, much like the author herself. Her character development was so realistic that the readers often found themselves emotionally involved with the story.

By 1932, Zora returned to Florida working in the Creative Literature Department of Rollins College. Professionally she prospered but personally an excruciating stomach ailment that plagued her throughout life reared its ugly head. Obviously her physical illness hampered Zora's work, she wrote a New York benefactor Charlotte Osgood Mason that she had "little food, no toothpaste, no stockings, needed shoes badly, no soap." There seemed to be no even keel for Hurston, she was either doing very well or virtually destitute.

Zora spent considerable time in New Orleans studying with a hoodoo doctor while researching parts for a book. Hoodoo is folk magic based on herbs, roots, minerals, animal parts and personal possessions. Shortly after her sojourn in New Orleans, Zora married her second husband, Albert Price III. The wedding took place at Fernandina Beach and the groom was fifteen years her junior. It did not appear that the marriage was a profoundly happy one, it was suggested that Zora used some of the spells she had learned while studying hoodoo against Albert.

New York called to Zora again in the winter of 1940-1941 in a quandary over what to write next. A publisher suggested Zora write her autobiography, she vehemently resisted the idea. Soon she moved to California with a rich friend, Katharine Mershon and found work as a consultant at Paramount, then began working on the autobiography. Ever the wanderer, Zora put on her traveling shoes once again and headed for Florida.

Zora settled in St. Augustine where she began work at Florida Normal and Industrial Institute and began revisions on her autobiography. It was spring of 1942 and her rental house was only a mile from the college at 791 West King Street. While at Florida Normal, Zora managed to turn bad cafeteria food and a crowded dorm into a national crisis.

The United States War Department had given the college $500,000 to initiate a Signal Corps Civilian Training program. Because of sluggish enrollment numbers, the school desperately needed financial support. The Signal Corps program was meant to bring blacks into the war effort industry during World War II. Zora accused the War Department officials of choosing schools who could not financially afford to turn down the program because they did not want the Signal Corps to succeed.

Students recruited into the Signal Corps program complained about the cafeteria food, overcrowding in the dormitories and non-existent hot water due to ancient water lines. In protest, the students organized a boycott of the school cafeteria. The college president, William Gray, Jr. expelled some of the protesters who refused to apologize to the lady in charge of the cafeteria. The lady was in fact Gray's wife. Zora was incensed, she could pardon the presidents inability to manage the Signal Corp program but narcissism and conceit was inexcusable. Zora received great criticism from the black leaders of the time and decided it was time to move on. President Gray took the protests in stride and eventually began to institute improvements at Florida Normal after obtaining a second grant of seven hundred thousand dollars. However, Gray left the school too soon. He became the President of Florida A & M at Tallahassee in 1944.

"Dust Tracks on a Road", her autobiography, was published in November 1942. Critics were brutal in response to her offering. Many concluded that Dust Tracks on a Road was the "best fiction she ever wrote." Zora landed this time in Daytona Beach. She finally purchased a home, of sorts. The *Wanago*, a houseboat, satisfied her desire to have a home and be able to move on when the urge took hold. Zora enjoyed frequent trips up and down the Halifax and Indian Rivers. During this time she read, fellow Florida emigrant, Marjorie Kinnan Rawlings's Cross Creek. The work impressed Zora and she began a pen-pal relationship with the author.

Zora divorced Albert in November 1943. She continued to write but received only rejection letters in response. Scribners, who represented her friend Rawlings, took an interest in her work. By 1947, Scribners published one of her novels and took an option on a second. " Seraph on the Suwanee" was published the next year to a good public response, though the critics were confused. The work was quite different from any other work Zora had ever offered ~ it was about white people. Again her professional life was on the upswing; however personally, Zora was about to enter a low era from which she would never completely recover.

The lowest point in Zora Neale Hurston life began on September 13, 1948. She was arrested and charged with committing an immoral act with the ten year old son of her landlord, two years previously. Zora was at once able to prove the allegation false, she had in fact been out of the country at the time this crime was to have been committed. The charges were eventually dropped, unfortunately the press managed to gain access to the story and the sensational headlines cared not for guilt or innocence. Zora was devastated, she declared to a friend,

> "I care nothing for anything anymore.... My race has seen fit to destroy me without reason, and with the vilest tools conceived of by man so far.... All that I have ever tried to do has proved use less. All that I have believed in has failed me. I have resolved to die.... I feel hurled down a filthy privy hole."

Zora did live through the humiliation; she left New York and refused to communicate with her friends. Scribners bought another novel and she continued to publish articles. By 1950, she was working as a maid in south Florida. Zora said she was researching a piece on domestic workers, but the cold hard truth was she needed the money. Sporadic sales of magazine articles brought in some money but over the next ten years she continued to take odd jobs to support herself. Zora managed to purchase a small one-room cabin, her stomach ailments continued to plague her health and money was a constant concern.

She eventually filled the position of librarian at Patrick Air Force Base but was fired in less than a year for apparently being too educated for the post. In 1957 she became a reporter for the black weekly newspaper, the Fort Pierce Chronicle and then worked part-time as a substitute teacher at Lincoln Park Academy. None of these humble positions managed to dampen Zora's spirit. Always determined, proud and confident she trudged on; when asked in an interview what she wanted out of life, characteristically Zora replied, "I want a busy life, a just mind and a timely death."

She was forced by circumstances to enter the Saint Lucie County Welfare Home when she suffered a stroke on October 29, 1959. Zora Neale Hurston died alone there of hypertensive heart disease on January 28, 1960, strangely enough forty-four years to the day this article was written. Her remains were interred at the Garden of the Heavenly Rest, a segregated cemetery in Fort Pierce. Zora's resting-place went unmarked; her funeral was paid for by charitable donations.

Though she died without a penny, she had lived a very rich life. Zora fought for everything she believed in and had no regrets. She rose from nothing to become a member in good standing of the American Folklore Society, American Anthropological Society, American Ethnological Society, New York Academy of Sciences and the American Association for the Advancement of Science; she was listed in Who's Who in America for 1937.

The University of Florida today offers the Zora Neale Hurston Fellowship in Anthropology and the City of Orlando named a building in her memory. Perhaps the greatest honor came in 1973, when noted author Alice Walker[21] placed a stone at Zora's gravesite. It reads,

ZORA NEALE HURSTON "A GENIUS OF THE SOUTH"

1901 – 1960

NOVELIST, FOLKLORIST, ANTHROPOLOGIST

Zora was 69, 59, 58 or 57 at the time of her death. Regardless of her age, Zora Neale Hurston's work has stood the test of time.

MARKLAND

Markland, the Anderson family home has been a local landmark since 1843. Dr. Andrew Anderson, a prominent civic leader, laid the foundations of the coquina shellstone house in 1839, just before his death in a yellow fever epidemic. The original house, which forms the east wing of the present building, was completed by his widow, Clarissa Anderson.

His son, the second Dr. Andrew Anderson, developed the Markland orange grove, which extended from present-day Cordova St. west-ward to the San Sebastian River, into one of the most famous groves in Florida after the Civil War.

As a friend and business associate of Dr. Anderson, Henry M. Flagler purchased the eastern portion of the grove in the 1830's for the site of his Hotel Ponce de Leon. After the death of Dr. Anderson in 1924, the house was purchased by St. Augustine mayor Herbert E. Wolfe who sold it to Flagler College in 1968.

102 Kings Street, St. Augustine
SJ12 ~ GPS Coordinates: 29.891867, -81.316838

Markland is an exceptional historic site considering that for its more than one hundred sixty-five years of existence there have been a mere three times that ownership has changed hands. Originally the property belonged to the Anderson family for one hundred seven years, the Wolfe's held the deed for three decades and since 1968 Flagler College has claimed ownership. Rarely do historians see so little change for a property as significant as Markland. The story is fascinating.

Dr. Andrew Anderson arrived in St. Augustine from New York with his wife Mary and their two young daughters in December 1829. Mary's ill health had precipitated the move, because physicians at this time believed the semi-tropical climate was conducive to good health. His intent was to hang out his shingle and practice medicine; however, other opportunities soon caught his eye. Dr. Anderson realized the potential for commerce was great here and St. Augustine already had two physicians, Dr. Seth Peck and Dr. Simmons. Dr. Anderson was soon importing goods for resale from his brother Smith Anderson in New York. Brick, hay, beef, corn, oats and butter arrived on sailing vessels and in trade Dr. Anderson sent pine lumber and fire wood north to New York.

His acquisitions quickly grew to include real estate and a small orange grove. Though Dr. Anderson knew nothing about growing citrus, he resolved to expand his holdings. Dr. Simmons reported that orange farms could support one hundred trees per acre and each tree would potentially produce ten dollars annually. Dr. Anderson was delighted with the prospects.

Since 1834 the family lived on the property. The doctor acquired lots at what is today Cadiz Street and Artillery Lane. It was during this time that Dr. Anderson began calling his expanding estate Markland and the ever-present bayonet hedge appeared. These hedges remained well into the 1870s. The two daughters had been sent north for schooling during this time and a third daughter was born. Mary's health was still declining but financially the move south had been a profitable one. Until…

Four days of devastating cold in February 1835 ended all hopes of an orange harvest for that year. The temperature dropped to ten degrees on that cold February night. The temperature never rose higher than twenty-one degrees over the three frigid days. The unripened fruit hung like solid greenish orange balls of ice from the heavily laden trees. During the following days the blackened fruit littered the ground and trees looked as though a blaze had decimated entire groves. Few trees survived the killing freeze.

Undaunted, Dr. Anderson continued to find ways to recover from the great freeze. He believed that the mulberry trees and silk worms might aid in rebuilding, thus he pursued the new venture. He recovered financially enough to move the family to better accommodations on Hospital Street, now known as Aviles. Mary Anderson, however, was declining and obviously she realized that the end was near. She wrote to a widowed friend, Clarissa Cochrane Fairbanks and asked if she might travel south to help care for the Anderson family. Dr. Anderson repeated the request only two months later when Mary Anderson died at the age of thirty-seven. Clarissa Fairbanks sailed south from Boston to answer Mary's last request.

By 1838 Dr. Anderson acquired almost twenty acres of property and a new wife. Clarissa Fairbanks became the second Mrs. Anderson. Within the year Andrew Anderson was reporting considerable economic difficulties to his brother, Smith. As an afterthought he added, "my dear wife presented me with a fine boy on the 13th of March…He is a knowing one for his age."

Within the year, Dr. Anderson planned a grand mansion complete with an innovative communication or intercom system throughout the house. The cornerstone was laid without much fanfare and building had only just begun when the next tragedy struck St. Augustine. A yellow fever epidemic raged through the population and the first to be laid low was the town's doctor and Anderson family friend, Seth Peck. Dr. Anderson had no choice but to pick up his medical bag and return to his previous profession. Unfortunately, on November 7, 1839, Dr. Andrew Anderson succumbed to the yellow fever he valiantly fought.

Over the next several decades the story of Markland revolves around Clarissa Cochrane Anderson. She was determined, despite pleas from her Boston family, to continue Dr. Anderson's dream for success in St. Augustine. Unfortunately her endeavors first met with a rocky start. The mulberry trees that Dr. Anderson thought were certain to recover his loses from the orange groves after the great freeze left the family virtually destitute. The largest shipment of mulberry trees was slated to bring twenty thousand dollars the family coffers. When the precious cargo arrived at the New York harbor the entire lot was rejected as unclaimed and the shipment was consigned to the muddy water of the Hudson River.

Because of her dire circumstances Clarissa Anderson was forced to stop construction on their Markland home. Though within a years time she had accumulated enough money to resume building but on a much lesser scale than the original plans had detailed. The innovative intercom system proposed by Dr. Anderson was eliminated in favor of a much cheaper house bell system. By 1841, Clarissa Anderson and young Andrew were finally able to move into the home. The orange trees were heavy with bright globes of citrus, bringing new hope to Markland for the coming year. To supplement her income, Clarissa was forced to "rent" out her slaves to other farms; this action resulted in severe criticism and threat of eternal damnation from her Presbyterian minister brother.

Just when the oranges appeared to be recovering a new complication arose. This time it took the form of orange *coccus* or scale insect. Mrs. Anderson, along side her workers, personally scrubbed the trunks of every tree and sprayed the branches with whale oil soap mixed with kerosene. This remedy and many more were tried to no avail. Within weeks virtually Markland's entire orange grove was infested. Clarissa was forced to ask Sarah Peck, widow of Dr. Anderson's long time friend Dr. Seth Peck, for a loan offering the mortgage on Markland for collateral. Again, Clarissa Anderson was begged to move north; again, she refused to give up.

Markland became a hotel and Clarissa Anderson its weary host. Her days involved tending the house, keeping the animals, the vegetable garden and medicating her orange grove. In addition, she now added care for her "extended family," which is how she referred to the paying guests. Eventually, Markland provided a room for school lessons where five-year-old Andrew would first attend classes.

The process took ten years but slowly Markland recovered. Clarissa was able to pay off the loan from Mrs. Peck and save enough money to travel north with Andrew, now 14 years old. The purpose of the trip was to enroll Andrew in a proper school. Phillips Academy in Andover, Massachusetts was chosen to prepare Andrew for college. Clarissa remained north with relatives while Andrew attended school. Meanwhile Markland was in the care of C. C. Meeker, a "guest," who maintained the estate for a number of years in the absence of its owner.

Mr. Meeker quickly initiated a number of improvements, the first of which was to hire a gardener. Mr. Bodenhoff, whose first name was never given, was said to have been gardener for the King of Denmark for several years. His influence was very beneficial and Markland quite literally, blossomed. Bodenhoff added roses, black-berries and tomatoes to the estate and Bodenhoff began extensive restoration of the sickly orange groves.

By 1858, after twenty years at Markland, Clarissa Anderson pondered the thought of selling the estate. Rejecting the idea, she initiated construction instead. A separate house was built for the servants who had always slept in the attic of Markland. They included Matilda, housekeeper and gardener; Lettie, who tended the house and "hennery"[22]; Annie, the cook and her daughter, Lena. The four women were all taught to read and write and were all provided for when Clarissa Anderson drew her Last Will and Testament in 1860.

In 1858 Markland received a its first coat of paint to the bare coquina walls. The color was not specified, therefore the original color scheme is unknown. The idea delighted Andrew, who kept up to date of the happening on the estate through constant correspondence with his mother. In fact, it is that very correspondence which allows for such a detailed accounting for life on the estate.

Andrew finished college in 1861 and made his way home. With the dawning of the Civil War he joined the St. Augustine Blues. When Andrew departed for New York and medical school at Columbia University's College of Physicians and Surgeons, he paid a local youth to serve in the Confederate Army in his place. By 1863, the Civil War raged and the orange trees blossomed at Markland. Seemingly the restoration of Mr. Meeker and Bodenhoff paid off. The orange groves were heavy with fruit and Markland prospered. Dr. Anderson was now practicing medicine at St. Luke's Hospital in New York.

Dr. Andrew Anderson returned to Markland in 1866, much to the delight of his lonely mother. Though as joyous as Andrew's return was, this was the end of their detailed correspondence. Strangely enough Andrew had not long returned to St. Augustine when he heard the call of more lucrative endeavors. Like his father before him, medicine was vastly less appealing than business and agriculture. So repeating history, Andrew chose not to prac-tice medicine but became a gentleman farmer.

Markland was again expanded in 1870. It was not until 1884 that the first mention of a sanitary system was made. The estate was spruced up in sufficient time to welcome notables such as Sydney Lanier and General Ulysses S. Grant.

Clarrisa Cochrane Fairbanks Anderson fulfilled her final wish when in June 1881, after forty-three years at Markland; she died quietly in her bed. After a fitting memorial service at the estate, Andrew Anderson deter-mined that he could not stay at the plantation alone and resolved to travel for a time. The estate was left in the capable hands of Richard Nateel, a former slave who had learned the orange trade at the hands of a master, Clarrisa Anderson. Even though Andrew returned from time to time checking on the management the estate he never stayed at Markland. Though the house was lovingly restored and rented.

During 1885, Andrew Anderson met and befriended a man who would if not change his life certainly make a drastic impact. Henry Flagler and his wife traveled south for her health and after spending the day in Jacksonville, traveled on to St. Augustine. Flagler and Anderson became friends almost immediately, the relation-ship would last the remainder of their lives. In fact, determined to build a resort hotel, Flagler enlisted Anderson's help in finding suitable property in which to build. Eventually the Ponce de Leon Hotel was built adjacent to Markland; some of the estate property was actually sold to Flagler in order to amass enough property for the vast construction.

Andrew Anderson frequently stayed at Flagler's hotel while tenants came and went at Markland. Over the years as Flagler's interest turned to the south, Anderson often traveled with his friend to Ormond, Palm Beach and on to Miami. Flagler's influence seemed to spur Anderson's life to take a number of different directions. His real estate holdings flourished and so did his love life.

On January 29, 1895, Andrew Anderson wed Elizabeth Smethurst. The first time groom was fifty-six years old. Wasting no time at all, the couple had two children. Clarissa, named for her grandmother, was born in November 1895 and her brother Andrew just one year later. For the comfort of his family and to fulfill a long awaited dream, Andrew Anderson began the modernization and rebuilding of Markland to the standard first set forth by his father fifty-three years earlier. Dr. Anderson, Senior would have been proud of the modern upgrades added to the structure, such as heating insulation made of seaweed an innovation never imagined by the elder Anderson. The restoration took five years to complete but the Anderson family happily welcomed the dawning of a new century, 1901 by moving into their new/old home.

Over the next ten years Markland was the site of many social occasions. Mrs. Anderson took great pleasure in entertaining and her home was indeed a show place. Unfortunately over the years her health began to decline and her social obligations took a back seat. Elizabeth Anderson died in September 1912. Andrew was left alone, both children now teenagers, were away at school. He began numerous projects to fill the empty days and turned the running of the household over to his sister-in-law, Mary Smethurst.

In keeping with the times, Andrew purchased an automobile and built a garage to house it. The Hupmobile was often seen on the streets of St. Augustine but Dr. Anderson refused to learn to drive, leaving that responsibility to someone else. Determined to leave his mark on St. Augustine, a series of gifts were presented to the city. First the memorial bronze flagpole was given on Armistice Day 1921 to be placed at the newly created Anderson Circle and dedicated to war veterans and notables in Florida history from Ponce de Leon to Flagler. Two years later Anderson donated a statue depicting Ponce de Leon for placement at the plaza. Last and most importantly, in 1924, was the gift he was never to see in place. Italian sculptor F. Romanelli designed and created a pair of lions fashioned from Carrera marble. These lions were to be placed at the new bridge access to Anastasia Island, which was to be called "The Bridge of Lions." Dr. Andrew Anderson died on December 2, 1924, having lived eighty-three of his eighty-five years at Markland. His legacy for all time, "The Bridge of Lions" opened in the spring of 1927.

Markland remained in the Anderson family until it was sold in 1939. One hundred seven years of Anderson ownership had come to an end. Herbert and Virgie Wolfe purchased the property. More modernization came to Markland in the form of air conditioning, bathroom facilities and actually a freight elevator with access to the driveway. As with Elizabeth Anderson, Virgie displayed the grandeur of Markland with magnificent parties ranging from fifty to three-hundred guests. One of the Wolfe's pet projects happened to be the historical heritage of St. Augustine, to this end they helped to establish the Historic St. Augustine Preservation Board. Herbert Wolfe became its first chairman and remained so for ten years.

By 1967, Markland became more house than the couple really needed. Therefore after almost thirty years in 1968, Markland was awarded to its final owner, Flagler College. Extensive restoration work was again done. Establishing Markland as a fond welcoming hall. Classes upstairs continue to echo with the voices of students even today.

LINCOLNVILLE
HISTORIC DISTRICT

Once the site of Indian villages, colonial plantations and orange groves. Lincolnville began as a settlement of emancipated slaves in 1866. African-Americans, who trace their origins to the City's 16th century founding, played an integral role in the history of St. Augustine for centuries before the forced segregation of the late 1800's led them to create their own community institutions. Here, they built churches, schools, and a vibrant business center surrounded by residences that displayed the ornate architecture of the age. By 1930, Lincolnville had become a major part of the city, encompassing both the African-American community itself and the adjacent white residential areas that had grown up with it. In 1964, civil rights demonstrations organized in Lincolnville attracted nationwide attention and influenced the Congressional debate that led to the passage of the Civil Rights Act of 1964. Today, the fifty-block Lincolnville neighborhood still contains the Ancient City's largest concentration of late Victorian Era buildings, most of them private homes. The Lincolnville Historic District was listed in the Nation Register of Historic Places in 1991.

Intersection of Bridge and M. L. King Streets, St. Augustine
SJ13 ~ GPS Coordinates: 29.888767, -81.315783

Lincolnville, originally known as Africa, was a prominent black community within the city of St. Augustine. Former slaves founded the neighborhood named for President Abraham Lincoln in 1866. The citizenry was affluent and politically active.

Washington Street was the virtual center of the business district. Domingo M. Pappy, Republican representative of the Lincolnville district, encouraged the growth of black business. During the elections of 1877 Pappy carried an amazing landslide vote and with his support commercial endeavors of the Lincolnville businessmen flourished in St. Augustine. Pappy ran on the "People's Ticket" becoming a highly effective leader in the Lincolnville community.

Flagler established the Hotel Ponce de Leon as a playground for wealthy white patrons, Lincolnville was an elite address for the prominent black members of St. Augustine society. The reflections of those socialite countenances were captured in the haunting images of a little known photographer named Twine.

Richard Aloysius Twine was born in St. Augustine on May 11, 1896. He pursued a photography profession for five years from 1922 to 1927. Twine's vision with the camera was superb, the clarity and personality he portrayed with his work has few rivals before or since. The most famous event caught in his lens was the Emancipation Day Celebration in 1922.

Twine virtually disappeared into history and his work went unheralded. When a demolition crew was assigned the task of taking down the Twine home in 1988, a miraculous discovery was made. Hidden away in the Twine attic were one hundred three glass negatives. The subjects were for the most part residents of Lincolnville. The negatives were carefully restored and are today safeguarded by the St. Augustine Historical Society.

Dr. Robert Hayling, a Lincolnville dentist and NAACP[23] representative, became a leading proponent of the budding Civil Rights Movement in St. Augustine. Strangely enough the city that first claimed a society for free people of color and escaped slaves at Fort Mose was now quite possibly the most segregated city in the United States. Hayling initiated protests aimed at businesses catering to the white tourist industry and urged representatives of the White House to decline an invitation to participate in the 400th celebration of the founding of America's oldest city, St. Augustine. When both endeavors met with negative responses, Hayling called in reinforcements.

At Hayling's request, the SCLC[24] recruited volunteers from New England colleges to stage demonstrations in the northeast Florida city in March 1964. Lincolnville residents provided room and board for the visiting protestors. After a few short days the police had arrested more than one hundred locals and volunteers for illegal demonstrations including a group of New York rabbis and the seventy-two year old mother of Massachusetts' governor. Vigilantes struck under the cover of darkness those businesses that dared cater to black patrons.

The SCLC realized a need for higher profile representation. On June 9, 1964, Dr. Martin Luther King, Jr. stood on the steps of a Lincolnville church and pledged his support at a sit-in to be staged at Monson's Motor Lodge the very next day. Baseball legend and hero Jackie Robinson spoke at a civil rights rally later that same month. Because of the enormous publicity toward St. Augustine, Congress was forced to accelerate passage of the Civil Rights Act. The historical edict became law on June 20, 1964, just eleven days after Dr. King stepped up to the podium at Lincolnville.

Many of the white St. Augustine business owners refused to acknowledge the Civil Rights Act. Monson's manager threw acid into the hotel swimming pool when African American's dared utilize the amenity. He then had the pool drained and stationed guards around it. Civil Rights protestors took advantage of the new law to prove a point. The group waded in the waters of the Atlantic on a formerly segregated beach to the horror of the white sunbathers. Vigilantes attacked not only the demonstrators but the policemen sent to protect them. Eventually tempers cooled. Acceptance was a gradual process. The process is slow and in some aspects is still developing.

Lincolnville harbors the highest concentration of Victorian construction in St. Augustine. The styles are varied and beautiful including the Italian Gothic of St. Mary's Missionary Baptist church to Gothic Revival of St. Paul's AME[25] church. Yallaha Plantation House on Bridge Street is one of the oldest homes in Florida. Black artisans and carpenters built most of the residences in Lincolnville. Though historic from the start, Lincolnville has proven itself to be a very progressive community. The heritage of this neighborhood should be a source of great pride. Lincolnville remains an active community today.

FLAGLER MEMORIAL PRESBYTERIAN CHURCH

(Side 1)

St. Augustine had no Protestant church when it became an American town in 1821. At first a united Protestant church was favored. Many denominations sent missionaries such as Presbyterian Eleazer Lathrop, who first arrived in 1821. By October 1823, the few resident Presbyterians had decided to build their own church. Rev. Wm. McWhir arrived to organize the congregation. In 1824, the First Presbyterian Church was constituted and a cornerstone was laid for a structure. That church, which was located on St. George Street, housed Florida's first formally constituted Presbyterian congregation until 1890.

HENRY M. FLAGLER

(Side 2)

Henry M. Flagler, whose efforts greatly aided the opening of the east Florida coast for development, built the Memorial Presbyterian Church in memory of his daughter, Jennie Flagler Benedict, who died tragically in 1889. He presented the magnificent Venetian Renaissance style structure to the First Presbyterian Church. Upon moving into the new building in 1890, the congregation took the name Memorial Presbyterian Church in honor of their benefactor. The remains of Henry Flagler lie beside those of his first wife, Mary, and his daughter in the mausoleum.

Sevilla Street, St. Augustine
SJ14 ~ GPS Coordinates: 29.893833, -81.316500

It was only three years after Florida became a United States territory that the First Presbyterian Church was founded in St. Augustine. Reverend Doctor William McWhir organized the development of the fledgling congregation. At the time, June 10, 1824, there were twelve-charter members and two elders. Theirs was the first Presbyterian congregation in Florida.

Reverend McWhir was of Scottish descent, born in Dublin, Ireland. He traveled to America in 1783, settling in Alexandria, Virginia. It was there that he came to know and become a confidant of George Washington. Reverend McWhir was the headmaster of the academy that Washington's nephews/wards attended and where Washington served as a trustee for ten years. The men corresponded throughout the remainder of their lives. One of those letters is on display at Flagler Memorial Church today.

McWhir only remained in St. Augustine a short time, returning to Georgia to attend his duties as head of the Sunbury School, a position, which he held for more than thirty years. Reverend Doctor William McWhir died at the age of ninety in Savannah, Georgia. He had served the Presbyterian ministry for more than sixty years.

The church was left in the most capable hands of Reverend Eleazer Lathop. It was Lathop who managed

FLAGLER MEMORIAL PRESBYTERIAN CHURCH

to raise the funds required for the construction of the first Presbyterian sanctuary. The cornerstone was laid on January 1, 1825 at South St. George Street. In fact the location of the church had met with some debate. Two church elders each insisted that the edifice be constructed within the shadow of their own homes. Because it was impossible to satisfy both, the church was built halfway between the two homes as a compromise. Unfortunately, the solution did not satisfy either party and as the years passed it was noted that neither the location nor construction of the building was ideal.

The First Presbyterian Church was constructed of local coquina mined from nearby Anastasia Island. Construction took nearly five years. The church was formally dedicated in 1830. Membership increased and even slaves were allowed a place within the congregation, though kept separate from the white membership. In 1842 a notation in the church session minutes records regarding slave membership thus: "every such instance require satisfactory evidence that the application is made with the knowledge and permission of the owner or master recognized by law."

Frederick Marquand, Esquire, made a valuable donation to the church in 1854 in the form of a finely toned bell. Mr. Marquand stipulated that should the church be dissolved or otherwise disbanded that the bell be returned to him or his heirs. Strangely enough the large bell was stored by order of the Church trustees for thirty years in the basement of the church, it was never returned.

During the Civil War, the First Presbyterian Church like so many others ceased to conduct services as a great number of her congregation fled to safer locales. While Federal forces occupied St. Augustine the Union Army used the church for various purposes. The sanctuary suffered very little damage. After the south's surrender at Appomattox Courthouse, church trustees met to reconvene services and call a new minister. It was decided that Reverend C. D. Reynolds of Green County New York, a Yankee minister, would be asked to lead the Presbyterian congregation. To further shock the membership, the trustees decided to withdraw from the Georgia Presbytery and join the Presbytery of Philadelphia. Reverend Reynolds only remained in St. Augustine for just over a year when ill health forced his resignation. His tenure was highly praised for uniting all elements of the church and fostering prosperity during his ministry.

In 1870 a wooden chapel was built primarily to serve the ever-expanding Sunday School population. A tower was built adjoining the old church to house the bell generously donated by Mr. Marquand. The tower reportedly drained the church coffers of three thousand dollars, an enormous amount given the time period. In 1877, Indian prisoners moved the chapel to a location behind the post office facing Cordova Street. This move allowed closer accessibility to the Sunday School classes and made attending the evening worship services more attractive to the St. Augustine Presbyterian congregation. The final move of the First Presbyterian Church came in 1888, when services were held at North City near the city jail. In 1889, Henry Morrison Flagler made an offer that the Presbyterian trustees could not refuse. In exchange of the deed to the old church and manse[26] on St. George Street, he would erect a virtual cathedral for worship. The First Presbyterian Church was on the threshold of a new era.

I pause a moment here to introduce the reverse side of the Flagler Memorial Presbyterian Church historical marker concerning Henry M. Flagler and his role in establishing this magnificent structure. The information following will only tell the story of Henry Flagler's grand memorial and the circumstances involving this gift. To chronicle his life would be and has been the subject of countless volumes of text. Flagler's life was extraordinary. Other stories concerning this force of Florida history can be found throughout the book.[27]

Henry Morrison Flagler earned quite a reputation in Florida by 1889. He was in the prime of his life, his wealth was blossoming and his beloved daughter Jennie Louise was about to make him a grandfather. Jennie Louise reminded her father so much of his dearly departed wife, Mary Harkness, who had passed away seven years previously. Flagler had been devoted to his wife and was devastated at her passing. The Flagler's were blessed with two children, Jennie, the oldest and a son named, Harry. Unfortunately, Harry and his father never found a common bond.

Jennie Flagler had been married previously to John Arthur Hinckley and upon his death knew the grief of a widow. The family was overjoyed when Jennie met and married wealthy Wall Street Broker Frederick Hart Benedict. On February 9, 1889, the couple welcomed a daughter, Margery. The tiny little girl lived only a matter of hours. When Jennie's health failed to improve, her physician suggested that she be transported south to Florida for rest and recuperation. Her father-in-law offered his yacht *Oneida,* fully staffed with a doctor, nurses and round the clock attendants.

The passengers set sail. Traveling with Jennie was her husband, Frederick Benedict and brother Harry. Henry Flagler was so anxious to see his Jennie that he traveled from St. Augustine to Charleston to intercept the yacht. As soon as the ship signaled Charleston harbor, Flagler hired a launch to take him to Jennie. He boarded the *Oneida* only to find his beloved daughter lying dead in her cabin. Jennie Flagler Benedict had quietly passed away just as the yacht sighted Fort Sumter in the Charleston harbor. Henry Flagler was shattered with grief.

Upon his return to St. Augustine, Flagler believed that only God had the power to offer comfort in the shadow of such sorrow. He knew that the First Presbyterian Church wished to expand their facilities and to that end he proposed to build the edifice with the understanding that it be a memorial to his beloved Jennie. The church trustees agreed without any idea of the grandeur or speed with which Flagler intended to proceed.

Flagler engaged noted architects, Carrere and Hastings[28], who had gained an outstanding reputation in designing the Flagler hotels. Their mission: to create a living memorial to inspire parishioners to lead a good and faithful life in the service of the church. The partnership was prolific until Carrere's tragic death. Carrere was mortally wounded as a result of a massive collision between the taxi in which he was riding and a speeding street-car in 1911.

The firm's designs were baroque in nature, very formalized and quite overscaled. This style is magnificently evident in both the Presbyterian Church and the Ponce de Leon hotel. Henry Flagler was attracted to the firm for their willingness to engage advanced technology from structural steel to electrification, even centralized vacuum cleaning. Their construction never compromised the functionality of the interior spaces. Carrere and Hastings resume included such noted construction as New York Public Library, the eastern facade of the U.S. Capitol building, as well as the House and Senate Office Buildings in Washington DC. After Carrere's life was tragically cut short, Hastings went on to design the Arlington Cemetery Tomb of the Unknown Soldier and residences for such names as Guggenheim, duPont and Vanderbilt.

Contractors McGuire and McDonald, Flagler's official builders, were given the task of completing the massive, elaborate structure. Materials and furnishings were ordered from all over the world and round the clock expert craftsmen were employed from distant lands. It is difficult to imagine that in a time before modernized building methods, advanced tools and swift transportation options that the sophisticated workmanship was completed within the span of just one-year.

The building is an eclectic merging of various architectural styles. The popular term being Venetian Renaissance but with touches of Byzantine, Spanish, Romanesque, Greek and Gothic as well as the personal touches of the architects and builders completing the overall picture. Regardless of the style, the structure is impressive. The church is in the form of the Latin cross, its central Venetian dome rising more than one hundred feet and crowned by a Greek cross which adds an additional twenty feet. The dome is glistening copper atop solid octagonal masonry. Twenty-four arches form the dome's arcade supported by pillars of red terra cotta. The facade is highly ornamented using antique gold and stark white terra cotta embraced in Roman brick masonry. The more diminutive bell towers are featured at the front of church, their open weave design in white terra cotta.

The interior of the sanctuary is basked with richness and symbolism. The interior furnishings were imported from Santo Domingo. Every pew, panel and door was carved from mahogany especially for this church. Double cruciform bronzed chandeliers of interlacing floral design hang from high vaulted ceilings while torchiers of Venetian bronze illuminate the aisles. Above the rostrum[29] and behind a magnificent carved screen is the choir loft. From this vantage the choir sings and the organ fills the hall with celestial music. The acoustics of the Sanctuary, corrected in 1920, as the generous gift of Henry Flagler's life long friend Dr. Anderson. When the choir sings and the organ plays due to their positioning and the exceptional acoustics, it sounds as if the music is drifting down from the angelic heavens. Twelve plaques of breccia[30] marble were placed among the floor tiles symbolizing the twelve apostles.

One of the most note worthy features of the sanctuary is perhaps the exquisite windows. Reverend John

N. MacGonigle, then pastor of the church, along with Dr. Andrew Anderson were responsible for the planning of the windows. Mr. T. Schladermundt of New York was commissioned to provide the sketches. Much planning went into the development of these windows, the church committee along with the architects considered the window subjects and what their relation would mean to the church, the colors of each window and their cast on both the inside and outside of the church. It was decided to use the Apostles' Creed so that people of all denominations could appreciate the creation. Protestant, Catholic and Orthodox all recognize the Apostles' Creed. The architecture featured narrow lancet windows making it impossible to use full pictures, therefore the composite symbolism was decided upon. A constant color scheme of the ten narrow windows kept the sanctuary awash in a single color tone. The two broader windows and the rose window are independent of the others.

The illustrations feature traditional symbolism of the church and those of nature. Each window has a prominent panel with the article of the creed used in the illustration. All of the windows have an incredible story, for example: The window depicting the "Crucifixion" has the inscription "Was crucified, dead and buried;" the church symbol above it is the excelsus[31] red cross, the purple passionflower is a symbol from nature. The passionflower is said to contain all the symbols of the Passion. The central column is a reminder of the scourging and the spear-shaped leaf is symbolic of the weapon. The flower blooms for three days signifying the time Jesus was in the tomb.

Henry Flagler funded the purchase, production and installation of the windows. Mr. Schladermundt was an exceptional artist, he was also commissioned to design the Library of Congress building in Washington, D.C. Other memorials that can be seen in the church were given at the time of its dedication, including: Jennie's husband, Frederick Benedict gave a flesh colored Baptismal Font caved from a single slab of Sienna marble, it is inscribed: "In memoriam-F.H.B. to J.L.B.-March 25th, 1889"-"I will be a God unto thee and thy seed after thee." Jennie's attending physician at the time of her death, Dr. George G. Shelton donated a black leather bound Bible with hand-wrought silver. The inscription reads: "In Memoriam G.G.S. to J.L.B., March 25, 1889." The Scripture for worship has been read from that Bible from that date forward.

The dedication service took place on March 16, 1890. Almost one year to the date that Jennie passed away. The ceremony was well attended, because of the enormous crowd many were forced to stand outside. Mrs. Benjamin Harrison, the wife of the United States President as well as the Vice President and his wife came to pay their respects. Henry Flagler attended with his second wife, Alice[32], son Harry and Jennie's husband. During the ceremony a silver winged plate engraved with "Henry M. Flagler," was affixed to pew number twenty – the Flagler family pew. It remains in place today.

Dr. John R. Paxton, minister of West Presbyterian Church of New York City, an old friend of the Flagler family preached an eloquent service on the Lord's Prayer. The Jacksonville Times Union printed the entire sermon in the daily news. The Reverend E. K. Mitchell offered a moving invocation, in all, eight ministers took part in the ceremony. Dr. Paxton brought his entire New York City choir with him to dedicate Flagler's Memorial to Jennie. Reportedly, Paxton described Flagler Memorial Presbyterian Church as,

"A house of prayer beautiful enough to move a savage's wonder or make an atheist pray."

Unfortunately the years were unkind to the beautiful memorial. The building suffered due to the depression in the 1930s until after the conclusion of World War II. The interior was damaged due to the failure to waterproof the structure and funds were not available for repairs. The efforts of then pastor, Dr. Howard Lee and trustees Howard Hawkins, Frank Upchurch, Sr. and W. F. Clark, Jr. funds were raised, the sanctuary repaired and the endowment program was greatly strengthened.

In 1957, full time guides were hired to lead tourists through the magnificent structure. An honorable mention certainly is due Mr. John Drexel Mays who served as the curator for the church for forty years. The fragrant gardens of jasmine, gardenias and beautiful bird of paradise plantings amidst landscaped walkways and handmade tiles were due to the generosity of Jean Flagler Matthew, Henry's granddaughter. Mr. and Mrs. H. M. Johnson, long time members of the congregation met a grave need in the church by replacing the failing organ. Their gift was the finest organ in the southeast, rivaled only by those at Lincoln Center, the Mormon Tabernacle and the National Presbyterian Church in Washington, D. C. The organ was installed in 1970.

Henry Morrison Flagler died on May 20, 1913 in his amazingly beautiful estate, Whitehall at Palm Beach, Florida. His body lay in state in the grand Rotunda of the Ponce de Leon Hotel until the funeral procession carried him to his final rest at the Flagler Memorial Presbyterian Church. The stately marble mausoleum shelters the crypts of his dear first wife, Mary Harkness; beloved daughter, Jennie Louise with baby Margery held safely in her arms; and finally Henry Flagler, himself.

Today more than two hundred thousand visitors tour the church and grounds each year. Their donations are largely responsible for the maintenance and upkeep of the facility. Flagler's cathedral for Jennie is an amazing tribute of love from father to daughter. The Memorial Presbyterian Church certainly remains a sight to behold. The verse Flagler had chiseled in stone above the east doors says it all,

"Thy memorial, O Lord, is throughout all generations."

VILLA ZORAYDA

The Villa Zorayda was constructed in 1883 as the winter home of Franklin Smith, a Boston millionaire who was so impressed by the magnificence of the Alhambra Palace which he saw during a visit to Granada, Spain, that he decided to build his house as an exact replica of one wing of the palace at one-tenth of the original size. The 12th century palace had been built by the Moors who had ruled Spain for six centuries before being expelled in 1492. Smith, a gifted amateur architect, designed the house himself, using the innovative technique of constructing the building with poured concrete reinforced with crushed coquina stone. Many other materials used in finishing the residence were imported from Spain. In 1913, Abraham S. Mussallem bought the building. In 1922, it became a nightclub and gambling casino, which closed in 1925 when Florida outlawed gambling. In 1936, it was opened as a tourist attraction called the Zorayda Castle, exhibiting items fitting the architectural theme of the building. The property was listed in the National Register of Historic Places in 1993.

83 King Street, opposite Flagler College, St. Augustine
SJ15 ~ GPS Coordinates: 29.891867, -81.315183

Franklin Waldo Smith was born on October 9, 1826 in Boston, Massachusetts. He rose to prominence in various business ventures and dabbled in architecture. By his side was his wife, the former Laura Bevan of Baltimore, Maryland. During a European tour in 1882 the couple rented a chateau near Lake Geneva, Switzerland. It was at Lake Geneva where Franklin Smith first encountered the use of poured concrete as a building material.

Around 1883, the couple decided to build a winter home at St. Augustine. Of course, not just any home would do the imaginative amateur architect, Smith. Villa Zorayda would be an exact one-tenth-scale replica of a wing in the Alhambra, which was an immense palace that once sat on a hilltop gazing over Granada, Spain. The Alhambra was built during the thirteenth century by Ibn al-Ahmar, originator of the Nasrid dynasty. The citadel type castle was a city unto itself, comprising the royal residence, governmental chambers, a roman bath and a mosque. Square by design, all rooms opened toward a grand courtyard either at ground level or via balconies and terraces. Heavily influenced by Moorish schemes visitors were captivated by the special combination of the slender columnar arcades, fountains and light-reflecting water basins found in the courtyards. It was said that the Lion

Court was a physical realization of Paradise described in Islamic poetry.

Smith quickly realized that to build with wood was unwise considering the location but no stone existed within reach or did it? Fossilized shell deposits mixed with sand and water had long been mined at nearby Anastasia Island and this stone combined with poured concrete would be used to fortify Villa Zorayda. To be located on King Street, the Villa was the first building in Florida to use this unique form of construction. Villa Zorayda was constructed of layer upon layer of the poured concrete mixture. Builders formed and poured one layer allowing it set then formed and poured the next until the full height was obtained. Villa Zorayda was also the first cast in place concrete building in the United States.

Some considered Villa Zorayda pretentious while others described it as one of the loveliest private homes in St. Augustine. The Moorish influence blended well with the Spanish décor prevalent around the city. The red and gray cement walls and Spanish tiled roof proved to be an asset to the St. Augustine cityscape. At night the Villa was illuminated by soft colored lamps, which were placed on the outside. Forty various shaped stained glass windows allowed the lamps outside to cast a rainbow glow to the interior of the Villa.

Franklin W. Smith also envisioned a resort hotel to be built nearby. However it would be January of 1888 before the Cordova became a reality. The Cordova employed the same Moorish themes utilized at Villa Zorayda resulting in a beautiful effect. Nearly fifteen years later, Smith would share his innovative ideas with Henry Flagler. The magnificence of Villa Zorayda convinced Flagler that the concrete mixture was the ideal material for use in his proposed St. Augustine ventures. Today, such construction has become commonplace all over the world, but it was Franklin Smith who used it for the first time in the construction of his Villa.

Smith's progressive ideas led the way for the construction of the Hotel Ponce de Leon as well as the slightly lower scale Alcazar Hotel. The Ponce de Leon was to be the largest concrete structure in the world. The Cordova Hotel was sold to Henry Flagler shortly after its completion. The Cordova eventually was renamed, the Casa Monica Hotel. With this acquisition, Flagler opened the triumvirate to the public:

VILLA ZOYRADA

The Ponce de Leon, the Casa Monica and the Alcazar all designed in the Spanish tradition and centrally located in St. Augustine. The trio bordered an avenue of oaks called the Alameda. Flagler eventually paved this dirt packed path, which had long been called Lover's Lane. Today it is known as King Street.

It was Franklin Smith who soon realized the preservation of what was old and lovely was of vital importance to the city. He proposed a committee of architects be formed to control all future construction in the City of St. Augustine. Franklin Waldo Smith died in 1911.

Abraham S. Mussallem purchased Villa Zorayda just two years after Smith's death. In 1922, "Castle Zorayda" became a nightclub and gambling casino. Unfortunately the endeavor did not last, Florida outlawed gambling in 1925. In 1936, the facility was opened as a tourist attraction called the Zorayda Castle, exhibiting items fitting the architectural theme of the building. Today the castle houses many treasures such as a two thousand three hundred year old Cat Rug, the court of lions and harem quarters, as well as a mummified foot.

It is said that the magnificent windows are varied in shape and size adhering to the legend that spirits may depart through these portals but would encounter much difficulty finding their way back in.

PONCE DE LEON
HOTEL

The magnificent structure was erected between 1885 and 1887 by Henry M. Flagler, the hotel and railroad magnate whose activities contributed greatly to the development of Florida's eastern coastal area. Designed by the New York architectural firm of Carrere and Hastings, the building reflects the Spanish Renaissance style throughout. The hotel was the first major edifice in the United States to be constructed of poured concrete, a mixture of cement, sand, and coquina shell. The interior is decorated with imported marble, carved oak, and murals painted by Tojetti and George W. Maynard. Its stained glass windows were created by Louis Tiffany of New York. The Ponce de Leon Hotel was the flagship of the Flagler hotel system, which soon extended all along the east coast of Florida. Located in the "Winter Newport," this resort hotel entertained celebrities from around the world, including several U.S. Presidents. During World War II, the hotel served as a Coast Guard Training Center. In 1968, this historic landmark was converted into Flagler College, an accredited liberal arts institution. Independent and coeducational, the college serves students from across the nation.

74 King Street, Flagler College, St. Augustine
SJ16 ~ GPS Coordinates: 29.892112, -81.312957

In 1882, Henry Flagler, New York entrepreneur and cofounder of Standard Oil, developed an interest in the historic city of St. Augustine and its potential as a winter resort. Flagler's subsequent development of transportation and resort facilities along the eastern coast of Florida created vast opportunities for expansion. A prominent feature was Flagler's Hotel Ponce de Leon.

Henry Flagler was 53 years old when he wed Ida Alice[33]. The couple traveled to St Augustine to escape the frigid north winter and enjoy a delayed honeymoon, which would last three months. The temperature in New York was a frozen ten below zero compared to St. Augustine's balmy sixty degrees. During the visit Flagler first encountered Dr. Andrew Anderson, who was to become his life long friend. Anderson worked as Flagler's agent in St. Augustine once the couple returned to New York. The arrangement enabled Flagler to procure property he required for his budding dream. The couple was destined to return to the ancient city only one year later. Flagler's intent involved making St. Augustine the "Newport of the South." Newport was at that time the most famous resort community in America.

Friend and business associate William Warden, owner of the home that is today the odditorium housing Ripley's Believe It or Not Museum. He said to Flagler of his venture: "Flagler, I was asked the other day why you were building that hotel in St. Augustine and replied that you had been looking around for several years for a place to make a fool of yourself in, and at last selected St. Augustine as the spot."

Within the hour of his arrival to St. Augustine Henry was investigating an innovative type of construction he had recently heard rumors of and the scene sparked ideas in his ambitious mind immediately. He was introduced to a Boston capitalist and amateur architect, Franklin W. Smith, who was building his winter home Villa Zorayda utilizing a poured concrete process.

Henry Flagler's Hotel Ponce de Leon was to be the largest poured concrete structure in the world. He first bought a grove of unproductive orange trees, hired an architect and planned the first of his St. Augustine triumverant ~ the Ponce. Originally the idea was for Smith to assume a quarter of the financial responsibility to build the establishment, estimated at two hundred thousand dollars. Unfortunately Smith was unable to raise the capital and Flagler continued on, funding the entire project alone.

To begin the incredible undertaking required numerous property transactions. First Flagler purchased the Sunnyside hotel, which he had relocated, then proceeded to buy several other properties. Though Dr. Anderson supported Flagler's dream, his three half-sisters did not. In fact the ladies brought suit against Henry Flagler in an attempt to block the sale of the Anderson property he required to complete the Ponce de Leon. In the end Flagler made a financial settlement to each of the three women. Only one property remained, the Ball estate, that sale was made in short order.

In 1887 Flagler hired two young architects from the prominent New York firm of McKim, Mead, and White, to design the hotel. With the design of the Ponce de Leon, John Carrere and Thomas Hastings launched a new architectural firm, Carrere & Hastings, which would gain national prominence. Hastings was in fact the son of Flagler's New York pastor.

News of the project swept through New York City financial circles. The publicity spurred Florida's real estate frenzy and Flagler was swamped with offers, most of which he declined. The *Jacksonville News Herald* interviewed Flagler asking him why he went into the hotel business. Flagler told this story: An elderly church deacon was asked to explain a sudden unaccountable bout of drunkenness. The deacon related to his pastor that he had spent all his days up to this point in the Lord's service and now he was finally taking one for himself. For the last fourteen years Flagler had devoted his life to business and now he was pleasing himself.

Building this hotel was not an easy task; malaria was rampant in the hot and humid climate and the amount of local rock to be quarried required a government waiver. When the transaction to obtain the needed coquina rock became too complicated, Flagler's builder James McGuire bought a quarry on Anastasia Island. It took nearly eighteen months to build the five hundred forty-room hotel. Flagler oversaw the entire process including unloading the furniture along side the crew.

Flagler chose the Spanish Renaissance Revival style so that the hotel's design would compliment its historic surroundings. Louis C. Tiffany was retained to decorate the interior of the hotel using stained glass, mosaics and terra cotta reliefs on the walls and ceilings; several grand murals were commissioned. The structure was to amass four and half acres with an additional acre and a half for the dining hall and other buildings. The grand entrance led into an open courtyard allowing the warmth of sun to supplement heating during the winter months.

Twin towers rose above the main structure accented by four terracotta balconies, each weighing five tons. Arched windows reflected the Moorish influence. The towers however were not just for effect, they each stored sixteen thousand gallons of water for fire protection.

Flagler often dropped by the construction site unannounced. On one occasion he walked very nonchalantly up to the site smoking his usual stogie; there he found his entry blocked by an unknowing guard. The guard pointed out the "No Smoking" signs posted every where and informed Flagler that there would be no trespassing on the construction site. When Flagler protested that he was the owner, the guard was unconvinced after all there had been a good many "Flaglers" presenting themselves in an attempt to get a peak at the ongoing construction. The unwavering guard had thrown out every one. Flagler was still trying to talk his way onto the site when the general contractor showed up and began to chastise the guard for not recognizing the boss. Flagler interceded; he was pleased by the guard's commitment. He then proceeded on his way under a full head of smoke.

The interior of the hotel was more personal in nature as opposed to the elaborate of the exterior. The lobby featured a three-storied rotunda, to the left was a grand parlor which was divided into five areas by means of arches, portieres[34] and screens. Stairs from the lobby led to the men's bar and the ladies' saloon both flanking the dining room. All of the luxuries popular during the era were to be included in the hotel. Public rooms consisted of a writing room, barber shop and even ladies' sporting room. In addition to electrical power from four Edison direct current dynamos throughout, five hundred-foot deep artesian wells provided sulfur water filtered through fountains for the hotels' use. The water had an unpleasant aroma but many physicians felt it contained medicinal properties. Later a fresh water pond to west of town was piped in to allow hotel guests to have more palatable drinking water. However the one area lacking in the grand hotel were private bathrooms. Flagler's suite claimed the only one throughout the hotel, an oversight that was soon rectified.

When manager Osborn D. Seavey welcomed the first guests to the Ponce de Leon on January 10, 1888, it was proclaimed by the national press as superior to most United States hotels. Seavey continued in the managerial position until the 1895 season. No special ceremony marked the inaugural debut of the hotel. Ironically considering Flagler's future endeavors to bring rail transportation to southern Florida, in early January the first vestibule train ever to reach St. Augustine brought the Ponce de Leon's first guests. Socialites flocked south to experience this opulent haven. Even the cheapest room had electric lights and boasted a cost of one thousand dollars each to decorate. Flagler insisted that no detail be overlooked. At one point he had an entire wall eliminated so that the telephone operator could have access to a window.

The president's wife, Mrs. Benjamin Harrison, Vice President and Mrs. Levi Morton hobnobbed with the Astors, Vanderbuilts, Rockefellers and Wanamakers. The impressive Ponce de Leon soon claimed the entire roll of the Social Register. At a time when common laborers were paid approximately forty dollars per month, rates of the Hotel Ponce de Leon ranged from thirty-nine dollars to seventy-five dollars per night.

The popularity of "the Ponce" and its style strongly influenced the architecture of southern Florida for the next fifty years. The Ponce de Leon's major competition would come from Flagler's former associate Franklin Smith with his Cordova hotel. In April 1888 Henry Flagler purchased the Cordova for three hundred twenty-five thousand dollars and changed the name to the Casa Monica.

The popularity of his hotel spurred Flagler to begin a companion hotel adjacent to the Ponce, the Alcazar. This establishment allowed guests of more modest means to enjoy grand surroundings. The Alcazar was to feature a grand casino, recreation and amusement area. Fearing public scrutiny, Flagler did not advertise the attributes of the hotel/casino. The first floor hosted a shopping arcade, three hundred guestrooms and a restaurant offering an inexpensive European meal plan. Social functions included dances, plays, musicals, and water polo, concerts, bowling and tennis matches. Two amazing pools, artesian and saltwater, offered guests a wonderful means of entertainment and exercise. The saltwater pool featured a bandstand perched above it. Roman, Russian and Turkish baths were luxurious ascents for patrons of the Alcazar.

Flagler and Ida Alice took a suite in the Ponce and declared St. Augustine their permanent winter home. He basked in the popularity of his hotel, in the success of the venture and the new ideas flowing through his brain. This time was probably the highest point in his life thus far but with great highs come a great fall.

His greatest low, aside from the loss of his first wife Mary, came when tragedy struck and his first born Jennie Louise died enroute to his side to mourn the loss of her new born daughter. To Jennie he built a cathedral. Then continued on his mission to develop the prime real estate of Florida's East Coast. The success of the Hotel Ponce de Leon was wavering, immediately contending with a yellow fever epidemic and the worst freeze known in state history in 1895. St. Augustine's weather proved not to be as tropical as other resort areas further south along the Florida peninsula. The city never quite blossomed into the winter resort Flagler expected.

However, tourists did flock to the city during the first twenty years of Henry's residence. The Ponce de Leon was the only one of three Flagler Hotels to survive the Great Depression. Following a lull in tourism during World War II, the hotel attracted large crowds for several years, but the decline resumed. In 1967 the hotel closed and was sold to Flagler College. The former Hotel Ponce de Leon was extensively renovated yet today retains most of its original integrity, beauty and charm.

THE PONCE DE LEON HOTEL
TODAY FLAGLER COLLEGE

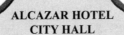

ALCAZAR HOTEL
CITY HALL

Built by Henry Flagler, the Alcazar Hotel opened as a companion to the Ponce de Leon in 1888. The building, one of the first multi-storied structures in the county constructed of poured concrete, was designed by John M. Carrero and Thomas Hastings who modeled its facade after a Moorish palace in southern Spain. The hotel remained closed from 1932 until publisher O. C. Lightner purchased the building from the Florida East Coast Hotel Company in 1942 and deeded it to the city for use as a museum for his extensive collection of Victorian memorabilia. In 1969, the voters of St. Augustine approved a bond issue to renovate the structure to house the museum and also municipal offices. After remodeling the building was dedicated as St. Augustine City Hall on April 27, 1973. The Lightner Museum opened to the public August 12, 1974.

79 King Street, St. Augustine
SJ17 ~ GPS Coordinates: 29.892433, -81.313667

The second St. Augustine hotel born to Henry Flagler reflected the same Spanish Renaissance Revival style used in the construction of her sister the Hotel Ponce de Leon just across the street. The royal palace of Seville, Spain, an Arabic word meaning "royal castle," inspired the Alcazar. Indeed with her twin towers, gothic spires and blazing crimson terracotta roof tiles, the Alcazar Hotel presented a regal portrait. In their day the huge square towers dominated the cityscape and offered a majestic view unavailable anywhere else in St. Augustine.

The Alcazar shared many things with its older, more opulent sister; the same architect, builders, workmen, in most cases the very same building materials and furnishings. The two young architects, Carrere and Hastings, later designed the New York Public Library and the U.S. Senate office building.

Though smaller than the Ponce, only occupying one city block, the structure boasted four stories embracing a common courtyard. Salons, shops and restaurants all opened to covered promenades supported by intricately carved columns and curvaceous arches. The courtyard provided a vista of hues brandished by tropical flowers, lacy palms and gurgling fountains.

Secluded in the rear, sheltered from the prospect of moral criticism, was the casino and "sporting section" of the hotel. Indoor sulfur and salt-water pools, one hundred twenty feet long, fifty feet wide and deepening from three to twelve feet depths, were warmed by the strategic placement of skylights even in the extreme of winter. Separate dressing facilities for both men and women were at opposing ends of the pools. Though it was possible from the male point of entrance to swim into the main portion of the pool, the more modest feminine area was closed off so that they could enjoy the recreation without the glaring attention of their male counterparts. A gallery overlooked the entire scene and often orchestras provided music for the gallant waltzes of the day.

The casino also offered Turkish steam baths and several skilled masseuses, creating the first vacation spa in Florida. Amusement courts and game rooms rounded out the entertainment mecca and were very popular tourist attractions. No grand foyer or opulent dining room was built for the Alcazar. The cost, including the casino totaled approximately half of what the Ponce de Leon had demanded. Though definitely second to her older sister, the Alcazar was spoken of in glowing terms by visitors from all over the world. Many felt she was just as beautiful. The final determination came down to a matter of personal taste and the bulk of ones pocketbook.

The Alcazar Hotel received her first guests on Christmas Day 1888 with seventy-five rooms awaiting occupancy. Unfortunately over the years, the hotel's business was extremely unstable until the Alcazar was finally forced to close her doors in 1932.

In 1946, Chicago newspaperman and publisher of Hobbies magazine, Otto C. Lightner appraised the Alcazar; he was so impressed with the potential of the building that he chose to relocate his Chicago-based collection of Victoriana to St. Augustine. After purchasing the former hotel from the Flagler estate in 1947, he immediately turned it over to the city in trust. The first Lightner Museum opened its doors two years later.

Otto C. Lightner passed away only three years later. The former Alcazar Hotel sadly succumbed to the elements of time and Mother Nature. The drastic corrosion of the iron framework that reinforced the structure and the brittle terracotta roof tiles bore the brunt of the damage. The city of St. Augustine accepted the challenge in 1968 and began renovations on what was to be the new city hall. On April 27, 1973 the St. Augustine City Hall was dedicated. The following year the second Lightner Museum open on the second floor.

Through the support of grants from the Florida Department of State's Division of Historic Resources and the dedication to preservation by the City of St. Augustine, the regal Alcazar again reflected the grandeur of Flagler's Era. The beautiful structure is one St. Augustine's most prized treasurers and their commitment to her preservation is to be commended.

The Lightner Museum today displays a vast collection of art and memorabilia cleverly linking the beauty of centuries past to the uniqueness of present day creation. The Lightner Museum is open from 9 a.m. to 5 p.m. every day except Christmas and the St. Augustine City Hall is obviously a public building open during business hours. A small admission is charged for the museum.

The sisters have indeed married well ~ Hotel Ponce de Leon to academia and Flagler College; Alcazar to the arts with the Lightner Museum and civic duty in St. Augustine's City Hall.

SPANISH DRAGOON BARRACKS

A first Spanish period two-story coquina, shingle roofed structure, 33' x 19', erected on the east side of this lot became the barracks for the Spanish dragoons in 1792. Each story had two rooms. One upper room contained a rack for 20 muskets and 40 pistols, another rack for saddles and bridles, a table and two benches. A detached kitchen, coquina curbed well, stable and privy were located adjacent to the barracks. In the yard, a cultivated vegetable garden, orange, lemon and fig trees flourished. By 1822 the barracks had deteriorated and was razed.

64 Cordova Avenue, St. Augustine
SJ18 ~ GPS Coordinates: 29.894200, -81.314367

The Spanish Dragoons were equivalent to what Americans know as cavalrymen, though much more dramatic. Their responsibilities entailed not only their mounts but also the cattle and other livestock providing food and income for the settlement. The protection of a specific area of land was also considered a part of the troop's mission. This two-storied barracks served as their home and base of operations in St. Augustine. Most of the dwelling was devoted to the storage and safe keeping of their weaponry and horse tack.

The usual uniform for a Spanish Dragoon bore the colors of the Bourbon livery introduced in Spain with the accession of King Felipe V in 1700. Their wardrobe was particularly dashing with blue coats, waist coasts and breeches, red cuffs, trim, collars, cockades[35] and stockings, which were sometimes white. Brass or gilt[36] buttons and buckles adorned the outfit giving it a regal appearance.

The Dragoon barracks was identified as a third era fort. Though these fortifications are important, the garrison would have less than thirty men at service. Many such barracks held only a dozen or so men. This third era fortification existed only in support of the Castillo de San Marcos and for the protection of the Spanish missions at St. Augustine. One must understand that with the exception of St. Augustine and Tallahassee to the west, the remaining Florida territory was wilderness frontier occupied by the Native American tribes and virtually no one else. The Spanish Dragoon barracks existence was considerably short-lived. By the early 1800s, no detachment remained on site. In 1822 the property had deteriorated to the point that the fortification was put to the torch.

The Spanish Dragoon barracks, located at 61 Cordova Street, became the modern day home for the Security First Building. Today the site is home to the Thompson Baker Agency. John Thompson and Harold Ryman founded the agency in 1925. Their original location was a former tailor shop in the Old Cordova Building. The agency has occupied many prominent addresses during its tenure but after extensive renovations in 1990, the owners settled into the former location of the Spanish Dragoon barracks.

SITE OF THE
SPANISH DRAGOON BARRACKS TODAY

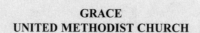

GRACE
UNITED METHODIST CHURCH

Grace United Methodist Church is a reminder of the tremendous physical impact Henry M. Flagler had on St. Augustine. This complex of structures resulted from a compromise between Flagler and the congregation of Olivet Church. That group of northern Methodists agreed to exchange the land on which their church and parsonage stood for a new complex designed by John M. Carrere and Thomas Hastings. Flagler, in turn, employed the same architects in designing his Alcazar Hotel, which rose on the former Olivet Site. Construction began in 1886 and was completed in late 1887. Grace Methodist Episcopal Church was dedicated in January 1888. The church and parsonage are excellent examples of the Spanish Renaissance Revival Style of architecture, and the decision to execute the design in poured concrete resulted in unusual and aesthetically pleasing structures which have stood the tests of time and the elements. Grace United Methodist Church was entered in the National Register of Historic Places on November 29, 1979.

Intersection of Cordova & 8 Carrera Street, St. Augustine
SJ19 ~ GPS Coordinates: 29.894979, -81.315262

The Methodist Church in St. Augustine first began with the help of George L. Adkins, owner of the Florida House, in 1881. The first pastor was Reverend Samuel D. Payne and the congregation gathered at the black Methodist Church on St. George Street. Eventually the black congregation would build their sanctuary on what is today Bridge Street calling it the Trinity United Methodist Church. The white congregation organized the Olivet Methodist Episcopal Church in 1884 on King and Tolomato Streets, today the street is known as Cordova.

As Henry Flagler watched the land being prepared for the construction of his Alcazar Hotel, he realized the need for additional property. Olivet Methodist stood adjacent and Flagler realized that the addition of this acreage was needed to build what was in his mind's eye. Because the Methodists wielded major influence in the community he realized the importance of remaining on good terms with them, therefore, in true Flagler fashion, he offered the congregation a proposal. In exchange for the deed to the property at King and Tolomato, he would build them a sanctuary in the location of their choosing.

The congregation met to discuss the proposal and all assumed Flagler would deal fairly with them and spend at least five thousand dollars in constructing the new edifice. In fact the Olivet property with existing structures was worth no more than four thousand dollars. Not only did Flagler deal fairly with the parishioners but he employed the same architects, John M. Carrere and Thomas Hastings, to design the structure. The same builders, McGuire and McDonald, were contracted to build Flagler's elaborate hotel Ponce de Leon for the rich and powerful of the era were hired for the church project as well. He utilized many similar materials for the construction, however his generosity did have limits. When Flagler noticed workers using prime muck filler for the church lot he stated, "Use the country sand, it is good enough for them."

The Methodist church was built in the same Spanish Renaissance style with nuances of Moorish flavor as many of St. Augustine buildings constructed during this period. The two-story edifice wore coquina masonry blended with salmon hued brick featuring a square turret, conical roof, picturesque terracotta moldings and spire. The light golden wood finishing the interior gives a golden glow throughout the sanctuary, making it one of the most beautiful churches in St. Augustine.

Grace Methodist Church welcomed the new year in 1888 with open doors. Henry Flagler had built the church and parsonage at a cost of eighty-four thousand dollars. With a glad heart, he gave the Methodist congregation the official deed to their new home.

E. C. Kenyon and Professional Restoration were awarded the contract for an exterior facelift of Grace Methodist Church in the year 2000. Most of the work concentrated around the terra cotta bell tower, moldings and spire. The expertise of these artisans makes it difficult to distinguish the restored features from the original. The church continues to this day with an active congregation. Tours of the sanctuary are available at select times.

TOLOMATO CEMETERY

During the First Spanish Period, prior to 1763, this site was occupied by the Christian Indian village of Tolomato, with its chapel and burying ground served by Franciscan missionaries. The village was abandoned when Great Britain acquired Florida. In 1777 Father Pedro Camps, pastor of the Minorcan colonists, who had come to St. Augustine after the failure of Andrew Turnbull's settlement at New Smyrna, obtained permission from Governor Patrick Tonyn to establish this cemetery for his parishioners. Father Camps was buried here in 1790; ten years later his remains were re-interred in the "new church", the present Cathedral. The first bishop of St. Augustine, Augustin Verot (d. 1876), is buried in the mortuary chapel at the rear of the cemetery. The last burial took place in 1892.

Cordova Street, St. Augustine
SJ20 ~ GPS Coordinates: 29.897017, -81.314833

The Tolomato Indians established a village long before Europeans arrived to call the area St. Augustine. Early maps refer to the site as "the church and village of Tolomato." During the initial Spanish period the primary colonization goal was to bring the Natives to Christianity. The Spaniards arrived with Cuban monks and Franciscan missionaries assigned to bring their plan for the Native Americans to fruition.

Though the Tolomato tribe spent a number of years dwelling in the St. Augustine area. That village was neither the beginning nor the end of the Tolomato's journey. The Native Americans were first known to inhabit St Catherine's Island on the Georgia coast. Eventually raids by other Native American tribes forced them from their homeland to seek the safety of Florida shores. The Tolomato and Spanish seemed to coexist though there are reports of Spanish enslaving of the Native Americans.

When the British from the Carolinas and Georgia attacked St. Augustine in 1702 the hostile invaders burned every village from Amelia Island southward along their trek to St. Augustine including Tolomato. Daunted but not defeated the Tolomato rebuilt. However, in 1763 when the British assumed control of Florida, the Tolomato joined their Spanish compatriots and fled to Cuba. The sacred ground of Tolomato Cemetery was the last North American mainland home of its namesake villagers.

The old Drug Store in St. Augustine bears a remnant of the Native Americans in a carved headstone placed for Seminole Chief Tolomato. The crude epitaph reads:

"NOTIS. This werry elaborte pile is erectted in memery of Tolomato a Seminole Ingine cheef whoos wigwarm stuud on this spot and sirroundings. Wee cherris his memery as he was a good harted cheef. He wood knot take yoour skalp without you begged him to do so or pade him sum munny. He always akted more like a Christsun gentle man than a savage Ingine. Let him R.I.P."

Father Pedro Camps, who was the pastor to the much-maligned Minorcans who immigrated to St. Augustine from the persecution of New Smyrna, successfully kept their faith alive both there and in refuge at St. Augustine during the American Revolution. Fourteen hundred three Minorcan citizens sailed from the Spanish island huddled aboard eight ships and due to the reported ill-treatment of New Smyrna founder Dr. Andrew Turnbull only four hundred seventy-three survived to make it to the sanctuary of St. Augustine in 1777.

Father Camps insisted on staying with the sick at New Smyrna yet by summer of 1777 all of those in ill health had set sail north to freedom. Dr. Turnbull refused to release Father Camps until November. Upon arrival in St. Augustine, Father Camps wasted no time establishing a new parish, the only one in St. Augustine at the time. Meetings were held on the first floor of a parishioner's home near the city gates. The parish was called San Pedro. Later in 1777, Father Pedro Camps, requested and received permission to use the former Tolomato village as a cemetery. Tolomato Cemetery continued to be St. Augustine's Catholic cemetery until 1892.

By 1783, Father Camps was suffering from ill health and requested retirement. Because the British were about to relinquish possession of Florida to Spain, getting a replacement priest was extremely difficult. Two Irish priests were sent but neither spoke or understood the Minorcans language, two Spanish speaking priests arrived but neither of these men could communicate in the specific Minorcan dialect. The faithful priest remained at his post and put his need for retirement aside. Father Pedro Camps died on May 19, 1790. His Minorcan flock as well as the entire Spanish community cherished his memory. He was buried in Tolomato Cemetery.

Felix Varela was born to Cuban parents and when his mother died tragically young, Felix was sent to St. Augustine to be raised by his maternal grandfather, who was highly placed with the Spanish government. He was Lieutenant Colonel Bartolome Morales, Commander of the City of St. Augustine. As a young adult, Varela returned to Cuba to attend the Seminary College of San Carlos and San Ambrosio. He was a dedicated student and excelled in his studies. Eventually joining the priesthood, Father Felix Varela spent his life vocally proclaiming issues of human rights in regard to Cubans and Native Americans. His progressive ideas were unpopular with the Spanish government. In 1823, the Spanish Crown condemned him to death.

Varela retired to St. Augustine, continuing his abolitionist work. His shadow frequently fell at Tolomato Cemetery where his devoted Aunt Rita Morales and his mentor Father Miguel O'Reilly, Vicar of East Florida were buried. Father Felix Varela peacefully passed away in the quiet of the east courtyard of the Cathedral Parish of St. Augustine on February 25, 1853.

The Tolomato Cemetery Chapel Monument stands at the end of a long, narrow walk leading to the rear of the cemetery; it was constructed the year of his death to cradle his remains. Reports state that in 1911 some of his "leftovers" were transferred to the University of Havana where Father Varela was once a noted professor. The balance of the noted priest's body is said to still occupy the monument at Tolomato Cemetery. In 1876, Jean Pierre Agustin Verot, the first bishop of St. Augustine, was initially buried in the chapel alongside Father Varela. Bishop Verot was eventually relocated to the center of the cemetery where he rests today.

The "positio," an official document outlining the "life, virtues and holiness" of Father Felix Varela was presented to the

TOLOMATO CEMETERY

Vatican's Congregation for the Saints in 2003. The pope's approval will bestow on Father Varela, whose status has been "servant of God," the title "venerable." One proven miracle attributed to Father Varela would make him eligible for beatification or religious exaltation above others; two miracles would clear the way for his canonization to sainthood.

Many sightings have been reported over the years of shadow like spirits inhabiting the venerable burial ground. A dancing lady in a snowy white dress twirls among the gravestones; a impish young boy is perched on an oak branch, watching as visitors pass by; and the figure of a somber man stands attentively at the door of the Chapel Monument at the back of lot. Benevolent specters all, Tolomato Cemetery remains a peaceful haven of silence and rest.

Today, Tolomato Cemetery is closed to the public.

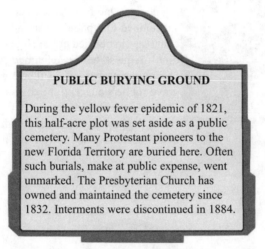

PUBLIC BURYING GROUND

During the yellow fever epidemic of 1821, this half-acre plot was set aside as a public cemetery. Many Protestant pioneers to the new Florida Territory are buried here. Often such burials, make at public expense, went unmarked. The Presbyterian Church has owned and maintained the cemetery since 1832. Interments were discontinued in 1884.

Visitor Center, north of cemetery, San Marco Avenue, St. Augustine
SJ21 ~ GPS Coordinates: 29.897350, -81.313500

St. Augustine's "Publik Burial Ground" is also called the Huguenot Cemetery. Referring to a group of French Huguenots who sought sanctuary at Fort Caroline in 1564 from the atrocities of the Spanish Inquisition. The Huguenot settlement did not survive for long. Don Pedro Menendez de Aviles massacred the inhabitants at Fort Caroline with very few survivors.

Florida was sold to the United States in 1821. It was then that the Spanish departed for the last time. On July 10, 1821 with full military regalia the United States troops took possession of the territory. Unfortunately St. Augustine would soon suffer much darker days.

Northerners began flocking to St. Augustine and due to Seminole uprisings settlers living in outlying areas now moved into the safety of the city walls. The population began to swell. An increasing population required an abundance of supplies. It is said that one epidemic began when casks of fresh water arrived from Havana contaminated with mosquito larvae carrying yellow fever.

Yellow fever, also known as "the black vomit," was virtually always fatal. One-third of the population succumbed to the deadly disease during the 1821 epidemic. It was during this time that another need was brought to light. Because of the vast Catholic population, a cemetery had long been established for those parishioners; non-Catholics, however, could not be interred there. The need for a Protestant cemetery was pressing and the Publik Burial Ground was established.

The half-acre plot is situated just outside the City Gates. It was feared that burial within the city might bring on more disease from the decaying corpses. In 1832, local Presbyterians were finally deeded the property. Strangely enough, the oldest grave is that of George Bartlett whose stone reads a death date of June 29, 1811. Only four marked graves are etched with the year of death 1821, which would coincide with the yellow fever epidemic responsible for the establishment of the cemetery.

PUBLIC BURIAL GROUND

The cemetery embraces one hundred known graves. It is suspected that many more unmarked plots and possibly mass graves are hidden beneath the loamy soil. Among the more notable graves are those of Gideon Barstow, United States Representative from Massachusetts and member of the state legislator and Congressman Charles Downing. Burials were discontinued in 1884 due to lack of available ground.

Nightly ghost tours often linger near the iron gate of the cemetery and speak in hushed tones of the mists and spirits hovering about. One favorite speaks of Judge John B. Stickney who succumbed to typhoid fever and died in 1882. The noted politician was first buried at the Huguenot Cemetery but at his children's request, he was exhumed and shipped to Washington D.C. During the process of disinterring the body, obviously desperate grave robbers attacked the diggers and stole the gold teeth from Stickney's skull. Many say that in the dark of night the Judge still walks the garden of the dead with his head focused on the ground below searching perhaps for his missing teeth.

**PRISONERS OF WAR IN
ST. AUGUSTINE DURING
THE AMERICAN REVOLUTION**

From the onset of the American Revolution in 1775, the British Crown Colony in East Florida was a Loyalist bastion. In its capital, St. Augustine, the British lodged as prisoners many American Patriots and their French allies. Most of these prisoners were given the liberty of the town, but some were held in Castillo de San Marcos. A few captives rented quarters, but most of the men were housed in the unfinished State House which stood near this spot. By the end of 1780, these prisoners included three signers of the Declaration of Independence—Thomas Heyward, Jr., Arthur Middleton, and Edward Rutledge. On July 4, 1781, the Patriot captives celebrated Independence Day.

**Plaza at corner of King & St. George Streets, St. Augustine
SJ22 ~ GPS Coordinates: 29.892233, -81.312333**

During the siege of Charleston in 1780, the British managed to capture five signers of the Declaration of Independence. Though the men were not charged with treason, if so they would have surely been hanged, they were considered prisoners of war. The five signers captured were Richard Stockton, George Walton, Thomas Heyward Jr., Arthur Middleton and Edward Rutledge.

These men were fortunate to have been captured and taken to St. Augustine. While most undoubtedly as prisoners they suffered, conditions were much better than those of most regular Continental troops. Continental troops captured were generally taken to prison ships at anchor in the Charleston harbor. More than a third of their number perished aboard the retched ships from denial of food, bedding, clothing and general harassment. Few cases of torture were noted but those incidences appeared to be exceptions. Deaths occurred more from neglect rather than the intentional infliction of suffering. However in making that statement denial of the essentials of life should be considered torture in and of itself.

The five signers were considered rebel political leaders and the British made it well known that indeed there was a price on their heads. This knowledge certainly would have shaken the men, knowing that at any time the British could make good on their threats. Stockton, Walton, Heyward, Middleton and Rutledge were held at St. Augustine until prisoner exchanges exacted their release in the summer of 1781.

Sir Henry Clinton of Britain took Charleston by storm and claimed possession of the city on May 12, 1780. The political prisoners upon arrival at St. Augustine were addressed concerning their circumstance by a British officer, saying:

> "Expediency, and a series of political occurrences, have rendered it necessary to remove you
> from Charleston to this place; but, gentlemen, we have no wish to increase your sufferings; to all,
> therefore, who are willing to give their paroles, and not to go beyond the limits prescribed to
> them, the liberty of the town will be allowed; a dungeon will be the destiny of such as refuse to
> accept the indulgence."

Judge Thomas Heyward had commanded a battalion during the preceding battle and was taken prisoner. During his absence Heyward's home was demolished and his slaves seized. Though a good many of the slaves were later recovered, one hundred thirty were sold by the British to Jamaican sugar plantations.

After being held for just over a year, the prisoners were exchanged and shipped back to Philadelphia. Strangely enough, Thomas Heyward survived prison only to narrowly cheat death on his voyage to safety. While onboard ship, Heyward by some twist of fate found himself over the side and fighting for his life in the murky darkness of the ocean. He managed to keep himself afloat by clinging for dear life onto the ship's rudder. Sailors finally managed to rescue the grateful would be drowning victim.

Judge Thomas Heyward, Jr. returned to serve as a circuit court judge and state legislator. He died in March of 1809 at the age of sixty-four.

Arthur Middleton was actively engaged in the defense of the city of Charleston. Upon the surrender of the city he was taken prisoner and along with the others transported by sea to St. Augustine. He was exchanged in July 1781 and shipped to Philadelphia where Governor John Rutledge appointed him representative in Congress for South Carolina. One year later Middleton won the seat by election but opted to return to his family whom he had not seen since before the siege of Charleston. His estate was in ruins as a result of the war. He managed to rebuild his home and enjoyed retirement there in the embrace of his family. Arthur Middleton died on January 1, 1787.

Edward Rutledge, like the others, participated in the siege of Charleston and was taken to St. Augustine as a prisoner of war. After his release, he remained in Philadelphia until the British relinquished Charleston. Upon returning home, Rutledge practiced law and was elected as chief magistrate of South Carolina.

Ill health forced Rutledge to temper his participation in public office. Even so, he continued to serve in the state legislature and was elected Governor of South Carolina. He suffered from severe attacks of gout but it was a foolish exposure to wind and rain that resulted in a deadly bout of influenza. Edward Rutledge died while still occupying the Governor's office on January 23, 1800.

While Heyward, Middleton and Rutledge are certainly central figures, another individual, General Christopher Gadsden was a man among men. As lieutenant governor of South Carolina, Gadsden was forced to sign the surrender of Charleston. He was later arrested by order of Lord Cornwallis and transported to St. Augustine. Parole was offered each man in exchange for allegiance to the British crown. Undoubtedly each man refused the offer and was detained; though it was thought that the proposition was generally accepted.

General Gadsden not only refused the offer but did so in such a way that the British were determined to crush his spirit. Gadsden was no young man at this time but no consideration was given for either his station or age mainly due to his own goading words. He was placed in solitary confinement, in a small dark cell with only his mind to relieve the mundane passage of time.

General Gadsden concentrated his efforts on activities of the mind, diligently refreshing his memory in the study of the Hebrew language. While his jailers expected Gadsden to suffer under the penalties of his actions, he rose to the challenge and defied them once again.

When Major John Andre was arrested as a British spy, the governor of the Castillo, Colonel Glazier advised Gadsden that should Andre be executed, the British would retaliate. Glazier made it clear that Gadsden would forfeit his life, to which he replied that he was always prepared to die for his country. He realized it was impossible for Washington to yield, by the law of war, to fear or affection, yet he would not shrink from the sacrifice. Gadsden stated that he would rather ascend the scaffold than purchase with his life the dishonor of his country.

America and the cause of freedom were truly fortunate to have such a breed of men. When the country longed for civil and religious liberties, her citizens rose to the challenge with wisdom, fortitude and patriotism. Without these brave souls and countless others unknown to us, we as a nation would never know the meaning of life, liberty and justice for all.

TRINITY PARISH CHURCH
EPISCOPAL

The Church of England was established in Florida during the British occupation (1763-1783). The Reverend John Forbes held services first in the Spanish Bishop's House then on this site. Later, the ancient Spanish church a short distance south on St. George street was renovated and renamed St. Peters. There Anglican worship continued until the Spanish returned to Florida in 1784.

Shortly after Florida became a United States Territory in 1821, the Reverend Andrew Fowler of Charleston, South Carolina founded the Protestant Episcopal Church in St. Augustine and held first services in the Government House. The cornerstone of the original church, which forms the north transept of this building, was laid June 23, 1825. The church was enlarged to its present form in 1902.

223 St. George Street, St. Augustine
SJ23 ~ GPS Coordinates: 29.892153, -81.312150

The Church of England or Anglican Church got off to a rocky start in Florida. The Spanish influences, of course, made it impossible for the Anglicans to found a congregation. A small church was established by Anglican missionaries during the first brief British period beginning in 1763, however the Spanish regained control of Florida in 1783 and the tiny church congregation was abolished.

John Forbes was born in 1740 at Descrie, Scotland. Reverend John Forbes came from Scotland to America in 1764, as Judge in the British Admiralty at St. Augustine. Forbes married Dorothy Murray in Massachusetts on February 2, 1769 and the couple had three sons. Shortly after his arrival Reverend Forbes became minister of the Anglican Church. He conducted services in the old Spanish Bishop's house until a more suitable location could be found. The ancient Spanish church a short distance south on St. George Street was renovated and renamed St. Peters. It was there that Anglican worship continued until the Spanish reclaimed Florida in 1784.

Hoping to avoid any confrontation with the Spanish government, Reverend John Forbes sailed for Scotland by way of England in 1783. Accompanying Reverend Forbes was his eldest son, James Grant. Reverend John Forbes, the first Anglican clergyman of Florida, died in Scotland September 17, 1783.

In 1789, the Anglicans requested missionary services from the newly formed Protestant Episcopal Church of the United States. Church services would be dependent for many years on circuit rider ministers. Reverend Andrew Fowler of Charleston, South Carolina founded the Protestant Episcopal Church in St. Augustine and held its first services in the Government House on October 7, 1821. From that time the Trinity Episcopal Church became an active parish and the first Episcopal Church to be formed in Florida.

Episcopalians established an American extension of the Anglican Church at St. Augustine in the very year Florida became a United States territory, 1821. Reverend Fowler made such progress in building a strong foundation for the local parish that the construction of the first edifice was necessary. The cornerstone of Trinity Parish Church was laid in 1825. The first church was but thirty-six foot by fifty foot in size and occupied the present site in 1830. Other cities soon followed the "ancient city's" lead, congregations formed at Mandarin, Tallahassee and Jacksonville.

In 1833, thanks to the energetic leadership and fund-raising abilities of the Reverend Raymond Henderson the parish rolls swelled to one hundred sixty communicants. These numbers made Trinity Parish the largest single new faith in the territory. The Florida Diocese was founded January 17, 1838 at Tallahassee having seven parishes. A constitution and rules of order were drawn up and submitted to the General Convention. The General Convention of the Protestant Episcopal Church recognized the new growth of the Florida Diocese on September 7, 1838.

The shear size of the Florida Diocese meant there was little communication between the churches, no continuity and even travel between the parishes could take up to a month to complete. Without a resident Bishop and a shortage of clergy, the Diocese struggled. Difficult economic times hindered many parishes and by 1851, there were no more than two hundred sixty members in the entire diocese. However, change was on the horizon. The election of Reverend Francis Huger Rutledge as Bishop of the Diocese of Florida in October 1851, saved the Florida Episcopalian diocese.

Bishop Rutledge worked tirelessly, visiting churches, raising funds, recruiting new clergy and organizing the diocese into an effective operation. Gradually, the parish flourished not only in membership but also financially. Tiffany stained glass windows were installed, hand carved pews, an organ was purchased and a steeple with a bell was erected, all of which added to the opulence of the Episcopal parish. The monies were raised by the women of the church through bazaars, fairs, teas and ice cream socials. A major restoration was undertaken in the late 1800s, completely reorienting the church to the position where it remains today.

By the dawn of 1861 the new Florida Christian denominations, joined by the relatively few surviving members of the long-positioned Roman Catholic Church, were anxiously engaged in justifying the enslavement of the state's sixty thousand African-Americans. The slavery issue, together with other regional claims, would come to a tragic boil on January 10 of that fateful year when the independent "nation of Florida" withdrew from the American Union, the third state in the newly organized Southern Confederacy to do so.

As the Civil War drew to a close, the defeated South and Florida's churches were left in terrible shape.

Four churches had been torched, the rest abused, neglected and in disrepair. Many clergy had fled for their lives, funds were almost nonexistent and it appeared that all Bishop Rutledge had built might be lost.

At the 1866 Convention, it was decided to withdraw from the Confederacy and return to the Constitution and Cannons of the Episcopal Church in the United States. One year later, the Reverend John Freeman Young became the second bishop of the diocese and the churches came back to life. The South's reconstruction was still "a struggle for life" following the war.

Bishop Young traveled extensively throughout the diocese, but going from Jacksonville to Key West might take a month or more. But in 1880 he could report that "eleven churches built or in progress in one year." Bishop Young died in 1885 and the following year the Reverend Edwin Gardener Weed was elected Bishop of the Diocese of Florida. He oversaw continued growth and changes as the state and the diocese continued to grow. It was apparent that the state must be divided. This approach was approved in 1892 and the missionary jurisdiction of Southern Florida came into being.

Today Trinity Episcopal Church is a thriving parish. The church provides something for everyone and every age. Once again, the ladies of the parish play an important role and are very much involved. They have two Episcopal Churchwomen groups, a growing youth organization and a dedicated Altar Guild. There are several prayer groups and many educational classes at all levels for parishioners. For the men, The Brotherhood of St. Andrew has become a reality. The Diocese of Florida today has seventy-five congregations, fifteen parochial schools, more than fourteen thousand households represented in twenty-five northeast Florida counties.

DR. PECK HOUSE

The stone walls of this building date from before 1750 and were a part of a house owned by the Royal Treasurer late in the First Spanish Period. During the British Period it served for a time as the home of Governor John Moultrie. In 1837 Dr. Seth S. Peck purchased the house and rebuilt it using the old walls and adding the frame second-story. It remained in the Peck family until willed to the City in 1931. A generous grant from the Flagler Foundation permitted extensive restoration in 1968.

143 St. George Street, St. Augustine
SJ24 ~ GPS Coordinates: 29.892820, -81.312488

The exact date of construction of the house at 143 St. George Street is unknown. The facts that are documented date the house to precede 1741. When Juan Estevan de Pena arrived from Spain the next year, he moved into the already established residence. The location was described as bordering the East Side of the street leading to the land gate and on the south side of an alleyway leading to the bay. Today we would detail the location as the corner of St. George and Treasury streets. The ownership of the dwelling has been well noted over the years and provides a fascinating story of St. Augustine history.

Unlike many of the other dwellings dating to the same period the house featured flat roofs and a loggia[37]. The loggia was particularly important because it faced southeast to absorb the cooling breezes in the summer and warmth of the winter sun. The roof tiles were notched at the edges to drain rainwater and carefully spaced so that persons entering the dwelling were not soaked from the run off. The living area of four or five rooms opened directly off the loggia. Obviously much thought went into the construction of this residence.

The house was identified as the "Treasurer's House," which in fact it was for many of the twenty years that Juan Estevan de Pena lived in St. Augustine. However, other statements naming it "the old Treasury" or "the Spanish Treasury" are false. In fact the Spanish treasury was held safely ensconced within the walls of the Castillo.

Juan Estevan was a bachelor when he left Spain, but by the time of his arrival in St. Augustine he had with him a wife. Dona Maria Antonia Odriasola joined Juan Estevan from her home in Havana, where he ported during his voyage from Spain. Even with his elevated governmental stature, Juan Estevan felt his accommodations were less than ideal. The couple never had children but accepted the responsibilities as godparents to a number of St. Augustine children. Because of their social standing it would be very prestigious to have Juan Estevan and Dona Maria Antonia as godparents.

Juan Estevan's status in St. Augustine society was second only to the governor in importance. His duties were vast involving food and pay for the garrison, the support of widows and orphans, dealing with the native Americans as well as all of the pomp and ceremony required of a government liaison. The governor found Juan Estevan de Pena to be ingenious and industrious having "a friendship of those partisans to us and to attract the non-aligned."

Even still, with all of Juan Estevan's successes in St. Augustine he did not like his adopted home. He considered it, "one of the most miserable settlements in all of the Indies." Even though Estevan tried, with the governor's support, to leave the settlement a number of times it would take twenty years and the invasion of British soldiers to finally allow his departure.

The Spanish inhabitants of St. Augustine knew dark days during the war with England. However, Juan Estevan de Pena knew with the signing of the Peace Treaty relinquishing Florida to England in January 1763 more desperate days were ahead. Evacuation and transportation for more than three thousand had to be coordinated. The British agreed to allow anyone who wished to remain in Florida permission to do so, however, Spanish officials were determined to leave no one behind to betray their Catholic way of life.

Amazingly those leaving St. Augustine were not all Spanish. A number of the immigrants were runaway slaves, free men and women of color and any native American wishing to leave Protestant soil. Aside from these other travelers included the dearly departed whose families refused to leave loved ones buried in English ground. Can you imagine the fragrance of the departing ship?

Because of the expediency of the evacuation, little time was left to dispose of St. Augustine property. Juan Elixio de la Puente and Jesse Fish were assigned the task of selling the remaining property and forwarding the proceeds to the rightful owner. It is believed that these deals were rarely done to benefit the landowner and many times the profits were simply pocketed by Fish.

On January 21, 1764, Pena finally left St. Augustine in the company of the Spanish governor. The duo left on the last vessel to depart for Havana. Only one signature baring the name Juan Estevan de Pena remains in St. Augustine today, that of the deed transferring ownership of the Treasurer's House in 1763.

The next owner was to be John Gordon of Carolina. Gordon never bothered to move to St. Augustine though it is believed that the house was let out[38] during this time. During Gordon's ownership, English botanist John Bartram noted extensive restoration work to the Treasurer's House, including glass windows, the detached kitchen was connected to the residence and four chimneys were added for heating purposes. Heating made the house more desirable for one of the house's more prominent inhabitants to date: John Moultrie, of the governor's council. Moultrie gave up his lease on the Treasurer's House in 1778; however, the residence did not remain uninhabited.

Because of the deplorable condition of the Government House in St. Augustine, Governor Patrick Tonyn moved with his family to the quarters. Though the residence was not considered grand, it was certainly suitable for the Governor's needs. By this time the owner, John Gordon had passed away and willed the property to his nephew Thomas Forbes. Forbes, along with his business partner William Panton moved into the house. During this time many of the Spanish real estate sales came into question by the British government. The validity of each transaction was carefully examined, including that of the Treasurer's House. To ensure a proper deed was in hand, Thomas Forbes quickly sold the property to attorney Henry Yonge whom then in turn sold the property again to Forbes and Panton. The transaction was completed for no other reason than to ensure the new owners had a clear title to the property.

By 1783, Governor Tonyn received the distressing news that Florida would again be transferred to Spain. The English would evacuate just as the Spanish had nearly twenty years earlier. Forbes and Panton, both bachelors, made the decision to remain in Spanish Florida. When Spain's new Governor of Florida, Vicente Manuel de Zespedes, assumed leadership ownership of the Treasurer's House was challenged. Don Antonio Fernandez arrived from Havana with a power of attorney in hand from Pena's widow claiming that the residence was only left in trust to John Gordon and never had in fact been sold to him. After investigating the matter Zespedes determined that Panton and Forbes' title to the house was valid, but less than one year later while the two men were away from St. Augustine on business, Governor Zespedes ruled that the property had been abandoned and seized it for the Spanish Crown.

Florida came under the leadership of Juan Nepomuceno de Quesada in 1790 and it was he who ordered a full accounting of all Spanish property. So detailed was the inventory that a full reporting of the condition of the house listed as No. 89 in Square No. 10 is available. The house was described as being a "rubble work masonry house with lot. The description included "accurate dimensions" of the kitchen, garden and boundary walls as well as the entire house. It was noted that the roof was in deplorable shape. Occupants were listed as Joaquin Sanchez and others; the others were probably his wife and two children.

From April to November 1791 the house changed hands amazingly enough three times. Eventually ownership would come to Francisco Xavier Sanchez, whose family would retain the property for thirty years. Francisco Sanchez was a remarkable entrepreneur and his personal life was incredibly interesting. He had married Maria del Carmen Hill, the daughter of his neighbor, in 1787; the girl was seventeen compared to his fifty-one years. The age difference was not out of the ordinary for this time but what is amazing is that he then merged both a legitimate and illegitimate family with what appeared to be little animosity. Sanchez had long maintained a relationship with a free mulatto[39]; Beatriz Piedra from Charleston who bore nine children all acknowledged by Sanchez. In fact, Sanchez' legitimate heirs continued to provide for Piedra's children even after their father's death. Over the years both branches of the Sanchez family would call the Treasurer's House home.

By the time of Sanchez death in 1807 the house had deteriorated noticeably. The residence went through a full inventory and evaluation as a result of probating the Sanchez estate. The roof tiles, which drained water from the flat surface, were all but absent and three of the four chimneys were gone as well. The entire estate consisting of the main house with kitchen, shed, a stable, fencing, water closet and a grove of fifteen orange trees had a noted worth of three thousand six hundred thirty-eight Spanish pesos, ranking third in the whole of Sanchez' nine holdings. Converted to American money by today's standard the worth of the Treasurer's house would have been equivalent to approximately three hundred thirty dollars. In 1807 this was a considerable amount of money.

Finally on March 1, 1821 after thirty years of ownership the Sanchez family sold the property to Jose Mariano Hernandez. Hernandez paid sixteen hundred pesos (approximately one hundred sixty American dollars) for "some walls of stone covered with shingles and very deteriorated." Hernandez was a remarkable man of Minorcan heritage. His father after escaping the torture of Andrew Turnbull at New Smyrna had risen to become the chief master carpenter of St. Augustine fortifications. As a young man Jose was allowed the privilege of education in schools at Savannah and Havana.

When the Adams Onis treaty was signed finally ceding East Florida to the United States in 1820, St. Augustine citizens were given the option to choose to become American citizens. Jose Mariano Hernandez became a citizen of his adopted country. In 1822 all of Florida became a part of the United States. Hernandez was bestowed the title brigadier general of the East Florida Volunteers of the newly instituted government by old friend Governor William P. Duval. By now he was known as Joseph M. Hernandez, an Americanized version of his Spanish name. This choice was made upon Hernandez entrance into political life when he filled the unexpired term of the territory's first delegate to Congress upon the death of James Bronaugh. He then served in the House of Representatives and was appointed to Florida's legislative council by President James Monroe.

Unfortunately as adept as Joseph Hernandez was in the political arena, financially left much to be desired. Eventually Hernandez lost title to the Treasurer's House. In 1833, James Heilbron of South Carolina was the title-holder of record. Little is known of Heilbron or by what means he obtained the dwelling, possibly Hernandez owed a debt he was unable to resolve. Regardless Heilbron sold the property to Hernandez' friend, Daniel L. Griswold for eleven hundred dollars. Four years later the property again changed hands and became the property of New Englander, Dr. Seth S. Peck. Dr. Peck was determined to transform the rubble into a suitable dwelling for his family.

Dr. Peck ordered what supplies he required to restore the house that he could not barter for locally. Much of the labor and materials came to him in kind for medical services rendered. The restoration wed a strange couple, one of Spanish descent and the other from colonial Connecticut. The original structure was very much like that of the days when Pena walked the tabby flooring but for the new upstairs addition a more somber, proper New England attitude permeated. A northwest room off of Treasury Street was rented to Isaac Avery of Groton, Connecticut to house his general store and at the other end of the building was Dr. Peck's medical office. Perhaps the Peck Building was a mini-mall long before its time.

Dr. Seth Peck's opinion was respected politically both locally and in the territory. Everyone sought his medical services from slaves to government officials. It was with sadness that death claimed him on July 21, 1841, only four years after acquiring the Treasurer's House. Strangely enough 1841 marked one century since Juan Estevan de Pena first came to the house and Dr. Seth Peck would be the first owner to die with its walls. The Treasurer's House from this point forward would be known as the Pena-Peck House.

The house now belonged to Dr. Peck's widow, Sarah and so it would remain until 1879 when Sarah Peck died shortly before her eighty-eighth birthday. The dwelling was left to daughters Rebecca and Mary. Little is known about the sisters other than they kept house, read and occasionally attended various social functions. Neither woman ever had children or married for that matter.

In 1888, modernization in the form of gas lighting and cooking came to the Pena-Peck House. Within five years regular postal service warranted the need for permanent addresses, therefore the latest moniker denoting the house would be 143 St. George Street. Miss Rebecca died suddenly in 1910 leaving the responsibility of the house and an aging Miss Mary to niece Anna Burt. Others in the home at this time were the "colored persons" who maintained the household. Emmeline Warren oversaw the kitchen, Louis Whaley kept up the house and grounds and John Burns cared for the stables and drove the buggy.

Anna Burt led a quiet life at the Pena-Peck House. She cared for her aunt, carried the responsibility of treasurer for the Woman's Exchange and was secretary of the Free Public Library Association. Anna served on the Executive Committee of the Library Association, one of only a very few St. Augustine women to obtain the prestigious elected role.

Two years after the death of her sister Rebecca, Mary died at the advanced age of ninety-five. Now Anna Burt was sole owner of the house where she had been born sixty-two years earlier. She lived alone in the dwelling with the exception of her ill-tempered parrot, Polly. Polly, a Jamaican green parrot, was a gift from close family friend Dr. Andrew Anderson.

Anna continued to care for those loyal servants to the household the remainder of their lives. Louis Whaley was given Dr. Peck's old office even when he was no longer able to care for the house and grounds. The former stable across the street was extensively refurbish for Emmeline Warren, their cook for over a half century. Unfortunately Emmeline was afraid to live in the little house by herself so Miss Anna promptly found accommodations more toward her liking.

Toward the end of her life Anna Burt was somewhat distressed over what might happen to the St. George Street home after her death. There were no relatives that she trusted to care for the home and its future. Through

THE DR. PECK HOUSE

Dr. Andrew Anderson she had heard public speeches denoting the importance of historic preservation in St. Augustine. To this end as Anna Burt put her affairs in order through the Florida National Bank trust department. With the assistance of William Hardin Goodman of Florida National Bank, Anna willed the Pena-Peck House to the city of St. Augustine. Her stipulation was that the house was "to be maintained as an example of the old ante-bellum homes of the South." Her affairs in order, the home of her birth safely preserved, Anna Gardner Burt died in May 1931. Like many others of her family she had ascended to an impressive eighty-one years when she passed away quietly in her beloved home.

The city of St. Augustine was at first thrilled with Miss Burt's gift, however, after further research into the financial requirements of maintaining the home their ardor cooled somewhat. Eight months after Anna Burt's death, the city of St. Augustine formally rejected the heartfelt bequest. The citizens of St. Augustine were aghast at the city's actions, under pressure of public outcry the city commission scheduled reconsideration. The Woman's Exchange had the city attorney draw up a proposal in which they would assume the responsibility of the "Burt Property." Within twenty-four hours the proposal was accepted unanimously.

Since 1932, the Woman's Exchange has cared for, preserved and ran the Pena-Peck House. Beginning with an admission price of twenty-five cents, the residence continues to house the largest collection of original antiques to date in a Spanish Colonial home. A Flagler Foundation grant allowed needed restoration work to be accomplished in 1968. Today the wonderful house museum remains open in a way that would have made Miss Anna Burt and her ancestors very proud. A minimal admission charge helps to maintain the residence, which is open for tours daily.

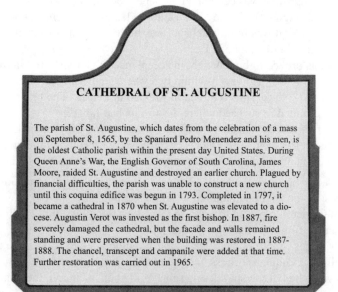

CATHEDRAL OF ST. AUGUSTINE

The parish of St. Augustine, which dates from the celebration of a mass on September 8, 1565, by the Spaniard Pedro Menendez and his men, is the oldest Catholic parish within the present day United States. During Queen Anne's War, the English Governor of South Carolina, James Moore, raided St. Augustine and destroyed an earlier church. Plagued by financial difficulties, the parish was unable to construct a new church until this coquina edifice was begun in 1793. Completed in 1797, it became a cathedral in 1870 when St. Augustine was elevated to a diocese. Augustin Verot was invested as the first bishop. In 1887, fire severely damaged the cathedral, but the facade and walls remained standing and were preserved when the building was restored in 1887-1888. The chancel, transcept and campanile were added at that time. Further restoration was carried out in 1965.

38 Cathedral Place, St. Augustine
SJ25 ~ GPS Coordinates: 29.893398, -81.312694

Don Juan Ponce de Leon was the first European to make landfall on northeastern Florida soil. He had sailed from Puerto Rico in April 1513 in search of riches. Because he sailed without a priest no religious rites could be performed. He returned eight years later at the behest of Spain's King Charles V and this time was accompanied by a religious contingent. Charles V gave instructions to convert the natives to the Catholic faith "as best you can." Ponce de Leon's first mission attempt was a dismal failure. After an intensely brutal attack by the Native American, an injured Ponce de Leon fled to Cuba where he died only a few days later of wounds sustained during the altercation.

A plethora of Spanish explorers followed Ponce de Leon's lead. However, all were doomed to failure due to diminished provisions, disease and the savagery of the local Native American tribes. It wasn't until the arrival of Adelantado Pedro Menendez de Aviles under the auspices of King Philip II of Spain that a permanent and lasting settlement was established.

Menendez was charged with the establishment of a village, mission and elimination of the Frenchmen who preceded him at Fort Caroline. He met his goals against the French quite swiftly, with much bloodshed. Matanzas, the name of the inlet at St. Augustine, quite literally means, "massacre." Menendez was accompanied by "four secular priests with faculties to hear confessions," Francisco López de Mendoza Grajales, Rodrigo García de Trujillo, and Pedro de Rueda, the fourth name remains unknown.

Menendez' flotilla met a brutal storm along the planned course, which forced his nineteen ships to return to Cadiz on the first attempt to reach American shores. The second attempt proved more fruitful and fateful as it were, Father Lopez reported a sign from God saying,

"...God showed us a miracle from heaven... About nine o'clock in the evening, a comet appeared, which showed itself directly above us, a little eastward, giving so much light that it might have been taken for the sun. It went towards the west — that is, towards Florida, and its brightness lasted long enough to repeat two Credos."

The first mass at St. Augustine was celebrated on September 8, 1565. Father Lopez met Admiral Menendez carrying a cross and singing the hymn 'Te Deum Laudamus.' Menendez knelt, kissed the papal symbol and the first parish of the New World was born. A chapel was built at the site of the mission called Nombre de Dios, cradling an image of María Santísima de la Leche.

The Native Americans proved to be reluctant in acceptance of Christianity. In the next year the Jesuits arrived to help build diocese missions. However, within two weeks Father Pedro Martinez was martyred and none of the missions survived. In 1572, the Jesuits returned to Mexico in defeat. The Franciscans arrived the next year, in small numbers at first, determined to succeed where the Jesuits had failed.

No record of the parish church remains, we do know that during Sir Francis Drake's marauding raid of 1586 the sanctuary was reduced to ashes. The Franciscan monastery succumbed to a molten blaze on March 14, 1599. The friars were forced to take residence in Governor Canzo's newly built hospital. The friars moved into Nuestra Señora de la Soledad[40] hospital, the United States' first medical facility, and Governor Canzo built another hospital. Over the course of the next one hundred years the Church continued to grow. Nearing the end of the century, Gabriel Diaz Vara Calderón reported to Spanish Queen Mariana that thirteen thousand Spaniards and Native Americans had been confirmed in the New World.

English Governor James Moore of Carolina viciously bombarded St. Augustine in 1702. The entire city sought refuge in the Castillo; the coquina fortress bore more than fifty days of torrential cannonade. Moore withdrew in frustration, in his wake he left the smoldering ruins of the parish church, the mission Nuestra Señora de la Leche, friary, the Franciscan chapel and most private domiciles. Only the hospital and twenty residences escaped the fiery breach. The hospital chapel became the parish church until, by treaty, the English took St. Augustine in 1763.

During the English period, the Spaniards were offered freedom of worship. Though within a year less than ten Catholics remained throughout Florida. All of the resident priests had fled to Havana. The Catholic parishioners removed all of their ultramontane[41] possessions including the pews on which they sat and the bones of their deceased Spanish governors.

During this time, Dr. Andrew Turnbull of London began amassing a group of colonist from the Isle of Minorca to provide "indentured labor" for his Florida Plantation. Turnbull managed to gather fourteen hundred three indentured servants. Men, women and children accompanied by Father Pedro Camps, a thirty-eight-year-old secular priest with a doctorate in theology, who would be the pastor of the new colony, and Father Bartolomé Casanovas, an Augustinian, as assistant pastor. The voyage was tumultuous and more than one hundred forty of the would-be servants perished.

The wretched journey was but a glimpse of the trouble that would befall the Minorcans once they arrived. Substandard provisions and meager shelters accompanied by lack of proper clothing, cruel punishments, disease and slave labor in the fields brought about the deaths of nearly a third of the Minorcan's number, in 1768, as many as fifteen people perished per day. Father Casanovas was deported in 1774 under a charge of insubordination. Apparently, the assistant pastor dared to question Andrew Turnbull concerning the treatment of the Minorcan people.

The Minorcans fled Turnbull's oppressive authority in March of 1777 upon the realization that they would never fulfill their indenture or claim the promised land. The people sought sanctuary at St. Augustine and were granted asylum by the governor. Father Camps remained behind for a time to care for those unable to travel. Father Camps finally arrived in November and set to work immediately to establish a chapel and cemetery. The first services were held at the little stone house on St. George Street where Father Camps lived. The cemetery was established at the site of a former Native American settlement called Tolomato.

When Spain reclaimed Florida in 1783, St. Augustine was found in deplorable condition. The Old Spanish parish church was said to be a "useless pile of masonry." Father Thomas Hassett chose to use the upper floor of the old bishop's house as the best location for a temporary church. Unfortunately the arrangement was not ideal. Older parishioners were unable to maneuver the stairs and the lower floor served as a guardhouse for the soldiers keeping watch. Another peculiarity concerned the fact that often prisoners were held at the guardhouse, therefore, since the guardhouse was literally "under the Body of the Church," the captives could claim religious sanctuary.

Father Hassett convinced the governor of St. Augustine of the need for a new sanctuary in October 1784, but it wasn't until 1793 that the cornerstone was finally laid. The architect for the new church was Mariano de la Rocque and contractor, Don Miguel Ysnardy. The church took four years to build and was finally dedicated on December 8, 1797. Father Michael O'Reilly, new pastor and Vicario of East Florida, carried the Blessed Sacrament from the old bishop's house accompanied by the church parishioners.

Sadly, Father Pedro Camps did not survive to see the new church. He had died seven years before its completion and was buried at Tolomato. Father Narciso Font, who died only one year after his arrival, succeeded him. Both priests were disinterred at Tolomato and placed in brick vaults provided under the sanctuary of the newly constructed church. The contractor Don Miguel Ysnardy had also provided a place for himself there and was laid to rest in April of 1803.

The next transition for St. Augustine occurred with the signing of the Adams-Onis treaty of 1819, granting Florida to the United States. The Catholic citizens of St. Augustine were shocked to find that the church, the cemetery, the bishop's residence, the Mission Nombre de Dios and the old Franciscan friary were listed as property of the King of Spain. Therefore all of the property legally belonged to the United States. Things turned from bad to worse when, in 1822, the Bishop of Havana suddenly relinquished jurisdiction to the ill prepared Bishop John England of the Diocese of Charleston. Their pastor, Father Michael Crosby, died the same year, and his assistant Father Juan Nepomuceno Gómez, returned to Cuba the following year. The Catholics of St. Augustine were left without a church or a shepherd.

The church was embroiled in a battle of will over the next several years. Newly appointed Father Edward Francis Mayne and Church Warden Alvarez disagreed over the burial of a parishioner. José M. Sanchez, a former treasurer of the church Board of Wardens, had been a member of the Free Masons and according to Alvarez, could not have a funeral service in the church. Of course the fact that Sanchez had defeated Alvarez in a municipal election only a year before his death, surely did not affect Alvarez' opinion. The two men battled continually until Father Mayne convinced the Board of Wardens to toss out Alvarez. Undeterred, Alvarez returned as president of the board the very next year and retaliated by dismissing Father Mayne due to "lack of funds."

Rome appointed Fathers Nicholas Bourdet and Frederick Rost to serve St. Augustine. Neither man lasted the year. Father Bourdet did not understand nor speak Spanish, so he quickly departed. Father Rost became involved in serious "parochial intrigues" and was asked to leave. Father Mayne returned once again, but his domineering ways over various other diocese resulted in his final removal only two years later. Bishop England of Charleston recorded the incident as "termination of this miserable and unfortunate little schism[42]."

Battles over the rightful ownership of the church and cemetery began in 1823. It would be fifty years before the Mission Nombre de Dios site came to the church once again. However, the Franciscan friary has never been returned and remains to this day property of the federal government. Today the friary houses the Florida National Guard.

Father Augustin Verot was ordained bishop in April 1858 and arrived in St. Augustine on June 1 to attend his flock. Father Verot managed to secure seven additional priests to join the three already in place. His vicariate[43] included the entire state east of the Apalachicola River. He also recruited five sisters of the Order of Mercy and three Christian Brothers to provide an education for the diocese children.

When the Civil War began in April of 1861, Father Verot was given the additional responsibility of the Savannah diocese. Unfortunately this appointment involved his moving to the Savannah area. By 1865, he had obtained eight Sisters of St. Joseph from France to offer instruction to the newly emancipated slave children. By 1870, Bishop Verot requested a return to St. Augustine. Perhaps one of his greatest gifts to the St. Augustine diocese was his recovery of the nearly complete registers of the Spanish parish from Havana, Cuba. Bishop Verot continued to serve the St. Augustine Church until his death on June 10, 1876.

Bishop John Moore was ordained on May 13, 1877 to succeed Verot. During the twilight of April 12, 1887, fire engulfed the St. Augustine Hotel. The blaze rapidly spread consuming everything in its path. The St. Augustine Cathedral sounded her bells in alarm but to no avail. The Cathedral was completely devoured. Eerily during the entire ordeal, the clock situated high above the façade continued to sound the hour until the death knell struck at 5:30 when the resounded peel would be heard no more. Henry Flagler stood that morning with a devastated Bishop Moore and pledged to help rebuild.

Morning light illuminated the charred destruction, which left only a shell standing. Remarkably the walls and façade were salvageable. James Renwick, architect for the famed New York St. Patrick's Cathedral, just happened to be visiting St. Augustine at the time of the fire. Renwick offered his service for the restoration of the majestic cathedral. Less than one year later, the doors of the St. Augustine Cathedral were opened to parishioners for Easter services on April 1, 1888. It would be several years later before the altar and other parts of the interior were completed.

Today the first Parish finds itself exploring new technology and making it part of their ministry. The progressive church has instituted an online community. The computer age technology is used to "provide the means for everyone who visits, regardless of their religious affiliation, to pursue their own personal exploration of faith in a tranquil and restorative space." The Cathedral-Basilica of Saint Augustine has been part of the community's history for more than four hundred thirty years. Today, they continue to grow and meet the needs of their parishioners as an ever-changing constant offering faith and love to all who pass through her doors.

CATHEDRAL OF
ST. AUGUSTINE

PUBLIC MARKET PLACE

The first public market was established in this Plaza by Governor Mendez de Canzo in 1598. Here, for the first time a standard system of weights and measures was introduced in this country for the protection of the consumer. On this site a market for the sale of meats and produce was erected in 1824, and in use until 1878. This structure was rebuilt by the City in 1888 following a disastrous fire in this area April 11, 1887.

Plaza at Charlotte & St. George Streets, St. Augustine
SJ26 ~ GPS Coordinates: 29.892450, -81.311500

Strangely enough for a place that has been in existence for more than four hundred years, except for one brief interval, there is very little written about the Public Market Place. What is clearly written about concerning the Public Market Place is the fact that although it is often referred to as the "Old Slave Market" there is no evidence that slaves were ever sold here.

Gonzalo Mendez de Canzo became the Governor of St. Augustine in 1597 and was very enthusiastic about his newly appointed position. His intentions for the city included a much-needed revitalization resulting from the 1593 fire, which burned the entire city to the ground. The Governor was determined to establish public service facilities in the Spanish settlement. His first goal was the construction of a medical system. The first hospital in America was constructed in St. Augustine in the year of Menendez' arrival 1597, called Nuestra Senora de la Soledad or Our Lady of Solitude.

Menendez wrote to Spain's King Philip II on February 23, 1598, concerning the construction of the small frame hospital which adjoined a wooden church. He explained the need for the structure by giving examples of the many soldiers and Native Americans who been treated for fevers at the institution the previous summer. He also took the opportunity to request that King Philip declare the giving of alms to defray the five hundred-ducat[44] deficit, which had drained St. Augustine's coffers.

Construction of the first Government house began the next year in 1598, as did the Public Market Place. Governor Mendez was very progressive in his ideas. The Market Place was to be the first commercial source of goods to be offered utilizing a standard system of weight and measures to ensure that the consumers of St. Augustine received fair quantities.

The city now claimed more than one hundred twenty homes, though most were crude dwellings built of palmetto fronds. Governor Mendez continued to institute urban improvements with a horse-drawn gristmill and to the south of town, a residential development. The Public Market Place and Plaza that surrounded it became St. Augustine's center, a gathering point for her citizens to share news of the settlement, trade and bring goods to sell.

The year 1599 brought disaster upon the citizens of St. Augustine. First a fire brought to ruin Nuestra Senora de la Soledad and then a torrential hurricane flooded the city on September 2, very nearly washing what was left of it into the sea. Though these were not the first catastrophes St. Augustine faced, they were quite daunting. Governor Mendez was not to be defeated, he rebuilt the hospital and it remained well into the 17th century. St. Augustine recovered from the disasters and survived.

By 1602 questions loomed concerning the fate of St. Augustine. Official hearings were held to decide her fate, whether it was best to maintain the city, relocate it or abandon the settlement. Of course, Governor Gonzalo Mendez de Canzo fought for the city with relish. At the conclusion of the hearings the decision was made to keep the settlement at its present location. The city would serve as a haven for shipwreck survivors and a strategic military position guarding against marauding pirates continually preying on Spanish treasure galleons.

The Public Market Place at the Plaza continued to exist though over the years deteriorated substantially. The facility was finally razed and rebuilt in 1840, surviving for almost fifty years only interrupted by the demand of Civil War. After the war the Public Market Place on the Plaza again came to prominence and continued to serve the citizens of St. Augustine. On April 11, 1887, fire consumed the Plaza. From St. George to Charlotte Streets, the blaze left blackened smears of ashen remains where homes, churches and the beautiful plaza once stood. Again, the Public Market Place on the Plaza was rebuilt.

Thousands of tourists visit each year and pose for pictures on the steps of the Public Market Place unaware of the history that lies beneath their feet. The site has endured the test of time and remains today a place where citizens of St. Augustine share news of the city, sell goods and gather in celebration.

FLORIDA
The Sunshine State

Colonized by Spaniards, 1559 – Site of first permanent settlement in U.S. 1565 – Acquired by U.S. from Spain, 1819 – Admitted as 27th state, 1845 – Now nation's fastest growing state – 1963 population 5,639,900 – State song – "Old Folks at Home" – State bird – Mockingbird – State tree – Sabal Palm – One of world's great resort areas – 30,000 named lakes – 600 varieties of fish – Over 1,000 miles of sandy beaches – Site of famed Cape Kennedy moonport – Boasts versatile and expanding economy based on its factories, forests, farms, and mines – Manufacturing employment has doubled in last 10 years.

Charlotte Street, St. Augustine
SJ27 ~ GPS Coordinates: 29.892317, -81.311500

Florida spans some fifty-eight thousand five hundred sixty square miles with a length from the St. Marys River to the southern most tip of Key West, four hundred forty-seven miles. That is precisely the route I have taken with "Get Off the Interstate," unfortunately by means of Florida highways the distance is about five hundred thirty-seven miles. She has six hundred sixty-three miles of white sand beaches and her longest river, the St. Johns, traverses two hundred seventy-three miles. The Sunshine State is dotted with approximately seven thousand seven hundred lakes and thirty-three springs. Florida's largest county is Palm Beach and largest city is Miami-Fort Lauderdale, the line between the two has long since been smudged.

St. Augustine was the first permanent European settlement founded in 1565 by Spanish Commodore Pedro Menendez. Twenty-three years after becoming a United States territory in 1821, Florida became the twenty-seventh state. During the last census, taken in 2000, Florida ranked fourth in population throughout the United States at nearly sixteen million.

Florida's state animal was actually chosen by the school children of the state, the Florida Panther. The Panther and its primary food source the white-tailed deer share the very same habitat. Unfortunately population expansion has pushed the large cat to the endangered list for more than thirty years. The common mockingbird is Florida's state bird. The songbird and mimic has a pleasant voice and will sing through the night during the cool spring evenings. Actually Florida shares the warbler with Arkansas, Mississippi, Tennessee and Texas.

Sea Cow, Big Beaver or Mermaid, whatever the name, the Manatee is Florida's marine mammal. The flippers appear from a distance like hands, then add the rounded tail and the mermaid legend of ancient mariners was born. In fact the mammal belongs to the order called Sirenia defined as siren or mermaid. The manatee is listed as an endangered species, however because of the Florida Manatee Act limiting the speed of boats in known manatee areas, chances for their survival are good. Is the porpoise or dolphin Florida's saltwater mammal? Well in true political fashion, Florida is sitting the fence; the response is: "porpoise, also commonly known as the dolphin." Well, not quite, but OK. Over the years, sailors have claimed the presence of porpoises is a sign of good luck.

When one hears the words orange juice they immediately conjure up an image of the Sunshine State. In fact, orange juice is the state beverage. During World War II frozen orange juice concentrate was developed and an industry was born. The fragrant orange blossom is the state flower. The tiny white flowers fill the air with a light perfume throughout most of the state.

The moonstone was selected as the state gem in deference to NASA, the Kennedy Space Center in Brevard County and the brave astronauts who landed on the lunar surface. The moonstone is not natural to Florida and was not found on the moon. Its hard to imagine any other state having a state soil, but Florida does; and to no one's surprise it is sand. With one thousand, one hundred ninety-seven miles of coastline, what other type soil could it possibly be?

The state seal in use prior to 1985 had numerous errors, these were corrected by Secretary of State George Firestone that year. The new seal represented a Seminole Indian woman rather than the Western Plain Indian previously portrayed; a steamboat used on the second seal was much more accurate and the state tree, the sabal palm replaced the cocoa palm. The state song, "The Suwanee River" written by Stephen C. Foster in 1851 represents the Suwannee River flowing from Georgia's Okeefenokee Swamp to the Gulf of Mexico. Foster chose the name Suwanee because it fit in the two-syllable cadence he required for the tune he had composed. It could not have been a love for the river that inspired Florida's state song because Stephen Foster never visited the state.

World War II instigated a tonic into Florida's economy. The semi-tropical climate allowed year round training for soldiers, sailors and aviators. Because of the military influx, transportation became a priority in Florida. Highway and airport construction began in earnest and by the end of the war residents and tourists utilized the new advantages in droves. The warm climate attracted an increase in population, retirees flocked to the balmy peninsula state, young people looking for work in the tourism industry and the wealthy seeking out the posh addresses along the coast. The tourism, cattle, citrus and phosphate industries were joined by more modern enterprises involving electronics, plastics, construction, real estate and banking.

Floridians have a long, exciting history to be proud of. By preserving the past, the youth of today is ensured to have a legacy in the future.

SEGUI
KIRBY SMITH HOUSE

The Segui-Kirby Smith House is one of only 36 Spanish Colonial houses remaining in St. Augustine. The house dates from the late 1700s. The site on which it is situated has been continuously occupied since the late 1500s. In 1786 it became the home of Bernardo Segui, a prosperous merchant of Minorcan descent who was also baker to the garrison and a Spanish militia official. Judge Joseph Lee Smith, first Judge of the Superior Court for East Florida, rented the home about 1823 from Segui's heirs, and in time the family purchased it. Edmund Kirby Smith was born here in May 1824. A West Point graduate, he became at 38 the youngest lieutenant general in the Confederate Army and was the last Confederate general to surrender his command. When General Kirby Smith and his sister sold the home in 1887, it became a boarding house with offices. The small building on the west was the kitchen and dining room. In 1895 John L. Wilson and Frances Wilson, gave the lot and building in trust to a private organization for use as a free public library. Today the St. Augustine Historical Society holds the property under this trust as its historical research library.

Artillery Lane, St. Augustine
SJ28 ~ GPS Coordinates: 29.891567, -81.311767

The house at 6 Artillery Lane was originally built during Spain's second round of occupation at St. Augustine during the late 18th century. It has since been named for its two more noted owners, Bernardo Segui and Edmund Kirby Smith.

Bernardo Segui was a member of the Minorcan society so ill treated at the village of New Smyrna. After the Minorcan's fateful immigration to St. Augustine in 1777, Segui became a garrison baker and later gained notoriety with the Spanish militia. He purchased the residence at 6 Artillery Lane in 1786.

The Segui families' journey to prominence continued with a grant from Spanish Governor Coppinger of the former Indian settlement recorded as Gray's Place in 1818. Today we know that particular tract as the city of Palatka. Segui held the property for less than one year before selling it, at an enormous profit for the day, to George Fleming for twelve hundred dollars.

Secretary of War John C. Calhoun appointed Colonel James Gadsden and Bernardo Segui, second generation St. Augustinian, Treaty Commissioners in April 1823. Their mission was to move the Seminole Indians south of Tampa Bay. However, a survey of the Everglade property revealed that the Native Americans could not sustain life south of the Charlotte Harbor. Eventually Calhoun was convinced of the unsuitability of the southern property and expanded the reservation boundary northward.

Heirs of the Segui family rented their first St. Augustine home to Joseph Lee Smith in 1823. November 2, 1824, Bernardo Segui became Mayor of St. Augustine. Smith was an American lawyer who had gallantly served in the War of 1812, rising to the rank of Colonel. Judge Smith presided over the first court of Jacksonville on December 1, 1823 before a crowd of more than two hundred settlers gathered at the corner of Market and Forsyth Streets.

Edmund Kirby Smith was born at the Artillery Lane address on May 16, 1824. In the proud tradition of family soldiers, Edmund graduated from the United States Military Academy at West Point in 1845 and promptly joined an infantry troop. Assigned under Generals Zachary Taylor and Winfield Scott, Edmund marched off to the Mexican War. Distinguished for gallantry, he quickly rose in rank to first lieutenant and later captain.

Ephraim, Edmund's older brother by seventeen years, met his final end at Molino del Rey while serving under General Worth. General Worth was ordered to attack and take the foundry used for casting cannon and destroy any munitions found. Worth incorrectly assumed that the Mexicans had abandoned the buildings when no one was sited there. He sent a detachment of only five hundred men out of a total strength of twenty-eight hundred. When Worth's men approached the Molino, Ephraim among them, six pieces of field armory and six thousand muskets met the brave American front. Within minutes more than two hundred fifty men lay dead and dying on the gently slopping hill of the Molino. The full power of the American Infantry advanced in retaliation of their fallen brethren, the Mexican foundry was taken under the thick fog of acrid smoke and hail of musket shots. But like so many others, Ephraim Kirby Smith did not survive to taste sweet victory.

Ever the soldier, Edmund served as a cavalryman against the Native Americans on the brutal Texas frontier. By 1849 he had returned to West Point, as the assistant professor of mathematics. During his time in the western backcountry, Edmund wrote extensive botany reports. The Smithsonian Institute later published these meticulously compiled works.

In 1861, Edmund Kirby Smith resigned his army post to join the Confederacy. Much to his dismay, his nephew, Joseph Lee Kirby Smith took the Union side. Unfortunately, much like his father Ephraim, Brevet-Colonel Smith met his end at the battle of Corinth. He was twenty-six years old.

Promoted to Lieutenant General, Edmund nearly met a similar fate during the vicious first battle of Manassas at Bull Run. He took a bullet to the chest, which only briefly stayed the brave combatant in 1861. Upon his triumphant return to duty, Edmund was dismayed to find he had been assigned to the small western theater of war that offered little chance for glory.

Edmund, however, found a way to notoriety. While supposedly defending Chattanooga with General Braxton Bragg during the summer of 1862, thirty-eight year old Edmund concocted a plan to invade Kentucky. During his rout of Union troops at Richmond, Kentucky, his detachment captured four thousand soldiers, ten thousand weapons and a wagon train of much-needed supplies. Edmund saw action at Perryville and Murfreesboro, moving on to Lexington and Frankfort.

His success garnered Edmund yet another promotion and command of the Trans-Mississippi Department. There he served from February 1863 until the fall of the Confederacy. The Mississippi territory was dubbed by the Confederate soldiers as "Kirby Smithdom." It is said that during his time there, Edmund considered resigning his post and entering the ministry.

Even General Smith's heroics and adept soldiering skills could not save the Confederate Army from defeat. On May 26, 1865, General Edmund Kirby Smith surrendered his troops. His was the last major Confederate regiment to submit.

After the war, Edmund prospered as the president of Atlantic and Pacific Telegraph, president of the Western Military Academy, chancellor of the University of Nashville and later, professor of mathematics at the University of the South at Sewanee, Tennessee. Edmund Kirby Smith died at Sewanee on March 28, 1893. He was the last surviving full General of either the Union or Confederate Armies. True to the end, the last man standing.

General Smith and his sister sold the house at 6 Artillery Lane in 1887 to philanthropist John L. Wilson and his wife, Francis. The Wilson's also purchased what is today known as the St. Francis Inn in 1888, built homes on St. Francis and St. George Streets. The St. George Street residence was gifted to their daughter, Emily. Wilson donated a residence on Aviles Street to be used as the city's first public library with a stipulation, Emily was to be named librarian. That's certainly one way to guarantee the kid has a job. In 1899, the Segui-Kirby House became the home of the St. Augustine Evening Record. Simply known as The Record, this newspaper remained at the Artillery Lane location until 1906. Few actual copies of the newspaper are in existence today.

Today the St. Augustine Historical Society utilizes the locale as it Research Library. Open to the public Tuesday through Friday from 9:00 am until 4:30 p.m., the library offers a wealth of Florida history. The library is graciously adorned with the work of artists obtained at the request of Henry Flagler. Information provided by the St. Augustine Historical Society Research Library has been truly invaluable during the research phase of this book. I can not express enough gratitude for Mr. Tingley and his staff.

**GONZALEZ-ALVAREZ HOUSE
THE OLDEST HOUSE**

For more than three centuries this site has been occupied by St. Augustinians. Beginning about 1650, a succession of thatched wooden structures were their homes. This coquina stone house was built soon after the English burned St. Augustine in 1702, and originally was a one-story rectangle with two rooms. As times changed during the Spanish, British and American occupations, a wooden second story, an off-street porch, and other features were added. Preserved by the St. Augustine Historical Society since 1918, the house became a registered national landmark in 1970.

**14 St. Francis Street, St. Augustine
SJ29 ~ GPS Coordinates: 29.888000, -81.310183**

The Gonzalez-Alvarez House has long been noted as the Oldest House, which is quite a feat due to the constant raids by the English during the early days, later pirates found the community beyond temptation and plundered as well. In defiance of the turmoil all around, the house has stood the test of time and has been continuously occupied by Europeans and Americans since the early 1600s.

The initial construction was a crude hovel of logs with a palm frond thatched roof. It is understandable that this structure met an early demise due to fire in 1702. Eventually the dwelling evolved to become a flat roofed, single story abode, still a very simple home.

The real story begins with the first known occupants, Tomas and Francisca Gonzalez Hernandez. Tomas was an artilleryman at the Castillo de San Marcos and moved his family to St. Augustine sometime before 1727. We know that the family was in residence in 1727 because church records reflect that one of Francisca babies died in the home that year.

The lodging was a two-room coquina[45] structure having a flat roof and a tabby floor. The dwelling was still really rustic and small. Even so Tomas and Francisca raised six children in the home, though ten children were born to them only six lived to adulthood. The home contained sparse furnishings, sleeping mats and only those essential items required for everyday life. It seems the family was quite impoverished, however it is obvious to the keen observer that their needs were very simple and easily satisfied.

The family remained at the St. Francis Street address until the English seized St. Augustine in 1763. All Spanish residents were forced from their homes, including a now elderly Francisca. She wearily packed her belongings gathered throughout her entire married life, assisted her adult children and with sorrow, left her home of more than sixty years. The destitute family emigrated to the nearest Spanish speaking community possible, Havana.

The British brought new ownership to 14 St. Francis Street when Major Joseph Peavett, paymaster for the English military force, bought the former Gonzalez home in 1775. The meager abode was not up to the standards of an important British officer, so it was refurbished to meet the new owner's taste and position. A second story was added to the home at that time, as well as a shingled roof. The Peavett's designed the structure so that they could live and entertain upstairs and the couple opened a tavern downstairs in the Gonzales family's old living area. Maria, or Mary as she was called, was quite an important person in her own right; she served the tiny community in the much sought after position of midwife. Together Joseph and Mary Peavett accumulated a considerable amount of property, slaves and money. Joseph Peavett died in 1786 leaving Mary a quite wealthy widow.

Mary continued to live at the St. Francis Street home following Joseph's death. She decided to remarry several years later, unfortunately her choice cost her all she and Joseph had amassed. Mary married John Hudson, who turned out to be a scoundrel and compulsive gambler. Hudson's debts mounted and by the time Mary died in 1792, she was nearly broke.

Mary's life was memorialized in the late Eugenia Price historical fiction novel, "Maria". A detailed description of the Gonzalez house was given in the work. Many recount that the upstairs of the house leaves visitors with the feeling that Mary Peavett still silently moves through her house. It is easy to imagine her sitting in the parlor reading from one of her many books. The rooms appear as though Mary has simply stepped out to the public market to buy the makings for dinner.

Maria's home and belongings were auctioned off to the highest bidder in order to settle John Hudson's extensive gambling debts. Geronimo Alvarez, a baker for the government hospital, purchased the home. Though by this time Tomas and Francisca were long dead, their son, Hipolito Gonzales witnessed the transfer of ownership of his long ago family home.

Geronimo moved his young wife, Antonia Venz and their children Antonio and Teresa into the house, which would be henceforth known as the Gonzalez-Alvarez House. The dwelling underwent another alteration with the addition of wooden railroad siding applied to the upstairs walls. Unfortunately, Antonia was unable to enjoy her new home for long.

Tragically, Geronimo's young bride died shortly after moving into the St. Francis Street home. Geronimo was forced to hire help in order to care for his children due to his political aspirations in St. Augustine. Antonio, his son was eventually politically active in the city as well. He served several terms as city treasurer and mayor. Geronimo Alvarez died in 1846. His legacy was not only left with the house at 14 St. Francis Street, but also at his church. The bell in the topmost niche at the Cathedral of St. Augustine was his gift to all St. Augustine citizenry.

The Gonzalez-Alvarez house changed hands several times over the next four decades. Modern conveyances were added over the years including the kitchen outbuilding. The separate structure provides a glimpse of a little-remembered fact concerning early houses: Namely that the kitchen was often placed in a separate building, to reduce the risk of fire and, in the South, to maintain a tolerable temperature in the main house during the summer months. This example is quite well appointed for such a kitchen; its oven was rather modern for its day.

The St. Augustine Historical Society obtained the Gonzalez-Alvarez House in 1918. Since that time the Society has presented the dwelling as a family home with an amazing story to tell for its four hundred years of life in St. Augustine. The Historical Society oversaw an extensive restoration, Victorian embellishments were removed from the home's exterior and from all but one room inside. Upstairs, the influence of its various owners can also be seen; the house has been carefully decorated and appears much as it would have during each period in its vast history.

The garden paths invite visitors to cool off in the shade and enjoy a moment of imagination on what it might have been like to live through the history of the house. The rhymic sound of horses' hooves tapping along the streets as sightseeing carriages amble by, brings to mind a time long ago when citizens traveled on horseback or on foot. A tour guide, noted historian of St. Augustine and friend, Kellie Sharpe, described the Gonzalez-Alvarez House, "It is the best place I have found in St Augustine to get as close as possible to the people who helped make the city survive and live to tell its own stories." Kellie's vision of St. Augustine was an incredible gift during the writing of this book, as is her friendship.

A small fee is charged to visit St. Augustine's Oldest House, though St. Johns County residents are exempt. Family packages offer a savings on the admission price.

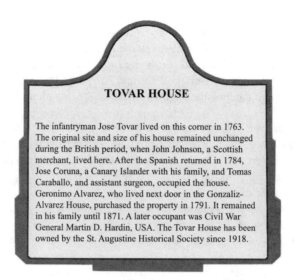

TOVAR HOUSE

The infantryman Jose Tovar lived on this corner in 1763. The original site and size of his house remained unchanged during the British period, when John Johnson, a Scottish merchant, lived here. After the Spanish returned in 1784, Jose Coruna, a Canary Islander with his family, and Tomas Caraballo, and assistant surgeon, occupied the house. Geronimo Alvarez, who lived next door in the Gonzaliz-Alvarez House, purchased the property in 1791. It remained in his family until 1871. A later occupant was Civil War General Martin D. Hardin, USA. The Tovar House has been owned by the St. Augustine Historical Society since 1918.

22 St. Francis Street, St. Augustine
SJ30 ~ GPS Coordinates: 29.887950, -81.309967

The first noted resident of the Tovar House, neighbor of St. Augustine's Oldest House, was Spanish infantryman Don Jose Tovar for whom the house was named. The residence was a typical Spanish dwelling listed as built of tabby and later recorded as constructed of coquina, which is by far the more likely material used. The first floor featured living space of four rooms located at the address known today as 22 St. Francis Street.

The house appeared to be more of a rental property than that of a historical family home due to the constant turn over of occupants. It was stated that Geronimo Alvarez purchased the property, probably to extend his St. Augustine holdings and as an investment. The residence reveals few amazing occurrences within its walls but the amazing inhabitants residing there proved to be very dynamic individuals indeed.

One of the most colorful tenants was a man known as Jesse Fish. Initially from New York by way of England, his father sent Jesse to St. Augustine at the tender age of twelve. He was a child left to his own devises without knowing the language or a single adult to turn to in times of need. Jesse Fish was to become an expert in Spanish customs and language, establishing a place in society so that his father's employer, the Walton Company, could continue to supply goods to the Spanish government. By the age of twenty-three, Jesse Fish was well ensconced in the Spanish government and working closely with officials. In 1764, he was living in the Tovar House and business prospered. During the years of the French and Indian War, the English laid siege to Florida numerous times. Finally the Treaty of 1763 was signed bringing an end to the war thus beginning the British Period in Florida for the next twenty years.

The Spanish were forced to leave St. Augustine in the face of British rule therefore they left their property holdings in the hands of trusted friend, Jesse Fish. He received a "general power of attorney" to sell their property and goods then forward the profits to the owners in Havana. Fish became a real estate tycoon overnight, selling more than twenty-two houses, various businesses and twenty-one vacant lots formerly owned by Spaniards. The remainder of the Spanish property was leased to northern Tories escaping the ravages of the American Revolution to British held Florida and Minorcans escaping the deplorable conditions of Dr. Andrew Turnbull at New Smyrna to the south. He also acquired a ten thousand-acre estate on Fish Island, today known as Anastasia Island. Few of the Spaniards ever saw any profits from their Florida property, however, Jesse Fish' coffers swelled considerably.

Fish married a young seventeen-year-old girl named Sarah in 1768. Sarah proved to be very out-going, to put it politely and middle aged Jesse had a hard time keeping up with his young bride. In order to escape public humiliation and rampant gossip, Jesse built an elaborate two-storied house on his Fish Island estate called El Vergel or "The Garden," and lived there the remainder of his days. Jesse Fish might have been down but he certainly was not defeated, prominence was again right around the corner.

As rumblings of war began to emanate through the colonies and reach British held Florida, Jesse Fish was hard at work establishing one of the first orange groves in the Americas. El Vergel was true to its name and provided fertile soil for growing citrus, date palms, olives, indigo, as well as raising cattle, all cash crops Fish experimented with. Oranges proved to be the most profitable out of all the initial crops. By the time the Revolutionary War was blazing full force throughout the colonies, Jesse Fish was shipping oranges to London in bulk, barreled as juice sweetened with sugar cane and as an orange flavored spirit.

The American Revolution drew to an end in 1783 and again the Spaniards assumed dominion over the Florida territory. This turn of events was not welcome news to Jesse Fish, because finally his swindling of Spanish money would now come to a reckoning. By the time the Spanish were again well ensconced in Florida, Fish filed a petition of bankruptcy with the King of Spain. The reason for his financial losses was listed ironically as corrupt business management of his affairs by a relative of his wife's. Jesse Fish died at El Vergel in February of 1790 and was buried on the island named in his honor. Soon grave robbers desecrated the once wealthy landowner's burial site based on a rumor that gold had been buried with the body. In fact, Jesse Fish was destitute when he passed away.

El Vergel was sold at public auction in 1792 in order to repay Spanish debts, the estate was purchased by his son. Unfortunately the young man died unexpectedly, Jesse Fish's widow filed a petition to reclaim the entire ten thousand acres of Fish Island. Her request was approved in 1823, however she abandoned the property and the land reverted to the Spanish crown.

The only remembrance of Jesse Fish in existence is Fish Island Road, which is not located on what was known as Fish Island. Other than this obscure reference, very few are aware of his amazing story or Jesse Fish' historical influence in the area. Eventually the remains of Jesse Fish were carefully boxed and delivered to his family's burial plot in England away from his beloved El Vergel. During the last several years a drive has been initiated to recover the remains of El Vergel plantation and bestow on it the historic recognition it certainly deserves.

One of the last private residents to live at Tovar House was Union General Martin D. Hardin. During the Civil War General Hardin commanded the IC[46], selected because he had only one arm, assigned to the Union First Division. The Invalid Corps called IC was often confused with the food designation "Inspected-Condemned," therefore the name was changed to the VRC[47]. Having six regiments, the VRC consisted of twenty-seven thousand, nine hundred seventy-four men. Their orders ordinarily involved guarding Union prisoner of war camps and garrison guards throughout the northern states.

When tragedy struck on April 14, 1865 with the assassination of President Lincoln, the VRC was to receive its most distinguished orders for the duration of the unit's existence. As the President's body made its mournful journey by funeral train to Springfield, Illinois, his final resting-place, the Veteran's Reserve Corps escorted his remains with General Martin D. Hardin leading the way. General Order one hundred forty disbanded the Veterans Reserve Corps in 1866. Brigadier General Martin D. Hardin passed away in 1923. His body was interred with full military honors at the St. Augustine National Cemetery.

The St. Augustine Historical Society retained stewardship of the Tovar House in 1918. Today the site is used as the Museum of Florida's Military. The museum features artifacts illustrating the longest standing militia in the United States, since its inception in 1565. The Tovar House displays include antiques from the Spanish, English and American eras ranging from 1565 until present day. The museum is open daily, except for major holidays with a small admission charged to support the constant maintenance required of historical buildings. The St. Augustine Historical Society does an exceptional job in maintaining, preserving and restoring the many sites under their care.

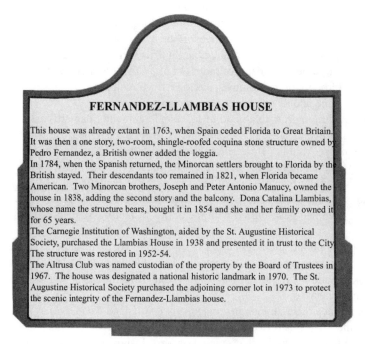

FERNANDEZ-LLAMBIAS HOUSE

This house was already extant in 1763, when Spain ceded Florida to Great Britain. It was then a one story, two-room, shingle-roofed coquina stone structure owned by Pedro Fernandez, a British owner added the loggia.

In 1784, when the Spanish returned, the Minorcan settlers brought to Florida by the British stayed. Their descendants too remained in 1821, when Florida became American. Two Minorcan brothers, Joseph and Peter Antonio Manucy, owned the house in 1838, adding the second story and the balcony. Dona Catalina Llambias, whose name the structure bears, bought it in 1854 and she and her family owned it for 65 years.

The Carnegie Institution of Washington, aided by the St. Augustine Historical Society, purchased the Llambias House in 1938 and presented it in trust to the City. The structure was restored in 1952-54.

The Altrusa Club was named custodian of the property by the Board of Trustees in 1967. The house was designated a national historic landmark in 1970. The St. Augustine Historical Society purchased the adjoining corner lot in 1973 to protect the scenic integrity of the Fernandez-Llambias house.

31 St. Frances Street, St. Augustine
SJ31 ~ GPS Coordinates: 29.887933, -81.309967

Suffice it to say that the Fernandez-Llambias House is a St. Augustine treasure. The former residence is noted as one of the oldest restored original buildings in the city. Records date the structure to the final year of the first Spanish possession, 1763. The coquina abode was then a one-story Spanish dwelling owned by Pedro Fernandez.

By 1771, the home was occupied by Juan Andreu, Sr. Andreu was a native of Mercadal, Spain located on one of the Minorcan islands. He, along with his family, had immigrated to New Smyrna led by the promise of a better life. Unfortunately what the Minorcans found in the remote colony was cruelty, hunger and death.

Three Minorcans (one a later owner for which the house is named, Llambias) managed to escape the bonds of virtual slavery at New Smyrna. The men braved the Atlantic and swam most of the way to the Matanzas Inlet. This was an enormous feat. The journey took nearly three days. Upon arrival in St. Augustine, the three men sought out Governor Tonyn, who charitably fed them and offered them dry clothing. They told their depressing tale of woe. The governor was so moved by their sad story, he offered sanctuary to their people.

The men returned to New Smyrna and secretly made plans to relocate to St. Augustine. Ninety people gathered in April 1777 and marched north on King's Road to St. Augustine. On May 5, 1777, Governor Tonyn took depositions. Within the month six hundred Minorcans moved from New Smyrna to St. Augustine.

The house remained in the Andreu family until after the cession of Florida to the United States. Joseph Juan Andreu was born in St. Augustine on July 5, 1801. He married Maria Dolores Mestre and was known to be the Jailer in St. Augustine in 1844. Andreu was appointed keeper of the St. Augustine Lighthouse on Anastasia Island on April 11, 1854. Five years after assuming the keepers job, Andreu fell sixty feet to his death while painting the lighthouse tower when the scaffolding gave way. The newspaper announcement of his death states,

"Mr. Andreu was highly esteemed for his many hospitable and social virtues. He was followed to the grave by a numerous concourse, and buried in the Holy and Solemn form of the Catholic Church."

Andreu's wife, Maria, was made keeper of the Lighthouse within days of his death. We have no record of how long Maria served as keeper, but do know that during the Civil War the light was extinguished to avoid giving any aid to Union gunboats. Joseph and Maria had nine children. One of the children, Margaret, was born in St. Augustine on August 5, 1822. Margaret Andreu is said to be the first white child born in St. Augustine after Florida was ceded to the United States from Spain, thus making her the first United States citizen of St. Augustine.

In addition to the nine children of Maria, Joseph also had an illegitimate son with Antonia Lorenzo. Matias Ramon was born on February 20, 1831, later with permission of the courts, he was legally permitted to use the name of Andreu. Matias grew up to become a rather distinguished citizen of St. Augustine. In 1853, he was appointed Clerk of the City Council and owned a dry goods store at the corner of St. George and Picolata Streets. Matias was listed as the publisher of the St. Augustine Examiner weekly newspaper in 1859 and in 1867, he became a real estate auctioneer and broker.

Peter and Joseph Manucy, whose father came to New Smyrna from Mahon Harbor, Menorca on the Balearic Islands of Spain purchased the home. The Manucy brothers are listed as a being employed by the Patrols of the City of St. Augustine in 1839. The patrols were under the instruction of the mayor and served as follows:

> The Captain will organize his Patrol into two parties, one of which will patrol, from the Market, North, and the other from the Market, South. The Patrol will apprehend all slaves, or free persons of color, who may be found in the streets after the ringing of the Bell, without having a proper pass from their masters or guardians.
> The Patrol will quell all riots or improper conduct in the streets; and are authorized to enter any lot where there is any improper noise and to report the offenders the next morning to the Mayor.
> The Captain of the Patrol will report all absentees to the Mayor, together with all infractions of the Patrol Ordinances of this City.

> F. L. Dancy, Mayor

In 1854, the Manucy's sold the property to Catalina Usina Llambias. The Llambias family heirs retained the house for sixty-five years. The Usina family, Catalina's maiden name, were also Minorcan who arrived in St. Augustine from New Smyrna in 1777. Many of their descendants remain in St. Augustine today. Since the 1900's, the Usina family has been operating St. Augustine Scenic Cruises. Offering St. Augustine tourists a unique view of the city only available from the water. The narrated cruises are given by third and fourth generation captains, providing an interesting and enjoyable cruise on the St. Johns while viewing the historical landscape and unique points of interest.

In 1954, the St. Augustine Restoration and Preservation Association completed restoration of the house. Later, in an agreement between the Carnegie Institution, the City of St. Augustine and the St. Augustine Historical Society, the Society assumed all responsibility for the maintenance and interpretation of the house and grounds. The restoration brought the original appearance back to the Fernandez-Llambias House. The coquina exterior walls are covered with stucco with the street level floor having a tabby facade. Obvious in several locations of the house is the superimposed coats of paint, which have been unveiled. The residence serves as a supreme example of restoration techniques as they should be used to restore other Spanish Colonial structures. The original building techniques were expertly employed in its restoration.

The Altrusa Club of St. Augustine assumed stewardship of the Fernandez-Llambias House Museum in 1967. The site is available as a rental for weddings, receptions, parties, meetings or any event planned by your organization. The public is invited to share The Llambias House and Grounds on the third Sunday of each month when the Altrusa Club hosts an Open House with refreshments and free tours from 2:00 to 4:00.

The club also sponsors a number of other worthy projects including the sale of United States Flags flown on the Bridge of Lions. Because of northeaster winds, the life of the flags is limited. Rather than destroy them, the Altrusa Club offers the flags for sale including a written statement of the flag's history. The tradition began when flags were flown on the Bridge of Lions in honor of the sixty-two hostages held in Iran.

ST. FRANCIS BARRACKS

These coquina walls were once part of the Franciscan chapel and triary of Our Lady of the Immaculate Conception, established by missionaries from Spain. Before these walls rose, thatch roofed wooden buildings on this site were burned in 1599, rebuilt and again destroyed by fire in 1702, when English forces from South Carolina burned the town.

The coquina buildings known for years as the St. Francis Barracks were used as military housing by the British from 1763 to 1783, by the Spanish, 1783-1821 and then by the United States. In 1907, the property was leased to the State of Florida for its military headquarters. The main building was gutted by fire in 1915, but the coquina walls were unharmed. In 1921, by act of Congress, the St. Francis Barracks were turned over to the State of Florida. Today the Barracks and the military reservation house the Headquarters, Military Department State of Florida and Headquarters Florida National Guard.

86 Marine Street, St. Augustine
SJ32 ~ GPS Coordinates: 29.886367, -81.309400

The dawning of late summer in Florida on September 16, 1565 saw a newly established Spanish military settlement named St. Augustine. The first militias served the Spain crown for a total of two hundred thirty-six years, the flag of Great Britain flew over the harbor city for twenty years and the Confederate States of America banner waved for a war engulfed five years. The St. Augustine militia has defended against the French, Native Americans, English and a bevy of pirates, scalawags and ne'er do wells who threatened her shores.

The Spanish first developed the sight at today's 86 Marine Street as a Franciscan Monastery and Convent serving the mission called Our Lady of the Immaculate Conception. Constructed in 1588, the crude buildings were pieced together with only those materials at hand, oak log walls with palm frond thatched roofs and dirt floors. The friary was left untouched by the devastating raid of Sir Francis Drake's English invasion in 1586. The friary was not so fortunate when fire swept the city in 1593; the buildings were reduced to a smoldering heap of ashes. The buildings were rebuilt only to be consumed again by an uncontrollable blaze in 1599 and all evidence of the Monastery and Convent were washed out to sea by a tropical hurricane that same year.

Walls of coquina rock replaced the flammable wooden structure of the Monastery when construction began in 1724 and was finally completed in 1739. The solid rock building was one hundred sixty-eight feet in circumference having eighteen-foot tall walls. The magnificent view spanned the Matanzas River. The interior boasted twenty-five cells[48], which proved to be more than enough, at the time only ten Franciscan monks remained in St. Augustine. The friary's time was running short, Florida was ceded by treaty to England in 1763 and the Monastery no longer held any religious connotations. For the next twenty years British troops lived, served and trained at the facility known as St. Francis Barracks.

Florida again became a Spanish possession in 1783 but the monastery was never restored. Though one effort was made to use the facility as a monastery. When Spanish Governor Vicente Manuel de Zespedes protested saying, "the troops (are) without shelter, God (is) without a temple, and I (am) without a home," the suggestion was dropped. The English had added a wooden barracks alongside the coquina structure, however, as was common fire had taken the rooms and only the chimneys were left standing.

The building served as the military headquarters for the second Spanish period. When the United States assumed control of Florida in 1821, St. Francis Barracks became the United States Army military post. During the dawning days of the Civil War Captain John W. Starke's home at 22 Water Street was used as a military hospital until an adjoining structure, built between 1864 and 1867, was constructed at St. Francis Barracks. The structure was intended for use as a Union Military Hospital. However, the facility was largely utilized to house wounded Confederate troops as they painstakingly returned to their homes during the aftermath of the Civil War. It is said that bloodstains remained on the parlor floor of the Starke home well into the 1930s.

Confederate General E. Kirby Smith, who was born and raised in St. Augustine, had a black manservant by the name of Alex Darns. After the war, in appreciation for his life long service, the general paid for his former servant to attend medical school. Alex Darns later became a successful doctor in Jacksonville. St. Augustine was occupied by Union troops in 1862 and it is said that General Smith's mother was a known Confederate spy. She, with assistance, cut down the flagpole so the Union flag would never wave in the breeze of the Matanzas Inlet from the flagpole of the city arsenal (now the National Guard headquarters).

In the early 1900s, the United States Army sold the adjoining building to a local boat builder and his family. He moved the building across the street to its present location on the bay front. During that time, a railway extension ran from that sight out to deep water for loading and unloading boats in the Matanzas Bay.

In 1907, St. Francis Barracks was leased to the Florida National Guard for the sum of one dollar per annum. The facility would serve as the state military headquarters. Fire again claimed the wooden structures associated with St. Francis Barracks in 1915. Governor Sidney Catts, elected in 1916, deemed it necessary to move the state military headquarters to Tallahassee in 1917. The act was interpreted as a slap in face to St. Augustine citizens.

Citizen outcry was so vocal that eventually the legislature appropriated forty thousand dollars to reconstruct the barracks in 1921. The coquina walls were left standing so the outward appearance of the structure remained much the same. When the restoration was completed, the state military headquarters was returned to St. Francis Barracks. The patch representing the Florida National Guard is depicted as yellow and red rays referring to the Spanish settlement of St. Augustine and subsequent rule of Florida; the white and red rays symbolizing twenty years of English occupation and the blue ray which alludes to the final control of the United States. The Barracks are situated on Marine Street and face the magnificent Matanzas Bay.

The property adjoining St. Francis Barracks was bought out of foreclosure in 1921 and converted to an apartment house. The spacious waterfront apartments have housed many generals, officers and families, and remained in use as an upscale apartment house. Villas on the Bay was lovingly renovated in 1996, creating a unique option for luxury short-term apartment rentals in St. Augustine's historic downtown area and on the bay front.

The Army is the oldest and largest branch of the Florida National Guard, with nine thousand nine hundred fifty-one assigned as of 2001. The Florida Army National Guard maintains seventy-two armories and is represented in sixty-three communities. The Florida National Guard is provided for by the Florida State Constitution. As Commander-in-Chief of the Florida National Guard, the Governor looks to the Adjutant General to provide military organizations trained and equipped to function when necessary in the protection of life and property, and in the preservation of peace, order and the public safety. Today the Florida National Guard stands ready in any crisis from natural disaster to national defense.

MAJOR DADE
AND HIS COMMAND MONUMENTS

On December 28, 1835, during the Second Seminole War, a column of 108 U. S. Army soldiers dispatched from Fort Brooke (Tampa) to relieve the detachment of Fort King (Ocala) was surprised by a strong force of Seminole Indians near Bushnell in Sumter County. Except for three soldiers and an interpreter, the entire column of 108 men, led by Major Francis Langhorne Dade, perished in battle that day. On August 15, 1842, Dade and his command, as well as other casualties of the war, were re-interred here under three coquina stone pyramids in a ceremony marking the end of the conflict. Among those buried with Dade are Captain George W. Gardiner, U.S. Military Academy (U.S.M.A.) 1814, first Commandant of Cadets at West Point, and Major David Moniac, U.S.M.A., 1822, a Creek Indian and first Native-American graduate of the Military Academy.

104 Marine Street, St. Augustine National Cemetery
SJ33 ~ GPS Coordinates: 29.885228, -81.309133

The year was 1835, as Christmas drew near Brevet Major[49] Francis Langhorne Dade led a force of one hundred men and eight officers bound for Fort King. The column was made up of the 4th Infantry, Companies of the Second and Third Regiments of Artillery and accompanied by a guide, surgeon and teamsters[50]. The troops were enroute from Fort Brooke, today known as Tampa, on December 21; little did the contingent realize that they would never live to see the New Year.

Major Dade was told be ready for hostilities for as the men traveled toward Fort King their route would bring them through the heart of Seminole country. The transfer was necessitated by a vague request for re-enforcement from Fort Brooke dispatched from General Clinch; the request was erroneously taken to mean that Fort King was under siege and needed immediate aid. In fact the real reason for the request was a lack of provisions.

Once the column reached the pine barrens, Major Dade believed that there would be little trouble the remainder of the way. In the past the Seminoles had always attacked from the hammocks[51] of Florida, mainly due to the camouflage offered by the dense vegetation. Christmas day came and passed without incident. The soldiers were obviously exhausted, wet and cold. In an effort to bolster morale, Major Dade spoke these encouraging words on the morning of December 28, 1835:

> "Have a good heart; our difficulties and dangers are over now and as soon as we arrive at Fort King you'll have three days to rest and keep Christmas gaily."

During the next eight hours, only three soldiers would survive the battle that would mark the beginning of the Second Seminole War.

Nearby at Wahoo Swamp Chiefs Micanopy, Alligator and Jumper laid in wait for the column bound for Fort King. The location was one of several sites in the pine barrens around the swamp chosen because the Seminoles knew that the United States forces did not expect to be ambushed there. Osceola, who was expected to join the attack, was late; Micanopy made the decision to begin the offensive at Wahoo Swamp. The swamp's muck and mire bordered Major Dade's flanks. The column had only one choice, to fight.

The Seminole band had covertly watched the military detachment for many days and knew that their guard was down. Normal procedures required the enlisted men carry their muskets inside their greatcoats or store them on the wagons to keep moisture from the weapons. Unfortunately this order led to the destruction of Dade's men. Hidden amidst the pines and palmettos, one hundred eighty Seminoles quietly waited.

The initial musket volley at point blank range killed or wounded half the command; Major Dade and Captain Upton S. Fraser were the first officers to go down. Three of the six surviving officers were wounded. Assuming command, Captain George W. Gardiner rallied the men and returned fire with their six-pound cannon.

The Seminoles withdrew a short distance to regroup. The soldiers hastily took advantage of the lull in battle to build a small breastwork made out of logs in a triangle. They tended the wounded as best they could and collected ammunition from the fallen. The Seminoles second attack lasted until early afternoon when all the firing from the breastwork was finally silenced. Most of Dade's command was dead. The Seminoles, followed by their black allies, cautiously closed in. Three wounded soldiers Edwin DeCourcey, Joseph Sprague and Ransom Clark managed to escape and make it to Fort King alive. Dade's black interpreter, Louis Pacheco, was taken captive. The Seminoles lost only three warriors and five were wounded. As the sandy ground soaked up the blood of the massacred soldiers, the Seminoles retired to Wahoo Swamp to dance in celebration of their victory.

The grisly scene of the ambush went undisturbed for seven weeks. On February 20, 1836, an expedition under General Edmund P. Gaines discovered the site. The decomposing bodies were identified and given proper military burials. The officers' were interred on the east side of the trail and the ninety-eight enlisted men were buried in two mass graves within the log breastwork they had built. The six-pound cannon was retrieved from a nearby pond where the Seminoles had tossed it away. The cannon was mounted and placed muzzle down at the head of the officers' grave as a monument to the dead.

Six years later on August 14, 1842, Major Dade and his command were laid to rest at the National Cemetery in St. Augustine. The elaborate ceremony and military burials were made possible by contributions from the officers and men of the army. The massacre of Major Dade and his command was one of the most terrible defeats ever suffered by the United States Army at the hands of Native Americans. The engagement is second only to Custer's Last Stand.

Among those buried with Major Dade are Captain George W. Gardiner, who was the first Commandant of Cadets at West Point and Major David Moniac, the first Native American graduate of the Military Academy. Captain Gardiner lost his life at Wahoo Swamp along side Major Dade. Major Moniac met his end under the command of Governor Richard Call, also during the engagement at Wahoo Swamp. The men are buried beneath three coquina pyramids erected as a monument to their brave sacrifice.

**ST. AUGUSTINE
NATIONAL CEMETERY**

WARDEN WINTER HOME

The Warden Winter Home was built in 1887 for William G. Warden of Philadelphia. A partner with Henry Flagler and John D. Rockefeller in the Standard Oil Company, Warden was also the President of the St. Augustine Gas and Electric Light Company and Financial Director of the St Augustine Improvement Company. One of the most imposing private residences in the city, it was a center of winter social activity. Its Moorish Revival architecture and elaborate interior reflect the exuberance of the Gilded Age and St. Augustine's role as a winter resort. It remained in the Warden family through the 1930s. In 1941 it was purchased by Norton Baskin and remodeled as the Castle Warden Hotel. Baskin and his wife, Marjorie Kinnan Rawlings (author of The Yearling), had an apartment on the top floor. Many writers and other distinguished visitors came here during its decade as a hotel. Locally known as Warden Castle, it has served as Ripley's Believe It or Not Museum since 1950.

19 San Marco Avenue, St. Augustine
SJ34 ~ GPS Coordinates: 29.899698, -81.314518

The unique structure located at 19 San Marco Avenue in St. Augustine was built by entrepreneur William Grey Warden in 1887. The Moorish Revival mansion was to be the Warden summer cottage, not a full time residence. The house consists of eighteen thousand square feet of living space, covers an amazing three stories and was referred to as "Castle Warden." Richly veined marble flooring and impressively hand carved woodwork adorn each of the three floors. The most modern conveniences for the time were installed and the view from the penthouse afforded a splendid panorama of St. Augustine. I would say that the house was a little more than a simple "summer cottage."

William G. Warden originally hailed from Philadelphia. His move to St. Augustine resulted from Warden's business association in the Standard Oil Company with John D. Rockefeller and of course, Henry Flagler. Henry Flagler had encouraged his partner to join him in a substantial venture most called "Flagler's Folly." The venture involved opening up Florida to development with the addition of a railway system. After Warden visited the area he believed Flagler to be in over his head. Warden felt that Flagler would never be able to complete an undertaking of this magnitude. William Warden was perhaps a little more cautious than Flagler after all Warden had a family of fourteen to support. William Warden declared he would not invest a penny in the railroad. Instead he vowed to build a home in St. Augustine and watch Flagler go broke. Obviously William Warden instincts were wrong on this account.

After Warden's death, Elizabeth Warden Ketterlinus sold the home in 1941 to Norton Baskin and his wife, Marjorie Kinnan Rawlings. Rawlings was a Pulitzer Prize winning author best known for her book, "The Yearling." The couple converted the vast mansion into a hotel and lived in a penthouse apartment on the third floor for a time.

All was well until one fateful morning in April of 1944, when acrid smoke and scorching orange blazes poured from the third story windows. Attempts to fight the fire proved futile, little could be done as the blaze seared its way down the third floor corridor. When the pyre was at last squelched, it had claimed two souls. The damage was extensive and required complete renovations to the penthouse. From that day forward it was said that those two brave members of the staff have kept a watchful eye on Castle Warden.

Baskin and Rawlings owned the home for five years. It was sold in 1946 to a guest who often stayed at the hotel when he visited St. Augustine. This was the end of "Castle Warden's" days as a residence. The new owner had long tried to purchase the home and was none other than well-known adventurer and cartoonist, Robert Ripley. Ripley had much broader plans for the stately mansion.

Robert Leroy Ripley was born on Christmas day in 1890. His family lived in Santa Rosa, California at the time. At the tender age of 16, young Robert had become a very talented self-taught artist. Life magazine recognized his skills and purchased one of his first drawings.

Though obviously a gifted artist, Robert's passion was baseball. Often referred to as a natural athlete, he played semi-professional baseball at the age of 18 but began supporting himself and his family with his art. Robert's father had passed away in 1905 and his mother became increasingly dependent on her eldest son.

After a move to New York in 1912, Robert was determined to play baseball professionally and tried out for the New York Giants. Unfortunately his dreams were dashed when during practice he broke his arm and the New York Giants never offered him a contract. Robert Ripley was crushed with despair. The next year he sought an escape to soothe his tragic loss, it was then that he made the first of many trips abroad. His first travels took him to Europe.

By 1918, Robert Ripley was working as a sports cartoonist for the New York Globe. It was during this time in his life that his most noted adventures began. Over the next forty years, Ripley explored one hundred ninety-eight countries collecting fascinating and strange oddities throughout his travels. His travels were initially financed by the publication of his "Champs and Chumps" cartoon, which were soon renamed at the insistence of his editor. Thus "Ripley's Believe It or Not!" was born. The cartoons were instantly popular.

Robert Ripley amassed his amazing discoveries to become a traveling sideshow. His collection always attracted vast numbers people curious to see everything from shrunken human heads to medieval torture devices. Over the next thirty years the collection grew to become the largest accumulation of oddities in the world.

Robert Ripley died in 1949, leaving the sideshow in the care of a board of directors due to the fact that Ripley had no heirs. He had been married only once, but unfortunately the union lasted a total of only three months. In 1950, Ripley's Believe It or Not! Odditorium finally found a permanent home. Robert Ripley had often described the Warden mansion, where he had spent a great deal of time, as the "ideal showplace" now it would shelter his famous collection.

The St. Augustine museum opened in 1950. Not only are animal oddities, incredible miniatures, full size wax figures of the tallest, biggest, smallest and most unusual human beings, works of art in unusual media and unique artifacts represented, but most of Ripley's personal estate is sheltered in St. Augustine. The museum contains over eight hundred exhibits, Believe it or not!

The Warden mansion is today Ripley's Believe It or Not museum, located at 19 San Marco Avenue, is open three hundred sixty-five days a year. A modest admission fee is charged to view the amazing collection. New to the museum are two new interactive galleries with challenging puzzles and exhibits that are fun, entertaining and educational for all ages. Tourists can ride in a vacuum air chair, experience-moving sound, catch their shadow on a wall and create music on a foot piano. The Cargo Hold Gift Shop allows visitors to purchase a small replica of Ripley's dream for their very own.

WARDEN WINTER HOME
TODAY
ATTRACTION "RIPLEY'S BELIEVE IT OR NOT!"

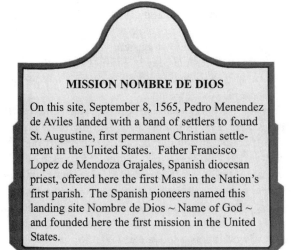

MISSION NOMBRE DE DIOS

On this site, September 8, 1565, Pedro Menendez de Aviles landed with a band of settlers to found St. Augustine, first permanent Christian settlement in the United States. Father Francisco Lopez de Mendoza Grajales, Spanish diocesan priest, offered here the first Mass in the Nation's first parish. The Spanish pioneers named this landing site Nombre de Dios ~ Name of God ~ and founded here the first mission in the United States.

San Marcos Avenue on grounds of Prince of Peace Church, St. Augustine
SJ35 ~ GPS Coordinates: 29.904102, -81.316896

The Spanish discovery of 1492 brought with it a need to convert the Native American inhabitants to Christianity. The Spanish crown claimed America as its own. They concentrated their efforts to colonize the new territory on the peninsula they dubbed La Florida. However, the Spaniards consider the territory extending from Key West in the south to Newfoundland, Canada northward and westward to the plains to Texas. This was no small tract of real estate. By 1526, it became apparent that the construction of Catholic missions was necessary to tame the aboriginal inhabitants of Spanish Florida.

The Spanish King, Philip II dispatched his most reliable General, Don Pedro Menendez de Aviles and on August 28, 1565 his crew sighted land. The date was known on the Spanish Catholic calendar as the feast day of Saint Augustine, Bishop of Hippo, and therefore the community to be established at the landing site was naturally called, St. Augustine. Captains Andres Soyez Patino and Juan de San Vincente, led two companies of infantry to shore. Timucua Indians welcomed the Spaniards without fear. The Native Americans went so far as to provide a large dwelling, belonging to their chief, for temporary shelter. The lodge was situated in a prime location near what was called the Seloy River[52]. Members of the company were immediately ordered to build an entrenchment around the lodge. The men had no digging tools, however the task was expediently completed. Twenty-four canon of varying caliber were delivered from the Spanish Fleet at anchor then strategically placed around the fortress for defense.

Father Francisco Lopez de Mendoza Grajales, a Catholic priest, disembarked on the evening of September 7, 1565 in preparation of Mass when General Menendez and the crew officially claimed the territory the next morning. The priest had a rustic altar constructed and a crude cross fashioned from fallen timbers.

The General ceremoniously disembarked on Saturday, September 8th. He had donned full military regalia in keeping with his status as supreme military attaché and Governor of the newly created St. Augustine. Glorious banners snapped in the wind, trumpets sounded the Governor's arrival and artillery exploded in salute. The priest shouldered the cross and sang the hymn *"Te Deum Laudamus"* as he led the procession to meet Governor Menendez. He strode to the cross and beside the holy symbol took to his knees and embraced the roughly honed timber. The Timucua who had gathered in great number watched intently, aping the movements of Spaniards as they knelt in prayer. On Sunday the Governor assumed formal possession of the country in the name of King Philip II.

It is said that the first shrine to the Catholic Holy Virgin was constructed around 1615. Much to chagrin of few historians, at least four missions preceded *Nombre de Dios* in La Florida. The Spanish name translates to English as "Name of God." However, none of the preceding missions flourished into settlements, all were quickly deserted. *Nombre de Dios* alone carries the distinction of the longest surviving mission in the New World. The mission was prominent the forty-two years before the first English settlement at Jamestown, Virginia; fifty-five years before English Puritan pilgrims landed at Plymouth Rock, Massachusetts; and close to two hundred years prior to the establishment of any California mission.

The shrine was dedicated to *"Nuestra Senora de La Leche y Buen Parto"* translated to mean Our Senora of Milk and Good Pregnancy. A small structure erected at the mission sheltered the statue of the Holy Virgin Mother cradling in her arms the nursing infant Jesus. The depiction is one in the most ancient of all Catholic rites; in fact the very same theme is represented in several painted examples on the walls of Rome's catacombs. The popularity of the Catholic faith and devotion of Our Lady spread throughout the sixteenth century, the first settlers at St. Augustine embraced the ideal and ensured the survival of the mission *Nombre de Dios* with their support.

The mission church would minister to more than two hundred Timucuan Indians at the onset and served as a home base for priests venturing forth to establish other missions throughout the New World. For more than two hundred years, priests traveled the famous Santa Fe trail across northern Florida through Georgia, the Carolinas, Alabama, Mississippi to the great Mississippi River building mission sites along the way.

The shrine of Our Lady that is seen today is in reality the fourth site to be constructed. The ravages of war destroyed the first shrine; the second site was obliterated when pirates plundered St. Augustine and the third locale succumbed when Mother Nature released her fury with a massive hurricane bluster. The fourth shrine was built in 1915 and consequently called "America's Most Sacred Acre." The statue of Our Lady of La Leche is today a replica of the ancient one shattered during hostilities at the mission. Recent archeological excavations have unearthed what is believed to be the foundation of the first stone chapel built on the grounds of the mission during the seventeenth century. Careful examinations continue to date the site and preserve artifacts found there.

The shrine of Our Lady of La Leche continues to provide a serene place of contemplation for tourists, local residents and a pilgrimage haven mothers-to-be praying for a healthy delivery. At the center of the sanctuary is a small stone chapel and beyond the chapel is an altar of palmetto logs representing the location of the Mass offered by Father Francisco Lopez de Mendoza Grajales on that fateful September morning. A two hundred eight foot cross is brilliantly reflected in the clear water pool beyond and a winding pathway leads visitors past the statue of Father Lopez's out stretched arms reaching to heaven, the mission plaque, the shrine of Our Lady Guadalupe, Saint Francis of Assisi, the Byzantine shrine and Saint Joseph's prayerful depiction.

"America's Most Sacred Acre" is open to the public without charge, though a donation box is in place. Donations are used to assist in the maintenance of the peaceful site. A visit to the Mission of *Nombre de Dios* offers a comforting place of prayer for those seeking religious strength and continues to provide a place of quiet reflection unwavering during her more than four hundred year history.

MISSION NOMBRE DE DIOS

EL PUEBLO DE GRACIA REAL
DE SANTA TERESA DE MOSE

On the shore of Robinson Creek, ¼ mile east of this marker, was the site of a
Spanish mission for Indians left homeless during Queen Anne's War. Since 1688,
Negro slaves from the English colonies had found refuge in Spanish St. Augustine.
On March 15, 1738, Governor Manuel de Montiano freed them in the name of the
King and later formed a village for them named Gracia Real at Mose. Here the
freedmen would cultivate the ground and learn the Catholic religion. For their
protection, a moated earthwork was created, called Fort Mose.
In 1740 during the British attack against St. Augustine, the freedmen evacuated
Mose and Scotch Highlanders occupied it. At daybreak June 26, in a decisive
blow the Spaniards ejected the enemy from the fort and later demolished it. The
freedmen resettled the village and rebuilt the earthwork in 1752 and later formed a
militia company. The British dismantled Fort Mose during their rule in Florida.
After their return the Spaniards rebuilt defenses at Mose in 1792. The East Florida
Patriots occupied the deserted site in 1812 during their ill-fated attempt to over-
throw the Negro militia and Indians forced them to withdraw.

Saratoga Boulevard, St. Augustine
SJ36 ~ GPS Coodinates: 29.928033, -81.325217

Ponce de Leon, in the early days of the sixteenth century, had among his crew Africans Juan Garrido and Hernando Cortez. Obvious by the names they bore, Spain had a certain influence in their upbringing. Later African Esteban joined explorer Panfilo de Narvaez on his travels along the Gulf Coast and throughout the Southwest.

Spanish Conquistadors and Adelantados solicited Africans for their skill as artisans, seamen, navigators, black smiths, carpenters, cattle ranchers and military technicians. One of every five Spanish crewmembers was a free person of color. Rather than slaves, some arrived as poor men who obligated themselves as indentured servants. The Africans melded comfortably with the Spanish colonists.

The Spaniards needed cheap labor to build new world settlements; therefore, they began to enslave the local Native Americans. In 1672, Queen Regent Mariana of Spain and Florida's Governor Cendoya commissioned the construction of a coquina fortress. The Castillo de San Marcos was necessary to protect the settlement of St. Augustine from the advancing English colonists and merciless pirates. The vast project would require much more labor than the Spaniards had available, to resolved this dilemma the Spanish began to include Spanish prisoners, as well as escaped Africans from the English colonies of Carolina and Georgia.

Bartholomew de Las Casas, a Spanish priest, was so opposed to the idea of slavery that he immediately penned a letter pleading with the King and Queen of Spain to cease the enslavement of local citizenry. The King and Queen were so moved by the impassioned letter of the Priest, that they ordered the conquistadors to cease the enslavement of natives. Not to be without their free labor, the Spanish began to bring in slaves from the Caribbean and Africa. Father Bartholomew was horrified; this result was not what he had in mind at all. The good Padre continued to fight the injustice of slavery the remainder of his days. Father Bartholomew de Las Casas is known in many circles as the creator of the human rights movement in America.

St. Augustine inhabitants were affected very little by this change. Those taken into slavery by the

Spaniards were more or less adopted into the community. Spanish slaves were allowed to own property, they were more indentured than enslaved because it was very possible to buy their freedom, they were able to take legal action against their owners or others should the need arise and it was unlawful for families to be separated.

Escaped English slaves were offered freedom in exchange they were to be baptized in the Catholic religion and swear an oath to fight alongside the Spanish against their enemies, the English. Because the Africans were accepted into the community and the Catholic faith, excellent records of marriages, births and death were kept. Even though as a community the Africans were treated well, they longed for a community set apart from the Spaniards. Gracia Real de Santa Teresa de Mose or Fort Mose was built in 1681.

Located two miles north of St. Augustine, Fort Mose was surrounded by farmland and homes of the freedmen. A shallow moat embraced the garrison with pointed stakes and thorny cactus impeding a breach. The hand hewn log walls were reinforced with an earthen berm. Thatched palmetto huts housed approximately one hundred men, women and children. The majority of the people who would live there had been born in the western half of Africa. Fort Mose, a maroon community[53], was legally sanctioned by the Spanish Government. Thus Fort Mose became the first free African settlement to legally exist in the United States.

King of Spain, Carlos II, issued a Royal Cedula[54] on November 7, 1695 encouraging bound people to rise up against English enslavement. He said in part:

> "Giving Liberty to all ...the men as well as the women...so that by their example and my liberali
> ty others will do the same..."

The English were incensed at the audacity of King Carlos to put such ideas into the heads of slaves. England berated the Spanish King; the loss of slavery and inexpensive labor would destroy the English economy. English slaves began to revolt in droves; stealing horses, boats and running for miles to escape their bondage.

Newly appointed Spanish Governor, Antonio de Benavides silently disagreed with the King's edict and refused to follow its direction. When refugees arrived in St. Augustine after having escaped their enslavement seeking sanctuary, Benavides would betray their trust and return them to the auction block. Benavides initially said his actions were guided by a wish to keep the peace with England. When the English saw no money returned for their lost chattel everyone involved realized that he was lining his own pockets with the profit.

Once Spain's King was informed of Benavides deception, two Spanish edicts were issued. The first Cedula ensured that Britain would no longer be reimbursed from Spanish coffers for runaway slaves and no slave could be sold to any private citizen. The second Cedula commended the African community for their bravery against the British enemy and stated that any slave wishing to find safe sanctuary in Spanish Florida would serve four years of military service before receiving emancipation papers.

Francisco Menendez, born in Mandinka, western Africa, escaped from his bonds in Carolina, arrived in St. Augustine and embraced freedom around 1724. He eventually earned the respect of the Spaniards and people of Fort Mose. In 1728, he led the Black Militia. Menendez vowed "to shed their last drop of blood in defense of the Spanish Crown." Slave rebellions continued throughout the English colonies, Spain refused to budge on their position to offer sanctuary and the situation was about to turn ugly.

Those at Fort Mose realized the danger in store as a result of English aggression. Many turned to the walls of St. Augustine, others joined the Native American tribes and some refused to be displaced from their homes within the fort. Within the year, Spain and Great Britain would clash; Fort Mose would pay the price.

General James Edward Oglethorpe, founder of the Georgia British colony to the north, marched on St. Augustine in May of 1740. His first stop however was Fort Mose. After a token defense the remainder of the African American inhabitants rushed for the safety of St. Augustine's Castillo de San Marco.

Trying to starve the Spaniards out in June, it became painfully obvious to Oglethorpe that the Castillo could not be taken. Oglethorpe sent an armed force of more than one hundred thirty men to ensure no one escaped the confines of the great fort. The attack combined forces of the forty-second British Regiment, the Scottish Highland Independent Company of Foot, the South Carolina militia, Georgia volunteers and various Indian allies.

Captain Hugh Mackay officially led the troops whom by now had settled in the abandoned fort. Colonel

John Palmer, having operational control, was constantly at odds with Captain Mackay. The British held the fort, but the fighting among themselves was nearly as brutal as their battles with the Spanish. For six long months the battling British remained in the fort, it must have been miserable, but what followed was much worse.

The Spanish Regulars, Black Militia and their Native American allies made plans to retake Fort Mose. What followed has been recorded in English history as "Bloody Mose." Colonel Palmer having fought against the Yammasee Indian, which were staunch Spanish allies, knew that the attack would come under a cover of darkness in the early hours of morning. He sounded reveille at 3:00 a.m. each day to prepare for the attack. By mid June, the fort heard Indian war drums in the distance and fear swept through the camp. Captain Mackay downplayed the incident as if the raging rant were nothing more than rain dances and Native Americans at play. Still Palmer insisted the men rise before the sun and be prepared, but because of the infighting between the two leaders Colonel Palmer was ignored. The soldiers went back to bed. The attack came suddenly before the dawn on June 26, 1740.

Colonel Palmer's plan of attack involved waiting until they were fired upon then firing a barrage in shifts, while one team fired the other reloaded. The British were unprepared and taken totally unaware, the surprise attack caused great confusion. The Indians made a quick and decisive assault from several different vantage points. Colonel Palmer continually yelled encouragement to the British troops that is until he was decapitated. When the smoke cleared the Spanish had taken thirty-four prisoners and sixty-eight lay dead but Fort Mose was a smoldering ruin. The Spaniards won the ground but lost the fort in the end.

The former residents of the fort were forced to live in make shift huts in the settlement until a second Fort Mose could be constructed. Still under the leadership of Captain Menendez, this community was larger and included a Catholic chapel. Menendez wrote a letter to the King of Spain demanding that his militia be paid for their services to the crown, however his audacious petition went unheeded. Fort Mose continued to support the African community until 1764, when Spain finally ceded Florida to the British. The Spanish subjects, including most of those at Fort Mose, were evacuated to Cuba. Among those listed was Captain Menendez, his wife and four children. The family resettled in the Matanzas Province.

During the Revolutionary War, British East Florida became the last loyalist stronghold in North America. Florida reverted back to the Spanish at the end of the war but only for a short time. Florida became a United States territory in 1821.

Over the next century, Fort Mose gradually returned to the marsh from which it was built. In the late 1800s during the construction of Henry Flagler's grand Hotel Ponce de Leon in St. Augustine the ground that was once Fort Mose was used as fill muck for the foundation of the structure. Eventually with road construction and changes in the water table the former site sank into the murky waters of history.

A team of archaeologists from the University of Florida investigated the second site of Fort Mose in 1984. Much to their delight in a simple grouping to trees amidst the marsh grass they began to discover the evidence of a long dead village. Buttons, utensils, weaponry and glass told a story little known in Florida history.

Unfortunately this brave group of Africans are not thought of when discussing the history of civil rights and equality among all people. This history has gone virtually unnoticed but today a group of local citizens have formed the Fort Mose Historical Society in an attempt to rectify this gross oversight. Reenactments tell the story of a courageous group of people, their military leader and a determination to live as free men and women in a community of their choosing. The Fort Most Historical Site offers a lesson to us all.

OGLETHORPE BATTERY PARK

From this site, General James Oglethorpe, Commanding military troops from Georgia and Carolina bombarded Castillo de San Marcos from June 27 to July 20, 1740. The Castillo's modern coquina walls absorbed the cannon shot and damage was slight. Florida's Spanish Governor Manuel de Montiano, returned the fire but the exchange was ineffective. Provisions arrived from Havana just in time to relieve a critical shortage, which would have caused St. Augustine to surrender. Frustrated by the military stalemate and the oncoming hurricane season. Oglethorpe withdrew to Georgia.

Oglethorpe Boulevard, Anastasia Island
SJ37 ~ GPS Coordinates: 29.895573, -81.299707

General James Oglethorpe, with the permission of the British parliament, founded the English colony of Georgia in 1733. Oglethorpe selected the potential settlers from families doomed to the English workhouses for financial hardships. It was Oglethorpe's opinion that these people deserved a second chance. Parliament took the stance that the new world conditions were so difficult with disease, hunger and hostilities from native peoples that if the workhouse incarcerated succumbed to the harsh conditions little of consequence was lost.

Spain claimed the majority of the land Oglethorpe dared to colonize and at St. Augustine the expected hostilities were quick to come. The War of Jenkin's Ear was the first altercation with Spain, this atrocity supplied all the reasoning General Oglethorpe needed to attack St. Augustine. Oglethorpe led the march from Fort Frederica on St. Simons Island, Georgia in May of 1740. The Georgia battalion consisted of nine hundred British regulars combined with Scottish Highlanders as well as eleven hundred Native Americans.

A troop of fifty-seven manned nine cannon, which laid siege on Fort San Diego just nine miles to the north of St. Augustine, taking the fort with ease. A runner arrived at Fort Mose with a warning of the approaching British troops, the garrison abandoned their post for the safety of St. Augustine's walled city two miles to the south. General Oglethorpe sent word demanding they surrender the city. The unconditional surrender was immediately refused. Oglethorpe prepared to attack the city by land and sea.

Oglethorpe suddenly realized that his ships would be unable to draw near enough to support the forces attacking by land. The original plan was abandoned and a long-range naval siege began. The General knew his first course of action would be to blockade the city. The blockade designed to keep Oglethorpe out of the city also allowed nothing to come in. There would be no supplies, military reinforcements or messages of warning. The Spaniard had enough ammunition and supplies to last twenty-one days.

Matanzas Inlet was barricaded first, allowing nothing to get through by sea and Colonel Palmer was ordered to take his men on patrol blockading the perimeter by land. General Oglethorpe's orders were clear patrols should be very obvious; all deserters and spies should be captured immediately; to over emphasize the number of troops on the march; and most importantly never to camp at the same location for more than one night. Colonel Palmer failed to obey General Oglethorpe's specific orders and spent three nights camped at Fort Mose.

The Spaniards received word that a regiment of British soldiers was camped at Fort Mose and in the stillness of the early morning hours as the men lay sleeping, the Spanish attacked. Colonel Palmer's failure to obey a direct order cost more than sixty-eight men under his command their lives, thirty-four were taken prisoner and the

Spanish regained control of Fort Mose. Colonel Palmer was one of the sixty-eight dead; it was reported that he was decapitated. General Oglethorpe was faced with fighting the Spanish but struggles within his own camps. Though it was Palmer's disobedience that proved to be the turning point of this siege; it allowed an open passage for supplies to be brought into St. Augustine.

General Oglethorpe was left little choice now but to take St. Augustine by storm. Cannon fire against the Castillo de San Marcos was virtually useless but for twenty days the siege continued. The Cuban fleet arrived with supplies and reinforcements on the twenty-first day much to the relief of Governor Manuel de Montiano. Oglethorpe's men were sick, the climate was taking a toll and the Native Americans began disappearing into the forest by the dozens restless from the idle days waiting for an opportunity to attack. General Oglethorpe was also unwell. One last attack was planned.

It was reported to Governor Montiano that a British deserter had been captured and was willing to talk. He told the Spanish Commander that Oglethorpe planned a night assault in two days and that the British had withdrawn to blockade the Matanzas. Believing the report, Montiano knew that six Cuban ships loaded with supplies were waiting just beyond the inlet to bring in much needed provisions. Montiano was none the less cautious and waited an entire week for an attack that never came. Relieved, he dispatched five small ships out to bring in some of the needed supplies determining the way was safe. However as the boats reached the inlet, British sloops opened fire and the fight began. The cannon fire continued through the night until the British sloops returned to their squadron. The supply ships quickly slipped through the lines.

By this time General Oglethorpe, sick, in fear of the approaching hurricane season and feeling defeated, sailed north. By July of 1740, Oglethorpe had returned to Fort Frederica. Four hundred fifty men were lost and four forts were now securely in the hands of the Spanish. The experience resulted in the realization of the Spaniards that the wooden tower at Matanzas Inlet must be replaced with an almost invincible coquina structure. Engineer Pedro Ruiz de Olano was ordered to begin work on the new structure to the south of the Matanzas Inlet in the fall of 1740.

Another significant realization from this altercation was the result of a report by Admiral Edward Vernon who addressed a general order to all British Naval Captains and surgeons on August 4, 1740. Admiral Vernon recounted that the Navy having such harsh restrictions on its personnel offered only a daily ration of rum to ease the morale of its sailors. The rations were often abused resulting in incidences of drunkenness that could not be tolerated. Admiral Vernon proposed that the rum ration be diluted by fifty percent to ease the intoxication, the proposal was accepted throughout the British Navy. Strangely enough the Admiral's nickname was Old Grog, based on the cloth his coats were made from Grogram[55]. The diluted rum ration became known as Grog in reference to the Admiral and remained a Navy tradition until 1970.

ST. AUGUSTINE ALLIGATOR FARM

The St. Augustine Alligator Farm is one of the oldest continuously operated attractions created specifically for the purpose of entertaining visitors to Florida. Its origins date to the early 1890s, the first decade of St. Augustine's emergence as a popular tourist destination. Alligators were initially used to attract visitors to a small museum and souvenir shop on St. Augustine Beach at the terminus of a tram railway that ran across Anastasia Island. The owners soon discovered the public's fascination with the reptiles and in 1909 incorporated the South Beach Alligator Farm and Museum of Marine Curiosities, which they moved to its present location in 1920. W. I. Drysdale and F. Charles Usina purchased ownership in 1936 and, after a disastrous fire, began at once to rebuild the facilities, expand the collection, and create national publicity for the attraction. Thousands of servicemen who visited the Alligator Farm during World War II helped to broadcast its popularity. The collection of alligators and other animals in a controlled environment has provided a unique opportunity for scientists who have conducted research in cooperation with the institution. The St. Augustine Alligator Farm's role in the development of tourism in the state was recognized in 1992 with its listing on the National Register of Historic Places.

999 Anastasia Boulevard, Anastasia Island
SJ38 ~ GPS Coordinates: 29.884652, -81.291171

By 1893 St. Augustine began to attract northern tourists. Just five years earlier Henry Flagler had opened his spectacular Ponce de Leon hotel playground for the rich and famous, tourism began to flourish. Entrepreneurs saw a market by bringing the Everglades north displaying alligators caught in local swamps. The secret was that many of these modern day dinosaurs were captured at the depot of the tram railway that extended across Anastasia Island. The attraction proved popular, in 1909 the South Beach Alligator Farm and Museum of Marine Curiosities was born. This was not the first wildlife adventure attraction in Florida; Hullam Jones had opened the first with his glass bottom boat tours at Silver Springs in 1878.

The attraction was moved in 1922 to the location it claims today at 999 Anastasia Boulevard and eventually renamed, St. Augustine Alligator Farm. Though it can not claim to be the oldest Florida attraction, the Alligator Farm is the oldest tourist venue in continual operation within the state of Florida. After celebrating one hundred years of existence in 1993, it was determine that the venture is definitely a success.

The attraction was sold in 1937 to Co-owners State Representative F. Charles Usina and W. Irving "Driz" Drysdale. These two civic-minded men were certainly the driving forces behind the St. Augustine Alligator Farm. It was under their management that the present facility and buildings were made a reality. Drysdale and Usina's contribution within the attraction gates and beyond continues to leave a lasting mark on the city of St. Augustine to this day.

Charles Usina was born and educated in St. Augustine. His Minorcan family has deep roots extending more than two hundred years in Florida's sandy soil. Usina served constituents for eleven terms in Florida's House of Representatives; he was active in the political realm, community service, charitable organizations and civic leadership. Upon his passing the Florida State Senate memorialized Representative Usina as "a man of unquestioned integrity and devotion to his family and church, a good companion to his friends and fellow members of the Legislature… an inspiration to those who follow in his footsteps." A man of those qualities is rare indeed.

Partner W. Irving "Driz" Drysdale embodied the very same dedication and commitment to St. Augustine. Obviously extremely respected among his peers, whenever his name is spoken a certain amount of esteem creeps into the tone. Driz Drysdale was also responsible for another of the city's most valuable landmarks, the St. Augustine Amphitheater. This site also has a historical marker.

Nearby Camp Blanding provided thousands of servicemen during World War II, looking for just such an attraction. Word of mouth advertising quickly spread and soon St. Augustine's Alligator Farm became a national treasure. The post war years brought throngs of auto bound tourists on an annual pilgrimage to the Sunshine State and the Alligator Farm was a must see.

Together, Usina and Drysdale published a book in 1949 called, *"Alligator!"* The Alligator Farm, has in fact, has become a family affair for the Drysdale's. The Alligator Farm has become an annual pilgrimage for most Florida families as well as a host of others, including mine. Today Driz Drysdale's son, David, owns the park.

The wonderfully done exhibits and an extremely knowledgeable staff of St. Augustine's Alligator Farm and Zoological Park make a great outing for tourists and locals alike. The featured exhibit is of course, the Land of Crocodiles. This park is in fact the only place in the entire world where the viewing of all twenty-three species of crocodilians is possible.

The "Gomek Forever!" presentation became necessary when the park's star performer passed away. Gomek, a giant salt-water crocodile, was billed as the largest reptile in the Western Hemisphere. He was first captured in New Guinea in 1968 and he became a St. Augustine citizen in 1990. He quickly achieved stardom when on command Gomek would explore from his pool and feed on "pre-killed" nutria[56]. Sadly the giant performer died on March 6, 1997 of cardiac failure resulting from heart disease. It was said that he lived a full eighty years. The giant beast will certainly be missed. Much to the delight of fans around the world Gomek's presence in the park continues, his remains were expertly taxidermied and are respectfully displayed in a personal exhibit depicting his natural habitat.

Although it would be impossible to replace Gomek, the St. Augustine Alligator Farm welcomed Maximo and his gal, Sydney in the summer of 2003. Natives of Australia, the couple relocated to Florida in order to fill the vacancy left after Gomek's demise, two for one. Maximo is also a "Saltie"[57] weighing in at a hefty twelve hundred fifty pounds and fifteen feet, three inches long at last report. He is still a growing boy, a mere toddler at thirty-three years old; Maximo could quite possibly live to the ripe old age of eighty continuing to grow every year.

Exotic Birds make up yet another exhibit. Native species as well as South American Macaws across the spectrum to "Laughing" Kookaburras are on display. The wonders of nature regale the crowd with their rainbow hues and audible delights from the smallest tot to the avid bird watcher.

The most recent exhibit at the Alligator Farm features albino alligators. The amazing alligators were long thought to be no more than a folk legend told in the bayou's of Louisiana. However, today several of the species are now on display at St. Augustine. When you first look at these creamy white creatures, they have the appearance of wax figures. However, they are very much alive and enjoying their special shrimp boat house enclosure with Cajun music in the background to make them feel right at home.

The park is not however limited to alligators and exotic birds. From every corner of the earth come monkeys, snakes, lizards, giant tortoises and kangaroos. For the little tykes and big kids too, the petting zoo allows visitors to cuddle and feed a bevy of barnyard animals. A hand wash station is nearby; some of the locals can be messy eaters.

The Alligator Farm is a must when visiting St. Augustine. The park is historical, educational and entertaining with fascinating alligator, reptile and bird shows taking place throughout the day. Alligator feedings are done each afternoon. The nature walkway allows patrons an up close view of alligators in their natural habitats and multitudes of water birds nesting in the trees. During the season within a few feet of the wooden walkway are nests with eggs and young chicks, closer than you would ever imagine. Though it seems a dangerous spot to raise young chicks, the alligator population in fact protects the small birds from natural predators.

Conservation is of the utmost importance to the management and staff. Thirty-one species of endangered animals are on exhibit. Recently the Anastasia Island Conservation Center was opened on the grounds of the park to offer training to interning zookeepers on how to care for reptiles. The facility was dedicated in honor of W. I.

"Driz" Drysdale and F. Charles Usina.

Refreshments are available at the snack bar and a wonderful gift shop is available for guests to purchase a memento of this special place. The St. Augustine Alligator Farm Zoological Park is open every day from 9 a.m. until 5 p.m. During the Summer Park hours are extended to 6 p.m. each day. Admission is charged, discounts are usually offered on the official website

SENTINELS OF THE COAST

Since early times, coastal towers were important in the defense of St. Augustine. From the wooden lookout here in 1586, Spanish sentries warned of approaching English raiders under Sir Francis Drake. Later the tower was built of stone. It served during the 1740 siege, was converted to a lighthouse in 1823 and used until it was lost to the sea. The present light replaced it in 1874.

Lighthouse Park, Anastasia Island, St. Augustine
SJ39 ~ GPS Coordinates: 29.881885, -81.283516

Since the 16th century the northern portion of Anastasia Island has been the location for various defensive watchtowers and maritime signaling stations. In 1586, early Spanish settlers built the first wooden watchtower in an effort to defend the settlement from attack. It was from this vantage point that the ships of English privateer, Sir Francis Drake was spotted as he approached St. Augustine. Ironically it was the sight of that same watchtower, looming on the horizon, which led Drake to St. Augustine. In fact when put to the torch, the tower provided a signal fire seen for countless miles.

St. Augustine was then the largest Spanish settlement in the New World and one of the few safe havens for free African Americans. The homes and public buildings were generally constructed of wood and clay leaving them vulnerable to hostile fire. On May 28 and 29, 1586, St. Augustine suffered a devastating attack.

Sir Francis Drake and his men caught sight of the beacon tower that stood upon four masts towering over the beach of Anastasia Island from their fleet. Drake landed nearby leading his men along the river toward town. Three of the men boarded a small skiff and scouted the area, but found the town abandoned. A sound in the distance unnerved the men yet offered some encouragement in their quest. The sound was that of a fifer playing a tune known to be anti-Spanish. If the fifer could be found, the English soldiers knew they would find a person who hated the Spanish as much as they did.

The fifer was Nicholas Borgoignon, a Frenchman who had recently escaped from the Spanish after six long years of captivity. With his help, Drake and his men formed a plan to attack St. Augustine. The newly built Spanish fort situated upon huge standing tree trunks on top of which was a platform supporting fourteen brass cannon. Nearby was a chest holding the garrison's pay, equaling about two thousand English pounds.

The one hundred fifty Spanish troops said to be guarding the fort were nowhere to be found. The townspeople had evacuated the settlement cowering in the underbrush of the forest for safety. It was said that in their haste to flee the English invaders, the Spanish actually left behind a small child in the fort. The English, unwilling to ransom her or take her back to England, returned the child to the Spanish after the attack on St. Augustine. This was the only humane act Drake ever accomplished.

The unnatural quiet of the fort was suddenly broken with the sound of Spanish sniper fire. Anthony Powell, second to Drake in command of the English infantry, located a Spanish horse and galloped in pursuit of the gunmen. The Spanish marksmen took careful aim and shot him in the shoulder knocking him from the horses' back. The Spanish soldier descended on him with fury, finishing Powell off with the thrust of a sword. Drake called in his men, refusing to allow them to seek out the hiding Spanish. Instead Drake ordered that the fort and settlement be set to the torch after plundering for any tools or implements useful to English colonists up the coast in Virginia. Drake also seized a dozen brass cannon before boarding his ship and sailing north.

During the late 17th century, a second guard house and lookout tower was built on the site of the original wooden watchtower. This structure would prove to be far more difficult to obliterate. Constructed of coquina, quarried near the northern end of Anastasia Island, this distinctive material was most resilient and impervious to fire. Coquina is formed from donax shells in large deposits, which have become cemented by calcium carbonate over the ages and found in the coastal regions of Florida and Cuba.

Though the attack on St. Augustine by the English was a devastating blow, the city remained under Spanish control and rebuilt. Yet the battle between the Spanish and English continued. The northern end of Anastasia Island remained a strategically important location constantly fought over throughout the colonial period.

In 1739, the Spaniards accelerated the hostilities with the English by landing a party of men on Amelia Island. Spanish troops descended on two unarmed men gathering wood for their cook fires, brutally beheading the men and mangling their bodies. After the senseless murder, the Spaniards calmly boarded their boats and returned to St. Augustine. Georgia's founder, General James Edward Oglethorpe was notified of the attack and in retaliation called out a thousand soldiers and cavalrymen, a regiment of fierce Scottish Highlanders pursuing the Spanish assassins. Oglethorpe and his troops drove the Spaniards back to St. Augustine but the fighting had only just begun.

Oglethorpe returned to Frederica to gather forces and in May 1740, he again made the trek toward St. Augustine with nine hundred men and eleven hundred Indians. He captured Fort San Diego, nine miles west of St. Augustine, with fifty-seven men and nine cannon. Fort Moosa[58], an African American stronghold two miles from St. Augustine, was abandoned warnings of the British approach. The entire garrison retreated to the walled city. General Oglethorpe called for the St. Augustine commander's surrender. The commander replied: "I will be glad to shake hands with Oglethorpe in the castle."

Oglethorpe planned to attack the city by both land and sea. After drawing the infantry up and giving the signal for attack, it was found that the ships could not get close enough to the city to offer cover fire for the invading force. The plan to storm St. Augustine by land was abandoned and the hail of cannon fire began from the ships at anchor.

In order to prevent Spanish reinforcements into the city, Oglethorpe ordered his second in command, Colonel Palmer, to take a battalion and scour the country; to never be idle, revealing his position along the way; to pick up stragglers, cut off all supplies, deceive the enemy as to the strength of his force, and not rest any three nights in the same place. Colonel Palmer disobeyed this last order and remained three nights at Fort Moosa. The Spanish heard rumors of this occupation and managed to ambush Palmer's men early one morning. Twenty of Palmer's men were killed and the Spanish recaptured Fort Moosa. The victory was significant for the Spanish who suffered for the lack of food and medical supplies, with Fort Moosa again under Spanish control the supply route was again open.

Oglethorpe was determined to take St. Augustine and resolved to storm the city. For twenty days his batteries threw shot and shell into the city, lighting the sky with the barrage. Finally, a fleet from Cuba arrived bringing much needed reinforcements to the Spaniards. Oglethorpe soldiers suffered from heat exhaustion, the Timucua were growing restless and the General himself was unwell. St. Augustine was reluctantly abandoned and the English returned to Fort Frederica in Georgia, July 1740. General Oglethorpe had lost four hundred fifty men and four forts.

St. Augustine remained in the hands of the Spanish until 1763, when England gained control for about twenty years, by treaty. The English erected a coquina tower resembling that of the Spanish adding an additional cannon to sound a warning of approaching ships. Spain regained control of the city for the final time in 1784. During this occupation the East Florida governors made numerous land grants of property on Anastasia Island. The land surrounding the watchtower and guardhouse was granted in 1793 to Spaniard Lorenzo Rodriquez. Rodriquez, a sea captain and bar pilot cultivated the lands known which he called "Buena Vista" for several decades.

In 1821, Florida became a territory of the United States. The tower site proved to be the logical place to construct the first lighthouse in St. Augustine. The light was placed on the existing tower and stood only thirty feet tall. First lit in 1824, the tower was raised twice during its history eventually reaching a height of fifty-two feet. The federally controlled lighthouse continued in service until the Civil War when all southern lighthouses were extinguished to ensure no aid was given to Union ships. Following the Civil War, the St. Augustine lighthouse again brightened the Anastasia Island coast.

Though the lighthouse stood a half a mile from the sea when it was constructed, Mother Nature was determined to reclaim the area as beachfront property. A jetty was created to waylay the erosion but alas the lighthouse was eventually undermined. The St. Augustine lighthouse collapsed into the sea on August 22, 1880.

When it became apparent that the 1824 lighthouse would be consigned to the sea, the United States government purchased an additional five acres of the Rodriquez grant in 1871. Construction began on the new lighthouse and Keeper's Quarters immediately. The structures were placed near the original site, yet further from the water and on much higher ground. The tower was completed in 1874 with the red brick keeper's cottage in front. Hezekiah H. Pittee, a native of Maine, was placed in charge of the St. Augustine light. Pittee later served as superintendent of construction of the United States Lighthouse Bureau along the Atlantic Coast. The one hundred sixty-five-foot St. Augustine lighthouse still stands today and has never been threatened by beach erosion.

For eighty years, lighthouse keepers and their families kept the light ablaze. At times as many as fifteen adults and children occupied the keeper's cottage but in 1955 the light was automated and a keeper was no longer needed bringing to an end an era of American history. The carefully manicured grounds that had been so lovingly tended eventually began to suffer neglect and in 1970 the keepers' cottage was set aflame by arsonists. The Junior Service League of St. Augustine spent fourteen years dedicated to the restoration of the lighthouse and keepers' cottage.

The first-order Fresnel lens is still in operation today as an active aid to navigation and stands eighteen feet tall. In 1986, a fourteen-year-old boy shot out the lens with a high powered rifle. The Coast Guard decided to remove rather than replace the shattered lens, but the Junior Service League again came to the rescue of the St. Augustine light. The organization raised the half million dollars required to replace the damaged prisms and had bulletproof glass installed on the outside.

St. Augustine Lighthouse is said to be the first official lighthouse built in Florida. The daymark[59] is black and white spiral bands with the top of the tower painted red. The lighthouse was given a fresh coat of paint in March and April of 2000. There are two hundred nineteen (I climbed them) exhausting steps to the top. The lighthouse is the tenth tallest in the United States and is truly a sight to behold. The view from the tower is breathtaking and the light from the beacon can be seen for twenty-five miles at sea.

The Junior Service League continues to devotedly care for the displays and buildings, hosting more than one hundred thousand visitors each year. The lighthouse is open to the public every day. Young children are not allowed to climb to the top of the tower due to the fact that it is not enclosed except for the railing. Though a special tour is provided for younger children including a fascinating story all about what it was like to be a lighthouse keeper. There is a charge to climb the lighthouse and tour the facilities; the fees are used for maintenance and upkeep for the buildings and grounds. The keeper's cottage serves as a gift shop and museum.

Though if you should visit keep your senses about you in the museum, it is said that a melancholy spirit still haunts the former keeper's home and the ghostly specter of a young girl sometimes materializes on the third floor. Others say the pervasive smell of a strong cigar drifts through the fuel house, though no one is there. While in the tower, it has been reported, that voices, footsteps and an unseen apparition carrying a bucket signifies that a former lighthouse keeper still cares for the St. Augustine beacon.

173

THE ST. AUGUSTINE AMPHITHEATRE
(Anastasia Island State Park)

This 2,000 seat theatre is built on the site of the royal Spanish quarry, where the native shellstone called coquina was dug and ferried across Matanzas Bay for the construction of Castillo de San Marco and many other early structures in colonial St. Augustine. Here on June 27, 1965, the Paul Green symphonic drama CROSS AND SWORD was first presented to commemorate the 400th anniversary of the founding of St. Augustine, Florida.

Off of A1A, Anastasia Island State Park
SJ40 ~ GPS Coordinator: 29.875283, -81.284683

Noted businessman Irving "Driz" Drysdale, co-owner of the St. Augustine Alligator Farm, envisioned an amphitheater on Anastasia Island in the early 1960s. The construction of the some two thousand seat capacity facility took several years, however was quite ready for St. Augustine's four hundredth year anniversary.

Driz' son, David remembers his father traveling all about the south to every outdoor performance he could find, today we would call it test marketing. He convinced Pulitzer Prize winner Paul Green to write a drama to be featured at the amphitheater. In fact, I was told that Green spent a good amount of time sequestered in the Drysdale home while gestating the play. The play called *Cross and Sword*, was to tell the great historical story of St. Augustine and its survival for more than four centuries.

The drama was such a success that former State Legislature A. H. "Gus" Craig pursued and eventually attained the title Official State Play in 1973 for the production. Gus Craig, in addition to the eighteen years of public service in Florida's House of Representatives, has always been an active leader in the community through cultural endeavors, historic preservation and social services. He was instrumental in gaining the initial funding for the amphitheater that was built at Anastasia State Park. Why did Gus Craig offer such amazing support to this project? Simply out of respect for Driz Drysdale and Paul Green; his dedication and personal commitment to the community were important factors as well.

"*Cross and Sword*" celebrated opening night on June 27, 1965. Essentially a reenactment of St. Augustine's founding and her earliest noteworthy figures including Pedro Menendez, Jean Ribaut and Father Lopez. The play involved expansive musical productions, expressive dance, pantomime and heart felt poetry. The drama was performed ten summer weeks every year. The play was an expensive endeavor and as the theater aged upkeep costs continued to rise. Unfortunately tourism was declining and state funding was dwindling away. After a denial of state supported funds in 1997, "*Cross and Sword*" was forced to close after thirty-two years of summer productions due to low attendance.

In 2005, the St. Augustine Amphitheater will celebrate forty years with a complete makeover, fitting for middle age. The facility is now under a long-term lease from the state to St. Johns County. The renovations include an addition of some twenty-five hundred seats, doubling the former capacity of the amphitheater. Experts say the increased size is required to attract name performers.

Five million dollars in renovations and expansion funded new furniture, fixtures, equipment, modernized lighting and sound convinced performers that was this a much-desired venue. The opening date is set for late summer of 2004. While undergoing renovations, the amphitheater has continued to be used for other things. Possibly the *"Cross and Sword"* can be revived, if for nothing else the celebration of St. Augustine Amphitheater's forty years of community service, education in its simplest form. The event would make Driz Drysdale proud.

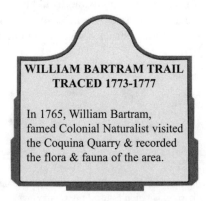

WILLIAM BARTRAM TRAIL
TRACED 1773-1777

In 1765, William Bartram, famed Colonial Naturalist visited the Coquina Quarry & recorded the flora & fauna of the area.

At the St. Augustine Amphitheater, St. Augustine
SJ41 ~ GPS Coordinates: 29.874496, -81.282371

The history of coquina use in the United States reportedly extends for as much as four hundred years. Of course the most famous and extensive use of the porous stone is St. Augustine's Castillo de San Marcos in 1671. Because mining the quarries required an abundant labor force, transportation was difficult and the whole process very expensive, approval for construction of the stone fort from the Spanish government required almost one hundred years of debate.

The first vein of coquina was located on the north end of Anastasia Island. Once the stone was cut it was loaded on oxcarts to the river where the stone was then placed on barges then again unloaded to oxcarts and taken to the work site. The most abundant labor force was Native Americans provided by the Spanish missions. Unfortunately through this virtual slavery market and the introduction of European diseases, for which the Indians had no resistance, the source of labor quickly began to dwindle. African slaves were then used to supplement the labor need.

It has been estimated that approximately three hundred Native Americans were used in the construction of the fort at any one time, supplemented by Spanish prisoners and Africans. The workers would remove any topsoil, working in teams to separate the coquina blocks then proceeding with the difficult task of transportation. Once the blocks arrived on the work site, they were left to cure for up to a year. The curing process involved all of the moisture leaching and evaporating from the stone. After the water is removed the stone hardens, suitable for use in construction.

The Castillo virtually depleted the entire first vein of coquina and soon a second quarry was opened on Anastasia Island. The second quarry allowed the now very popular building material to be used in public and residential construction. Once the British came into power in 1763, a third coquina vein was opened very near the inlet. Several large churches were built of coquina during the second Spanish period. It was during this time also that the porous stone was used as tombstones replacing traditional wood grave markers.

By this time workers were using more modern implements in the mining process; crow bars, picks and jump bars were all in use but no written evidence exists explaining their mining techniques. Even though the tools were modern speculation was that the mining methods could be traced to the Egyptian pyramids.

The quarries became a tourist attraction by the late nineteenth century. The Flagler railroad allowed visitors easier access and the construction of the Ponce de Leon, Cordova and later the Alcazar hotel. Tourism flourished. Flagler used a mixture of poured concrete and coquina for his various construction projects, the idea was taken from Villa Zorayda where the process was first used. Eventually the main quarries were closed to mining. However, coquina is still taken today from various East Florida quarries in limited quantities. Chain saws were wielded in an attempt to fashion modern statuary from coquina, though this form of art never really found an avid audience.

Were it not for coquina the appearance of St. Augustine would be drastically different today. Many of the buildings still standing from the Spanish era, including the regal Castillo de San Marco owe their longevity to the durable building material. The preservation of these structures goes hand in hand with the continued safekeeping of the history of St. Augustine.

OLD SPANISH CHIMNEY AND WELL

These ruins are all that remain of what was probably a Spanish barracks which housed the quarry overseer, master masons, and stonecutters who were involved in the construction of the Castillo de San Marcos. The quarry, located directly across the road from this site, contained rich veins of coquina which the Indian workers shaped into rough blocks. Under the supervision of the quarry overseer, Alonso Diaz Mejia, the blocks were transported by wagon and then by raft to the site of the Castillo. Completed in 1695, the great fortress was the keystone of the Spanish system of defense of Florida.

Anastasia Island, Highway A1A turn beside Anastasia Baptist Church to Old Beach Road (right), St. Augustine
SJ42 ~ GPS Coordinates: 29.864600, -81.280383

During the early days, St. Augustine was a Spanish outpost, a port along the trading routes bringing sailors from all parts of the world. The beginnings were hard, but the determined Spanish settlers stuck it out in spite of hurricanes, drought, Englishmen, Indians and pirate attacks, cold and disease. The settlers had very little, the only implement available to them was their hands. Palm fronds were woven into thatch roofs and timbers were honed by hand to construct the crude hovels the settlers called home. They ate whatever they could kill, catch or coax from Florida's sandy soil. The Spanish colony proved to be an easy target.

Time and again the little colony was attacked and burned. But the villagers persisted and fought to maintain their grasp on Spanish La Florida. After the malicious pirate Robert Searles and his vicious crew fired the city in 1668, the citizenry of St Augustine realized that they must devise a way to protect themselves.

Using the slave labor of local Indians, Spanish convicts and captured Europeans construction began on the Castillo de San Marcos in October of 1672. It took three years to cut and move enough coquina from Anastasia Island to actually build a structure of that magnitude. Labor had always been a problem but the Native Americans were easily duped into supplying manpower and the forced labor of prisoners provided the remainder of the workforce. Florida Governor Manuel de Cendoya and his staff chose the location and design, ground was broken and construction began.

The walls of the mighty fort began to rise. The fort was completely self-contained. Within the compound a well provided fresh water and the parade grounds inside the fortification walls lent a safe haven for families and their livestock until the danger of invasion or weather had passed. Most of the rooms inside the fort are connected through a catacomb system making it possible to travel the perimeter without ever having to leave the safety of the twelve foot thick walls. The gun deck overlooks the water and the bastions at each corner allow for observation without leaving the observer vulnerable to canon fire below. It remains a large, secure structure, however, one must remember that the entire town and its livestock huddled together there in times of trouble. Today, the fort green is lovely and manicured. In 1740, when General James Oglethorpe arrived from Georgia to take St Augustine and bring Castillo de San Marco to its knees, the fort was a dark, filthy place. But it did provide a safe haven and that was the reason for its construction.

Eventually the Native Americans were decimated beyond recovery and all but died out completely. In the search for cheap labor, St. Augustine turned to enslaved Africans. Though St. Augustine had always been a haven for free men of color now the government embraced slavery to take the role Native Americans had previous filled. Life was hard on the workforce; those that survived the grueling hard labor often succumbed to disease and many were worked into an untimely death.

The fort itself tells a different story. Those who lived within the walls left an indelible mark. One of the rooms, a military bunkhouse, reveals pictures scratched into the walls by perhaps a homesick Spanish soldier longing for the site of his own beloved shore. One of the most popular rooms in the Castillo is the Chapel of St Mark. The chapel leaves each visitor with a feeling of serenity and peaceful reflection. Imagine the St. Augustine villagers who brought a heavy heart to that chapel long ago, bringing their troubles to an altar of stone.

The Castillo has stood solid and firm, cannonballs simply absorbed into the coquina sides, plucked out after dark and fired back at persistent raiders. Fireproof and solid in any storm the mighty fort sustained for days on end and remains steadfast today. Unfortunately time has been the most pervasive enemy to the Castillo de San Marcos. Impervious to pirates, European raiders, Indians and severe storms yet time is taking its toll. The ancient walls show cracks and the foundation is returning to sand. Impenetrable for over three hundred years if handled with care the majestic edifice will remain for generations to come.

The National Park Service manages the fort today. The site is open for visitors daily with a small entrance fee charged to assist with the care and maintenance of the great Castillo de San Marcos.

OLD SPANISH WELL

OLD SPANISH QUARRIES

(Side 1)

About 200 yards south-east of this point are the remains of the King's Coquina Quarries. (Coquina, a type of limestone composed of mollusk shells and sand, is found along the north-east coast of Florida.) Coquina was used in the building of many early colonial structures in St. Augustine, including the fortress Castillo de San Marcos (1672-1696).

OLD SPANISH QUARRIES

(Side 2)

On July 21, 1821, Major General Andrew Jackson, Florida's first Territorial Governor, established St. Johns County, with St. Augustine as the county seat. It contained all of Florida east of the Suwannee River, approximately 39,400 square miles, with over 1,100 miles of coastline. Since 1821, more than 2/3 of Florida's present 67 counties have been carved from St. Johns' original boundaries, reducing it to 609 square miles of land area.

Anastasia Island State Recreation Area, Highway A1A, St. Augustine
SJ43 ~ GPS Coordinates: 29.862423, -81.272857

Most structures in the early days of St. Augustine were constructed of local wood with palmetto frond thatched roofs. The dwellings and forts were rustic and hardly durable. Repeatedly Spanish St. Augustine fell victim to the burning torches of European raiders and later pirates set the torch to the settlement. Eventually the Spaniards realized that a more defensible building material had to be found.

The answer was found in what amounted to their own backyard. On nearby Anastasia Island, the Spaniards discovered an immense amount of the soft deposits comprised of bits of broken shell. The rock is comprised of tiny shell fragments and quartz grains bound together by calcium carbonate. These formations began during a time when sea levels were higher and today's coast was in fact underwater. Sand and shells bound together forming a hardened sand bar. Later, during a glacial period approximately one hundred twenty-five years ago, the sea levels dropped. The sandbars were left exposed to the air and natural elements. Rain dissolved the shells and calcium carbonate resulted then forming a sort of cement. The loose ground shell sediment was fused into rock and that hardened rock was coquina. The word *coquina* literally means "tiny shell" in Spanish.

The earliest structure known to have been built of coquina at St. Augustine was a gunpowder storage magazine. The building was constructed around 1598. Unfortunately the Spanish had a small labor force and limited engineering skills required utilizing coquina on a larger scale. That problem was about to change.

As time progressed, the labor force increased with the addition of Native American's enslavement, Spanish convicts and European prisoners of war. By 1671, the coquina quarries were in full operation. Anastasia Island was called *Cantera*, Spanish for "quarry". The quarries were ablaze with activity as the workmen hauled blocks of coquina rock from the depths of the pits. Using hand tools, they pried out squares of the soft shell-stone and once the squares were loose along natural layers in the rock, the blocks were then loaded onto ox-drawn carts and ferried onto barges crossing Matanzas Bay to St. Augustine. The blocks were used to construct the Castillo de

San Marcos as well as many other public and private buildings.

Coquina rock is relatively soft and easy to cut while in the ground, when exposed to air and the water drains away, the rock hardens. The Spanish learned to preserve the rock from erosion, waterproofing was required. Stone walls were coated with plaster and painted sealing the porous rock. Surprisingly, the Spanish found that coquina possessed a unique feature making it ideal for fort construction. When Georgia founder General James Edward Oglethorpe bombarded the Castillo for twenty-seven days, it was discovered that the coquina walls simply absorbed the cannon balls. The Castillo de San Marcos was never captured in battle.

Coquina continued to be a prized building material not only for the Spanish, but also later to the British from 1763 to 1783 and then the Americans in 1821. By the late 1700s, the Native American population had been decimated and new source of quarry workers had to be found. St. Augustine had long been a haven for free men of color but coquina mining brought enslaved Africans to Anastasia Island.

The site at Anastasia Island Recreation Area is only one of several quarries on the island. The St. Augustine Amphitheater location was another active quarry. Coquina rock is part of a sedimentary formation that underlies much of the Atlantic shore of Florida. It is usually covered by sand with exceptions along some stretches of beach in Flagler, Martin and Palm Beach counties. Washington Oaks Gardens State Park at Palm Coast and Blowing Rocks Preserve at Jupiter are excellent places to see coquina outcroppings. Small amounts of coquina continue to be quarried today in Flagler County.

The Anastasia quarry was listed on the National Register of Historic Places in September 1970. The distinction serves to protect this unique area and no further mining will ever be permitted. Because of the protected status nothing may be removed from the quarry area. The area is open to the public for viewing.

COQUINA QUARRIES

Note: The second side of this marker discusses the founding of St. Johns County. Because this information is repeated on four additional different historical markers, the story will only be told once. The other locations include: CR 203, in front of Ponte Vedra Inn & Club, Jacksonville Beach; Side Two of the Public Market Place marker, Charlotte & St. George Streets, St. Augustine; and the reverse side of New Switzerland, 2159 Mandarin Road at the Volunteer Fire Department, Mandarin.

TREATY PARK

In 1823, two years after Florida was acquired by the United States, leaders of the Seminole and Miccosukee Tribes met with government officials on the banks of the creek near this site to settle conflicting claims to Florida lands. After twelve days of negotiation, they signed the treaty of Moultrie Creek on September 18, 1823. The tribes were to occupy a four million acre reservation of the interior peninsula extending roughly from Lake George to the Everglades. The Government was to assist their relocation and help support them there for a period of twenty years. Failure on both sides to comply with the terms of this and later treaties led to the Second Seminole War (1835-1842). The longest, most costly of American Indian wars decimated the Seminole and Miccosukee Tribes and led to the surrender of most of the survivors for transportation to the reservations in the West. Some of the surviving natives escaped this forced migration by taking refuge in remote areas of the Everglades. Today their descendants still maintain the Seminole and Miccosukee cultural identity and contribute to Florida's diverse ethnic heritage. The exact site of the treaty signing is unknown. This park is dedicated in commemoration of that historic event.

Treaty Park on Wildwood Drive, St. Augustine
SJ44 ~ GPS Coordinates: 29.823686, -81.351202

The fight for dominance between the white man and Native Americans in Florida had the distinction of being the longest continuous war in United States history until the dark days of the Vietnam conflict. No other event deterred the growth of the Florida territory and hampered their efforts toward statehood like the Seminole Wars. The conflicts began more than one hundred years before the Seminole Wars began and the initial responsibility lay in the hands of the British.

The British, in an attempt to drive out the Spaniards in Florida and later to defeat the colonists during the American Revolution, allied themselves with the Native Americans. Of course, the British failed on both accords but the fate of the Seminole people was sealed. As more and more white men encroached on Native American lands, the Seminole were forced to fight to defend their homes.

The Seminole did not actively participate in the Creek Wars to the north in Georgia, but sought what they thought to be the safety of Florida's inland plains. The tribes embraced European ways introduced by the Spaniards. Native Americans began farming wheat and raising cattle, most of which was the wild stock left after Spain's retreat. Colonists looked for ways to discredit the Native Americans, often accusing them of stealing cattle. Though what angered the settlers most was the fact that the Seminole welcomed runaway African American slaves. That is not to say the Seminole were completely guiltless of molesting the white settlements, but the white settlers did strike the first blow.

When Florida finally became a United States territory in 1821, the first Governor Andrew Jackson considered the seven thousand Seminole in Florida a major problem. In September 1823, Governor William F. Duval, who succeeded Jackson, met Seminole representatives at Moultrie Creek on the St. Johns River. Duval proposed a treaty, which would create a reservation south of Ocala. The elder tribal chiefs were convinced to accept a treaty written in English that they could neither read nor understand. In fact, the old chiefs were simply lied to about the contents of the treaty making it appear to be much more appealing than the terms actually provided for. The younger, more suspicious, militant braves never complied with the Treaty of Moultrie Creek.

These braves had already been forced from their traditional hunting grounds, had changed their way of life from farming to cattle and the thought of any form of confinement stirred their blood. Neamathia, a Mikasukis from North Florida, challenged Duval:

"Do you think . . . I am like a bat, that hangs by its claws in a dark cave, and that I can see noth ing of what is going on around me? Ever since I was a small boy I have seen the white people steadily encroaching upon the Indians, and driving them from their homes and hunting grounds . . . I will tell you plainly, if I had the power, I would tonight cut the throat of every white man in Florida."

Neamathia's fears were realized when a drought in 1827 forced the Seminole outside their reservation boundaries in search of food and fresh water. The Florida Legislature beseeched Congress to remove the Seminole from their territory. In 1829 the newly elected President, Andrew Jackson, issued a plan to relocate all of the troublesome tribes to reservations far away, west of the Mississippi River.

The Seminoles were given a tourist tour of only the most desirable areas of the Oklahoma reservation. Seminole interpreters bribed by Government agents did not explain that the lands would be shared with other tribes who had historically been the sworn enemies of the Seminole people. Further the Seminole were never told that the Oklahoma land would not support crops traditionally grown by the Seminole to feed their people.

The next year Congress passed the Indian Removal Act and three years later, Micanopy, a Seminole chief accepted the Treaty of Fort Gibson. The adoption of the Fort Gibson Treaty led to the Second Seminole War. This war proved to be the most costly both in money and blood of the three Seminole Wars. The action brought forth a young Native American whose name will be forever linked with Florida history, Osceola.

Osceola was born in Georgia around 1800. Reportedly, his father was a white man by the name of William Powell, his mother a Creek Indian. The Creeks were known as Red Stick Seminole. Osceola's resentment toward the white man was said to erupt when his wife and four children were seized. Whatever the reason was, he arrived in eastern Florida to become a voice for Indian rights. There are many views pertaining to Osceola's effectiveness as a leader, both good and bad. By 1835 random attacks and selective killings lead to a grisly massacre, the beginning of the end for Osceola.

On December 28, 1835, Major Francis Dade and his regiment of one hundred eight soldiers were ambushed and brutally murdered in one of the most heinous massacres in history only short of Custer's last stand. The two companies under Dade's command had been trekking from their former post at Fort Brooke near Tampa to their new assignments at Fort King near Ocala. Meanwhile at Fort King, Indian Agent Thompson was taking a leisurely evening stroll after dinner when he, as well as others accompanying him, were murdered. These two events resulted in a warrant issued for the arrest of Osceola. In 1837, he was captured under a white flag of conference. Osceola was first sent to the Castillo de San Marcos at St. Augustine. Later he was taken in chains to Fort Moultrie outside of Charleston, South Carolina. Osceola died in bondage on January 30, 1838. His severed head was paraded around Charleston on a pike. Thirty-three other Seminole, including Principal Chief Micanopy and Wild Cat, were tricked into surrender and imprisoned the same way.

The five thousand United States troops continued their efforts against the Seminole until their dismissal on August 14, 1842. Colonel Worth announced at Cedar Key that on that day the Second Seminole War was finally over. The total cost of the war was estimated at forty million dollars and resulted in approximately sixteen hundred military deaths, ironically the Florida Seminole probably never numbered more than fifteen hundred warriors. The United States had sent some of their most qualified soldiers to win this war, including "Old Rough and Ready" Zachary Taylor and "Old Fuss and Feathers" Winfield Scott.

The Seminole were scattered; the few remaining Seminole in Florida were driven into the uninhabitable Everglade Swamps. The Native Americans were adjusting to a new way of life, even some of their cultural activities changed for survivals sake. Some Seminole Natives intermarried into the last remaining Calusa tribe; adopting an economy based on hunting and fishing in the swamps.

The Second Seminole War had left only about five hundred Florida Seminole. A two and one half million acre "hunting and planting" preserve was established in the Lake Okeechobee area. The principal Chief was Holatta-Micco or known by the English as Billy Bowlegs and Sam Jones could be called the second in command.

The brutality of war notwithstanding, there was certain gains for Florida at the expense of Native American losses. The improvements included: considerable exploration and mapping; many trails and roads established throughout the state; and many forts that served as starting points for various towns. Money was spent directly and indirectly through employment of civilians, payments for rent, food, supplies and relief. Another Florida benefit as a result of the Seminole Wars was the Armed Occupation Act of 1842. The Occupation Act allowed white civilians to obtain homestead rights.

In December of 1855 a party of United States reconnaissance surveyors were mapping the Seminole reserve in the Big Cypress. They passed by a Seminole farm and for some reason destroyed all the banana trees; at least they were the ones blamed.   The farm owner, Chief Billy Bowlegs, retaliated by wounding and killing several soldiers as well as the officer in charge. Billy rejected federal bribes of five thousand dollars plus one hundred dollars per surrendered Indian, but when his granddaughter was seized, he was forced to surrender. On May 4, 1858, the last of the famous Seminole warriors met the soldiers at Billy's Creek and was sent forever from Florida. Billy Bowlegs and one hundred sixty-three others had been sent west. Sam Jones remained hidden in the Everglades with about two hundred men, women and children.

The Seminole Wars had delayed Florida statehood for thirty years. The Seminole never surrendered, each individual was allowed to decide whether or not to accept a treaty. Now the frontier was ready for settlement and only the Civil War would delay the potential growth of this last frontier. Billy Bowlegs served in the Union Army during the Civil War.

By 1908, the Florida Seminole population was noted to be approximately two hundred seventy-five individuals. Since the Native Americans were no longer a threat, being broke and having very little land of value; the hate, greed and prejudice against them began to dissipate. By an act of Congress in June 1924, all "Native Americans" were given "American" citizenship. The Florida Seminole people were divided into those who lived near Lake Okeechobee, the Cow Creek division and those who lived in the Big Cypress, Everglades and Tamiami Trail, the Cypress division. Approximately two-thirds of the Seminole people were located west of the Mississippi River.

MASSACRE OF THE FRENCH-MATANZAS INLET

In 1565 some 300 French castaways, under Jean Ribault, were massacred here by Spaniards, crushing their attempt to occupy Florida. The French ships, sailing from Fort Caroline to attack St. Augustine, were driven ashore by a storm. At this inlet most of the survivors were put to the knife by Don Pedro Menendez. Hence it was named Matanzas, meaning slaughters.

200 ft. North of Matanzas Inlet Bridge, West side A1A, Summer Haven
SJ45 ~ GPS Coordinates: 29.711017, -81.229767

French Huguenots, lead by Captain Jean Ribaut were dispatched to the New World in the 1560s to establish Protestant settlements to escape religious persecution. Ribaut's expedition traveled the St. Johns River, in search of a location to establish a colony.

Sovereign Philip II of Spain heard rumors of the French intrusion and dispatched his most trusted General Pedro Menendez de Aviles to ward off the invasion. The Spanish Crown had previously claimed *La Florida* and Philip regarded the French as Protestant heretics trespassing on land under the protection of the Catholic Church.

Menendez sailed from Spain in command of eleven ships supported by more than one thousand Spanish soldiers under orders to oust the French from *La Florida*. By the time Menendez reached his destination the Spanish fleet had been reduced to five ships, the remainder was blown off course and feared lost during the crossing. Included in those lost at sea was Menendez own son. The Spanish fleet made land fall on September 4, 1565 but it was several days later on September 8th before the Spaniards actually set foot on the Florida shore.

Meanwhile, Ribaut divided his forces leaving a small number of troops under the leadership of Rene de Goulaine de Laudonniere to construct a garrison dubbed Fort Caroline. Ribaut sailed south with plans to attack the Spanish troops as they landed at St. Augustine. Hurricane winds shredded their canvas sails and reduced the French ships to driftwood. One by one the ships wrecked leaving two hundred gasping French survivors sprawled upon the Florida shore.

While Ribaut and his men fought the forces of nature, Menendez attacked Fort Caroline. The inhabitants of the fortress were butchered without regard. Men, women and children were brutally slain, only a small number of the French Protestants managed to escape the slaughter. As Ribaut struggled to reach what he thought was safety at Fort Caroline, Menendez returned to St. Augustine.

On Friday, September 28, Menendez was awakened by a group of Native Americans gesticulating a message. Through signs Menendez was informed of the shipwrecked Frenchmen. Without delay, the General ordered a scouting expedition of fifty soldiers to evaluate the situation. General Menendez impatiently paced, unable to hold out until the scouting report returned he ordered the remainder of the encampment to travel with him down the river.

General Menendez led the flotilla of small boats men each containing twelve men in each boat, two of which were Timucua guides. The General eventually ordered his troop to abandon their boats and march through the thicket in search of the scouting party. After traveling the entire day and deep into the night, much to the delight of the Spanish soldiers, Menendez located his scouts.

Menendez ordered two Spanish soldiers to advance and find on the French contingent. When the men returned they reported that the French were on the opposite side of the river, Menendez ordered the retrieval of their boats left downstream. The Spanish quietly crept toward the huddled mass of Frenchmen, lying concealed between the sand dunes the Spanish spied on the French camps' activity.

Menendez who was fond of speeches made the following proclamation to his men:

> "I intend to change these [clothes] for those of a sailor, and take a Frenchman with me (one of
> those whom we had brought with us from Spain), and we will go and talk with these Frenchmen.
> Perhaps they are without supplies, and would be glad to surrender without fighting."

Menendez set his plan in motion, quickly summoning a representative of the French encampment. One of the men swam the river toward Menendez, the Frenchman told the sad tale of their shipwreck and distress. The men had not eaten except for what little they were able to gather from the sea for ten days and most were in a sorry state indeed. Menendez sent him back saying that the French crew must surrender and give up their arms. A French sergeant returned expediently with their reply, all would surrender on the condition that their lives should be spared. Menendez refused saying, in part, 'that he could make no promises, that they must surrender unconditionally, and lay down their arms. If he spared their lives, Menendez wanted them to be grateful for it, and if they were put to death, there should be no cause for complaint.'

The sergeant soon returned with the French arms and flags surrendering the French encampment without choice. General Menendez ordered that the entire French contingent be put to the sword. Father Francisco Lopez de Mendoza Grajales, who traveled as religious council with Menendez, pleaded for the lives of any among them that might be Christian. The General agreed and the priest left to investigate.

Captain Jean Ribaut and approximately one hundred fifty of his men were ferried across the river. Of these men only sixteen were spared, four of them professed the Catholic faith and the rest were said to be fifers, drummers and trumpeters. Some two hundred of Ribaut's men escaped into the thick underbrush of the forest to take their chances with the hostile natives known to inhabit the area. One hundred fifty Frenchmen including Captain Jean Ribaut met their death, by Spanish sword, staining red the sand of Anastasia Island. Ribaut was said to have been stabbed in the stomach with a sword, run through the chest with a pike and finally beheaded.

News of the massacre reached France on October 10, 1565. Two years later, in June of 1567, Dominique de Gorgues with the assistance of the Timucuan Indians led by Chief Saturiba avenged the massacre of Ribaut and his men as well as the slaughter of those at Fort Caroline. San Mateo, as Fort Caroline was then known, was viciously raided and reduced to mere rubble. Every Spanish soldier captured was hung. Though the retaliation was complete, Florida remained under Spanish control almost continuously for the next two hundred fifty years.

HASTINGS
POTATO CAPITAL OF FLORIDA

In 1890 Thomas Horace Hastings, a cousin of Henry Flagler, founded the settlement of Hastings. He built the first house and constructed greenhouses to raise early winter vegetables for Flagler's hotels. The post office was established in 1891. Mr. Charles Dupont taught the first school in 1897. Hastings received its town charter in 1909. With the development and irrigation of the clay subsoil land in this area, a new era in Florida agriculture began in the early 1920's. Pioneers in this effort were Messrs. U. J. White, W. H. Erwin, Frank Nix and John T. Dismukes. Modern machinery, fertilization and experiment brought potato growing into the realm of scientific farming. Early select potatoes are shipped from here every spring to markets all over the United States.

Main Street at the Community Building, Hastings
SJ46 ~ GPS Coordinates: 29.711700, -81.508233

In an effort to ensure the patrons of Henry Flagler's Ponce de Leon Hotel had the best of everything, the settlement of Prairie Garden was founded in 1890. Thomas Horace Hastings, Flagler's cousin, built the first home here and constructed greenhouses to cultivate winter vegetables for the elaborate dining tables of cousin Henry's St. Augustine hotels. The plantation consisted of more than fifteen hundred acres of prime real estate. Thomas Hastings requested that the Florida East Coast Railway, which of course Henry Flagler owned, connect the two areas making vegetable delivery a much simpler process.

The first post office was established in 1891 and six years later Mr. Charles Dupont began teaching basic education in a single classroom. The town received its charter in 1909 and was renamed in honor of Thomas Horace Hastings. Unlike the sandy soil of St. Augustine, Hastings' earth was lumped with clay. Pioneers in developing Hastings' rough loam included U. J. White, W. H. Erwin, Frank Nix and John Dismukes all who contributed to the development of irrigation systems allowing the sleepy St. Augustine suburb to make its mark in agricultural industry.

Modernization in machinery, chemical aids in fertilization and insect control has allowed Hastings to achieve the status as the tenth ranked nationally in the production of potatoes. Prime spuds are shipped from the small town all over the United States every spring. Approximately twenty-one thousand acres are devoted to the number one cash crop. In addition to potatoes, cabbage, St. Augustine sweet onions and hot Datil peppers are grown.

A great place to stop in Hastings is Tommy Lee's Bulls-Hit Ranch & Farm. Tommy is a potato farmer made good, his wonderful kettle-fried potato chips called "Bulls Chips," are quickly gaining national notoriety. Continue through town and follow the signs to tour Tommy Lee's potato chip factory. It is there with the help of his son Tater, who grows most of the potatoes used, that more than fifteen hundred pounds of spuds are processed every day. Tommy makes two types of chips: lightly salted and a Minorcan Datil pepper flavor. Stop by the farm Monday through Thursday for a great taste of local flavor.

Because of Tommy and others like him, Hastings has earned the title as "Potato Capital of Florida". Hastings, with a population of just over six hundred, still clings to small town values and integrity, lost in most metropolitan areas. The addition of a four-lane highway, State Road 207, has spurred a growing trend. Yet still the only traffic one contends with are tractors traveling from field to field slowing progress.

Flagler Estates in Hastings has been named the "Fastest Growing Subdivision" in ever expanding St. Johns County. The little city with great potential has much to offer.

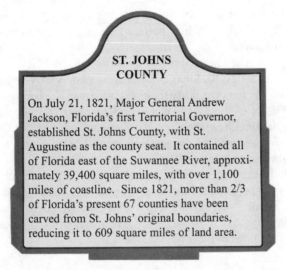

ST. JOHNS COUNTY

On July 21, 1821, Major General Andrew Jackson, Florida's first Territorial Governor, established St. Johns County, with St. Augustine as the county seat. It contained all of Florida east of the Suwannee River, approximately 39,400 square miles, with over 1,100 miles of coastline. Since 1821, more than 2/3 of Florida's present 67 counties have been carved from St. Johns' original boundaries, reducing it to 609 square miles of land area.

SJ1 ~ C.R. 203, in front of Ponte Vedra Inn & Club, Jacksonville Beach

*Note: This marker is duplicated a second time on the reverse side of the marker entitled New Switzerland located at 2159 Mandarin Road at the Volunteer Fire Department, Mandarin ~ SJ3

*Note: This marker is duplicated as Side Two of the Public Market Place marker located at Charlotte & St. George Streets, St. Augustine ~ SJ26

*Note: This marker is duplicated a third time on the reverse side of the marker entitled Old Spanish Quarries located at Anastasia Island State Recreation Area, A1A ~ SJ43

Named for the St. Johns River, the county was established in 1821. President James Monroe enacted a treaty proclaiming Florida part of the United States. The treaty was signed two years earlier in 1819, but was acted on until February 22, 1821. St. Augustine, founded by Pedro Menendez de Aviles in 1565, was to be and remains to this day the county seat.

President Monroe selected Seminole War hero Major General Andrew Jackson as the first Florida governor on March 20, 1821. Jackson reluctantly accepted the position but vowed he would remain governor only long enough to "set up shop." The state was divided into two counties: Escambia and St. Johns. Jackson had the distinction of being the first Florida governor, and was the sixty-seventh governor of the territory. However, Florida's line of governors is the longest in the United States.

The population during this period including approximately a thousand white Americans. This total is deceiving because many African Americans made Florida their home after escaping the bonds of slavery, though they were not counted as "citizens." The native Seminole Indians, eventually pushed into the Everglade swamps during the Second Seminole War, were overlooked in the count as well. The abundance of the white population centered around either St. Augustine or Tallahassee. The central region of Florida was considered, for the most part, uninhabitable swamp frontier. By the mid 1800s, cattlemen slowly began to establish homesteads in central Florida.

Major General Jackson's assignment had been to "collect and communicate" any information relating to Florida and its inhabitants to Congress. On August 4, 1821, after only four months, Governor Jackson sent a letter to President Monroe detailing his work in Florida. He reported that a state government had been established and the many problems facing the infant territory. Three months later Jackson considered his mission complete and resigned as Florida Governor on November 13, 1821.

Today St. Johns County has been pared down to a trim six hundred eight square miles. Bordered by Duval, Clay, Putnam and Flagler counties; St. Johns is lined to the east by fifty-five miles of Atlantic Ocean. The population has swelled to exceed one hundred thirty thousand citizens. The county offers great opportunities in education with the prominent Flagler College, St John's River Community College, First Coast Technical Institute, University of St Augustine For the Health Sciences and the Florida School for the Deaf and Blind.

The largest employers include medical services and ultimately the county's supporting industry, tourism. St. Augustine's vast historical presence attracts millions of visitors each year. Tourist flock to the magnificent Castillo de San Marcos, the whimsical Ripley's Believe It or Not! and the ever popular, St. Augustine's Alligator Farm to name but a few. History is celebrated throughout the year with the Menendez Day Celebration in February; Easter Week Festival, April; "Cross and Sword", June; Spanish Night Watch, June; Days in Spain Fiesta, August; and the Founding of St. Augustine in September. Of course not to be outdone, Hastings ~ St. Augustine's cousin to the west, is the state's leading producer of potatoes.

End Notes

[1] Submarine

[2] Land of Flowers

[3] Also listed as Don Diego Sinoza

4 Pronounced Fashow

5 Supplies required for the building of ships.

6 Tallahassee

7 An enclosed fort of sorts usually situated on long columns and assessable from a portal in the floor.

8 Ten thousand-eight thousand BC

9 Eight thousand to one thousand BC

10 One thousand BC to Nine hundred AD

11 Nine hundred to fifteen forty AD

12 Fifteen forty to the present day

13 St. Johns River

14 Wooden fencing, usually with a spiked top edge.

15 Brick and Clay

16 1763-1783

17 Partners according to one source.

18 Sometimes spelled "Vizente"

19 1849-1850

20 Today known as Morgan State University

21 Author of "The Color Purple" and many other wonderful works.

22 poultry farm

23 National Association for the Advancement of Colored People

24 Southern Christian Leadership Conference

25 African Methodist Episcopal

26 A Minister's home.

27 Begins Side 2 of this historical marker.

28 An interesting side note: Thomas Hastings' grandfather was a well noted songwriter, his most famous work being the Christian hymn *Rock of Ages*.

29 The speaking platform.

30 A rock containing fragments of stone.

31 A cross symbolically red with the Savior's blood.

32 Alice was slowly losing her sanity.

33 Ida Alice was 35 years old.

34 curtains

35 An ornament, usually a rosette, worn as a badge on a hat.

36 Gold colored.

37 A roofed open gallery.

38 rented

39 Having mixed ancestry.

40 Our Lady of Solitude

41 Of Catholocism

42 Formal division or separation from a church or religious body.

43 jurisdiction

44 A gold coin worth at todays equivalent to approximately $3.20

45 a native shell stone found across the bay on Anastasia Island

46 Invalid Corps

47 Veteran's Reserve Corps

48 bedrooms

49 Captain

50 Men in charge of the horses and pack animals.

51 Dense hard wood forest areas.

52 The St. Johns River

53 Term for fugitive slaves in the 17th and 18th century from the West Indies and Guyana or the descendants of such slaves.

54 royal proclamation

55 a material made from silk and mohair

56 Large rodent

57 Salt water crocodile

58 Most of the time listed as Fort Mose.

59 Color signature of the structure.

Flagler County

WASHINGTON OAKS GARDENS

Part of a Spanish land grant to Bautista Don Juan Ferreira in 1815. Developed as a plantation by General Joseph Hernandez, early Florida planter. George Washington, related to our first president, married Hernandez' daughter, Louisa, in 1844. They were given this land by Hernandez and remained here until 1856, developing the plantation and starting an orange grove. Louisa died in 1859, and George left, but returned in 1886, to live here the rest of his life. Purchased in 1936, by Mr. and Mrs. Owen D. Young, the gardens, groves, and plantings were expanded. In 1964, after Mr. Young's death, Mrs. Young gave the property to the State.

Three miles south of Marineland on A1A,
6400 North Oceanshore Blvd, Washington Oaks State Gardens at the Interpretive Center, Flagler
F1 ~ GPS Coordinates: 29.630600, -81.208883

WASHINGTON OAKS STATE GARDENS

Many years before European explorers arrived on the peninsula that is today Florida, Native Americans established sparse nomadic settlements throughout the state. The natives hunted the abundant game, fished in the more than seven thousand lakes and gathered the natural bounty offered from the sea. Mounds of oyster shells and various discards left from everyday form middens[1]. Those same "trash heaps" are integral to Archaeologists studying the way life of these ancient people. Truly one man's trash becoming another's treasure.

During the sixteenth and seventeenth centuries French, Spanish and English profiteers explored the area. The Spanish established a settlement at St. Augustine but few other villages existed outside the city gates. The first documented homestead at what we know today as Washington Oaks Gardens can be attributed to the Lieutenant Governor of East Florida John Moultrie. He gained the property through a British land grant in 1770. Moultrie utilized the vast middens of oyster shells to produce lime in kilns he had developed for that use, Governor Moultrie established the first orange grove on the property. He maintained the plantation until 1793 when a devastating fire destroyed everything within its path. The blaze was said to have been caused by a summer lightning strike.

Shortly after the fire left nothing more than charred remains, a Portuguese born merchant bought the property. He slowly restored the property, rebuilt the buildings and worked with the land to prepare them once again for planting. Rice was planted in the soggy bottomland and corn on the high ground. Unfortunately no record is available that reveals the Portuguese merchants name.

Jose Mariano Hernandez acquired the land through a Spanish land grant in 1818. Hernandez was of Minorcan descent, his family had escaped the brutality of Dr. Andrew Turnbull to arrive in St. Augustine where they thrived. He named the estate Bella Vista.

Only three years after receiving his land grant Florida became a United States territory. Hernandez was faced with a tremendous decision. Would he immigrate to Cuba with other Spanish subjects or remain in Florida? Not only did he choose to remain in Florida but swore allegiance to the new country and changed his name to

Joseph Marion Hernandez to blend in with his adopted land.

Though Bella Vista joined several of Hernandez other properties but it appears that he never developed the plantation as a working farm. Seminole Indians on a rampage in 1836 burned many of plantations along the Matanzas River. All of Hernandez's property with the exception of Bella Vista was destroyed. Bella Vista was not garrisoned by United States troops, therefore of any interest to the Indians. Many plantations along the Matanzas River never fully recovered.

Joseph Hernandez embraced the United States to the extent that he represented St. Augustine in state legislature. He eventually was elected as the first representative of Florida in the United States Congress. Hernandez accepted an appointment as Brigadier General and as such he organized as well as commanded the Florida militia during the Second Seminole War lasting from 1835 until 1842.

General Hernandez and his men were tasked with blazing a trail through east Florida for the purpose of establishing contact with self appointed Seminole Chief Osceola. His meandering path weaves through Brevard County to the Indian River County border. General Thomas Sydney Jessup ordered Hernandez to seize Osceola under a deceptive white flag of truce. On October 25, 1837 the capture was made; Osceola was forced to send messages to chiefs Miconopy, Jumper and Holatoochee, advising their surrender in exchange he would be allowed to contact his family. Osceola's advice was followed and he was allowed this one last contact with his family. Osceola was never allowed his freedom again, until death claimed him in a filthy Charleston prison. It is said his spirit still wanders about the Castillo San Marco where he was first held captive. Osceola appears to be searching for his head, which was paraded in the Charleston streets on a pike.

Joseph Hernandez bequeathed Bella Vista to his daughter Luisa. She married a North Carolina attorney named George Lawrence Washington in 1845. Washington was named for and a relative of President George Washington. Luisa and George lived nearby in St. Augustine, they never actually dwelled at Bella Vista. The property eventually went to one of Luisa's sisters.

It seems that George remembered the area fondly. After the death of his wife he built a small beach house on the property where he and his sons hunted, fished and raised citrus. At first his visits were only seasonal but eventually, in 1888, he purchased the surrounding property and the entire tract came to be known as "Washington Place."

He willed the property to one of his sons, who had very little interest in maintaining it. He sold the land to the developers in 1923. The collapse of Florida's real estate industry was the only thing that saved the plantation from becoming a cookie cutter subdivision called "Hernandez Estates." It seems the real estate collapse was beneficial in this instance.

Louise Powis Clark, a designer from New York, and her third husband, Owen D. Young purchased the plantation in 1936. Owen Young was chairman of the board of General Electric and RCA as well as advising the United States government in issues of international banking.

The couple expanded the gardens and built a summer home. The estate was dubbed "Washington Oaks." They eventually broadened the plantation to include much of the beach front property owned by their neighbors. For several decades their children and grandchildren (all from previous marriages) enjoyed vacationing at Washington Oaks.

Owen Young died in 1962 and anticipating her own mortality, Louise Young decided to donate Washington Oaks to the State of Florida. Louise had one condition, that the garden be maintained in their present state and be added to as funds became available. The Young's home became an interpretive center appropriately called "Young House."

Young House displays information concerning the flora and fauna as well as the history of Washington Oaks. Formal gardens provide a dazzling array of exotic plants from all around the world, most of which are labeled. Trails wander through the gardens featuring native azaleas, camellia and roses. The four hundred-acre park embraces A1A to the Atlantic Ocean. The ocean waves leaves a bevy of sea creatures clinging to the coquina rock strewn about the hard packed sand. Starfish and crab are often seen along the beach as sea birds swoop down to feast on the natural sushi buffet.

South of the gardens, high on a rocky bluff watching over the Matanzas River is the Washington Oaks picnic area. Century old live oaks shrouded with lacy Spanish moss, hickory trees dropping their nutty deposits along the shaded ground and huge magnolias emit a light fragrance as a cool breeze stirs glossy green leaves highlight the area. Florida's state bird, the Mocking bird, can be heard in the distance calling to friends across the way while ring tailed raccoons scurry in the undergrowth away from advancing footsteps. Washington Oaks Gardens is everything Louise Owens could have hoped for and more.

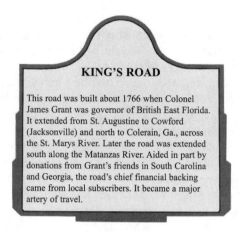

KING'S ROAD

This road was built about 1766 when Colonel James Grant was governor of British East Florida. It extended from St. Augustine to Cowford (Jacksonville) and north to Colerain, Ga., across the St. Marys River. Later the road was extended south along the Matanzas River. Aided in part by donations from Grant's friends in South Carolina and Georgia, the road's chief financial backing came from local subscribers. It became a major artery of travel.

S.R. 100 East of I-95 near Bunnell
F2 ~ GPS Coordinates: 29.475783, -81.182183

When the British acquired Florida their first priority was transportation. Florida was essentially divided into two colonies, East and West. The Apalachicola River was the dividing line between the two. Road transportation between the east and west was virtually non-existent while the only other alternative was sailing around the Florida Keys, which was quite a substantial distance.

Mimicking the thirteen original colonies, the two Floridas had a Governor appointed by the British Crown. James Grant was the governor first appointed. No one did more to supplement the population than Grant, other than perhaps Henry Flagler many years later. The Treaty of Fort Picolata was signed under his administration. This treaty established a boundary between the British and the Seminole. While cataloging the flora and fauna of Florida, botanists John and William Bartram proclaimed the natives peaceful and prosperous under Governor Grant's leadership.

Governor Grant managed to attract great numbers of European and Southern planters to East Florida. East Florida issued just under three million acres of British land grants versus three hundred eighty thousand acres in West Florida. The offer from the London Board of Trade was that any group of settlers willing to establish a village within ten years of issue would be awarded twenty thousand acres. Former British soldiers were given special consideration and southerners were encouraged with the allowance of slavery.

Of course when developing the roadway, like today, funding was a major concern. Governor Grant was given one fund, from which he was obligated to pay his entire staff including a secretary of state, attorney general, surveyor, title registrar, clergyman and two school teachers. If Grant was careful his staff could also fund a coroner, jailer, court clerk and several Indian agents. Miscellaneous requests for additional funds required six months for approval.

As the poorer classes of white Georgians and Carolinians crept across the East Florida border, stealing away livestock and slaves, the Spanish often cursed them with a word that sounded much like "Quaqueros." During the American Revolution, Governor Grant referred to the same thieves and border jumpers along the Kings Road as "Crackers."

Of course history can and does change over time with repeated story sometimes old folk tales are taken as fact. Sometimes fiction is accepted as factual events. These same "Crackers" were said to have come from Georgians driving stolen cattle cracking their leather whips. The British had Crackers long before the whip was ever used; in fact most Cracker settlers were too poor to own enough cattle to drive. Crackers never "cracked" a whip at all, rather the whip was "popped." Therefore, the origin of the title "cracker" is resolved.

End Notes

1 Native American trash heads, though sometimes middens were also sacred burial grounds.

Volusia County

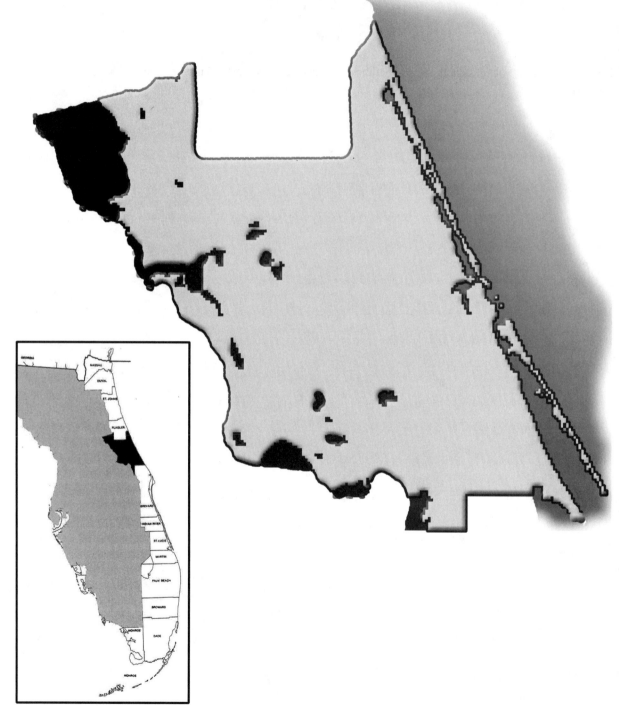

ORMOND TOMB

Near this site lies the tomb of James Ormond II. Ormond and his father, a Scot who immigrated to Florida via the Bahamas about 1804, made "Damietta," the family plantation, one of the most productive in the Halifax region. When Florida became a U.S. territory, Ormond became prominent in civil affairs, and during the Seminole War of 1836, commanded a platoon of the "Mosquito Roarers" at the Battle of Dunlawton. Ormond Beach was named for his family.

North of Tomoka State Park on S.R. 5A (Old Dixie Highway), Ormond Beach
V1 ~ GPS Coordinates: 29.385567, -81.131667

The Scottish trading firm, Panton, Leslie & Company employed Captain James Ormond. They were the first trading company to be established in Florida. Ormond ran an "Armed Brig" called *Somerset*, sailing from Savannah to Apalachicola and into the West Indies on trading expeditions for Panton, Leslie and Company. After retiring from the sea, he purchased a sugar plantation in the Bahamas called Exuma.

In 1783, England signed a treaty returning ownership of Florida to Spain. In order to encourage settlers to relocate to Florida, Spain offered vast land grants. Captain Ormond sold his Bahamian plantation and sailed to Florida. Like British plantation owners, Ormond was granted property in the Volusia County area around 1790. The first plantation was located in the New Smyrna area known as Spruce Creek. The other property, a two thousand-acre plantation Ormond named Damietta just south of Bulowville near the Halifax River.

James Ormond and his wife, Russell Walker were born in Scotland but left their home to establish a life in the new world. Captain James Ormond was shot and killed while walking with his son Emanuel in 1817. The assailant was an escaped slave, who thought Ormond was about to return him to his bonds. Ormond and eventually his wife, Russell, were laid to rest on their Spruce Creek plantation at Nordman's Point. Unwilling to remain in America alone, Russell returned to a son she had left in Scotland, James Ormond II.

James Ormond II was a junior partner in an ill-fated trading company. By this time his mother and brother, Emanuel had returned from America to add to his responsibility. When the trading company failed, Ormond II fled to the American plantation of his dead father in an attempt to avoid debtor's prison. After settling in, Ormond II sent for his wife Isabella and four children, Agnes, Russell, Helen and James III, in 1824. James Ormond II died in 1829 and was buried on the Damietta Plantation. His epitaph reads, "An Honest Man." After Ormond II's death the plantation was never the same. One last cotton crop was planted and harvested before Ormond Plantation was left to nature. Eventually Mother Nature reclaimed the land and the plantation was left to ruin. The plantation slaves were sold to the highest bidder, Cruger and Depeyster of New Smyrna to work sugar cane.

Unfortunately for James Ormond III his beautiful mother was a nervous sort. Isabella was said to have had captivating grey eyes, however when she suffered her bouts of anxiety she was unable to care for herself, much less her children. James III was often sent to live at the Bulow plantation when he was home from school in St. Augustine. The young man learned much about plantation management and life at the feet of John Bulow. While in the Bulow home, James III penned many an antidote concerning John Bulow's wild bachelor ways. Even though he was often estranged from his mother, he always described her as a talented musician and accomplished artist.

James III went off to join old friend Douglas Dummett in the Second Seminole War. Fighting the Native

Americans was most probably a conflicting emotion for James III; the settlers at Bulowville were friendly with chiefs King Philip, Billy Bowlegs and Coacoochee. The Ormond Family moved to Charleston, South Carolina in 1832.

The Ormond Plantation, Samuel H. Williams purchased Damietta after the Ormond's left for Charleston. He established Orange Groves throughout the grounds. By 1849, Williams was unable to pay the taxes and two-thirds of the plantation was sold at auction.

New Britain was renamed in 1890 in honor of the Ormond family. In 1950, both the mainland and peninsula side of Ormond became Ormond Beach. James Ormond II's tomb was badly vandalized and later restored by Maud Van Woy. The site was donated to the Park Service in 1945.

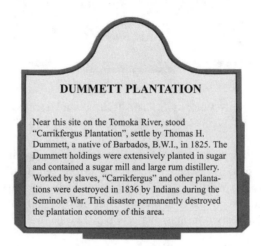

DUMMETT PLANTATION

Near this site on the Tomoka River, stood "Carrikfergus Plantation", settle by Thomas H. Dummett, a native of Barbados, B.W.I., in 1825. The Dummett holdings were extensively planted in sugar and contained a sugar mill and large rum distillery. Worked by slaves, "Carrikfergus" and other plantations were destroyed in 1836 by Indians during the Seminole War. This disaster permanently destroyed the plantation economy of this area.

Old Dixie Highway, south of Ormond's Tomb on the East Side of the road, Ormond Beach
V2 ~ GPS Coordinates: 29.354843, -81.106787

Originally the property that would eventually become known as Dummett Plantation was owned by a Brit, John Moultrie and called "Rosetta". Moultrie was Lieutenant Governor of Florida during part of the British period from 1771-1774. Though Moultrie never lived there, a plantation manor, outbuildings, barns and slave quarters were completed by 1777. John Moultrie had a manager run the entire place, which produced primarily, rice and indigo though corn, sugar cane and garden plants were also grown.

When Spain once again claimed the Florida territory Moultrie abandoned Rosetta and by virtue of a Spanish Land Grant John Bunch became the owner in 1804. In 1824 Bunch sold the property with all buildings plus two thousand, one hundred seventy-five acres of land and ninety slaves to Thomas Dummett. Thus the plantation became known as Dummett Plantation.

An officer of the British Marines, Thomas Henry Dummett purchased Rosetta with the intended purpose of producing sugar. Dummett left Barbados in the face of civil war to live briefly in northern Connecticut before eventually settling in Florida. His first several attempts failed miserably and he sent for a West Indies plantation manager to assist him with the production of sugar cane. Soon the large blades of sugar cane stalks began to flourish and entrepreneur Dummett built the first steam operated mill and rum distillery in the area.

Anna Dummett, Thomas' daughter, recalled the big log house with its thatched palmetto roof surrounded by acres of brilliant green Bermuda grass and majestic live oaks shrouded in Spanish moss in her diaries. She often told a story of accidentally falling into a cistern filled with molasses as a child as well as teaching many of the slave children to read.

Dummett's relationship with the Seminole was a good one and many worked the cane fields during the season. In fact Seminole leader Billy Bowlegs was considered a friend and as the government advanced on plans to remove the Native Americans from south Florida the two discussed the impending fight. Billy Bowlegs stated:

> "We (the Seminole) compare ourselves to a beautiful flower ...growing in poor soil. If that flower is transplanted...it will die."

In 1836, United States Army soldiers marched in and set up a defensive line in the Dummett Plantation sugar factory and kitchen of the plantation house. A cannon named "McDuffie" was placed on the roof and targeted enemy approaching from most directions. As solders ventured out in the dew of one early morning to collect firewood and sugar cane for early morning coffee, the Seminole ambushed the detachment. An attack on the makeshift fortification ensued, several soldiers were killed or injured, the Seminole retreated into the darkness of the forest to regroup but soon returned in force. After three days of unending battle the soldiers received word to retreat, the wounded were left behind in a quickly built wooden stockade. Imagine how these wounded soldiers must have felt knowing the fierce Seminole were about and having little or no way of defending themselves. They were rescued within the week, but it must have been a harrowing week for these men.

When the Seminole attacked no quarter was given even in view of their relationship with Dummett. All standing buildings with the exception of the slave quarters were left in smoldering ruins. It was a Seminole custom to leave the slave shelters untouched. When the attack was over Dummett Plantation was abandoned for the last time.

Thomas Dummett sold part of the plantation to a family named Addison who in turned sold the parcel to two brothers named Macrae. The Macrae sugar mill ruins are quite extensive and the fortified kitchen remains to this day, unfortunately it is misidentified on most maps as the "Addison Blockhouse." By the time the Seminole attacks occurred and the Macraes were forced to abandon their property, the Addison family was no longer alive. The Macrae site was partially rebuilt during the 1920s land boom but has long since been left to decay. The "Addison Blockhouse" and Macrae sugar mill ruins are restricted from the public.

All that remains today of Dummett Plantation are skeletons of the old sugar works and rum distillery. Today the area is called Bulow Creek State Park and is two miles north of the more popular Tomoka State Park. The area is opened to the public though it has no facilities.

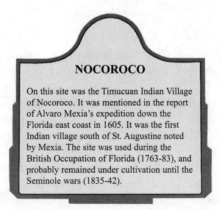

NOCOROCO

On this site was the Timucuan Indian Village of Nocoroco. It was mentioned in the report of Alvaro Mexia's expedition down the Florida east coast in 1605. It was the first Indian village south of St. Augustine noted by Mexia. The site was used during the British Occupation of Florida (1763-83), and probably remained under cultivation until the Seminole wars (1835-42).

Tomoka State Park, Ormond Beach
V3 ~ GPS Coordinates: 29.354250, -81.090000

Very near the convergence of the Tomoka and Halifax Rivers is the Tomoka Stone site. Shards of four thousand-year-old pottery as well as burial and trash middens that are even older have been located at the site. The Tomoka site is not open to public viewing, however Strickland Mound complex is a most interesting prehistoric site.

The Tomoka sites' lower level is underwater. However, archaeological data indicates that this site was once a year round encampment. The site was an excellent location for a settlement with an abundance of wild life as a food source, rich lagoons and an eastern barrier island providing a break for tropical storms.

It was here that the Timucua Indians made their home long before Europeans set foot on Florida soil. Spaniard Alvaro Mexia was the first to document the Timucua village located here known as Nocoroco. This village was perhaps the last Timucua settlement in existence. It was here that these noble people went about their daily living beneath the shade of ancient oaks draped in lacy Spanish moss blowing silently in the breeze. Their day to day living has been meticulously documented through the numerous middens found and excavated.

Richard Oswald purchased much of this site in 1763. Oswald, a British subject established a plantation here and clear-cut the land in order to produce indigo, rice and sugar cane. Though eventually nature reclaimed the land, wildlife returned and the forest began renewal. Unfortunately, the Timucua were lost forever.

Today the site is part of Tomoka State Park where a small museum is situated near a well-traveled trail. The works of Fred Dana Marsh are featured throughout the museum. The stone-faced Timucua Chief Ocalis greets visitors and the Fragile Little Cactus Girl offers a glimpse of how a Timucua maiden might have appeared.

Approximately sixty thousand visitors trek through Tomoka State Park each year. The park has much to offer including camping, canoeing, fishing, boating, picnicking and nature trails. The wonderful history combined with family recreation is available year round from 8:00 a.m. until sunset. A small entrance fee is charged.

OLD KINGS ROAD

The Old Kings Road crossed north to south near this site. First improved by the Spanish, and then constructed by the British as a road in 1763-1773 to connect St. Augustine and New Smyrna, Florida. Improved by the United States Army in 1827.

North Old Kings Road and Highway 40, Ormond Beach
V4 ~ GPS Coordinates: 29.279100, -81.080517

The Spanish began what we know today as the Old Kings Road, in 1632 when it was known simply as King's Way. The British realized when they came to power in St. Augustine a reliable road system was most important for moving plantation goods to the harbor, fostering the economy and moving militia. The road extended in a straight line directly from the St. Marys River to St. Augustine.

When Dr. Andrew Turnbull established his multi-cultural society at New Smyrna, he convinced the British Governor to extend the road southward. Turnbull volunteered his indentured servants as labor to widen the road to a full thirty feet through a tangle of dense forest. Unfortunately their efforts met with some roadblocks, so to speak.

British Engineers managed to map the road as far as what is known today as Flagler County, during that time it was known as Matanzas Swamp. The name was pretty self-explanatory. They had built bridges and causeways but could not ford Matanzas Swamp in order to extend King's Way to New Smyrna. The straight line down the Atlantic coastline was impossible from this point forward.

The British Governor was not easily deterred, he consulted a Native American by the name of Grey Eyes. The Indian was convinced he could map out the road. Grey Eyes followed the trails worn into the wooded swamp by game animals, he followed the ridges and curved his way through the swamp. King's Road was straight no longer but it did extended toward the intended destination of New Smyrna.

Even today the Old King's Road is still under construction. A half-mile section was recently added to connect the Matanzas Woods Parkway extension for the Interstate 95 overpass. Amazingly enough this small section was achieved at a cost of half a million dollars, more than the entire road cost from the beginning.

HOTEL ORMOND

Hotel Ormond, named for Volusia County pioneer James Ormond, was built in 1887 by John Anderson and Joseph Price. The large frame building was bought and enlarged by Henry M. Flagler in the 1890's. Operated by Flagler's Florida East Coast Railway, it was one of the first Flagler hotels in Florida. After 1890, the hotel and adjoining Ormond Beach Golf Club became major Florida tourist centers. John D. Rockefeller, a nearby resident, was a patron of both.

Corner of east Granada & John Anderson in park across from hotel, Ormond Beach
V5 ~ GPS Coordinates: 29.289367, -81.048100

John Anderson of Maine and Joseph D. Price of Kentucky began construction on a hotel in 1875 a few miles from Daytona on the Halifax River. Stephen V. White, owner of the St. Johns and Halifax River Railway and well-known Wall Street mogul, invested financially in the venture. It was White's financial assistance that made the hotel possible. The area was known as New Britain, it would be this hotel that put the city on the map, but not during the time of White's principal ownership. A local boy, fourteen years old George Penfield designed the entire first floor of the expansive wood frame hotel. Initially the managers were Dr. S. E. Churchill and his brother.

Henry M. Flagler purchased White's share of the failing venture in 1890, though both Anderson and Price maintained their interest, they assumed a managerial role in the hotel. New Britain became Ormond Beach, named for the Ormond Family. With his Midas touch, Flagler later purchased the entire hotel for one hundred twelve thousand dollars and revamped the entire operation. The location of the hotel was its greatest asset, so with that working in its favor Flagler went to work. The plain white-framed hotel became a spectacle to see in bright yellow with green trim. Flagler immediately doubled the room capacity from seventy-five to one hundred fifty rooms, ten years later Flagler would double the capacity once again. He added a casino, swimming pool, dormitory, laundry, beach pavilion, river pier and three elevators. The hotel grew to include eleven miles of corridors and over three hundred eighty rooms. The Ormond Hotel was listed as the largest wooden building in America in the early 1900s.

The landscaping was completely reshaped; the country look was replaced with a tropical ambiance. Although Flagler did not play golf, he saw the blossoming popularity of the sport and installed an eighteen-hole course on the grounds of the Ormond Beach Hotel. Flagler later bought out Anderson and Price's interest, however they remained managers until their deaths in 1911.

The Ormond Hotel attracted the social elite. R. E. Olds and Alexander Winston visited during the winter season of 1902. During their stay each participated in an automobile race across the hard packed white sand of Daytona Beach. The contest ended in a tie; the winning speed was a blinding fifty-seven miles per hour. One year later, Winston managed to be victorious at a world record sixty-eight miles per hour in their now yearly event. Of course these names are familiar in racing circles as Oldsmobile and the Winston Cup.

As a result of the newly established races across Daytona Beach, the Florida East Coast Automobile Association was founded. These activities fostered mechanical advancements in the automobile engine. To this day sections of Daytona Beach are still open to automobile traffic. Daytona is quite possibly the automobile racing capital of the world.

Because of the popularity of the area Henry Flagler extended his railway into the Daytona area. The railroad bridge was eventually remodeled so that wealthy hotel guests could actually bring their Pullman cars to the hotel's west entrance. As automobile racing gained acceptance, Flagler lowered the rates for hauling cars to Ormond.

Flagler business associate in Standard Oil, John D. Rockefeller spent several seasons at the Ormond Hotel. He obviously liked the area so much that he built his winter home, The Casements across the street. Local residents knew Rockefeller only as "Neighbor John". Every Sunday while in residence at the Casements he would attend the Ormond Union Church and after the services he would stand on the front lawn handing out bright new shiny dimes to all the children in attendance. Each child was told that saving their dimes would lead their way to fortune. Before boarding his private rail car at the end of each season, Rockefeller discretely gave the pastor of the Ormond Union Church an envelope. The envelope held the pastor's yearly salary and enough money to handle all the church expenses for that year as well.

Unlike Flagler, Rockefeller found great joy in the Ormond Hotel golf course. One well-known golfing partner, humorist Will Rogers, said upon losing one match, "I'm glad you beat me, John. The last time you were beaten, I noticed the price of gasoline went up two cents a gallon." John D. Rockefeller spent the last few years of his life at his beloved estate in Ormond Beach, the Casements. On May 23, 1937, at the age of ninety-eight, he passed away.

The hotel experienced financial difficulties again in the 1930s and 1940s. After Flagler's death the Ormond Hotel struggled to remain open under a series of several different owners. Competition was fierce as newer more modern hotels were built. Several other businesses within the confines of the hotel included a nightclub, a hotel management school and a retirement home for missionaries and ministers. Thomas J. Wetherell and T. T. Cobb purchased the hotel in 1957. Granada Avenue expanded in 1968 to four lanes necessitating the removal of twenty-four hotel rooms.

The hotel was listed on the National Register of Historic Places on November 24, 1980. The Ormond Hotel, a once regal Florida landmark, closed its doors for the last time on October 16, 1986 when it was decided that the wooden hotel was both a fire and safety hazard. In the Spring of 1987 the furniture was put up for auction, netting one hundred fifteen thousand dollars. The hotel was sold and demolished a decade later.

Today the Ormond Heritage condominium occupies the site long held by the Ormond Hotel. In recognition, a room has been established in honor of the hotel's contribution to the community. Flagler said of Ormond Beach, in part, "…you will see the Ormond Beach, return thanks to the Maker thereof, and refuse to use the rest of your railway ticket…" Today, the same is true.

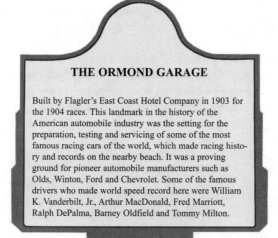

THE ORMOND GARAGE

Built by Flagler's East Coast Hotel Company in 1903 for the 1904 races. This landmark in the history of the American automobile industry was the setting for the preparation, testing and servicing of some of the most famous racing cars of the world, which made racing history and records on the nearby beach. It was a proving ground for pioneer automobile manufacturers such as Olds, Winton, Ford and Chevrolet. Some of the famous drivers who made world speed record here were William K. Vanderbilt, Jr., Arthur MacDonald, Fred Marriott, Ralph DePalma, Barney Oldfield and Tommy Milton.

113 East Granada at Sun Trust Bank, Ormond Beach
V6 ~ GPS Coordinates: 29.290267, -81.044183

James F. Hathaway was a retired businessman vacationing at the Ormond Hotel in 1902, when he noticed that bicycle tires left little or no impression in the hard packed sand of Ormond Beach. The automobile was readily gaining popularity and Hathaway distributed promotional materials to direct attention to his discovery. William J. Morgan, correspondent of Automobile Magazine, picked up the information. Ormond Beach would be the ideal place to hold automobile races.

Ormond Hotel managers, Price and Anderson, were always anxious to explore ways to lure patrons to their establishment. They asked Morgan to help stage an annual event encouraging the elite of the automaking industry to participate. Barney Oldfield, Alexander Winston, William K. Vanderbilt and Ransom E. Olds were all ready to accept the challenge and race at break neck speeds of more than fifty miles per hour along the sugar sand beach packed to a hard crust.

Within one month of Morgan's arrival in February 1903, the first time trails were held. The Daytona and Seabreeze Automobile Association was quickly formed and race time was set. The turn out was small but considering that the entire event was planned and executed in less than thirty days, the fact that it happened at all was amazing. Alexander Winston drove a racecar dubbed "Bullet Number 1" and in a separate class H. T. Thomas drove "Pirate" for Ransom E. Olds. Two days later in the First Annual Ormond Challenge Cup, the two men met on the sand. The race was very close, but in the end by one-fifth of second Bullet took the checkered flag. Ormond Beach became the "Birthplace of Speed" on March 26, 1903 on the hard packed sands of the beach.

A facility had to be constructed so that mechanics could make repairs and automobiles were stored. The Ormond Garage was built between the hotel and beach with enough room for one hundred cars. The garage was nicknamed "Gasoline Alley", America's first of many. The Florida East Coast Automobile Association built a clubhouse at the Silver Beach approach. The course was extended to Ponce Inlet then returning to Ormond Beach. Millionaires flocked to the races, William K. Vanderbilt, Jr. and Henry Ford were both frequently seen. Vanderbilt's Mercedes broke the first world speed record at a blinding 92.30 miles per hour.

The wealthy hired mechanics to do the greasy work and by 1906 the barracks had been built to house the men who were only allowed to use the back entrance of the Ormond Hotel. Fred Marriott drove a Stanley Steamer 127.66 miles per hour that year. In 1907, Glenn H. Curtiss set a speed on the Ormond Beach track of 136.3, however Curtiss was driving a motorcycle. It was reported that Curtiss often slept alongside his bike at the Ormond Garage.

Management decided that they no longer wanted repairs conducted at the Ormond Garage. A mechanic,

Robert E. Lowe, resolved the issue in 1919 by building a facility down the street from the original. The facility was also known as Ormond Garage. Today the facility houses an impressive collection of early racing memorabilia. Many wealthy men including Henry Ford, Louis Chevrolet and Ralph DePalma; sweated alongside mechanics in the new Ormond Garage.

Sir Malcolm Campbell drove his "Bluebird," an amazing two hundred seventy-six miles per hour in 1935. By 1940, automobiles were too powerful to be raced on beach. Bill France completed construction of the Daytona International Speedway in 1957. The Ormond Garage was reduced to a charred heap of molten metal on January 7, 1976. Ironically, the Fire Marshall determined that the blaze was due to stored gasoline that was ignited by an electrical spark.

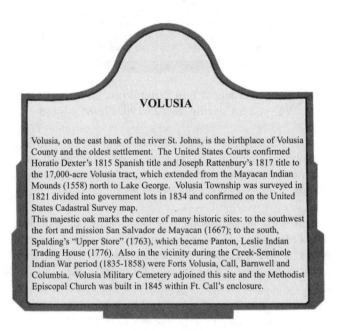

VOLUSIA

Volusia, on the east bank of the river St. Johns, is the birthplace of Volusia County and the oldest settlement. The United States Courts confirmed Horatio Dexter's 1815 Spanish title and Joseph Rattenbury's 1817 title to the 17,000-acre Volusia tract, which extended from the Mayacan Indian Mounds (1558) north to Lake George. Volusia Township was surveyed in 1821 divided into government lots in 1834 and confirmed on the United States Cadastral Survey map.

This majestic oak marks the center of many historic sites: to the southwest the fort and mission San Salvador de Mayacan (1667); to the south, Spalding's "Upper Store" (1763), which became Panton, Leslie Indian Trading House (1776). Also in the vicinity during the Creek-Seminole Indian War period (1835-1858) were Forts Volusia, Call, Barnwell and Columbia. Volusia Military Cemetery adjoined this site and the Methodist Episcopal Church was built in 1845 within Ft. Call's enclosure.

On east bank of St. Johns River, SR 40, Astor
V7 ~ GPS Coordinates: 29.168817, -81.520900

James Spalding, partnered with Roger Kelsell, saw the need for an inland trading post along the St. Johns River. In 1763, two businesses were established one called the "Upper Store" located at Astor, the other "Lower Store" was just south of Palatka. The site for store located at the community of Astor was chosen because three Indian trails intersected at that point. The location was a much-used canoe launching area for hunting and fishing parties. Governor Grant promised to assist in the establishment of a settlement at the site, an oath he failed to keep. But the fledgling community slowly came to be without Grant's assistance.

Indians raided the Astor trading post in 1774. Spalding was forced to retreat with his family to Shell Isle. Once it was safe to return James Spalding was intent on closing the store for the safety of his family. The Indian chief vowed to pay restitution for all damages in order to keep the trading post open. Spalding responded by selling the store to well known traders Panton and Leslie then leaving the area. Mr. Forbes purchased the store from Panton and Leslie until he abandoned the area because of Seminole uprisings. Eventually Fort Butler was built on the site to deal with the persistent Indian attacks. The crude wooden stockade and barracks was hastily built overlooking the river and during the next year a post office was established there. In 1843, after only five years the fort was abandoned due to rampant disease.

Governor Kindelan issued a land grant to George Petty on Lake George in 1815. Six years later the plantation known as Mount Royal was sold to noted settler Horatio S. Dexter and his wife, Abby. The transaction took place on May 21, 1821 and amounted to two hundred fifty dollars. Later when Florida became a United States territory, the Dexter grant was well enough documented that Horatio and Abby were able to maintain their homesite.

Barney Dillard moved with his extensive family consisting of wife and fifteen children to Astor in 1868. He discovered the remains of an early Spanish mission on the east side of the St. Johns River. The mission was believed to be the San Salvador de Mayaca built in 1657. Eventually a fort was also constructed in the same vicinity known as Antonio de Anacape built in 1680. Dillard also mapped the trails left by Spanish explorers connecting St. Augustine to Pensacola. Barney Dillard was said to have shared a number of his stories with noted author Marjorie Kinnan Rawlings. She used some of his accountings for the basis of her book, "The Yearling".

Determined to be fair, Dillard had his children draw lots to decide which plots of land they would inherit upon his demise. His daughter, Lillian Dillard Gibson utilized her inheritance to establish not only a homesite for herself but also the Volusia Museum. The Museum housed artifacts retrieved from local Indian mounds, historic documents, photographs and memorabilia of life along the St. Johns River.

In 1926, the first bridge crossing the St. Johns River was built. The construction was in fact a covered drawbridge with a tender house on the west riverbank. McQueen Johnson was given the job as the first bridge tender, opening and closing the bridge as needed twenty-four hours a day. His former position had been as ferry operator crossing the St. Johns River, once the bridge was complete the ferry was abolished but a new position was created tending the bridge and Johnson was hired.

Late one evening while Johnson went about his duties illuminated by only the light of the moon, a shot range out. When the smoke cleared McQueen Johnson lay dead, shot in back. He died where he fell in the very middle of the bridge. His head lay in Lake County and the remainder of his body was in Volusia County. A motive was never discovered but each county refused to claim jurisdiction. The vicious murder was never investigated, therefore never solved. To anyone looking for intriguing subject for a book, this true-life story is waiting to be told. The new bridge crossing the St. Johns was built in 1978, the bridge house was moved to the site in 1980.

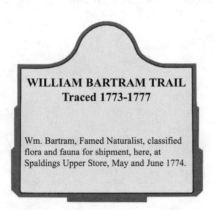

WILLIAM BARTRAM TRAIL
Traced 1773-1777

Wm. Bartram, Famed Naturalist, classified flora and fauna for shipment, here, at Spaldings Upper Store, May and June 1774.

On east bank of St. Johns River, SR 40, Astor
V7 ~ GPS Coordinates: 29.168817, -81.520900

When William Bartram first visited the Astor area in 1765 he was a young boy tagging alongside his father, renowned English Royal Botanist John Bartram. The duo spent several weeks in the area studying the flora and fauna using Spalding's Upper Store as their base of operations.

By the time of Bartram's lone exploration very few Native Americans actually remained in the area but there were sightings from time to time. Settlers were encroaching along the St. Johns River and the population began to develop in the area very slowly. James Spalding established his trading post some two years before the

Bartram father and son visited. The prime location was listed as being on the west side of the river above Lake George where Astor is located today. The area left such an impression on young William that he was to return nine years later in 1774 and remain in Florida just over a year.

Bartram explored the area known then as Indian country. The Seminoles struggled to establish villages and maintain life giving up hunting grounds as colonists pushed them further and further into the wilderness Everglades swamp. William Bartram was particularly amazed at the natural springs in the area, saying,

> "(it appears) . . . that you may without the least difficulty touch any one of the fish, or put your finger upon a crocodile's eye, when it is really twenty or thirty feet underwater."

It was during the visit of 1773-1774, that Bartram saw for the first time a Royal Palm amidst the pine forests and was enthralled by semi-tropical surroundings. Later, especially during the Reconstruction Era after the Civil War, people of all races sought what was thought to be the healing properties of central Florida springs. The area also attracted northerners intent on escaping brutal winters for the balmy climate and dreamed of making a fortune in the citrus industry. Most were very disappointed in this endeavor, citrus farming at best was an extremely risky venture and at worst could destroy an entire life savings with one fateful arctic blast.

William Bartram's observations of the area are extremely detailed and sometimes quite entertaining. His work remains one of the most complete, though not altogether accurate some poetic license was taken, details of Florida's appearance during his exploration. Bartram's work is still used as a reference today in many circles. He did catalogue some fascinating events including a battle between monstrous alligators that reminds one of the pre-historic dinosaurs.

In his book entitled "Travels," Bartram devotes seventy-two pages when describing the Volusia County area. His colorful wording illustrates Bartram's vision much better than I could hope to:

> "This blessed land where the gods have amassed into one heap all the flowering plants, birds, fish and other wildlife of two continents in order to turn the rushing streams, the silent lake shores and the awe-abiding woodlands of this mysterious land into a true garden of Eden."

ST. MARY'S EPISCOPAL

The Florida frontier remained relatively empty until after the Civil War. During the late 1860s, both northerners and native southerners perceived great potential in Florida. Among the places they settled was Tomoka, which became Daytona in 1871. Daytona settlers remained unchurched until various Protestant denominations established the Mission circuits so typical of frontier America. One early mission was St. Mark's begun in 1877. The parishioners of St. Mark's early felt the need for permanence and began planning a church building in the late seventies. Their efforts were crowned with success with the completion of St. Mary's, a Gothic Revival structure with board-and-batten exterior sheathing. St. Mary's has remained on its original site, growing with the community it serves. The structure has been enlarged several times to accommodate the expanding parish; however, the original St. Mary's remains the core of the present building, a visible reminder of Daytona's earliest years.

U.S. Highway 1 at Orange and Ridgewood Avenue, Daytona Beach
V8 ~ GPS Coordinates: 29.207267, -81.020967

Forty years after the Second Seminole Indian War, settlers began arriving in what was then known as the Halifax area. People came for the wonderful weather, because doctors advised the clean salt air for renewed health and many sought the frontier to begin a new life. When Bishop John Freeman Young first held serves at the Colony House, later called the Palmetto House, in 1871 the entire settlement attended.

The Reverend William H. Carter received the call to minister to the settlers from New Britain to Rockledge. New Britain later became Ormond Beach. Halifax became Daytona and the population grew to seventy settlers. Dr. Carter was in poor health and like others, this made his decision to accept the call to East Florida quite simple. He was required to travel the intracoastal waterway in a small sailboat stocked with a few prayer books and hymnals. Frequently his books were soaked through during times of rough intracoastal waterways. Constantly the good reverend was forced to retrieve his soggy gospels and lay them in the sun to dry for the next service.

Dr. Carter arrived at St. Mark's Mission in Daytona on May 20, 1877. That very day Carter held his first service at 220 South Palmetto Avenue, which was a white-framed schoolhouse, later that afternoon he led a second service. The quaint little schoolhouse was known as the Palmetto House. But the services varied in location sometimes William Jackson offered his store or Laurence Thompson would do the same. The ladies of the congregation prepared the altar with flowers from their gardens and the Huston family donated a silver cup and pitcher for offering communion.

When Dr. Carter was away serving the other ten settlements of his traveling ministry, Reverend Henry B. Stuart-Martin offered services in Daytona. By the end of the first year Bishop Young reported a windfall of two hundred dollars in the collection plate, eight burials, three marriages and three baptisms. By this time all services in Daytona were being held in the attic space above Laurence Thompson's store on South Beach Street.

April 25, 1883 was designated as St. Mark's Day in Daytona. To mark the occasion it was decided that this would be the day that the cornerstone for their new church building would be laid. While preparations continued and excitement swelled for the ceremony a marble block was ordered from a northern state to read "St. Mark's" and date for the much anticipated cornerstone. Finally the cornerstone arrived by boat, the heavy crate was unloaded and a crowd began to gather with great ceremony the wooden box was opened. As the straw was drawn away from the marble block, engraved on the stone were the words "St. Mary's". Even though the site was the oldest recorded mission in the entire area named St. Marks, from that day forward the church would be known as St. Mary's.

Built using board and batten sheathing by William and Tom Wetherell in a cruciform shape using the

ST. MARY'S EPISCOPAL CHURCH

Gothic design. Mirroring the growth of Daytona, St. Marys was enlarged periodically over the years. Reverend and Mrs. Palmer donated a copper bell for the church steeple in 1938. But perhaps the most dramatic change came in 1975 when stained glass windows were commissioned to enhance the beauty of the church.

Willet Stained Glass Studios of Philadelphia, Pennsylvania provided more than thirty of the wonderful visual effects. The studio also produced the chancel windows, which were installed in November 1984. Illuminated using artificial lighting along the east wall bringing back to the church a sense of its original appearance. One window represents the virgin mother, St. Mary. The figure is young and grieving, above her head are seven swords reflecting the scripture Luke 2:35, "Yea, a sword shall pierce thine own soul also." A white lily symbolizing purity adorns the glass as well.

It is said that during a time when the vast amount of working class people were unable to read, stained glass windows with their symbols, colors and pictures offered a picture book of sorts relating stories of God and his church. Even today the windows still offer inspiration to all that gaze upon them. The Memorial Garden was established in 1987. Offering a haven for peaceful reflection and prayer, the garden is embraced by a forty-foot half moon wall supporting a statue of St. Mary watching over those seeking serenity.

Today St. Marys Episcopal Church hosts an active congregation. On any given Sunday attendance averages two hundred twenty-five parishioners. Traditional values hand in hand with today's youth and enthusiasm offering modern ministries providing something for everyone in this church immersed in Florida history.

BLUE STAR
MEMORIAL HIGHWAY

A tribute to the Armed Forces
that have defended the United
States of America.

U.S. 1 & Hepburn Street, Daytona
V9 ~ GPS Coordinates: 29.194717, -81.014233

It was hurricane season, September of 1999. Hurricane Floyd was threatening the East Coast of Florida and citizens were advised to evacuate inland. The Navy ordered most vessels into safe waters to wait out storm, but the *USS John F. Kennedy* isn't just another Navy vessel and her crew was ready for duty.

United States Navy Aircraft Carrier *Kennedy* took a distress call from the *Gulf Majesty,* which was sinking. Their location was three hundred miles east of Daytona, also very near the eye of Hurricane Floyd. After it was determined that no other ship capable of withstanding the massive surf was in the area, the *Kennedy* turned and headed into the fury of the storm without hesitation.

They used modern technology to track an electronic signal marking the troubled craft. The *Kennedy* traveled at full speed into winds in excess of one hundred miles per hour. Waves crashed over the flight deck, which rises full sixty feet above the ocean surface. The floundering survivors looked like oranges floating in a churning washing machine. Without a thought to his own safety, Petty Officer 3rd Class Shad Hernandez leapt into the storm tossed sea to pull the survivors into a hovering helicopter fighting against the wind. Hernandez was attempting his first rescue. He succeeded with courage and professionalism.

The entire rescue, upon arrival, took an amazing eleven minutes. Relief flooded over the crew when Hernandez rode the hoist up with the final man. Unfortunately they were soon to learn that five other people were struggling to stay alive in the tumultuous surf. The first helicopter was low on fuel so a second took the call.

Once again the *Kennedy* arrived at the wreck site and rescue crews quickly located the remaining survivors. Again Navy divers plunged into the angry sea and again they emerged with the remaining survivors. Everyone made it home that night. When asked about the miraculous rescue the Navy Rescue Divers will tell you; "I was just doing my job." It is these men and women who care for our country. What is hero? They aren't hard to find, look into the wind; the Navy Rescue Divers and the *USS John F. Kennedy* are there.

BLUE STAR MARKER PRESERVED
IN SPITE OF OBVIOUS DAMAGE

FREEMANVILLE SETTLEMENT

Founded soon after the U.S. Civil War, the settlement that would become "Freemanville" was established by Dr. John Milton Hawks, an abolitionist and Union Army surgeon, along with other Union Army officers and the Florida Land & Lumber Company. In 1866, roughly 500 former slaves, many of whom had fought for the Union during the war, and their families initially settled here. An additional 1,000 freed slaves would arrive via steamboats in the following months. Of the 3,000 blacks that made Florida their home, roughly half settled near the Halifax River, thus making this area the most populous in Volusia County at that time. In 1867, Dr. Hawks named the settlement Port Orange. Due to harsh farming conditions and poor supplies, the settlement, the Florida Land & Lumber Company, and the integrated school, disbanded in 1869. Many of the settlers returned to their home states or headed for area citrus groves looking for work. However, a few of those original freed slaves stayed. Over time, the settlement became known as "Freemanville." Mt. Moriah Baptist Church is the last remaining structure from the pioneering African-American community in Port Orange known simply as Freemanville.

3431 Ridgewood Avenue, Port Orange
V10 ~ GPS Coordinates: 29.149164, -80.990213

Florida was the Promised Land for emancipated slaves at the conclusion of the Civil War. Hundreds flocked to the state offering what we think of as the American dream yet the dream was elusive. Freedom was guaranteed; prosperity was a luxury not extended to all.

Most of the families had endured a great deal to get to this place but ease was not to be. They toiled under unrelenting heat with very little to sustain them. These people lived in temporary huts until they could build more permanent homes, tried to raise crops to feed their families and all the while they built sawmills then worked in the mills to earn their keep.

The Homestead Act of 1866 offered government land to freedmen in Florida as well as Arkansas, Mississippi, Alabama and Louisiana. Approximately three thousand homesteads were issued with more than half of these being settled in Volusia County. The Florida Land and Lumber Company planned to begin a sawmill operation using the labor of these freedmen, men who were accustomed to the back breaking work in the fields and sweating under the blaze of the Florida noon-day sun.

Though the settlement was a good concept in theory, the colony failed rather quickly. In a very short time, strong and proud men could be found in tears on the dirt streets, begging strangers for food to nourish their families. These same men would walk for miles to get some scrap to feed their children.

A New Hampshire couple, John Milton and Esther Hawks, were white abolitionists who spent the majority of the Civil War in South Carolina. They arrived to manage Freemanville. Both were physicians, during a time when it was unheard of for a woman to be a doctor. John Hawks, along with several fellow Union officers commanding black regiments, formed the Florida Land and Lumber Company.

The settlement was named Port Orange, today known as Ponce Inlet. The settlement was moved twice eventually ending up where Port Orange is found today. Of course, the colony would depend on the success of the sawmill, which had yet to be built. They would rely on the lumber to build their homes and businesses. The Freedmen's Bureau was to provide food and supplies but alas due to greed and corruption within the agency, they failed in the tasks.

Dr. Esther Hill Hawks established the first integrated school. She taught adult classes to those unable to read or write and combined the classes of both white and black children. The students were taught in the open air sometimes before an open fire for warmth. The sawmill was delayed so building a school had to wait while most of the homesteaders had no more than lean-to shelters in which to live. In spite of the less than ideal circumstances, the school was a mediocre success; many of the children suffered from illness probably due to lack of proper nutrition and sometimes rampant disease; also during planting and harvest seasons the children were required to work the fields. Eventually the white parents began to complain about the desegregation and most removed their children.

Many other problems existed in the community. These former slaves knew how to work the soil but Florida's sandy loam, semi-tropical climate and lack of seeds, tools and supplies were major obstacles. Again the corruption of the Freedman's Bureau prevented success. Instead of supplies, ships arrived constantly bringing more mouths to feed and no way to feed them. In January of 1867, General Ralph Ely showed up from Charleston with one thousand more settlers. Ely and S. C. Osborn, Freedman agents, were both accused to selling supplies meant to feed the swelling settlement. Then to add to the awful conditions, the treasurer of the Florida Land and Lumber Company, G. A. Purdie embezzled all of the companies' funds. By spring only two hundred fifty-one settlers remained and more than one hundred were children. They were forced to subsist on wild coutee[1], palmetto cabbage and any fish they managed to snare. The colony had failed.

Dr. Esther Hawks continued to teach but moved the school in an effort to remain near her students. Unfortunately this also brought her in closer contact with the white settlers who were now openly hostile. A new schoolhouse was built but within a month, someone set the little wooden structure ablaze. Esther could no longer tolerate the prejudice and with a broken heart returned to New Hampshire to practice medicine.

The black population was now quite sparse, only eighty-three remained out of more than three thousand original settlers. Most took work in the citrus groves, others returned to the plantations of their birth for little more than food and shelter. Despite the hard times, a few settlers remained. Henry and Hannah Tolliver owned land in northwest Port Orange. They offered a haven there to some of the former settlers. In fact, the little haven was dubbed Freemanville.

Henry was a successful farmer of corn, sweet potatoes, peas, beans, cotton and sugar cane. His sugar cane mill produced two hundred fifty gallons of molasses. Hannah was a seamstress. Emma Overstreet, said to have been Tolliver's stepdaughter, married a man named George Freeman (hence the "Freeman" in Freemanville). The couple had fifteen children raised next door to Henry and Hannah. The Freeman's purchased the lot from the Tollivers for one dollar. John Tolliver, Henry and Hannah's son, was one of two black elected officials who voted to incorporate Daytona. John later accepted a contract from the Daytona town council to build a number of roads including a main thoroughfare Ridgewood Avenue.

Freemanville grew to include residences both east and west of US 1 in the 1920s. Eventually a school was built, but unlike Esther Hawks' school the institution was segregated. Freemanville remains to this day, although greatly diminished. All that remains of the original settlement is one historic home and Mount Moriah Baptist Church. Mount Moriah has soothed the souls of Freemanville since 1911.

BATTLE OF
DUNLAWTON PLANTATION

During the First Seminole War, 1836, the Mosquito Roarers, a company of Florida militia under Major Benjamin Putnam, engaged a large band of Seminoles pillaging Dunlawton, a sugar plantation on the Halifax River. Heavy fighting ensued, but the militiamen were unable to disperse the Indians. The extensive system of sugar plantations on Florida's east coast was eventually destroyed by Seminole raids and the sugar industry in this area never recovered.

950 Old Sugar Mill Road, Port Orange
V11 ~ GPS Coordinates: 29.140655, -81.006520

Historians have long told us that the Dunlawton Plantation site was once the site of an old Spanish mission. Many of these Franciscan missions were extensions of the mother mission at St. Augustine established in 1625. However, official Spanish records indicate that no mission was ever established in this area.

In 1804, Patrick Dean was awarded a Spanish land grant of nine hundred fifty-five acres. When an Indian killed him, the plantation was willed to his sister who in turn sold the property to Charles Lawton in 1830. He named the plantation Dunlawton, Dun in honor of his maternal grandfather.

It is a strange coincidence that the name Dunlawton has remained attached to the plantation for almost

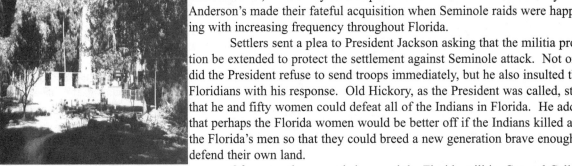

one hundred and seventy-five years when Charles Lawton only owned the property for approximately two years. James and George Anderson bought the property in 1832. The pair had originally owned a plantation near the Tomoka River, which they sold to purchase Dunlawton. Unfortunately the Anderson's made their fateful acquisition when Seminole raids were happening with increasing frequency throughout Florida.

Settlers sent a plea to President Jackson asking that the militia protection be extended to protect the settlement against Seminole attack. Not only did the President refuse to send troops immediately, but he also insulted the Floridians with his response. Old Hickory, as the President was called, stated that he and fifty women could defeat all of the Indians in Florida. He added that perhaps the Florida women would be better off if the Indians killed all of the Florida's men so that they could breed a new generation brave enough to defend their own land.

DUNLAWTON RUINS

Of course, those words incensed the Florida militia, General Call responded that in fact his men fought with distinction enduring all manner of hardship and for their trouble the government[2] cheated the militia out of their just pay. Continuing the back and forth verbal war Old Hickory replied, "Let the damned cowards protect their own country." In response the Florida Herald published the following in March of 1836:

"We belong to no political faction, have few party predilections, and neither fear the frowns of the court, the smiles of the Whig or democrat; but we belong to Florida…. Our character and interests are identified with hers; and no man, or set of men, however, high in office, or any party, shall trample with impunity upon her rights, or wantonly on her honour, without receiving merited censure."

The wives of militiamen hosted a grand tea in honor of their soldier husbands sending a message to the President that they were very happy with their brave husbands.

At Dunlawton Plantation, then known as the Anderson Place, in 1836 the Seminole Indians and a band of escaped slaves led a vicious rampage against the white settlers south of St. Augustine. Eighteen plantations were set to the torch from St. Augustine to New Smyrna and all that was left was charred ruins and destroyed lives. The residents of Dunlawton Plantation put up a valiant effort but their fight was for naught as Coacoochee led a superior raiding party against the poorly armed and frightened settlers. Every building on the estate and most of the sugar mill was laid to waste. The aftermath of the malicious Second Seminole War led to the famous Trail of Tears. Most of the Seminole, as well as other tribes were forced to move their entire villages to reservations west of the Mississippi River. Many died along the way; others after they arrived to live in horrendous conditions yet still others refused to be corralled like cattle and escaped into the Florida Everglades. From that time forward the proud members of the Seminole tribe were only seen in ghost like glimpses, their song of tradition heard in the wind as it swept the saw grass marshland.

John J. Marshall of South Carolina purchased the burned out plantation in 1846. He rebuilt the sugar mill and set stalks to grow sugar cane. Marshall abandoned sugar production within ten years. During the Civil War, Confederate soldiers camped at Dunlawton Plantation and used the sugar mill to grind salt.

In 1948, a Florida doctor named Sperber came up with an idea to take advantage of the blossoming tourism industry to open a theme park featuring virtually life-sized dinosaur sculptures made from concrete, a Seminole village and various animal exhibits. The park's mascot was a baboon named Bongo; thus the park was called Bongoland. The park was only open for four years but generations of children have climbed the huge sculptures and imagined the very natural appearance of the dinosaurs coming to life.

J. Saxton Lloyd acquired the property and completed an extensively landscaping project. In 1963, he donated the former Dunlawton Plantation to Volusia County. Today the park is known as Sugar Mills Garden where the remnants of Bongoland still pose a menacing stance along the garden path

BONGOLAND REMAINS

**BLUE STAR
MEMORIAL HIGHWAY**

A tribute to the Armed Forces that have defended the United States of America.

US 1, Port Orange
V12 ~ GPS Coordinates: 29.144413, -80.987941

Four acres in the midst of Ormond Beach were set aside in 1946 as a memorial to those who fought and died for America. An oasis reserved as a War Memorial. The lush tropical garden has in its midst a obelisk honoring those who served.

The original plaque bore one hundred forty-seven names of World War II veterans donated by Cincinnati residents Claus and Elsa Wiedemann who wintered every year in Ormond Beach. While it was certainly a moving tribute, unfortunately the list was incomplete. You see the plaque only honored those white men and women who served. Because of segregation the African American veterans were recognized on a separate memorial hidden away in the old Reading Room located at U.S. 1 and Tomoka Avenue. Unfortunately when the Reading Room was demolished, the plaque listing the seventy-seven African American veterans went down with the building and was lost forever.

Andrea Hall, granddaughter of forgotten veteran James Lewis Hall, worked tirelessly for twenty-five years to bring due recognition to the African American veterans. All of these veterans white and black fought side by side with uncommon valor and bravery. This memorial was to reflect the dedication to duty for those that sacrificed a great deal for their country and some that paid the ultimate price with their lives. In 1999 she achieved her goal and the seventy-seven names were listed in their rightful place beside fellow brothers and sisters in arms. After fifty-three years the injustice was made right. The monument also features a tablet representing three Ormond Beach men who gave their lives during World War I.

On the grounds is also a Museum founded and paid for with donations from Ormond Beach residents. The collection represents "creative freedom and equality of all persons regardless of race, sex or social status." It is a fitting tribute to those veterans who served their country, fighting for those very ideals. This park was the first of its kind in the state of Florida.

The Art Museum features the work of local artists as well as others throughout the world. The continually changing exhibits ensure that all aspects of media are represented and the public is treated to an ever-changing exhibition. The Museum provides a permanent home for a collection of work by artist, Malcolm Fraser.

A nominal donation is required for adults visiting the museum. Members, senior citizens and children are admitted without charge, though the Museum is supported solely by donation. The Museum is open daily at 78 East Granada Boulevard, Ormond Beach.

GAMBLE PLACE

In 1898, James N. Gamble, of the Procter and Gamble Company and a longtime winter resident of Daytona Beach, bought this land on Spruce Creek for use as a rural retreat. In 1907, he built a small cracker cottage with an open front porch and a breezeway connecting a separate kitchen and dining room, which he named "Egwanulti," a Native American word meaning "by the water." At the same time, he rebuilt an existing packing house to process citrus from his grove. In 1938, Gamble's son-in-law, Alfred K. Nippert, completed the "Snow White House," a Black Forest style cottage inspired by the Disney animated film classic Snow White and the Seven Dwarfs. The house is surrounded by a Witch's Hut, the Dwarfs' Mine Shaft, and an elaborate network of rock gardens. Collectively, these buildings and grounds form a historic landscape now known as Gamble Place. This property was listed in the National Register of Historic Places in 1993.

1819 Taylor Road (off S.R.431), Port Orange
V13 ~ GPS Coordinates: 29.093955, -81.047750

English candle maker, William Proctor and Irish soap maker, James Gamble first teamed up when they married the Norris sisters, Olivia and Elizabeth. The infamous Proctor and Gamble Company was born in 1837 near Cincinnati. Begun with an initial investment, most of it from their father-in-law Alexander Norris, of seven thousand dollars by 1859 total sales from soap and candles reached an amazing one million dollars. The company claimed only eighty employees.

Gamble's son, James, directed the eastward line crew of the transcontinental telegraph project. He and his men reached the convergence with the westward crew at Salt Lake City, Utah on October 24, 1861. Meanwhile in the east, the Civil War had begun. Proctor and Gamble did their part for the war effort in favor of the Union Army by supplying soap and candles to the fighting force. Very little of the goods actually made it to the men on the battle lines and quite a bit was sold on the black market or made its way south via blockade runners.

As the Civil War came to its inevitable end, the new Union was in the grips of reconstruction. Business for Proctor and Gamble flourished as word spread on both sides of the Mason Dixon line of their high quality goods. The end of the war also opened the supply lines to the south for raw materials essential for the manufacture of many Proctor and Gamble products.

James Gamble, Jr., develop a staple of the Proctor and Gamble line in 1879; a cheap white soap. The newly created product possessed a feature never before seen and taken for granted today, the smooth white bar floats. In fact the quality was developed quite by accident when a soap mixer in the Proctor and Gamble factory went on his lunch break forgetting to turn off his machine. Air whipped into the soap, resulted in the bar floating in the bath. Afraid of being fired, the soap maker said nothing and the batch of soap was sold – Proctor and Gamble knew nothing of the groundbreaking discovery.

Customers were soon clamoring for the soap that floats, company official were initially confused then finally amazed at the popularity of the "accidental" product. William Proctor's son, Harley found the perfect name for the product one Sunday while reading a biblical phrase, "out of ivory palaces." A perfect fit for the white soap's purity, gentle cleaning and longevity. Proctor and Gamble began advertising Ivory soap nationally in 1882.

James Gamble Jr. began wintering at Daytona Beach in 1862. His father passed away in 1891 and the company belonged solely to the second generation of the Proctor and Gamble Families'. Imagination, innovation and advertising led to the development of more than thirty different soap products. Their research laboratories cre-

213

ated a flaked powder for the newly invented mechanical washing machines. In the process an experimental fat product to be used in the production of soap lead to the first ever all-vegetable shortening, a substitute for lard, called Crisco.

James Gamble bought a 150-acre hunting and fishing retreat on Spruce Creek from George Leffman in 1898. He named the property "Egwanulti," an Indian term meaning "by the water." Gamble built a modest "cracker-style" house in 1907 and a citrus packing barn becoming a gentleman farmer. The house was only accessible using horse and cart or by way of Gamble's yacht, the *Seabreeze*. In order to bring the *Seabreeze* up Spruce Creek, Gamble was forced to dismantle a railway trestle, which he owned, that crossed the water.

Many affluent guests made their way to the Gamble retreat including John D. Rockefeller, H. J. Heinz and even former President William Howard Taft. James N. Gamble passed away in 1932 and Egwanulti was left to his descendents. His son-in-law, Judge Alfred K. Nippert built a playhouse for the children's wonderment and the adult's childlike delight in 1938 emulating Walt Disney's Snow White scenery. Disney was actually a guest at the retreat that very same year. The mirrored set was complete with a chalet looking amazingly similar to Snow White's cottage, a Witch's hut, the Dwarfs' Mine Shaft and an elaborate network of rock gardens. Walt Disney was flattered by the construction and for years the families' children were enchanted with the fantasy playland.

The Gamble heirs donated the property to the Nature Conservancy in 1983 with the stipulation that they be allowed visitation. Today the Museum of Arts and Sciences manages what is called Gamble Place and the surrounding Spruce Creek Preserve. Self-guided nature walks, pontoon boat trips along Spruce Creek and historic tours are said to be available by reservation only through the museum. The area has an abundance of rich natural beauty, various woodland creatures, birds, flora and fauna all native to Spruce Creek.

DELAND HALL
BUILT 1884

The oldest building in Florida in continuous use for higher education and the first building on the Stetson University Campus. Originally housed the library, chapel, classrooms, gymnasium and offices. Later used as a women's residence, kindergarten, school of music and the administrative center of campus. Listed on the National Register of Historic Places in 1983.

503 North Woodland Boulevard, Deland
V14 ~ GPS Coordinates: 29.035051, -81.303544

DeLand Academy was Florida's first private institution of higher learning. Founded by and originally named for New York entrepreneur Henry A. DeLand in 1883, four years would pass before the state approved the charter allowing instruction to begin. DeLand Hall was the first building to be constructed on the campus. The stately edifice is to this day the oldest building serving continuous higher education concerns still standing in Florida.

DeLand Hall was constructed in the American Heritage Stick architectural style featuring two and a half stories. Looming above the second story was the bell tower that once summoned students to lessons and sounded out significant proclamations. DeLand Hall initially comprised the entire university but as the institution grew and new buildings were constructed the Hall eventually was claimed for a time by every educational department. The School of Music settled in and remained at DeLand Hall for thirty-two years. Many of the structures built subsequently to DeLand Hall were the products of many well-known architects during that era. The picturesque campus features handsome structures at every turn, revealing an interesting lesson in beautiful historical architecture. Generously Henry DeLand bequeathed the grand hall to the university.

In 1889, the university name was changed in honor of DeLand friend and generous school benefactor John B. Stetson. His dedication to the school rivaled only that of DeLand himself and both men served the school for the remainder of their lives as trustees. Elizabeth Hall was built in honor of John Stetson. The grand edifice was modeled upon Philadelphia's Independence Hall.

John B. Stetson was ailing with tuberculosis when he left the cold weather of Philadelphia for Colorado. Like others he had heard gold was to be had for any man willing to work for it and Stetson was willing to do whatever he had to do to gain his fortune. Once he arrived in the Colorado wilderness Stetson realized not only was gold not so easily obtained but life in this undeveloped land was rugged and hard. His health declined rather than improved and soon Stetson was seeking means just to survive the elements, never mind gaining any fortune.

John Stetson began trapping beaver pelts and tanned the hides to felt, a skill taught by his haberdasher[3] father. He made tents out of the pelts and then began work on some personal protection from the elements. Stetson experimented and discovered that a big air pocket between the head and a hat's crown trapped body heat, this kept the head not only dry but warm. A wide brim kept rain off the face and made good handles for carrying water. You see the pelts were waterproof so hauling vital water was easily done with a Stetson hat. This element led to the legend of the ten-gallon hat, although the hat could only carry about a half-gallon of water at a time. When an old mule driver offered John Stetson a five dollar gold piece for the used hat right of his head, the ambitious young man knew he had found his calling. The first of Stetson's famous hats, which still exist today, was born.

Stetson returned to Philadelphia with only one hundred dollars in his pocket and invested every cent of it into founding a hat factory. He was the entire staff; Stetson made the hats, then wore them everywhere he went advertising his wares. His was not an overnight success but within twenty years he employed four thousand workers and was selling two million hats a year. Stetson's factory was one of the first to utilize the industrial revolution when he transformed hat making from manual to machine assisted production.

Stetson's hat was said to be heavy enough to knock a man down in a fight and was heralded by keeping its shape after being shot by twenty bullets. Hollywood did their part in making the Stetson a legend when heroes only wore white and the black hats they sported identified villains.

Even though Stetson took great pride in the quality product that bore his name, he should be well remembered for his humanitarian endeavors as well, John B Stetson was one of the first wealthy tycoons to offer worker benefits. He gave free health care to employees and factory shares as rewards for work well done. Stetson's philanthropy to his community as well as others far over shadowed his industrial success. He built the Philadelphia hospital and gave generously to Stetson University among many other endeavors.

Stetson University today offers the community culture, the arts as well as a beautiful historical campus at the heart of DeLand. The School of Music introduces more than two hundred concerts each year by well-known artists as well as faculty members and students. The oldest collegiate acting company performs in the historic Stover Theater offering a different play each quarter. The Gillespie Museum of Minerals exhibits one of the largest private mineral collections in the world and the Duncan Gallery of Art shows works by students, faculty and visiting artists in residence. Most of these fascinating tourist attractions and informational gems are supported by the generosity of donation.

The first president, Dr. John F. Forbes, set standards of excellence still demanded today. Students are selected based on talent, leadership skills, personal growth and their personal support of the community in which they live. Students, faculty and staff are encouraged to bring creativity, enthusiasm and a general love for knowledge to enhance their experience at Stetson University.

In 2002 DeLand Hall endured an extensive revitalization including repairs to the wooden window seals, siding and exterior doors. Handicap access was added to comply with current regulations then the structure was brightened up with a brand new coat of paint. A state grant provided part of the funding. The National Register of Historic Places recognized DeLand Hall in 1983 and today the building provides spacing for the administrative offices of the ever-prestigious Stetson University.

SAUL'S HOUSE SITE

Central Florida opened to settlers at the end of the 2nd Seminole War. The creation of Mosquito (later Volusia) County in 1843 signified rising interest in the area. George and Adaline Sauls were among those who came to Volusia County in the 1850s. Sauls built a two-room home near the road from Enterprise to the East Coast in an area, which became known as Saulsville. He added a second floor and other rooms as his family increased. After the 1880s, population centered on the railroad town of Osteen. Sauls family members remained in their home until the early 20th century. The Sauls house stood for over 100 years until fire destroyed it in 1972.

Osteen Memorial Gardens Cemetery, Mountain Way off SR 415 (follow the signs), Osteen
V15 ~ GPS Coordinates: 28.892393, -81.155290

George Sauls obtained a tract of land in what was Mosquito County, Florida in the late 1840s utilizing the government letter patent program. It was there that he brought his family from their Georgia home to become Florida pioneers. George with the help of local Seminole Indians built his sparse two-room home, which would eventually come to be known as the Sauls mansion.

Constructed of heart-pine timber, the house was a work in progress for many years. The log construction consisted of log timbers some of them eighty feet in length, held together with wooden pegs; in fact, very few homemade square iron nails were used in the building and those were only found in the additions of the stairway and porch. Obviously well built, the structure stood for almost one hundred fifty years. Eventually the second story was added; so the "mansion" consisted of four large rooms, a detached kitchen common during the era to prevent the destruction of the home resulting from cooking fires and a wide expansive porch embracing the entire structure.

Imagine the history surrounding the Sauls home and involving the family. George Sauls was a trailblazer. He established a small town site that came to be known as Saulsville, which no longer exists today but evolved to become Osteen. George first grew indigo to support his family and later joined the trend to become an orange grower. He, along with neighbors H. E. Osteen and Ora Carpenter, created the community with the establishment of a church and the first educational system. The school involved a tutor traveling from family to family.

The Sauls home was a way station for the stagecoach. Built with a substantial overhang to shelter travelers from the elements when alighting the stage, the porch was actually the site of history in the making. As the Civil War was ending, Confederate Secretary of War James Cabell Breckenridge managed to escape prosecution as a war criminal by fleeing via the stage. His travels delivered Breckenridge to the stage depot at the Sauls home where he was hidden from Union patrols for several days. He remained in seclusion until the arrival of a ship at nearby Mims, which was bound Cuba and safety from prosecution.

Over the years the Sauls mansion was transferred to a series owners. The last residents were Dr. and Mrs. W. R. Hutchinson, though a great number of Sauls' descendants remain throughout Florida to this day. Eventually the house was sadly left empty. The dwelling was unprotected from the molestation of teenagers who repeatedly vandalized the site and adults with no regard for the importance historic preservation. Local sheriff officials admitted in a 1972-newspaper article that they were aware that the house was a teen hangout but obviously did little to protect the more than one hundred-year-old historical treasure.

In 1971, plans were in progress to restore the ill-used Florida pioneer family homestead. Funds had been allocated to begin the tedious process of renovations, when carelessness and neglect brought disaster. In the early morning hours of New Years Day before the dawning of first light on January 1, 1972, acrid smoke filled the air and flames turned history to ashes. Teenagers, partying in the abandoned home, recklessly set the place ablaze and within moments the Sauls mansion was fully engulfed. The home that George Sauls lovingly built for his family that had withstood the test of time and the elements was gone. No one was held accountable for the desecration of history; possibly those present that night still feel the shame of their actions more than thirty years later. I certainly hope so.

**SAULS HOMESITE MARKER
THEFTPROOFED**

Eventually the Sauls homestead was memorialized with this historical marker. Unfortunately it too was subject to vandalism; the large bronze sign denoting the significance of the historic site was stolen. In the meantime, the home site property was sold to developers intent on creating a housing subdivision in area. The historical marker was later recovered and embedded in a virtually theft-proof boulder of native coquina rock. The marker was placed at Osteen Memorial Gardens Cemetery where George and Adaline Sauls found their final rest.

In late 2000, the Sauls family name again made history in Florida and lingered in the news media throughout the world. Judge N. Sanders "Sandy" Sauls was selected to preside over the controversial 2000 Presidential Election. Known to be both cautious and quick-witted, Judge Sauls was given an impossible task any decision he made was bound to be contested by the losing side. The United States Supreme Court eventually upheld Judge Sauls' decision. In 2002, the National Press Club honored Judge Sauls in Washington DC saying, "much like King Solomon, (he) entered the breech, and with a sense of fairness and justice settled the political war...." With distinction and dignity the Sauls family name is carried on.

Even though the historical marker no longer stands at the Sauls homestead site, the pioneering spirit still remains in the area. Neighbors of the lot where Sauls' mansion once stood often catch a fleeting glimpse of George and Adaline Sauls strolling hand in hand amidst the grounds. The Sauls are perhaps contemplating the changes that have come to pass in Saulsville or wandering the area searching for the home entrusted to the future, unfortunately that trust was betrayed.

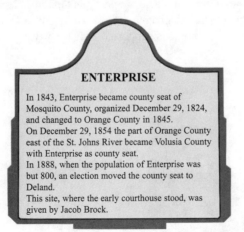

ENTERPRISE

In 1843, Enterprise became county seat of Mosquito County, organized December 29, 1824, and changed to Orange County in 1845.
On December 29, 1854 the part of Orange County east of the St. Johns River became Volusia County with Enterprise as county seat.
In 1888, when the population of Enterprise was but 800, an election moved the county seat to Deland.
This site, where the early courthouse stood, was given by Jacob Brock.

**Intersection 3ʳᵈ & Main Streets in front of Enterprise Elementary School, Enterprise
V16 ~ GPS Coordinates: 28.870909, -81.266082**

Cornelius Taylor, a cousin of President Zachary Taylor, visited the area near Lake Monroe in 1841. From

St. Pablo, Florida, he had been a timber agent and was impressed with the strategic location of the property. On the opposite bank of Lake Monroe was Fort Mellon, a settlement here would provide a link to Jacksonville by way of the St. Johns River.

Taylor applied for a one hundred sixty-acre homestead in 1842. Within three years the population warranted the establishment of a post office with Ora Carpenter serving as postmaster. During the elections of 1843, Cornelius Taylor was elected state legislator. Serving his own interest, he introduced a bill making Enterprise the county seat of Mosquito County. The county seat moved to Mellonville when Mosquito County was divided and Orange County was formed. When Volusia County was formed, Enterprise was again the county seat.

A typhus epidemic swept through the county and Taylor's household was not exempt. His thirteen-year-old daughter succumbed and nine African slaves were lost to the merciless disease. Polly Taylor was the first white colonist to be buried south of St. Augustine. Cornelius Taylor decided to withdraw to California and set sail. Unfortunately, he never reached the West Coast, Taylor drowned in 1849.

Dr. James Starke acquired the property and upon his death, it passed to his son John W. Starke in 1867. Enterprise had blossomed now having a dry goods store, bowling alley, two-story hotel, courthouse and a blacksmith shop. Enterprise began attracting those in ill health to her three sulphur springs. The Lower Salt and Green Springs still exist today, however the Upper Salt Sulphur Spring disappeared when an earthquake struck on August 31, 1886. The hunting and fishing opportunities drew sportsmen from all over the United States to Enterprise. Overlooking Lake Monroe, Starke built a plantation called "Bueno Retiro." Oddly enough the location he chose on a knoll above the lake also bore the marble headstone marking the gravesite of Polly Taylor.

In 1870, Jacob Brock donated a lot for the construction of a new courthouse. But shortly after construction was completed Enterprise began a slow and steady decline. Within twenty years the county seat would be moved to Deland, which was enjoying a growth spurt. The relatively young courthouse was sold to the Board of Public Instruction for three thousand nine hundred seventy-five dollars for use as the Enterprise Elementary School. By 1916, the population had declined to a point that the school had to be closed. The building was carefully torn down in 1917, the lumber was retained for construction of a two-story replacement in Deland financed by Henry Deland.

Enterprise has virtually returned to its original state. The intersection of DeBary Road and Main Street mark the town's center. Into the 1980s, the Enterprise post office was still a room in the postmistress' home. Though little is left of Enterprise, one occupant is a great source of pride: the Florida Methodist Children's Home on Lake Monroe.

Children arrive at the home victims of abuse, neglect, personal problems, drug abuse or lack of available family for whatever reason. The kids there are given a safe haven, counseling and some normalcy to their harried young lives that is certainly missing. The home is supported 85% by private funding. Enterprise has every reason to be proud.

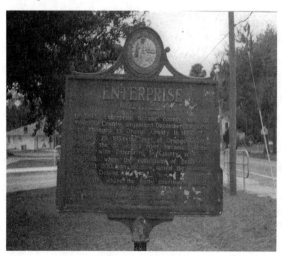

ENTERPRISE HISTORICAL MARKER

THE RAID ON ENTERPRISE
THE SUGAR MILL RAID

On March 14, 1864 Acting Ensign Sanborn, commanding the USS Columbine of the Union fleet, which was patrolling the St. Johns River into Lake Monroe, landed at Enterprise and sent Mr. Davis and a squad of men from the 48th New York Infantry to destroy a Sugar Mill, 2 miles from the town of Enterprise. They proceeded to destroy the grater part of the Mill, took sugar & molasses, and impressed slaves, cattle, and wagons to transport the goods. Before their duties were complete, a Home Guard of 30 to 40 Confederates chased them back to their ship. The contraband was put aboard the captured Confederate State steamer General Sumter. No lives were lost. Two months later, on May 23, 1864, the USS Columbine was captured and destroyed at Horse Landing, near Palatka, by Capt. J. J. Dickison of the 2nd Florida Cavalry.

ALL SAINTS EPISCOPAL CHURCH

All Saints' Episcopal Church was founded in 1881, and first met on this Lakeshore at the Brock House Hotel. The first Vicar rowed across Lake Monroe from Sanford to conduct services in the parlor. Baron Frederick de Bary donated the lumber to build what is now Volusia County's oldest "Florida Gothic" Church in 1883. The Church retains an active congregation, and has been listed in the National Register of Historic Places since 1974.

All Saints Episcopal Church, 155 Clark Street, Enterprise
V17 ~ GPS Coordinates: 28.871460, -81.267664

Union side wheel tug *Columbine* was assigned to the South Atlantic Blockading Squadron off the South Carolina shores when she received orders in February of 1864 to make way toward Jacksonville, Florida. Upon arrival she was to support the flotilla defending against Confederate forces on the St. Johns River.

The *USS Columbine* was built in New York around 1850, originally named *A. H. Schultz*. The Union Navy purchased her on December 12, 1862 and employed Howe & Copeland to outfit the side-wheel tug for use in naval warfare. Acting Master J. S. Dennis was initially given command. She weighed in at one hundred thirty tons amassed in a length of one hundred seventeen feet with a girth of thirty-six feet. The *USS Columbine* bore a compliment of twenty-five men; she was armed with two twenty-pound musket-loading rifle cannon.

On May 22, underway with commanding officer Acting Ensign Frank W. Sanborn, *USS Columbine* was sent to assist the *USS Ottawa* that was under intense enemy fire. The *USS Ottawa* was severely damaged from land artillery at Brown's Landing and rendered motionless for more than thirty hours. Confederate Captain James Jackson Dickison turned his attention to a new prey when he saw *USS Columbine* purportedly coming to the rescue. Dickison commanded Company H of the Second Florida Cavalry.

When the *USS Columbine* moved to within sixty yards of the shore, Dickison ordered an attack. The two cannons were fired and sharpshooters from his cavalry units aimed at the wheelhouse. After an intense forty-five minute exchange of gunfire, the *USS Columbine* drifted aground and the acting commander, Ensign Frank W. Sanborn, surrendered the vessel. Only sixty-six members of the one hundred forty-eight-member crew were alive when the vessel was surrendered. The vessel was stripped of its cannon and provisions then set ablaze to guarantee against rescue from the *USS Ottawa*. The *USS Columbine* burned to the waterline and sank.

This was actually the first battle to take place between a cavalry unit and a gunboat. The Battle at Horse Landing was also one of first times a new weapon was utilized, the floating torpedo or mine. Ensign Sanborn was rowed ashore and officially gave up his ship to the Confederate States Army. In addition to the lost lives during the battle, a great many men drowned when they jumped ship in an attempt to swim toward safety; the Confederates suffered no losses. The Union dead were buried on the west shore of Horse Landing in unmarked graves.

Seven Union officers, nine seamen and forty-seven enlisted Negro soldiers were taken prisoner. The officers were taken to Macon, Georgia; the seamen and enlisted men were transferred to the Georgia hellhole known as Andersonville Prison. Only one *USS Columbine* prisoner was specifically listed among the dead interred at Andersonville: J. H. Ellis who died of typhus on July 9, 1864; his grave is number 3064.

Rear Admiral Dahlgren reported the following:

"The loss of the Columbine will be felt most inconveniently; her draft was only 5 or 6 feet, and having only 2 such steamers, the services of which are needed elsewhere, can not replace her."

At the conclusion of the Civil War, it is quite possible that the wreck of *USS Columbine* was salvaged. Nothing has been substantiated but some indications are that the wreck was only partially submerged in shallow water. In later years, the remainder of the Civil War wreckage was covered in mud left by dredging during the 1960s construction of the cross Florida canal.

The *USS Columbine* was rediscovered by sport scuba divers in 1971. The site was looted extensively and a great number of the artifacts could be found in private collections. Very few of the artifacts found their way into museums, the majority of the relics were lost to time, the river and the elements.

ALL SAINTS EPISCOPAL CHURCH

During the late 1800s steamboats became common on the St. Johns River. Enterprise was the final port along the river and home to Jacob Brock. Brock, a former sea captain, established a hotel along the banks of the St. Johns where it converges to become Lake Monroe. The Brock House came to be a haven for the wealthy seeking a winter retreat, away from the hustle and bustle of larger towns.

The Brock House sitting room became a sanctuary on Sunday's for the All Saints' Episcopal Church, which was founded in 1881. The Vicar of Holy Cross Episcopal Church in Sanford, Reverend Samuel B. Carpenter, rowed across Lake Monroe to hold services. Many of the worshipers had considerable wealth and soon they determined that building a church was a priority.

An orange grove owner by the name of Lester Clark donated the property on which the sanctuary was to be built. Baron Frederick DeBary, the Brock Family and Frank Storer all donated generously to the construction. DeBary, though not of the Episcopalian faith, donated most of the virgin pine and cypress lumber. Storer eventually became to first treasurer for the congregation.

Construction was completed in 1883 and the parishioners moved into the edifice at the corner of Clark Street. The church was built in a form known today is as Florida Gothic embraced by a hint of classic Americana, the white picket fence. For more than one hundred years, All Saints has stood virtually unaltered with the exception of a small sacristy[4] in the 1950s and a front porch with a handicapped ramp in 1971.

In the mid 1940s membership at All Saints began to decline. About this time a hurricane tore through Enterprise leaving the church considerably damaged by an upended ancient oak. Right Reverend Henry I. Louttit and Reverend Mark Carpenter saved All Saints from demolition by utilizing funds left by Frank Storer in memory of his mother. Restoration was quickly completed and the church was reopened. All Saints Episcopal Church has been opened continually since that time.

The Convention of Episcopalian Diocese of Central Florida admitted the church as a full parish on November 15, 1974. From the beginning days of services in the Brock House until this very day, All Saints has provided a spiritual haven for all of Volusia County. The congregation continues to this day as an active and involved member of the rapidly growing communities.

DeBARY HALL
FLORIDA FEDERATION OF ART, INC.

Built in 1871 by Baron Frederick de Bary. Born 1815 in Germany of Belgian descent, de Bary came to New York in 1840 as agent for Mumm's Champagne. His estate of many hundred acres here in Florida was a hunting and fishing preserve and his family's winter home, where many notables of the day were entertained. Presidents Grant and Cleveland and members of Europe's royalty were guests. He died in 1898 in his 84th year, and his son Adolphe inherited the property. De Bary's residence here was during the steamboat era of the St. Johns River, and his interests included ownership of a steamship line.

FLORIDA FEDERATION OF ART, INC.

Organized 1927 in Orlando for the purpose of promoting, developing, and advancing art in the State of Florida. DeBary Hall, with about five acres of land, was given to the Federation in 1959 by the Property Owners Association of Plantation Estates and became the Federation's State Headquarters and Art Galleries. In 1967 the property was acquired by the Florida Board of Parks and Historic Memorials, which then leased it to the Federation for its continued use. The Federation Committee that negotiated this sale and lease was Mrs. G.J. Brooks, Chairman; Mrs. Willard Bielby, Secretary; Dr. and Mrs. A. E. Brandt; Mr. William Daniell; and Mrs. Mabel Bullis.

210 Sunrise Boulevard, DeBary
V18 ~ GPS Coordinates: 28.874459, -81.296567

The end of the Civil War spurred an influx of northern travelers seeking milder climates. Ironically, recovery of the south from the devastation of war was largely paid for by northern dollars. Steamboats traveling two hundred miles along the St. Johns River from Jacksonville made inland Florida accessible. Enterprize[5] was a little known resort community hidden away on the banks of Lake Monroe.

Samuel Frederick de Bary was German born in 1815 and it was one of those very steamboats that brought him to the little resort town. Baron de Bary came to live in New York in the 1840s as a friend of the G. H. Mumm family to establish the only American franchised distribution company for Mumm's Champagne. De Bary was recently widowed and looking for a change in scenery when he arrived in Florida, the state captivated him immediately. Ever the outdoorsman, de Bary resolved to spend the winter in the semi-tropical locale and indulge his hobbies. He checked into the Brock House, which was known for the amenities the hotel provided and hunted through the season.

By the time April showers brought May flowers, de Bary had decided to build a winter hunting retreat at his new discovered haven. He purchased four hundred pine-covered acres and began construction of his "modest" twenty room-hunting lodge in 1871. The Colonial style structure that incorporates Italianate and Victorian nuances was constructed of cypress shipped by way of the St. Johns River by the Fox Lumber Company in Georgia. The windows bore hand-blown crystal panes and a veranda embraced the home on three sides. The flooring was a gleaming pale heart pine, kept immaculate by a bevy of live-in staff. The latest technology was used both in the construction of the dwelling and the mechanisms installed. A unique bell was system was placed in each room to summon servants at the whim of every guest. When the bell was pushed in the room upstairs, a peel sounded in the kitchen and a staff member was on the run.

De Bary was very proud of his quaint hunting lodge and entertained frequently. His guests often remained for weeks or even months to enjoy the quiet solitude of Florida's sparse landscape. De Bary Hall, as the mansion was called, enjoyed grand parties during the 1880s. The guest list included Presidents Grant and Cleveland, European royalty and American socialites. It is said that so much champagne was served during parties at de Bary Hall that the bottles were used as decorative edging along drive and in the gardens.

Guests who received and accepted invitations to de Bary Hall were those that shared Count[6] de Bary's passion for hunting, fishing, swimming and outdoor activities. The estate harbored a spring-fed swimming pool, which maintained a constant seventy-two degrees year round. But it was the hunting that drew most of his guests. Game managers kept the pine forests baited attracting bounties of quail and dove as well as more exotic fowl, which were kept in cages until the hunt was initiated. Taxidermied kills coated with arsenic, to hamper insect infestation, can still be seen today in a glass case in the library.

De Bary set aside four hundred acres to grow oranges. He obviously did not need the money, for contrary to popular rumor de Bary did not arrive in Florida with only fifty dollars in his pocket, quite possibly fifty dollars in cigars were there but he was by this time a millionaire. He seemed to enjoy a challenge and citrus production was indeed a risky venture. Of course to be a proper orange producer, all of the newest equipment was essential including an orange-crate maker and fruit sorter; both mechanisms can still be seen today in the restored barn. The winter of 1894-95 brought a devastating freeze that killed most of the trees. The grove looked as though a blazing fire had swept through and left only the sad charred branches. De Bary retired as an orange grower and turned the acreage into pasture for cattle grazing. He also built a sugar mill on the east bank of the creek on the north end of the property; today the waterway is called de Bary Creek and is located where Interstate 4 crosses the St. Johns River.

De Bary Hall represents the modernization of Florida. The flourishing tourism industry, transportation innovations including steamboating, train travel and the early days of passable road construction as well as the blossoming yet unreliable orange industry. In 1875, de Bary purchased the steamboat *George M. Bird* to transport his oranges to buyers, the next year he added to his fleet with the side-wheeler, *Frederick de Bary* establishing the de Bary Merchants Line. Several years later he merged with the Baya Line and acquired thirteen additional steamboats. De Bary then joined the Clyde St. Johns River Line in 1889, more steamboats increased tourism tenfold.

He continued to winter at de Bary Hall until 1898 when Baron Samuel Frederick de Bary passed away, he was eighty-three. His beloved hunting lodge was willed to his two children, Adolphe and Eugenie. In the 1930s the property passed to his great granddaughter, Leonie. Unfortunately Leonie perished when an airplane she was traveling in tragically crashed. Leonie left no heirs and de Bary Hall was sold to V. F. Proctor's Paco Land Company.

George Stedronsky purchased the property in 1945, becoming the first person to live in de Bary Hall not related to the original owner. Stedronsky sold the estate two years later to Plantation Estates, Incorporated. The residence was used as a retirement community clubhouse.

The house was purchased and restored by the Florida Federation of Art, Incorporated in 1959. They utilized the former de Bary residence as the Florida Federation of Art's state headquarters. The Federation was founded in Orlando in April 1927. The organization offered promotion and art appreciation for artists throughout Florida. The house has been recognized as both a state and national historic site.

A small town developed the surroundings de Bary Hall property called Plantation Estates in the 1950s. Three developers were determined to establish a community that would be irresistible to northerners seeking relief from brutal winters. Eventually the city's name was changed to DeBary and was incorporated in 1993.

De Bary Hall is open for tours Thursday through Sunday until 4:00 p.m., a nominal fee is charged. The beautiful facility has provided an incredible backdrop for weddings, small festivals and corporate retreats; rental information is available through their business office. Special programs are offered each month to the community.

For more than one hundred years a huge sago palm planted on the front lawn of de Bary Hall has kept a silent vigil. Imagine the changes, people and activities that the brilliant green fronds have beheld over the years. All the while the old hunting lodge called de Bary Hall, so beloved by the Baron, continues to preside majestically.

DR. ANDREW TURNBULL
Dec. 2, 1720 - March 13, 1792

Founder of the Largest Colony under British rule ever to come to the New World the New Smyrna Colony of Florida. 1768 – 1778

Sams Avenue, in front of City Hall, New Smyrna Beach
V19 ~ GPS Coordinates: 29.026619, -80.922832

Andrew Turnbull was born at Annan, Dumfriesshire Scotland on December 2, 1720. He found success as a physician, amassing quite a fortune.

In 1763, after more than two hundred years of Spanish rule, Florida became a British province. To encourage settlements, the British Crown offered large land grants to anyone willing to establish an agricultural venture. The production of cotton, hemp, indigo and silk fueled the Industrial Revolution in England and other such colonies had proven successful in both Virginia and Carolina.

The wealthy Scotsman was intrigued with the idea and excited by the possibility of immense power and wealth. He traveled to the new colony at once, finding the semi-tropical climate and fertile soil much to his liking. Turnbull imagined a multi-cultural settlement along the Mosquito Inlet, today called Ponce de Leon Inlet, which would rival the Virginia colony of Jamestown. He managed to acquire, with the help of other investors, a vast amount of prime property; now a suitable labor force had to be impressed to work the land. The New Smyrna Colony was founded in 1768.

His wife, Maria Garcia Dura Bin, whom he had met while traveling in Asia Minor, joined Turnbull in Florida. Maria was the daughter of a wealthy Smyrna merchant in Greece. The colony was to be named in honor of her birthplace. The couple sailed for Greece with plans to offer a new life in Florida in exchange for seven to ten years of indenture. Upon fulfilling their obligation each family would be given fifty acres of land per adult and five acres per child.

Upon arrival two hundred mountain tribesmen were quickly recruited and then the party moved on to Corsica where an additional one hundred ten indentured servants were signed on. Turnbull and Maria sailed for Mahon, Minorca reaching their destination on February 1, 1768. After three years of famine, crop failure and starvation, the Minorcans were anxious to join Turnbull. The muster expanded by one thousand ninety individuals.

The first European mass migration to the New World sailed on March 31, 1768. Greeks, Italians, Spaniards, Corsicans, English and even an Irishman numbered one thousand four hundred three settlers eager for a better life. There were farmers and fishermen, stonemasons and blacksmith, as well as shopkeepers and sailors; virtually every walk of life was represented on the eight ships bound for New Smyrna.

The journey was tumultuous, a rough crossing that took just over three months. By the time the ships made landfall at St. Augustine, one hundred forty-eight souls had been consigned to the briny deep in watery graves. Most of the casualties had succumbed to scurvy, the rest dying of sickness; one thousand two hundred fifty-five emaciated souls staggered off the ships in Florida. After a few days of rest, about half of the travelers were loaded back on the ships to sail toward New Smyrna, the remainder of the sea weary settlers opted to walk the seventy-five miles.

Once the ailing and exhausted wayfarers arrived in Turnbull's settlement it became glaringly obvious that provisions were not sufficient for the entire party. They had only planned for a group of up to six hundred, however the people that arrived more than doubled that figure, food was in short supply from the beginning.

An epidemic of malaria, conflict between varying cultures and the backbreaking drudgery quickly took its toll on the population. The settlers, so accustomed to close knit communities, were put into isolated cottages. The distance added to their homesickness and loneliness, no sense of society was ever established. Turnbull left the everyday working of the plantations to his overseers, who he continually failed to provide adequate food or medical support for the indentured. The overseers were cruel, brutal and heavy handed in the treatment of the indentured. Within two years, seven hundred four adults and two hundred sixty children perished under the strain of the appalling conditions.

In spite of the terrible conditions, amazingly in the third year a successful harvest was made. Indigo yielded forty-three thousand, two hundred eighty-three pounds over the next five years for export from New Smyrna. Indigo, used in the production of blue dye, was highly demanded in England. In fact indigo brought one dollar a pound, more than the going price for gold. Turnbull's colony was a financial success, but the windfall would not last.

The sheer magnitude of this endeavor, cultural differences among the settlers, Britain's loss during the American Revolution and the eventual return of Florida to Spain all played a part in the failure of New Smyrna. Political scheming, financial irresponsibility and the finalization of a portion of the indentures also had something to do with the demise of the immense plantation. However, probably the most viable cause for failure was neglect, brutality and slave-like conditions perpetrated by the overseers and allowed by Turnbull.

Father Casanovas, the settlement priest, approached Turnbull with the hardships and complaints of the beleaguered workers. When Dr. Turnbull refused to speak with the priest, he took the problem to the Spanish authorities in St. Augustine. Xavier Pellicer led ninety colonists on the seventy-five mile escape to refuge at St. Augustine in May 1777. Once they arrived Governor Patrick Tonyn initiated an investigation into their claims, twenty-one depositions were taken and in the end Turnbull was accused of cruelty and murder.

Governor Tonyn released the colonists from their indentures and the majority of the settlement was abandoned. The Governor offered land grants in a small area of St. Augustine for the new arrivals. Turnbull was arrested for failing to meet his financial obligations. Dr. Andrew Turnbull intended that the ill-fated New Smyrna Colony would be a profit-making venture, but largely due to his own irresponsibility it ended in a tremendous financial loss to his investors. Father Pedro Camps meticulously recorded the story of the Menorcans in the annals of the Catholic Church. His work, "The Golden Book of Menorcans", is the most complete record of early Menorcan history in Florida available.

The failure of New Smyrna Colony resulted in Turnbull expulsion from Florida. He sailed for Charleston, South Carolina on May 7, 1781. Dr. Turnbull returned to the medical profession. He became one of the founders of the South Carolina Medical Society, which led the way for the American Medical Association. Dr. Andrew Turnbull died in Charleston on March 13, 1792.

Investors purchased the deserted site of New Smyrna in 1837. The fertile land continually attracted ships to the harbor. The Menorcan meanwhile became a strong and integral part of the St. Augustine community. For two hundred years, the descendants of these brave people held tightly to their culture and heritage. In 1987, the Menorcan Cultural Society was founded. Today more than ten thousand ancestors of Menorcans arriving in Florida in 1768 live in the St. Augustine area. Recipes like Datil pepper sauce, pilau and clam chowder are all Menorcan standards passed down through the years and are still held dear.

New Smyrna is known today for its beach and port as well as sport fishing and water sports. The community retains a touch of Florida from years past, a quiet refuge illuminated with tropical sunshine and glistening white sand.

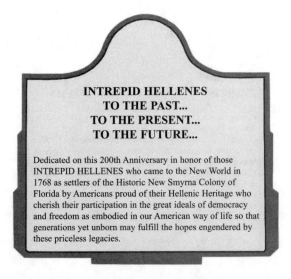

**INTREPID HELLENES
TO THE PAST...
TO THE PRESENT...
TO THE FUTURE...**

Dedicated on this 200th Anniversary in honor of those
INTREPID HELLENES who came to the New World in
1768 as settlers of the Historic New Smyrna Colony of
Florida by Americans proud of their Hellenic Heritage who
cherish their participation in the great ideals of democracy
and freedom as embodied in our American way of life so that
generations yet unborn may fulfill the hopes engendered by
these priceless legacies.

**Sams Avenue, in park across from City Hall, New Smyrna Beach
V20 ~ GPS Coordinates: 29.026856, -80.922429**

Hellenes[7] are an ancient people who have for centuries immigrated to foreign lands in search of a better life. The regal people have most often founded communities where emphasis has been placed on arts, sciences, commerce and sociology. The Hellenic ingenuity and tradition was part of every neighborhood created.

History records that a Cretan man called Pedro accompanied Pizarro, a Spanish conquistador who traveled along the American coast, to the New World. When Dr. Andrew Turnbull began his New Smyrna colony in 1768, the adventuresome Hellenes joined the procession. Many staked their hopes and dreams on this venture but unfortunately, a grand future was not to be found at New Smyrna. For ten years, the overseers of Andrew Turnbull kept the Hellenes like the Minorcans and others, in virtual slavery. By the time the people of New Smyrna escaped the tyranny of Dr. Turnbull only seventy-five of nearly five hundred Hellenes survived.

One of the few survivors was Dimitrios Foudoulakis, who settled in St. Augustine. He was part of the crew that built a one room, log schoolhouse that survives today as the Oldest Schoolhouse. Of course for the Hellenes establishing new homes in foreign lands was far from a novel idea.

In recent years, the Pancretan Association of America and American Hellenic Educational Progressive Association joined forces to create a monument to honor those that had gone before. The New Smyrna Odyssey Memorial was constructed at a cost of approximately two hundred thousand dollars. The beautiful Hellenic memorial was dedicated on November 18, 2000. Their brave ancestors would be proud, not only for the amazing tribute but the tradition that has been kept within the hearts and minds of Hellenes for generations.

HELENIC MONUMENT

1768
BRITISH COLONY OF NEW SMYRNA

During Florida's British Colonial Period, 1763-1783, Doctor Andrew Turnbull established the largest North American Colony at this site. Approximately 1300 Minorcans, Greeks, and Italians comprised the colony named after Smyrna, Asia Minor the birthplace of Dr. Turnbull's wife.

The colony experienced success in producing indigo dye, rice, help, and other crops for shipment to England.

Buildings, wharfs and a canal system still visible today were constructed.

Despite successes, after nine years, the colony failed approximately 600 survivors of the colony relocated to St. Augustine where many descendants reside.

North Riverside Drive, New Smyrna Beach
V21 ~ GPS Coordinates: 29.027150, -80.921871

The stories of the New Smyrna colony are varied in the details but what is certain are the tales of hardship, pain, neglect and death. When Spain ceded Florida to Britain in 1763, the British were determined to increase the population through colonization. To this end they offered considerable land grants.

One such transaction took place by a group of wealthy men who managed to secure a considerable amount of land. Scottish born Dr. Andrew Turnbull, Englishmen Sir William Duncan and Sir Richard Temple formed a partnership to develop a plantation. Turnbull selected an area on what was then known as the Hillsborough River for the development of the colony of New Smyrna, named for his wife's Grecian home.

He traveled to Greece, Menorca and a number of other locations to secure colonist to work the land. By the time eight ships sailed from Mahon, Minorca in March 1768, they bore three times the number of persons anticipated. They buried one hundred forty- eight at sea during the tumultuous three-month voyage. Once the settlers arrived it was glaringly evident that the colonists had been deceived.

There was never enough to eat, disease was rampant and the work was back breaking. Turnbull had planned to use five hundred African slaves for the most strenuous work; however, their ship was lost off the coast of the Florida Keys with no survivors. At the end of the first year another four hundred fifty of the indentured had succumbed to the harsh conditions. Death was a daily occurrence.

By late summer of the first year, rivaling cultures resulted in rebellion. The Greek and Italians scaled an uprising for three days. When calm was once again restored, the three leaders were taken to St. Augustine for a trial presided over by Governor James Grant. The trio was found guilty. Two men were hung, the third man was ordered to serve as their executioner. For this service the third man was pardoned. He was so ostracized once he returned to New Smyrna, that he eventually took his own life.

The colonists were indentured for seven to ten years. The first indigo was shipped to England in 1771. After nine years of brutal treatment, left to the overseers by Turnbull who had no hands on management of New Smyrna, the settlers were determined to escape their bonds. The overseer had a modest home located where today US 1 crosses Murray Creek, but Turnbull had two plantations. One supposedly located at in the midst of New Smyrna, the other some five miles to the north.

Francisco Pellicer led approximately ninety colonists in April 1777 to St. Augustine and asylum. Governor Tonyn granted the immigrants a small portion of the city as a haven. New Smyrna was all but abandoned and Tonyn had Turnbull arrested for financial irresponsibility. The irrigation canal dug by the New Smyrna colonists was filled in 1925. Today a sidewalk follows the route of that canal.

Turnbull lived the remainder of his life in Charleston. The colonists immersed themselves into St. Augustine society. Eventually they would become an important part of the community and to this day those surnames appear throughout the city. The New Smyrna colonists withstood the hell of servitude and endured.

Commemorating the Memory of
ZELIA WILSON SWEETT
1897-1980

Local historian and a leader in the cause for preservation of the historical sites in Volusia County.

North Riverside Drive, New Smyrna Beach
V21 ~ GPS Coordinates: 29.027150, -80.921871

Zelia Mary Wilson was born to Cornelia "Cora" Jane Sams and Lawrence Edward Wilson on December 10, 1897. She was the third child and only daughter. The family lived in New Smyrna. Their ancestors were one of the founding families of New Smyrna, after the failure of Turnbull's atrocities there, having moved there from Philadelphia.

She married Sergeant Jasper Sweett from St. Simons Island, Georgia on January 1, 1920. Zelia Wilson Sweett was instrumental in founding the Jane Sheldon Chapter of New Smyrna's Daughters of the American Revolution. She was the Organizing Regent and active in the chapter for most of her adult life.

Mrs. Sweett wrote two volumes of New Smyrna history: *New Smyrna, Florida, Its History And Antiquities*, publishing in 1925 and *New Smyrna, Florida In the Civil War*, published through the Volusia County Historical Commission in 1963. Zelia Wilson Sweett died on April 4, 1980, at the age of eighty-three. She was buried along side her husband in the place of her birth that she had devoted a lifetime to, New Smyrna.

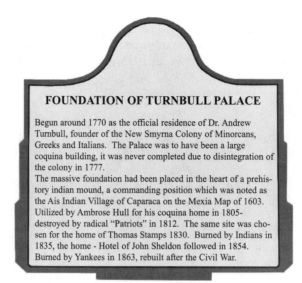

FOUNDATION OF TURNBULL PALACE

Begun around 1770 as the official residence of Dr. Andrew Turnbull, founder of the New Smyrna Colony of Minorcans, Greeks and Italians. The Palace was to have been a large coquina building, it was never completed due to disintegration of the colony in 1777.

The massive foundation had been placed in the heart of a prehistory indian mound, a commanding position which was noted as the Ais Indian Village of Caparaca on the Mexia Map of 1603. Utilized by Ambrose Hull for his coquina home in 1805- destroyed by radical "Patriots" in 1812. The same site was chosen for the home of Thomas Stamps 1830. Burned by Indians in 1835, the home - Hotel of John Sheldon followed in 1854. Burned by Yankees in 1863, rebuilt after the Civil War.

North Riverside Drive, New Smyrna Beach
V21 ~ GPS Coordinates: 29.027150, -80.921871

The first inhabitants of the property located at today's North Riverside Drive in New Smyrna were probably Ais Indians. A seventeenth century Ais village called Caparaca has been uncovered by archaeologists after examining a midden[6] on the property. Excavations also show evidence that a far older group of people first lived in the area around 500 AD.

The site has always been questionable. Some reports point to a Spanish fort possibly built in the late 1500s. Certainly the remains of thick coquina walls are consistent with the style fortress' built by Menendez de Aviles, founder of St. Augustine, during this time. Others suggest that the three-foot thick walls are symbolic of perhaps an early Catholic Church. This would be in keeping with the Ais village, which could have been a Catholic mission.

The ruins measure approximately 40 x 80 feet and are in keeping with the dimensions of Dr. Andrew Turnbull's large two-story stone house as well. When the New Smyrna colony failed due to financial mismanagement, cruelty, cultural diversity and disease, the majority of the settlers escaped to St. Augustine. By the fall of 1777, Dr. Turnbull, his family, overseers and a few Africans slaves were the only persons inhabiting the community. In December of that year, forty Seminole raided the Turnbull home. Turnbull retreated to Charleston, South Carolina and once again began to practice medicine. New Smyrna was left a ghost town.

Spain regained control of Florida in 1783 and like the British before, they offered land grants to encourage settlements. Dr. Ambrose Hull of Wallingford, Connecticut, an Episcopal minister obtained almost three thousand acres including the former home of Dr. Turnbull. Hull built a sugar and cotton plantation in 1801.

Dr. Hull built yet another two-story house on supposedly the very same foundation. Zealot patriots during the War of 1812 drove the Hull family out of their home. The home was set to the torch and once again only the coquina foundation remained. Dr. Ambrose Hull moved his family to St. Augustine.

Thomas Stamps of South Carolina purchased the ruins in 1830. He built a modest plantation house on the site and remained there for five years. In 1835, the plantation was burned to the ground at the beginning of the Second Seminole War. There seemed to be a disastrous pattern at the site but the story continued.

John Dwight and Jane Sheldon purchased the ruins of Stamps plantation in 1854. Within five years, they had built a two-story forty-room hotel; said to be the largest hotel south of St. Augustine. The Union steamer, *Oleander* fired on the Sheldon Hotel on July 9 and 11, 1863. The hotel was so badly damaged that a complete restoration had to be done.

Jane Sheldon[7] rebuilt the hotel out of driftwood collected from the beach. Later the building would contain the New Smyrna post office, port collector's office, newspaper office and a shoe shop. Dolph Sheldon and M. L. Childs eventually added a general store to the hotel. The building was demolished in 1896; finally surrendering to the fates, no other construction has occupied the foundation since. Today it is a noted Florida historic site.

FOUNDATION OF TURNBULL PLANTATION

1863-1963

To commemorate the one hundredth anniversary of the shelling and burning of the Sheldon House on this site July 26th during the War between the States by Union Gunboats Oleander and Beauregard.

North Riverside Drive, New Smyrna Beach
V21 ~ GPS Coordinates: 29.027150, -80.921871

John and Jane Sheldon were two of only a few people to remain in the New Smyrna area during the Second Seminole War. They bravely faced the Native American attacks, as plantations were routinely torched. The couple refused to be displaced from their home. When Civil War erupted, one of their sons chose to fight in the Army of Virginia and another, who was handicapped, operated a Union blockade in order to procure supplies for the community. John died in 1861, leaving Jane to face the ugly days of war alone. Jane was a hardy sort and again met the challenge courageously.

Jane Sheldon became the community doctor, she doled out medicines and with the assistance of her daughters, wrapped bandages for the Confederacy. The wooden Union side-wheel steamer *Oleander* fired on the Sheldon home and hotel. It was this ship that was responsible for the destruction of Jane Sheldon's home and business. During the final assault on July 11, 1863, the Sheldon Hotel was burned to the ground.

By the end of the month the *Oleander* returned shelling the entire town and capturing a sloop loaded with cotton. The Confederates burned several vessels to prevent capture and a large number of buildings in New Smyrna were destroyed during the Union barrage.

Jane Sheldon was the epitome of courage and perseverance. She rebuilt her home from driftwood collected along the shore. She nursed the sick, was New Smyrna's first Postmistress and continued to run her hotel until age forced her retirement. The Sheldon home and hotel was demolished for the last time in 1896. Jane Sheldon died on June 7, 1903.

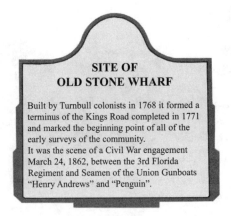

SITE OF
OLD STONE WHARF

Built by Turnbull colonists in 1768 it formed a terminus of the Kings Road completed in 1771 and marked the beginning point of all of the early surveys of the community.
It was the scene of a Civil War engagement March 24, 1862, between the 3rd Florida Regiment and Seamen of the Union Gunboats "Henry Andrews" and "Penguin".

Corner of Clinch Street & South Riverside Drive on the riverfront, New Smyrna
V22 ~ GPS Coordinates: 29.019370, -80.918223

Dr. Andrew Turnbull's indentured servants brought to New Smyrna to establish a multi-cultural settlement, built the Stone Wharf. Constructed in 1768 out of native coquina, the wharf marked the southern terminus of the King's Highway. The two pillars representing the wharf are located at what is today South Riverside Drive at the foot of Clinch Street.

The wharf was essential for the import and export of produce from New Smyrna to ports both domestic and foreign. Highway transportation had not been fully implemented at the time, the King's Highway would be extended to New Smyrna at a later date, but in the beginning water transportation was vital.

During the Civil War the Stone Wharf was the site of a battle between the Confederate 3rd Florida Regiment and the Union gunboats *Henry Andrews* and *Penguin*. New Smyrna happened to be one of the busiest blockade running ports in the South. The handicapped son of John and Jane Sheldon managed the blockade.

The Union gunboats were ordered to break the blockade and capture any vessels baring contraband. The Florida Regiment was stationed at New Smyrna to receive supplies brought in from the Bahamas and guard the cotton stored there awaiting export. The Union intended to confiscate a large stockpile of lumber stored at Ponce Inlet.

On March 23, 1862 the 3rd Florida Regiment fired on six Union landing craft baring forty-three men. The Union suffered seven losses with seven men wounded and two of the wounded taken prisoner. Only two Confederates received minor wounds.

When the tide is low at the foot of Clinch Street, remains of the old stone wharf are still visible. One can only imagine the way it must have looked when the indentured of New Smyrna laid the stone, remnants of their presence still remain.

End Notes

[1] Starchy roots of a native plant, similar to turnip roots.

[2] Meaning President Jackson

[3] Hat maker

[4] A room near the altar where priests vest for the service; the room where the communion vessels and vestments are kept.

[5] The spelling was later changed to Enterprise.

[6] Count was more a title of endearment rather than distinction, de Bary in fact should have been correctly called "Baron" meaning nobleman of various rank.

[7] Greeks

[8] Burial and/or disposal mounds.

[9] John Sheldon passed away in 1861.

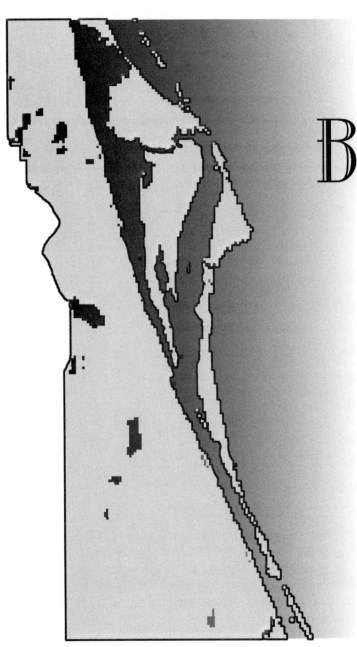

Brevard County

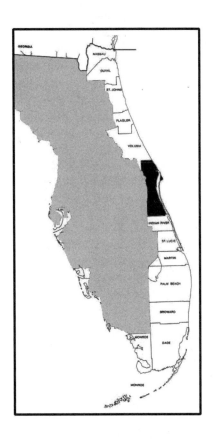

HARRY T & HARRIETTE V MOORE
MEMORIAL HOMESTEAD

This property is the former homesite of civil rights activists Harry T. and Harriette V. Moore, two people whose lives were committed to help Florida's Negro communities unite to form a collective identity. Mr. Moore was a Brevard County educator who became a full-time civil rights activist. After being fired for demanding equal pay, he worked to equalize the salaries received by Negro teachers with that of their white counterparts. He organized the Progressive Voters League of Florida, and his efforts to open the Democratic Party to Negroes provided new political opportunities for minority citizens all over the state. Mr. Moore organized the first Brevard County Branch of the National Association for he Advancement of Colored People in 1934, and served as its president for five years. From 1941-1946, he served as president of the Florida State Conference of the Branches of the NAACP, and then as the executive director until his death. Mr. Moore and his wife were murdered when a bomb was planted beneath their house on Christmas night in 1951.

2180 Freedom Avenue, Mims
BE1 ~ GPS Coordinates: 28.654983, -80.845383

Harriette V. Simms was born in the little town of Mims on June 19, 1902. Three years later, the man who was to be her soul mate for more than two decades was born in Houston near Tallahassee on November 18; his name was Harry Tyson Moore. Together the pair would change the course of history and become martyrs to the Civil Rights Movement. Their story is heart wrenching, inspirational and thought provoking well deserving of a prominent place in the education of generations to come.

Raised in a household where education was essential, Harry Moore was brought up by a widowed mother who supported the family as a teacher. He attended both Florida Normal and Bethune-Cookman Colleges, graduating with the credentials to enter the classroom as an educator. On December 25, 1936, Harriette and Harry were married.

THE ACTUAL MARKER

The couple had grown up in rural Florida where drinking from a "White" water fountain, using a "White" restroom or daring to enter a "White" restaurant could result in a disturbance charge and time in the local jail. The Ku Klux Klan deterred Black Americans from speaking out for freedom and justice with hideous violent attacks.

The Moore's taught the Black children of Mims in a cramped three-room schoolhouse. Harriette, in addition to her teaching duties, prepared lunch in a tiny closet; this meal was for most of the children their only hot meal of the day. Harry and Harriette experienced the racial separation first hand within the Florida educational system when supplies and facilities for Black schools were limited to second hand materials and barely inhabitable shacks. Additionally, Black teachers routinely earned only a fraction of the pay their White counterparts received.

Though Mr. and Mrs. Moore were unassuming, soft-spoken people, they accepted the call to oppose the long accepted segregation and inequality. Within the year, Harry Moore founded the Brevard County Branch of the NAACP[1]. He began to gather evidence to prove that Black teachers were being discriminated against. Sixteen years before Brown vs. Board of Education had brought about desegregation of schools. Harry Moore launched the first lawsuit to challenge payment schedules for black versus white teachers in Florida. The case was thrown out of court but led the way for future legislation equalizing teacher's salaries.

Unfortunately, his work on behalf of the Black teachers cost Harry his job as principal of the three-room elementary school in Mims. Eventually the all white Brevard County School Board would strip Harry Moore of his teaching credentials altogether making it impossible for him to return to the classroom as a teacher anywhere.

Undaunted, the Moore's traveled the state starting new chapter of the NAACP along the way. The work was treacherous, however Harriette Moore insisted on being at her husband's side should anything happen to him along the way. Their daughters, Evangeline and Annie, remembered the terror as the family traveled remote country roads. Their car was often closely followed and sometimes bumped slightly by menacing, faceless tormenters only to have them disappear into the darkness as the county line approached. Though never injured on these trips, the message was clear: "Get out this county and stay out."

The Moore's family life was sacrificed to endless NAACP meeting, letter writing, investigations and lawsuits. In 1941, Harry Moore accepted the presidency of the Florida Chapter of the NAACP. Moore was virtually anonymous in Mims until he ascended to the state post and death threats became a common occurrence. Tragically, in 1944, a horrendous case involving Lake County Sheriff Willis V. McCall sealed the fate of Harry and Harriette Moore.

Sheriff McCall was known as one of Florida's most powerful politicians. Certainly a powerful example of a man, McCall was six foot two with thick broad-shoulders topped off by a towering ten-gallon white Stetson that added another foot to his already massive stature. He believed his office was above the law and was investigated more than thirty-seven times for civil rights violations; McCall was never cited in any of these cases. In fact his office featured signs declaring a "White Waiting Room" and "Colored Waiting Room" until a federal judge forced their removal in 1971. Regardless of the signs' removal, everyone knew where they stood, or didn't stand, in Sheriff McCall's jail.

In 1949 a case of police brutality was brought to Harry Moore's attention for investigation. The particulars involved a 17-year old white girl from Groveland located in Lake County, who accused four young black men of rape. Sheriff McCall led a huge posse of men from the three surrounding counties in search of the suspects. Ernest Thomas, one of the accused, was chased down in a field. Thomas' body was so riddled with bullets he was almost unrecognizable as human. The other three suspects were arrested after being brutally beaten by Lake County deputies. Their trial was a travesty.

During the trial no medical evidence was ever offered to prove the rape, the defense was not permitted to offer testimony of police brutality also the young men were denied legal counsel for almost a month. The all white male jury took ninety minutes to find the three men guilty, one of young men was only sixteen years old. The United States Supreme Court overturned the conviction two years later.

Sheriff McCall was sent to the state penitentiary to bring the men back to Lake County for a new trial on November 6, 1951. He claimed to have had a flat tire and while changing it allowed the men to go to the bathroom along side the road. Even though the men were manacled together, McCall stated that the men attacked him with a flashlight and he opened fire with his pistol. One of men managed to survive by playing dead. The surviving man stated that minutes later, Sheriff McCall's deputy arrived and discovered that he was not dead, then shot him again in the neck.

Harry Moore demanded that Sheriff McCall and his deputy be prosecuted for murder. The NAACP raised money for the remaining defendant, brought the case to light in the media across the country and finally, approached Florida's governor. On December 2, 1951, Governor Fuller Warren received the following dispatch from Harry Moore:

"Florida is on trial before the rest of the world. Only prompt and courageous action by you in removing these officers can save the good name of our fair state."

On December 25, 1951, after spending a delightful evening celebrating the Moore's twenty-fifth wedding anniversary with both their mothers and daughter Annie, the couple returned home. Annie and her grandmother Moore had retired to bed, while Harry and Harriette closed up the house and prepared for the next day when daughter Evangeline would arrive from Washington DC and the family would celebrate Christmas. The house was festive with brightly wrapped presents awaiting the family gathering. By 10:00 p.m. the Moore's were asleep as well.

The house violently shuddered when a bomb exploded about 10:20 p.m. on Christmas night. The explosive force hurled the Moore's bed through the pine plank ceiling before it crashed back to the ground. Harry and Harriette Moore were buried under a mass of debris from the splintered remains of their room. Nothing resembling the room was left, wood from the structure was thrown as far as fifty yards. The windows in the master bedroom had been blown out of their frames and dust floated through the heavy fog.

Master Sergeant George Simms, Harriette Moore's brother, was home on leave from Korea and was first to arrive on the scene. Soon a second brother, Arnold Simms, arrived and the two carefully placed the couple into the car to transport them to the Sanford hospital thirty miles away. Annie and her grandmother were unharmed. No ambulance would transport blacks in Brevard County and the Sanford hospital was the closest facility to accept them. The men observed the state of Harry Moore, "He didn't feel like there was an unbroken bone in his body."

Harry Tyson Moore died on the way to the hospital in his mother's arms. Harriette Moore was in excruciating pain but suffered through it, leaving the hospital only long enough to see her husband's body at Burton's Funeral Home in Sanford. The FBI questioned her daily all the while Harriette was wracked with pain and the devastating grief of Harry's death.

Funeral services for Harry Moore were held at the St. James Missionary Baptist Church in Mims on New Years Day 1952. The church was selected because the Methodist church where Mr. Moore was a member was too small to accommodate the hundreds of people in attendance. State investigators and family members scanned the church for explosives before the service. Flowers were delivered from Miami to cover Harry Moore's casket because local flower shops refused to deliver them to a black funeral.

On January 2, 1952, the FBI continued to interrogate Mrs. Moore. Harriette V. Simms Moore died of her injuries on January 3, 1952, two days after her husband was buried. The Moore's were laid to rest side by side. The brutal assassinations were recorded on the front pages of newspapers around the world.

The Moore's murderers were never brought to justice. The FBI focused its investigation on the huge Orange County Ku Klux Klan. They spied and tapped phones and were eventually able to come up with three suspects. One of the suspects committed suicide after being questioned by the FBI and the other two suspiciously died of "natural causes" within a year of the murders. The case is listed to this day as unsolved. In 1978, Raymond Henry, Jr. confessed to devising the bomb that killed Harry and Harriette Moore. During his confession, Henry implicated Sheriff Willie McCall, other lawmen, grove owners, ranchers and businessmen. To date, the FBI has refused to release the taped confession, saying there is not sufficient public interest.

The Brevard County Commission, in 1993, named the new courthouse for slain civil rights leaders. The Harriette and Harry T. Moore Justice Center is named as well as a Multicultural Center on the Brevard Community College Cocoa campus in remembrance of their sacrifice. A park at the Moore homesite will be a living memorial in Mims.

A plaque at the site reads:

"Harriette and Harry T. Moore are unique in American history as being
the only husband and wife team to have sacrificed their lives through
assassination, for championing the ideals we as Americans have been taught
is our birthright. It remains a matter of pride that they are from Brevard, but,
equally, it is a matter of shame that they were slain here. Those responsible
for this terrible crime were never brought to justice."

The story of the Moore's life and subsequent death remains undisclosed in most of the Florida history books. Even the Civil Right Movement seldom recognizes their martyrdom for the cause. Slowly the story is coming into the public forefront and Brevard County has recognized their native son and daughter. Appreciation for this couple who gave their lives to bring equality and justice to blacks in America is mainly due to the unswerving efforts of those that knew and loved them.

LAGRANGE CHURCH

On March 6, 1942, a historic marker was placed in front of the oldest church between New Smyrna and Key West in Florida. LaGrange Church and Cemetery, located on Old Dixie Highway just north of Titusville, was built in 1869, and was the social center for the early settlers. The LaGrange church first begun in 1869, is the oldest church between New Smyrna Beach and Key West and the oldest Protestant church between St. Augustine and Key West.

1575 Old Dixie Highway, Titusville
BE2 ~ GPS Coordinates: 28.639341, -80.836887

J. N. Feaster, J. C. Feaster and B. J. Mims built LaGrange Church in 1869. It is listed as the most aged religious edifice from New Smyrna to Key West and the eldest Protestant church from St. Augustine southward. By the time LaGrange was constructed David Carlile and his wife had populated the area with ten grown children and were joined by a host of other families. The community rolls can be read quite easily by strolling through the LaGrange Church cemetery, the townships population is well documented there.

The settlers of LaGrange used the religious edifice for more than services; it provided a social hall for the community as well. People of all denominations gathered there for meals and fellowship. Dinner on the ground it was called, like a picnic where every family brought various dishes to be shared. Typical entrees included wild boar, deer, turkey, duck, mullet with side dishes to include indigenous vegetables and fruits like cabbage palm, oranges, mangoes and fresh made lemonade to wash it all down. Sweet potato pie was a favored desert of the day.

Reverend William Chaudoin came to the LaGrange community in 1871, for thirty-three years he devoted his life to serving the LaGrange Church congregation. In honor of Reverend Chaudoin's service to the community upon his death in 1904 Stetson University dedicated Chaudoin Hall in his memory.

In an effort to preserve history LaGrange Church and Cemetery Association was formed. Their efforts included restoration of the edifice and burial ground. Application was made and in 1995, LaGrange Church and Cemetery were listed on the National Register of Historic Places. The third Saturday of each month, except during the summer, the church is open and free tours are conducted from 10:00 am until noon. Special tours and lectures are often hosted for groups.

Merritt Island Wildlife Refuge SR 3, Merritt Island
BE3 ~ GPS Coordinates: 28.656612, -80.707822

When the Dummett family arrived to homestead in south Florida few had come before them. Thomas Henry Dummett established a sugar plantation in the area around 1825, but soon the venture took a downward turn. Virtually bankrupt, he turned over his holdings to son Douglas and moved the remainder of the family to St. Augustine. Douglas lived in St. Augustine for a time but eventually decided to try his hand at citrus farming in Volusia County. Douglas left his wife, son and daughter without a backward glance and was gone. The separation was consensual. It was said, Mrs. Dummett was not too heartbroken over his departure.

Douglas Dummett planted sour orange trees that were said to be taken from rootstock of Dr. Turnbull's colony at New Smyrna. The orange trees originated from Spain. He sold his first crop very successfully in 1828. The oranges were transported on flat boats called Minorcan Sailors; the name derived from the colonists at New Smyrna. The produce was shipped out to vessels bound for foreign shores waiting at the Mosquito Inlet.

Unlike the other scattered coastal plantation owners, Douglas Dummett refused to leave his holdings during the treacherous days of the Second Seminole War. In the face of danger he helped establish a local militia company. The regiment was dubbed "Mosquito Roarers". They were organized to protect the remaining settlers, their homes and families from the continual threat of the merciless Seminole Indians.

Following the war, Douglas took advantage of the Florida land program to expand his holdings. Utilizing a new grafting technique in which he infused buds from sweet orange trees onto sour orange bark resulting in a hybrid frost resistant stock. Douglas Dummett's vision virtually single handedly established the largest orange producing region in the state. The technique, known as top-grafting, resulted in a 1859 crop of more than sixty thousand oranges. Dummett supplemented his grove income by selling budwood to other orange growers in the region.

As outstanding member of Mosquito County, Dummett held numerous civic offices including judge, justice of the peace and appraiser of the Union Bank. When Florida was granted statehood in 1845, Dummett became the first state representative from Titusville. Socially Douglas Dummett was a pariah because he openly lived with one of his slaves. Leandra Fernandez was Dummett's common-law wife. Fernandez bore him three daughters, which Dummett openly claimed giving each his name.

A wonderful historical novel details the conflicts both socially and within Douglas Dummett's own heart entitled "Canaveral Light" by author Don Argo. Though it seems Dummett is devoted to the love of his life, he also supports the right to own slaves creating a great contradictory struggle in his own mind as well as his position in society. He did nothing to disguise his domestic situation, which was widely known. The public turned a blind eye as if Leandra and her daughters did not exist.

On April 23, 1860, Douglas Dummett's legitimate sixteen-year-old son Charles was killed in a hunting accident. While young Charles was walking through the forest with a friend, he stumbled over an exposed root. As he fell to the ground his rifle was discharged tearing through his body and ending his life. The tragic accident was interpreted by his distraught father as recompense for his sin in living with a slave and fathering her illegitimate children. Douglas Dummett had his son interred in a sarcophagus on the spot where he breathed his last. The marble slab is etched with the words, "Sacred to the Memory of Charles Dummett, Born August 18, 1844, Died April 23, 1860". Today the grave site of Charles Dummett can still be found splitting the asphalt of Canova Drive in New Smyrna Beach, which was paved around the crypt.

Douglas joined the Confederacy in the early days of the Civil War as the highest-ranking officer in the area. He was appointed Collector of Customs. He sold most of his slaves and paid little attention to his orange groves during this time. Leandra and her daughters were given their freedom. Brevard County was virtually untouched by the Civil War. Dummett embarked on the production of salt, which was a bustling industry during the Civil War. Huge iron caldrons were filled with seawater boiled to evaporation leaving the much-needed salt. Brevard County became a safe harbor for blockade-runners dealing in illegal contraband trading.

Douglas Dummett died in 1873, leaving a legacy of what was to become one of the most widely recognized orange producing areas in the United States. His contributions both politically and economically overshadowed his social indiscretions. His beloved groves were seriously damaged by the hurricane of 1893 and left in total devastation following the killing freezes of 1894-95.

Little changed in the Titusville area over the next twenty years until the Florida population explosion of the 1920s. People began flooding in buying every particle of property available. The great depression and failing of the stock exchange brought a sudden halt to the economic boom. The area went stagnate until World War II. During this time the United States began looking toward the stars with the idea of traveling beyond the horizon.

The United States government began searching in the 1950s for a site to establish a missile test range that would have no impact on populated areas. The area to the east of Titusville, known as Cape Canaveral, was chosen due to the length of the range, available land and isolation from the public. Another important factor was the proximity of support services such as the facility at today's Satellite Beach, which was then known as the Banana River Naval Air Station.

The initial base at Cape Canaveral was activated to safe guard the shipping lanes utilizing Martin patrol bombers in October of 1940. Nine years later President Truman enacted orders directed toward all branches of military service for a test facility. The mission was later modified and the entire base turned over to the Air Force. The facility was named in recognition of Major General Mason M. Patrick; hence Patrick Air Force Base was created.

Space exploration became the aim of the 1950s and plans were first implemented for the launch program at Cape Canaveral. NASA[2] arrived at the Cape in 1958. The first missions involved communication, weather and scientific study satellites and with the full support of the President an exciting era began. President John F. Kennedy vowed that within the next ten years the United States would put a man on the moon. The federal government acquired more land on Merritt Island and a new fifty-two story Vertical Assembly Building was constructed.

The new mandate brought with it scientists, military members, engineers and all manner of support personnel. The workers came with their families and within a very short span of time the population of Brevard County tripled. However Cape Canaveral was very isolated to purchase groceries, see a doctor, go to school or meet any basic family needs, residents were required to travel as far as Orlando. The demand quickly spurred the construction and establishment of housing developments, medical facilities, schools, civic services, utilities and shopping. With the buzz of space launches came tourists and a completely new industry was born.

Although the Space industry has suffered several cut backs over recent years, Brevard County still flourishes. The emphasis now, rather than expansion, is conservation of the natural resources on the unspoiled coastal areas. The county places great importance on the historical environment, archaeological sites and continues to heed the call of community development. A beautiful unspoiled beach, rich history, vast economic and agricultural areas, civic services, education and the latest in modern technology, Brevard County is today a well-balanced community. Douglas Dummett would be amazed.

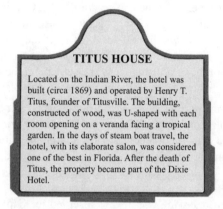

TITUS HOUSE

Located on the Indian River, the hotel was built (circa 1869) and operated by Henry T. Titus, founder of Titusville. The building, constructed of wood, was U-shaped with each room opening on a veranda facing a tropical garden. In the days of steam boat travel, the hotel, with its elaborate salon, was considered one of the best in Florida. After the death of Titus, the property became part of the Dixie Hotel.

402 Indian River Avenue at park, Titusville
BE4 ~ GPS Coordinates: 28.611350, -80.806667

The circumstances surrounding the birth of Henry Theodore Titus are as controversial as the life he led. Reportedly he was born between 1815 and 1823, the most accepted date being February 13, 1823 in Trenton, New Jersey; though other reported life activities support an earlier birth date. He grew into an adult, moving to the Oklahoma Territory but soon returned to Jacksonville, Florida.

On Wednesday, March 10, 1852, Henry wed Mary Hopkins in Darien, Georgia. Her father, Edward Hopkins led a highly successful political life in northern Florida serving as a member of the legislature, Mayor and customs collector. He eventually ran for Governor but was defeated in his pursuit. Henry and Mary Titus set up housekeeping at Sand Point where they eventually had eight children. The couple established a mercantile and soon a settlement developed in the area.

Henry Titus sought adventure in the wilds of Kansas, where some say he chose to become soldier of fortune and other accounts list him as a Confederate officer. The Confederate Army has no record of his enlistment. Titus did serve as Adjutant for Earl William Walker in Nicaragua and later Adjutant General in Pennsylvania. It was during this time that he began using the title Colonel. It was noted that Colonel Titus opposed Abolitionist John Brown during an episode noted as Bleeding Kansas.

Reports of Bleeding Kansas stated that Colonel Henry T. Titus accepted a commission in the Second Regiment, Southern division, Kansas Militia on August 6, 1856. He took an active role in what was called the "Sack of Lawrence." Titus and his men destroyed the abolitionist-supported presses of the "Herald of Freedom" and the "Free State". The type set machine was thrown into the river. The abolitionists retaliated under a cover of darkness in the wee hours of the morning when a party of "Free-State" men attacked the Titus home. Seven cannon balls fashioned from the metal of the destroyed presses retrieved from the river blasted through the house. Colonel Titus was wounded in the head and shoulder then captured. He was treated quite humanely, made comfortable and given medical attention. The remainder of the prisoners were confined in the "Herald of Freedom" building that Titus' men had earlier attacked. After his release, Colonel Titus spent the waning days of the Civil War as a blockade-runner.

After his return to Sand Point Titus continued the operation of the family mercantile. Titus was a busy man, he later he established a pony express line to Enterprise, an insurance agency, a sailboat mail route to Daytona and a mule transport team which hauled passengers, farm produce and mail to and from the St. Johns River. He purchased considerable amounts of property and joined the ranks of citrus growers in Florida. The groves were very successful and the Titus' fortune was made.

By this time Sand Point's population had swelled to approximately two hundred fifty. Colonel Titus played a friendly game of dominoes with Captain Rice though the stakes were considerable. The victor would have the honor of renaming their ever-expanding settlement. Colonel Titus met the challenge and won the day ~ Titusville was born. He donated the property for the construction of St. Gabriel's Episcopal Church and the Brevard Courthouse as well as additional acreage for schools, churches and civic buildings. Colonel Titus stipulation was that if the county seat were ever moved from Titusville, all of the donated land would be returned to his rightful heirs.

Though Titus was generous in the establishment of the settlement, he was not well received by the entire population. His fellow citizens hated his pro-slavery stance and wanted to restrict his power in the community. Colonel Titus owned a hack[3] those transporting passengers from boats at Salt Lake and Lake Harney into town.

Colonel and Mrs. Titus built a hotel dubbed the "Titus House" utilizing a tropical design in keeping with their semi-tropical surroundings. The construction consisted of a large one-story wood framed building with expansive wings on either side forming three sides of a square. The courtyard featured a lovely garden and next door an ornate gold guilded saloon offered food and spirits to patrons. Rooms were let at Titus House for three dollars per night.

The southeast corner room of one wing was always reserved for Captain Mills O. Burnham, the lighthouse keeper at Cape Canaveral. Burnham would often arrive for a stay accompanied by his crew aboard the impressive sailing vessel, *Osceola*. The lively group brought a great deal of excitement to town. By this time Colonel Titus was confined to a wheelchair suffering with considerable pain from rheumatoid arthritis. Town folk reported that he often sat in his chair on the raised porch of the Titus House with a shotgun across his lap. History does not reveal that he ever actually shot anyone from his sentry post, but it kept patrons of his hotel in line.

Titus granted an interview, which appeared in print on Sunday, August 7, 1881, detailing his feeling for the settlement he had founded. He stated, "Titusville is the grand center of all trade and will so continue to be. Her motto is to live and let live." Four days later Colonel Henry Theodore Titus passed away. The "Tallahassee Floridian" eulogized, "There are few men more widely known in this state than was the deceased gentleman." Obviously Colonel Titus was quite a character."

ST. GABRIEL'S EPISCOPAL CHURCH

In 1887, construction of a church was begun on land donated to the Titusville Episcopal mission by Mary Titus, wife of the town's founder, and J. Dunlin Perkinson, lay reader of the mission. The name of the church was changed from St. John's to St. Gabriel's with the gift in 1888 of a stained glass window depicting St. Gabriel. The neo-Gothic style reflects a trend in Episcopal Church architecture in central Florida during the late 1800's. This style was spread through the efforts of Edwin G. Weed, third bishop of Florida. The church, which is on the National Register of Historic Places, contains a fine collection of Victorian stained glass.

South Palm Avenue & Pine Street, Titusville
BE5 ~ GPS Coordinates: 28.610650, -80.809217

J. Dunlin Perkinson, a lay minister at the Titusville Episcopal mission and the widower of Titusville founder, Mary Evalina Titus, each donated the land for use as the site for an Episcopal Church. The congregation utilized the services of Edwin G. Weed; the third bishop of Florida, to design the Gothic Revival sanctuary and L. R. Decker was hired to construct it. Donations for building expenses were solicited from many sources including Captain R. P. Paddington, master of the steamer *Rockledge*, Captain Paddington. The church was to be built at Sand Point, today known as Titusville. The edifice was to be named St. Johns Episcopal Church.

The plans called for a gabled roof, tall spired steeple and arched windows meeting at their apex in a point. Construction was completed in 1888. The wooden framed sanctuary embraced a dark paneled interior. The edifice featured breathtaking stained glass windows, initially imported from England. The windows were finished in New York by famed designers Gorham[4] and Tiffany[5] with the exception of the St. Luke pane originated by Lamb[6]. Completed between the years 1888-1890 the windows depict ecclesiastical as well as local themes. One particular locally inspired portal is dedicated to Mills Burnham, an early lighthouse keeper for the Cape Canaveral beacon and a second window was to bring change to St. John's forever; the St. Gabriel's window was donated in 1888 prompting the membership to change the name of the church to St. Gabriel's Episcopal. These magnificent Victorian stained glass panes illuminate the dim interior of the sanctuary with streams of multifaceted prisms. St. Gabriel's windows are considered to be one of the finest examples of Victorian stained glass on the eastern seaboard.

In 1892 the previously vacant steeple was adorned with the assistance of St. Gabriel's ladies. The women of the church donated a bell, which was known to be the largest in Brevard County. The initial plans for the church grounds included a cemetery, however, one was never established. The proposed burial ground met with resistance from both local citizens and the city commission who objected to a cemetery within the city limits. The first rectory was established in April 1895 and five years later the Parish House and Sunday School were added.

A much-needed expansion in 1960 resulted in double the seating capacity for parishioners. Riverboat steamers often delivered near capacity crowds to St. Gabriel's special services and social functions held by its Guild from towns up and down the river. The church underwent cosmetic restoration at this time as well. In the early 1970s St. Gabriel's sanctuary was deservedly added to the National Register of Historic Places. By 1992 it became obvious that the sanctuary required some extensive restoration work. The support beams were sagging, the roof had been patched beyond repair and the paint on the exterior of the building had begun to flake under the harsh strain of Mother Nature's elements. A state grant, the community and congregational donations made the desperately needed restoration project possible. Today St. Gabriel's Episcopal Church continues to host an active congregation. The historic church and congregation carries on a sense of tradition in the Titusville community offering spiritual guidance.

BLUE STAR

A tribute to the Armed Forces that have defended the United States of America.

Harrison & US 1, South of Titusville
BE6 ~ GPS Coordinates: 28.584617, -80.801200

This particular marker was placed as a result of the community service provided by the Titusville Garden

Club. The club, whose motto is "Come Grow with Us," was established in 1933 and is itself a historic treasure for Brevard County. The TGC[7] Center is located at 5275 Sisson Road situated between State Road 405 and State Road 50.

The TGC continues to hold dear their time-honored objectives. The club's aim is to instill an adoration of working with the soil and the horticultural knowledge to grow and cultivate plants and trees. Further the club promotes the preservation of our natural resources and the importance of a clean environment. While working toward these objectives the club maintains a close knit relationship with the community.

The club projects involve maintaining the landscape surrounding the "Welcome to Titusville" signs, this seems to be a fitting vocation for the community orientated group. However it is only a small portion of the work they do. The club was actively involved in the establishment of a bird sanctuary in the Sand Point area, they also maintain floral arrangements at Astronaut High and the Cape to honor the crew lost in the Challenger tragedy.

Education is a large part of the coupling between the community and the club. Master gardeners host plant clinics on a weekly basis and the club sponsors local students with scholarship programs and Camp Wekiva. The civic-minded club's endeavors widely range from community clean up campaigns to Christmas decorations for the library and public buildings. The club introduces area youth to the joys of gardening and the responsibility of preserving our invaluable natural resources; as well as providing a touch of cheer for those ailing or in the care of Hospice. Of course the Blue Star marker program honoring those that have fought and died in the military service of our country is quite possibly one of the Garden Club's most rewarding efforts.

In keeping with the tribute to those that have served and died for our country, I would also like to recognize the World War I Memorial located at the flagpole on the old courthouse lawn at 506 Palm Avenue in Titusville. Originally dedicated on May 12, 1921 in honor of those that died in service to our country during the First World War. The bronze plaque was initially installed in the vestibule of the courthouse; nothing exists to state why the memorial was moved to its current location.

U.S. 1 at King Street, State Road 520, Cocoa
Intersection of Airport Road, at Old Dixie Highway, Titusville
BE7 ~ GPS Coordinates: 28.355833, -80.733017

Joseph M. Hernandez was assigned several impossible tasks in late 1837. First he was directed to bring in the Seminole renegade Osceola and secondly, to simply use his detachment as a work force to build a road. Capturing Osceola and returning him to St. Augustine into the hands of his superior officer General Thomas S. Jesup proved to be the easier assignment. Hernandez was now to begin work on the second set of orders.

Joseph Hernandez was born in the St. Augustine area in 1792. He remained there for much of his life except for the periods when his position as Brigadier General of the Army called him away. One such occasion occurred when he was given the assignment to build a road. The road or trail would exist to connect the fortifications along the Atlantic coast making transportation to the southern reaches of the territory easier for those seeking to homestead the area. The trail would also aid in the removal of hostiles, hence the Seminole people were driven-from their homes. Specifically the road was to be sixteen feet wide and more than two hundred miles long. The girth would ensure that mule trains and ox carts could effortlessly traverse the trail and the two hundred-mile trek leading travelers from St. Augustine to Fort Pierce was established in 1738.

Many obstacles existed in the road building project. First of all, Hernandez men were armed with only hand tools to make their way through the dense vegetation and fashion a reasonably level road. In their favor, it was winter so the men were not forced to toil under the baking semi-tropical sun. Also during this season lessened the swarms of malaria-carrying mosquitoes delivering their infectious sting resulting in the debilitating disease. Other dangers certainly existed. The Second Seminole War was at it height and the native Seminole were adept at blending into the scenery then ambushing unsuspecting prey. Likewise animal predators would lie silently in wait. Florida panthers were not yet hunted to virtual extinction and presented a potential hazard while soldiers gnawed their way through the forest. Through marshland regions, the powerful jaws of alligators caused great fear in the hearts of cautious workers.

A great deal of the terrain was high and dry along the tops of sand dunes, which are now protected by law. The roadway path, running along the region known to geologists as the Atlantic Coastal Ridge, is west of what is today U.S. Highway 1. Portions of the road had been blazed some twelve years before under the direction of Colonel James Gadsden. Gadsden had taken the trail south to the St. Lucie River and General Hernandez was ordered to take the roadway to Fort Capron. Both Gadsden and Hernandez had the benefit of following the hunting trails used by the Seminole as well as the vanquished Ais and Timucuan tribes. These warriors would travel by horse and on foot along the Rio de Ais, known to us as the Indian River.

Other than the soldiers at Fort Pierce, who remained until 1842, the military rarely used the road. Settlers began flocking to the southern territory once the Army spread the word that the Seminole Indians had been defeated, many driven into the saw grass marshes of the Everglades. At first the homesteaders arrived directly from the Atlantic Ocean by way of the Indian River Inlet. With the creation of what was noted on the hand drawn maps of the era as the Hernandez, Capron or Hernandez-Capron Trail, made Fort Pierce more readily accessible by land.

As time passed the Haulover Canal was established in 1854, easing river travel. Later Flagler's railroad slowly made its way south opening up the area to the flood of expansion and paved roads during the early days of the 20th century. The railroad all but erased the Hernandez Trail from the map. Cattle drives continued to take the trail as late as the 1940s. From the sky, in aerial photography, some sections of the old Hernandez Trail remain visible to this day. General Joseph M. Hernandez would be proud to see his hard work has stood the test of time, at least in part after more than one hundred fifty years.

HERNANDEZ TRAIL Marker #2 - On June 28, 1928, a second marker was placed at the intersection of Airport Road, at Old Dixie Highway in Titusville, with the cooperation of Florida Board of Parks and Historic Markers. The bronze marker was originally encased in a large boulder of native coquina rock, (mixture of shell fragments and quartz grains bound together by calcium carbonate).

BLUE STAR

A tribute to the Armed Forces that have defended the United States of America.

Florida Avenue & US 1, Rockledge
BE7 ~ GPS Coordinates: 28.337383, -80.726600

Few people in Brevard County know the story behind Bennett Causeway or Emory L. Bennett Veterans Memorial Park. Most have never thought of who Emory L. Bennett was or why he deserved the recognition of a park and bridge named in his honor.

Emory L. Bennett was born on December 20, 1929 in New Smyrna Beach. After his father lost the family business, the family had moved from New Smyrna to Indianola on Merritt Island. Bennett's father took work with the state road department and later managed a family-owned seafood business. Because of their meager circumstances the family lived above the business, remaining there for fourteen years. Travis Hardware today occupies the building that once housed the seafood business. Emory worked his way through school and after graduation continued to work in order to amass enough money to attend college.

When hostilities broke out in Korea on June 25, 1950, Emory enlisted in the Army and shipped out to basic training one month later. He was interested in pursuing an education with the Army engineers but when the fighting in Southeast Asia escalated Emory was transferred to the infantry and sent to the front lines. Bennett was assigned to Company B, 15th Infantry Regiment, 3rd Division and given a position as an Automatic Rifleman. He was quickly promoted to PFC[8] and earned the Combat Infantry Badge for his performance in battle. Company B was soon dispatched to Sobangsan, Korea.

In the wee hours of the morning on the eve of the first complete year of hostilities in Korea, two enemy battalions descended on PFC Bennett's company. From their defensive position Company B put up a gallant effort but the enemy fighters continued to press the American perimeter. Bennett quickly sized up the situation and realized that the odds were against them. An order was passed through the ranks to fall back. With the enemy steadily advancing it became obvious that Company B would suffer great losses. PFC Bennett, although wounded, continued to stand his post against overwhelming odds until he took a fatal bullet.

Private First Class Emory L. Bennett paid the ultimate price in the service of his country on June 24, 1951. For his sacrifice, Bennett was awarded the Congressional Medal of Honor posthumously. He was finally returned to his beloved home where PFC Emory Bennett was laid to rest at Pine Crest Cemetery.

Through impact fees and grants, construction of a park began, but it would take ten long years before the park was completed. In a ribbon-cutting ceremony on July 25, 2002, Bennett was recognized for his bravery and valor in the face of certain death. The opening ceremony was well attended by dignitaries from every walk of life, countless military veterans and a very special guest, PFC Bennett's only surviving brother, John Bennett.

Today the park spans two hundred ten acres. The facilities include three ballfields, a playground, hillside walking paths and family picnic areas. The main feature is a large multi-purpose field, which can be used for a variety of purposes. PFC Emory L. Bennett would be proud.

FLORIDA AGRICULTURAL COLLEGE

In 1869, Gleason purchased 10,000 acres of land along the Indian River originally known as Arlington. He renamed the place Eau Gallie which comes from two French words: "Eau" for Water and "Gallie" which is a corruption of the word Galet meaning gravel or small rounded rock. In 1872, he persuaded the Florida Legislature to locate the state agricultural college to Eau Gallie and gave 2320 acres of land. Gleason stated a two-story building with ten classrooms and offices made out of coquina in 1878. No students ever attended the college because I March 1877 the republican government lost control and the democrats moved the college to Lake City. In 1886 the college moved to Gainesville and became the Univ. of Florida. The original building that was bought from the state by Gleason and the land deeded back to him 1884. The building was used as the areas first hotel called the Granada Hotel. The hotel was used by steamboat passengers and was destroyed by fire on July 8, 1903.

Pineapple Avenue, between Law Street & Aurora Road, Eau Gallie
BE9 ~ GPS Coordinates: 28.136083, -80.628933

Governor Thomas Brown signed a bill supporting the state of Florida's university education programs on January 6, 1853. The first school under this mandate was to be EFS[9] located in Ocala. Unfortunately the hostilities of the Civil War called to service, according to record, all of the students and faculty of EFS thus forcing the school to close its doors for the duration of the war.

EFS reopened for classes in 1866 but the school was moved to Gainesville. The original school was housed in what would later be the Methodist Church in Gainesville. Epworth Hall, named for Methodist founders John and Charles Wesley's home in England, is one of the original EFS buildings and is still in use today. EFS in Gainesville began what would be a continuous journey of more than one hundred fifty years as one of the world's most prestigious universities, Florida Agricultural and Mechanical University.

Florida Agricultural College was to open in Gainesville but due to financial constraints, plans and politics changed. Eau Gallie became the new site and construction began on the facilities in 1872. Once several of the buildings were in place, political genuflecting caused the entire project to fall apart. It was soon obvious that Florida Agricultural would never open its doors in Eau Gallie. The college site was changed once more and this time to Lake City.

Florida's first land grant college began matriculation as Florida Agricultural College at Lake City in 1884. The school temporarily changed its name in 1903 to the University of Florida. The Buckman Act of 1905 brought radical changes to the public university system in Florida, all public higher education facilities in the state would come under the same umbrella.

BREVARD COUNTY'S FIRST SCHOOL LOCATED TODAY AT FLORIDA AGRICULTURAL COLLEGE

Andrew Sledd was selected as the first president of the new University System, though his tenure was inundated with controversy from the beginning. Most believed his standards were much too lofty and the system under his tutelage was destined to failure. He refused to incorporate extracurricular activities such as athletics believing that students would be distracted from academics. Andrew Sledd was forced to resign in 1909.

The Buckman Act resulted in four major schools being established in Florida: the University of Florida, catering to white males; Florida State University, serving only white females; Florida Agricultural and Mechanical University, for all African American students; and the Florida School for the Deaf and Blind. The Buckman Act was abolished in 1909. Eventually desegregation forced all schools to open their doors to all students regardless of gender and race. Later the Disabilities Act also created opportunities in higher education facilities for handicapped students.

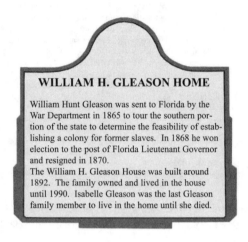

WILLIAM H. GLEASON HOME

William Hunt Gleason was sent to Florida by the War Department in 1865 to tour the southern portion of the state to determine the feasibility of establishing a colony for former slaves. In 1868 he won election to the post of Florida Lieutenant Governor and resigned in 1870.

The William H. Gleason House was built around 1892. The family owned and lived in the house until 1990. Isabelle Gleason was the last Gleason family member to live in the home until she died.

Law & Pineapple Streets, Eau Gallie
BE10 ~ GPS Coordinates: 28.135117, -80.628567

William H. Gleason left the War Department at the conclusion of the Civil War to enter political life in Florida. Gleason was the sitting Lieutenant Governor when impeachment proceedings were initiated against Governor Harrison Reed. When the Florida legislature adjourned on November 7, 1868, the Senate had failed to begin the impeachment trial. None the less, Lieutenant Governor Gleason laid claim to the Governor's office. Reed's supporters refused Gleason entry to the capitol but that did not deter him from establishing an office and issuing proclamations signed as Florida's Governor.

The Florida Supreme Court ruled on November 24 that Governor Reed had never been officially impeached and Gleason had no right to the office. Governor Reed, some say motivated by revenge, had Gleason removed from the Lieutenant Governor's office based on the fact that he failed to meet the required three year residency stipulation to hold the office.

Gleason and his family were living in Dade County during this time. In 1872, he reentered public service by defeating "Pig" Brown for the state legislature. William H. Gleason was known to dissenters as that "Miami Carpetbagger". Everyone remembers the Florida election controversy of 2000 but practically no one knows of the Florida election fiasco nearly one hundred and twenty-five years previously. While the rest of the United States was embroiled with the Presidential election of November 7, 1876 between Republican Rutherford B. Hayes and Democrat Samuel J. Tilden, Florida's Dade County was preoccupied with local affairs. Dade County held the national election in limbo while they hashed out their own problems.

The Florida legislative election, especially in Dade County, had some complications. The first declared results were Stewart 34; Varnum 18; Brown 27, and Gleason 24. Incidentally, but of little interest to most Florida voters, the presidential results were Tilden state electors 28 and Hayes 27.

Before the official election tally was released on November 17, William H. Gleason registered to contest the proceedings. By doing so the presidential count from Dade County would not be sent to Tallahassee until the controversy was settled. Unknown to most of the electors in Dade County, the presidential election was as heated and controversial as their own. Samuel Tilden had gone to sleep on election night believing that he had been elected. The next day, the New York Tribune declared: "Tilden Elected".

Incredibly a New York Times reporter, John C. Reid, did some quick arithmetic and realized that three states had not submitted their electoral count. Florida, South Carolina and Louisiana were holding up the entire United States final count and Hayes could still win. Before long national interest focused solely on Florida, where on November 27th, the official tally had begun by the state canvassing board. The state was given ten days to determine the results of the election because Florida's four presidential electors were required by law to cast their votes on December 6th. As the chairman read each county return, one side or the other challenged. On the first reading it appeared that Hayes had a slim forty-three-vote majority. But another important factor remained - Dade County's returns were missing!

Accusations of fraud and intimidation flourished throughout the United States. Rumor of corruption ran rampant in Florida. Canvassers of Dade County met to consider William Gleason's case. Gleason alleged that irregularities and illegal voting took place at the Sears Precinct. One irregularity listed was that Simeon Frow voted after dark. Secondly, A. F. Bracklin and R. H. Thompson were foreigners by birth and did not present their naturalization papers. Third, Gleason alleged that certain ballots had fallen to the floor in the Sear district and when they were retrieved a number of them had been changed. The allegations were supported with eight pages of depositions by various individuals supporting Gleason's claims.

The canvassers threw out the Sears Precinct results. With those results discounted, Gleason had 7 votes, Brown 4, Stewart 6 and Varnum 5. Stewart died on his return trip home to Lake Worth. The Hayes electors were victorious over Tilden 8 to 5. On Friday, December 2nd, Gleason finally delivered the Dade County returns to Tallahassee. He had managed to not only to elect himself, but also deliver Florida for the Republicans. The nation did not know who was elected president until the evening before the inauguration. The headlines read, "The Last Straw for the Democratic Camel, Dade Comes in with a Republican Majority". Though Tilden certainly had grounds to further contest the controversial returns, he chose to concede the election and help restore faith to the last three states ~ Florida, Louisiana and South Carolina.

Gleason suffered enormous financial set backs and moved his family to Eau Gallie. Eventually he recovered the lost wealth and rose to prominence in the community. William Hunt Gleason died in Eau Gallie on November 9, 1902.

CORNER OF HIGHLAND & LAW STREET

The three story building on the corner of Law and Highland was built by the Gleason Family 1910. The third floor was the Masonic Temple. The building was built on some of the highest ground in the area and still had an artesian well with enough pressure to supply water to the third story restroom. The second floor housed the Gleason Brothers land office. The lower floor was the State Bank of Eau Gallie, which remained open until the depression in the 1920's.

The house on the northwest side of Law Street was the Florida East Coast Railway Agent's house, built sometime around 1900. S. K. Watts, Station Agent, and his family lived there.

The Thomas Shave house located at 1695 Highland was built in the Folk Victorian Style in 1903. Shave owned turpentine stills, the Carter House at 668 Law Street was built around 1900.

Highland Avenue & Law Street, Eau Gallie
BE11 ~ GPS Coordinates: 28.134583, -80.629367

Originally this area was known as Arlington, named by John C. Houston for his families' homesite near Jacksonville having the same name. When William Hunt Gleason arrived in the late 1860s, he renamed the area Eau Gallie in honor of Eau Claire, Wisconsin founded by the Gleason family. Observing the coquina strewn Indian River shores, the name was derived from "Eau" the French term for water and "Gallie" from "Galet" meaning gravel loosely translating to rocky water thus Eau Gallie.

William H. Gleason was infamous in Florida politics, more information detailing his political exploits can be found in the article "William H. Gleason Home". Gleason generously offered the state more than two thousand acres for use as a state agricultural college. The offer was accepted but was stopped under governmental opposition after one building for the college was constructed. Eventually Gleason made use of it as the Granada Hotel. Today state agricultural college is located today in Tallahassee and is known as the Florida Agricultural and Mechanical University.

Gleason's sons, William H. Gleason and George G. Gleason, inherited both their father's business and political acumen. Together they built a land development company and William continued his father's law practice. The brother's were licensed steamship pilots offering intracoastal shipping and having dry-docking facilities.

Grandson William Lansing Gleason was heavily involved in real estate law and substantially increased the families' Florida land holdings. Continuing the family commitment to public service, he served as the Eau Gallie mayor in the 1930s. The Gleason family was never far from public life and was always in the mix of Eau Gallie political life. The Gleason endowment included property deeded to the city of Eau Gallie that was protected with a reversionary clause. Ten members of the family signed the Gleason deed. The clause states that if the property ever ceases to be used for the public good then it will revert back to the Gleason heirs.

A proposal was put before the city council in 2002 that part of the Gleason property be used as the site for a child care facility. But in keeping political aspects questions were raised about this use meeting the intent of the endowment. Because the signers of the original deed were deceased, the only way to verify the proviso would be contact all of the surviving descendants or have a circuit court approve the project. Neither option was easy or inexpensive. After much controversy and considerable effort the project was approved. The political double talk and lawyer wrangling, began. It was finally decided that childcare could be considered "for the public good". Thus the Gleason family legacy continues to enrich Eau Gallie to this day.

DR. W. J. CREEL & HIGHLAND AVENUE

This home was built around 1914 for Francina Houston Hancock, a descendant of Eau Gallie's founding family, the Houston's.
In later years, Dr. W. J. Creel and his family bought the house and lived in it until his death in 1970. The Creel's, who came to Eau Gallie from College Park, Georgia in 1910, First lived in the house at 1667 Highland Avenue before moving across the street. He was the only doctor between Cocoa and Fort Pierce when he came to Eau Gallie. During the depression, he would receive payment for his services in the form of fresh eggs, pies, lawn work, or whatever a person could pay. One summer Dr. Creel delivered 35 babies for $38.
He practiced medicine for 54 years until his retirement.
The house to the north was built around 1890 for Carroll Houston. The next house further north was built around 1900, originally with a widow's walk on the roof. Dr. E. E. Macy, a homeopathic physician, owned the house.

1634 Highland Avenue, Eau Gallie
BE12 ~ GPS Coordinates: 28.133700, -80.628900

William Jackson Creel was born in Carrolton, Georgia and attended medical school at Emory University in Atlanta. He first practiced medicine at Bayard, Florida leaving to become a "railroad doctor" at the little settlement of Eau Gallie.

Dr. W. J. Creel literally backed into his job at Eau Gallie. He bought a Flanders Studebaker automobile from a man in Rockledge but something went wrong. Dr. Creel was driving along the dirt road that was US 1, when the car shuddered to a stop and refused to budge in any direction but backwards. Not to be deterred Dr. Creel just backed his way to town. The most severe illness he dealt with was typhoid. He was one of the first to campaign for area residents to stop using drinking water from ponds and shallow wells as a means of preventing the disease. Digging deeper wells would resolve the problem and Dr. Creel advocated their use throughout the county. According to his son Earl, one of the most difficult house calls Dr. Creel made was out to see Mike Simmons on the opposite side of Lake Winder. To get there he was forced to swim the horse and buggy across the shallow lake.

Dr. Creel had two offices, one at Watts' drugstore on the corner of Highland Avenue and Ninth Street (now Eau Gallie Boulevard) and another in Melbourne. The fact that he kept offices did not preclude patients from knocking on the door at his home on Highland Avenue. A local lady, Mrs. Ozaki was badly burned and because there was no local hospital at the time, Dr. Creel cared for her in his home until she recovered enough to go home. From that time on the Ozaki family, farmers by profession, kept the Creel family stocked with vegetables in payment and gratitude.

When patients required hospitalization they had to be sent to Riverside Hospital in Jacksonville. The invalid would travel on a cot in the baggage car of the Florida East Coast Railroad to the hospital. Often Dr. Creel would travel with patient when the illness was severe enough. Many times a boat was sent from Merritt Island to fetch the doctor, often patients from Sebastian or Grant sent letters asking Dr. Creel to come.

Dr. Creel was a three-term mayor of Eau Gallie and served one term in the Florida legislature in 1927. He worked as a canal digger with shovel in hand at Sebastian Inlet and from Lake Harney to Titusville. Eventually he tried to gracefully retire from the medical profession but never quite left it behind. He never did make a living with medicine but this was possibly because he never sent anyone a bill. His most profitable summer came when he delivered thirty-five babies and earned thirty-eight dollars.

In his waning years Dr. Creel enjoyed fishing for pompano but preferred to eat mullet. Today when a great number of doctors take a moment of relaxation on the golf course, Dr. Creel found solace in the orange groves. He would spend an afternoon working amid the fragrant groves and the world would seem miles away. Dr. William Jackson Creel left an indelible mark on Brevard County. His legacy was the lives he saved, children he brought into the world as well as his active interest in his church, the school system and the political working of the community he loved.

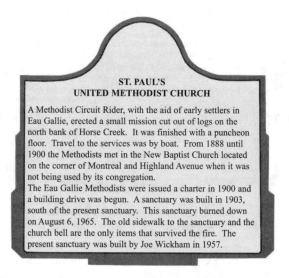

ST. PAUL'S
UNITED METHODIST CHURCH

A Methodist Circuit Rider, with the aid of early settlers in Eau Gallie, erected a small mission cut out of logs on the north bank of Horse Creek. It was finished with a puncheon floor. Travel to the services was by boat. From 1888 until 1900 the Methodists met in the New Baptist Church located on the corner of Montreal and Highland Avenue when it was not being used by its congregation.
The Eau Gallie Methodists were issued a charter in 1900 and a building drive was begun. A sanctuary was built in 1903, south of the present sanctuary. This sanctuary burned down on August 6, 1965. The old sidewalk to the sanctuary and the church bell are the only items that survived the fire. The present sanctuary was built by Joe Wickham in 1957.

Highland Avenue, Eau Gallie
BE13 ~ GPS Coordinates: 28.132500, -80.628117

The history of St. Paul's United Methodist Church spans more than one hundred years. The foundation comes from a group of individuals known as circuit riders. When central Florida first began attracting settlers, the Methodist Church assigned circuit preachers to minister to the sporadically placed communities. Most small groups of parishioners gathered in private homes, local inns or community buildings. Eventually when the numbers warranted, a small church would be built on donated property and more permanent clergy sought.

The South Carolina Methodist Conference dispatched circuit riders to service the area. The circuit riders, often called saddlebag preachers, traveled a typical route covering from two to five hundred miles. He was tasked to complete the circuit usually within four weeks. The itinerate preachers slept in various homes of the parishioners. Because of this method of traveling preachers, Methodism became known as the "frontier faith."

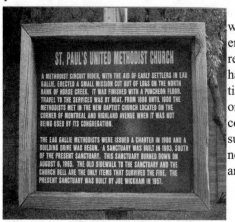

THE ACTUAL
MARKER

The typical circuit rider was a young, single man; usually with a responsible career such as carpentry, shopkeepers, school teachers or blacksmiths who at some point had been profoundly affected by a religious experience. Circuit Riding was a very hard life. More than half of these young men died before their thirty-fifth birthday. The initial building used for the Methodist congregation was a small log cabin on the banks of Horse Creek. The walls and floors featured a split log construction left natural on one side and sanded smooth on the interior surface. The congregation reorganized in 1900, building a more permanent modernized structure. An educational building was constructed and then dedicated on Palm Sunday in 1957. Unfortunately the new structure burned to the ground only eight years later. The only remnants of the Methodist

Church were the bell and sidewalk.

Today the St. Paul's United Methodist Church on Highland Avenue has an active congregation. The programs and services offered by the church continue to support the community as it has for more than one hundred years.

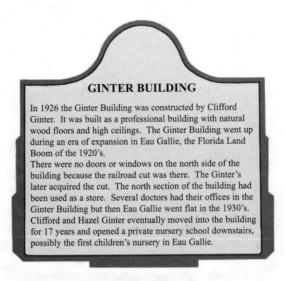

GINTER BUILDING

In 1926 the Ginter Building was constructed by Clifford Ginter. It was built as a professional building with natural wood floors and high ceilings. The Ginter Building went up during an era of expansion in Eau Gallie, the Florida Land Boom of the 1920's.

There were no doors or windows on the north side of the building because the railroad cut was there. The Ginter's later acquired the cut. The north section of the building had been used as a store. Several doctors had their offices in the Ginter Building but then Eau Gallie went flat in the 1930's. Clifford and Hazel Ginter eventually moved into the building for 17 years and opened a private nursery school downstairs, possibly the first children's nursery in Eau Gallie.

St. Clair Street & Highland Avenue, Eau Gallie
BE14 ~ GPS Coordinates: 28.131967, -80.627967

As one approaches the northwest corner of Highland Avenue where it intersects with St. Clair Street, a two-story building comes into view. The building has graced this particular corner since 1926. Construction was initiated by Clifford Ginter and will forever be known to locals as the Ginter Building.

The building featured glowing wood floors and high ceilings in keeping with the tradition of the day. However, strange for the construction was the fact that the northern section held no openings of any kind. The reason for this unique architectural concept was the location of the railway. Being solid, the wall would baffle some of the din heard when steam locomotives would chug down the tracks. Originally built as an apartment house, imagine living in a space that would shudder as the great steel wheels rolled on down the line. Sleeping must have been difficult at best and certainly a plate or two succumbed the tremble of the train passing.

The Ginter Building sheltered numerous people over time and served several different purposes. The building evolved, beginning as an apartment house and later a department store. Several doctors actually saw patients there but eventually the decline in population during the 1930s at Eau Gallie resulted in the Ginter Building being vacated.

Hazel and Clifford Ginter realized that the building would have worth for a new unique concept. In fact, they established what was most likely the first nursery school in the area. During the late 1930s childcare outside the home was a very new concept unlike today when four out of six children attend daycare, according to Parents magazine.

The concept of nursery school came to public view with initiatives from the highest office in the land, President Franklin Delano Roosevelt. In 1935, the President signed Title V of the Social Security Act providing funding for emergency nursery schools. Title V became necessary to serve children from low-income families, whose mothers were forced into the work force due to the depression and later in support of the war effort during World War II.

The federal government offered monetary grants to provide child care services and research in the area as well. The Works Progress Administration provided jobs for women in desperate need of work. By 1943, the

Lantham Act funded childcare for women working in factories manufacturing goods for World War II. The war ended, the factories closed and the funding for childcare quickly evaporated into the ethereal. Even though the war was over, a new trend had begun and women largely remained in the work force. Nursery schools became a part of everyday reality for most and the Ginter Building was used in this capacity for seventeen years.

HIGHLAND & ST. CLAIR

The Florida East Coast Railway arrived in Eau Gallie on May 20, 1893. The first engine arrived on June 24, 1893. A ticket from Jacksonville to Eau Gallie was $7.00. Eau Gallie was the terminus while construction continued to Miami. A "Y" was built in downtown so that trains could turn around and head back north. A spur line ran down to the Indian River where the Library and City Park are located. Cargo was transported onto the steamboats for transportation south for three years thus creating a short lived land boom in Eau Gallie.

The large hole in back of the Ginter Building on the north side of St. Clair Street (1540 Highland Avenue) was the cut out for the railway. The hole has been filled in over the years. A wooden bridge was built over the cut out on Highland Avenue so cars could travel over the tracks.

Highland Avenue & St. Clair Street, Eau Gallie
BE15 ~ GPS Coordinates: 28.131850, -80.628000

When the railroad arrived in Eau Gallie on May 20, 1893 it was known as the Atlantic Coast, St. Johns and Indian River Railroad. For the years previously steamboats had provided the mainstay of passenger and produce transport but with Flagler's ever extending rails, times were a-changing. The railroad offered a faster, more reliable system of travel and in doing so its lonesome-whistle sounded the death knell of the majestic steam driven ships traversing the gently rolling intracoastal and river waterways.

Two years after the railway made the scene of Eau Gallie, Henry Flagler officially changed the name to the Florida East Coast Railway. In doing so, the Eau Gallie inland spur became part Florida's history and Flagler's railway to the sea. The steamship companies tried unsuccessfully to keep abreast of the railways forward march, even coordinating travel schedules to ensure continuity in travel. However, unwittingly the more reliable railroad soon displaced the steamships and they slowly disappeared into history.

Invariably the railway brought northern travelers in great numbers. The impact on Brevard County's economy was immediate. Traveling was now much more comfortable for passengers, which was often weather dependent on the waterways. The movement of local produce and products was much easier, faster and more cost efficient. The speed of the new mode of transportation decreased the amounts of spoilage experienced previously. In effect the increase in suitable products increased profits.

Businesses in complement to the rail industry began to pop up. Dozens of ice houses, packing plants and canneries were founded along the railroad tracks. The expansion explosion came to a decisive halt with the devastating freezes of 1894 and 1895. The citrus industry was virtually destroyed in Brevard County and people were forced to seek alternative money making prospects. The devastation to the economy was sudden and decisive, some growers were ruined for life.

OLD CITY HALL COMPLEX

Brevard Art Museum was at one time City Hall, Police, and Fire Department of Eau Gallie. Whenever there was a fire, a siren, located on top of the three story roof, would inform all the local volunteers they were needed. Local businessmen on Highland would push the fire truck out of the station onto Highland.

During the depression the City did not have enough money for a new battery for the fire truck. The volunteers would push the truck down Bud Yeager Drive and pop the clutch to start the engine. This was how they got the truck started for about a year before a new battery was purchased. The fire truck always started and arrived at each call.

Early residents had to be careful where they walked. A revised Eau Gallie ordinance in 1907 state under Section 3, "No horse, mule, or other animal shall be ridden, led or driven, or be allowed to stand on any of the sidewalks of the town."

Highland Avenue, Eau Gallie
BE16 ~ GPS Coordinates: 28.131417, -80.627550

The site of the old Eau Gallie City Hall, located on the east side of the main old town thoroughfare Highland Avenue, is only one block from Indian River and the heart of the historic district. The site has served many purposes over the years. The majestic old building during its life span was the location of most civic services in the early 1900s. Aside from its responsibilities as City Hall, both the Police and Fire Department once called the scenic site home. The building rose two stories and the City Hall called the site home in 1910.

The Old City Hall site was transformed into the Brevard Museum of Art, which opened its doors on March 14, 1978. Three galleries welcomed visitors to browse among the artist's treasures. Within a very short span of time, it became obvious that the wealth of cultural exhibits bulged the seams of their existing quarters. A larger modernized museum space was procured in 1986, expanding the visitor's space to more than seven thousand square feet including seven galleries.

Today, only one block from the picturesque Indian River and at the heart of Brevard County's historic district, the Brevard Museum of Art and Science provides a cultural educational center benefiting local residents and tourists alike. The commitment to the preservation, appreciation and display of the visual arts is evident in amazing exhibits featured within the confines of the museum. Local talent as well as nationally and internationally known artisans displaying a myriad of styles, eras and media is shown in both permanent and revolving exhibitions.

Featured events involving specific themes and individual artists are often showcased throughout the museum, which because of numerous facilities can be presented simultaneously. Eight to ten momentous occasions are planned each year in addition to permanent displays and additionally long-term exhibits from private collectors and corporate holdings. Docents lead informative gallery tours while available guides and videos offer assistance with self-guided tours.

In 1995 the museum was expanded to include an impressive Science Center and was aptly renamed, the Brevard Museum of Arts and Science. The facility offers wonderful hands on exhibits displaying the amazing facets of the physical sciences. One of the most popular exhibits allows visitors to the museum to discover the constellations in the Brevard County night's sky.

The Brevard County Museum of Arts and Sciences includes the Harris Auditorium, two Museum Shops, the Foosaner Educational Wing, Science Center and Art Galleries. Museum Shops stock various gift items and souvenirs to commemorate your visit. Their unique inventory of everything from original works of art to educational toys set the museum shops apart from local gift stores. The museum is an amazing asset to the community and visitors alike, it continues to offer cultural enlightenment in the form of educational camps and classes to students of all ages. The facility is open Tuesday through Sunday, charging a small admission. Amazingly if you plan your excursion for a Thursday afternoon, admission is free.

OLD EAU GALLIE POST OFFICE AND SURROUNDING AREA

This building was the Eau Gallie Post Office circa 1900-1925. Before the advent of automobiles, old-timers recall tying their horses and buggies to the big oak tree in the back. The building just south of the Post Office was Eau Gallie's first theater, operated by Harry Sample. Movies, stage plays and minstrel shows were shown here and the Eau Gallie School. Located at that time across the street, used the theater for theatrical productions.
The two-story building on the corner of Highland and St. Clair Street was originally built by Clifford Ginter as an apartment house.

1596 Highland Avenue, Eau Gallie
BE17 ~ GPS Coordinates: 28.131167, -80.627567

The building used as the Eau Gallie Post Office was originally built in the 1890s. The building was utilized as a post office for some twenty-five years, though the postal history of Eau Gallie began many years before. Just after the Civil War left its mark on the country, a black freedman by the name of Peter Wright became the legendary sailing mailman.

Peter Wright, a founding father of Eau Gallie, sailed a regular mail route from Titusville to Malabar delivering posts to the riverside communities. A true wilderness, the waterway was precarious but provided the easiest access to settlements along the coast. Today a plaque commemorating Wright's service resides in a small park overlooking the Indian River Lagoon.

Possibly the first established post office was in the DuNil Hotel owned by pioneer John Green. Eau Gallie was at the time thought to be the final destination of Flagler's railroad, though he later expanded until the railroad reached the southern most United States point at Key West. Taking advantage of the railways promise to bring wealthy Yankees south, the DuNil Hotel resort was established. The resort featured a large hotel, private cottages, a fresh water pool, tennis, lawn bowling, running water and an impressive horse stable. Green named the settlement Sarno for a city in India and opened a post office there in 1895, it closed only one year later. After Green died the resort never turned a profit and eventually was closed. The facility was later used as the Kentucky Military Institute.

Constructed at 1596 Highland Avenue the Eau Gallie Post Office was built using rusticated block common in Art Deco, Georgian Revival, Italian Renaissance and Classicism styles. Rusticated can be defined as masonry cut into large blocks separated by deep ingrained joints. The architecture is given a bold, exaggerated look to the lower part of an exterior wall, the frame of a door or window.

Convenient to patrons, it was a common sight to see countless horses and buggies tied to the enormous oak tree behind the building. During this time postal patrons were obliged to come to the office to gather their mail. Home delivery of the post had not yet been established, rather the mail was brought to the post office twice a day. For many in the community it was a treat to drive their buggies into town once a month intent on gathering mercantile supplies and visiting the post office. The postal facility was where locals congregated to share the news of the area and had a festive atmosphere. The postmaster was a revered member of society because he provided a link to the outside world where few ventured beyond the close confines of their homes. Many people at this time died without ever traveling more than ten miles from the place of their birth.

J. P. Varnum, was the first Postmaster of Eau Gallie, as well as the founder of the "Jacksonville Times". Later, Varnum purchased the Jacksonville Union and combined them into the present great daily, The Times-Union. Today, heirs of J. P. Varnum can still be found inhabiting the original Varnum homestead amassing a sixteen-acre tract near the later-day High School.

A new uncharted chapter in postal history was created in 1959 known as Missile mail. The *USS Barbero*, a Navy submarine ported out of Norfolk, Virginia, assisted the United States Postal Service in the search for a faster, more efficient means of delivering the mail. Only one such mission was ever attempted, shortly before noon on June 8, 1959. It took exactly twenty-two minutes for the dispatched Regulus missile to launch three thousand pieces of mail to reach their destination. Two official postal mail containers replaced the submarine's nuclear warhead. The mail consisted of envelopes containing a picture or story relating to the historic event. The posts were address to President Dwight Eisenhower and community postmasters. United States Postmaster General Arthur E. Summerfield signed the letters. This was a brief but impressive chapter in postal history.

Just south of the Eau Gallie Post Office was Harry Sample's theater. The facility was the first of its kind, offering entertainment in the form of minstrel shows, new fangled silent moving pictures and frequent stage productions. An organ off to stage right provided additional musical accompaniment. Students of the nearby Eau Gallie School often performed amateur productions at the Eau Gallie Theater. Theater patrons were treated to silent film stars such as Mary Pickford in 'Pollyanna', Douglas Fairbanks in 'The Mask of Zorro' and the westerns of William S. Hart. The most popular traveling musical stage shows of the day were Minstrel Shows. These shows embodied racial segregation with both white and black performers donning blackface. Ironically audiences of all races enjoyed them.

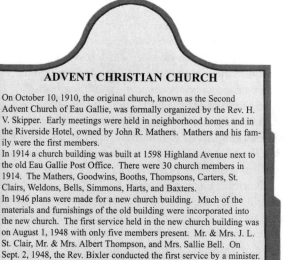

ADVENT CHRISTIAN CHURCH

On October 10, 1910, the original church, known as the Second Advent Church of Eau Gallie, was formally organized by the Rev. H. V. Skipper. Early meetings were held in neighborhood homes and in the Riverside Hotel, owned by John R. Mathers. Mathers and his family were the first members.

In 1914 a church building was built at 1598 Highland Avenue next to the old Eau Gallie Post Office. There were 30 church members in 1914. The Mathers, Goodwins, Booths, Thompsons, Carters, St. Clairs, Weldons, Bells, Simmons, Harts, and Baxters.

In 1946 plans were made for a new church building. Much of the materials and furnishings of the old building were incorporated into the new church. The first service held in the new church building was on August 1, 1948 with only five members present. Mr. & Mrs. J. L. St. Clair, Mr. & Mrs. Albert Thompson, and Mrs. Sallie Bell. On Sept. 2, 1948, the Rev. Bixler conducted the first service by a minister.

1596 Highland Avenue, Eau Gallie
BE17 ~ GPS Coordinates: 28.131167, -80.627567

Advent is Latin for coming, appropriate in that the Advent Christian Church is based on the Second Coming of Jesus Christ. The Right Reverend H. V. Skipper assembled the initial congregation on October 20, 1910. Before construction of the first church meetings were held in parishioner's homes and John R. Mathers' Riverside Hotel. Within four years the membership had saved enough money to build a sanctuary.

There were thirty recorded members in 1914 and among them very prominent founding families of Eau Gallie. The facility remained next to the Eau Gallie Post Office for just over thirty years when plans for a new sanctuary took form. Preserving the materials of the initial church building, the materials were reused in 1946. Construction took two years, unfortunately by this time the membership had dwindled due to the economic difficulties of the time.

Originally sects of Second Adventists, based on the teachings of William Miller, met in Albany, New York. Miller spoke on the belief that the end of the world would come to pass in 1843, when that failed to happen Miller predicted the return of Christ in 1844. Of course that prophecy proved false as well. In 1845, the leadership adopted a belief that Christ would return at an indefinite time and the dead would be resurrected. Just prior to the outbreak of the Civil War, the largest and best-known sect was founded and called Advent Christian Church. This branch was formed as a result of a controversy over the question of the soul's immortality.

Today, the Advent Christian Church has a membership in the United States of over thirty thousand. Other sects of the original include the Seventh-Day Adventists and the Church of God whose combined membership is in the millions.

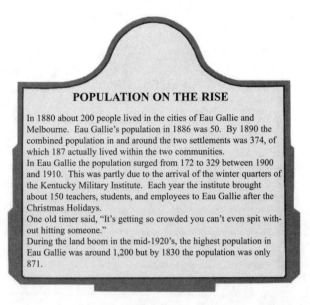

POPULATION ON THE RISE

In 1880 about 200 people lived in the cities of Eau Gallie and Melbourne. Eau Gallie's population in 1886 was 50. By 1890 the combined population in and around the two settlements was 374, of which 187 actually lived within the two communities.

In Eau Gallie the population surged from 172 to 329 between 1900 and 1910. This was partly due to the arrival of the winter quarters of the Kentucky Military Institute. Each year the institute brought about 150 teachers, students, and employees to Eau Gallie after the Christmas Holidays.

One old timer said, "It's getting so crowded you can't even spit without hitting someone."

During the land boom in the mid-1920's, the highest population in Eau Gallie was around 1,200 but by 1830 the population was only 871.

Pineapple Street in front of Public Library, Eau Gallie
BE18 ~ GPS Coordinates: 28.131833, -80.626717

Grand changes were taking place in the United States in the 1920s. The country was experiencing a time of great economic and social expansion enabling thousands of Americans in all walks of life to flock to warmer climates. This period changed forever the Florida wilderness into a tourist mecca.

Benefits including paid vacations and pensions were, for the first time in history, offered to working Americans. Therefore a great portion of the American population now had the time and money to travel. The other end of the financial strata arrived in droves to seek employment in the service industry to provide for the arriving tourists. Though the railroad at the beginning of the century opened the lines of transportation south, the emerging automobile made the trip much more comfortable and simple.

Entrepreneurs realized the possibility of riches by investing in Florida real estate. Ready capital was not a problem; credit was easy to obtain. Sudden winter migratory Northerners known as "Snow Birds" began having an enormous impact on the Florida economy. The elderly and ailing sought the warmer climate to soothe their frozen countenance. The rich and middle class saw an opportunity in the ever-flourishing landscape and the poor saw a means to improve their station in life.

The Republican administration of President Warren G. Harding proposed lower taxation and increasing business assistance programs. The conservative Florida government now began borrowing funds to maintain the constant growth necessary to meet the influx of new residents and tourists.

The land of white sand beaches was glamorized in the northern presses with exaggerated tales of land investors doubling profits within months. Real estate firms realized that selling property at auction rather than simply advertising set pricing could fatten coffers significantly. Investors bidding on a prized location often drove selling prices through the roof, much to the delight of real estate tycoons.

Occasionally land speculation was less than successful, but for the most part during the Florida Land Boom riches were there for the taking. One story reported in a 1920s Florida newspaper told of an elderly gentleman who was committed to a sanitarium by his children for "squandering" his entire life savings and their inheritance on Florida property. He spent seventeen hundred dollars for a tract of Florida land. In 1925, the value of the property ballooned to three hundred thousand dollars. The gentlemen's attorney secured his release from the sanitarium in order to file suit against his ungrateful kids!

**EAU GALLIE
PUBLIC LIBRARY**

This library is the second oldest library in Brevard County. It
was founded by the members of the Avilan Club in 1898. Its first
location was in the Eau Gallie Post Office (see marker on
Highland Avenue).
The Eau Gallie Woman's Club took over the function of the
library about 1939. The library was then located in Ella
Rossetter's Insurance office on ninth street (now Eau Gallie
Boulevard.)
The library at various times has been located in a restaurant, the
City Hall and the Civic Center on Highland.
The first permanent home of the library was erected on this site
in 1962. Books were moved down the hill from the Civic Center
by a "Book Brigade" of concerned citizens.
This building was erected and dedicated in 1998.

1521 Pineapple Avenue, Eau Gallie
BE19 ~ GPS Coordinates: 28.132083, -80.626267

The historical marker dedicated to the Eau Gallie Public Library details the history of the facility very well. In 1939, while the Eau Gallie Woman's Club saw to the library resources, the collection consisted of twenty-five books. Other locations that served as the library in addition to Ella Rossetter's Insurance Office were Ada Stabler's restaurant, the Eau Gallie City Hall and even the Civic Center located on Highland Avenue. Of course the first permanent facility was constructed in 1962 and was completely renovated in 1999.

Honors of the first library in Brevard County go to the facility at Cocoa Village founded in 1895. The library was in a rented one-room cabin, leased for five dollars a month. The books and furnishings were donated by local patrons, who paid one dollar per year for membership. Ladies of the village volunteered to serve as the librarian for a week at a turn.

For fifty years the library system of Brevard County expanded from its start at Cocoa Village to Cocoa Beach then Eau Gallie, Melbourne and Titusville. Money received from the state enabled the system services to become available to all county citizens. The population significantly increased with the work of NASA and the space program. In response the state increased funding for many things in Brevard County including the library system. The facility number increased from five to nine facilities and with the cost of maintenance and a boost in book price the money was put to good use.

Today sixteen libraries serve Brevard County representing more than a million books as well as an abundance of media items including videos, recordings and various periodical files. Programs such as tax assistance, educational seminars, book discussions and signings, lectures and classes are hosted for patrons. Children's events are carefully planned to foster, at an early age, an appreciation for books and reading. Disabled citizens are provided with services to make the libraries of Brevard County accessible and beneficial to all. Completing a transformation to a modern age, computers and the Internet has made using the library as easy as signing on from ones' home computer. Free classes in using the Internet and computers are offered at various facilities.

HARBOR CITY HOTEL

A spur track for the Florida East Coast Railway was once located on the north side of this site. The track went out on a dock where freight and passengers were loaded onto river boats for the journey south.

In 1902, the East Coast Lumber and Supply Co. built its planing mill and novelty works at this site. A waterwheel powered by an artesian well created electricity for the mill.

In 1925, the Harbor City Hotel was built here, estimated cost of the building was $150,000. The name was changed to Oleanders Hotel a few years later and eventually it became known as the Imperial Hotel. In the 1970's it was known as River House. The aging building was razed in 1991.

Corner of Pineapple Avenue & Eau Gallie Boulevard, Eau Gallie
BE20 ~ GPS Coordinates: 28.131267, -80.626217

In 1991, an aged Eau Gallie landmark became a footnote in history after almost seventy years of hosting visitors. When it fell victim to demolition, little of the former glory of what was known as the River House remained. Unfortunately few details of this tourist mecca can be found.

Originally the structure was built in 1925. Called the Harbor City Hotel, the inn welcomed its first guests on May 8. The initial construction cost an estimated one hundred fifty thousand dollars, which was a considerable sum for this time. The structure must have been quite elegant. The grand hotel had a tropical and distinctive Spanish influence adorned with grayish-white stucco. Noted Eau Gallie resident, Dr. W. J. Creel was president of the firm who commissioned the hotel's construction. J. L. Allen managed the Harbor City Hotel.

One month after the grand opening of the hotel, Mrs. George Thorne of Chicago, Illinois purchased it. The selling price was two hundred fifty thousand dollars, this was an amazing hundred thousand-dollar profit for Dr. Creel's firm. The considerable amount of money was but a drop in the bucket for Mrs. Thorne, whose husband was one of wealthiest men in Chicago at the time. George Thorne was co-founder of a wildly successful business in 1872 with partner Aaron Montgomery Ward. Of course the venture was Montgomery Ward & Company; they sold dry goods by mail. The company got its start by sending out a catalogue featuring everything from corn planters to windmills and underwear to Knickerbockers suits. According to most folk, if you could not find it in the Montgomery Ward catalog you really didn't need it.

The Harbor City Hotel experienced many changes over the years including modernization. However, it transformed under several different monikers. The second name bestowed on the establishment was Oleanders, which remained until 1958 when it became the Imperial. Finally ending with the River House, it was under that calling that the majestic gray stucco hotel last graced the northeast corner of Pineapple Avenue and Eau Gallie Boulevard.

Preceding the hotel years, the lot was home to the novelty works and planing mill of the East Coast Lumber and Supply Company. The company was founded in Eau Gallie on May 15, 1902 and began business under the hot July sun of the same year. George F. Paddison was named president and built a home some six blocks to the south. A water wheel powered by an artesian well on the property provided electricity for the lumber business as well as Paddison's home.

From the beginning the East Coast Lumber Company relied on local fruit and vegetable growers for business. To that end, the company developed ready to assemble crate kits. The kits contained wooden slats, wire and even tissue paper to wrap the produce, which the crates were used to transport. Unfortunately Florida growers suffered numerous set backs during the seasons of 1914 and 1915 due to extreme weather conditions and eventual crop failures. By this time East Coast Lumber had established enough business to record a five-percent profit.

The company cooperated with the United States government when World War I demanded that all non-essential construction, materials and millwork be halted. The company supplied products for the Army Air Stations during the war years. By the war's end in 1918, the Eau Gallie location was dismantled and moved to Ft. Pierce. Although its days in Eau Gallie had come to an end, the East Coast Lumber and Supply Company is still in business today after more than one hundred years from its start at the northeast corner of Pineapple Avenue and Eau Gallie Boulevard.

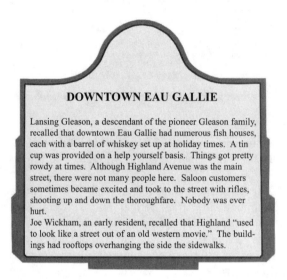

DOWNTOWN EAU GALLIE

Lansing Gleason, a descendant of the pioneer Gleason family, recalled that downtown Eau Gallie had numerous fish houses, each with a barrel of whiskey set up at holiday times. A tin cup was provided on a help yourself basis. Things got pretty rowdy at times. Although Highland Avenue was the main street, there were not many people here. Saloon customers sometimes became excited and took to the street with rifles, shooting up and down the thoroughfare. Nobody was ever hurt.
Joe Wickham, an early resident, recalled that Highland "used to look like a street out of an old western movie." The buildings had rooftops overhanging the side the sidewalks.

NE corner of Eau Gallie Boulevard & Highland Avenue, Eau Gallie
BE21 ~ GPS Coordinates: 28.130683, -80.627083

Downtown Eau Gallie, in the early days, was somewhat wild and wooly. Appearing like a scene from one of silent screen star William S. Hart's westerns, Eau Gallie featured an abundance of saloons and fish houses. Barrels of homemade distilled whiskey were strategically placed around the downtown area with a tin cup that everyone shared when they imbibed on special occasions without charge. Then came the national prohibition of alcohol in 1920-1933, it was a drastic change.

Prohibition was implemented to reduce crime and corruption, reduce the social problem of public drunkenness, relieve the tax burden created by prisons and poorhouses as well as improve the health and hygiene of Americans. These were lofty goals for what was called the "noble experiment". It was soon discovered that alcohol was not an integral part of social problems as was first imagined. The alcohol prohibition experiment was a miserable failure on all accounts.

Most rural salt of the earth Floridians accepted prohibition as law without question, but urban communities disliked the unpopular edict immensely. Tourists traveled south to the Sunshine State to have a good time and prohibition hampered the party atmosphere. Because of Florida's close proximity to the Bahamas and Cuba, where alcohol was legal, demand for spirits created a new source of supply. Locals knew that if a wine bottle appeared on a windowsill of a house or business then white lightning, moonshine, illegal hooch, bathtub gin or whatever name attached to it was sold secretly out of the backdoor after dark.

Nassau and Grand Bahama flourished as rum smuggling centers. Florida's vast coastline was wide open to illegal hooch. Despite the fact that Florida locals were just a short boat trip away from a cocktail, they had to devise a means keep tourism dollars within the state. The result ~ Florida's Rum Run, began in 1921.

Alcohol smuggler's developed what was known as "Bimini Boats" to make their rum runs. These boats were built for speed with large cargo holds and designed to detect Coast Guard vessels. The Bimini boats were also built with shallow drafts to navigate close to shore. Devices were included to ditch cargo into the sea should advancing Coast Guard patrols threaten the mission. By 1927, the Coast Guard introduced newer, faster cutters and curtailed a significant amount of the smuggling.

CORNER OF HIGHLAND AND EAU GALLIE BLVD.

The First State Bank building was open for business on the south side of Eau Gallie Boulevard in 1883. One day in 1896, the cashier of the First State Bank was seen boarding a northbound train with two large suitcases. He was never heard from again, nor was any of the bank's cash found when the directors went to open the bank the next morning. The large brick building on the southeast corner of Highland and Eau Gallie Blvd. Was the State Bank of Eau Gallie, built in 1925. South of the bank, in the middle of the block, was the Airdome Theater which was a tin building – hot in the summer and cold in the winter.

NE corner of Eau Gallie Boulevard & Highland Avenue, Eau Gallie
BE22 ~ GPS Coordinates: 28.130333, -80.626950

It was an inside job, a normal banking day in 1896 when the heavy doors opened for business but by closing a clerk and two large suitcases filled with the days receipts were on a northbound train never to be heard from again. The robbery forced the bank to close its doors for a time but seventeen years later was reorganized. William H. Gleason was named president and once more the First State Bank was vital again.

Gleason had come to Eau Gallie from Miami after a series of financial reverses and aimed to begin again. He set his sights on regaining prominence in the new community. It was during the 1920s that Florida experienced a population boom. Historically, while the Spanish welded great influence on southern Florida, settlers from Georgia more along the lines of English planters seemed to dominate northern Florida. The semi-tropical climate, diversity, industrialization, media promotion, sun and sand attracted seasonal visitors, tourists, the ailing and opportunists to Florida. The First State Bank moved into new facilities in 1925.

Unfortunately this boom was soon followed by economic depression. By 1928, the First State Bank closed its doors for a final time. Eventually the economy would turn around and prosperity returned to Florida. Eau Gallie would remain a small, quiet town engulfed by her larger sister city Melbourne.

KARRICK'S GROCERY

Karrick's Grocery opened in 1918 in a small 16x30 ft. building with an inventory worth $800. Sugar was selling at 28 cents a pound, butter 60 cents a pound, rice 15 cents a pound, and flour $2.35 for 25 pounds. The U. S. was engaged in World War I.

In July 1924, Jesse Karrick constructed this building as a "General Merchandise Store & Grocery." In 1933, he added a $500 stock of dry goods. The whole family assisted Karrick in the business until the senior Karrick retired in 1947 and then his son operated the business until closed in 1983.

Jesse Karrick became the first fire chief since his business was near the fire station. On August 11, 1916 the first pumper, mounted on a trailer, was purchased. If a car could not be found then men walked or pulled the trailer. Karrick said, "It seldom made it. One time the fire truck overturned in Horse Creek. Another time it fell into Elbow Creek, and it burned one time. Actually, the hand bucket brigade did a better job."

1490 Highland Avenue, Eau Gallie
BE22 ~ GPS Coordinates: 28.130333, -80.626950

The Karrick family grocers opened their doors at Eau Gallie in 1918 at the brink of Florida's land and population explosion. Obviously the family managed the business well, not only did it prosper but lasted an amazing sixty-five years. The operation employed the entire family in some capacity. After the elder Karrick retired in 1947, his son assumed the helm.

By virtue of proximity, Jesse also became Eau Gallie's First Fire Chief. The selection was simple; he was closest to the fire station every day while managing his store. Fire fighting was an unimproved notion in those days. When the fire bell sounded, four to six men, whoever heard the alarm would pulled the first pumper truck down the sandy streets to fight the fire. The truck often sank in the sand and refused to budge. Often, because many of the buildings were constructed of highly flammable heart pine, when fire threatened little could be done but watch them burn.

Of course during the course of the sixty-five years of Karrick's Grocery operation, some changes were bound to take place. For instance when Jesse Karrick opened the business a Hershey Candy Bar cost a hard earned three cents. But Florida economy was on this rise. People poured into the Sunshine State from places all over the country and every walk of life. Previously only the wealthy had the means and opportunity to travel, now the face of America had changed and families began taking vacations. The automobile made travel easier and more comfortable; labor laws meant paid vacations, pensions and benefits. Americans were skilled, educated and working hard for the fringe benefits coming their way.

Winter migrations of northern tourists had an enormous impact on the Florida economy and summer family vacations became common place. Inexpensive accommodations flourished and businesses like Karrick's Grocery in Eau Gallie did quite well. President Warren G. Harding promoted lower taxes and small business opportunities. The state of Florida responded by employing droves for state road improvements and public services to attend the arriving masses. The interest rates were high but no matter, credit was easy to obtain.

Unfortunately everything that rises must also fall. Florida's economy took a down turn before the great depression gripped the rest of the country. Weather changes brought crop failures to the citrus industry, which played an enormous part in the state's economy. Several destructive hurricanes left entire towns devastated and the tourist began to stay home. This was by no means the end and bravely the state endured, recovery would be no simple feat.

Karrick's Grocery closed their doors for the last time in 1983. The same Hershey Candy Bar was then cost an exorbitant sixty-five cents. A dollar bought a lot less, but a minimum wage was established and pay increased considerably. Times, they were a changing…and continue to do so today.

FIRST BAPTIST CHURCH

The First Baptist Church of Eau Gallie originally met at this location. The land was given by W. H. Gleason. Completed in 1888 and organized in 1889, the First Baptist Church is the oldest Baptist Church in Brevard County. Trees were felled on the south bank of the Eau Gallie River, ferried across on a barge to the saw mill near the railroad and hauled to the church site by ox cart.
The building was used as the public schoolhouse for almost five years. According to some early settlers, it was also for a brief period the town hall.

Montreal & Highland Avenue, Eau Gallie
BE23 ~ GPS Coordinates: 28.129400, -80.626583

Before there was any established Baptist Church in Eau Gallie there was a small gathering of devout individuals who congregated along the banks of the Indian River to pray and gather for fellowship. The assembly committed to constructing a building and organizing a formal congregation in 1888. The process required over a year of labor and diligence to bring the dream to reality. The First Baptist Church was dedicated in March of 1889.

Initially the church experienced lean years financially with only a small congregation to support the church. The membership numbers fluctuated from a high of sixteen to a low of only one lone soul in 1904. The ensuing years were difficult for the church as well as the whole of the United States through the times of the first World War and hardship of the Great Depression. The austere times brought a return to the church. The First Baptist Church's membership swelled to a congregation of more than one hundred members in 1951.

During the next era Brevard County experienced a population explosion with the arrival of the space industry. The church continued to thrive with the influx of people. An increase in membership meant that First Baptist coffers were healthy. The assets allowed for the construction of additional buildings to meet the needs of the growing congregation. Bringing the message to the community, two missions were established Bowe Gardens and Lakecrest.

Steady growth and continual financial stability allowed the church to consider the benefits of expansion in 1997. A Building Committee was established and a long-range plan adopted, which allowed the First Baptist Church to be relocated, after more than one hundred years in the same location. A new seventeen-acre site was purchased to the west of Eau Gallie Boulevard.

The Eau Gallie First Baptist Church moved into their new facilities in the spring of 2001. On May 29th the dedication service was held, officiated by Pastor Ralph M. Nygard. The forty thousand-foot facility was constructed to provide enough space for a membership of eight hundred parishioners. The attendance for the dedication service numbered at eight hundred twenty. The multitude of church programs serves all aspects of the membership from children to the elderly. The congregation and community are flourishing with the spiritual support provided by the historical Eau Gallie First Baptist Church.

The Ais tribe lived predominately along the Indian River on the southeastern coast of Florida. The name has no known English or Spanish translation and is often erroneously said to be a derivation of the Choctaw word "isi" for deer. Their language was very similar to that of the Calusa, which was believed to be relations of the Muskhogean tribes. The Ais have been noted as the most important and populous tribe in southeastern Florida. It was for the Ais tribe that the Indian River was named.

The first reports of the tribe came from a Biscayan called Pedro who was held prisoner during the sixteenth century and managed to learn the language fluently. The Ais warred with the Spaniards who strove to bring them religion. Peace finally came in 1570 and during the next three decades the tribe flourished. In 1597 Spanish Governor Mendez de Canço traveled the Atlantic coast from St. Augustine to the Florida Keys, he reported that the Ais chief had more Indians under him than any other tribe. Unfortunately the peace did not last when the Ais killed a Spaniard and two Indians. The Spaniards demanded revenge and decimated an Ais village of unprotected women and children. Relations finally cooled between the Spanish government and the Ais but efforts to bring them to God never came to pass.

Little is known of the Ais tribe, however in 1605 Lieutenant Alvaro Mexia was dispatched to the Titusville area in order to negotiate with the Native Americans. Mexia's mission was to convince the Ais Chief to squelch their attacks on the Dutch, French and English ships. The second point of terms involved securing an agreement with the Ais to assist Spanish shipwreck victims to safety and the authorities at St. Augustine. The Ais agreed but still refused to accept the Christian way of life, in 1675 the Bishop of Cuba toured the Ais villages and reported that they still clung to their heathen ways.

English Quaker, Jonathan Dickinson was shipwrecked with his family and a number of others off the Florida coast in 1696. The group was taken prisoner by the Ais, whom Dickinson referred to as Jece. Dickinson wrote of their predicament in detail. He spoke of the cruel treatment they received at the hands of the Ais, kept virtually naked and starved. Dickinson stated that the Ais lived in flimsy wooden framed lean-to huts with palmetto leaf thatched roofs. He described the people as cruel, warlike and lacking in religious teachings despite more than one hundred years of Spanish influence.

By the time the English took possession of the Florida territory the Ais were all but extinct. Disease, war and loss of their traditional hunting grounds slowly killed off the tribe.

EAU GALLIE BRIDGE TO THE BEACH

The First wooden bridge from Eau Gallie to "Eau Gallie Beach" was started in 1924. The bridge was formally opened in February, 1926. Soon after, John R. Mathers began plans to build a bridge from the barrier island to the tip of Merritt Island, that bridge, spanning the Banana River was completed in 1927.

The Eau Gallie Bridge frequently caught fire. Joe Wickham, who was Chief of the Volunteer Fire Department, recalled that during one period the bridge caught fire 16 times in a two week period. The fire engine" brakes failed on one occasion as it went across the bridge, it slammed into the palmettos on the other side.

Wickham resigned as Fire Chief after having his sleep disturbed so frequently.

The first wooden bridge was replaced with a bridge/causeway in 1955 and dedicated to Dr. W. J. Creel, a pioneer physician. The present bridge was completed in 1988.

On West end of Eau Gallie Causeway, Eau Gallie
BE25 ~ GPS Coordinates: 28.144922, -80.598374

THE ACTUAL MARKER

Grover Fletcher completed construction on the Eau Gallie Bridge in early 1926, the causeway was opened to traffic on February 22. Located about four miles north of Melbourne, the Eau Gallie Bridge was meant to relieve some of the beach bound traffic across the Melbourne Bridge. The wooden bridge constantly caught fire from carelessly flung cigarettes, cigars and men using kerosene lanterns to fish off the bridge at night. Fire Chief Joe Wickham responded to sixteen fires on the Eau Gallie Bridge at one point within a short fourteen-day period. Chief Wickham resigned under the stress.

Ten years earlier in 1917, a wooden bridge fording the Indian River connected Merritt Island and Cocoa. In those early days cattle roamed free on Merritt Island. Cow hunters rounded up and cared for the herd. The men were known as cow hunters rather than cowboys due to the heavy palmetto scrub and difficult hammock. Laws requiring that the cattle be fenced forced the cow hunters, who did not own the grazing land and could not afford the fencing materials even if they owned the land, to sell their herds.

Hiram and Jerome Platt, Brevard County cattlemen, agreed to buy the Merritt Island cattle under the condition that the cows were delivered across the new wooden bridge. When the County Commissioners were approached with the proposal their permission was conditional on the Platts posting a twenty-five thousand-dollar bond. Simple men, the Platts did not understand what exactly a bond was but put their mark to a personal check to cover the replacement of the bridge if it was damaged.

The cattle were herded into groups and held at what is today the Winn Dixie Plaza. The plan was to drive the cattle across the bridge through Cocoa Village and to an open range. The first few groups crossed the bridge without a problem, that is until the last group of cattle were spooked by something unknown. Pandemonium broke out, the cattle scattered to the four winds. Some of the cattle leapt from bridge into the water and had to be pulled to safety; one frightened animal tore into a local restaurant, today known as the Black Tulip, then had to be dragged out; and one of the big bulls rushed into the Buick Garage, today the Wine Experience. It was a wild time in Cocoa Village that day for sure.

John R. Mathers constructed a toll bridge in 1927 from the mainland to Merritt Island. Initially known as the Mathers' Bridge, when improvements were made the bridge was renamed for Dr. W. J. Creel. The waterway narrows at the point that the Eau Gallie Bridge fords the Indian River. The shores on either side are naturally landscaped with palmettos, Brazilian Pepper tress, water oaks and mangroves. The call of pelicans and water birds can often be heard above the din of traffic whizzing across the bridge. If one takes a moment to gaze into the murky depths, rolling mullet can be seen rippling across the water's surface.

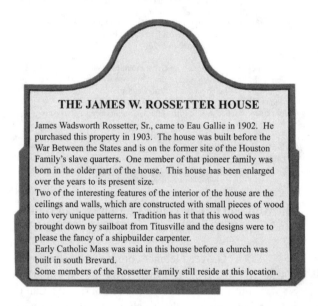

THE JAMES W. ROSSETTER HOUSE

James Wadsworth Rossetter, Sr., came to Eau Gallie in 1902. He purchased this property in 1903. The house was built before the War Between the States and is on the former site of the Houston Family's slave quarters. One member of that pioneer family was born in the older part of the house. This house has been enlarged over the years to its present size.

Two of the interesting features of the interior of the house are the ceilings and walls, which are constructed with small pieces of wood into very unique patterns. Tradition has it that this wood was brought down by sailboat from Titusville and the designs were to please the fancy of a shipbuilder carpenter.

Early Catholic Mass was said in this house before a church was built in south Brevard.

Some members of the Rossetter Family still reside at this location.

1328 Houston Street, Eau Gallie
BE26 ~ GPS Coordinates: 28.128567, -80.626067

Before the Civil War one of the first families of Eau Gallie built a small one-floor residence to shelter their slaves. The Houston family hired local shipbuilders, to construct the house during their idle time. Shipbuilders were known for their exemplary construction skills. Some thirty-five years later the house would become home for an Eau Gallie prominent family, the Rossetter's. The house was so expertly built, the Rossetter's were glad to make the former slave quarters their home.

James Wadsworth Rossetter, Sr. moved his family from their Jacksonville home in 1902 in order to pursue a new career. After settling in Eau Gallie, Rossetter became the Standard Oil distributor for Brevard County. Another side job involved shipping fish bedded down in ice to customers in the north. He purchased the former Houston slaves quarters in 1903 and immediately implemented additions including a second story and modernization. It is said that this location was the site of the first Catholic mass held in Eau Gallie.

In 1992, two Rossetter daughters Caroline and Ella donated their family home to the Florida Historical Society for use as a house museum. Philip Nohrr, attorney representing the Rossetter Trust and Rossetter House Foundation, put the proposals before the town council. The house and gardens were to be restored to the structure's awesome appearance of the 1920s for the pleasure and historical record of the public.

Restoration clues for the site were to be taken from the extensive journals kept by Ella Rossetter. Ella worked daily in her gardens, no display of the house and grounds would be complete without close attention to this very prominent detail. Problematic in the restoration was modernization and the placement of today's city streets.

When the home was constructed building and sanitary codes were nonexistent. The placement of the home in a residential environment made it difficult to open it as a public facility without disturbing residential neighbors.

Many decisions would have to be made before the Rossetter Home could be opened to the public. Public rest rooms and parking were the major obstacles to be worked out. The support and belief in this project from everyone involved would see this undertaking to a successful conclusion. Financial commitments are often a stumbling block, though efforts continue toward keeping the museum an admission free exhibit.

Recently I visited the Rossetter site, which had not yet been completed. Progress seemed to be marching forward. As I walked about the place I found one of the most marvelous sites I had ever seen, a Staghorn Fern. This sounds so simple; the massive plant was so enormous it would take a crane to move and was as large as a standard living room. The history that must have occurred during the growth of this substantial specimen is amazing considering the years of its existence. I can hardly wait to return to see the finished home and gardens ~ won't you join me.

**THE ROSSETTER HOUSE
DURING RESTORATION**

**THE AUTHOR VIEWING AN
AMAZING STAGHORN
FERN IN THE
ROSSETTER GARDEN**

267

ROESCH HOUSE

The exact year the Roesch House was built is unknown. It was probably constructed sometime after 1892. It was constructed by William Russell Roesch. Roesch was made City Treasurer of Eau Gallie in 1887, Roesch was also Mayor of Eau Gallie numerous times. He served from 1896 through 1897, from 1908 through 1909, and from 1924 through 1926.

President Woodrow Wilson appointed W. R. Roesch as the Postmaster for Eau Gallie in 1913. President Wilson reappointed him again in 1918. In 1921 President Warren Harding reappointed him to this position. Roesch also was a member of the local fire department and was a seller of fruits.

Today, most of the house is original, containing original wires and flooring. The house is used as an office by the Florida Historical Society.

1320 Highland Avenue, Eau Gallie
BE27 ~ GPS Coordinates: 28.128417, -80.626117

Although no exact date is on record for the construction of the Roesch House, building most likely would have taken place between 1890 and 1901. William Russell Roesch, noted Eau Gallie citizen, initiated the home's construction. Roesch wore many hats in the community including: editor of the Eau Gallie Record, auxiliary member of the fire department, citrus vendor, City Treasurer, first Eau Gallie mayor[10], reelected several terms, as well as receiving the appointment as Postmaster by two United States Presidents.

The Roesch House, as it will forever be known, occupies the northwest corner of Highland Avenue and Old Oak Street. The construction was completed in the frame vernacular style of architecture popular during the turn of the twentieth century era. Like a great number of houses built in harbor towns the home features fish scale adornment and shiplap siding. Caroline Rossetter, whose family owned the historic home just across the street, also purchased the Roesch in house 1945. Generously, Caroline Rossetter donat-

THE ROESCH HOUSE
FORMERLY
THE
FLORIDA HISTORICAL
SOCIETY

ed the family home to the Florida Historical Society in 1992. Until recently the historical society has used the house as their state headquarters.

The original Historical Society of Florida was organized in 1856, although the society eventually dwindled away, it was reorganized as the Florida Historical Society on November 26, 1902. The charter was registered three years later, stating their mission as:

"The collection, arrangement and preservation of all materials pertaining to the history of, or in any manner illustrative of Florida . . . [and to] prepare, edit and publish articles, sketches, biographies, pamphlets, books and documents, descriptive or illustrative of Florida."

In accordance with the Society charter the "Publications of the Florida Historical Society" book was first published in April 1908. Today the volume is published four times per year as the "Florida Historical Quarterly".

The Florida Historical Society continues to this day as the foremost proponent of historic preservation in the state. The organization remains dedicated to the charter under which it was founded. Added responsibilities include scholarly research, maintaining historical records, preservation of historic sites and educating children on the history of the state.

The Roesch House has now been turned over to the Rossetter Foundation for use as the organization's headquarters. The Rossetter House across the street will be opened in the future as a museum and gardens; the Roesch House will serve as the administrative offices. Because of Caroline Rossetter's philanthropic bequest the Roesch House will continue to be maintained in the manner that this wonderful historic home deserves.

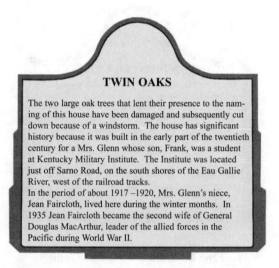

TWIN OAKS

The two large oak trees that lent their presence to the naming of this house have been damaged and subsequently cut down because of a windstorm. The house has significant history because it was built in the early part of the twentieth century for a Mrs. Glenn whose son, Frank, was a student at Kentucky Military Institute. The Institute was located just off Sarno Road, on the south shores of the Eau Gallie River, west of the railroad tracks.
In the period of about 1917–1920, Mrs. Glenn's niece, Jean Faircloth, lived here during the winter months. In 1935 Jean Faircloth became the second wife of General Douglas MacArthur, leader of the allied forces in the Pacific during World War II.

Highland Avenue & Shady, Eau Gallie
BE28 ~ GPS Coordinates: 28.128050, -80.626050

Mrs. Glenn commissioned the home dubbed as Twin Oaks in the late 1890s to be near her son. Frank Glenn attended the nearby winter facilities of the Kentucky Military Institute. Like other parents in similar socio-economic circles, Mrs. Glenn chose to winter in Brevard County.

G. C. Restone converted the DuNil Hotel to serve as the winter facilities for the Institute in 1907. John Green founded the town known as Sardo, named for a city in India, in the late 1800s. Unfortunately, Flagler's railroad continued south and the area never developed as the tourist mecca that Green had envisioned. Sardo was a ghost town when the Kentucky Military Institute decided to call Eau Gallie home. The hotel was renamed the Military Inn and more than three hundred students arrived each year for winter classes. The institute burned down in 1921 and never reopened here.

Each winter from 1917-1920, Jean Faircloth joined her aunt at Twin Oaks. Certainly is not unusual to have visitors arrive to enjoy Florida's semi-tropical climate escaping the frozen north, Jean was an adventuresome young woman who never minded traveling alone, which was unheard of at that time. While alone on a trip to Asia, Jean met and fell in love with a dynamic military man known to the world as General Douglas MacArthur.

The tiny woman from Murfreesboro, Tennessee became Jean Faircloth MacArthur on April 30, 1937. She embraced military life with complete devotion and throughout their married life referred to her husband as "Sir Boss" or "The General." Their only child, Arthur named for his Civil War hero Grandfather was born in Manila, Philippines in 1938. Three years later the Japanese attacked and forced the family to seek safety on the nearby island of Corregidor.

Mrs. MacArthur was never shy and often represented her husband at official and social functions when his schedule did not permit him to attend certain events. She was completely devoted to her husband both publicly and privately. After General MacArthur's death in 1964, she proudly continued to represent "The General" as she had during his life and was named honorary Chairman of the General Douglas MacArthur Foundation. President Ronald Reagan awarded her the Presidential Medal of Freedom in 1988 for her life's work and devotion to her country both on her own and alongside General MacArthur.

Mrs. Jean Faircloth MacArthur passed away on January 22, 2000 she was 101. Mrs. MacArthur was laid to rest beside her husband at the MacArthur Memorial in Norfolk, Virginia. She was buried on what would have been General Douglas MacArthur's one hundred twentieth birthday.

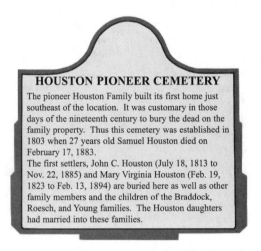

HOUSTON PIONEER CEMETERY

The pioneer Houston Family built its first home just southeast of the location. It was customary in those days of the nineteenth century to bury the dead on the family property. Thus this cemetery was established in 1803 when 27 years old Samuel Houston died on February 17, 1883.
The first settlers, John C. Houston (July 18, 1813 to Nov. 22, 1885) and Mary Virginia Houston (Feb. 19, 1823 to Feb. 13, 1894) are buried here as well as other family members and the children of the Braddock, Roesch, and Young families. The Houston daughters had married into these families.

1266 Houston Street, Eau Gallie
BE29 ~ GPS Coordinates: 28.127950, -80.626017

John Carroll Houston and his brother left North Carolina in search of the great American dream. John ventured to Florida and his brother made his way to Tennessee. The Tennessee brother was to go down in history as the father of Texas legend General Sam Houston. The Florida Houston's would be instrumental in settling the Spanish Florida territory, their name will be forever linked as a founding Florida family.

Initially the Florida Houston's settled in Mayport near Jacksonville and it was there that a son, eventually known as Captain John Houston was born on April 3, 1842. Captain John was to be an early pioneer of the Indian River region. A Houston man fought valiantly on every battleground that shaped the country as well as the wilderness yet to be tamed called Florida.

The Houston family has left an indelible mark on much of mid eastern Florida but none so dramatic as that of Melbourne and particularly the Eau Gallie area. Many of the descendants of John C. and Mary Virginia, the pioneering Houston's remain in the area to this day.

The quiet little cemetery sits amid the residential neighborhood originally called the home place by the Houston family. A shaded grove filters brilliant sun light for the final resting-place of distinguished Florida pioneers. Annie Laura Houston Braddock, a wonderful family biographer, left a remarkable written legacy of her family history. In the work she referred to Port Everglades as "the Giant Oak that has grown from the tiny acorn planted by a true pioneer, just one of the many to whom we owe so much for their courage and ability to fight back when the odds were against them." The quotation could easily be used to note the Houston's influence on Eau Gallie, Brevard County and the state of Florida.

SITE OF FIRST HOUSTON HOMESTEAD

The first hickory log cabin built by John C. Houston, original settler of Eau Gallie, was erected in this area.

Houston came here in 1859 with his older sons and 10 slaves. He had served in the U.S. Army during the Seminole Indian Wars and had been stationed at an Army fort in Enterprise.

When the large cabin was completed (Houston had 8 children) the pioneer went to get his family. It took 3 weeks to drive the covered wagons and the herd of cattle and horses from Enterprise to the new home site.

Houston made friends with the Seminole Indians living in the area and they exchanged otter skins, alligator hides and fresh wild pork for sugar, coffee and other items the new settlers offered. Having no fishing tackle the Houston family built a skiff and found that by burning a torch in a bucket of sand and poling around in the creek, the fish intrigued by the light, would jump into the boat. The Houston's grew sugar cane, rice and their own vegetables. They had a sugar cane mill (oxen powered) and a "salt mine" south of their home at what is now known as sunny point.

1266 Houston Street, Eau Gallie
BE30 ~ GPS Coordinates: 28.127817, -80.625250

His grandmother, in her Jacksonville hotel, raised John Houston for nine of his formative years while his father struggled to carve a livable territory out of the Florida wilderness. The hotel was often a stop over for those traveling south along the Florida coast. Grandmother was the widow of Major Taylor, her second husband and step-grandfather to John. Taylor's cousin was the former United States President Zachary Taylor.

At the age of sixteen, young John left his grandmother to join the Seminole Indian Wars. By 1859, John joined his family at their hotel in Enterprise near Sanford. Father and son traveled together down the old Capron Trail named for Fort Capron at Fort Pierce. The duo reached a site along the Indian River that the elder Houston dubbed Elbow Creek, for the river's shape and it was there that they founded what was later to be known as called Eau Gallie. Only one other family inhabiting the area was that of Captain Paine, a military officer at Fort Pierce.

The elder Houston acquired a long-standing Spanish land grant and it was there that building began on the first family homestead. The initial dwelling was made of crudely hewn local lumber and with the help of ten slaves, the structure was completed. The abode required enough expanse to accommodate the considerable Houston clan. Once the homestead was established crops were planted to assist in the families' survival. Sweet potatoes, corn, sugar cane and various vegetables as well as beef and pork were grown to sustain the family and slaves. Because refrigeration was not an option at this time, meat was preserved with salt harvested from the ocean nearby. Every aspect of nature could be and was used to survive the wilderness. The younger Houston traveled by oxen to Lake Winder where he boarded a boat sailing to Jacksonville or Sanford for staple supplies, cloth for clothes and various provisions the family could not grow or produce.

Mills were established to cook off cane sugar and syrup as well as another mill to grind corn for grits and meal. Wild game and fowl including turkey, quail, duck, deer and bear among others, were taken from the forest to supplement the family larder. The Houston men soon discovered that lighting a pine knot torch in the dark of night would entice fish to actually jump into the boat without line or bait. The family subsisted largely off the land. Just before the family established the new homestead at Elbow[11], their number increased by one. On September 5, 1860, the younger John C. Houston married a LaGrange lass by the name of Susan Stewart and a new generation of Houston's was soon to come. The pioneering name and spirit continues to this day.

BRECKENRIDGE LANDING

Following the Civil War, Confederate Secretary of War, John C. Breckenridge, and his entourage came down the Indian River in a sailboat on their journey Cuba where Breckenridge knew he would be safe from prosecution by the United States Government.

After leaving Titusville, his boat sprang a leak. Breckenridge saw John C. Houston's dock, which was located about where the dock at Ramshur Tower is now located. Breckenridge stopped to ask Houston's assistance in caulking the leak and making repairs. Houston, a Confederate sympathizer, gave his assistance. Breckenridge made his escape to Cuba.

1279 Houston Street, Eau Gallie
BE31 ~ GPS Coordinates: 28.127683, -80.625150

John Cabell Breckinridge[12] was born near Lexington, Kentucky in a small settlement called Cabell's Dale on January 16, 1821. He would never really know his father, who passed away when the boy was only two.

Young John was well educated, eventually attending the College of New Jersey[13]. He completed the study of law near his home at Transylvania Institute and was admitted to the bar in 1840 at the young age of nineteen.

The Mexican War loomed large in 1847 and Breckinridge accepted a commission as Major of the Third Kentucky Volunteers. His political life began shortly thereafter as a Democratic Representative for Kentucky later an election to Congress. When James Buchanan attained the Presidency in 1856, John C. Breckinridge achieved the office of Vice President; amazingly Breckinridge was only 36 years old.

He made an unsuccessful bid for the Presidency during the next election and settled for the United States Senate. The Civil War loomed large on the horizon, fragmenting the nation's government. Breckinridge was expelled from the Senate on December 4, 1861, however the action was for naught; he had already accepted an appointment as brigadier general of the Confederacy. Eventually, John C. Breckinridge would be named Secretary of War in President Jefferson Davis' Cabinet of the Confederate States in 1865.

General Robert E. Lee realized the end of the war was eminent and surrender was eminent. Before an exchange between the two great Generals Grant and Lee, the Confederate President evacuated Richmond with his Cabinet on April 1, 1865. Nine days later, General Lee would lay down his sword at Appomattox Courthouse. Escaping with President Davis was John Breckinridge, Secretary of War; Judah Benjamin, Secretary of State; John Reagan, Postmaster General; George Trenholm, Secretary of Treasury; Stephen Mallory, Department of the Navy; and George Davis, Attorney General. Provisions included a half million dollars from the Confederate Treasury in coins and the deposits from Richmond banks.

The escape route would take the band from Richmond along the back roads and dusty pathways through the Carolinas, Georgia and Florida. Travel was difficult at best and the group soon parted ways. Jefferson Davis clung to the idea that the war could still be won if only he could reach Mississippi and gather fresh Confederate forces to rejoin the fight.

Breckinridge remained with Davis, serving as his voice of reason. John C. Breckinridge adeptly convinced Jefferson Davis of the importance in bringing the conflict to an honorable conclusion and in the process saving countless lives. The Confederate Cabinet disbanded at Washington, Georgia on May 5, 1865. The two men parted company, Breckinridge to the south into Florida and Jefferson Davis heading west through Georgia. Davis now considered the safety of his family the most prominent concern. John C. Breckinridge made plans to flee through Florida to Cuba then on to England and settling in Canada, the longest way around.

The former Confederate Secretary of War attempted the daring and perilous escape by small boat toward Cuba when as the fates would have it, water began to flood the vessel. Luck was with him on several accounts, first he just happened to be near the dock of the Houston homestead and secondly, John C. Houston was a Confederate sympathizer. Houston gave aid to Breckinridge and soon he was on his way once again.

After three years abroad, President Andrew Johnson issued a proclamation of amnesty to Breckinridge in 1868. Finally able to return to his Lexington, Kentucky home, Breckinridge resumed his law practice. He later became Vice President of the Elizabethtown, Lexington Big Sandy Railroad Company. John C. Breckinridge passed away on May 17, 1875 and was buried at the Lexington Cemetery.

The question remains whatever happened to the Confederate treasury? Rumor has it that some of it was used for the troops and supplies, though this is doubtful. Others say the North confiscated some of the money and Georgia raiders stole some one hundred seventy thousand dollars in gold, this story is very plausible. Another story relates:

> "... the stolen treasure ... was never seen again. Locals years hence told of friends who removed to Missouri and California with sudden fortunes, never to return."

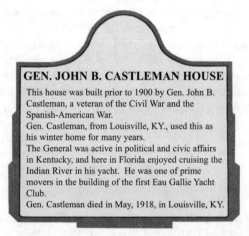

GEN. JOHN B. CASTLEMAN HOUSE

This house was built prior to 1900 by Gen. John B. Castleman, a veteran of the Civil War and the Spanish-American War.
Gen. Castleman, from Louisville, KY., used this as his winter home for many years.
The General was active in political and civic affairs in Kentucky, and here in Florida enjoyed cruising the Indian River in his yacht. He was one of prime movers in the building of the first Eau Gallie Yacht Club.
Gen. Castleman died in May, 1918, in Louisville, KY.

Corner of Sunny Point Drive and Young Street, Melbourne
BE32 ~ GPS Coordinates: 28.127150, -80.624067

John Breckinridge Castleman was born in Fayette County, Kentucky on June 30, 1842. He grew to become a noted military man whose career was highlighted with issues varying from greatness to in the Union eyes treasonous. He was first commissioned as a cavalry company captain under General John Hunt Morgan. Later, it was said, Castleman became the junior partner of Major-General Thomas H. Hines in the notorious Northwest Conspiracy.

The Northwest Conspiracy involved Northern Confederate sympathizers called Copperheads led by Confederate officers. The men planned to rob gold from United States banks located at the furthermost northern border with Canada. Further they would lay siege to such cities as New York, Chicago and Philadelphia leaving them in smoldering ruins. Assassination plots were also in the works against select government officials. Though the plan was developed in much detail, the Northwest Conspiracy never came to fruition. It was later speculated that this conspiracy inspired another that was successful in the assassination of President Abraham Lincoln.

John B. Castleman was captured during September of 1864 in Indiana. He spent the remainder of the

Civil War incarcerated in a Union prison speculating that any day he would be executed for war crimes. The most serious charges included lurking and acting as a spy as well as conspiring to destroy government property.

Judge Samuel Breckinridge, a maternal uncle of Castleman, held an important position for the Union in Missouri. He regularly gave anti-secessionist speeches turning many in the state in favor of the Federal government. Judge Breckinridge knew President Lincoln and used the relationship to intervene on behalf of his nephew.

The president secretly gave Judge Breckinridge the following handwritten note with instructions that it be used in a state of emergency. The note read:

"Major General Hovey, or
Whomsoever may have charge:

Whenever John B. Castleman shall be tried, if convicted and sentenced, suspend
execution until further notice from me, and send me the record. A. Lincoln"

John B. Castleman was released and ordered to leave the country forever. After Lincoln's assassination, President Johnson rescinded Castleman's exile and allowed him to return home to Kentucky. A Louisville, Kentucky newspaper called the "Farmers Home Journal" held a meeting on April 7, 1891 and as a result the American Saddle-Horse Breeders' Association was founded. John B. Castleman was appointed the first Association President. He was instrumental in the preservation of documented pedigrees of American saddle horses. He was commissioned General during the Spanish-American War and it is said that Castleman precluded the possibility of another Civil War in Kentucky as a result of the 1900 state election. The governor's election was hotly disputed and one of the candidates was brutally killed. It was General John B. Castleman as Adjutant General of Kentucky using level headed arbitrary skills that saved Kentucky from major upheaval.

Castleman was eventually named President of the Board of Parks Commission on Louisville, Kentucky. It was under his leadership that the city's park system was established. A statue in tribute for all that Castleman had given to Louisville was placed facing Cherokee Park in 1913. General John Breckinridge Castleman passed away on May 23, 1918. He was buried at the Cave Hill Cemetery, Louisville, Jefferson County, Kentucky.

BALLARD HOUSE ON SUNNY POINT

This home was started in Dec., 1915, for the S. T. Ballard Family, owners of the Ballard Flour Co.

Ginter Brothers had the construction contract and it was said the house cost $40,000 to build.

The Ballards were from Louisville, Ky., and they brought their yacht, "Sunshine," from the city by railroad freight car.

Going farther back in history, in the 1860's, this area of Sunny Point was owned by John C. Houston, Eau Gallie's first settler. This site was the "salt mine" where river water was boiled in a high iron pot until it condensed, then the salt was spread out on cypress log slabs for drying.

From here, westerly, surrounding the creek, rice was planted. And it was in this area the Houstons had their sugar cane mill, propelled by a horse, or sometimes oxen.

South end of Sunny Point Drive, Eau Gallie
BE33 ~ GPS Coordinates: 28.126150, -80.624067

Before the dwelling at Sunny Point was ever a part of the Ballard Family estate, Eau Gallie forefather John C. Houston laid claim to the area. It was on this site during the years before Civil War divided the country that Houston mined salt on this site. Salt was soon to become an extremely important commodity.

This was a time in history, before the advent of refrigeration, when food was being transported sometimes long distances to troops in the field. Salt was used to preserve food from spoilage. The demand of salt quickly influenced the price, which rose to soaring heights. Early opportunity taking advantage of supply and demand set up crude seawater evaporators to produce the popular commodity. In venturing down to the seas' edge, these enterprising men were taking their lives in hand. If spotted from ships just off the coast it was very possible that mortars would be fired their way or soldiers on patrol duty along the shore would shoot first and ask questions later.

Salt making was a difficult, tedious process. When seawater was evaporated in salt pots, the result is unrefined "yellow salt." The yellowed color came from smoke being utilized to remove impurities. Meats and fish could not be properly cured using the yellow salt. Professional salt works were required to finish the salts by crystallization turning out table quality or palatable salt. These professional salt works were located along the shore, usually made of brick, which is the explanation for the shards of broken old brick found on the beach.

Samuel Thruston Ballard, founder and president of Ballard & Ballard Flour Company, was Lieutenant Governor of Kentucky. Ballard purchased the site of the salt mine from the Houston heirs. The family home was completed there in 1915. The Ginter Brothers Construction Company won the contract to build the Ballard house, reportedly costing S. Thruston Ballard forty thousand dollars.

Though a man of considerable wealth, it seems Ballard conducted his life and managed his business with considerable acumen. One story revealing Ballard's astute business sense follows:

> While in the process of hiring a man, Ballard noticed as the man went
> about signing his name that he had no eraser at the end of his pencil.
> Ballard asked, "Why haven't you got an eraser?"
> The man responded, "I don't make mistakes."
> Taken aback, S. Thruston Ballard finalized, "Then I can't use you. Because
> if you don't make mistakes, you won't do nothing."

Samuel Thruston Ballard passed away on January 18, 1926, the homesite was left to his heirs. In 1952, Pillsbury purchased the Ballard Flour Company. It was this buy-out that allowed Pillsbury to expand into the area of packaging and refrigerating unbaked biscuit dough. Located at the end of Thomas Barbour Drive, Ballard Park was created in memorial to the Ballard Family. The park features a playground, picnic area, boat ramp and tennis courts with a scenic vista overlooking the Indian River lagoon.

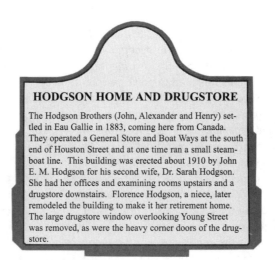

HODGSON HOME AND DRUGSTORE

The Hodgson Brothers (John, Alexander and Henry) settled in Eau Gallie in 1883, coming here from Canada. They operated a General Store and Boat Ways at the south end of Houston Street and at one time ran a small steamboat line. This building was erected about 1910 by John E. M. Hodgson for his second wife, Dr. Sarah Hodgson. She had her offices and examining rooms upstairs and a drugstore downstairs. Florence Hodgson, a niece, later remodeled the building to make it her retirement home. The large drugstore window overlooking Young Street was removed, as were the heavy corner doors of the drugstore.

Young & Houston Streets, Eau Gallie
BE34 ~ GPS Coordinates: 28.127183, -80.625217

Some twenty-four years after the establishment of the Eau Gallie settlement the Hodgson Brothers arrived with their families to begin a new life. Originally from Canada John, Alexander and Henry opened a mercantile business, boat ways and steamboat line. The businesses were successful and the Hodgsons' quickly became an integral part of the ever-growing Eau Gallie community.

John Hodgson built what is called the Hodgson home and drugstore around 1910 for his second wife Dr. Sarah Hodgson. Because of the scarcity of physicians in frontier location Dr. Hodgson was often the only option available. Historically still only six percent of the doctors in America were women in the early 1900s. Like today the majority of her patients were women and her duties were consisted mostly of midwifery. John Hodgson built the home to house Sarah's office and examination room upstairs with a pharmacy downstairs. There was a large glass window looking out over Young Street at the front and solid wooden double doors entering the establishment.

Even though her position as a physician was predominately considered unsuitable, Sarah Hodgson was accepted by Eau Gallie society. Most of the time a doctor's position on the social ladder is a high rung that is if the doctor were a man. By virtue of simply being a woman, Sarah had selected an occupation when women were thought of as simply keeping her home, husband and children. Townswomen often whispered behind her back, socially she became a pariah. Slowly with persistence, working long, hard hours as her reputation grew; Dr. Sarah Hodgson became a well-respected physician for all.

Even as late as World War I women continued to be discouraged in the practice of medicine but by World War II females were often recruited for medic duty. Though after the war this medical training support for women disappeared and only seven percent of America's doctors were women in 1960. There was actually a quota that medical schools set to admit only a small percentage of women in each class. In 1970, a discrimination suit was brought against the medical society by the Women's Equity Action League. This litigation opened the medical school doors to women, forcing the institutions to consider all applicants on an equal basis regardless of sex. By the year 2000, forty-six percent of new medical school students were women.

Florence Hodgson, a niece of Sarah and John, later assumed responsibility for the Hodgson pharmacy and medical facility. She remodeled the building into a retirement home for herself. The large display window was removed and the heavy wooden corner doors were replaced.

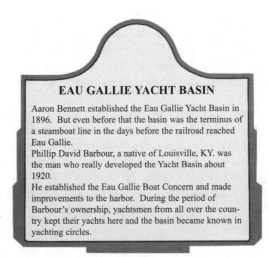

587 Young Street, Eau Gallie
BE35 ~ GPS Coordinates: 28.126350, -80.624750

Captain Aaron Bennett founded a boat yard and basin around 1885, which would eventually become
known as the Eau Gallie Yacht Basin. The site chosen was ideal for the use Captain Bennett intended, the yacht
basin would be located at the safest deep water harbor on the eastern coast of Florida. Eau Gallie acquired the
moniker "Harbor City".

During the population explosion, Eau Gallie's notoriety grew largely due to her accessibility as a superb
port. The fact that transportation was dependent on travel by water during this time encouraged the popularity of
the Eau Gallie Basin. Shortly, another entrepreneur arrived on the scene. Captain T. J. Lund brought a steamboat
called *Pioneer* to the Indian River port. Some questioned the productivity of this notion because, regardless of the
growth in inhabitants, only some two hundred fifty persons lived between Eau Gallie and the southern most tip of
Florida during this time.

It may be cliché but people lived off the land; farming, fishing, hunting, raising cattle and subsiding off of
the fruits of their labor. Because of Eau Gallie's location on the Indian River, learning to sail came shortly after
walking in the scheme of things. The arrival of the steamboat, *Pioneer* also brought change to the area. The
Pioneer made runs from Jacksonville to Enterprise during the Civil War, some say bringing supplies inland and
others say the steamboat did a bit of smuggling.

At the conclusion of the war, the Indian River Steamboat Company began operating seven steamers. One
of these was a magnificent one hundred thirty-six-foot side-wheeler called *Rockledge*. She was a luxury craft featuring elegant dining facilities, staterooms and a brass band performing on deck. The *Rockledge* traveled between
Eau Gallie and Titusville delivering supply essentials, luxury items and visitors in a fraction of the time previously
experienced.

Piers reached like fingers into the lagoon to aid the delivery of goods and passengers. Visitors to the Eau
Gallie shores enjoyed a resort atmosphere. When evening boats arrived, the shoreline would be a blaze with burning torches to light the way, dancing flames greeting the travelers. As the passengers strode down the gangplank,
their senses were assailed with the pungent odor of burning insect powder. Vicious flying teeth otherwise known
as sand gnats and swarming, disease-carrying mosquitoes made the noxious perfume of bug repellent a necessary
evil.

The Jacksonville, St. Augustine and Indian River Railroad steamed into Eau Gallie in 1893. As the train
chugged its way south it brought both progress and the end of an era. The railroad, later known as the Florida East
Coast, virtually edged the steamship industry out. Rail travel was certainly faster to one destination but settlers

were hesitant to give up the more tranquil river steamboats.

The Eau Gallie Yacht Basin received a much-needed makeover in 1920 under the hand of Phillip David Barbour. The Louisville, Kentucky native made vast improvements in both the basin and the harbor. With Barbour at the helm, yachtsmen from all over the United States ported their impressive vessels at Eau Gallie. The basin became very popular; soon the lustrous teakwood and gleaming white of opulent yachts came to be an everyday site in the Eau Gallie harbor.

One of the most respected and successful marine surveyors throughout the country came to Eau Gallie in the 1932 and became a partner in the Yacht Basin. Eventually, when World War II was declared, Buster Chadwick was to become President and General Manager. His accomplishments were many ranging from the construction of the Cat Cay lighthouse in the Bahamas, which still stands to this day, to vessel conversions and repairs for the Coast Guard, Army and Navy. Chadwick left Eau Gallie for Daytona in 1948 and from there went to Fort Lauderdale. Buster Chadwick left his indelible marks not only on Eau Gallie but the state of Florida as well.

The Eau Gallie Yacht Basin remains to this day a popular port of call for pleasure craft. For more than one hundred years the basin has stood the watch.

FIRST EAU GALLIE YACHT CLUB

The Eau Gallie Yacht Club was organized in 1907 and this building for the club was built some time after that.
The death of the last charter member of this club occurred on April 1934, when Alexander R. Hodgson passed away.
The Eau Gallie Yacht Club's present headquarters is located on the east shore of the Indian River in the community of Indian Harbour Beach.

South end of Houston Street, Eau Gallie
BE36 ~ GPS Coordinates: 28.126050, -80.624700

The membership rolls of the Eau Gallie Yacht Club has been like a who's who of prominent Brevard County founders. Organized in 1907, the club is the fourth oldest in the state. Originally the club claimed only three hundred members, as the Yacht Club approaches the century mark it claims more than three times that number today. The original building was approximately the size of a two-storied residential home. The change in location, amenities and increased membership necessitated the facilities expansion as well.

The Eau Gallie Yacht Club traversed the Intracoastal Waterway to its new location in 1960. Located now on the Indian Harbour Beach, the new site allowed the club to spread wide its wings on nearly five and half acres. The deep-water marina at the mouth of the Banana River allows for the safe mooring of yachts up to an amazing fifty-five feet. The harbormaster is on duty full time and ready to assist with boating needs or charting a course for distant shores.

Growing from merely a social club for yachting enthusiasts, at last count the one thousand forty-member organization hosts a wonderful array of amenities. Facilities encompass an impressive clubhouse; luxury as well as casual dining opportunities featuring award winning chefs; a swimming pool offering lessons for children during the summer months; and six clay tennis courts, lighted for evening enjoyment. The nearby pro shop provides everything from helpful tips for improving your game to hosting tournaments to soothe the competitive spirit. The experience of the main dining room for lunch or dinner is without equal. The view overlooking the marina provides an ambiance to patrons from the majesty of the moored yachts to the slow setting of the evening sun.

Banquet facilities provide the perfect setting for that dream wedding, social events or impressive business gatherings.

Of course at the heart of the Eau Gallie Yacht Club is boating. The club provides instruction for children as well as planning regattas, weekend cruises and group trips to provocative locales. Active for more than ninety-five years, the club continues to provide enjoyment for its membership today.

The success of the club resulted in the ability to retire its mortgage in 1996, largely due to the superb efforts of the dedicated management and staff. Members and their guests are treated with the utmost hospitality and attention. The Eau Gallie Yacht Club combines outdoor fun with indoor elegance and continues to be a mainstay of Brevard County society.

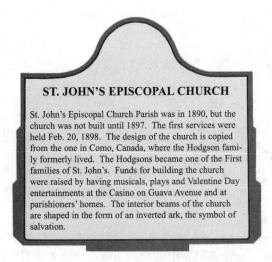

ST. JOHN'S EPISCOPAL CHURCH

St. John's Episcopal Church Parish was in 1890, but the church was not built until 1897. The first services were held Feb. 20, 1898. The design of the church is copied from the one in Como, Canada, where the Hodgson family formerly lived. The Hodgsons became one of the First families of St. John's. Funds for building the church were raised by having musicals, plays and Valentine Day entertainments at the Casino on Guava Avenue and at parishioners' homes. The interior beams of the church are shaped in the form of an inverted ark, the symbol of salvation.

610 Young Street, Eau Gallie
BE37 ~ GPS Coordinates: 28.127150, -80.627483

When the Hodgson brothers arrived from Como, Ontario Canada in 1885, Alexander and Henry were determined to establish a legacy for the family in Florida as well. Later, John Edwin, their younger brother joined the duo to rough out the terrain. The Hodgson brothers purchased property from the founding Houston family and the dynasty began.

The Florida Episcopalian diocese experienced a profound growth by 1888. Eighty parishes and missions comprised the diocese. The Missionary Jurisdiction of Southern Florida was created and the Right Reverend William Crane Gray was appointed Bishop. The missions served a wide variety of parishioners including Native Americans, African Americans and immigrants new to the growing frontier.

St. Johns was organized in 1890 with five members. Mary Houston Young donated property for a sanctuary but the building was not constructed for another seven years. During construction parishioners met at the Truetler Hotel on Hyde Park Lane and shared the sanctuary of the First Baptist Church. Mrs. Young donated other property in the vicinity; eventually the street was named in her honor. St. Johns was the second church to be established along the street. The architectural design was taken from a sister church in the Hodgson's Canadian hometown. The interior of the church was created to resemble an inverted ark, taken from the biblical story of Noah. The ark serves as a symbol of salvation.

Church rolls were comprised of only five members at 610 Young Street. Bishop William Crane Gray was called upon to consecrate the church. Part of the consecration ceremony involved "beating the bounds," in which the Right Reverend walked the boundaries of the churchyard, stopping at each corner to pray. Reverend B. F. Brown of Titusville was chosen to be the first St. John's vicar. Bishop Gray traveled to Eau Gallie quarterly from his Orlando home until his retirement in 1910, though records indicate he continued to visit the diocese circuit.

The congregation saw a need for a new parish house, which was built in 1957. The membership increased by 1962 enough to require a new edifice. The old sanctuary moved to the back of the lot and a modern addition was built to the front. St. John's Episcopal Church continues to this day with an active congregation, serving the community and caring for the spiritual needs of those that gather there.

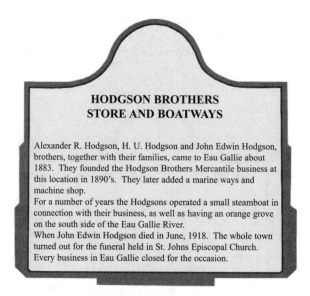

HODGSON BROTHERS
STORE AND BOATWAYS

Alexander R. Hodgson, H. U. Hodgson and John Edwin Hodgson, brothers, together with their families, came to Eau Gallie about 1883. They founded the Hodgson Brothers Mercantile business at this location in 1890's. They later added a marine ways and machine shop.

For a number of years the Hodgsons operated a small steamboat in connection with their business, as well as having an orange grove on the south side of the Eau Gallie River.

When John Edwin Hodgson died in June, 1918. The whole town turned out for the funeral held in St. Johns Episcopal Church. Every business in Eau Gallie closed for the occasion.

South end of Houston Street, on northern shore of Eau Gallie River, Eau Gallie
BE38 ~ GPS Coordinates: 28.127083, -80.627900

The community of Eau Gallie was founded in 1859 and soon a post office, school and civic offices were established. Misters Hill and Olmstead opened stores bringing steamers to the Indian River shores laden with supplies. The town was platted in the early 1880s, a sawmill built; Eau Gallie began to prosper. It is said that the first of the Hodgson family, brothers Alexander and Henry arrived in Eau Gallie around 1883. However, records show that R. W. B. Hodgson was a land surveyor in the area as early as February 1859, according to a land deal between Richard K. Call and Blaney Johnson.

John Edwin M. Hodgson arrived from the family home in Como Ontario Canada in 1885, two years following his brothers. John was the eldest brother, at the age of thirty-five, according to the 1885 Brevard County Florida State Census. Accompanying him was his wife, eight-year-old daughter and six-year-old son. The Census further states that as of that year, both Alexander and Henry were unmarried. All of the Hodgson brothers were listed as Fruit Growers.

The Hodgson's purchased property from the Houston's, early Eau Gallie settlers. Called Windmill Grove where the Hodgson's lived in a close knit family compound on the northern shore. Soon the family established a boat way, mercantile and steamboat businesses. By 1888 the brothers operated a steamer service using their ship, the *Kathleen*. The Hodgson Mercantile sold dry goods and groceries at the south end of Houston Street; the marine ways built, repaired and chartered boats as well as hauling small craft out of the river; also at the foot of Houston Street was a Hodgson operated telegraph office.

The Hodgson's worshiped alongside other Eau Gallie families as an Episcopal congregation organized in 1890. They first met at the Truetler Hotel located on Hyde Park Lane and utilized the First Baptist Church facilities as well. The first sanctuary was completed in 1897, obviously with great contributions from the Hodgson's. The edifice featured overhead beams reminiscent of the interior of an ancient ecclesiastical ark, the symbol of salvation for the Episcopals. The design resembled the Hodgson's home church in Como Ontario Canada. W. H.

Gleason donated the property for the sanctuary just as he had done for the Baptist edifice. St. John's Episcopal Church donated proceeds from their collection plates to assist in the construction of the first wooden Eau Gallie Bridge. Special services were held at St. John's for the cadets of the Kentucky Military Institute.

In 1911, adjacent to Hodgson Mercantile, was the main building of the Eau Gallie Yacht Club established in 1907. George Paddison, who was the owner of the East Coast Lumber Company, donated the site and was made the first club commodore. Noted as one of the oldest yacht clubs in Florida, the organization rolls appeared as if a whose who member of Eau Gallie's social elite. Alexander Hodgson was listed as a founding member. Facilities included a men's cigar room, women's bridge hall, a reception center and a grand ballroom. The northern shore was soon dotted with boathouses, businesses and elegant homes. Just beyond the Yacht Club was the Eau Gallie River beacon watching over Sunny Point, the Ballard family home. The Ballard's were known as Eau Gallie socialites. Today what was the main building of the Eau Gallie Yacht Club is a private home.

Because the river was the most prevalent means of transportation, sailboats became the center of attention for not only transportation but also for employment and recreation. Settlers from surrounding river communities would gather at Eau Gallie for sailboat races on festive spring and summer weekends. Boat building became a major industry for the community. The Hodgson Boatyard was on the northern shoreline and just beyond was Bennett's Boatyard and the Yacht Basin. River traffic was quite congested until the railroad arrived and subsequently good roads were constructed.

At the corner of Young and Houston Streets, John Hodgson built a home in 1910 for his second wife, Dr. Sarah Hodgson. The home was constructed to meet the needs of the doctor wife having a pharmacy downstairs with offices and examination rooms upstairs. The home was left to a niece, Florence Hodgson who had the home remodeled to remove the drugstore window and large double entrance doors converting the house to a more private home in appearance. The entire house was demolished in the 1930s.

The elder brother, John Edwin M. Hodgson passed away in June of 1918 at the age of sixty-eight. His services were conducted at St. Johns Episcopal Church and the entire town lined up to pay their respects. It is said every business in the Eau Gallie community closed their doors displaying a black wreath in recognition of the circumstance.

BLUE STAR

A tribute to the Armed Forces that have defended the United States of America.

Sunset & US 1, Melbourne
BE39 ~ GPS Coordinates: 28.125333, -80.630200

David McCampbell was born in Bessemer, Alabama and grew up around West Palm Beach, Florida. His education began at Staunton Military Academy in Virginia and later he attended Georgia Tech in Atlanta before being appointed to the United States Naval Academy at Annapolis. While at Annapolis, McCampbell was a championship swimmer and diver. He graduated in 1933 with a Bachelor's degree in Marine Engineering.

Ten years later, having achieved the rank of Commander, McCampbell was billeted as Landing Signal Officer Instructor at NAS[14] Melbourne. Quickly rising in rank, the next year Captain McCampbell was Commander of Air Group 15. His cognizance included fighters, bombers and torpedo bombers aboard the aircraft carrier *Essex*. His squadron saw almost six months of continuous combat and participated in two major air-sea battles, the first and second battles of the Philippine Sea.

By October 1944, Captain McCampbell shot down nine enemy planes in one mission. When he landed his Grumman Hellcat, his six machine guns had only two rounds to spare and only ten minutes of fuel remaining.

Captain McCampbell received the Medal of Honor in recognition of the October fight. The citation reads, in part:

> "During a major fleet engagement . . . assisted by but one plane, [Captain McCampbell] inter cepted and daringly attacked a formation of 60 hostile land-based craft approaching our forces. Fighting desperately but with superb skill against such overwhelming air power, he shot down nine Japanese planes and, completely disorganizing the enemy group, forced the remainder to abandon the attack before a single aircraft could reach the fleet."

Thirty-four victories made Captain McCampbell the armed services' fourth-leading ace of all time behind three Army Air Forces pilots. In addition to the Medal of Honor, other awards included the Navy Cross, the Navy's second-highest award for valor; a Silver Star; and the Distinguished Flying Cross.

After World War II, Captain McCampbell commanded the carrier *Bon Homme Richard* and served a tour as Plans Division Chief for the Joint Chiefs of Staff. Captain David McCampbell retired from active duty in 1964.

The Navy's all-time leading ace passed away on June 30, 1996 at the age of 86. Medal of Honor recipient Captain David McCampbell was laid to rest with full military honors at Arlington National Cemetery.

BLUE STAR

A tribute to the Armed Forces that have defended the United States of America.

Seminole & US 1, Melbourne
BE40 ~ GPS Coordinates: 28.082733, -80.605583

Although the Blue Star marker program specifies that the plaques are placed in tribute to members of the Armed Forces, I would feel remiss leaving out a vital group of individuals who work in the space industry. Brevard County is commonly known as the Space Coast and with this I pay homage to those who have tragically given the ultimate sacrifice in support of the space program.

The Astronauts Memorial Foundation (AMF) was formed as a result of the Challenger accident in 1986. Five years later President George Bush and Congress designated a national memorial called the Space Mirror Memorial located at the Kennedy Space Center. The memorial stands to recognize all United States astronauts who lost their lives either during missions or while in training on American Space Ships. Sadly, twenty-four astronauts are honored with this memorial.

The AMF receives no funding from NASA but is fully approved. Their purpose is to build and maintain two facilities at the Space Center's Visitor Complex. The lion's share of the funding is provided from Florida's Challenger automobile license plates; fifty percent of the state sales are allotted. Corporations, foundations and individual contributions support the facilities and programs as well.

The Space Mirror Memorial represents a blending of art and science. More than seven hundred fifty architects vied for the chance to design what was to be an amazing tribute. The only memorial to attract more architectural attention was the Vietnam Veterans Memorial in Washington DC. Standing an amazing forty-two and a half feet tall and stretching fifty feet wide, the memorial is comprised of ninety polished granite panels. The panels are two inches thick and are a hefty five hundred pounds.

Each name is carved through the granite and filled with clear acrylic to allow light to illuminate the lettering. Bright rays of sun pass through the sculpture during daylight hours and beams of artificial light illuminate the memorial as the sun slips below the horizon. Vice President Dan Quayle provided a moving dedication introducing the Space Mirror Memorial in 1991.

The last names added to the memorial came in 2003 when all seven Columbia astronauts perished during reentry of the earth's atmosphere. Our prayer is that the memorial is complete and no other names will appear. The Space Mirror Memorial stands as a bright, shinning beacon to those brave men and women who like their brothers in arms gave all for their country.

ICE PLANT

This building was started in December, 1926, by the Florida Power and Light Co., as a 150-ton ice plant. The plant was to be built in units, with the first unit a 50-ton capacity. Cost of the building was about $100,000. Before this ice plant was built, the one in Fort Pierce used to ship ice to Melbourne on the Florida East Coast Railway. Someone would meet the train with a horse and wagon and deliver ice door-to-door. Those who wanted to make ice cream in home ice cream freezers would often bury the ice in a hole in the ground until Sunday rolled around. Then they made ice cream for the whole family.

1604 South Harbor City Boulevard, Melbourne
BE41 ~ GPS Coordinates: 28.082717, -80.605683

THE ICE PLANT TODAY

Florida Power and Light Company was founded in the dawning days of 1925. The state was experiencing the most significant population explosion to date and electrical power excited the public dreaming of appliances in the future. The company traces its lineage from General Electric founded by Thomas Edison, which in turn evolved into the Electric Bond and Share Company then American Power and Light.

December 28, 1925 is the official birthday of Florida Power and Light, whose expansion shows a direct correlation with the growth of the state. The list of businesses springing forth as a result of electrical power was amazing. Everything from the obvious electrical plants to sponge fishing boats using the Ice Plant in Melbourne.

Construction consisted of a two-storied establishment, built of masonry with stucco embellishments. The building was completed in 1927 and became a mainstay in Brevard providing businesses and residential customers with block ice. Refrigeration was rare and the ice created an innovative way to preserve foods as well as aid the local fishing trade bringing their produce to market. Of course other much more fun uses for the ice came to

283

be during this time as well. Sunday Ice Cream Socials were very popular and shaved "Snow Cones" became a wonderful childhood treat, I dare say the adults came to love the sweet delicacies as well.

The Florida Power and Light Ice Plant was placed on the Historical Register in 1982. The plant was eventually closed and went for many years uninhabited. Today the site is under construction and will be deemed the Ice Plant Office Center. MAI Engineering Construction Services, Incorporated was hired to restore the old building without disturbing the historical architecture of the structure. Certainly this endeavor to preserve a long-standing piece of Melbourne history is commendable.

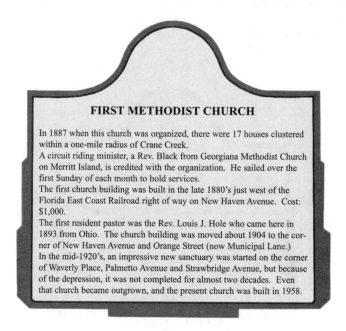

FIRST METHODIST CHURCH

In 1887 when this church was organized, there were 17 houses clustered within a one-mile radius of Crane Creek.

A circuit riding minister, a Rev. Black from Georgiana Methodist Church on Merritt Island, is credited with the organization. He sailed over the first Sunday of each month to hold services.

The first church building was built in the late 1880's just west of the Florida East Coast Railroad right of way on New Haven Avenue. Cost: $1,000.

The first resident pastor was the Rev. Louis J. Hole who came here in 1893 from Ohio. The church building was moved about 1904 to the corner of New Haven Avenue and Orange Street (now Municipal Lane.)

In the mid-1920's, an impressive new sanctuary was started on the corner of Waverly Place, Palmetto Avenue and Strawbridge Avenue, but because of the depression, it was not completed for almost two decades. Even that church became outgrown, and the present church was built in 1958.

110 East New Haven Avenue, Memory Park, Melbourne
BE42 ~ GPS Coordinates: 28.081933, -80.612533

Reverend Black from Merritt Island recognized the need for a permanent Methodist congregation in 1887 as Melbourne grew to some seventeen families. The pastor ministered to the Georgiana Methodist Church regularly made the trip to the Melbourne church only once a month. Lay ministers conducted services between Reverend Black's visits. He would board his small sailboat the first Sunday of each month for services at the Melbourne Methodist Church.

One year later the first sanctuary was built at the New Haven Avenue site. The congregation raised one thousand dollars to build the simple white wooden religious edifice. Located to the west of the Florida East Coast Railroad track, the train shook the building as it steamed down the rails.

Finally, five years after the church was built a permanent pastor was installed. Reverend Louis J. Hole traveled with his wife from Ohio to accept leadership of the Methodist congregation. A novice author, Reverend Hole wrote "Melbourne Sketches: A Souvenir of Melbourne on the Indian River" in 1895. The work was reprinted due to demands for book in 1980.

The church was moved one block west in 1904. The new location was the corner of New Haven and Orange Street, which is today known as Municipal Lane. By the mid 1920s construction began on a new sanctuary. Much more elaborate, the edifice was to be situated at the intersection of Waverly Place, Palmetto Avenue and Strawbridge Avenue. When the depression drew the entire country into financial disaster, construction on the church was halted. The building took approximately twenty years to complete. By the time the new edifice was built it was already too small for the congregation, so in 1958 construction on a third sanctuary was initiated. The first service was observed at this location on April 6, 1958, as well as every service since that date. The location at New Haven Avenue and Orange Street has welcomed the Emmanuel Baptist Church later known as Grace Baptist Church and the Presbyterians at the very same site over a span of more than one hundred years.

MELBOURNE PUBLIC LIBRARY

The library began in Mrs. Campbell's store, called the bazaar, on lower New Haven Avenue, in 1918.

It soon outgrew the store, moved to a building on the corner of New Haven Ave. and Vernon Place, then across the street to the display room of the Ford Motor Co.

In 1922, the books were moved to the office of Dr. I. K. Hicks, upstairs over the Ford Motor Co.

Outgrowing Hick's office, the books were stored in a feed store on Melbourne Court for a time.

The first library building came into existence in 1924 on the corner of Palmetto and Waverly, where the parking lot of the Sun Bank is in 1989. Cost of construction: $2,500.

There were 3,000 books

In 1954, under the leadership of the Civic Improvement Board. A building was completed on this site, with subsequent enlargements made in 1959 and 1974. That building was razed in 1988 and the present library dedicated in September 1989.

540 East Fee Avenue, Melbourne
BE43 ~ GPS Coordinates: 28.078756, -80.618876

Cocoa Village was home to the first library in Brevard County in 1895. However, as the county experienced an influx in population the need for a library in Melbourne became glaringly evident. Mrs. Campbell volunteered a section of her store on New Haven Avenue in 1918 to serve as a library. Basically the library consisted of a few books donated by local inhabitants and two chairs in a corner of Mrs. Campbell's store.

Over the next six years the Melbourne library had four different homes. Once library inventory outgrew Mrs. Campbell's store, the books were carted down the street to a little shop on the corner of New Haven Avenue and Vernon Place. With generous bequeaths from library patrons the ever-expanding collection soon required additional space and moved to the display floor of the Ford Motor Company. Dr. I. K. Hicks had his office above the Ford show room as well and soon the library spilled over into his dealership space. Then a local feed and seed store allotted space for the library but by now it had become glaringly evident that a permanent home was vital.

The library found a home of its own in 1924, when facilities were built at the corner of Palmetto and Waverly. Florida Statute 150 provided the funding necessary for construction at a cost of twenty-five hundred dollars. In order to qualify for the financing the library was required to serve all county residents from Mims to Melbourne. The library had an inventory of more than three thousand varying volumes. This site would serve as the Melbourne Public Library for more than sixty years. Two subsequent additions were added to the library in 1959 and 1974 before it became evident that a new modernized facility was required. The first permanent home of the Melbourne Library was demolished in 1988.

The new library was located at 540 East Fee Avenue and was dedicated in September 1989. The information and services provide a wealth of opportunities to the Brevard County residents. Enrichment classes ranging from book presentations to the Art of Belly Dancing offers a wide variety of programs for everyone. Services have been modernized and blossomed to include audio/visual materials, computer usage, literacy programs, meeting facilities, services for the handicapped and various children's programs. The Melbourne Public Library continues today as an integral part of the Brevard County community. Take the time to go in and discover the wealth of information available at the Melbourne Public Library.

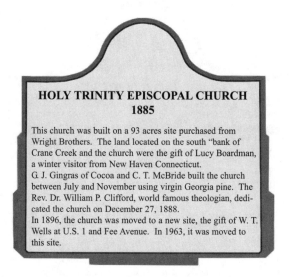

HOLY TRINITY EPISCOPAL CHURCH
1885

This church was built on a 93 acres site purchased from Wright Brothers. The land located on the south "bank of Crane Creek and the church were the gift of Lucy Boardman, a winter visitor from New Haven Connecticut.
G. J. Gingras of Cocoa and C. T. McBride built the church between July and November using virgin Georgia pine. The Rev. Dr. William P. Clifford, world famous theologian, dedicated the church on December 27, 1888.
In 1896, the church was moved to a new site, the gift of W. T. Wells at U.S. 1 and Fee Avenue. In 1963, it was moved to this site.

50 West Strawbridge, Melbourne
BE44 ~ GPS Coordinates: 28.080350, -80.622783

Across from Grant Place on what was the south side of Crane Creek lay the original site of the Holy Trinity Episcopal Church. The first services were held in the dining room of the Goode family home in 1884. The Right Reverend John Freeland Young, the second bishop of Florida, conducted those first services.

A Connecticut native, Lucy Boardman, donated the property, which was to become the site of the first Melbourne church of any denomination. She gave one thousand dollars, which was an enormous amount of money in 1886, for the building fund. C. J. Gingras and C. T. McBrice were hired to build the tiny frame building made of durable Georgia heart pine floated down the St. Johns River for construction.

The very first service, preached by Reverend William Porcher DuBose, was held on December 27, 1886. Parishioners arrived on sailboats, small fishing boats, long canoes, wagons and buggies near the church site. But unfortunately could only dock on the opposite shore. After finally arriving it was as if crossing an obstacle course; a rickety plank and rope bridge, swayed precariously in the blowing wind. By the time parishioners crossed over they had prayed for safe arrival for hours, of course then prayer for the return trip was necessary. A trip to church once a month was sufficient to make up prayer for the entire period. Lucy Boardman donated property once owned by one of Eau Gallie founders, Wright Brothers, equaling some ninety-two acres and Holy Trinity was moved to a more centralized location. Fortunately the location on U.S. Highway 1 in 1895 was on the western side of the intracoastal waterway making the trip to church a much easier experience. Though it must have been quite a sight to see the little wooden church being floated across the intracoastal waterway onboard a barge.

When the population swelled additional space was desperately needed so a lot at 50 West Strawbridge was purchased. Seven classrooms, a conference room, two offices and a kitchen were built and by 1958, the Holy Trinity Parish Day School was opened, relieving the overcrowded public school system.

The Episcopal Church Women's organization labored for five years to raise funds to have the original chapel structure moved to the Strawbridge Avenue location. The building, which is almost one hundred twenty years old, is still very much in use today. The immaculate condition of the structure is a wonderful example of historical preservation. The credit is due the Episcopal Women's organization that the facility is still in such wonderful condition today.

The Day School was then serving more than four hundred students. New offices, a library and the Episcopal Counseling Center became a reality in 1980 under the leadership of Reverend William G. Lewis. Lewis Hall, named in the Reverend's honor, was purchased in 1999 and was completely remodeled three years later.

Holy Trinity Episcopal Church continues to have a very active congregation. The church continues to provide services for their congregation as well as the community. The following statement sums up their philosophy:

> Holy Trinity opens wide its doors in the name of Jesus Christ and says "Welcome"...
> to all who feel joy and wish to celebrate,
> to all who are weary and need rest,
> to all who seek God's desire for their lives,
> to all who mourn and wish comfort,
> to all who pray and to all who sometimes struggle to pray,
> and to all who are looking for a community of fellow pilgrims.

**ACTUAL MARKER AT
HOLY TRINITY
EPISCOPAL CHURCH**

**LINCOLN HOTEL
(Now the Florida Air Academy)**

The south side of this building was originally built in 1923 as the home for the Ernest Kouwen-Hoven Family. During the year they lived in it, it was the scene of many spectacular parties, as well as more down-to-earth "Crab-Boils" held on the spacious lawn.

Purchased in 1926 by the Widrig Brothers, additions were made to the building and it became the Lincoln Hotel. The hopes of the Widrigs to make Melbourne another Palm Beach with their beautiful hostelry did not materialize.

In 1957 the hotel was sold to A. J. Rimer who renamed it the Barcelona Hotel. It operated under this name until 1961 when it was sold to Jonathan Dwight to become Florida Air Academy.

**1950 South Academy Drive, Melbourne
BE45 ~ GPS Coordinates: 28.079535, -80.628195**

Ernest Kouwen-Hoven arrived in the Melbourne area around 1915. As he surveyed the picturesque surroundings, Ernest had an epiphany. He could develop the area as an exclusive beachside resort and eventually his dream came to pass. He created a tract known as "Indialantic-by-the-Sea." Only one complication inhibited the resort's success, the only way to reach the lovely vacation spot was by ferry crossing. Well, Ernest had another inspiration, he would build a bridge.

The bridge concept became known to locals as "Kouwen-Hoven's Folly," most believed that the construction would never be finalized. The process took just over three years but in 1921 the first motorized vehicle crossed the wooden bridge to Indialantic. The bridge was only sixteen feet wide and the steel draw lifting the bridge for boats was operated by hand. It took fourteen minutes to raise and lower the bridge and that did not include the slow moving boats passing through, patience was a necessity. Kouwen-Hoven collected a ten-cent toll for each car to pass and fines for those failing to adhere to the ten miles per hour speed limit. The bridge suffered many shortcomings, travelers were known to bring along hammers to pound in loose nails across the span. To ensure safe passage across during the evening hours, the way was lit with kerosene lanterns. Unfortunately the idea was not as safe as it sounded. Whenever a strong wind swept through the area, the lanterns would be blown to the bridge floor and it would burn. It was said that during a two week span the bridge caught fire six times, resulting in the fire chief resigning his position so that he could get a good night rest.

Ernest built a home for his family at Melbourne in 1923. The five-bedroom residence was called Magnolia Manor, but the Kouwen-Hoven family only resided there for one year. The house was sold to Bob Widrig and his brother in 1926. The Widrig Brothers renovated the house and added additional wings creating the Lincoln Hotel. The hotel welcomed guests for almost thirty years.

The Lincoln Hotel was sold to A. J. Rimer in 1957 and the name was changed to the Barcelona. Rimer, who was once the owner of the Green Bay Packers, only held the property for four years. In 1961 the Barcelona was sold to Jonathan Dwight, a teacher from New Jersey who had definite ideas for the property. Dwight founded the Florida Military Academy on the site. The proud tradition of the Florida Military Academy continues today under the guidance of Dwight's sons and daughter. The main building of the former Lincoln Hotel is today known as the Hall of Flags and a Spanish style residence that once housed the Dwight family is today known as Dwight Hall.

The Florida Air Academy is an exemplary facility noted as one of the finest military academies through-out the south. Excellence in academics, athletics and flight training for the all-male student body is a continuing goal. The course curriculum is geared toward military bearing and self-discipline. Students are offered the oppor-tunity to pursue flight training while attending the academy.

In 2004, the Florida Air Academy celebrated their forty-second class of graduates. Included in this class was the grandson of founder Jonathan Dwight. Kyle Dwight Powers is the third generation of the founding family to receive his diploma. He gave a rousing valedictory address before the Class of 2004, their families, underclass-men and guests.

MELBOURNE NAVAL AIR STATION

This site was the 129th building Naval Air Station con-structed at the Melbourne Municipal Airport at the begin-ning of World War II. It was commissioned as Operational Training Unit #2 on October 20, 1942 and closed on February 15, 1946. The Station was used for training newly commissioned Navy and Marine pilots. There were over 2,200 pilots who trained in Grumman F4F Wildcat and F6F Hellcat fighter planes. Of the pilots trained there, 63 died in aerial accidents and two enlisted men died in ground-related accidents. The location served more than 310 officers and 1,355 enlisted personnel. Today the area is operated by the City of Melbourne Airport Authority.

Across from Melbourne International Airport in mobile home park, Edie Allen & Playhouse Streets, Melbourne
BE46 ~ GPS Coordinates: 28.091483, -80.630650

The United States was forced into World War II and suddenly high-ranking military leaders realized that pilots and aircraft were in short supply. Immediately the Grumman Corporation was given the go ahead to build F6F Hellcats and cadets had to be quickly trained. To resolve the situation eight new Naval Auxiliary Air Stations would be created to handle the wave of future pilots reporting for operational training.

The Melbourne-Eau Gallie Airport was first dedicated in 1941 but just one year later the facility experienced a profound metamorphosis. From the airport facility NAS[15] Melbourne, Florida was commissioned and designated a day fighter Station on October 20, 1942. Navy personnel would be trained to become "top gun" fighter pilots, flying the F6F Hellcats.

All the while German U-boats[16] patrolled the Melbourne coast. Eventually the United States sunk several ships just off the Melbourne beach. The beaches of Brevard County became sticky black with burned oil, debris could be found for miles and the water was polluted with the remains of the wrecked U-boats. Because of the offshore German U-boats blackouts were ordered within a mile of the beaches and alerting sirens signaled sightings. The Department of the Army set up coastal towers along the beach as spotting stations for aircraft, ships and rescue efforts. Volunteers manned the stations in six-hour shifts. The volunteers were required to attend classes in aircraft identification before standing the watch.

Life at NAS Melbourne was not all training and U-boat sightings. Actually a festive atmosphere also seemed to permeate the community. Organizations hosted parties and social events for the flying aces. The Casino Club served as the petty officers club and the Bahama Beach Club offered a large artesian well pool and cabana, which both proved to be popular gathering places for Naval personnel. Of course part of the excitement of the Bahama Club was the thrill of crossing the old wooden bridge to the beach. Dilapidated at best, the bridge became increasingly unsafe but due to the war building a new bridge had to be delayed until the war's conclusion; finally being completed in 1947.

Rumor during the waning days of the war passed that Churchill and Roosevelt were to meet at Neptune Hall on Melbourne Beach to devise the plan for their D-day invasion. President Roosevelt was said to be arriving by aircraft landing at NAS Melbourne and Britain's Prime Minister Churchill was to arrive aboard a submarine.

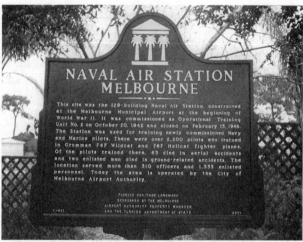

THE ACTUAL MARKER

By the end of World War II, the Department of the Navy returned the NAS Melbourne facilities to the city. Eastern Airlines became the first commercial carrier to serve Melbourne in 1953. Change seemed to be continual when by the 50s and early 60s the space program began to progress. The Brevard County shore became known as the Space Coast. The Brevard Engineering School was founded in 1958 and had its first classes in a wooden barracks building previously used at NAS Melbourne.

Further detailed information on NAS Melbourne is available from a first hand source, William R. Barnett. Ensign Barnett completed fighter operational training with the F6F Hellcat while at NAS Melbourne. His book "US Naval Air Station, Melbourne, Florida WWII" is available at most bookstores.

MELBOURNE'S FIRST SCHOOL

This building was erected in 1883 by John Goode, an early settler. About 800 yards south of his home, called Fountain Heights, on the Indian River. This area is now South Riverview Drive.

The schoolhouse served both white and black students and the first two teachers were Maude Goode and May Valentine.

The school was painted red from the very beginning. A hand-operated pump stood outside the door and long benches served as the only seats inside. There were no desks. The students wrote on slates. The school term was only about five or six months in the summer time.

Florida Institute of Technology, in the botanical garden, Melbourne
BE47 ~ GPS Coordinates: 28.066433, -80.623400

Located on the bank of the Indian River in the area that is today known as South Riverview Drive was the first schoolhouse for the children of Melbourne. The school was built at the homesite of John Goode in 1883. The structure was a small nine by twelve-foot wooden building. At the risk of being cliché it was indeed a little red schoolhouse, but eventually the building's façade would fade to brown. When the South Brevard Historical Society began restoring the building, they decided on a "russet" red. It has been said that years ago when livestock and various other animals were slaughtered for food, the blood would be saved for use as paint. Blood turns brown over time, creating the color of many old buildings, therefore explaining the use of the russet paint.

Teachers Maude Good and May Valentine served both white and black children though the children were not allowed to mix at the same sessions. White students were said to have attended classes during the morning hours and the black students in the afternoons. Some say the students were combined during some classes but this is highly unlikely. The first class had four graduating students.

After six years the schoolhouse was abandoned for more modern facilities. Eventually the little schoolhouse became home to a single family during the World War II when their home tragically burned. It was later used for a storage shed that is until the South Brevard Historical Society discovered the historic significance of the schoolhouse in 1969. Over time the little red schoolhouse was stored in the school bus barn in South Melbourne and carefully preserved. The Inter-Fraternity Council had the schoolhouse moved in 1971. The wooden structure was placed on the coquina rock foundation that was part of Florida's first land granted university, Florida Agricultural College. Later the college became Brevard Engineering and eventually Florida Tech as it remains today.

Ironically the oldest school had served both white and black students; many years later Brevard Engineering had enrolled two African American students in opposition to a noted county official. The school president was ordered to turn away the black students or face eviction. The college chose to move their classes rather than bend to the unfair edict.

Originally the campus of Florida Tech along Crane Creek was known as "Cathead." The name came to be for the abundance of wild cats and panthers frequently seen in the area. Locals told tales of circling around an evening fire while bright yellow eyes peered from the edge of the eerie dark forest. They waited patiently to pounce on unsuspecting prey. In the morning paw prints would be found at the perimeter of the campsite as the great cats staked out, waiting for an opportunity to pounce. No attacks were ever recorded in the area. The shadows of the great cats would often be seen in the forest but seldom close except when roadways began to invade the wilderness and bloodied carcasses would be found on the highway. The cat's numbers dwindled as modern motorized vehicles increased. Today the Florida panther is nearly extinct.

Melbourne's oldest schoolhouse was placed in what the Florida Tech students lovingly call, "the jungle." Dent Smith, a long time supporter of the school, accumulated the largest collection palm trees ever amassed in the United States; the result was the jungle. A trail through the hardwood hammock and palms was named in Dent's honor. According the university's deed the jungle must be preserved. Along the trail is a Seminole chikis[17], strangely enough many of the professors can be found there during office hours in the cool, quiet shelter of the beautiful, lush green, tropical garden harboring the oldest schoolhouse.

SITE OF
FIRST PERMANENT LOG CABIN

Richard W. Goode, wife, Jessie Goode and three small children arrived in the area of Crane Creek in 1877. The came here from Evanston, Illinois.

Goode explored the area on foot and by boat, while his family remained in the small settlement of Eau Gallie. He finally selected this site on the banks of Crane Creek for his first log cabin.

He purchased a homestead of 153 acres, stretching from this area westward through what is now Country Club Colony. The purchased from the United States Government cost him $3.85.

The Goode Family was living at this site in 1890 when straws were drawn thereby selecting the name of the small community as Melbourne. John Cornthwaite Rector, a settler from Australia, suggested the name Melbourne.

Melbourne Avenue just west of Roxy Street, Melbourne
BE48 ~ GPS Coordinates: 28.076400, -80.615383

Richard Walter Goode, originally from Scotland, married wife Jessie and with her immigrated to Evanston, Illinois. Eventually the Goode family, parents and the three small children, arrived at a serene spot only a mile west of Crane Creek's origin. The Goode patriarch instinctively knew that they were at last home.

Thomas Mason held a Spanish land grant in the area that Richard Goode meant to claim as his own. However, Mason had long since abandoned the property and Richard applied for homestead rights from the United States Government. The homestead grant was approved for one hundred fifty-three acres for which Richard Goode spent three dollars eight-five cents. The Goode homestead spanned from what is today Hickory Street, traveling west to Country Club Colony. Richard built a fine family log cabin, said to be first permanent dwelling in Melbourne, near the modern day intersection of Melbourne Avenue and Roxy Lane.

Jessie Goode described the area as a hunter's mecca where both white hunters and Seminole braves hunted all manner of wild life from turkey to bear. The acreage was commonly called "Cathead," referring to the abundance of feral felines including panthers that roamed the dense forest. Today the Florida panther is listed on the endangered species list as a result of being hunted to the brink of extinction and the loss of natural habitat.

Jessie and Richard Goode gave Melbourne the first structure built solely for use as a schoolhouse. The one room, cypress building cost an exorbitant twenty-five dollars to erect. It was located east of Riverview Drive and south of Line Street. Today the little red schoolhouse stands on the grounds of Florida Tech, which was at one time part of the Goode homestead.

In 1897, Goode was listed as Melbourne's seventh postmaster. In addition, Richard operated a real estate office. He returned north for a visit to Evansville and Chicago in 1912, it was there that Richard Goode met his end. While walking along the train tracks, Richard Walter Goode was killed by an elevated railroad train.

HENEGAR SCHOOL COMPLEX

The western most building of this complex was built in the period 1919-1921 and the first high school graduating class graduated May 12, 1921 with 13 students.
The building was soon overflowing and six "shacks" were built to care for the surplus students.
The high school building (eastern building) was completed in 1926. William Christen was the architect.
Even that was insufficient and the "primary" building (now destroyed) was erected in 1928.
The year 1920 when this complex was started there were two streetlights, three churches, and few houses. No paved streets and one or two general stores in Melbourne.

635 East New Haven Avenue, Melbourne
BE49 ~ GPS Coordinates: 28.078567, -80.610417

Proudly standing at 635 East New Haven Avenue is a memorial to one of Melbourne's most respected educators. The Henegar Center was dedicated March 12, 1963, named in tribute to Hazel Ruth Henegar. She was a beloved high school teacher, assistant principal and principal in the Melbourne school system for some twenty-six years. The only school to rival Henegar in longevity is the first schoolhouse built by the Goode family in 1883, which now can be seen on the campus of Florida Tech.

The first of several buildings constructed in what would later be dubbed the Henegar Complex was completed in 1919. Architect William Christian was responsible for the design, the subsequent secondary and primary grades buildings were not finished until 1926 and 27 respectively. Two years after the construction of the initial edifice the first group of thirteen students graduated as the Class of 1921.

The school was in use for more than forty years; however, the facilities never seemed to meet the demand of the ever-increasing population. Small huts were set up to accept the overflow until it became glaringly obvious more modernized facilities where imperative. During the late 1960s the west building was put to use as the Brevard Junior College, unfortunately the facility closed in 1975. Sadly, the Henegar School Complex was left to disintegrate into time, suffering from the effects of Mother Nature.

Concerned citizens with an eye for preservation of the communities historical buildings were no longer able to watch as the Henegar Center was lost to time and the elements. The group formed Brevard Regional Arts in order to revitalize the Henegar School Complex. The Brevard County School System graciously donated the buildings to BRAG and as a result the Henegar Center for the Arts was born.

More than two and a half million dollars were raised to complete the extensive renovations. Tradesmen generously volunteered their services for the project, which resulted in an amazing state of the art facility. The edifice was unveiled in 1993. At the heart is a four hundred ninety-three seat capacity magnificent theater designed by a known Tony Award winning Broadway set designer. The impressive stage is adorned with the original curtain taken from the Broadway production of "The King and I". The lighting and sound system rival any used New York's finest stage productions.

The Henegar Center for the Arts has wonderful facilities for meetings, seminars, conventions and venues for any special event planned. Meeting rooms are suitable for groups of ten to the Grand Ballroom, which will seat up to one hundred twenty persons. Of course, theatrical productions, concerts, exhibits and special appearances are the heart and soul of the center. Schedules are posted regularly advertising the cultural festivities offered at the Henegar Center.

It is often said that mysterious noises, moaning sounds, can be heard echoing through the hall; props appear in awkward places; and a vague figure silently watches the activities from high in balcony. An apparition dubbed "Jonathan" was perhaps a student whose life ended tragically short or the tortured soul of an actor unable to leave behind the stage. Regardless to those who have seen the eerie specter say the benevolent spirit is definitely an avid patron of the arts drawn to the marvelous facility.

TIN CAN TOURIST CAMPGROUND

Almost this entire block was a campground for Tin Can tourist in the years 1919-1923.
Travelers from all over the country camped here in tents, homemade trailers and even wooden shelters built on the backs of Model T Ford trucks. Out houses and hand pumps provided sanitary facilities and water. People washed in outdoor tubs, and cats, dogs, and chickens roamed the campground.
"Gospel Cars" often came to the campground, bringing with them 'Hell - Fire and Collection Plates."
Campers would also gather around a big campfire for hotdog roasts, other activities included pine needle craft and palmetto weaving by the women. The campground was the official meeting place for the local chapter of the Tin Can Tourist. A formal organization with headquarters in Tampa and a stated purpose of providing "Fellowship" for its members.

712 East New Haven Avenue, near Waverly Place intersection, Melbourne
BE50 ~ GPS Coordinates: 28.078550, -80.608333

Florida, the Sunshine State, in 1919 was experiencing an economic, population and tourism boom never seen before in the state. Use of the automobile made transportation comfortable and easy, money was readily available either on hand or by credit and people were flocking to the land of sunshine in droves. Some travelers came south and never left, while others just came to wiggle their toes in the sandy soil for a little while. To this end, the era of the Tin Can Tourist was born.

The Tin Canners Club actually began at Desota Park in Tampa around 1919, deriving the name for the heavy metal cans containing gasoline and water carried for spare by tourists. Many of the travelers crept along the unimproved highways in caravans while other vehicles carried several families piled in alongside the tents, food supplies and extra fuel. Towns along the Florida roadways began catering to the new breed of tourists with camps having recreational facilities and group entertainment.

This was a new day for tourists in Florida. These people weren't searching for the high priced accommodations or expensive restaurants, they were not the rich but middle income and sometimes poor subsiding on what a day of work here or there could provide. Another suggestion concerning the name "Tin Canners" stemmed from the fact that many of the families ate little more than vienna sausages, pork and beans or canned hash easily carried, prepared and nourishing all the same.

The Tin Can Tourist Camp in Melbourne located on East New Haven Avenue had a relatively short existence. The camp was active only four years but during that time thousands arrived with tents, homemade trailers and crudely built wooden huts mounted in the beds of Ford Model T trucks. The atmosphere around camp was fun and carefree, people shared food, gathered round wash tubs and telling stories by the light of an evening campfire. Women crafted small trinkets out of shells or woven palmetto fronds, sometime selling them along the roadside to tourists for pocket change.

Later the "Tin Canners" evolved to include pull behind campers and new fangled pop up tents. All the while the spirit of the group remained the same: safe and clean camping areas, wholesome family entertainment and high moral values. Often cars and trucks were seen rolling down the roadway with tin cans welded to the radiator cap, signifying membership in the Tin Canners Club. Unfortunately the camp at Melbourne fell victim to the great depression and declining Florida economy in 1923. By 1926, the Florida population boom came to an abrupt halt. Money for travel was no longer available, people were simply trying to survive and easy credit was a thing of the past. Several severe hurricanes further deterred tourism and the Great Depression loomed eerily on the horizon. The Sunshine State clouded but eventually the golden rays would return.

The tourism boom brought more to the state than fleeting travel dollars, the Florida legislature moved to build new, improved roadways that would eventually bring tourists back to her sandy shores. The Tin Can Tourists would eventually claim more than one hundred thousand campers on their membership rolls. Most of the tourist areas gave way to formal campgrounds and economy hotels sprang up like weeds along the roadside. Eventually the club slipped into obscurity, no record exists of its actual demise. But for a brief time, Tin Can Families gathered in Melbourne singing around the campfire and roasting hot dogs. It was a simpler time and perhaps we have lost much more than a happy campground, along the way.

MELBOURNE TIMES

Emmett David Oslin founded the Melbourne Times in a small shop on Front Street in 1894.
The four-page newspaper was printed on a hand press and subscription price was $1 per year. That same year the lighthouse at Cape Canaveral was built.
Around 1914 the Melbourne Times moved to the Myles Building on New Haven Avenue, west of the railroad tracks. About four years later it again moved a few doors west.
In 1920, the newspaper built a two-story concrete block building on Vernon Place, where it was published until merger with the Melbourne Journal took place in 1927. It then move to a building on Waverly Place, just north of the present building.

2015 South Waverly Place, Melbourne
BE51 ~ GPS Coordinates: 28.078550, -80.608333

The "Melbourne Times" began as a small print shop located on Front Street in 1894. The small newspaper was founded, written, edited, published and sold by Emmett David Oslin; for a number of years the paper was a one-man operation. Published weekly at a subscription cost of one dollar per year to local residents, the population totaled one hundred fifty-seven at that time.

Only a portion of the population could actually read, some were children and others were rural farm workers with very little, if any formal education. Yet everyone was excited when the editions arrived hot off the press. Groups would gather outside Hodgson's Mercantile or later Karrick's Grocery and revel in every word of the paper. Rural folk sat in the cool breeze of the evenings after the days work was done and supper finished, listening while the stories from the paper were read. It was a simpler time. The newspaper was entertainment before television surpassed the written word and lifestyles became so hectic that little time was left for quiet pleasures.

The Times was actually the second newspaper to go to print in Melbourne. The editions consisted of four pages covering for the most part local interest stories in the beginning. The processing was tedious at best, with each paper individually printed using a hand-operated press.

In 1914, the "Melbourne Times" took up residence in the newly constructed Myles Building just west of railroad tracks. The newspaper only remained at 919 East New Haven Avenue address for four years, though the next location was only a few doors down. Two years later, in 1920, the "Melbourne Times" packed up again. This time a brand new two-storied building built of concrete block on Vernon Place became home to the paper, which remained there for seven years. A new communications era began in 1927 when the "Melbourne Times" and the Melbourne Journal merged. The newspaper offices moved again and finally moving a short distance north to the location where they can be found today at 2015 South Waverly Place.

Eventually the "Melbourne Times" was acquired by the communications conglomerate, Gannett Publishing. Still covering local news, the "Melbourne Times" is a division of the expansive daily "Florida Today". Everything from world issues to community events is reported within the pages. Each section currently encompasses more than the original four pages of the "Melbourne Times".

But the days of the community gathering to hear the stories of the day around town square, in the mercantile or at the barbershop is a thing of the past. The newspaper has expanded from four to thirty or more pages and on most days the bad news outweighs the good. There's no longer a farm report; those visiting the community or traveling to tend their sick aunt is no longer news; there once was a hospital report when there were twenty beds or less in hospital; and fishing was always good somewhere. Progress has marched forward, growth is present all around.

ORANGE SPOT INN

The original hotel on this site was built in 1884 on property, which Richard W. Goode purchased from Thomas Mason first white settler of Melbourne. Mrs. R. W. Goode operated the "Rooming House." She called it the Goode House.
In 1894, the Campbell Family purchased the property, enlarged the hotel and changed the name to the Bellevue Hotel. A water wheel and a cement pool were added.
In the early part of the twentieth century, tennis matches were held on the Bellevue's tennis courts and the entire population of Melbourne came out to watch.
In 1920, Harry Baisley bought the Bellevue Hotel and changed the name to Orange Spot Inn.
The Inn was destroyed by fire January 12, 1927.

Melbourne Avenue & Melbourne Court, Melbourne
BE52 ~ GPS Coordinates: 28.076950, -80.605550

The first hotel in Melbourne was known as the Goode House, built by founding father Richard W. Goode. Though known as the first hotel the much more formal Carleton Hotel, owned by Emma Strawbridge, was built about the same time. Mrs. A. W. Goode managed the "Rooming House" with an outstanding view of the Indian River area known as Crane Creek.

Often the twelve rooms were filled to capacity with persons waiting to board the ferry to Melbourne Beach located just across the crushed shell road. Patrons arriving between 10:00 a.m. and 6:00 p.m. on Sundays would find the hotel abandoned. The Goode family took this time each week to spend the day together, fishing and swimming at the riverside.

C. J. F. Campbell purchased the hotel in 1894. Under the Campbell family ownership the Goode House became the Bellevue Hotel. Renovations began immediately with a cement swimming pool, a water wheel supplying indoor plumbing to the hotel, a pulley system hauled guest's luggage to the second and third floor rooms and clay tennis courts completed the hotel amenities.

The water wheel became a fascinating tourist attraction, a penny a wish, for years to come. The Bellevue hosted tennis tournaments on their beautifully done clay courts, the social events were eagerly attended by all of Melbourne's population. Melbourne's first telephone switchboard was installed in the Bellevue's downstairs front room in 1906. Maxie Goode, who knew everyone in town and was related to most, served as the first operator. As in movies of the 1920s and 30s, the telephone operator was the most informed person in town.

A Detroit native named Harry Baisley purchased the Bellevue in 1920 and promptly changed the name to the Orange Spot Inn. The hotel became a popular retreat for northern tourists. Melbourne was in the midst of a tremendous population explosion people were flocking south. Guests of the Orange Spot Inn came for the tropical weather, warm ocean waters and brilliant sun shinny days. Visitors enjoyed the tennis courts and relaxing on the picturesque banks of Crane Creek watching the graceful sails navigate the Melbourne Harbor.

The hot water boiler tragically exploded on January 12, 1927, lighting the sky with wicked orange flames and destroying the majestic Orange Spot Inn completely. The site is today the northwest corner of Melbourne Avenue and Melbourne Court, home to the Melbourne Harbor Place apartments.

CRANE CREEK PROMENADE AREA

Melbourne's founding fathers were three black men: Peter Wright, Balaam Allen and Wright Brothers. They came to the Crane Creek area a few years after the end of the Civil War. Brothers and Allen homesteaded land on the south side of Crane Creek, while Peter Wright bought land on both sides of the creek, building his home on the bluff, at the top of the Trysting Steps. Brothers and Allen made their living through agriculture, mostly citrus growing. Wright also went into agriculture, but he was also an early mail carrier, transporting the mail in his small sail boat from Titusville to St. Lucie.

The Fish House on the south side of Crane Creek was probably built in 1919 by John Brechwald and has been operated as a fish house (wholesale and retail) since that time.

According to Jessie Goode, early Melbourne settler, Crane Creek was an area where "white sportsmen and Seminole Indians came to hunt blue herons, ducks, marsh hens, bear, deer, wild turkeys and quail." The headwaters of Crane Creek (campus of Florida Tech) was an area inhabited by panthers and was commonly referred to as "cathead."

Crane Creek Promenade Park, East Melbourne Avenue, Melbourne
BE53 ~ GPS Coordinates: 28.077495, -80.603232

During the early days of the Civil War, the sparsely populated area then known as Crane Creek hosted a training field for drilling soldiers of the Confederacy. Many of the men were attracted to the area, which was bordered by the Indian River and just beyond is the Atlantic Ocean. Inland was the wild frontier forest rarely touched by man with the exception of the natives who were very nearly part of the landscape and once called this land home. The river yielded fish and water fowl; the ocean provided all manner of crustaceans and salt water life; the beaches brought oysters, crab, mussels and whelk; and still beyond that the forest was home to enough bear, deer,

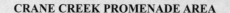

wild fowl and small mammals to keep a family plentiful in meat year round. The mild temperatures meant longer growing seasons for fruits, vegetables and sugar cane, which could be grown in abundance. A family would want for little. Yet living here was desolate and lonely far from established cities, travel was hard going.

When the war finally ended, land on the vast Florida peninsula could be had for five cents per acre for anyone willing to work the land and homestead. The Crane Creek name denoted the importance of the fresh clear water creek flowing into the saltwater lagoon beyond. It was three freed men of color who chose to homestead this area; they were Peter Wright, William (Balaam) Allen and Wright Brothers. They came to the area in the early 1870s. Allen and Brothers purchased land on the south shore of the creek while Peter

CRANE CREEK PROMENADE PARK

297

Wright purchased land to the north and south. The Clohecys and Bradleys were the first white families to claim land, arriving in 1874 and 75. The Goode family came from Chicago in 1877 and Cornthwaite Hector deserted his wife and children in Australia, arriving the very next year.

Peter Wright became known as the sailing mailman when he began maneuvering his small skiff, *Nellie*, to deliver the mail to coastal settlements from Titusville to St. Lucie. Wright sailed the river twice a week for fourteen years until a permanent post office was established in 1880. However, in order to have an official government post office the community must be given a proper name. In the most politically correct by the book process, the name was chosen. They drew straws. The possibilities were Fountainhead, Villa Ridge and Melbourne to name a few and in the end, Melbourne, the home Hector had abandoned, won out.

Eight years later, on the morning of December 22, twenty-three men met and by voice vote incorporated the Village of Melbourne. By the time the sun slid beyond the horizon, elected officials had been chosen and a city seal established. The seal bore a pineapple plant, the symbol for welcome; the crane, in respect of the original Crane Creek name and the abundant palmetto tree, whose fronds had been woven to provide primitive shelters.

Today, more than one hundred years later the Crane Creek Promenade Park resides in downtown Melbourne. Located west of the Melbourne Causeway, just off Melbourne Avenue. The park was officially dedicated to the memory of the legendary sailing mailman, Peter Wright. The lovely ten-foot wide promenade meanders along the Indian River. Picnic tables and benches provide a quiet respite to sit and watch the river roll on past. During the fall and winter months the manatee call the warm waters home and the Crane Creek Promenade provides an exceptional view of the gentle beasts. Though any time of the year it is nice to take a moment to drink in the beauty of the river feed the ever-hungry seagulls and gaze at the boats in the harbor.

Close your eyes and imagine Peter Wright sailing past aboard his sailboat *Nellie*. With a wave of his hand and shout he would call a greeting to everyone he passed, maybe stop and chat a moment passing a story or two from one river community to the next. Then Wright would continue on his route to next riverside settlement bringing the mail and the news.

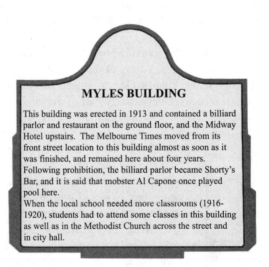

MYLES BUILDING

This building was erected in 1913 and contained a billiard parlor and restaurant on the ground floor, and the Midway Hotel upstairs. The Melbourne Times moved from its front street location to this building almost as soon as it was finished, and remained here about four years. Following prohibition, the billiard parlor became Shorty's Bar, and it is said that mobster Al Capone once played pool here.
When the local school needed more classrooms (1916-1920), students had to attend some classes in this building as well as in the Methodist Church across the street and in city hall.

919 East New Haven Avenue, Melbourne
BE54 ~ GPS Coordinates: 28.078317, -80.605500

The Myles Building was constructed in 1913 in what is today the downtown historic district of Melbourne. The Art Deco buildings adorning the block have withstood many transformations. The Myles Building has been home to a hotel, newspaper, school classrooms and even a billiard hall.

Rumor has it that when the billiard parlor became Shorty's Bar, several gaming tables were always running, often the notorious Al Capone stopped in to play when he was in the area. The gossip is quite possibly true, evidenced by the following quote attributed to Al Capone:

> I am going to Florida, tomorrow. Let the worthy citizens of Chicago get their liquor the best they can. I'm sick of the job-it's a thankless one and full of grief. I've been spending the best years of my life as a public benefactor.

The FBI listed Capone as public enemy number one. As the United States floundered under the burden of the great depression, Capone's mobster ties, contracted killings, bootlegging and various other dark criminal activities were well hidden from the government's eagle eye. Eventually a Federal Court found Capone guilty of tax evasion and sentenced him to eleven years in Alcatraz.

After serving seven years, Al Capone was released in 1939. He was ravaged by advanced syphilis, emerging from prison a sick and broken man. Capone returned to Florida to live out his remaining days in the tropical sunshine. His mental faculties were slowly slipping into oblivion when Capone contracted pneumonia in his weakened state. He seemed to rally by his 48th birthday but one week later on January 25, 1947 at 7:30 p.m., the nefarious Al Capone succumbed to a stroke brought on by the advanced stages of the disease.

He was pronounced dead in a guestroom of his Palm Isle, Florida home. To keep away the prying lens of the media cameras Capone was moved from his bed to a room removed from view. His bedroom was windowed all around to allow the view of the breath-taking Gulf of Mexico. Al Capone died sequestered in secret, much like he lived.

KEMPFER GROCERY STORE

Kempfer's was founded in 1923 on this site. William Kempfer was the original owner, his nephew, Robert Kempfer, took over the store in 1935.
This store had the first commercial air conditioning unit in the city of Melbourne (installed sometime prior to 1953).
Geiger's Ford Agency was next door to Kempfer's (west) until the agency moved to Prospect Avenue. There are still old gasoline tanks buried beneath the sidewalk here.

918 New Haven, Melbourne
BE55 ~ GPS Coordinates: 28.078383, -80.605383

The Kempfer Family is well established with deep roots firmly set in the sandy soil of Brevard County. Kempfer Grocery was only one of many endeavors flourishing under this distinguished Florida family name. In fact the entire area cradling Kempfer Grocery was known as the Geiger-Kempfer Block. Located to the north side of New Haven Avenue, the section lies between Municipal Lane and Melbourne Court. When the building was constructed in 1923 it became home to several businesses. In addition to William H. Kempfer's Market and Grocery was C. J. Denham's Dry Goods and Gents Furnishing Store. The building still stands today.

Deer Park became the home base of the Kempfer family. A twenty-five thousand-acre tract was purchased in the late 1800s. An extensive cattle ranch was founded on the property. The Kempfer men were part of that historical class of Florida Cracker Cowboys. Eventually the family diversified into other areas such as saw milling and timber production, farming, sod harvesting, leased hunting property, native Florida plants, as well as dirt and shell mining. The Kempfer family realized that living from the bounty of the earth continued to be a great responsibility. Their attention to conservation, scientific advancement and commitment to environmental issues is the most impressive aspect of this successful family's accomplishments.

Savannah native Carolyn Reed became the bride of George Kempfer and with the vows came tremendous responsibility. The young Georgia girl was up to the task and proved her metal when George passed away in 1962. Carolyn Kempfer was left with four teenagers, a thirty thousand-acre cattle ranch and sawmill as well as a well-established commitment to the community. Because George had always kept his wife actively involved with the workings of the ranch and mill, she was well prepared for the huge endeavor. Under her exceptional influence Deer Park not only continued to operate but prospered.

The matriarch of the Kempfer clan had her priorities firmly in place always putting the responsibility to her family and the ranch first. Amazingly she assumed the additional responsibility to fill her husband's seat on the Osceola County School Board, being reelected for two additional terms on her own. She served as director of the Brevard County Hospital Guild for ten years; became the director of the Osceola Art and Culture Center; all the while continuing as an active parishioner at the Eastminster Presbyterian Church.

Caroline Reed Kempfer was deservedly recognized as "Woman of the Year in Agriculture" for 1988. In 1987 she was awarded the "Outstanding Agriculturist Award" and the "First Lady of the Year" in Osceola County for 1979. Perhaps she was proudest of the recognition concerning the Kempfer Family as the "Outstanding Farm Family" in Osceola and Brevard Counties.

Today the fourth generation of Kempfer's expertly manages the family endeavors with skill and love learned by example. Under their leadership the family businesses continue to flourish. The next generations of Kempfer children and grandchildren continue to be taught the lessons necessary to carry on these remarkable family traditions and legacy.

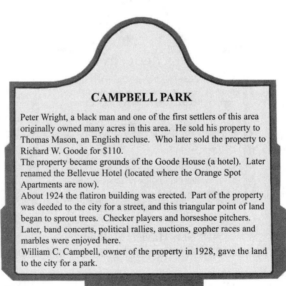

CAMPBELL PARK

Peter Wright, a black man and one of the first settlers of this area originally owned many acres in this area. He sold his property to Thomas Mason, an English recluse. Who later sold the property to Richard W. Goode for $110.

The property became grounds of the Goode House (a hotel). Later renamed the Bellevue Hotel (located where the Orange Spot Apartments are now).

About 1924 the flatiron building was erected. Part of the property was deeded to the city for a street, and this triangular point of land began to sprout trees. Checker players and horseshoe pitchers. Later, band concerts, political rallies, auctions, gopher races and marbles were enjoyed here.

William C. Campbell, owner of the property in 1928, gave the land to the city for a park.

At intersection of Melbourne Court & New Haven Avenue, just west of Florida East Coast Railroad tracks, Melbourne
BE56 ~ GPS Coordinates: 28.078233, -80.605133

At the heart of Melbourne's historic district is a small park representing so much more than the tiny space it occupies. Named for William C. Campbell, who donated the small triangle of land to the city in 1928, the little piece of solace is at the heart of a bygone era. Several benches and flowers offering brilliant splashes of color adorn the comfortable surroundings, which for more years than most can remember has been a gathering spot for locals and visitors alike.

Originally the area belonged to Peter Wright, a free man of color who came to central Florida looking for a home and made one out of the beauty of the wilderness that was Crane Creek. Wright was known as the legendary Sailing Mailman, delivering posts from Titusville to Malabar regularly. He sold the property to an odd English recluse, Thomas Mason for thirty dollars. Mason in turn sold the property to Richard W. Goode for one hundred ten dollars ~ a substantial profit for any day or time.

William C. Campbell, who purchased the Goode House (later known as the Orange Spot Inn) in 1894, came to own the property and around it Melbourne Village was established. The Flatiron Building was constructed around 1924, which still stands today at 927 East New Haven Avenue utilized as office suites. By this time several shops had opened their doors along the avenue and generously Campbell gave Melbourne what was to be a small park named in his honor.

The site is perfect for outdoor events including band concerts, politicians sounding off atop their soapboxes, auctions as well as a Sunday afternoon gopher race or kids kneeling in the dirt for a game of marbles. Many was the day that old men spent a beautiful Spring afternoon playing checkers with wooden discs painted red and black in friendly competition for bragging rights. The news spread between far removed neighbors from new babies to visiting cousins, fish tales and hunting bounties, crop successes and failures alike; everyone caught up on the news at the square on their usual once a month trip into town.

Though times have changed, it seems as one walks down the avenue just west of the railroad tracks, a quiet serenity comes to mind of a simpler time, an innocence lost so long ago. The pace slows to meld with the relaxed surroundings visitors long to embrace. There is no atmosphere of gaudy tourist trappings found in so many places but souvenirs are readily available. Quaint shops specialize in art, antiques, books and candles. Lovely bistros and cafes provide a respite for the hungry. It isn't to say that modern times have left the avenue behind, which is not the case at all but rather today has been embraced by yesterday and left a wonderful feeling of history brought into modern day.

Take a moment and sit in the shade of Campbell Park. Let the breeze brush past and tell you the story of more than one hundred years of history. Enjoy the surroundings and visit the shops, turn off the cell phone and ignore the beeper ~ Melbourne Village and her beautiful little park offers an opportunity to enjoy a less hectic day.

FLORIDA EAST COAST RAILROAD

Henry M. Flagler, Florida East Coast Railroad owner, was influenced to extend his railroad south from Rockledge by a Melbourne Resident: E. L. Branch.
The railroad tracks were built into Eau Gallie about 1892.
Considerable delay was experienced in building the railroad bridge over the Eau Gallie River.
The tracks reached Melbourne June 1893, and the first train reached Melbourne July 3, 1893 (a Monday), the same day that the Melbourne State Bank opened its doors. The day before, the first service had been held in the New Congregational Church of Melbourne.
Until Flagler could complete his rail line into Miami and later Key West, the F.E.C.R.R. connected in Melbourne to steamboats, which carried passengers and freight down the Indian River.

At New Haven Avenue Railroad Crossing, Melbourne
BE57 ~ GPS Coordinates: 28.078167, -80.604667

Flagler's railroad was just the catalyst required to blossom the state of Florida into the beautiful flower the Spaniards intended with the name. E. P. Branch convinced a reluctant Henry Flagler to extend his railroad south from Rockledge. Branch would later go on to serve as postmaster for Melbourne when Richard W. Goode was killed, ironically by an elevated railroad train on a visit to his native Chicago.

Railroad tracks were laid in the sandy soil of Eau Gallie in 1892, but tremendous delays were incurred while attempting to construct a railroad bridge crossing the Eau Gallie River. Ferryboats had, until this time, been the mainstays of transportation to the barrier islands. Mail, food and other supplies continued to be delivered this way from early in the 1880s through 1920. Of course, the heavy iron of the steam engine brought change down the tracks.

The Atlantic Coast, St. Johns and Indian River Railroad constructed a spur from Enterprise to Titusville in 1885. The railway was continually moving south. After the spur was built Flagler leased the line adding to his Jacksonville, Tampa and Key West Railroad. More railroad names were bandied around than could be reasonably kept up with. It was hard to tell whose engine was steaming down the track until the name came into view along the side.

Finally the tracks of the Flagler owned Jacksonville, St. Augustine and Indian River line reached Melbourne in June of 1893. The first engine arrived on Monday, July 3rd. By this time Flagler was determine to set tracks for Miami and on to Key West, the railroad was going to sea. Steamboats still brought passengers and freight down the Indian River to points south, but rail travel was more convenient and faster by far. Soon the steel wheels rolling along the rails edged out the romantic era of steamboats yet travelers still protested leaving the elegant old ships behind.

The railroad consisted of a push car transporting everything from produce to people. The Melbourne Station was a small, whitewashed building ~ hot in the summer and cold in the winter, typical of most in Florida. Henry Flagler changed the name for a final time in 1895 to one that still exists to this day, the Florida East Coast Railway.

Melbourne's businesses were soon drawn to the rails where loading and unloading freight was easily accomplished. The shops were eagerly awaiting travelers as they stepped down from the train. New Haven Avenue became the business district of Melbourne and the train the center of attention. As residents heard the sound of the southbound steam whistle in the distance calling, "trains a comin', trains a comin'" a crowd would gather. People came just to see who would arrive and marvel, as if it were Christmas, at the various produce and products being unloaded. All manner of "delights" arrived from far off places and with them a link to the outside world like never before.

Titusville also experienced change with the construction of a railroad wharf on the banks of the Indian River. The steamships brought goods and passengers from the south then transferred them to rail to be delivered to points north. It became much easier to get Florida's chief exports of fish and fruit to northern markets. Businesses suddenly sprang up in response to the new mode of industry; ice plants, packinghouses and canneries were established. Unfortunately with a great rise, comes an eventual fall. Mother Nature struck a brutal blow during the icy winters of 1894 and '95 bringing devastation to the citrus industry in Brevard County and statewide. The region was forced to explore other avenues of income to improve the downward economic trend.

G. W. Hopkins founded the Union Cypress Sawmill and Railroad in 1912. Located in South Melbourne, which was then known as Hopkins, the line ran westward eighteen miles to Deer Park. In 1919 much of Melbourne was destroyed by fire but immediately rebuilt adjacent to the Florida East Coast Railway depot.

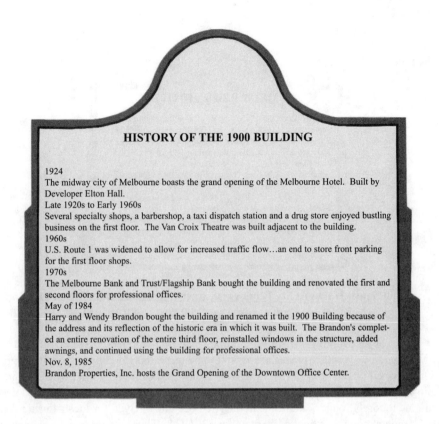

HISTORY OF THE 1900 BUILDING

1924
The midway city of Melbourne boasts the grand opening of the Melbourne Hotel. Built by Developer Elton Hall.

Late 1920s to Early 1960s
Several specialty shops, a barbershop, a taxi dispatch station and a drug store enjoyed bustling business on the first floor. The Van Croix Theatre was built adjacent to the building.

1960s
U.S. Route 1 was widened to allow for increased traffic flow...an end to store front parking for the first floor shops.

1970s
The Melbourne Bank and Trust/Flagship Bank bought the building and renovated the first and second floors for professional offices.

May of 1984
Harry and Wendy Brandon bought the building and renamed it the 1900 Building because of the address and its reflection of the historic era in which it was built. The Brandon's completed an entire renovation of the entire third floor, reinstalled windows in the structure, added awnings, and continued using the building for professional offices.

Nov. 8, 1985
Brandon Properties, Inc. hosts the Grand Opening of the Downtown Office Center.

1900 South Harbor City, Melbourne
BE58 ~ GPS Coordinates: 28.079017, -80.603683

The 1900 Building, dubbed for the address at 1900 South Harbor City, was the result of work by developer Elton Hall. Hall was the son of railroad man turned real estate mogul hailing first from Fellsmere and later moving on to Fort Pierce.

Originally built to accommodate tourists as the Melbourne Hotel during the land boom of the 1920s. The Grand Opening was the social event of 1924. The entire town turned out for the festivities as well as a great number of dignitaries from throughout the state. The hotel evolved to include specialty shops as well as a pharmacy, a barbershop and taxi stand. Today the 1900 Building still stands after eighty years at US 1 and New Haven Avenue. Owned by Harry and Wendy Brandon, the structure has been extensively renovated. The building is utilized for office space under the care of Brandon Properties, Incorporated.

The Brandon's are not only the caretakers of the 1900 Building but active in the community as well. Wendy Brandon is a former president of the Henegar Center for the Arts and the Melbourne/Palm Bay Area Chamber of Commerce. Their names are often linked with the concerns of historical preservation in the state of Florida. The 1900 Building could not be in better hands.

MELBOURNE HOTEL

The Melbourne Hotel was first opened on the evening of September 23, 1924, with several hundred guests in attendance. Elton Hall was the promoter of the hotel and celebrated his 36th birthday on the day of the opening.

That same year (1924), the Melbourne Municipal Band was organized (D. P. Barber, Director), the Melbourne State Bank opened in the "Banking Rooms of the Hotel." Prize Fighter Jack Dempsey stopped at the Maddox Café in Melbourne, and a bear was killed near the city by hunters.

Electric power (furnished by the Melbourne Utilities Co.) was unpredictable and if one of the two boilers was inoperative, the town, as well as the new hotel, could be without lights for several nights.

1900 South Harbor City Boulevard, west side of building, Melbourne
BE58 ~ GPS Coordinates: 28.079017, -80.603683

The year 1924 was an eventful one for Melbourne. The first wooden bridge to be constructed over the St. Johns River near Melbourne was violently washed away by the torrential flooding rains of a storm during the year the Melbourne Hotel opened its doors. Located at what is today the northwest corner of US 1 and New Haven Avenue, the building was constructed by developer Elton Hall. The Melbourne Hotel provided accommodations for tourists and so much more. Soundly built, the hotel often became a haven for locals during threatening storms.

The gala Grand Opening was held on September 23, 1924. There were hundreds of guests in attendance, the opening coincidentally fell on what was Elton Hall's 36th birthday. Guests wandered about the elegant gardens to strains of the orchestra playing a new George Gershwin tune called "Rhapsody in Blue." Gossip passed of Calvin Coolidge and the up coming presidential election.

Later that same year, the Melbourne State Bank opened an office on the first floor of the hotel. Small shops, a pharmacy, barbershop and taxi stand added to the amenities. Visitors were often treated to flower shows, teas and even an occasional celebrity appearance. Sidney Platt began his employment at the hotel only months after its opening and within five years ascended to the position of manager; he held the job for more than thirty years.

Boiler powered electrical lights courtesy of the Melbourne Utilities Company, were installed in the hotel. Though the electrical system was often unreliable. Many nights the town was suddenly plunged into total darkness when the boilers failed. Eventually Florida Power and Light consolidated the various small electrical companies and service became a more reliable commodity. Service during the 1920s cost an average of eight cents per hour, whereas today the premium has risen to more than three times that amount.

In May 1984, Harry and Wendy Brandon purchased the former Melbourne Hotel. Though in a sad state, the Brandon's saw great potential in the structure, renaming it the 1900 Building. After extensive renovations, the Grand Opening of the Downtown Office Center was unveiled on November 8, 1985. During a time of disposable everything, the Brandon's are to be commended for revitalizing a wonderful part of Melbourne history.

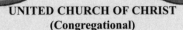

UNITED CHURCH OF CHRIST
(Congregational)

The First Congregational Church of Melbourne was organized December 6, 1889. It was the southernmost Congregational Church in the United States at that time.

For almost four years, public services of the church were held in the Methodist Episcopal Church alternating with those of the Methodist Brethren.

In 1892, a decision was made to erect a permanent church building. W. H. Powell gave the lot and the Congregational Church Building Society gave $500 for the building of the sanctuary was completed and the first service held on the first Sabbath in July 1893. Almost the entire population of Melbourne attended that service.

The building was considered the best and probably the most beautiful church building on the Florida east coast, south of Daytona Beach.

1824 South Harbor City Boulevard, Melbourne
BE59 ~ GPS Coordinates: 28.079917, -80.603900

The First Congregational Church of Melbourne celebrated its centennial year on December 6, 1989. Though for several years the Congregational parishioners had no formal sanctuary. The Methodist Church was graciously extended for services of the United Congregational Church parishioners.

The congregation donated and raised funds through bake sales for the construction of their own sanctuary, which began to take shape in 1892. William H. Powell noted community figure and United Congregational parishioner generously gave the lot at what is today South Harbor City Boulevard and additionally, five hundred dollars for building materials. The edifice took just over a year to build and services were held on the first Sunday in July 1893. Regardless of religious affiliation, all of Melbourne turned out in support of the dedication ceremony. The sanctuary was said to be the most beautiful church south of Daytona on Florida's East Coast.

John and Nannie Lee sponsored many ice cream socials and dinners in support of the Congregational Church at their home known as "The Terrace." Today the home is known as the popular Melbourne restaurant "The Strawberry Mansion".

The United Congregational Church enjoys a relatively new sanctuary erected in 1957. Still located in a beautiful edifice, the parishioners continue to have an active and growing congregation known as the United Church of Christ.

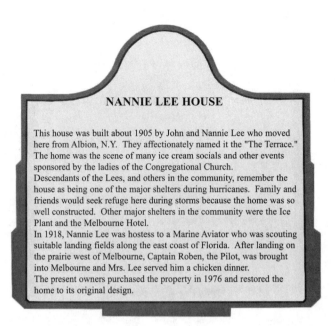

NANNIE LEE HOUSE

This house was built about 1905 by John and Nannie Lee who moved here from Albion, N.Y. They affectionately named it the "The Terrace." The home was the scene of many ice cream socials and other events sponsored by the ladies of the Congregational Church.

Descendants of the Lees, and others in the community, remember the house as being one of the major shelters during hurricanes. Family and friends would seek refuge here during storms because the home was so well constructed. Other major shelters in the community were the Ice Plant and the Melbourne Hotel.

In 1918, Nannie Lee was hostess to a Marine Aviator who was scouting suitable landing fields along the east coast of Florida. After landing on the prairie west of Melbourne, Captain Roben, the Pilot, was brought into Melbourne and Mrs. Lee served him a chicken dinner.

The present owners purchased the property in 1976 and restored the home to its original design.

1218 East New Haven Avenue, Melbourne
BE60 ~ GPS Coordinates: 28.081400, -80.602867

Clark County, Illinois was the birthplace of Nannie McBride in 1847. On July 10, 1894 she wed John B. Lee in Milwaukee, Wisconsin. The blushing bride was forty-seven years old. The couple made their home in Albion, New York traveling south each year to avoid the harsh northern snows.

So taken with the Melbourne area, the couple eventually purchased property near the elegant Carleton Hotel, where they often stayed. The Lee's made the acquaintance of Claude Beaujean, whose family had a long history in town. Beaujean was known as an exceptional carpenter, having spent many years in the boat building industry and being raised along the shore. The Beaujean family ran the Atlantic Ferry Service, which crossed the Indian River five times each day. Claude Beaujean's qualifications were well known and he was hired as lead carpenter for the Lee's mansion.

The family arrived in 1905 and the mansion was completed soon thereafter. They affectionately called it, "The Terrace." The house was a magnificent dwelling and Claude Beaujean's influence was evident throughout. His expert skills are displayed in the intricate beauty of the oak staircase, bay window and detailed gingerbread trim. The Lee family now had a home to come to each winter. However, after John B. Lee's death Nannie chose to remain in Melbourne permanently and raise their adopted daughter, Lillian (Lily) in the quaint little town.

"The Terrace" was the place to be seen in Melbourne society. The local newspaper continually reported various events including ice cream socials, Sunday School meetings as well as fabulous parties and dinners at the Lee House. Nannie Lee was known far and wide for her chicken dinners. Because of the sound construction, "The Terrace" became a haven in the eye of vicious storms. When hurricanes threatened, the house sheltered family and friends, keeping everyone within safe and warm.

Sadly Nannie Lee died in January 1929; she was eighty-two years old. She was memorialized in the Melbourne Times as follows:

"A splendid character, a loving, motherly woman, whose kindly ministrations gladdened many hearts during her life, and whose passing will be mourned by many."

Eventually Lily came to live in the mansion with her husband Frank Tidwell. The home was later used as a group home for single businesswomen, for it would be improper for them to live alone unchaperoned. The home was also utilized as a rehabilitation center for troubled youth. When the cost of upkeep became unbearable, "The Tidwell House" was abandoned. For three years the lovely mansion stood empty an easy target for abuse and vandalism.

Bob and Sue Brown along with Pete Wynkoop had a vision for the beautiful but neglected mansion. They purchased "The Tidwell House" in 1975 with the idea that it become an unpretentious thirty-seat restaurant. Renovations began throughout and the house received a shiny new coat of glowing white paint. By chance the Brown's noted a house located in Atlanta featured in the Smithsonian magazine and were drawn to it at once. With this design in mind, the couple had "The Tidwell House" repainted to resemble the Atlanta home. Colors displayed were strawberry, peanut shell, red and salmon with a copper colored roof, the restaurant could be seen from quite a distance. The newly applied paint was the talk of the town for weeks. The restaurant was dubbed "Strawberry Mansion" and opened to guests in 1981. Strawberry Mansion serves lunch and dinner six days a week, closing on Mondays. Lovely facilities are available to add elegance to any special occasion.

Due to popular demand, the Strawberry Mansion was expanded in 1986. The new restaurant includes romantic ambiance in the secluded garden. The less formal restaurant, called "Mister Beaujean's Bar & Grill" was named in tribute to the expert builder of Nannie Lee's house. "Mister Beaujean's" offer breakfast, lunch and dinner seven days a week. The setting has a beautiful garden ambiance where the lovely semi-tropical climate can be enjoyed beneath the ivy shade, for those less inclined or when weather turns somewhere less than perfect inside accommodations are also available.

The owners of Strawberry Mansion are in a bitter fight to preserve the historic beauty of downtown Melbourne threatened by a grotesquely huge Causeway Center. Developers, with little regard for the lovely historic appeal of the riverfront, want to modernize the area bringing steel and concrete in place of the warm feeling of heritage and times long past. Losing this last vestige of the "Bluff Walk" would be a detriment of the historical feel, from which Melbourne could hardly recover.

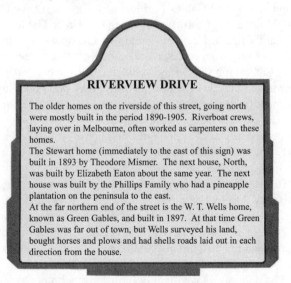

RIVERVIEW DRIVE

The older homes on the riverside of this street, going north were mostly built in the period 1890-1905. Riverboat crews, laying over in Melbourne, often worked as carpenters on these homes.

The Stewart home (immediately to the east of this sign) was built in 1893 by Theodore Mismer. The next house, North, was built by Elizabeth Eaton about the same year. The next house was built by the Phillips Family who had a pineapple plantation on the peninsula to the east.

At the far northern end of the street is the W. T. Wells home, known as Green Gables, and built in 1897. At that time Green Gables was far out of town, but Wells surveyed his land, bought horses and plows and had shells roads laid out in each direction from the house.

1811 Southview Drive, Melbourne
BE61 ~ GPS Coordinates: 28.080533, -80.602350

Throughout history, much like today, property along the Indian River was very valuable. The reasons denoting value vary greatly. When homesites were first established along today's Riverview Drive the primary concern was convenience of transportation and supply lines. The river served as the main conveyance system before the railroad came to town. Most riverside homes had docks extending out to receive guests and goods. The public dock, not too far in the distance, was used for those not owning private facilities. However the vast number of homes still standing along the scenic drive were those built during the population explosion of 1890 through 1905.

Families such as the Stewarts and Wells' built homes along the waterway. Construction workers were often hired from riverboat crews waiting in Melbourne for their next call to duty. The men hung out at local taverns or on the corner of the sandy street where builders often stopped and shouted, "who wants to work today?" Men looking for a little jingle in their pockets would follow along to the construction site. The men worked for just a few coins a day, enough for a meal or two and possibly a bed for the night. Many of the men were skilled carpenters. A great number of riverboat men often worked the shipyards building boats; therefore, they knew a thing or two about swinging a hammer.

The first Stewart family settler arrived during the Civil War from LaGrange to Eau Gallie. Jonathan Stewart set up homesteading south of Horse Creek. Brother Israel, who called his homesite "Bonaventure", closely followed Jonathan to Eau Gallie. Israel fathered six children, several established prominent names for themselves in the county. Son Quincy became the first Brevard County Sheriff and Alexander, the first Deputy Clerk of Brevard County. Alexander A. "Aleck" Stewart served as Deputy Clerk for an amazing forty-three years. The first Court sessions in Brevard County were actually held at Aleck's home, beneath the trees in his yard. The Stewart home on Riverview Drive was built in 1893, many of the distinguished families' descendants still remain in the area.

William T. Wells and wife Nora first came to Melbourne in 1894 as tourists. So enamored with the town, the Wells family returned for the next two seasons until 1897 when they decided was made to make Melbourne their permanent home. William T. Wells purchased one hundred fifty-two acres and readied the lot to build a home for his family. Wells went about clearing the land and constructing shell roads to allow easier access. These roads, though not in the city proper during those days, make up many of the existing streets of Melbourne today.

The Wells house was built between what is today Riverview Drive and Hibiscus Boulevard on the eastern side of US 1. The home was dubbed "Green Gables". Modern for its time, the construction contained the second indoor bathtub ever installed in Melbourne. Construction began on "Green Gables" in 1897.

William T. Wells was hardly finished with his home when he donated property for the construction of the Holy Trinity Episcopal Church. Turning from ecclesiastical endeavors to intellectual pursuits, he founded the first high school and invested in The Canary Inn. All of this took place during his first year in Melbourne.

The first classes of the new high school were held in R. W. Goode's building on New Haven Avenue until Wells could have a more permanent facility constructed. Unfortunately, few Melbourne children were ready for advanced education and the school closed its doors only two years later. A private school was held for a time in the Canary Inn, which also served the city as the public meeting house. Wells had an auditorium built which resembled an upturned ark and brought the Chautauqua there. William T. Wells donated another tract of land to the city in 1921. Today the property is named in his honor, Wells Park.

The Brevard County Board of Commissioners began discussions concerning the endowment of the Wells House in August of 1999. Two very different opinions were voiced. It was noted that the Wells House was an incredible property and a suggestion was made that it be purchased by the city in conjunction with the state for use as a historic site as well as offered for weddings and special events. The opposing position stated that such property requires extensive maintenance and upkeep, usually resulting in a burden to the taxpayers. The negative voice suggested that if the Historical Society wished to preserve the property that they find a way to do so. Amazingly the William T. Wells home still held the well loved family furnishings with books laying in wait of an inquisitive mind and beds ready for the night's slumber. It would be unfathomable to allow this valuable representation of a historical era with the original furnishings, books, linens and cooking vessels to fall victim to a soot billowing bulldozer.

Today Riverview Drive is crowned with a beautiful sixteen-acre park on the Indian River Lagoon. The wonderful family recreation area includes a conservation site and a very popular windsurfing spot. The shoreline at the park is an ideal location for fishing along the picturesque riverbanks, a one lane boat ramp is available for non-motorized craft. Families can enjoy hours of play on the kid's playground and volleyball court. The park pavilion may be reserved, accommodating up to one hundred people.

Riverview Drive has evolved over the years from a sandy lane to paved street. The landscape has changed though some of the homes remain as they have for more than one hundred years. As the days have progressed to years and centuries have passed one constant survives while others fade with age. The Indian River, a wondrous panorama for which Riverview Drive was named rolls on.

CARLETON HOTEL
IDLEWYLDE HOTEL

The first Carleton Hotel was built on this site about 1887, under the ownership of Jennie and Emma Strawbridge, sisters, who were natives of Sharon, PA.
That hotel burned in 1904. At the same time, the Idlewylde Hotel, to the north, also burned.
The Carleton was rebuilt almost immediately by John Ferguson and was managed by his wife, Lillie Robinson Ferguson, until 1915. It was then sold to L. G. MacDowell.
On a March night in 1925, the night policeman saw a blaze in the Carleton's kitchen and ran to rouse the hotel guests. He fired his revolver several times as an alarm. Chief of Police Joe Brannen rounded up the firemen, but the blaze was already out of control. There was one loss of life: a laundress died in the flames.

1825 South Riverview Drive at the corner of Strawbridge Avenue, Melbourne
BE62 ~ GPS Coordinates: 28.079578, -80.601479

Three free men of color arrived at Crane Creek shortly after the Civil War. They were Peter Wright, William Allen and Wright Brothers. All of the men managed to purchase land in the area and earn a profitable living growing citrus. Peter Wright bought land on both sides of the creek but it was on a high bluff beside the Indian River where he chose to make his home. The lot would later become the site of the Carleton Hotel, today known as the corner of Strawbridge Avenue and Riverview Drive.

In addition to his agricultural endeavors, Peter Wright became the legendary Sailing Mailman. Wright delivered mail to coastal towns in a small sail boat traveling from Titusville to St. Lucie. The mail was delivered as they say, in rain, sleet, snow or hail and even in the dark of night; well, snow was never an issue but large swells and storm tossed seas could delay the post a bit.

Sharon, Pennsylvania native, Emma Strawbridge found her way south in 1887. She purchased land high on the bluff, which had belonged to Peter Wright. Emma convinced fine northern carpenters to travel south to build her dream. Her dream was an elegant three-story hotel called "The Carleton".

Emma's hotel was the stylish place to stay for well-heeled clientele. News of the Carleton's popularity quickly spread among the wealthy. The hotel hosted everyone from sport hunters to society ladies especially those escaping the cruel winter months of the northern states. Patrons often gazed at the river with excitement as Indians paddled their dugouts from the headwaters of the St. Johns River with venison, plume birds and panther hides to sell to the white mercantiles. White hunters flocked to the Florida wilderness to hunt wild turkey, bear and fowl.

Emma with her sister Jennie, who helped operate the hotel, was elated with the success. Soon a smaller, less formal hotel was built just next door. "The Idlewylde" catered to what we would call the middle income crowd but it was a handsome retreat all the same. For many years the sister hotels enjoyed prosperity.

Suddenly their hopes went down in flames on a fateful night in 1904, when both hotels burned to the ground. The Carleton refused to die an easy death and like the phoenix rose from her ashes; the hotel was quickly rebuilt. Unfortunately the Idlewylde was never reconstructed. By this time another captain manned The Carlton's helm, John Ferguson and his wife, Lillie Robinson, managed the hotel. The Ferguson's were Carleton innkeepers for eleven years, but sold the illustrious Melbourne locale in 1917 to L. G. MacDowell.

One scenic site just beyond the Carlton drew visitors and locals alike, the Trysting Steps and Bluff Walk. The wooden steps and walk were built around 1886 over an Indian midden. The thoroughfare gave means for foot traffic to travel from Front Street to the Carleton and residences beyond. The famous moniker came when young lovers discovered that this was a most romantic spot to while away a glorious evening, strolling arm in arm. Of course, sand gnats and mosquitoes along the wooden boardwalk sometimes looked upon this as a fabulous afternoon buffet. The wooden walkway and steps eventually fell victim to Mother Nature and Father Time. In 1938, the Trysting Steps were replaced with a concrete recreation.

Late in the evening of a cool March night in 1925, an observant policeman was making his rounds. As he checked doors along his route, often stopping for a moment to test the locks, he noticed an unusual disturbance near the river. The policeman quickened his pace heading toward what appeared to be an orange horizon. As he approached the realization struck, the Carleton was engulfed in flames.

Astutely he sounded the alarm, three shots in the air from his revolver. Chief of Police Joe Brannen rounded up the Melbourne firemen and headed toward the blaze. Meanwhile, the hotel guests were quickly ushered to safety. Everyone was out, but were they? By the time the Melbourne firemen and bucket brigade volunteers arrived nothing could be done but watch the as inferno reduce the once beautiful hotel to a molten mass and charred skeleton. Sadly everyone did not make it out of flames, a Carleton employee ~ the laundress died on that March night in 1925. The Carleton did not rise from the ashes this time. The site was later occupied by a car wash then a Melbourne attorney located his office there, but wistful days of wealthy patrons at Carleton Hotel were done. A Melbourne era came to an end.

For the past several years developers have looked upon the site where the regal Carleton once stood with dollars signs in their eyes. A proposal was put before the city for the construction of three multi-storied buildings to be located at Riverview Drive and Strawbridge Avenue. Plans are to dispose of the last presence of the Trysting Steps, bulldoze flat the Indian Midden and demolish two older homes that impede their modernization progress. A Historic Preservation Committee was selected to advise the city concerning these issues. However, thus far concerned citizens have stood their ground and protected the former home of Melbourne's original settler, Peter Wright. Court actions have been filed and the valiant fight goes on, with any luck historic preservation will win this battle.

EARLY POST OFFICE SITE

The first 14 years of postal service in Melbourne saw the mail arriving twice weekly by sailboat from Titusville. A black man by the name of Peter Wright brought the mail in a boat named the "Nellie".

The first post office was in John Cornthwaite Hector's store at Hatterman's Point (the end of Front Street). Hector was appointed postmaster on June 17, 1880.

About 1897, when Richard W. Goode became postmaster the post office was relocated to this building. Goode was Melbourne's seventh postmaster. He also operated a real estate office in this building.

On a visit to his native Chicago in 1912, Goode was killed by an elevated railroad train. Edward P. Branch succeeded him as postmaster.

Eastern end of New Haven Avenue, Melbourne
BE63 ~ GPS Coordinates: 28.079700, -80.601083

There was little in the way of settlements in what was then known as Mosquito County before the Civil War. Postal service was all but non-existent, mail only arrived by passing ships. Douglas Dummett was the largest landowner, the rest of the population was sparse and well dispersed. The area was untamed wilderness as well as the ongoing threat of the warring Seminole. Life was harsh, transportation was not easy; overland travel was virtually impossible with thick maritime forests just inland, swampland throughout with only animal and Indian trails making the way somewhat passable at all. The majority of travel was by way of the river or ocean going vessels, though even this had its own perils.

Possibly the most important transport system in the area is the Indian River. At the northern end just south of what was Fort Ann was a man made canal completed in 1854. The canal linking the Mosquito Lagoon and Indian River was dug about one third of a mile in length, ten to twelve feet wide and only three feet in depth. The haulover canal as the name implies was meant for shallow draft boats and could be forded by foot if necessary.

With the development of Fort Ann, a small community was formed called Sand Point. It was a meager settlement but in 1859 the government established the first post office there. Settler Shubel G. Luffman was appointed as postmaster but due to the remoteness and primitive living conditions the post office lasted less than six months. By 1860 the population soared to an all time high of two hundred forty-six. Most settlers lived in simple hand cut log cabins with wood shuttered window cut outs, others lived much like the native Americans in chickees having log frames covered by woven palmetto fronds. During the Civil War Sand Point became a convenient hide out for blockade-runners carrying black-market supplies to the Confederacy.

Three black men, Peter Wright, William (Balaam) Allen and Wright Brothers first established the settlement at Melbourne, then called Crane Creek. They homesteaded on land adjoining the creek and made their way by growing citrus fruit. Peter Wright assumed the position as mail carrier though he was never appointed postmaster. He sailed his small skiff called Nellie to coastal settlements from Titusville extending south to St. Lucie twice weekly delivering the mail. He maintained this route for fourteen years.

Although most texts list the post office located at John Cornthwaite Hector's store at Hatterman's Point the first post office, that is not entirely true. It was the first post office to endure. Hatterman's Point is located, as we know it today, at the end of Front Street on the shores of the Indian River. On June 17, 1880, Hector was appointed postmaster. He was also responsible, by means of the longest drawn straw, for naming the settlement

Melbourne after his Australian home.

Richard W. Goode became postmaster around 1897 and at his convenience the office was moved to his place of business at the eastern end of New Haven Avenue. Goode managed and owned a successful real estate office from this site. While visiting family at Chicago in 1912, Richard Goode was struck and killed by an elevated railroad train.

Edward P. Branch was appointed the next Melbourne postmaster. Mail service at this time still involved patrons traveling into town to receive their posts. Usually the settlers made this trip on a monthly basis. Melbourne's postal service was slow to modernize, it was not until June of 1949 before rural postal routes were established. The first routes covered a distance of fifty-seven miles, two days per week. The typical letter mailed from Melbourne to New York would generally take six to eight weeks to arrive. Today we can pay for next day delivery or fax the post for arrival in a matter of minutes from our home. Time and technology do have a tendency to change things.

FRONT STREET

Front Street was the original business section of Melbourne. It came into existence in the 1880's as Dry Goods Stores, Grocery Stores, a Fish House Boat building and the Post Office were located along the waterfront.

In 1894, Melbourne's second newspaper, the Melbourne Times, was founded in a building on Front Street. The population of the town at the time was 157.

The Riverside Hotel was on the East Side of Front Street. A City Dock extended 1,400 feet into the river and steamboats stopped here. The southern end of Front Street was originally called Hatterman's Point, then Stewart's Point, and later Vorkeller's Point.

Fire destroyed all of the commercial buildings along Front Street in 1919 because the fire engine became bogged down in sand and never made it to the fire. A citizen's bucket brigade was unable to cope with the blaze.

Northern end of Front Street near Indian River, Melbourne
BE64 ~ GPS Coordinates: 28.078450, -80.600150

By the late 1800s, before the railroad, most of Melbourne centered around the Indian River shores. Wooden shops, fish houses and even the Post Office occupied places along what was then and is today Front Street. Today Melbourne extends from the mainland across the lagoon to the barrier island, but in the early days little besides cattle occupied that outlying property. Transportation across the waterway was difficult at best. During prehistoric days the lagoon connected to the Atlantic Ocean. Over time those connections have virtually all filled with sand on the incoming tide. Currently a few inlets and the manmade Sebastian Inlet at the south end of Brevard County are the only connections to the sea.

On July 15, 1969 an election resulted in the consolidation of Melbourne and Eau Gallie. Though the merger passed, it seems the public is not always too fond of the idea. The two sections of the city are currently the same yet divided. Sharing services, utilities and the like does not a merger make. Eau Gallie will always have her unique history and civic pride; Melbourne embraces a more modern appearance. Each has something to offer and are glorious in their diversity.

Combined, Melbourne encompasses over thirty-five square miles of central eastern Florida landscape. The population exceeds seventy-three thousand people and growing by leaps and bounds as visitors discover the wonderful area, often refusing to leave. The Melbourne area ranked very high as one of the most affordable places to live by the National Association of Home Builders. Money Magazine listed Brevard County as seventh across the nation in 1998 as of the "Best Places" among medium sized Southern cities.

Front Street, at the heart of downtown Melbourne, suffered a devastating blow in 1919, which changed the face of the city forever. A guest in one of the downtown boarding houses in a drunken stupor casually tossed a lit kerosene heater out of his second-floor bedroom window. The tin heater crashed to the wooden sidewalk below and the flowing kerosene spread the flame. As the pine sidewalk quickly caught fire a strong gust of wind carried the destructive orange blaze to the buildings beyond. Black acrid smoke rising in the air and the alarm was sounded throughout town.

Shop patrons, owners and local citizens quickly ran to safety toward the river. The Melbourne firemen were on their way. A bucket brigade was formed but the meager pails were like fighting a forest fire with an eyedropper. The fire engine chugged down the street but became bogged down in the sand. Firemen pushed until their arms cramped and hung low with exhaustion. Every commercial building along Front Street was consumed by the unrelenting blaze. Businesses were eventually rebuilt and though scarred by the fire, Front Street came alive once again. Like Melbourne and Eau Gallie, Front Street was forever changed but in many ways much the same.

FIRST POST OFFICE SITE

Here at what was once known as Hatterman's Point, in the early years, John Cornthwaite Hector settled and had a store built. Completed in 1880 by carpenter U. D. Henderson of Eau Gallie.

Hector was described as "tall, heavy set, with white hair and a great square beard, he was strong as a bull." Most of the time he wore a ridiculous bowler on his head. This was influenced, undoubtedly, by his British origin.

In 1878, when Hector first appeared in the area, he was about 43 years old. He migrated here from Melbourne Australia, where it was reported he had deserted a common-law wife and five children.

Hector is credited with organizing the first community band in Melbourne, and became Melbourne first Postmaster.

2207 Front Street, Melbourne
BE65 ~ GPS Coordinates: 28.075833, -80.601383

America had a postal system well before we had an independent government. The British Parliament created an organized system of delivering post in 1711. By the time colonists arrived in America, a system of posts was in place. However, it was a privatized system, which operated only occasionally and the only concern were reports to the English crown of the progress or lack thereof in the Americas.

As colonists spread throughout the eastern seaboard post roads were established along Indian trails, so that news could be delivered from one settlement to another. Often the letters would be collected from English ships in port cities and delivered on horseback. Letters often took up to a year to arrive. Carrier service did eventually improve somewhat.

Penny postage stamps came available in the United States in 1847, followed by registered mail and in 1862, mail began being delivered by railroad. Of course, there were a few problems here. First of all the railroad did not extend to all cities, in fact at this time rail travel was still very limited, riders still had to be dispatched to collect the mail; secondly, the Civil War resulted in an almost complete halt to all postal traffic.

During the days following the Civil War, Brevard to St. Lucie Counties had mail service. Peter Wright, a free man of color, founder of Crane Creek as well as being the famous sailing mailman, sailed his small boat Nellie twice a week along his route. For fourteen years Wright delivered the mail to intracoastal communities.

Around 1870 an Australian immigrant named John Cornthwaite Hector arrived at Hatterman's Point. Of British ancestry, it was reported that he wound up in Australia due to bad debts like so many others during that time and when he left Australia, he deserted a common-law wife and five children. What we do know for sure is that Hector was about forty-three when he arrived on the scene. A bull of man, strong as an ox with stark white hair and a long squared off beard. He was often seen in a silly bowler hat, much to small for his ample head.

After Hector settled in, he employed U. D. Henderson of Eau Gallie to build a trading post. The store was completed in 1880 and was to house the first post office. But to qualify the city had to have a formal name. The towns' men drew straws, it is said, and Hector won the privilege to name the town. Melbourne was chosen in reference to his Australian home. John Cornthwaite Hector was appointed first postmaster and the post office opened for business on June 17, 1880.

Rural postal delivery began in various states in 1896 but most Floridians still had to travel to the local post office to receive their mail. Most rural post customers picked up their mail once a month when they traveled to town for supplies; city dwellers of course had easier access and received their mail more frequently.

Richard W. Goode became the seventh Melbourne postmaster in 1897. He served the post for fifteen years until, on a visit to Chicago, an elevated railroad train killed Goode. Edward P. Branch took over the postmaster duties. Limited airmail was instituted in the United States in 1918 but Melbourne remained behind the times. The first rural postal route originated in Brevard County on June 16, 1949. The route began at the Melbourne Post Office and covered fifty-seven miles.

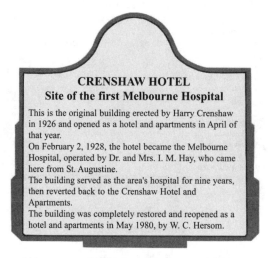

CRENSHAW HOTEL
Site of the first Melbourne Hospital

This is the original building erected by Harry Crenshaw in 1926 and opened as a hotel and apartments in April of that year.
On February 2, 1928, the hotel became the Melbourne Hospital, operated by Dr. and Mrs. I. M. Hay, who came here from St. Augustine.
The building served as the area's hospital for nine years, then reverted back to the Crenshaw Hotel and Apartments.
The building was completely restored and reopened as a hotel and apartments in May 1980, by W. C. Hersom.

Off U.S. 1, River Drive, Melbourne
BE66 ~ GPS Coordinates: 28.068250, -80.601233

The Crenshaw Hotel was constructed by and named for Harry Crenshaw in April of 1926. The hotel served both visitors and permanent residents. However, the hotel only remained open in this capacity for less than two years. Dr. Isaac Morris Hay came along with an offer to purchase the Crenshaw, which was readily accepted. Dr. Hay had much different plans for the hotel.

Located at what is today the south side of River Drive between Irwin Street and US 1, the Crenshaw Hotel morphed into the Melbourne Hospital. Dr. Hay and his wife, Lucille Elizabeth Hay, hailed from St. Augustine. He was a general practitioner and she the mother of three small children. The hospital opened its doors on February 2, 1928, Dr. Hay provided the medical services at the private institution. Meanwhile Mrs. Hay attended to the administrative and care taking duties as well as raising the children (her twins were only two years old at the time) and caring for their home. It seems perhaps, Dr. Hay had the easier tasks.

The hospital managed as the Great Depression gripped the United States in financial straits so dire most people had no means to pay for medical care. After nine years of service, the Melbourne Hospital merged with the Brevard County Hospital. An infusion of money cured their financial woes. The merger resulted in the hospital moving to nicer facilities and the Crenshaw became a hotel once again.

The Crenshaw Apartments still exist today. W. C. Hersom restored the complex in May of 1980. Dr. and Mrs. Isaac Morris Hay were honored by their daughter, Dr. Elizabeth Hay with the creation of a professorship at her alma mater. Dr. Elizabeth D. Hay is the Louise Foote Pfeiffer Professor of Embryology at Harvard Medical School. Certainly their children are a living tribute to the parents who helped so many.

OLDEN HOUSE

Constructed in 1912, the Olden House was first known as the Hopkins Hotel. A boarding house for white workers of the Union Cypress Sawmill, Mr. and Mrs. Olden operated the hotel. This building is one of the few building's remaining from the period of 1912-1924 when the Union Cypress Mill was one of the largest lumber concerns in Florida. In 1937, Martha Ann Hawkins purchased the hotel. She, and her daughters Laura and Phyllis Hawkins, picked beans in Pahokee, Fl., to earn enough money to purchase the 14-room house. Laura Hawkins married John Williams. They raised their nine children and one grandchild in the house. Hawkins and Williams descendants have lived in what became known as "The Big House" for several decades. Mrs. Hawkins converted the home to a rooming house for single men, and when she was sent to Africa as a missionary for her church, her family continued to operate it as a rooming house. Today it is owned by five of Hawkins' grandchildren and is still a rooming house.

Main and Mill Streets, Melbourne
BE67 ~ GPS Coordinates: 28.066750, -80.604633

In the early 1900s Melbourne may well have been an island for all the available access to the inner reaches of the peninsular state. Transportation was dependent on the coastal waters, though automobiles were increasingly more common; roads in Florida were not. The Union Cypress Company came to Melbourne in 1912 and with it brought many extra assets to the region.

The attraction for Union Cypress was a great stand of virgin timber known as the Jane Green Swamp providing vast amounts of hardwood. The company built a massive three storied facility housing a double band saw mill in Melbourne, George Hopkins owned the company. The mill hired more than five hundred employees and brought electric power to the city through the mill's power plant. Amazingly the tab for electrical power for the entire city was approximately what it would be for one household today.

Like so many other places a mill village was established and named after the founder of the feast so to speak, Hopkins. Mill villages were full service facilities with a post office, boarding house, infirmary, a church, theater, a ball field and swimming pool. Employees were paid with vouchers they could spend in the company store for groceries and clothing. The company store eventually became Kempfer's, the church was Macedonia Baptist and the boarding house was the Olden House.

In order to transport the timber to the mill, eighteen and a half miles of rails were laid crossing the St. Johns to Deer Park, which was the major logging town where the tracks spurred into the wooden vast lands. The

Union Cypress Mill Railway was in operation six years before the highway to interior Florida was created. The railway was responsible for various settlements to develop along the route. When the Kissimmee Highway, known today as US 192, was impassable for more than a year due to construction the Union Cypress Railway stepped in to fill the need. For a toll of one dollar per vehicle the train ferried automobiles serving as a detour.

Disaster struck in 1918, when a train engine wrecked near Deer Park and from there it seems a downward spiral began. Eau Gallie and Melbourne merged to become one but in February of 1919 the downtown district succumbed to a raging fire destroying everything in its path. The mill burned to the ground six months later. The fire had a devastating effect on everyone in the area because the town was without electricity for four very long months and more than five hundred workers were out of a job. Finally power was obtained from old Eau Gallie. George Hopkins managed to reorganize and begin construction on a new fire resistant sawmill. Unfortunately the seasons of unfortunate incidence were not completed, George Hopkins passed away in 1925 and the new Union Cypress Mill construction was never finished.

Three years later the Foshee Manufacturing Company assumed the operation of the mill, repaired the railway and the St. Johns trestle. Unfortunately the great depression gripped the entire United States and the mill was closed. All of the Union Cypress Company turned Foshee Manufacturing buildings and railway were demolished. The property was sold.

Today a few remnants of the old mill still remain. The Macedonia Baptist Church stands on what were the mill grounds. The Olden House remains a rooming house owned by descendants of Martha Ann Hawkins who purchased the hotel in 1937 with proceeds from picking green beans for truck farms in central Florida. Many of the old mill houses still stand, little more than tenement shacks. In places evidence of the railway can be found but modern day streets have replaced much of it. The Florida Institute of Technology boathouse is thought to be one of the old mill buildings and if not was likely created from materials salvaged from the demolition.

The Union Cypress Sawmill trestle at Mosquito Island's Little Sawgrass Lake was utilized by the St. Johns River Water Management Department built a weather station upon the old pilings. The cabin serves as a safe haven for boaters caught on the lake when the common sudden summer afternoon thunder and lightning storms arise with little warning. The simple construction is very well built, complete with lightning rods protruding from the roof. In the true spirit of recycling, the Union Cypress Railway has been made use of until the timbers are once again reclaimed by nature.

MACEDONIA BAPTIST CHURCH

The Florida East Coast Railroad had not reached Melbourne in 1891 when the first sanctuary of the Macedonia Baptist Church was built, at a site on East Brothers Avenue.
The first pastor, the Rev. Parson Miller, and a parishioner, J. E. Austell, transported the lumber to build the church from Titusville, bringing it to Melbourne by boat. About a dozen church members assisted the pastor in erecting the small, 20-foot square church building.
Groundbreaking ceremonies for this sanctuary were held in 1970, when church members marched from the old sanctuary on Brothers Avenue to this site, singing, "We've Come This Far By Faith." This church was completed in 1975 and dedicated August 17 of that year.

2729 Lipscomb Street, Melbourne
BE68 ~ GPS Coordinates: 28.032050, -80.603450

Sunday services for the Baptist congregation began under the protective boughs of a huge oak tree between the homes of William R. Brothers and Bettye Murray in 1889. This remained the location for more than two years. The church was officially organized as Macedonia Baptist in 1891 and a sanctuary was built.

Originally located on East Brothers Avenue, the first church pastor was active in its construction. Reverend Parson Miller and a member of the congregation, J. E. Austell, transported the lumber for the edifice on a flat boat from Titusville for building the church. The site was purchased from Melbourne's first black doctor, Dr. James Norris. The first sanctuary measured a meager twenty feet square. The pastor and twelve men from the congregation built the church with the labor of their own hands, sweat from their brow and all the love in their heart. Electricity brought artificial light to the edifice already filled with the golden glow of spirituality in 1918.

By the late 1960s the parishioners had outgrown the original little church and the need for a larger sanctuary became apparent. Groundbreaking ceremonies were held in 1970. The congregation marched from the sanctuary at East Brothers Avenue to the site of the new edifice to be located at 2729 Lipscomb Street. The new sanctuary was to be built upon the pillars of the old Union Cypress sawmill, which once occupied the site and employed a great number of the parishioners. Construction was completed in 1975 and the first services were held on August 17th. The Macedonia Baptist Church still has an active congregation today. From meager origins beneath the oaks, parishioners remain as faithful today as their predecessors more than one hundred years ago. Loyalty and devotion remain the watchwords for Macedonia Baptist Church.

End Notes

[1] National Association for the Advancement of Colored People

[2] National Aeronautics and Space Administration

[3] A taxi

[4] Gorham was best known for works chiefly in silver

[5] Tiffany's glass work was known worldwide

[6] Worked extensively with Tiffany

[7] Titusville Garden Club

[8] Private First Class

[9] East Florida Seminary

[10] Re-elected for numerous terms

[11] Later known as Eau Gallie

[12] The spelling of his name is often noted as Breckenridge, however the Congressional Record notes the spelling as Breckinridge

[13] Today known as Princeton University, School of Law.

[14] Naval Air Station

[15] Naval Air Station

[16] Submarines

[17] A native Seminole hut

[18] The Spaniard's first named the beautiful tropical peninsula "La Florida" translated as "The Flower".

[19] A chance for the community to gather for three to seven days to enjoy a course of lectures on a variety of subjects. Audiences saw classic plays, Broadway hits and heard a variety of music from Metropolitan Opera stars to glee clubs and bell ringers. Many saw their first moving pictures in the Circuit tents. Most important, the Circuit Chautauqua experience was critical in stimulating thought and discussion on important political, social and cultural issues of the day.

[20] huts

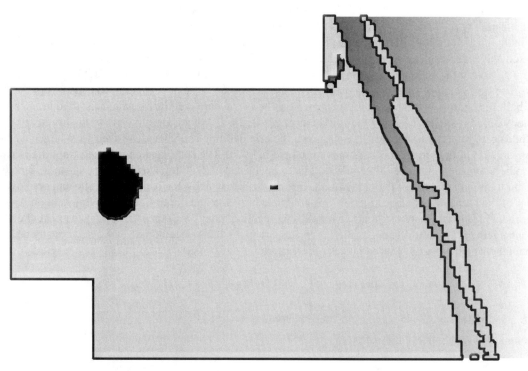

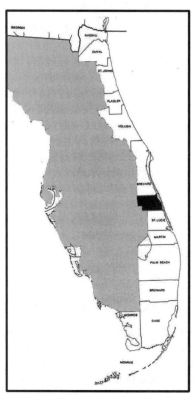

Indian River County

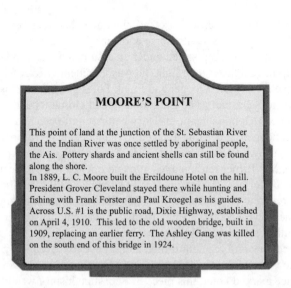

MOORE'S POINT

This point of land at the junction of the St. Sebastian River and the Indian River was once settled by aboriginal people, the Ais. Pottery shards and ancient shells can still be found along the shore.

In 1889, L. C. Moore built the Ercildoune Hotel on the hill. President Grover Cleveland stayed there while hunting and fishing with Frank Forster and Paul Kroegel as his guides.

Across U.S. #1 is the public road, Dixie Highway, established on April 4, 1910. This led to the old wooden bridge, built in 1909, replacing an earlier ferry. The Ashley Gang was killed on the south end of this bridge in 1924.

US 1, Park at northern Indian River County Line, Sebastian
IR1 ~ GPS Coordinates: 27.850367, -80.489633

The first inhabitants of what we know today as the Treasure Coast were the Ais Indians. The natives are noted as the most important Indian tribe in southeastern Florida as well as the most populous. The closest derivation of the Ais name is the Choctaw word "isi" meaning deer. The tribe lived from the bounty of the land and sea as hunter/gathers, they did not farm. It is said that the Indian River was named for the Ais people.

The Ais were exposed to Europeans for the first time with the arrival of Spaniards in the sixteenth century. It was not complete harmony at first. In fact the two groups suffered many altercations. The Spaniards' attempts to bring the Ais into their religious fold failed miserably. Unfortunately the Europeans did eventually conquer these proud people, not with might but by the diseases that the Native Americans had no immunities against. The Ais virtually were driven to extinction by the early 1700s.

Almost two hundred years later on land which still bore the artifacts of the vanquished people; Larry C. Moore arrived determined to build a future for himself. Known as a hard drinking man, Moore was never the less quite ambitious. He left Chicago for Sebastian to build his Ercildoune Hotel in 1889. Located on a picturesque bluff facing the convergence of the Sebastian and Indian Rivers, the elegant hotel was surrounded by sixty acres of fragrant citrus and beautiful landscaping. A royal poincinana planted by Larry Moore on the grounds of the Ercildoune grew to become the largest specimen of its kind in the country.

It is not known exactly how Moore came up with the hotel name, but was speculated that the origin may have been from "Ercil on the Doune," a European river. No matter where the moniker came from, the hotel was lovely and very well built. The building was constructed of weather resistant Florida cypress and pitch pine known to deter ruinous termites. The Ercildoune was painted a sunny lemon yellow along the flowing wings extending from each side. An elaborate lobby was at the heart of the structure highlighted with a magnificent coquina fireplace. The dining room and kitchen were hidden away on a lower floor on one end of the building.

A massive porch embraced the entire hotel ensuring that each room featured both a front and back porch with entrances from each direction. Should guests wish to take meals in the privacy of their rooms, they were discretely served from the back door. Though very luxurious for a frontier hotel, the Ercildoune had neither indoor plumbing nor heat. Hotel furnishings were delivered by ship from Chicago to the Florida location. Moore's furniture selections were odd in that they were elaborate hand carved pieces, not only ornate but so cumbersome that much of it had to be assembled in place. Each room had ten-foot ceilings and some of the furniture extended to the crown molding. Rooms rented for an exorbitant one-dollar per night.

After the railroad was extended as far as Roseland, the hotel chauffeur/bell hop/maintenance man/maid (well, you get the idea he did it all) met guests with horse and surrey to transport them to the Ercildoune. One guest, who wished to keep his visit private, registered under an assumed name. Town folk knew right away who the famous guest was for gossip travels faster than light, he was President Grover Cleveland. The president enjoyed the sportsmanship in the area. Paul Kroegel and Frank Forester served as fishing and hunting guides during the President's several visits to Sebastian. The Ercildoune Hotel closed its doors in conjunction with World War I. Though it never functioned as a hotel again, its story had not quite reached the end.

Once the hotel was abandoned, it became a haven for squatters and reprobates. A couple by the name of Turner was living at the Ercildoune when one fateful day Mr. Turner arrived home to find his wife in the arms of another man. In a jealous rage, Mr. Turner retrieved his gun and opened fire on the adulterous pair. It is not known if Mr. Turner was an accurate shot. A Georgia family known as Dill lived for a time in the caretaker's cottage and rented rooms in the Ercildoune to transients. By this time the rooms no longer contained furnishings so guests were obliged to bring their own bedding. Some food was available for sale including fruits, vegetables, live chickens and sometimes the Dills' barbecued wild razorback hogs. In addition, the Dills' dealt in a little illegal hooch or moonshine, which local law enforcement turned a blind eye to. Eventually, bit by bit the Ercildoune began to disappear. During the years of the Great Depression across the United States, locals pulled lumber from the hotel to build housing. Once a grand hotel, this piece of Sebastian history was literally spread far and wide.

Around 1911, a dredger working the canal from Lake Okeechobee to the Atlantic made a grisly discovery. DeSoto Tiger, son of a former Seminole chief, was identified as the victim of a brutal murder. A local thug known as John Ashley, the Swamp Bandit was accused of the crime. Before he could be brought to trial, Ashley escaped while being transferred from jail to the courthouse. Eventually he returned for trial and strangely enough the jury was deadlocked, it is believed that some of the panel members may have been bribed.

Ashley and his hoodlum gang began a robbery spree including a botched attempt to hold up the Florida East Coast railroad and eventually succeeding at the Stuart bank. Of course the gang did have certain standards, ever the gentlemen, they refused to rob women. During the bank robbery, cohort Kid Lowe accidentally fired a shot, which shattered Ashley's jaw and lodged in his right eye leaving him blind on that side. John Ashley was captured twelve miles southwest of Stuart; he pled guilty and was sentenced to seventeen and a half years at Raiford State Prison. In June of 1918, Ashley escaped once again but this time the cost was high. His brother Bob, who was also incarcerated for the bank robbery, was killed during the jailbreak.

Ashley hid out in the Everglades with girlfriend, Laura Upthegrove. She was a pistol-packing mamma, known as "Queen of the Everglades." They robbed numerous banks, businesses, trains, post offices as well as stealing dozens of cars to support their bootlegging enterprise. The gang commandeered a taxi in West Palm Beach for what was to be their last heist. Once they arrived in Deerfield, the Ashley Gang tied Wesley Powell, the cab driver, to a tree and left him with a warning to pass along to Palm Beach County Sheriff Bob Baker daring him to come after them.

The gang took the Pampano Bank for twenty-three thousand dollars. As the gang sped out of town, Ashley hung out the taxi window and shouted at Eugene E. "Gene" Hardy telling him, "We got it all, Gene!" A group of Pampano citizens gave chase but fortunate for them, they failed to catch the gang. Again the Ashley Gang escaped into the swamps, this time near Clewiston. In February of 1924 the gang was surrounded when an over aggressive deputy fired into a tent killing Ashley's father. Return fire killed Deputy Frank Baker, who happened to be the brother of Sheriff Bob Baker. Ashley hid out in Jacksonville at his sister Daisy's home.

Laura Upthegrove, in a snit because John Ashley left her behind, turned stool pigeon. She informed Sheriff Baker that the Ashley Gang planned to make a run for the Florida state line taking the Dixie Highway under a cover of darkness on November 1, 1924. Baker and St. Lucie County Sheriff J. R. Merritt planned an ambush at the Sebastian Inlet Bridge, which the gang would have to cross. A chain was strung across the road and a red lantern stopped all traffic at the roadblock. The deputies lay in wait along the roadside hidden by the undergrowth fighting off relentless mosquitoes buzzing in their ears and attacking all exposed skin, waiting for the notorious Ashley gang to make a break for it. At approximately 11:00 p.m. a long black touring car cautiously approached the bridge, the car came to halt but no activity came from inside the car. Alerted Sheriff Merritt shouted:

"Alright, Ashley, don't move, don't reach for your gun and don't say a word. Get out with your hands up!"

John Ashley along with Handford Mobley, Shorty Ray Lynn and Clarence Middleton emerged from the car as ordered. The events that followed have been hotly debated for years. Sheriff Merritt stated that while he returned to his vehicle for additional handcuffs, St. Lucie deputies kept watch over the prisoners at gunpoint. The deputies swore in a deposition that John Ashley produced a sleeve gun and attempted to escape. When the smoke cleared, the Ashley Gang's bullet riddled bodies lay dead on the bridge. Passersby claimed that the gang was safely in handcuffs when the deputies opened fire. No one except those involved will ever know the whole story of that dark evening on the Sebastian Inlet Bridge. The Ashley Gang died in much the same way they lived, violently and dead men tell no tales.

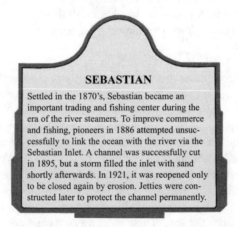

SEBASTIAN

Settled in the 1870's, Sebastian became an important trading and fishing center during the era of the river steamers. To improve commerce and fishing, pioneers in 1886 attempted unsuccessfully to link the ocean with the river via the Sebastian Inlet. A channel was successfully cut in 1895, but a storm filled the inlet with sand shortly afterwards. In 1921, it was reopened only to be closed again by erosion. Jetties were constructed later to protect the channel permanently.

U.S. 1 at Sebastian Inlet Chamber of Commerce, Sebastian
IR2 ~ GPS Coordinates: 27.817283, -80.468967

The early Sebastian settlement was cradled between the river and freshwater lagoon. The first European explorers dubbed the river the St. Sebastian. The reasoning is unknown. Perhaps the Spanish related attacks of the Native American Ais with the Saint who was pierced with arrows and eventually killed with a club or possibly the previous Spanish explorers who landed there on the feast day of St. Sebastian, January 20th. Regardless of how the river received its name, it was these bodies of water that attracted both Native Americans and later European settlers to the area.

The Ais had always taken their sustenance and trappings from the favor of the ocean. As the Spanish began sailing along the Florida shores the inevitable shipwrecks occurred. The Native Americans looked upon this treasure as any other bounty. Of course they knew nothing of the value of gold, silver and jewels beyond pretty colors and attractive ornaments. It was the 1715 sinking of the Spanish Treasure Fleet, for which the coastline obtained the nickname "Treasure Coast". The descriptive moniker has endured for nearly three hundred years.

Shipwreck victims and missionaries were another story completely. The pale skinned people were regarded with suspicion and concern. As the Spanish began to interfere with the Ais' way of life, bringing disease forced religion and enslavement that the Native Americans began to fight back. Unfortunately in the end the Ais were driven to virtual extinction. Some may have escaped to Cuba or were absorbed into other tribes but most were annihilated.

Settlers obviously had very differing view of the Sebastian area. Once beautifully described as:

"The thickly wooded shores, wrapt in silence and solitude, displayed to the view all the various shades of coloring which the imagination could fancy; and many green and sunny islands, clothed in gay verdure, and diversified by the richest and most luxuriant foliage in this southern clime, exhibited much of the picturesque, as we floated past with noiseless progress before the gentle and favoring breeze."

This view was possibly seen through the eyes of a dreamer, other settlers saw the area much differently based on their experiences. When trader John Barker was violently killed around 1848, his family abandoned the area in fear. The Indian River area received the following critique:

"There were few or no roads and no mail facilities or other medium of communication. Much of the country was an impassable swamp, and, during the last few years, the heavy and continued rains have almost broken up all travel in the southern part of Florida, and materially retarded the progress of the public (and private) surveys. In addition to those difficulties, which are formida ble enough, many of them (settlers) were in the neighborhood of a bloodthirsty and treacherous foe."

Indian uprisings and harsh conditions left the area virtually abandoned by the mid 1800s. Andrew P. Canova and Ed Marr arrived in the area around 1858 and though Canova left within a few years to join the army during the early days of the Civil War, Marr remained. The question remains, why did settlers keep returning to the Indian River area? The most apparent reason lay within the banks of the river itself. Opportunities derived from the proximity of the sea and the access to transportation as well as the bounty each provided. The sandy soil was unclaimed, fertile and supported an abundance of wildlife to feast upon. Yet even more, the southern frontier offered an escape, the chance to create civilization where no white man had ever dwelled as well as the possibility of a better life. All the same the Indian River area was far from tame at this point. Danger lurked from stormy seas to disease carrying mosquitoes; bear, panther and alligators were common then in addition to the occasional Indian attack or marauders running from the law. There were no conveniences living off the land meant just that.

Captain David P. Gibson later followed by Thomas New attempted to dig inlets across the barrier island but both quickly filled with sand and became useless. But by this time forty brave pioneers, determined to build a home here, settled just south of the St. Sebastian River. Finally by 1890, Sebastian was granted a post office. Then disaster struck with a killing freeze in the winter of 1894-95. The entire citrus and pineapple crops were lost to the winter's frigid temperatures. The settlers were steadfast and hardy they refused to be beaten and remained to persevere.

Every family owned at least one boat mainly because travel by land was virtually impossible. Mail was delivered, supplies purchased and even peddlers sailed the coast plying their trade. However, progress was coming on iron rails. The railroad arrived in Sebastian on December 11, 1893. Train number twenty-three of the Jacksonville, St. Augustine and Indian River Railroad opened the Indian River area to expansion. By the turn of the century Henry Flagler would purchase the entire line, which became known as the Florida East Coast Railroad. The railroad allowed commercial fishing to develop and in turn fish houses sprang up all over. Icehouses were need to preserve the catch, a new industry was soon inspired. Sebastian was now an established fishing village, small but prosperous.

The push for a usable inlet continued over the years. Gibson's Cut between the Atlantic and Indian River lagoon was reopened in 1895 but a violent storm washed in sand to close the inlet within a year. Roy D. Couch was the first to use a dredge in 1918 to open the sandy waterway and build a jetty to help keep it clear. This attempt was thwarted when a storm wrecked the entire project. Local fisherman joined with the Florida Legislature in 1919 to build and maintain a permanent inlet. Roy Couch was selected to head the Sebastian Inlet Tax District created to make the inlet a reality, he served in the position for thirty-two years. The inlet would con-tinually be opened then Mother Nature would intervene closing the gap. Finally in 1941 with the advent of World

War II, fear of German submarine attack forced the natural closure of the inlet to remain intact. Sebastian Inlet was reopened the final time on October 28, 1948 and has remained open to this day.

Many of the original founding families have remained steadfast in the community their ancestors worked so hard to tame. Familiar names appearing in history are still active today along the Treasure Coast. As long as the river continues to flow, the people who dared take the chance to build a life in the southeastern frontier will remain part of the history of the life giving shores.

HISTORIC
HARDEE OAK

This live oak tree was planted by Robert Hardee, Jr., in 1891. His mother, Emma Hardee, fought to save it when Main Street was paved in 1925.

Indian River Drive & Main Street, Chamber of Commerce, Sebastian
IR3 ~ GPS Coordinates: 27.817500, -80.468850

Robert A. Hardee and his wife, Emma, originally hailed from Quitman, Georgia. During the first days of the Civil War Hardee joined the Confederacy in Company H and rose to the rank of Captain. At one point Captain Hardee suffered a grievous injury after being shot from the back of his horse. Eventually he recovered from his wounds and returned home to Emma. The couple had a son, Robert G. Hardee. After the war, Captain Hardee moved his family to Hardeeville, today known as Rockledge, in search of a better life. He planted orange groves and raised cattle. Unfortunately a hard freeze wiped out his entire orange grove and killed the majority of his herd. Ever the optimist, Captain Hardee was determined to start again.

THE ACTUAL MARKER

Around 1891 the Hardee family moved once more to the tiny fishing village of Sebastian. Son Robert planted the Hardee Oak about seventy feet west of what is known today as Indian River Drive, the year of their arrival. The family purchased property and planted two orange groves. Father and son constructed a well built home. Later they would open a store, dock and fish house. Their endeavors in Sebastian were very successful.

The handsome son grew to become an important figure in the small community. At the age of twenty-three Robert G. (Bob) Hardee became a riverboat captain, operating his steamer from Rockledge. Bob owned a large sloop called *Dora*, which he and his future brother in law, Stanley Kitching used to haul shells from the huge Ais Indian midden at Barker's Bluff. The shells were used to build the first streets of Sebastian. He later built two substantial yachts the *Eagle* and *St. Sebastian*, ferrying passengers from Fellsmere to the beach and other places of interest. By July of 1894 the Florida East Coast Railway ran from Jacksonville to Lake Worth.

One of the Hardee boats, the *Jumbo*, was outfitted to serve as a floating fish house, the first of its kind in Sebastian. Smaller vessels would moor alongside bringing in the day's catch to be cleaned and put on ice to pre-serve freshness. The ice was delivered via the train and carted to the fish house by wagon. Often the Hardee men could be found standing in literally three feet of fish, after the sun slid low on the horizon torches were lit so that the men could continue cleaning fish and packing them in barrels in order to meet the midnight train to

Jacksonville.

Bob Hardee married Clarissa Kitching in 1900. Born in Warrington, England, Clarissa was the daughter of Mr. and Mrs. Sylvanus Kitching. Her father, while working as postmaster, changed the name of the settlement from New Haven to Sebastian on November 13, 1884. It has been said that the name was changed to simplify the process of canceling postage. Sebastian was derived from the St. Sebastian River named by Spanish explorers. Clarissa Kitching Hardee would later recall that while visiting her mother-in-law's home, Indians would arrive bringing turkey and venison to trade with the elder Mrs. Hardee for milk and eggs.

Bob Hardee became the first St. Lucie County Tax Assessor in 1905, a position he held for a number of years. Captain Robert G. (Bob) Hardee, Jr. died in 1947; he was seventy-five years old. The Hardee Oak was still standing thanks to his mother's efforts. When Sebastian's Main Street was paved in 1925, the city intended to do away with the tree. Emma Hardee fought to save it. Clarissa Kitching Hardee died in 1976; she was ninety-four years old. For ninety years she had remained in Sebastian. Clarissa Hardee was a devout member of the Sebastian United Methodist Church, the first Methodist church in Sebastian, which was founded by a group of ladies including both her mother and mother-in-law. The church was only one of many bequeaths left to the city of Sebastian by the proud Hardee legacy.

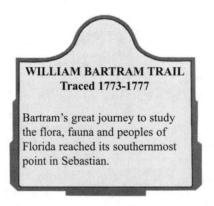

WILLIAM BARTRAM TRAIL
Traced 1773-1777

Bartram's great journey to study the flora, fauna and peoples of Florida reached its southernmost point in Sebastian.

US 1, Riverview Park, Sebastian Inlet
IR4 ~ GPS Coordinates: 27.808517, -80.465917

William Bartram was commissioned by the British crown to survey the flora, fauna and people of the American colonies. Bartram made his last trip south during the years 1773 through 1777. Several years before Bartram had accompanied his father, John, Botanist for the Crown along many of the same pathways. He left a detailed accounting of his southern travels entitled, "Travels through North & South Carolina, Georgia, East & West Florida, the Cherokee Country, The Extensive Territories of the Muscogulges, or Creek Confederacy, and the Country of the Chactaws." The work was first published in 1791 and was described as "the most astounding verbal artifact of the early republic."

Much of the time Bartram traveled throughout Florida he was gravely ill with what was thought to be typhoid fever and jaundice. Though sometimes incapacitated, William Bartram refused to let the illness interfere with his work. He chronicled weather conditions' including temperatures, well that is until one day while climbing up a tree after honey Bartram broke his thermometer. William Bartram wrote of the soil quality, artesian wells, newly discovered plants as well as the workings of an alligator's jaw and viciousness of the native rattlesnake, all in exquisite detail. His trails were the routes used for many modern day roads as well as suggesting suitable locations for placement of military forts. Bartram's observations of Native American customs, living conditions and burial rites continue to be referenced to this day. Something so simple as the Indians' preference for eating oranges doused in honey was detailed in William Bartram's writings.

His writings have been compared to poetry given the awe that comes shinning through from each page of his work. For example, when arriving at the southernmost point of his Florida travels Bartram described great mounds known as the Native American Ais shell middens:

> Southerly to the point of the peninsula of Florida, are to be seen high pyramidal mounts, with spacious and extensive avenues, leading from them out of the town, to an artificial lake or pond of water, these were evidently dignified in part, for ornament or monuments of magnificence, to perpetuate the power and grandeur of the nation, and no considerable one neither, for they exhib it scenes of power and grandeur, and must have been public edifices.

William Bartram captured glorious imagery of an untamed wilderness that is today southeast Florida.

THE KROEGEL HOMESTEAD

In 1881, Paul Kroegel was 17 years old when he came with his father, Gottlob, to build a house on top of a huge shell midden that was called Barker's Bluff (a/k/a Two-Mile Bluff). This mound was over 40 feet high towering above the Indian River. In 1889, title to 143 acres including the midden was formally granted to the Kroegel family under the Homestead Act. In 1908, the shell in Barker's Bluff was sold to St. Lucie County for road material. The Kroegel Homestead and the midden site are located on Indian River Drive south of this site.

PAUL KROEGEL (1864-1948)

Paul Kroegel was a skilled carpenter and boat builder. In 1899, he built his house on the Kroegel Homestead and in 1900 married Ila Lawson. From his father's old house on the shell mound, he had observed the disturbance and wanton killing of birds in the island rookery across the river. With others, Paul waged a persistent campaign to protect the nesting area - a tiny island called Pelican Island. In 1903, President Theodore Roosevelt signed an Executive Order establishing the Pelican Island Wildlife Reservation, the first National Wildlife Refuge. Paul Kroegel was appointed its first warden.

Riverview Park by the pier, Sebastian
IR5 ~ GPS Coordinates: 27.809300, -80.463983

C. F. Gottlob Kroegel left Chemnitz, Germany around 1871 accompanied by his two young sons, Paul and Arthur. The trio immigrated to Chicago and remained there for ten years. After hearing about the Homestead Act, which was to be enacted the very next year Gottlob set out for Ohio where his brother had settled. Once there he settled twelve-year-old Arthur with his uncle then Gottlob and seventeen-year-old Paul set out on foot for a place in the far south called New Haven. The name was changed in 1884 to Sebastian.

The Homestead Act allowed settlers up to one hundred sixty acres of land provided that five acres be cleared, retained for five years and that the owner be an American citizen. Gottlob Kroegel complied and filed for the homestead, which was awarded on June 21, 1889 signed by President Benjamin Harrison. A littler over one hundred forty-three acres of the property was on dry land while the remainder was in the Indian River. Kroegel's was the first land patent requested from the Indian River area.

Their first home was a palmetto frond shanty that a hurricane laid flat shortly after it was built. A short time later, Gottlob built a more substantial wooden frame house on top of a forty-foot shell midden left by the Ais Indians. Soon Gottlob discovered the ground to be very fertile and he had a knack for growing things. He planted the first orange grove in the area and raised an abundance of winter vegetables including Valenti beans then built one of the first packinghouses to accommodate his produce.

In 1885, at the age of twenty-one, Paul began studying navigation and earned his Captain's license. Paul built a boat shop where he constructed boats of very fine quality. On Saturday evenings, he would often board one of his vessels possibly the thirty-five foot *Irene* or the fifty-foot *Wanderer* and travel up and down the coast to play his accordion for barn dances. In addition, young Paul tended his own citrus grove, assisted his father and brother with construction projects and cared for one hundred beehives. Honey was sold from a little hut near his home. Gottlob Kroegel made headlines in the May 21, 1889 issue of the Indian River Advocate having shipped seventy-four crates of beans from his garden. This was a record for the largest amount of beans shipped from the Indian River by only one man.

While coming to age atop the high perch of the shell midden, Paul developed an affinity for the majestic brown pelicans, which came to land on a small island in the Indian River adjacent to their home. He often watched in horror as plume[1] hunters approached the rookery awash in pelicans, egrets, herons and spoonbills. During this time these plume feathers were very highly valued in the fashion industry for hats, boas and trimmings. Paul Kroegel often took out in his skiff armed with a ten gauge double-barreled shotgun to patrol the lagoon warning off hunters and vandals. But having no authority to keep the hunters away unless he was willing to shoot someone, Paul's warnings went unheeded. He knew it was time to take action.

Paul Kroegel spoke to anyone who would listen in concern for the beautiful brown pelicans, which were now virtually being hunted to extinction. Knowing his quest, Mrs. Latham of Latham's Oak Lodge resort in nearby Micco frequently informed Paul when guests were expected who could possibly help his cause. It was through her that Paul met Dr. Frank Chapman, an ornithologist[2], who was prominent in the Audubon Society and the American Ornithologists' Union. Dr. Chapman was easily convinced to work with Paul in saving what came to be known as "Pelican Island."

The pelican campaign went on for several years, seemingly to make headway only to fail once again. Meanwhile, Paul married Ila Lawson in October of 1900, then built a house for his new bride behind the bluff. All the while he remained active in the pursuit to save the brown pelican. The Florida State legislature finally enacted a law in 1901 protecting non-game birds. The law opened the door for the Florida Audubon Society to hire four wildlife wardens for enforcement. Paul Kroegel was one of these wardens, hired to protect his beloved Pelican Island.

The pay for this important job was a meager twelve dollars per year to start. Unfortunately, Paul had to supplement his income with boat building and farming. But happily it was the warden's position that he most cherished, now he had a badge to go along with his boat and shotgun. He was given a large American flag to fly on Pelican Island once it became protected, however, quite astutely Paul placed the flag on the bluff instead. As boats approached they would blow their horns in respect for the flag, this was Paul's signal to jump into his sailboat and head 'em off at the pass. Ila was concerned for her husband's safety on his patrols but Paul would not be deterred. Even after the birth of a daughter Frieda, Paul continued his vigil. Two of the four wardens hired by the Audubon Society were murdered while protecting the plume birds; still Paul Kroegel refused to give up his quest.

Dr. Chapman finally convinced environmentally conscious President Theodore Roosevelt to sign an executive order protecting Pelican Island. Five days after Ila gave birth to a son they named, Rodney; President Roosevelt enacted the following, in part:

> "It is hereby ordered that Pelican Island in Indian River . . . is hereby reserved and set apart for the use of the Department of Agriculture as a preserve and breeding ground formative birds."

Pelican Island became the first unit of the National Wildlife Refuge System. The Kroegel sons began construction on a new home for their father, now elderly, on the north side of the midden in 1908, which he moved into upon completion in 1910. The old house atop the midden was demolished and the mound was sold to St. Lucie County for the shell. A railroad spur was built to the mound where the shell was loaded and carted away for use in paving the road from Micco to Stuart. When a massive hurricane pummeled the area in 1910 the birds on Pelican Island moved to another location nearby only to return a few years later. By 1913 the shell midden was completely leveled. Unfortunately most of the Ais Indian historical artifacts contained within the midden were scattered from Micco to Stuart.

The Pelican Island Wildlife Refuge came under attack by commercial fisherman in 1918. The fishing community claimed that the pelicans were consuming the food fish thereby threatening their way of life. They insisted that the ban on killing these birds be lifted. Federal Bird Reservations Inspector, B. J. Pacetti studied the situation and concluded that pelican only eat surface fish where with only one exception food fish are bottom dwelling. The exception was mullet and he further found that pelicans mainly feed the young small bony fish not fit for human consumption. Warden Paul Kroegel responded to the allegations as follows:

> "Regarding the reduced catches of fish, this is caused mainly the fishermen's own greediness. There has been no law framed yet that the fishermen have not broken… The size of mesh in nets has been steadily reduced until now they are catching fish unfit for market, and unless something is done soon, the fishing business will be a thing of the past."

Fishermen responded by taking children out to Pelican Island and instructing them to kill the baby birds in their nests. Three hundred chicks were bludgeoned to death; no charges were ever filed.

Gottlob Kroegel passed away in 1923. Paul and Arthur were known to have visited their Dad every Sunday throughout his life to share a beer together. Every father should be so fortunate.

Though Paul Kroegel had the authority to control poachers and vandals, he could not control the pelicans' nesting habits. In the fall of 1923 the pelicans flew the coop once again, this time they did not return. With the island bare he had nothing to protect so after three years of waiting for the birds to return, Paul Kroegel was terminated as warden of the Pelican Island National Wildlife Refuge in 1926. It was a devastating blow, but one he knew was coming. He lived in Sebastian for the remainder of his life, waiting for the birds to return to his beloved Pelican Island. Paul Kroegel died in 1948 at the age of eight-four. Once again pelicans came home to roost on Pelican Island adjacent to Kroegel's home and remain there today.

Indian River County eventually purchased the Kroegel site where Arthur Rodney Kroegel once lived. Paul's photo studio and two workshops containing all manner of memorabilia from his days as warden of Pelican Island stand just beyond the house. A bronze memorial of Paul Kroegel proudly stands gazing across to the island he loved; a pipe in his mouth, a brown pelican at his feet and beautiful Riverview Park all around. As you look into his face the word contentment comes to mind. The National Register designated Pelican Island as a historic landmark in 1963, another first in history. The island draws more than thirty thousand visitors each year.

The Pelican Island National Wildlife Refuge celebrated one hundred years on March 14, 2003. The theme for that celebration was "One Man Can Make A Difference." Paul Kroegel was one man who made a difference and left a legacy for us all.

BROWN PELICAN

PAUL KROEGEL MEMORIAL

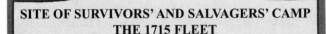

SITE OF SURVIVORS' AND SALVAGERS' CAMP
THE 1715 FLEET

Late in July, 1715, a hurricane destroyed a fleet of eleven or possibly twelve homeward bound merchant ships carrying cargoes of gold and silver coinage and other valuable items from the American colonies to Spain. About 1500 men, women, and children who survived the disaster and reached the shore made their camp along the barrier island near the place where the fleet's flagship had sunk. Governor General Corcoles sent a relief party composed chiefly of Indian auxiliaries from St. Augustine to provide subsistence for the survivors. These auxiliaries also gave protection and aid to the salvagers who used the campsite while working to recover the valuable cargo from the sunken vessels. Archaeological work at the site revealed that the salvagers seem to have erected some temporary structures for use as storehouses for the recovered gold and silver. While the salvage operation was in process, Henry Jennings, an English pirate, sailed to the site, drove off the guards and seized a large quantity of the recovered coins which he carried away to Port Royal, Jamaica. But the great majority of the treasure was safely regained and moved to Havana by the Spanish salvagers.

Sebastian Inlet State Recreation Area, McLarty Museum, Orchid Island
IR6 ~ GPS Coordinates: 27.834083, -80.434417

The Spanish found an abundance of silver and smaller quantities of gold in the mountains of Mexico and South America. In order to retrieve the ore it was melted and formed into ingots and coins then shipped across the Atlantic. This is the basis for what we know today as the Spanish Plate Treasure Fleet. Each summer the Spanish ships set sail for home with the year's mountain of treasure including a stop in Cuba for other goods often rare Oriental finds. Warships accompanied the fleet for protection from pirates and privateers but nothing could save them from the ravages of a brutal sea when hurricanes stirred the water and wind ripped the sails.

The Spanish crossing of 1715 began without incident that is until the fleet left Havana heading north. As the twelve ships in the flotilla approached the Florida coast the skies began to darken and the winds churned the ocean into a white capped frenzy. The wooden hulls of eleven ships were shredded on the sharp rock of the shoals between St. Lucie and Sebastian Inlets then sank into the dark depths of a watery grave. The twelfth vessel was a captured French ship forced to travel with the Spanish fleet. She managed to escape the storms and returned to her homeland.

Fifteen hundred men, women and children struggled to shore while the treasure sank to the murky bottom. Thousands perished during the storm and many others succumbed to exposure of the elements and exhaustion after making it to shore. The date of the shipwreck was July 31. Imagine being stranded on a Florida beach exposed to the elements under the broiling summer sun, the stinging disease carrying insects and brutal tropical storms. The survivors scavenged for food and built make shift shelters out of debris from the wreck. These events will forever be remembered with the name, Treasure Coast.

Another fear gripped the survivors, the area Native Americans were thought to be quite brutal. However, the Spaniards were pleasantly surprised when the cautious Ais extended every courtesy providing sustenance and aid. The Ais knew how to survive from the bounty of the land and sea though they were not farmers. Baskets of game, edible plants, berries, fish and fowl were delivered to the famished survivors. In this instance rumor of the Ais' hostility were unfounded, the Spaniards later returned this kindness by driving the Native American tribe to virtual extinction through disease, enslavement and warring.

Don Juan del Hoyo Solorzano, Havana's Sergeant Major, took charge of the salvage operation that continued for four years. Spanish salvors and Ais divers recovered a great deal of the treasure. The treasure had no value to the Ais, who did not yet understand the European economic system. Those not involved with the recovery process were taken to Havana. Less than half of the ships' treasure manifest was reclaimed from the sea.

Notorious pirate Captain Henry Jennings attacked the encampment in 1716. He and his men made off with twenty-one tons of silver and more than six hundred thousand coins. This raid began an era of piracy throughout the Caribbean. However, the Atlantic had claimed much more than the Spanish or the pirates were able to lay hands on. The Atlantic refused to give up her bounty without a struggle.

Over the years Spanish ingots would sometimes wash ashore, teasing treasure hunters with a taste of what lay beneath the ocean's waves. In 1928, one of the Spanish ships *Urca de Lima* was found just off the Fort Pierce shore. But ironically the next clues were to be found on land. Kip Wagner discovered the base camp of the Spanish salvagers in 1950 after a hurricane unearthed clues previously hidden from view. Wagner reasoned that the site would be near the shipwreck and now had a place to begin searching for the lost fleet.

Wagner's search took more than ten years but in the end he was rewarded with an amazing find, another ship was located. The *El Capitana* wreck yielded silver pieces of eight, gold doubloons and bars, rare Chinese porcelain as well as common objects dating to 1715. Modern diving gear and dredging equipment certainly helped in the recovery. However the sea still had her secrets.

The *Nuestra Senora de la Regla* was found in August of 1988. To date she has given up more than three hundred thousand dollars in treasure. Salvagers estimate more than two hundred million dollars worth of silver, gold and various artifacts still remain on the ocean floor. Three of the ships from the Spanish Treasure Plate Fleet have yet to be discovered.

Today the McLarty Treasure Museum occupies the site of the 1715 Survivors and Salvagers Camp, which has been identified as a National Historical Landmark. Located within the Sebastian Inlet State Park, the museum is open seven days a week. Robert McLarty, for who the museum is named, was a retired Atlanta attorney living in Vero Beach. He donated the land to the state of Florida for the construction of the museum. A nominal fee is charged to view various artifacts recovered from the 1715 Spanish Plate Treasure Fleet at the McLarty Treasure Museum.

FELLSMERE

Is a dramatic account of floods, land "boomers" and land "busts". Named for E. Nelson Fell, Fellsmere was first incorporated in 1911, as part of St. Lucie County. The Fellsmere Farms Land Development Company promoted the area's rich soils and natural resources. By 1915, Fellsmere had a railroad, an electric company, two hotels and women could vote...a first in Florida. Overwhelmed by torrential rains and the Great Depression, Fellsmere struggled until the sugar cane fields brought prosperity. These cane fields are gone, but the soils and natural resources of the marshes still remain.

Intersection SR507 & SR512, Fellsmere
IR7 ~ GPS Coordinates: 27.767750, -80.600867

Fellsmere is just a little spot in the road but when it comes to heart and history, this small town rivals any metropolis. Located only three miles west of Interstate 95 on State Road 512, Fellsmere's population hovers around four thousand and covers a little over five square miles. Aptly, the city was named for a man who managed to put the small town on the map, E. Nelson Fell; in conjunction with the word "mere" meaning a great watery place.

E. Nelson Fell was born in Nelson, New Zealand in 1857. His father, Alfred, gained prominence and fortune through the wholesaling industry. As a youth Nelson was sent to several well-known schools to study engineering and mining. Brothers, Arthur and Nelson, worked closely together for the next thirty years. Nelson traveled all over the world at the behest of his brother supervising numerous mining and engineering projects.

During his travels Nelson met and married Anne Palmer, daughter of a New York Judge. Soon they were a family of five with the addition of two daughters and a son. In 1884, twenty-seven year old Nelson was sent to Florida. Nelson was determined to set down roots and did so in a city that would later be named in his honor, Fellsmere. Nelson quickly identified many improvements that could be made in the area and set about making his dream a reality. Roots came in the form of citrus and soon Nelson had a thriving grove but the good fortune would soon come to an end.

The winter of 1894 was unusually harsh and two days after Christmas the mercury plummeted to a frosty twenty-seven degrees. Freezing conditions lasted for almost three days. The younger citrus trees could not withstand the freeze and limb breaking ice. Older, well-established trees were stunted but a good many survived. Then the sun came out and warmed the earth in a bittersweet false spring. Citrus farmers watched as damaged orange trees responded to warmth with new growth and the fragrant scent of orange blossoms filled the air.

On February 7, 1895, Mother Nature struck her cruel blow again letting loose a devastating freeze across the entire state. The groves looked as if a massive fire had swept through leaving only the bare skeletons of dead trees and devastation to the economy.

Drainage Districts were organized in 1905 with the idea that millions of acres of wetlands could be drained to become viable building property. In 1910 Nelson Fell, with financial backing from Virginia engineer and philanthropist Oscar T. Crosby, purchased one hundred eighteen thousand acres at the headwaters of the St. Johns River. Fell set his engineers to the task of implementing the largest drainage system in Florida beginning with dredging and based on the principle of gravity. Florida's Governor Napoleon Broward challenged entrepreneurs across the country to create an "Empire in the Everglades." In response Fell and Crosby established the Fellsmere Farm Company; in 1912 the Indian River Farms Company was founded. The Florida real estate boom was at its height.

Young and ambitious Frank Heiser heard a rumor of cheap land in a place called Fellsmere where a midwestern upstart like himself could get rich quick. Heiser pooled his money with school chum, John P. Frommer and the duo purchased twenty acres sight unseen. The two young men left their Lafayette, Indiana home heading south for Florida. When they arrived, Heiser and Frommer realized that they had been duped. Rather than the cleared farmland they expected, what they saw before them was nothing more than drained swamp inundated with plow busting roots. Not to be deterred, they promptly went to work clearing their land. For John P. Frommer the promise of future riches was not worth the backbreaking labor.

Frommer abandoned Heiser and his share of the property after only two weeks. Frank Heiser was more determined than ever and worked doubly hard. He built a small cottage for himself, planting tomatoes and peppers to raise some money. The plants flourished and produced a very nice crop, unfortunately come harvest time everyone had tomatoes and peppers for sale. Heiser had no market for his goods, but he wouldn't go hungry. Still clinging to his never say die attitude, Heiser decided to take a real gamble. He planted citrus trees and hoped for the best in Fellsmere.

The Fellsmere Farm Company had since its inception supported the city of Fellsmere financially. In 1913 voters elected to create a commission form of government, still one year later the company continued to pick up the tab for the city. Nelson Fell had no one to blame for this predicament but himself. He had long assumed a paternal role in the city and cutting those apron strings proved to be rather difficult. For instance, when the city's tennis courts required maintenance the commission turned to the Farms Company with a request to pay for their upkeep. Nelson Fell was an avid tennis player and used the courts frequently so the company's executive committee approved the request. Of course the point was that a privately owned company should not be responsible for maintenance of city property.

On May 12, 1915, the city of Fellsmere was incorporated. The future appeared bright to the eight hundred ninety-six residents who saw progress all around. The first planned subdivision in St. Lucie County as well as a forty thousand-dollar public school facility was under construction. The Marian Fell Library, the first public library in the county, was expanding. City streets were paved using poured concrete including molded gutters and curbs, which was a new concept at that time. To the delight of everyone, the citrus groves planted after the 1913 devastating freeze were beginning to bear fruit. Among the firsts for Fellsmere was the city electorates' decision to allow women to vote five years before the 19th Amendment to the Constitution was passed in 1920.

Mother Nature struck with another cruel blow on Saturday, July 31, 1915. The skies were dark and dreary throughout the day, then in the early evening a slow steady drizzle began to fall. As the hours passed, the rains' intensity increased. When the sky finally cleared almost nine inches of rain had fallen. The drainage system failed, Fellsmere was completely flooded. Citizens were forced to abandon the area in boats searching for higher ground. Many Fellsmere residents never returned. The little hamlet of Broadmoor, five miles to the west, was evacuated. After the flood, Broadmoor never recovered becoming a ghost town overnight.

It was obvious that Fell and Crosby had severely miscalculated the amount of water the drainage system could handle. The paved streets looked much like the canals of Venice complete with poled boats. Years ago travelers would stop along the Dixie Highway, before the days of Interstate 95, asking for directions to Fellsmere; the answer was often given with a chuckle, "when you're knee deep in water, you're there!"

By late 1916 the Fellsmere Farms Company was bankrupt. Nelson Fell's ambition to create farmland and communities from Florida swamp had failed. The plan was perhaps too broad, money is always a factor and the outbreak of World War I played a part in the failure of Fell's company. The first day of the New Year 1917 the Fellsmere Farms Company assets were sold to the highest bidder on the courthouse steps in Fort Pierce.

Fell left his namesake city in 1917, never to return. He retired to the quiet solitude of his Virginia estate. His children were settled, daughter Marian was working to complete a translation of Anton Chekov's stories and plays; daughter Olivia, had recently announced her engagement; and Nelson, Jr. was attending Harvard. E. Nelson Fell died eleven years later in 1928.

However, Frank Heiser reemerges in our story around 1930 with a new concept for Fellsmere. Heiser overcame obstacles that would thwart the efforts of a lessor man including destructive weather conditions, nervous investors and even the federal government to create the Fellsmere Sugar Company. The company experienced many roadblocks but eventually it was the Fellsmere Sugar Company with Heiser at the helm that saved the city from economic ruin.

By 1933 the country was in the grips of the Great Depression. Twenty-five percent of American men were out work, families were starving and times were hard. However, thanks to Heiser, unemployment for Fellsmere citizens was almost nonexistent. It was company policy to hire only locals. In fact signs were put in place along the roadside leading to Fellsmere stating that the sugar mill did not hire outsiders. Imagine the lawsuits if someone proposed that today.

Puerto Rican sugar producers purchased the Fellsmere Sugar company in 1943. Though Heiser was invited to remain with the company, he turned down the offer. He sold his Fellsmere home to the new general manager and moved to Jacksonville. Heiser did return to Fellsmere from time to time, often consulting for the new owners. The Fellsmere Sugar Company went through a number of changes over the years until the Gulf and Western company purchased the property in 1967 but by that time the sugar operations had been moved to another location. Frank Heiser realized a dream for himself but perhaps his greatest accomplishment was his gift to the citizens of Fellsmere: providing jobs for more than thirty-five years. Heiser died in December of 1961. He did not live to see sugar production end at Fellsmere.

Fellsmere offers abundant fishing in the area lakes; the Stick Marsh is possibly the most popular site. Stick Marsh is noted as a catch and release lake. The city hosts an annual "Fellsmere Frog Leg Festival." The festivities begin the third week of January and last an entire weekend. The event offers carnival rides, arts and crafts, history booth and last but certainly not least, frog leg dinners. Several years ago the festival made the Guinness Book of World Records for the most frog leg dinners served in one day.

"Fellsmere Day" is celebrated each year on either the third or fourth Saturday in February. The usual festival activities abound beginning with a pancake breakfast provided by the local Lions Club. A parade highlights the days' events and is the only one of its kind in that the beginning meets the end. The Fellsmere Riding Club hosts an all out rodeo the first weekend in March. The rodeo is an excitement filled event with bull riding, calf roping and tons of other authentic rodeo attractions.

In the interest of historic preservation the Save Our Old School committee was formed in order to restore the old Fellsmere Elementary School. The lovely brick two-story school was built in 1916 and after nearly one hundred years is in desperate need of revitalization. The estimated cost is just over a million dollars. Fundraisers ranging from fish fries to ice cream socials have been hosted to solicit money. Seats in the school auditorium are being sold or visitors may have a room named in their honor or in memory of a loved one.

THE ACTUAL MARKER

SR507 & Oregon Avenue, Fellsmere
IR8 ~ GPS Coordinates: 27.769183, -80.601133

The pioneering members of the Methodist congregation conducted their first services inside the confines of a tent. Sweltering hot in the blazing Florida sun during the summer months, damp when the skies darkened and rain poured in, collapsing under the power of high winds tearing at the canvas and cold when the temperature dropped below the comfort zone, the tent was not a suitable sanctuary. Eventually the parishioners were allowed to utilize the pulpit of the Union Church on the first Sunday of each month, however the worshipers were still left with three Sundays crowded into the unpleasant temporary structure.

In 1922, local residents led by builder Corydon Nourse began construction of a permanent edifice. Nourse was a native of Ohio who, along with his wife Bertha and five children, came to live in Fellsmere. The church was to be located at 31 North Broadway Street on the northeast corner of what is today State Road 507 and Oregon Avenue. The structure was originally known as the First Methodist Episcopal Church of Fellsmere.

The majority of the building materials came from an apartment house, which had been torn down nearby. The edifice was constructed in a bungalow or craftsman architectural style commonly associated with the noted architect Frank Lloyd Wright. The style is usually identified as having a low-pitched gabled roof supported by square tapered columns and a wide front porch. Ordinarily construction materials such as brick, stone and wood were mixed throughout the structure. The interior would feature open rafters with very simple wood carved detail.

Construction was completed and the First Methodist Episcopal Church of Fellsmere was dedicated in

April of 1924. Graciously, the Community Methodist Church of Daytona Beach presented a fine toned bell to hang in the church spire. During a violent storm in 1955, the spire with its cross were completely destroyed. It became obvious in 1990 that the bell had to be removed before it came crashing down on its own. The Florida Department of State provided a grant for restoration of the exterior and spire soon after the bell was taken down. The church was rededicated as Fellsmere Historical Church on November 12, 1994. The structure was added to the National Register of Historic Places in 1996.

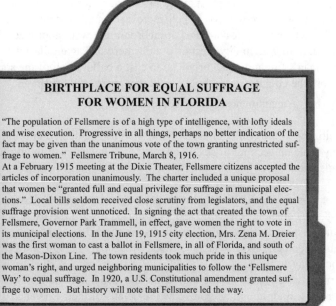

BIRTHPLACE FOR EQUAL SUFFRAGE FOR WOMEN IN FLORIDA

"The population of Fellsmere is of a high type of intelligence, with lofty ideals and wise execution. Progressive in all things, perhaps no better indication of the fact may be given than the unanimous vote of the town granting unrestricted suffrage to women." Fellsmere Tribune, March 8, 1916.
At a February 1915 meeting at the Dixie Theater, Fellsmere citizens accepted the articles of incorporation unanimously. The charter included a unique proposal that women be "granted full and equal privilege for suffrage in municipal elections." Local bills seldom received close scrutiny from legislators, and the equal suffrage provision went unnoticed. In signing the act that created the town of Fellsmere, Governor Park Trammell, in effect, gave women the right to vote in its municipal elections. In the June 19, 1915 city election, Mrs. Zena M. Dreier was the first woman to cast a ballot in Fellsmere, in all of Florida, and south of the Mason-Dixon Line. The town residents took much pride in this unique woman's right, and urged neighboring municipalities to follow the 'Fellsmere Way' to equal suffrage. In 1920, a U.S. Constitutional amendment granted suffrage to women. But history will note that Fellsmere led the way.

138 North Broadway, Fellsmere
IR9 ~ GPS Coordinates: 27.772834, -80.600411

The Sebastian and Cincinnatus Farms Railroad steamed to the headwaters of the St. Johns River in 1896. In order to attract settlers more than a thousand acres of swampland was drained to create land suitable for farming. Midwesterners flocked to the area and coincidentally the only way to reach their newly purchased property was by way of the railroad.

New Zealander, E. Nelson Fell retired to winter in the area in the early 1900s. A former engineer, ever active Fell sought a new project to fill his time. He purchased one hundred eighteen thousand acres and began developing the townships of Fellsmere (Nelson Fell's namesake), Broadmoor and Grassland. Grassland was destined to failure from the start and never made it to reality but both Fellsmere and Broadmoor flourished. Broadmoor was located just five miles west of Fellsmere and hosted a nine-block business district with a post office and a sizable residential community.

Soon tragedy struck and Broadmoor was drowned beneath sixteen inches of driving rain within the short span of forty-eight hours. The small town would never recover; in fact the post office building crumbled and was never found. However Fellsmere refused to be extinguished and survived the devastating flood.

Fellsmere not only recovered but blossomed. The population boomed to twenty-five hundred permanent residents. The city was surrounded by tremendous citrus groves, which are today known world wide as the most popular Indian River Citrus. Oranges and grapefruit made up the majority of the grove and by late fall of each year during harvest season the population will swell to more than double. Fellsmere Farms is by far the leading employers in Indian River County.

What the quaint little city lacks in population and land mass, it more than surpasses other cities in the county in progressive and forward thinking ideals. The rich legacy of Fellsmere is awash in historical firsts for Indian River County, including packaged sugar; first county library named for Marian Fell, which continues to provide services to the city today; the Fellsmere Subdivision, the first planned neighborhood; county firsts in Fellsmere also included a hotel, public school and railway depot. Progress included an electric plant and ice factory as well as the first concrete paved roads. Amazingly in the early days of electrical lighting each evening at 10:30 the lights would blink twice indicating that at the 11:00 hour, electric power would cease.

Without question the most progressive of Fellsmere's accomplishments occurred during the February 1915 town council meeting where the cities' articles of incorporation were approved. The document included an article giving women the right to vote in city elections. Fellsmere had again blazed a new path as the first community to acknowledge a woman's full and equal privilege to cast a ballot in all of the southern states. It would be more than five years before the country, as a whole would recognize equal suffrage.

On August 26, 1920, the 19th Amendment was ratified, reading in part:

> "The right of citizens of the United States to vote shall not be denied or abridged by the United States or by any State on account of sex. Congress shall have power to enforce this article by appropriate legislation."

One of the great mysteries of Fellsmere involves two gravesites at the Historic Brookside Cemetery. Established around 1888, the cemetery has white residents buried toward the front of the lot while after crossing a quaint little bridge on the western outskirts, black residents are tucked away near the back. The mysterious carved stones read Count Hugh Nuremberg, Born March 7, 1893, Died July 17, 1974 and Countess Kathleen Nuremberg, Born June 13, 1911, Died May 1, 1967.

The couple arrived in Fellsmere during the 1940s, moving into a modest home on Maple Street. The Countess was a virtual recluse and though no one knew the details of their existence, the Count was largely disliked. According to sources, he was self-declared ladies' man who had wandering hands for every woman he encountered. It was said that the Countess was quite ill, explaining her isolation. Rumors abounded concerning the reason this royal couple would choose to live in Fellsmere and the source of their income. They did not use local banking services and appeared to be just short of destitute.

Countess Kathleen Nuremberg died the way she lived, silently on May 1, 1967. He left town shortly after her death only to return for interment by her side in July of 1974, at the age of eighty-one. Their tenure in Fellsmere remains a mystery.

In more recent history, Fellsmere realized a shortcoming in 1990 involving recreational opportunities for the children. In an effort to provide funds to build facilities, the unique Frog Leg Festival was created. The festival has blossomed into quite an event. Fellsmere is noted in the Guinness Book of World Records for serving the most Frog Leg dinners in one sitting. Activities in support of the festival include everything from arts and crafts to an amazing parade.

Fellsmere, over the years has become world renown for the supreme bass fishing opportunities just beyond the St. Johns River marshes at Blue Cypress Lake or the Stick Marsh. These waters have yielded world record catches. Fellsmere caters to the sportsman by offering an abundance of fishing guides, bait and tackle shops, boat rentals and if fishing is not your forte; airboat rides are an exhilarating way to experience the St. Johns River marsh.

Perched on the edge of the beautiful marsh, only four miles from the speeding traffic of Interstate 95, Fellsmere remains a small town with a huge impact. The feeling of old world Florida creeps in as one travels about her one main street called Broadway. The impressive history changing progress has forever influenced her county, state and country. Fellsmere's depth lies just beneath a serene small town appearance.

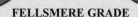

FELLSMERE GRADE

Fellsmere, the northernmost town in St. Lucie County in 1919, had a population of over 800 people. The county built the first public road to cross the St. Johns River marsh in St. Lucie County (now Indian River County). Promoted as the Fellsmere Tampa cross-state road, this road allowed travel between the interior and the coast. From 1919 until the 1940's, this road served as an important transportation route from Fellsmere, across the river to Kenansville, the sawmill at Holopaw, and the cattle markets of Kissimmee, but it never reached Tampa. During these decades it became a state road (SR 170) and provided a corridor to Central Florida and a recreational access to the St. Johns River marshes. The town of Fellsmere was dependent on the sportsmen attracted to these resources. In the late 1940's the bridges burned across the river and the Fellsmere Grade ended in the marsh six miles from this site. Today this road serves the public as a recreational access.

At Stick Marsh Boat Ramp Entrance, CR507, 4.2 miles north of CR512, Fellsmere
IR10 ~ GPS Coordinates: 27.822433, -80.607467

The iron rails of what would eventually be Henry Flagler's Florida East Coast Railroad reached St. Lucie County 1893. As the huge steam belching vehicle of progress chugged down the tracks with it came the availability of northern markets to fishermen, farmers and citrus growers as well as land developers infusing money into what was the Florida wilderness.

Fellsmere was founded in 1911. It encompasses approximately twelve hundred thirty five square miles and boasts a population of four thousand people. Well, that is in the off season. During the time of fruit harvest the inhabitants more than doubles.

A railroad spur was built linking Fellsmere to Sebastian some seven miles to the east. The first railroad depot of St. Lucie County was built in the tiny town. As the town grew it could boast many firsts including a hotel and public school, but that was just the beginning.

Fellsmere Grade was to be the southern most official road in the state, traveling from east to west. But unlike the chicken crossing the road, Fellsmere Grade never made it to the other side. The road did reach the deep interior of the state as far as the cattle markets of Kissimmee and a bridge fording the St. Johns River. Fellsmere Grade certainly made it easier for sportsman to reach the abundant fishing spots at the inner most reaches of the St. Johns River marshes. Unfortunately the bridge burned in the 1940s and was never rebuilt at this site. Today Fellsmere Grade ends at a very nice public boat ramp area that attracts fishermen from all over. But be warned, Fellsmere Grade has had few improvements over the years and traveling those six miles along the wash board dirt road is a very bumpy ride to put it mildly. In 2001, Field & Stream magazine named Fellsmere Grade one of the top spots for largemouth bass fishing.

SITE OF FORT VINTON

A few miles southwest of this marker is the site of Fort Vinton. As white settlers moved into Florida, demands increased for the removal of the Seminole
Indians to a western reservation. The Seminoles did not wish to leave, and in
1835 the conflict known as the Second Seminole war began. The 1838-39 campaign of that war was planned with the major objective of driving Indians away
from settled areas and into the southern part of Florida. New posts were to be
built where needed and others, such as Fort Pierce, were to be reoccupied.
Supply outposts were needed for field campaigns, and early in April 1839, such
a post, called Fort or Post No. 2, was constructed about twenty miles northwest
of Fort Pierce. This fortification was abandoned by or before 1842, when hostilities ended. Early in 1850, when another concerted effort to force the remnants of the Seminoles to emigrate got underway, it was reactivated as Fort
Vinton. The post was named for Captain John R. Vinton, who had served in the
area during the earlier conflict and had died in the Mexican War. Fort Vinton,
an outpost of Fort Capron at Indian River Inlet, was soon abandoned (May
1850) and is not known to have played a role in the hostilities of the later
1850's.

One mile west of Interstate 95 on State Road 60, Vero Beach
IR11 ~ GPS Coordinates: 27.639422, -80.533520

Soldiers began occupying the supply fortification called Post No. 2 on April 7, 1839. A Maine transplant, Captain Rueben Pinkham owned a river transport business and delivered goods to the post. He lived near Fort Pierce, running the trade boat from St. Augustine to Jupiter. It is said that Captain Pinkham planted the first orange grove in this area from crates of the fruit salvaged from ships lost at sea.

The location of the Post has been in question because of varying map drawings during the era. Research initiated by Pam Hall, the Indian River History Librarian, resulted in the most probable location at just south of what is today highway 60, west of the intersection of 122 Avenue. When the Second Seminole War ended in 1842, the post was abandoned.

A man known simply as Russell and his brother-in-law, John Barker established homesteads and a trading post on the bluff today known as Barker's Bluff. Along with their wives and children, the men began farming and dealing with the Seminole through their mercantile. Unfortunately, it seems they treated the Indians unfairly and were none to kind in the process. The Seminole grew increasingly frustrated over the treatment. Eventually the agitation turned to anger.

July 12, 1849 was a sweat wrenching day as Russell and Barker worked in their kitchen garden when two armed Seminoles appeared in the distance. They silently crept nearer and hailed a war whoop, discharging their rifles. The men were caught off guard and bolted for safety. As Russell and Barker fled the Seminole let go another volley. Russell was wounded but Barker lay dead at his feet.

The wives, hearing the commotion, gathered their children running as fast as their legs would carry them to their boat tied at the river dock. Though Russell was shot through the torso, he limped to his house and grabbed a weapon of his own. He returned fire and the Seminole retreated. They sailed to Hutchinson Island then began walking to Cape Canaveral, a forty-mile trek. The murder panicked the entire community and everyone crowded into Captain Pinkham's boat, headed toward the Cape. Russell and his family, along with Barker's widow and children were sent to St. Augustine. Soldiers were sent to Fort Capron to settle down the angry Seminoles.

Hostilities escalated, Post No. 2 was reactivated on December 19, 1849. The post was renamed on

February 25, 1850 for Captain John Rogers Vinton. Born in Providence, Rhode Island, Vinton graduated from the United States military academy and served in Florida and Mexico. He quickly rose in rank, receiving numerous honors for gallantry. He was killed near Vera Cruz, Mexico on March 22, 1847. Captain Vinton never served at Post No. 2.

As the Seminole threat waned, Fort Vinton was abandoned on May 22, 1850. The peace did not last and the Third Seminole War began in 1855. By January of 1856, the United States Army, Company L of the 3rd Artillery, manned Fort Vinton once again. When this conflict came to an end, Fort Vinton was once again abandoned never to be rearmed. The fortification succumbed to the elements and eventually nothing was left of the site. Today Fort Vinton is but a footnote in history. However, the existence of the marker and memorandums such as this will not let this important part of Florida fade into the unknown.

NAS VERO BEACH

Originally a small municipal airport with refueling and maintenance use by Eastern Airlines, this field became NAS Vero Beach in November 1942. Naval and Marine aviators as well as WAVES and women Marines trained here. NAS Vero Beach saw use as a Marine Air Squadron Base as well as a training facility for F6F Hellcat, SB2A Buccaneer, F4F Wildcat, and F7F Tigercat pilots.

In December 1944 the mission of the field changed to night fighter training using F6F and F7F aircraft. Witham Field in Stuart, as well as fields at Roseland, Sebastian, and Fort Pierce served as auxiliary sites. Air-sea rescue of downed pilots was provided from Fort Pierce. Over 237,100 hours of flight time occurred between 1942 and the base closing in 1946. Base personnel were quartered in the Beachland Hotel, The Sebastian Inn, and other facilities in the community.

This former NAS site serves today as the Vero Beach Municipal Airport and home to Piper Aircraft. Two WWII era buildings are presently in private use in the complex. In January 2000, a Florida Historical Marker was dedicated to the memory of the men and women who trained at this site.

Vero Beach Municipal Airport, On the flight line at Vero Beach Municipal Airport, 3400 Cherokee Drive
IR12 ~ GPS Coordinates: 27.654475, -80.421175

Bud Holman, the local Vero Beach Cadillac dealer, was instrumental in establishing the first airport for Indian River County. Air transportation became very prevalent by the late 1920s for commercial use. Holman saw the Vero Beach Airport dedicated in 1930. By 1932 Eastern Air Lines began using the airport regularly for refueling. Three years later, Eastern Air Lines instituted both mail and the all important passenger service out of the Vero Beach facility.

The ugly face of war peered over the horizon, but forward thinking Vero Beach developers had already begun vast improvements to the airport facility. Permanent runway lights were put in place as well as the purchase of a radio system and Teletype machines. Welfare recipients were given work when the Vero Beach Airport runways were extended in 1939 and again months later when the Civilian Aviation Administration implemented a quarter of a million dollars in other modifications. These improvements were the determining factor in the Vero Beach Airport becoming an important part of the United States military effort in World War II.

The world now focused all attention on the rising hostilities in Europe. The United States Navy officially commissioned the airport as Naval Air Station Vero Beach in 1942. The air station was outfitted to support crucial pilot training. The United States Government purchased fifteen hundred additional acres surrounding the original airport facility. Aviators began arriving in January of 1943; pilot training began within thirty days. During its most populous days, NAS Vero Beach hosted more than fourteen hundred service men and women as well as servicing some two hundred fifty airplanes.

As World War II wound down to its final dark days and slowly came to an end, NAS Vero Beach military personnel were drastically reduced. NAS Vero Beach was deactivated in 1947. Control of the facilities was returned to the city and the military installation became known as Vero Beach Municipal Airport.

It seems with the loss of the military personnel that Indian River County would suffer a sluggish economy until the area adjusted to the diminished population. Oddly enough just the opposite occurred. Personnel who attended classes at NAS Vero Beach seemingly fell in love with the place and many returned after their discharge to live in the county. A number of factors influenced people to make the decision to live in the beautiful county on the Treasure Coast, including: an abundance of available beachfront property, reasonably priced homes, low property taxes and last but certainly not least, the balmy subtropical weather. By the end of World War II, Indian River County boasted more than nine thousand year round residents, thirty-six hundred of those in Vero Beach.

After the war there was a question concerning what was to be done with the additional property turned over to the city. The answer came from an already familiar source. Bud Holman entered into extensive negotiations with the Brooklyn Dodgers to use the excess city property, once a part of NAS Vero Beach, as their spring training facility. In 1948, the franchise executives made it official, the Dodgers were coming to Vero Beach. One hundred nine acres would be utilized as the Brooklyn Dodgers spring training facility. Practice fields were laid out, dining rooms established, dormitories, medical office, training and fitness facilities. The spring training site is known as Dodgertown. Even though the Dodgers eventually left Brooklyn, the team still returns to Vero Beach each year. Four years after Dodgertown was founded, the stadium was renamed in honor of Bud Holman as Holman Stadium.

**BLUE STAR
MEMORIAL HIGHWAY**

A tribute to the Armed Forces that have defended the United States of America.

**Beachland Highway & A1A, Sebastian Inlet
IR12 ~ GPS Coordinates: 27.653451, -80.360502**

President George W. Bush faced a Joint Session of Congress only nine days after the tragedy of September 11, 2001 and then the public on October 7th. The speeches detailed the mission that would come to be known as Operation Enduring Freedom. The United States military was tasked with obliterating terrorist training camps and military strong holds within Afghanistan, the capture of al Qaeda leaders as well as bringing to a halt all terrorist activities in Afghanistan.

Blue Star Memorial Highway markers pay tribute to those serving in the United States Armed Forces. The brave military personnel who stand the watch to keep us safe. The following is a memorial, honoring Florida soldiers who have lost their lives in the war against terrorism. Unfortunately the war goes on, soldiers will continue to proudly serve though many will never return home to the loving arms of their families. Therefore this is only a partial listing but a nation's gratitude is extended to every soldier willing to fight and die for the United States.

Anderson, Army Specialist Marc A., 30, of Brandon, Florida. Killed in action in eastern Afghanistan during Operation Anaconda. Died on March 4, 2002.

Bourgeois, Navy SEAL Chief Warrant Officer Matthew J., 35, of Tallahassee, Florida. Bourgeois was killed while conducting small unit training at a remote site near Qandahar, Afghanistan. Died on March 27, 2002.

Crose, Army Sergeant Bradley S., 22, of Orange Park, Florida. Killed in action in eastern Afghanistan during Operation Anaconda. He was assigned to the 1st Battalion, 75th Ranger Regiment, Hunter Army Airfield, Georgia. Died on March 4, 2002.

Eggers, Army Captain Daniel W., 28, of Cape Coral, Florida. Eggers died in Kandahar, Afghanistan, when his vehicle hit a land mine. He was assigned to 1st Battalion, 3rd Special Forces Group (Airborne), Fort Bragg, North Carolina. Died on May 29, 2004.

Maltz, Air Force Master Sergeant Michael, 42, of St. Petersburg, Florida. Maltz died in an HH-60 Pave Hawk accident in Afghanistan. He was assigned to the 38th Rescue Squadron, Moody Air Force Base, Georgia. Died on March 23, 2003.

Mancini, Army Sergeant 1st Class Curtis, 43, of Fort Lauderdale, Florida. Mancini died west of Ghazni, Afghanistan, when a weapons cache prematurely exploded. He was assigned to the 486th Civil Affairs Battalion, U.S. Army Reserve, based in Broken Arrow, Oklahoma. Died on January 29, 2004.

Moehling, Army Chief Warrant Officer Timothy W., 35, of Florida. Moehling died in the weather-related crash of a UH-60 Blackhawk helicopter in Kuwait. He was assigned to 5th Battalion, 158th Aviation Regiment, Giebelstadt, Germany. Died on February 24, 2003.

Payne, Marine Corporal Ronald R., Jr., 23, of Lakeland, Florida. Payne died due to hostile action in the vicinity of Tawara, Afghanistan. He was assigned to 2nd Light Armored Reconnaissance, 2nd Marine Division, II Marine Expeditionary Force, Camp Lejeune, North Carolina. Died on May 8, 2004.

Pena, Army Specialist Pedro, 35, of Florida. Pena died in Kuwait. He was assigned to Headquarters and Headquarters Company, 1st Battalion, 64th Armor Regiment, 3rd Infantry Division, Fort Stewart, Georgia. Died on November 7, 2002.

Sledd, Marine Lance Corporal Antonio J., 20, of Hillsborough, Florida. Sledd died in Kuwait from wounds received in action while participating in an urban exercise as part of Exercise Eager Mace. He was assigned to Lima Company, 3rd Battalion, 1st Marines, 11th Marine Expeditionary Unit, Camp Pendleton, California. Died on October 8, 2002.

Wadman, Army Private First Class Brandon J., 19, of West Palm Beach, Florida. Wadman died in Afghanistan when his vehicle rolled over. He was assigned to 2nd Battalion, 265th Air Defense Artillery, Florida National Guard, West Palm Beach, Florida. Died on May 5, 2004.

Wood, Army Sergeant Roy A., 47, of Alva, Florida. Wood was fatally injured when the vehicle he was traveling in near Kabul, Afghanistan hit another vehicle. He was assigned to Company C, 3rd Battalion, 20th Special ForcesGroup (Airborne), Army National Guard, based in Starke, Florida. Died on January 9, 2004.

On a personal note:

I dedicate this passage to the following men who are each very dear to me: Master Gunnery Sergeant (Retired) Joseph W. Goddard, Lance Corporal Joseph William Dale and Reservist Christopher Ryan Pocock; three men who proudly wear the insignia of the United States Marines and Senior Chief (Retired) Jeffrey W. Howard of the United States Navy.

RIOMAR CLUBHOUSE
SAINT EDWARDS SCHOOL

The Riomar Club chose this site for its clubhouse which was completed and opened in 1930. Ladies were attired in flowing formal gowns and the men in strikingly-starched white linen suits. A center for social activities for the area, the club drew many permanent residents and winter visitors to Vero Beach. The building is a Spanish-design clubhouse reminiscent of the style of Palm Beach. The exterior is stucco with interior pecky cypress beams. Purchased in 1965 for the purpose of starting an independent school, affiliated with the Episcopal Church, Saint Edward's School opened with 33 students in Grades 5-8. In 1972, the Upper School campus was opened on A-1-A south of here, and the Riomar building continued to house Grades Kindergarten through Grade 6, adding Pre-Kindergarten in 1983. The building was renovated in 1988 with the exterior maintaining the original character. On November 3, 1988, Bishop William Folwell dedicated the newly renovated building, and with his pastoral staff he marked the threshold with the sign of the cross and gave a blessing.

2225 Club Dr. at Bay Oak Lane, Vero Beach
IR14 ~ GPS Coordinates: 27.640883, -80.356467

The Riomar Club first opened their doors in 1930. The atmosphere is reminiscent of Casablanca men in cool linen suits and women dressed to the nines sipping a cool drink as paddle fans stir the sticky humid air of a summer evening. Typical of a south Florida design, the exterior features stucco while the interior is decked out in exposed native cypress beams. The club, which is still in operation today as an exclusively private golf club, was the center for the Vero Beach social scene.

The original clubhouse was purchased in 1965 to serve the community as a grade school. The school was associated with the Episcopal Church and named Saint Edward's School. Thirty-one students were recorded on the original roster. Though the school has evolved in many areas over the years, traditions dedicated to the development of exceptional morals, dignified character, spiritual commitment and community responsibility remain constant goals for each student who passes though Saints Edward's corridors.

Saint Edward's bases their educational goals on individualized instruction, focusing on academic challenge, independent thinking and the personal development of each and every student. Alumni refer to the style of instruction and opportunities as the "Saint Edward's Advantage." The advantage is obvious in the success of the alumni, which is remarkable. In fact, many families actually move to the Vero Beach area so that their children can benefit from Saint Edward's phenomenal opportunities.

The school expanded in 1972 to include kindergarten through twelfth grade classes. The first Saint Edward's graduating class received their diplomas in 1974 and since that time claims more than fourteen hundred alumni. The student body blossomed through the years to number more than eight hundred fifty children. New facilities were constructed off of Florida A1A now totaling thirty-three acres near the Indian River lagoon. The programs are based on college preparatory instruction under the guidance of ninety-eight full time faculty members. The average class numbers a manageable seventeen students so that each child may receive individualized instruction. Saint Edward's efforts have been awarded with one hundred per cent of their student body being accepted into four-year college degree programs.

The extracurricular program at Saint Edward's is exceptional and completes a well-rounded education for each student. In addition adult education opportunities are always available in addition to summer day camps, which have been offered for more than thirty years. Saint Edward's continues to give back to the community each and every year with continuing education classes, cultural activities, theatrical performances and support of non-profit organizations. In addition to the incredible educational programs, Saint Edward's School gives something much more valuable ~ the future in the capable hands of their graduates.

CITY OF VERO BEACH
(Side One)

The pattern of community development which occurred in Vero Beach provides insight into some important aspects of Florida's history. Although the coastal waters in the region attracted fishermen, settlement of this area did not occur until the 1880's. During that decade, the problem of lack of transportation which had deterred settlers was solved by railroad construction. In 1891, a post office named Vero was established at the home of Henry Gifford who had settled on the site in 1888. When the railroad was extended south to Lake Worth in 1894, a depot was built at Vero. With the railroad came tourism and a growing interest in the area. At that time, large scale drainage of swamp land such as that which surrounded Vero was being undertaken in Florida. An example of the way in which investors took advantage of the newly recognized potential of swampy areas may be found in the creation of the Indian River Farms Company.

CITY OF VERO BEACH
(Side Two)

In 1909, Herman T. Zeuch of Davenport, Iowa visited the Vero area. He saw land that could be drained and sold to citrus farmers and cattle raisers. A corporation, the Indian River Farms Company, was chartered in 1912 with stockholders who were chiefly residents of Zeuch's home town. In 1913, the town of Vero was platted at the Company's direction. In 1915, the Vero Woman's Club was founded, an act which signified the vitality of the new community. A clubhouse, located near this marker, was built the next year on land donated by the Indian River Farms Company. The planned drainage program was completed in 1917. In that year, maintenance and extension of the drainage area was given over to the State of Florida. The name of the community was changed to Vero Beach in 1925, when the town became the county seat of newly created Indian River County. The Indian River Farms company was dissolved in 1936. Vero Beach has remained the center of this productive citrus growing region.

1534 21st Street, Vero Beach
IR15 ~ GPS Coordinates: 27.639850, -80.401217

A little village on the Atlantic Ocean was home to Henry T. Gifford in 1891 and he was determined to put it on the map. An application for a post office was completed but met with a little difficulty once the United States Postmaster received it. You see, the Postmaster scanned the paperwork and found what he thought was an error. A copy of the original application can be seen at the Indian River County Local History file in the Main Library, the name "Vero" was modified to "Zero".

The origins of the name "Vero" are many but most were totally false. The first story stated that Henry Gifford chose the name Vero after his wife's name, this rumor was dispelled because her name in fact was Sarah. The second explanation suggested that Sarah Gifford wanted to name the city Verona but because the Post Service required a four-letter designation the name was shortened to Vero; this was false, the Postal Service had no such requirement. Another tale related that Charles Gifford, Henry and Sarah's son, chose the name in honor of his mother's love of poetry, Vero is Latin for truth. Finally it was said that "Tie-pile near Milepost 228" was the city's first name for the railroad station on Flagler's line; this was also untrue, the station was not established until 1894. Regardless of how the name came to be, the post office was created at Vero in 1891.

Henry T. Gifford could be called the father of Vero. He left his appointed position as sheriff of Royalton, Vermont and purchased acreage west of the Indian River. He first laid out the town in 1888. Then attached a moniker to the little village, Vero, most likely for no other reason than he liked the name. The English and Spanish settlers in the early 1800s concentrated agricultural efforts on sugar cane. Later Captain Thomas E. Richards introduced another crop, pineapples. By 1920, reportedly more than fourteen thousand crates of the luscious yellow fruits were exported from Richard's farms. But the pineapple boom did not last; the semi-tropical climate was too unpredictable and often-cold weather spread its way down the coast. It was the citrus industry with oranges and grapefruit that prospered. Vero became a major shipping area for the sweet citrus. Henry Flagler unwittingly assisted the fledgling fruit industry when he extended his railroad and built a station at Vero.

Iowa Banker, Herman Julius Zeuch as well as his wife, Adelaide, and son, Warren, visited Florida some twelve times over three years before deciding to purchase a vast amount of property there in 1911. Once the family arrived Herman formed the Indian River Farms Company and hired civil engineer William H. Kimball to drain the land. Zeuch began construction of the town and the name was changed to Vero Beach in 1925. The streets were named for Indians and a city park was established called Pocahontas Park.

By 1912, Zeuch had sponsored the construction of a bridge extending across Indian River, which he later turned over to the county. His contributions to Vero Beach were immense including implementing mosquito control, building an electric light plant and the sizable hotel. The hotel was named in honor of an old Indian chief by the name of Sleepy Eye from Minnesota who claimed to have never raised arms in anger against the white man. The hotel was known as Sleepy Eye Lodge. Herman Zeuch died on October 13, 1937 at his home in Vero Beach, Adelaide lived to a ripe old age of 96.

Commonly seen along the sandy roadway were little lean to huts where families sold fruits, jams and jellies. A frame beach style cottage was built in 1915 and became the town library for more than forty years. The building was also home to one of the city's most enduring organization the Vero Beach Women's Club was also founded in 1915. A small group of Ohio winter visitors established a section of homes at the end of Ocean Drive called Riomar in 1919. A golf course and clubhouse was built to accommodate the Riomar area, today the area is known as St. Edward's School.

Riomar gained nationwide attention when President Warren G. Harding made an unscheduled stop upon learning that Vero Beach was the only golf course between Daytona and Palm Beach while vacationing. The 1920s brought tourism to Vero Beach. Vacation homes and winter resorts became the destination of those escaping brutal northern winters. Bud Holman, a local businessman, found a way to promote the area and utilize the Naval Air Station, which was deserted in the aftermath of World War II. In 1948 he invited the Dodgers, a major league baseball team to winter in quaint little Vero Beach. The result is today known as Dodgertown, spring training ground for the Dodger team and draws thousands each year to watch exhibition games. Two thirteen storied condominiums were built in the early 1970s along Vero Beach causing instant outrage among the citizenry. The construction resulted in stringent city ordinances against building the high-rises in an effort to preserve the old world Florida image of Vero Beach.

In spite of modernization and commercialism, Vero Beach has maintained its age-old atmosphere. The city is a lovely seaside community, which has much to offer. Lovely shops, wonderful restaurants, museums, theater as well as a multitude of outdoor sports are featured with pristine beaches and magnificent sunsets. What more could you ask?

MCKEE JUNGLE GARDENS

This is the original site of McKee Jungle Gardens, one of Florida's earliest tourist attractions. McKee Gardens was founded in 1932 by Vero Beach pioneer Waldo Sexton and Cleveland industrialist Arthur G. McKee. They engaged William Lyman Phillips, a landscape architect who designed Fairchild Tropical Gardens and Bok Tower Gardens, to enhance and develop 80 acres of dense tropical vegetation. The gardens contain a collection of native and imported tropical plants, an aviary, resident monkeys and an alligator named "Old Mac". One of the most impressive components of Phillips design was the magnificent Cathedral of Palms, a colossal stand of more than 300 royal palms planted in precise rows. At its height of popularity the garden attracted 100,000 visitors annually, but closed in 1976, unable to compete with the allure of new theme parks nearby. Most of the acreage became a golf course and condominiums. The remaining 18 acres, now known as McKee Botanical Garden, were saved from destruction by the Indian River Land Trust and the citizens of Indian River County, and serves as an example of environmental stewardship and horticultural inspiration.

350 US 1, Vero Beach
IR16 ~ GPS Coordinates: 27.607260, -80.382715

Local Vero Beach resident Waldo Sexton and northern born snowbird Arthur McKee joined forces in 1922 establishing the McKee-Sexton Land Company. For several years they speculated with a few small land deals, however their best was yet to come. The partners purchased an eighty-acre tract of wild tropical hammock on the Indian River in 1929. Their intent was to clear the land, planting a money making orange grove.

Together the men walked their recent purchase and discussed plans for the future. Sexton and McKee came to the same conclusion almost immediately; it would be a crime to ruin this tropical paradise. The problem was the McKee-Sexton Land Company had a good deal of money tied up in the property, how could they get a good return on their investment without destroying the natural beauty of the land? The answer lay right before their eyes, Florida's first tropical garden attraction to be opened for a small admission fee.

McKee and Sexton saw the property as a tropical paradise with all the trappings. Imagine walking scenic trails through a lush maritime forest, a myriad of colors displayed in delicate orchids strategically placed; the sound of splashing water, shrieking monkey and the call of a distant macaw; bathing beauties, water lily filled ponds, an animal petting barn whimsically illustrated were only a few of the features planned. Of course, they knew right away to bring the dream to reality professional help was needed.

William Lyman Phillips was enlisted to design the basic layout of the gardens, trails and waterways. Phillips was the landscape architect for Bok Tower Gardens located in Lake Wales, which was opened in 1925; after his work for McKee and Sexton was complete, Phillips designed Florida's Fairchild Gardens at Miami in 1938. While Phillips worked his magic, Arthur McKee and Waldo Sexton set out to assemble one of the most elaborate collections of orchids and water lilies said to exist in the world. Well, that may have been a slight exaggeration but certainly the most extensive in the United States. Phillips earned the title, Father of Tropical Landscape Architecture for his work on these three magnificent projects. An authority on orchids was hired away from the Missouri Botanical Garden to be the caretaker of McKee's precious orchids; he was Dr. David Fairburn.

Waldo Sexton had his own ideas about landscape architecture. He found an absolutely huge cypress stump that Sexton became so enamored with that he had it carted all the way across the state. Once it arrived,

"The Stump" as it was called was given a prized spot at the entrance of the gardens. The petting zoo barn featured a bevy of farm animals and fowl. Though it was the outside of the barn that attracted the most attention. Silly wall paintings gave visitors a little chuckle. Another picturesque location was the Stone Bridge. In fact more posed pictures were made here than anywhere else in the gardens.

It seems that Sexton was a master of discovering unique finds and oddities. One such object was a very special mahogany table. He originally spotted the table at the St. Louis Louisiana Purchase Exposition in 1903. It would be twenty years before Sexton was finally able to purchase the table and have it shipped backed to Vero Beach. In fact the table was so spectacular that a building was constructed just to house it. So…what was so special about this table? Its shear size for one, the table measures thirty-five feet, ten inches long and is an amazing five inches thick. Secondly, this huge piece of Philippine mahogany is one single slab, imagine the tree!

The building constructed especially to house the mahogany table was called the Hall of Giants. Built by Sexton, the hall was completed in 1940 of cypress and heart pine. The Hall of Giants hosted countless events during its thirty-six year history including various wedding receptions to a boy's only Saturday night cookout. Sexton advertised the featured table as follows:

"It was so huge that 10 mounted horsemen once stood on it side by side, accompanied by a couple of small boys, a dog, three kittens and a string of catfish."

Eventually the Hall of Giants became the garden gift shop. The magnificent mahogany table was used to display merchandise

Adjacent to the Hall of Giants was a beautiful structure called the Spanish Kitchen. From here weekend chefs would prepared countless steaks on the triple grill as smoke curled from the huge chimney filling the air with the aroma of grilled beef. Waiters decked out in white livery served massive trays to the Saturday night boys only crowd hosted by Sexton and McKee. They would have a few cocktails and tell the same stories over and over again as old friends do. Perhaps their only distraction was the occasional swat of a mosquito buzzing around their ears.

When Sunday morning rolled around, a repentant Waldo Sexton opened the garden gates to a local African American congregation, hosting gospel sings and services. Sexton often joined the congregation to hear the Sunday sermon. The beautiful lilypond was used as a baptismal font on many occasions. Imagine the sight of robed parishioners being led into the water amidst snow-white lilies and immersed to wash their sins away. It must have been a sight to behold.

Phillips crowning glory was the Cathedral of Palms. Row after row of Royal Palms numbering in the hundreds, planted meticulously and equally spaced in a precise graph. Unfortunately the palms were not indigenous. When the weather cooled in Vero Beach often the Royal Palms would suffer the effects of exposure to inclement weather.

McKee Jungle Gardens swung open its gates to a waiting public in 1932. The first attraction of it's kind and was very well received. Tourists flocked to see the lush tropical vegetation and enjoy a serene walk along the scenic trails. Within ten years more than one hundred thousand patrons strolled through the gardens annually. Sexton and McKee saw an amazing return on their investment; the garden was a hit!

Over the ensuing twenty years, McKee Jungle Gardens enjoyed much success. However, times they were a-changing. The buzz throughout Florida concerned coming attractions in the central part of the state. The construction of Interstate 95 drew travelers away from US 1 and businesses began to suffer. The first of Orlando's mega-attractions opened in 1971 and this was the beginning of the end for smaller enterprises unable to compete with the glitz and glamour of big money.

McKee Jungle Gardens was forced to close due to declining attendance in 1976. The garden gates were sold to a sentimental neighbor and the property was sold to an ecstatic land developer who realized his great fortune to obtain this prime real estate for only one million dollars. Former Los Angeles Dodger franchise owner Peter O'Malley purchased the great mahogany table.

The property fronting the Indian River was the most valuable portion and was the first section to be developed. A golf course as well as wall to wall condominiums stood where lush vegetation once graced the land. The eighteen acres along US 1 was left for Mother Nature to reclaim. The Hall of Giants, Spanish Kitchen, animal barn and Stone Bridge went virtually ignored except for pilferers stealing anything small enough to carry away. Boldly people trespassed onto the property with spade in hand and carted away countless unique flora specimens so carefully chosen and lovingly planted throughout the gardens. For twenty years the gardens faded as the wild natural Florida hammock reclaimed the beautiful garden.

By the mid 1990s focus shifted to the preservation of Florida's lost history. Astute citizens of Indian River County formed the Indian River Land Trust with the sole purpose of recovering an abundance of Florida landmarks set aside by time. Because so many had fond memories of visiting McKee Jungle Garden during its prime, the site was chosen as one of the Trusts' first projects. The public responded with interest; the Trust raised just over two million dollars to purchase what remained of the gardens including an additional eighty acres of Florida wetlands. On December 1, 1995 the sale of McKee Jungle Gardens was finalized for $1.7 million.

The firm of Wallace, Roberts and Todd provided the new garden design. The first order of business was a massive clean up and inventory of just what remained of the gardens. The beautiful Stone Bridge and lily ponds had been forgotten over time, imagine the excitement when volunteers made the discovery. Once the ponds were cleared of debris, the lilies responded with gratitude and rewarded the hardworking philanthropists with an amazing display of blooms. McKee's prized orchid collection was restored and miraculously many of Sexton's original pieces began to find their way back home.

The Indian River Land Trust has raised just over nine million dollars for the McKee Garden project, an astounding accomplishment. A formal dedication ceremony was held in November 2001. McKee Botanical Garden, after almost thirty years, welcomed visitors once again. The gardens are located at 350 US 1 in Vero Beach, opened Tuesday through Sunday, except for major holidays. A small admission is charged in order to maintain the garden. The Hall of Giants, Spanish Kitchen, Outdoor Patio and two classrooms are available for special events. The Director of Operations is available to schedule rentals on Tuesday and Thursday afternoons.

For lunch in the beautiful surroundings, sisters Janie Graves Hoover and Judy Graves welcomes guests to their Hibiscus Café. Both indoor and outdoor dining opportunities are available for individuals and small groups. One could say the McKee Gardens is a Graves family tradition, the ladies' aunt Gretchen Graves served as official hostess for the 20th anniversary celebration of the gardens in 1954. Open for lunch Tuesday through Sunday, guests may stop in for a bite without paying for admission to the garden. Though what a waste it would be not to take a serene stroll through the beautiful McKee Botanical Gardens.

The gardens became whole again after almost thirty years in February 2004 with the return of the handsome Philippine mahogany table to the Hall of Giants. Sexton's Stump, once greeting guests at the gate, today welcomes visitors to Vero Beach. Speaking of Sexton, Waldo died in 1967 at the age of 82 though sources say his spirit still remains in the places he loved. It wouldn't be hard to imagine hearing the laughter of old friends gathering for one of their Saturday steak nights, hovered around the huge mahogany table telling stories of the glory days long ago. Waldo Sexton and Arthur McKee would be proud. McKee Botanical Gardens has been exquisitely revived. Much of the credit for the successful return of the beautiful garden is due to the staff who is steadfast in their care and maintenance of the facility. It is definitely a site not to be missed when "getting off the interstate" to enjoy the true Florida.

WORLD WAR II
Java Arrow Rescue

On March 23, 2002, the Indian River County Historical Society dedicated a marker at this site to commemorate the German U-boat attack on the USS Java Arrow. Attacked on May 5, 1942, by the German submarine U-333, two crewmembers died and the rest abandoned ship in a lifeboat. The Kitsis, a thirty-foot fishing boat operated by Coast Guard Auxiliary volunteers, assisted in transporting these survivors to the Fort Pierce Coast Guard Station. Two other merchant ships were torpedoed that same evening off Fort Pierce by the U-333. Vero Beach author Rody Johnson tells the story of this rescue in his 1999 publication, Different Battles. Johnson's father, Kit, owned and captained the Kitsis during this mission.

A1A in south Indian River County at the St. Lucie county line, Indian River County
IR17 ~ GPS Coordinates: 27.561467, -80.323017

The Cape Canaveral Lighthouse within view lends a feeling of security to those ordered to patrol the Florida Straits. Though this was not the case in the submarine infested waters of World War II. In fact the Florida Straits provided the perfect target area. The channel was narrow and deep with nearly fifty miles between this site and the closest boat station.

Small Auxiliary Coast Guard vessels patrolled this area without the benefit of lighting. The risk was unfathomable. Chances were that the small boats would be rammed by merchant vessels, shot by Navy gun crews if mistaken for enemy vessels or sent to a watery grave as a result of damaging torpedo fire. The Auxiliary boats were ordered to patrol the shipping lanes from St. Augustine to the Jupiter Lighthouse from dusk to dawn, however to remain as close as possible to shore. Using these directives the Auxiliary could respond to distress calls and rescue survivors while maintaining the safety of their own vessel and crew.

German *U-boat 333* left port La Pallice on March 30, 1942 under the able command of Peter-Erich Cremer. Commander Cremer was under orders to the Bethel Shoal buoy. The mission was to sink United States and Allied ships using the seventeen torpedoes Cremer had at his disposal. The two hundred-foot German submarine arrived just off the buoy after four thousand miles and thirty-six days at sea. Commander Cremer searched the horizon through binoculars to observe a calm quiet sea. The solitude would not last; the calm was soon broken.

Kit Johnson volunteered with the United States Coast Guard Auxiliary along the shore not far from his home. His small boat, the *Kitsis*, was basically used as a ruse to have Germans believe Navy sub chasers heavily patrolled the area. The *Kitsis* was unarmed and had little idea what to do if he saw a German submarine conning tower break the surface. Though more importantly, Johnson and the *Kitsis* were to rescue sailors forced to abandon ship. Without regard for personal danger Auxiliary crews rescued more than one hundred fifty crewmen as a result of German submarine sinkings during a two-week period in May of 1942.

During the wee hours of the morning on May 5th, Kit Johnson observed magnificent sunbursts of light in the distance. At 0543 the unescorted *Java Arrow* was struck by the first of two torpedoes fired from *U-boat 333*. The first missile hit port side about fifteen feet above the keel just behind the bridge. The second torpedo slammed into the port side some ten feet above the keel completely destroying the engine room and killing two watch officers instantly. A call to abandon ship was sounded and within thirty minutes the surviving crew was loaded into two lifeboats.

Kit Johnson, without hesitation, hurried to the scene. Upon arrival Johnson and his crew hauled twenty-two burned and bleeding men into the *Kitsis*. By that time the *USS PC-483* had also arrived plucking the remainder of the survivors from the turbulent waters. The *Java Arrow* survivors were taken to the Fort Pierce Coast Guard Station. The overloaded *Kitsis* was very near sinking herself by the time they arrived at Fort Pierce.

The United States Coast Guard sent an officer to the *Java Arrow* to assess the damage and they determined that the tanker could be salvaged. Two tugs the *Ontario* and *Bafshe* were sent to bring her in with the assistance of fourteen crewmen. The anchor chain was severed using an acetylene torch and after nearly four days the *Java Arrow* arrived at Port Everglades. She was turned over the United State Maritime Commission for repair in June 1942. The *Java Arrow* returned to service the next year, however now she took to sea under a new name, the *Kerry Patch*.

In the North Atlantic just west of the Scilly Isles off the coast of England, *U-boat 333*'s luck at sea came to an end. The British sloop *HMS Starling* and frigate *HMS Loch Killin* dropped depth charges disabling the German submarine. *U-boat 333* would never see the surface again. There were no survivors. Commander Hans Fiedler and forty-five crewmembers were lost with her.

Peter-Erich Cremer spent the last days of World War II in British captivity, remaining there for a month after the surrender. He went on to become a respected businessman after the war. Kit Johnson eventually was held in a prison of his own, though not one of cells and bars. Alzheimer's Disease ravaged his brain until memories of his heroism and kindness could no longer be recalled. Fortunately Kit shared his memories of the *Java Arrow* rescue with son Rody who compiled them into a 1999 publication entitled, *Different Battles*. A wonderful tribute to a remarkable man; obviously written with love from his son.

End Notes

[1] feather

[2] study of birds

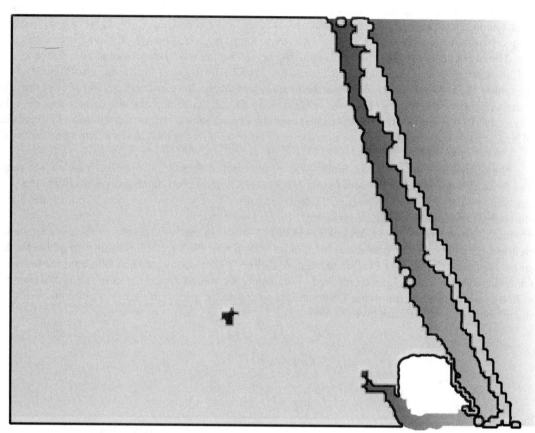

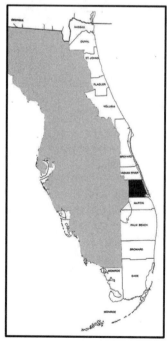

St. Lucie County

ST. LUCIE VILLAGE

Located on the Indian River opposite a natural inlet which shoaled about 1911. Pre-Columbian Ais Indians left numerous middens and mounds. After the Second Seminole War settlers homesteaded the area under the Armed Occupation Act of 1842. In 1849, a small band of Seminoles killed James Barker and looted his homes. Ft. Capron, established 1850-59, was the eastern terminus of military road called the Capron Trail. Active supporters of the Confederacy were led by James Paine. He and wife Johanna are buried in the St. Lucie School yard. The oldest standing house in St. Lucie County was built by Susan and William Russell in 1873. The railroad reached here in 1894 bringing politicians and sportsmen who built winter homes. In 1961 the Village was incorporated to protect residential character. Placed on the National Record of Historic Places in 1989.

Off US 1, Chamberlain Blvd, St. Lucie
SL1 ~ GPS Coordinates: 27.489717, -80.339600

St. Lucie Village did not begin as a settlement at all but as Fort Capron. The fortification, built in 1850, provided defense against the Third Seminole War. The Village extends along what is today Indian River Drive along the Indian River Lagoon, then to the FEC Railroad tracks and Chamberlin Boulevard.

No sign of Fort Capron remains today and the remnants of St. Lucie Village consists of thirty historical buildings. The structures vary with the scenery of 19th century Victorians to architecture referred to as Frame Vernacular. One can see throughout the neighborhood glimpses of the past still existing today. Indian River Lagoon provided much to the early settlers. Not only a source for food, they depended on the river system for transportation. The Ais Indians were perhaps the very first snow birds when they made winter camps at the mouth of what was later known as Barker Creek. Oddly enough the Ais would spend the hot summer months on the barrier islands where a constant sea breeze cooled the air and offered a respite from the sultry intercoastal. Then as the winter dawned, the season changed from thunderstorm ridden evenings to drier milder temperatures also then disease carrying mosquitoes were by far less numerous.

Major James Paine was stationed at Fort Capron for his last tour of duty. He became so enamored with the place, Paine decided to homestead there. He managed to obtain forty acres on the Indian River only one mile south of the fort. Paine sent for his family around 1857 and over the next twenty years began promoting St. Lucie as a "Sportsman's Paradise". Paine rented rooms to visiting sport enthusiasts for $3.00 per night.

Telephone inventor and gifted teacher of deaf, Alexander Graham Bell seeking solace brought his family to nearby Taylor Creek. In fact, the Bell and Paine families were neighbors. Soon others were attracted to the area including Mathew Quay, Republican Senator from Pennsylvania. His family was also neighbors of the Paines but their quaint little winter retreat was expansive. Quay added a private railroad stop to accommodate his wealthy friends. Representative Quay's associates began arriving aboard private railroad cars. Of course, as the great steam locomotives sped over the tracks just outside the fabulous retreat built for the wealthy, the entire dwelling would tremble with the vibration of the passing Pullman cars. Today much smoother diesel powered trains still rattle the china in the houses of St. Lucie Village.

Quay's cronies were so taken with the St. Lucie area that they formed the St. Lucie Club. Ten political allies joined together in 1902 to create the club, establishing St. Lucie as the headquarters for national Republican politics. Hattie Chamberlin arrived as a visitor from Kansas City, Missouri and was instantly taken with the area.

Immediately she had a vision of what the St. Lucie Village could be. It was the 1920s and the Dixie Highway had only recently been completed; Hattie imagined a bridge to North Hutchinson Island and set about making it a reality. Unfortunately while construction was still in process, the devastating hurricane of 1928 lay waste to her unfinished bridge and all of Hattie Chamberlin's plans collapsed. Her efforts were not completely wasted; St. Lucie Village had a boulevard extending to Indian River Lagoon. It was named in honor of Hattie Chamberlin.

Since Hattie's days development schemes have come and gone. The most traumatic being proposed a steel mill to be built on the bank of Indian River Lagoon. The inhabitants of St. Lucie Village banded together and in 1961, incorporated. They became the Town of St. Lucie Village and successfully defeated the steel mill proposal.

Though the village has thus far avoided transitions that would forever alter the ambiance of the neighborhood, change may be inevitable. Property values are steadily increasing along with taxes; insurance rates influenced by tropical weather systems continue to soar and all this combined make it difficult for the village to remain unchanged. Let's hope that St. Lucie Village can continue as it has for generations maintaining the quaint feeling of old world Florida, far too precious to lose.

FORT CAPRON

1850-1859
Erected July 4th 1925
By
Cora Stickney Harper chapter
Daughters of the American Revolution

Marking site of Fort Capron

At the foot of Chamberlain Blvd, on the Indian River, Fort Pierce
SL2 ~ GPS Coordinates: 27.490000, -80.336283

FORT CAPRON MARKER

Fort Capron was actually built during peacetime. Major Benjamin Kendrick Pierce was called upon to construct the fortification in response to the murder of a trader named Barker by the Seminole. Major Pierce, whose brother was to be United States 14th President Franklin Pierce, had been assigned to the area in order to escort the Seminole Indians to reservations in Oklahoma.

By this time Florida had endured two Seminole Wars and with the murder of Barker feared that the Indians were about to rise again. The Seminole were the only Native American tribe to never surrender nor sign a peace treaty with the United States government. The last Seminole War had ended in 1842, to waylay any attempted attacks Fort Capron was built.

The fort was located at what we call today St. Lucie Village on the banks of the Indian River four miles north of St. Lucie Inlet. Constructed of sabal and palmetto logs with a sweet water[1] spring nearby. Associated with the fort was the Capron Trail, which served to link Major Pierce's bastion to other military forts both to the west and south. Fort Capron saw no Indian uprisings but the Seminole erupted for one last stand in 1855. Largely the conflict was over land and the white man's constant encroaching on Indian territory pushing them further and further from the sea. By the time the Third Seminole War ended in 1858 less than two hundred Indians remained in Florida. Most disappeared into the Everglades and became shadow warriors.

The area of Fort Capron was said to be mild of climate, abundant with fruit, game and fish and very accessible to transportation along the river. The soldiers feasted on the bounty from the ocean: fish, oysters, and green sea turtles were staples in their diets along with large game such as deer and bear from the forest. Fowl including duck, turkey and snipe were plentiful at least during the winter months. The menu was quite extensive and though camp life is never easy, there was enough to eat. Most importantly it was said that there was absolutely no disease. Amazing compared to other semi-tropical locations where mosquitoes spread yellow fever bringing down entire communities. In fact it was said that a healing quality clung to the place.

Fort Capron with its pleasant climate and healthful atmosphere later became a haven for sportsmen and persons suffering from ill health. The climate expulsed all coughs, colds and rheumatism and the hills beyond the intercoastal waterway barred the spread of malarial and yellow fever so rampant near the fresh water swamps. The trade winds breathed a chlorinated vapor from the sea, which provided a unique sanitary source.

Fort Capron was much more than a soldier's base. It was a safe haven that protected life and provided for those it sheltered.

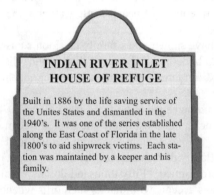

INDIAN RIVER INLET HOUSE OF REFUGE

Built in 1886 by the life saving service of the Unites States and dismantled in the 1940's. It was one of the series established along the East Coast of Florida in the late 1800's to aid shipwreck victims. Each station was maintained by a keeper and his family.

Atlantic Bach Blvd, across from Pepper Park, Fort Pierce Inlet Shores
SL3 ~ GPS Coordinates: 27.499365, -80.302780

The Indian River Inlet House of Refuge was built in 1885, according to the Department of Interior. Henry B. Archibald was named the second keeper on June 3, 1887. It was during his watch that one of the most fateful shipwrecks occurred, the *Panama,* fateful that is for the people living in the little town nearby.

It was deep into the fall on October 28, 1887, a Friday, when a four hundred fifty-foot Spanish merchant vessel went aground on the reef just two hundred yards off Sebastian in the wee hours of the morning. She departed New York with a crew of fifty-four, laden with fifty thousand dollars in cargo, destined for Havana and Central America.

The *Panama* listed at anchor as her crew worked feverishly to save their floundering ship. In an effort to free her from the coral snare, Master Luciana Alcatena ordered the entire cargo jettisoned into the briny deep. Sixty boxes of lamps, clocks, leather and calico; crates of dishes, cutlery, canvas and unbleached sheeting; even furniture, a sewing machine, a few barrels of whiskey and wine were included in the payload thrown overboard. One thousand barrels of potatoes, two hundred containers of lard, five hundred five-gallon cans of kerosene and turpentine, one hundred-fifty sacks of flour each weighing one hundred fifty pounds, several barrels of butter and apples were among the stores the crew was forced to toss. Various other items such as baled hay, pencils, one thousand syringes and one hundred forty-four gold watches completed the cargo manifest.

The wreckage would eventually extend along a four to five mile stretch of beach. As the goods began washing up on the beach, Henry Archibald was one of the first to arrive on the scene. As Keeper of the House of

Refuge, Archibald first noted that the *Panama* did not fly a flag of distress. But when he noticed the crew dispatching cargo, he quickly leapt to action.

Henry Archibald immediately issued an order that all non-perishable goods were to remain on the beach. Perishable items were to be taken from the surf first and would be sold. Salvagers began amassing the lost cargo to await the insurance agent. Thomas Eels, New York Insurance Company's agent would come from Jacksonville to manage the claim.

Before daylight, people began to gather on the beach and Archibald's edict went unheeded. Someone cracked a cask of wine and the party began. The people of this area were impoverished, they had little or nothing and to see the supplies washing up on the shore was like a gift from God. People came from far and wide, still in the dark of early morning. It was written in the local newspaper, "Folks dried the gingham (or calico) and used it for everything; clothes, curtains and tablecloths, everything looked just alike."

Henry Archibald was highly criticized for his handling of the shipwreck. Archibald described his duty thus, "My first duty at a wreck is to attend to the safety of human life. This I did, scarcely closing my eyes for forty-eight hours, and foremost man in the surf whenever a landing was made from the stranded vessel. The duty next in importance is to protect the revenues of the United States; but in this case no foreign goods were thrown overboard. Next it was my duty to protect as far as I could all property cast ashore. This I did as far as it was possible for one man to overlook four or five miles of beach while watching the stranded vessel and the safety of her crew."

Some of the salvaged items have shown up as family heirlooms passed down from generation to generation. The Kroegel family laid claim to bone-handled cutlery, "Ironwood" dishes of which plates and a platter remain in the family to this day. The Cain family managed the sewing machine, with it and the salvaged canvas made sails for Paul Kroegel's ships.

Just before sunrise the *Panama* managed to be freed from the reef. There are varying stories regarding how the ship managed to get off the rocks, but most likely she floated free at high tide. Once she was released from her rocky snare, a much lighter *Panama* without her cargo, set out for Havana.

While the shipwreck was certainly devastating for the *Panama* captain and crew, it was a windfall for local citizens. The local newspaper proclaimed, "Fifty thousand dollars worth of goods are not cast on the Indian River country every day, but she always accepts with thanks such gifts whenever given. Come again—if you must wreck."

Fortunately no lives were lost in this wreck and the only loser was most probably the insurance company. Henry Archibald and the House of Refuge did their jobs well; this time the shipwreck sailed free. The Indian River House of Refuse became part of the Department of Interior in 1948.

FORT PIERCE
1838-1842

Erected July 4th 1925 by Cora Stickney Harper Chapter, Daughters of the American Revolution. Marking the Site of Fort Pierce.

St. Lucie County Historical Museum, 414 Seaway Dr., Ft. Pierce
SL4 ~ GPS Coordinates: 27.459717, -80.316650

Born in Hillsborough, New Hampshire on August 29, 1790, Benjamin Kendrick Pierce hailed from a well to do Mayflower family. His father passed along to his eldest son his dedication to military duty with valorous missions at Bunker Hill and eight years of distinguished service to his country in the militia. Benjamin's younger brother Franklin emulated their father's civic duties. The Pierce patriarch served in the New Hampshire Legislature for thirteen years and was a two-term governor. Franklin Pierce began his political career as a state representative, senator, Brigadier-General in the United States Mexican War and the fourteenth President of the United States.

Benjamin Pierce enrolled at Dartmouth to study law. When the War of 1812 began, he immediately left school and enlisted in the United States Army as a Lieutenant of Artillery. Pierce distinguished himself and rose in rank throughout a thirty-eight year military career.

Though Benjamin Pierce met with success in the United States Army, his personal life was wrought with tragedy. From the age of twenty-six until forty-eight he married three times. Unfortunately all three wives died after a few short years of marriage. At the age of forty-eight, Pierce was responsible for the care of six children whom he seldom saw because of his military duties. Financial difficulties plagued the motherless family. His personal situation caused much inner strife and worry lasting many years for Benjamin Pierce.

Pierce received orders to the Florida territory three different times. The first assignment brought him to Fort San Carlos de Barrancas near what is today Pensacola. The United States had purchased the Florida territory from Spain two years before his arrival in 1821. Pierce was to establish forts to help protect the gulf coastline.

The second trip into the Florida territory was Fort Defiance near the Indian village of Micanopy in August 1836. Osceola was leading a war party and Pierce with his men defeated a band led by the chief. Governor Richard K. Call led the battle at Wahoo Swamp south of Withlacoochee River Cove. Colonel Pierce received high praise for the way he conducted himself during the engagement.

Benjamin Pierce received his third and final assignment to Florida in late 1837. The remaining Seminole refused to leave their native Florida and be displaced west; they were threatening soldiers and settlements. The army hacked their way through virgin forest resulting in passable trails, which later became roads. The United States Navy led by Lieutenant L. M. Powell joined Colonel Pierce to select a site along the Indian River to build a fortification. Pierce boarded Powell's ship and they sailed the river along with topographical engineer, Joseph E. Johnston and Dr. Leitner. They arrived at an ideal inlet on the last day of 1837 at four o'clock in the afternoon. The soldiers camped there for several days until January 2, 1838 when the group moved to the west side of the river four miles south. The first night in camp was described as:

"Nothing occured to disturb the quiet of the night, except the wolves in the neighboring forrest responding howl with howl as they threatened one another. At one time the reflection of the heavens of a distant Indian fire in the woods served to begile a few minutes of admiration, as the contrast between the part of the sky which was illumined, and that of the shade, was exceedingly beautiful."

A blockhouse was built and a crude wooden sign deemed the fortification Fort Pierce, for their revered leader. The fort remained active through the Second Seminole War ending in 1842. Then the fort was abandoned and was reduced to ashes in December of 1843. Ironically soldiers, William T. Sherman and Joseph E. Johnston, who would come to prominence during the Civil War, served under Colonel Pierce. Sherman would rise to the rank of an infamous Union General and likewise Johnston, on the opposing side, a Confederate General.

Benjamin Kendrick Pierce passed away in New York on April 1, 1850. He was fifty-nine years old. The fact that Fort Pierce was built to decimate the Seminole and in the shadow of a great Ais burial mound containing the remains of a vanquished people is ironic.

The site of Fort Pierce is today a park open daily, which can be visited at no charge. The state historical marker that designated this site for its great importance was repeatedly vandalized and eventually stolen. A replica has been placed at the St. Lucie County Historical Museum. The Museum is open Tuesday through Sunday, a modest admission fee is charged.

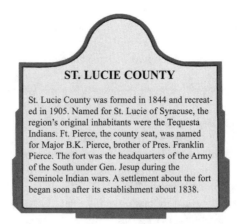

ST. LUCIE COUNTY

St. Lucie County was formed in 1844 and recreated in 1905. Named for St. Lucie of Syracuse, the region's original inhabitants were the Tequesta Indians. Ft. Pierce, the county seat, was named for Major B.K. Pierce, brother of Pres. Franklin Pierce. The fort was the headquarters of the Army of the South under Gen. Jesup during the Seminole Indian wars. A settlement about the fort began soon after its establishment about 1838.

200 Indian River Drive at Courthouse, Fort Pierce
SL5 ~ GPS Coordinates: 27.446583, -80.322567

Initially named for Saint Lucie of Syracuse or Santa Lucia by the Spanish in 1565, St. Lucie County has endured a long, interesting history. It is said that Pedro Menendez de Aviles bestowed the name in honor of the Roman Catholic feast day, December 13th in honor of Saint Lucia on which the original construction of a fort was built soon after their arrival.

As the Spanish Fleet sailed the coast in the seventeenth and eighteenth centuries the inevitable happened; savage hurricanes battered and bashed the great Spanish galleons until the ocean floor was a graveyard of broken ships and lost lives. Also scattered across the sandy bottom of the deep blue was an estimated three billion dollars in treasure. Imagine the white sand adorned with emerald green stones, shining diamonds, gold and silver. Of course, the name Treasure Coast came when the occasional silver coin or gleaming gem would wash up on the beach but over the years the vast majority remained undiscovered.

In 1964, famed treasure hunter Mel Fisher discovered the *Nuestra Senora de las Nieves* and approximately five million dollars in artifacts. It is well known that this is but a drop in the bucket. The tales of treasure laden ships call, like the sirens of mythology, to adventurers and divers some of whom spend their entire lives searching the murky deep for her bounty.

In 1810, St. Lucie County was simply called East Florida. For virtually the next one hundred years county lines and names varied so many times, it is wonder that any county citizen knew exactly where they lived.

Edgartown was the first settlement that would later become Fort Pierce. Named for Edgar Bowman, grandson of an early settler, the location would be today where North 2nd Street converges with Avenue D. The initial buildings were constructed from wood physically swam in by construction workers.

The Second Seminole War began in 1835 and it was to be one of combatants in that war who would lend his name to a newly established fort. Lieutenant Colonel Benjamin Kendrick Pierce, brother of President Franklin Pierce, commanded the 1st Regiment of Artillery and after spending several sleepless nights beside the river in 1838, his men were instructed to build a blockhouse or fort. Four miles south of the Indian River Inlet, the men erected a fortification from palmetto logs. In honor of their commander the site would bear his name, Fort Pierce. The fort was conveniently close to a natural fresh water spring and near an Ais Indian midden. Fort Pierce was abandoned at the conclusion of the war.

Dr. Weedon, a settler in the area, took control of the former Fort Pierce blockhouse as temporary housing for new arrivals. Unfortunately, a kitchen fire claimed the palmetto structure during the night of December 12, 1843 and it was never rebuilt.

Another community was established that very same year called Susanna. The settlement became the first county seat and was located some three and half miles from what would be present day Fort Pierce. This settlement lasted a little longer than the initial blockhouse but by 1849, due to Indian uprisings along the river, the settlers abandoned their homes and fled to St. Augustine in fear.

On December 29, 1900, a county notice was publicly posted summoning all registered voters to appear on February 2, 1901 to elect a municipal government. The first order of the day was incorporation; fifty-four of sixty-six men voted in favor of the effort. Fort Pierce was incorporated and named the county seat. St. Lucie County can lay claim to four Florida Supreme Court Justices, including Judge James Alderman who is the only person to have sat at all levels of the state court system beginning with County Judge.

Even today as visitors travel the byways of St. Lucie County, one can observe miles of grapefruit and orange groves. Countless family owned fruit stands have stood vigil by the side of road, some claiming the same spot of ground for fifty years. A bit of nostalgia creeps into your mind as you browse through Florida tourist souvenirs, fresh citrus and paper cups with a sip of orange juice to encourage sales.

St. Lucie County is a historical haven amidst lovely modern day shops, art galleries and delectable restaurants. Cattle ranches and citrus groves still dot the landscape of the interior while the intercoastal offers the calm of a river and the salty sea spray with white sand beaches of the ocean. Sun, surf, the tangy sweet smell of orange blossoms on the breeze as well as emerald green inland acres have something to offer everyone; a bit of old world Florida in the splendor of today.

ST. LUCIE ART DISPLAY

GOVERNOR'S HOUSE
DANIEL THOMAS McCARTY, JUNIOR

Was born in Ft. Pierce, St. Lucie County, January 18, 1912, was educated here and at the Univ. of Florida. He served in the 1937, 1939 Legislatures and was Speaker of the 1941 House of Representatives. In WWII, he was a Colonel in the U.S. Seventh Army. He was elected Governor in 1952 and died September 28, 1953. He attended St. Andrew's Episcopal Church across Indian River Drive and was buried from there in Palms Cemetery, Ankona.

300 Indian River Drive, on grounds of house, Fort Pierce
SL6 ~ GPS Coordinates: 27.445450, -80.322500

Born in Fort Pierce, Florida on January 18, 1912, Daniel Thomas McCarty was highly regarded both in his hometown and throughout the state. The young man attended public school at Delaware Avenue and excelled as captain of the football team, editor of the yearbook and vice-president of his senior class. McCarty's 1930 yearbook heralded the golden boy as "The captain of our school ship of state—and how able a captain." He went on to graduate from the University of Florida in 1934.

After graduation Dan McCarty returned to Fort Pierce as a cattleman and citrus grower. He settled into married life with Ollie Brown and the couple had three children. It was at that time the world was plunged into war. McCarty joined the United States Army and earned the rank of Colonel during World War II. With valor and bravery, he was decorated with the Bronze Star, Purple Heart, Legion of Merit and French Croix de Guerre.

After the war, Daniel McCarty returned to St. Lucie County and was elected to the Florida House of Representatives in 1937. He was reelected twice more and in 1941 at the age of twenty-nine became Speaker of the House. Known as a reformer, McCarty enacted major improvements for Florida during his tenure, including: educational scholarships for future teachers, restructuring the highway department, increased teacher salaries and pensions, advancement in programs for disabled citizenry and initiating a state construction plan. McCarty was known for his progressive ideas concerning state highway turnpikes, centralized spending and modernization.

McCarty threw his hat into the ring for Florida's highest office against incumbent Fuller Warren in 1948. Warren defeated McCarty with the assistance of fellow rural politicians in north Florida. The governor was eccentric but did manage to institute a sales tax to finance new public construction. Warren's good points were vastly overshadowed by his links to organized crime, which drew him to the brink of impeachment. By the end of his term, Warren had lost all political credibility. A defeated man, Fuller Warren crept away from Tallahassee frustrated and bankrupt.

McCarty easily won the next election as Florida's governor. He finally ascended the office in January 1953, unfortunately after little more than one month in office tragedy struck on February 25. The newly elected governor was stricken with a debilitating heart attack. He never recovered and on September 28, 1953 Florida's 31st governor passed away. Governor Daniel Thomas McCarty was laid to rest at Palms Cemetery near Ankona, Florida.

Daniel T. McCarty High School, built in 1954 at Fort Pierce, was named in his honor; deservedly so.

**THE GOVERNOR'S HOUSE
HISTORICAL MARKER**

End Notes

[1] Fresh water

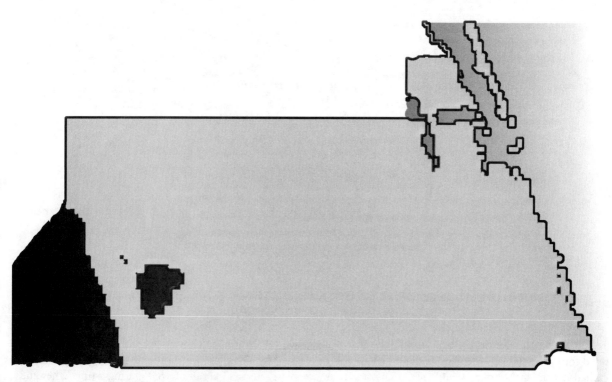

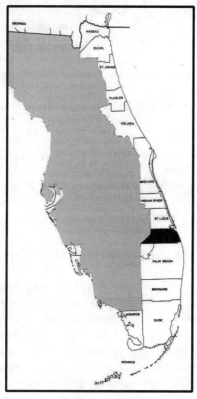

Martin County

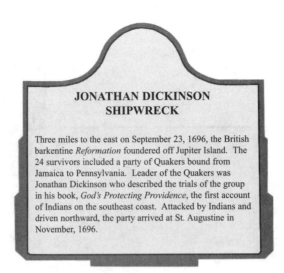

JONATHAN DICKINSON SHIPWRECK

Three miles to the east on September 23, 1696, the British barkentine *Reformation* foundered off Jupiter Island. The 24 survivors included a party of Quakers bound from Jamaica to Pennsylvania. Leader of the Quakers was Jonathan Dickinson who described the trials of the group in his book, *God's Protecting Providence*, the first account of Indians on the southeast coast. Attacked by Indians and driven northward, the party arrived at St. Augustine in November, 1696.

Jonathan Dickinson State Park (16450 SE Federal Hwy (US 1), in parking lot, Tequesta M1 ~ GPS Coordinates: 27.199650, -80.165817

Jonathan Dickinson, a youthful Quaker merchant, set out from Jamaica with his wife and infant son destined for Philadelphia. The trip, on the barkentine *Reformation,* would entail much more than the group had bargained for and the journey would take almost a year to complete. It was the fall of 1696 during a time when the weather channel did not report coming storms and many did not realize that fall was hurricane season.

Dickinson, his family and some twenty others aboard the *Reformation* struggled to weather a torrential storm when unfortunately their large barkentine began to break up. The ship's timbers moaned and creaked under the strain of the fierce storm. Waves crashed over the railing sweeping away anything unchained into the darkened abyss. As the barkentine surrendered to the fury of the tempest, consigned to the briny deep, her passengers clung to floating debris in an attempt to survive. The unlucky group washed ashore at Hobe Sound near Jupiter on September 23, 1696. Jonathan Dickinson meticulously recorded the events that followed the shipwreck recounting the horrors that the group endured.

The exhausted band managed to build a makeshift shelter, which provided barely more than respite from the blazing sun. They helplessly watched as Ais Indians pillaged everything of use from the Dickinson boat. Most of their clothing, with the exception of undergarments, was taken leaving the puritans all but naked against the elements. The group was herded like cattle into a leaky canoe, beaten with sticks at any hesitation. They were fed barely edible fare of dried fish and berries. Once the weary travelers arrived at the Ais Village, they discovered another band of shipwreck survivors. Five men and one woman had managed to make landfall from their doomed ship, *Nantwitch*.

The old Casseekey[1] was angered to find that the Dickinson's were Nickaleers[2] after examining their belongings. They denied their country in fear of their lives. A torrential rain flooded the village and the entire tribe including the band of shipwreck survivors were forced to relocate. The Dickinson party was continually tortured and starved when after approximately six weeks they were finally released. The thirty-one survivors began the arduous two hundred and thirty-mile trek to civilization at St. Augustine without food or adequate clothing. The weather took a frigid November turn, five members succumbed to exhaustion and exposure.

They managed to get several leaky canoes and hand made oars, easing their travel somewhat. After a week of travel, Dickinson's party arrived at an Indian town near what is today Cape Canaveral. Unfortunately, Indians made off with several of their canoes forcing the group to continue their journey at a much slower pace on foot. On November 15, the debilitated party arrived at the St. Augustine Lighthouse Keeper's cottage.

The Spanish governor took pity on the shipwreck survivors, allowing them to remain in St. Augustine for two weeks to recover from their torture and travel. They set sail for the St. Mary's garrison in Georgia where the Dickinson party sought shelter for several days. The traveler's journey included stops along the way at St. Catherine and Savannah until a brutal winter storm impeded their progress at Calibogue Sound in Carolina. By this time it was the eve of Christmas and South Carolina's Governor Blake took in the harried group. They were boarded in the home of Margaret Beamor near Charlestown.

On March 18, 1697, Dickinson and twenty-five shipwreck survivors finally continued their original pilgrimage to Philadelphia. The savage expedition took two additional weeks and claimed yet another life along the way. Dickinson returned to the mercantile business in Philadelphia and completed a journal detailing the shipwreck ordeal called, "God's Protecting Providence." This work was the definitive portrait of life in Florida for its time. Jonathan Dickinson died in 1722.

Today, Jonathan Dickinson State Park located north of Palm Beach pays tribute to the stranded family. Comprised of approximately eleven thousand five hundred acres, the park is alive with countless species of wildlife. Activities include camping, canoeing, hiking and bicycling, picnicking, fresh as well as saltwater fishing and guided tours of the Loxahatchee River. A small fee allows visitors access from 8:00 am until sundown, every day of the year.

**GILBERT'S BAR
HOUSE OF REFUGE**

Only one remaining of nine on Florida east coast commissioned in 1875 for the U.S. Life-Saving Service. Keepers provided shelter, food, clothing, and transportation to survivors of shipwrecks and storms at sea. In U.S. Coast Guard Service through WWI and WW II. Acquired as Maritime Museum in 1955 by Martin County Historical Society. Listed on National Register of Historic Places. Restored 1976.

**301 NE MacArthur Boulevard, Hutchinson Island
M2 ~ GPS Coordinates: 27.003700, -80.101633**

The Treasury Department issued an appeal for bids to build ten Life Saving Stations along the Florida East Coast in the summer of 1875. The deadline for applications was Tuesday, June 20. Albert Blaisdell was awarded the contract for five of the stations; Gilberts Bar House of Refuge was one of the five Blaisdell built.

Located at St. Lucie Rocks on Hutchinson Island, two miles north of Gilberts Bar Inlet; the station was completed at a cost of $2,900 on March 10, 1876. The station was often the deciding factor between survival and doom for shipwrecked travelers. When storms turned a tranquil sea into a boiling cauldron many a sailor found himself afloat and fearing the worst. The House of Refuge keeper would board his surf boat as the storm abated and search for survivors many times with only the light of the moon or an oil fed lantern.

Those fortunate enough to be plucked from certain death in the embrace of briny deep were given shelter at Gilberts Bar. A hot meal, tot of rum, warm blankets and a dry bed were provided for the unfortunate guests in the third floor dormitory. Most of the shipwreck survivors remained only a few days until other means of transport arrived.

Samuel F. Bunker was keeper at Gilberts Bar on April 19, 1886 when the brigantine *J. H. Lane* was stranded on the reef. Gale force winds tossed the three hundred seventy-one ton ship from Searsmont, Maine carrying a cargo of molasses worth over thirteen thousand dollars and she was compelled to anchor and wait out the storm. Fourteen and half miles from the Jupiter Lighthouse, her cable parted and the *Lane* found herself high and dry on the rocky bottom at low tide.

Bunker discovered the wreck at 9:00 am but was not able to reach the site until noon. Her crew abandoned the brigantine for a small skiff, which immediately capsized due to the swelling surf. The desperate crew clung helplessly to the overturned skiff, praying for rescue. Henry Whitlock, the ship's steward, exhausted from the ordeal lost his hold and vanished under the brutal waves; he was the only casualty. The *J. H. Lane* was a total loss; the weary survivors were sheltered at Gilberts Bar for six days.

Quite possibly the most popular of all Gilberts Bar keeper was in fact, the wife of Hubert W. Bessey, Susan C. Corbin Bessey or Aunt Sue as she was affectionately called. They were the first white settlers of what is today Stuart, serving as keepers of Gilberts Bar for twelve years, longer than any other in the position.

Aunt Sue made the House of Refuge a home and it was there that she entertained friends who arrived by boat for afternoon teas. She kept the Bessey family belongings all about her or her "pretty things" as they were called, lending a sense of comfort and calm to the often strained atmosphere. Some people say the welcoming spirit of Aunt Sue still clings to the House of Refuge at Gilberts Bar. Axel H. Johansen was to be the last appointed keeper when he served his second tenure from May 4, 1910 through November 22, 1918. The Coast Guard assumed responsibility of the station in 1918.

The Coast Guard continued active service of Gilberts Bar until 1941 when the Navy began utilizing the facility as a patrol station. However, due to lack of funding the Gilberts Bar Refuge Station closed its doors for the final time in 1945. The facility was turned over to the Department of the Interior in 1952.

Gilberts Bar House of Refuge is the last of its kind still standing on Florida's East Coast. Today the property is maintained and operated by the Martin County Historical Society as a museum. The house has been completely restored to reflect the cozy atmosphere of her most popular resident, Aunt Sue Bessey. The museum is open daily, except for major holidays, with only a small admission fee to assist with the maintenance and upkeep of the beautiful little cottage beside St. Lucie Rocks on Hutchinson Island. Gilberts Bar was a lifeline for many a sailor who might have otherwise been doomed to a watery grave.

End Notes

1 Ais Chief
2 English

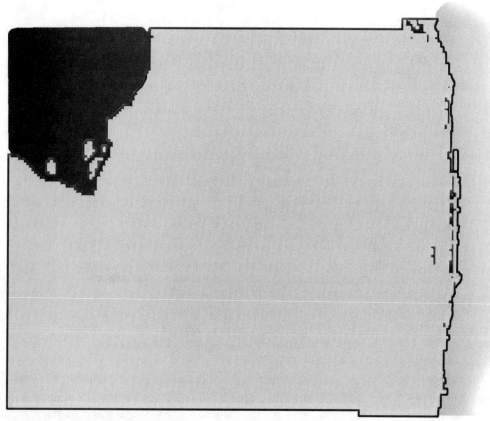

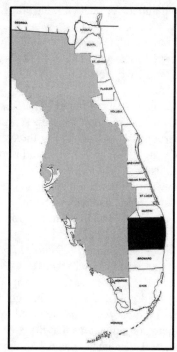

Palm
Beach
County

DIVE INTO HISTORY

These shipwrecked iron cannons and anchor were uncovered in July of 1987 just 2000 yards east of this spot in 10 feet of water off Jupiter Inlet.

Archives and research link these maritime remains to the Spanish "Aviso" vessel named "San Miguel de Archangel", bound for Spain, with its last port being Havana, Cuba. In December of 1659 the San Miguel foundered and wrecked off the river "Jeaga" (Jupiter Inlet). The thirty-three surviving sailors lived with the local "Jeaga" Native American until rescued by a vessel dispatched out of St. Augustine. The San Miguel de Archangel was one of the many ships lost carrying precious cargo of gold and silver to Spain. Modern archaeological recoveries include ships' rigging as well as Spanish coins and bullion. Mined and minted in Potosi, Bolivia: Lima, Peru; Mexico City; and Bogata and Cartagena Columbia.

Lighthouse Park, Jupiter
PB1 ~ GPS Coordinates: 26.950283, -80.084833

The voyage of the *San Miguel de Archangel* began with an edict from the viceroy of Lima, Peru demanding the aviso[1] to set sail for Spain. Under Spanish law an aviso could only carry cargo of up to sixty tons and then only governmental dispatches, military supplies and provisions. The *Archangel* was not a treasure ship. The viceroy's dispatch to Spain's King Philip IV was evidence of the gold and silver quality coins minted in the New World.

The ship set sail in November of 1659 making its last port of call in the Spanish stronghold Havana, Cuba. As the *Archangel* made its way north the skies turned ebony, the brutal wind tore at the sails and the tempest churned the waves until a massive wall of water crashed down on the wooden deck. The aviso hugged the coastline, moored tight to wait out the storm.

Suddenly the force of the storm snapped the lines and drove the vessel out to sea. The *San Miguel de Archangel* floundered in the gale, taking on water. There was a call to abandon ship, the crew scrambled to escape. As the aviso disappeared beneath the tumultuous ocean, survivors struggled to shore. Thirty-three exhausted souls lay on the sand at Jupiter Inlet gasping for air and choking on briny water. The crewmen would remain in the care of the Jeaga Indians until rescued by Spaniards arriving from St. Augustine.

On a hot July day in 1985, Jupiter Inlet lifeguard Peter Leo went for a swim that would change his life. During his leisurely exercise Leo discovered, gold and silver coins, silver bars and ancient Spanish artifacts. He realized right away that help was required and put together a salvage team then made a phone call. Leo called an attorney known in salvage circles as the Treasure Sultan, David Horan of Key West.

Horan had been linked with such recognizable names as *Atocha*, *Andreadoria*, *Santa Margarita* and *Titanic*. He is thought to be the attorney authority on admiralty as it applies to treasure recovery. Peter Leo was advised to meet with Horan and decide the terms of treasure division before any salvaging began. The attorney helped Leo establish Jupiter Wreck Inc. and soon more than ten thousand gold and silver coins, gold bars and various other artifacts were recovered. The coins were dated from 1652 through 1658, hand stamped by Spanish slaves. The wreck was verified as the *San Miguel de Archangel*. There are indications that the *Archangel* spent some time salvaging the Spanish galleon *Marvillas* just off the coast of the Bahama Islands based on some of the artifacts recovered.

During the recovery process two cannon and an anchor from the wreck were brought to the surface. Years of encrustation caked the artifacts. Generously, Peter Leo donated these fabulous finds to the city of Jupiter. The state of Florida's Bureau of Archeological Research, Conservation and Collection in Tallahassee would undertake the tedious steps to clean the artifacts. It would take two years for the cannons and anchor to be restored, sand-blasted then painted with primer and an industrial quality finishing paint to protect them. The *San Miguel de Archangel* artifacts are on permanent display at the Jupiter Inlet Lighthouse Park.

Dave Horan advises that should you discover a sunken or buried treasure immediately call an attorney who specializes in admiralty as it applies to treasure recovery, such as himself. On land, a deal must be struck with the landowner and the state; in water, a claim must be filed in federal district court to establish your claim to the treasure. Modern day pirates are well skilled in snatching treasure away from unprepared finders. Horan warns that sometimes the state plays the role of the pirate.

Oddly enough the majority of the people who discover treasure of any kind are not wealthy. Most have spent everything they have just to find the treasure. Dave Horan has said that in most cases his fee is taken from a predetermined portion of the treasure usually from one-half to seven and half percent. In fact he has received everything from silver spoons to cannon balls. Mel Fischer allowed Dave to select coins as his fee for representing the *Atocha* treasure. Wonder what prize came from the *San Miguel de Archangel*?

JUPITER LIGHTHOUSE

Designed by George G. Meade, later Federal commander at Gettysburg. First lighted July 10, 1860. Dark during the War Between the States and its mechanism hidden by Southern sympathizers. Relighted June 28, 1866, it has not missed a night in over 100 years. Early keepers: Thomas Twiner, J.F. Papy, Wm. B. Davis, James A. Armour, Joseph A. Wells, Thomas Knight, Charles Seabrook. Operated by the United States Coast Guard since 1939.

US Coast Guard Station inside a gated enclosure, Jupiter
PB2 ~ GPS Coordinates: 26.948467, -80.082433

The treacherous waters of the Loxahatchee at Jupiter Inlet where the river meets the sea became the graveyard for many a sailing vessel through time. It was decided that something must be done to warn ships of the perilous shoals. The first conversations of a lighthouse began as early as 1851. Within two years a site was chosen on the north shore of the inlet, part of the Fort Jupiter Federal Reservation. Congress appropriated thirty-five thousand dollars for construction and President Franklin Pierce signed the bill approving the lighthouse construction in 1854.

Area roads were little more than Indian trails through dense vegetation and transportation via the inlet from the ocean was dubious at best. The Loxahatchee River was frequently impassable due to sand,

JUPITER LIGHTHOUSE

363

silt and vegetation. More than five hundred tons of building materials including brick and the iron stairs were stranded in the narrow shallows. The impasse required shallow draft scows be brought down the river for the remainder of the thirty-five mile trip. The process was extremely tedious. The cargo had to be first moved from one vessel to another then taken down river, however the small boats could only accommodate ten tons of materials at time. Just delivering the construction materials required fifty trips and almost a month to complete.

It seems the project was destined for trouble from the start. Once the construction materials arrived on the site the next hurdle was getting them up the forty-eight foot hill that the lighthouse was to be perched upon. Archeologists later discovered that the site was not a natural knoll at all but an Indian oyster shell midden. The strength sapping heat made work on the site arduous but the insidious mosquitoes brought on what came to be known as "Jupiter fever". Today the disease would be diagnosed as malaria. As if hardship and disease were not enough, builders were the victims of several brutal Seminole attacks. The Native American aggression accelerated, 1st Lieutenant George Gordon Meade, who designed the lighthouse as part of the Bureau of Topographical Engineers, requested Washington send firearms for the protection of the construction crew. Meade would later rise to the rank of General and defeat General Robert E. Lee at Gettysburg during the Civil War.

Seminole hostilities and the third Seminole war brought work on the lighthouse to a halt from 1856 until 1858. Once construction resumed a keeper's cottage was added with thick coquina walls to protect residents and their families from Indian attack. Workers stepped up construction schedules and the lighthouse was finally completed in 1858. Costs exceeded the budget more than twenty-five thousand dollars equaling sixty thousand eight hundred fifty-nine dollars, fifty cents. The structure rose to one hundred eight feet plus another forty-eight feet of the mound making this the tallest lighthouse on the Florida coast. The conical tower was an unpainted natural brick, which remained for fifty years then painted bright red with a black lantern around 1910. The Henry-Lepaute Company in Paris made the rotating first order Fresnel lens. The guiding beacon could be seen for almost twenty-five miles across the azure waters. The Jupiter Inlet Lighthouse gleamed across the darkened sky for the first time on July 10, 1860.

Unfortunately the light was soon extinguished when the ugly face of war rose once again. The Confederacy requested that the Jupiter light be disabled in order to make it more difficult for the Union Navy to locate and apprehend blockade runners delivering supplies. The Union sympathizing head lighthouse keeper refused to douse the light. A group of citizens and the assistant lighthouse keeper crept into the tower removing parts of the lamp and revolving mechanism, rendering the lamp useless. The parts were secretly buried in Jupiter Creek.

Captain James Armour, pilot of the federal patrol boat *Sagamore*, was chosen as the new keeper. He was instructed to recover the light apparatus, once the parts were in hand Armour took them to safety at Key West until the light could again be put into service. On June 28, 1866 the Jupiter Inlet Lighthouse shined its brilliant beam across the ebony skies once again.

Captain Armour steadfastly served the lighthouse for forty-two years. When Armour married in 1817, his bride was to be the only white woman for a distance of one hundred miles. Their daughter Katherine, the first white child born in the area, she went on to marry the next lighthouse keeper. Life at the lighthouse was difficult. Food was often in short supply. The keepers were given a certain allotment of flour, which was to last the year, but worms and weevils infested the staple long before it could be used. The keepers would hunt, fish and trade with the Indians to supplement their larders. The monotony and loneliness were probably the worst burdens in this wilderness. A boat delivered supplies of oil, paint and essentials only once a year. Several times the tragedy of a shipwreck rendering gifts washed up on the shore from the force of a storm, such as a sewing machine and several dogs; on the other hand these same shipwrecks resulted in perhaps the worst part of a keepers job, recovering bodies. A silent testament to the harsh life at the lighthouse lay just beyond the luminous glow, side by side the tiny graves of the keepers' children.

A second keeper's cottage was built in 1883. Three years later the keepers were released from rescue duties when a life saving station was built. Telegraph services were added in 1898. A piece of history was lost when the main keepers' home was reduced to a smoldering ruin in 1927. Electricity was added to the lighthouse in 1928.

One of the fiercest hurricanes in recorded history slammed into south Florida in 1928. During the brunt of the storm the lighthouse went dark as the electrical plant failed. The keeper had an injured hand at the time so he was forced to send his sixteen-year-old son into the brewing tempest and certain danger. The young man employed the old style oil lamps rotating it by hand. Imagine walking round and round through the night, hanging on for dear life as the shear power of the wind swayed the entire lighthouse. The boy shielded his face as flying glass cut into the skin of his hand and arms. Windows burst and the bulls eyes section of the lens was shattered. The lighthouse looked much like a war zone when the skies finally cleared and the winds calmed. Months would go by before repairs could be made and the wounds faded from the brave boy's body and mind.

The brilliant beacon was dimmed during World War II by order of the Coast Guard. Sentries were stationed at the lighthouse to scour the waves for periscopes or the sight of a submarine conning tower breaking the surface. Even the adept attention of the Coast Guard could not deter all attacks. Several ships were torpedoed at Jupiter Inlet and many lives were lost.

The keeper's cottage was razed in 1959 and a modernized facility was erected. Fourteen years later the Jupiter Inlet Lighthouse Station was added to the National Register of Historic Places.

In September of 1999 major renovations began on the lighthouse. The original Fresnel lens was deactivated but an optic lens flashed in its place for the duration of the restoration. It was decided that the original brick would be left exposed, however the "firehouse" red paint was removed. It was discovered that many different colors of brick were used in construction. The paint issue was reevaluated and lighthouse was eventually painted a natural brick color. The restoration was expected to take approximately eight months at a cost of eight hundred thousand dollars. Both estimations were exceeded.

The city of Jupiter sponsored a relighting ceremony in April of 2000. Thousands attended the event and once again the guiding beacon of the Jupiter Inlet Lighthouse revolved across the water. The lighthouse is owned and maintained by the United States Coast Guard. The Loxahatchee River Historical Society lead programs and tours at the facility Saturday through Wednesday of each week. A moderate fee is charged for the tours. But beware as you walk through the lighthouse. Many have reported the feeling of an icy hand on their shoulder only to turn and find no one there. Perhaps one of the original lighthouse keepers wishes to lead the tour.

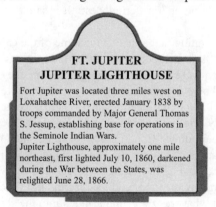

FT. JUPITER
JUPITER LIGHTHOUSE
Fort Jupiter was located three miles west on Loxahatchee River, erected January 1838 by troops commanded by Major General Thomas S. Jessup, establishing base for operations in the Seminole Indian Wars.
Jupiter Lighthouse, approximately one mile northeast, first lighted July 10, 1860, darkened during the War between the States, was relighted June 28, 1866.

800 US 1 at Bert Reynolds Park in front of Jupiter-Tequesta Chamber of Commerce, Jupiter-Tequesta
PB3 ~ GPS Coordinates: 26.940933, -80.084283

Major General Thomas Jesup defeated the Seminole Indians during the Battle of Loxahatchee with shear numbers. The men retired to a quiet spot to take a moment of respite and treat the wounded. Four days later they established Fort Jupiter on January 24, 1838.

A contingent of sixteen hundred bedraggled soldiers set up camp. The men were exhausted from cutting paths through dense semi-tropical vegetation. Most were without shoes, their feet cut and bleeding from the saw palmetto along the trail. The soldiers had little more than rags to cover their bodies, suffering the affects of exposure. General Jesup established his headquarters at Fort Jupiter but soon all hopes of healing were abandoned.

Jesup ordered his men to construct a bridge over the Loxahatchee River. The stockade surrounding what could loosely be called a fort was soon completed. The site is now known as Pennock Point and was chosen because it provided protection for the personnel on three sides. Tents soon dotted the landscape and dragoons supplied guard duty. Clothes, shoes, food and supplies arrived for the emaciated men on February 5, 1838. Unfortunately their recovery time was finished, the soldiers were ordered to take the field once again after the Seminole. They had little time to enjoy the essentials of life, which they now looked upon as luxuries. Heavy patrols covered the area from Fort Capron near New Smyrna to Fort Dallas in Miami. The route is still in use today, known as the Military Trail.

Inventor of the repeating rifle, Sam Colt showed up at Fort Jupiter on March 29, 1838. Colonel William S. Harney ordered fifty of Colt's rifles to arm his dragoons during their missions into the Everglades. Between February and March of 1838 approximately six hundred twenty-five Seminole were captured and held at Fort Jupiter eventually sending them to Oklahoma. Many of the Seminole did not survive the trip. Once Harney and Colonel William Lauderdale went after the Native Americans in the Everglades, Fort Jupiter was abandoned. Conditions were just too harsh to maintain troops in the area, when the inlet was closed with sand washed in by the force of a storm the fort was determined to be unhealthy and the troops were reassigned to other posts. The Seminole burned the fort one-month later.

On February 21, 1855 troops returned to the Jupiter area. A contingent of eighty-five officers and men were brought in for another Indian round up. In May the federal government set aside nine thousand eighty-eight acres to be known as the Jupiter Military Reservation. Part of the tract was designated for the construction of the Jupiter Inlet Lighthouse.

The original fort location was rejected and a new site was selected on a sandbar, high and dry because the inlet had been completely closed off for more than two years. The military contingent was first sent to the Jupiter area to protect the workers building the lighthouse from the rising Native American hostilities. Work on the beacon finally had to be suspended as the Third Seminole War was waged. Captured Seminole were brought back to Fort Jupiter and held there until they could be transferred west. It is said that several renegades were executed at the fort.

A story has existed for years stating that at one point some of the captive Seminole organized a stick ball game. Well into the game, with the guards distracted, several of the captives slipped away into the thick forest. It was some time before the missing men were discovered and by that time they had escaped to their hidden villages.

This second Fort Jupiter had no stockade fencing and appeared more like a tent camp than a fort. One building existed, a two-room cabin with cooking facilities that was to become the fort depot. Soldiers actually manned the second fort twice but only briefly in 1855 and again one year later. Fort Jupiter was quite possibly one of the worst duty stations a soldier could draw. Conditions were so harsh that the men often balked at having been ordered there. "Jupiter Fever" was rampant from the disease carrying mosquitoes. Today we know the disease as malaria. The horrible buzzing menace bred quite well in the often-stagnant water of the blocked inlet. The Third Seminole War ended in 1858 and Fort Jupiter was abandoned for the last time in May of that year.

Eventually every remnant of what was Fort Jupiter faded into the sands of history. Though for all purposes the fort was barely able to sustain day to day life, it was the first American "settlement" in what is now Palm Beach County. There is little mention of Fort Jupiter in the history books, however, it continues to be remembered whenever a history of the Jupiter Inlet Lighthouse is discussed. Today the historic site of Fort Jupiter is part of a modern day neighborhood. There has been a push in recent years to memorialize the site with a park.

JUPITER INLET MIDDEN I

Jupiter Inlet Midden I is an ancient shell mound built by Indians known as Jeaga. A description of these Indians by Jonathan Dickinson was first published in 1699. This shell mound is the site of the village of Hobe where the Dickinson Shipwreck victims were held captive by the Jeaga Indians in 1696.

9075 DuBois Road, Jupiter Inlet
PB4 ~ GPS Coordinates: 26.943233, -80.075367

In the days before Spanish occupation in southeastern Florida a peaceful Native American tribe went about their day to day routine. Their numbers were small, probably two thousand at the most, considering the great numbers that would come after them and they were called Jeagas[2]. Similar to their neighboring Ais tribe, the two were most likely related. Much of what we know of the Jeagas people comes from the vivid descriptions of Jonathan Dickinson's 1696 shipwreck later compiled into a published journal.

The Jeagas were was described as slight red skinned people, the men wearing their long ebony hair wound tightly in a bun behind their heads, securely held with pins of animal bone. Muscular bodies were naked to the sun except for a tiny patch of woven straw covering only their genitals and fastened from behind in a knot falling into a horsetail. The women wore very much the same attire leaving their breasts exposed to the heavens. Children were left naked, though babes were swaddled in crudely woven blankets, until such time as puberty demanded the slight covering. Modesty was unknown to the Jeagas people.

The Jeagas were foragers taking sustenance from whatever produce that could be gathered from their surrounding. Fish, crustaceans, berries and forest vegetation were the staples of their diet. Some indications show that they also hunted small game. The tribe members imbibed a strong black drink taken from a local herb called cassina, which was known to be very high in caffeine. Obviously used as a stimulant, Europeans dubbed the concoction as "Ilex Vomitoria," it seems they were not too impressed with the taste. Living accommodations were constructed of small poles anchored in the ground and bent together then tied securely with vines. After the arch was in place, the less than waterproof covering was fashioned from small palmetto leaves woven into large mats. It seems they were not great wanderers, remaining in close proximity of Hobe Sound area. Their territory extending from what we know today as Jupiter Inlet in the north to the southern realm at Lake Worth.

First impressions were that the Jeagas peacefully traded with the Spanish, but eventually the relationship changed. As the tribal elders realized that the foreign white skinned men intended to encroach on their lands, infect their people with unknown maladies and abuse their generosity; the peace quickly ended. In 1623 a dispatch to the Spanish King reads, in part:

" ... The Indians had risen and killed fifteen of the colonists, for the soldiers were exhausted with their journey thither, and the natives were so dexterous with their bows that they could discharge twenty arrows while the soldiers were firing a single shot. At first the colonists had driven them away but when the fort was completed a thousand Indians came down upon them, fought them for four hours, wounded the captain and the sub-lieutenant, killed eight soldiers, and shot six thousand arrows into the fort."

This recollection may have been a slight exaggeration, but in any case the Jeagas were no longer welcoming the Spanish. Soon, the Indian aggression made it impossible for the soldiers to hunt for food and starvation became foremost in their minds. Rations had dwindled to a pound of corn split among ten men; the emaciated soldiers began consuming snakes and rats, old fish and animal bones. When those barely edible scraps were gone they chewed belt and shoe leather like jerky. Eventually, it is said, to stay alive the men resorted to cannibalism, killing and eating French captives. Though this is not substantiated, when faced with certain starvation people have been known to resort to very drastic measures to stay alive.

During work on the Jupiter lighthouse it was discovered that the structure, always thought to have been built on a natural rise, was constructed atop a forty-eight foot Jeagas midden. Elsie Dolby Jackson described the midden in 1918 as,

> "A high ridge in the shape of a horse shoe is situated west of the mouth of the Jupiter Narrows. In the center of this ridge is a central mound. From the river to the convex side is, apparently, an approach ... Some have called this an amphitheater. Others have called it a fortification."

During renovations to the lighthouse, archeologists stepped in and conducted a dig at the site. Several three-foot by three-foot holes were excavated revealing a great deal of information to the scientists. Carbon dating suggested the origin of the midden to be around seven hundred AD. Pottery shards, shells, bone tools, a carved bone hairpin as well as large marine vertebrate suggests the midden was a Jeagas refuse dump. Of course, one man's trash is an archeologists treasure more than thirteen hundred years later.

Spanish enslavement and mistreatment as well as European diseases soon took their toll on the Jeagas people. By the early 1700s, none of the tribe remained. Perhaps Jeagas survivors were simply absorbed into other tribes, though the name faded into history. By 1716 the dominant tribe in Florida were the Seminole, who migrated from the Creek Indians of Georgia. The Europeans eventually drove these proud people to the edge of extinction as well. It is a tragedy that the cost of American civilization was so high and paid for so dearly by the Native American tribes.

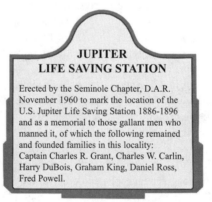

JUPITER
LIFE SAVING STATION

Erected by the Seminole Chapter, D.A.R. November 1960 to mark the location of the U.S. Jupiter Life Saving Station 1886-1896 and as a memorial to those gallant men who manned it, of which the following remained and founded families in this locality: Captain Charles R. Grant, Charles W. Carlin, Harry DuBois, Graham King, Daniel Ross, Fred Powell.

A1A, Carlin Park, Jupiter
PB5 ~ GPS Coordinates: 26.927667, -80.068500

At the site one mile south of the Jupiter Inlet, construction began on the Jupiter Life Saving Station in 1884 under the direction of Captain Charles R. Grant. Captain Charles W. Carlin was officially appointed the first keeper on November 27, 1885 before construction was completed the following year. The station was only active for little over ten years.

The mission of the Life Saving Station was simply to rescue victims of shipwrecks and others stranded at sea. Imagine setting out in a long rowboat giving aid to survivors in the same tempest which resulted in the ship's demise. Their motto was, "You must go out, but you don't have to come back". These men were some of the bravest souls ever to face danger and return to tell about it. In 1915, Life Saving Stations were combined with the Revenue Cutter Service to form the United States Coast Guard, which continues to this day to rescue, patrol, protect and defend our coastal waters.

Perhaps one of the most well known of the Jupiter Life Saving crew was a man by the name of Harry DuBois. Raised on a farm in New Jersey, Harry first ventured south at the age of sixteen to work in the citrus industry on Merritt Island. He eventually wandered further south on what we know today as the Intra-coastal Waterway to Jupiter Inlet. DuBois became enamored with a piece of property having a nice rise overlooking the water. He purchased twenty acres and proceeded to plant ten acres in pineapples. Soon he joined Captain Carlin's Life Saving Station crew.

He met Susan Margaret Sanders of Stuart on a blind date arranged by Charles Carlin, Jr. in 1898. The pair climbed the stairs to the top of the Jupiter Lighthouse to observe the magnificent view during their initial date. It was there in the moonlight beneath the luminescent beacon that Harry realized his heart was lost. He proposed on the spot and Susan accepted. The couple was married on September 15, 1898 at the home of her father in West Palm Beach. Susan resigned her teacher's position in Stuart, joining her husband in Jupiter.

Harry's gift to his beloved bride was a home atop the lovely rise built with his own hands and the assistance of Captain Charles Carlin. The DuBois Home is the second oldest in Palm Beach County. The one storied house featured a living room, dining room and bedroom built of Florida pine with cypress shingles. The tongue in groove pine interior was installed on the diagonal to reinforce its resolve against hurricane force winds.. The flooring was painted red in keeping with current fashion. The house was so well built that the hurricanes of 1926 and 1928 resulted in only twenty-eight panes of glass being broken and a little flooding to the second story addition.

Outside was a privy, cattle corral, chicken and duck coops as well as a woodshed. Due to the salt water aquifer there was no well, the river water was brackish so the only alternative for fresh drinking water was from the heavens. Rainwater would pour from the deeply pitched roof into a cistern on the eastern side of the house. The cypress tank would hold up to twelve thousand gallons of water.

Harry and Susan had four children all born in their home there atop the hill. A second story was built including indoor plumbing in 1903. Water was hand-pumped from the cistern to an upstairs tank for the toilets and faucets. The daily pumping to provide the water pressure was a task assigned to the children.

Harry DuBois was in his fifties when he passed away of pernicious anemia[3]. Susan lived another fifty-three years when she died of natural causes in 1977 at the advanced age of one hundred one years old. The home is surrounded by what is known today as DuBois Park just east of A1A and Jupiter Beach Road. The home is open on Tuesday and Wednesday afternoons except during August and September when the home is closed to the public. A small admission is charged.

Visitors are guided through the living and dining rooms among the couple's treasured things. Period furnishings and vintage clothing adorn the house just as it might have appeared during the days that the DuBois' raised their family. Harry and Susan continue to watch over their home smiling in their wedding clothes. Their portrait hangs in the honored place above the mantel. The Jupiter Life Saving Station was closed in 1900. Captain Charles Carlin transferred to the Bethel Creek House of Refuge on September 08, 1900. The station's buildings were inspected by the Board of Survey and condemned. The life saving station was sold in 1912. An era came to an end.

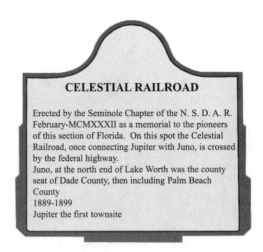

CELESTIAL RAILROAD

Erected by the Seminole Chapter of the N. S. D. A. R.
February-MCMXXXII as a memorial to the pioneers
of this section of Florida. On this spot the Celestial
Railroad, once connecting Jupiter with Juno, is crossed
by the federal highway.
Juno, at the north end of Lake Worth was the county
seat of Dade County, then including Palm Beach
County
1889-1899
Jupiter the first townsite

Juno Dunes Natural Area, Juno Beach
PB6 ~ GPS Coordinates: 26.884683, -80.054850

This story is possibly one of Florida's most wonderful legends and best kept secrets. The tale begins with the Jupiter & Lake Worth Railroad. The once upon a time covered a span of nine years originating in October of 1880. The hard labor of laying the iron rails could only begin after the materials were delivered via the cargo holds of steamships bound from Titusville. The delivery took numerous trips due to the limited space in the cargo holds.

The railroad is steeped in questions concerning its history. The initial run took place on Independence Day of 1892 or 1894[4] but most indications point toward 1892 so that will be the date I choose. Regardless of the year, the railroad was a part of the Jacksonville, Tampa and Key West Railroad Company founded to transport freight and passengers along its lines with Titusville as a hub. Jupiter was connected to Titusville by way of the Indian River Steamboat Company.

The steamboats docked at the Jupiter Inlet and it was there that the Jupiter and Lake Worth Railroad began. The line extended the seven and a half miles to the final conclusion at Lake Worth, today known as the Intra-coastal waterway. The narrow rails were only three feet wide to accommodate the large black engines and cars. The engine and tender were combined with one or two passenger cars.

The train ran two trips a day but was quite often late. The conductor was known to stop for anyone along the tracks who raised a hand, asking for a ride. Often the crew would bring the engine to a steamy halt to visit with friends along the line. Passengers paid a fare of ten cents a mile or seventy-five cents for the entire length of the rail. The fare was based on how far the passenger traveled. Oddly the train had no way to turn around once it reached the end of the line. On the return trip it appeared as though the freight cars were pulling the locomotive. I imagine it was quite a sight to see.

The first mention of the "Celestial Railroad" came in a March 1893 issue of Harper's New Monthly Magazine. An article written by Julian Ralph pointed out that the Jupiter and Lake Worth Railroad began in of course, Jupiter ending in Juno with stops along the way in Venus and Mars. Space travel by way of whistling steel rails. Jupiter and Juno continue to flourish to this day, however Venus and Mars are no longer a blip on the map. Mars was in fact little more than a wooden platform along the rails where passengers could get on and off the train, nothing more has been written about it. Venus on the other hand was said to have a population of three, one man and two cats. The felines did not appear on the census.

The Celestial Railroad's instant success became its eventual downfall. Henry Flagler offered to buy the line in 1893 to transport building materials to the site of his new resort at Palm Beach. The owners put a premium price on the line, however, Flagler realized he could expand the Florida East Coast Railroad southward for a much smaller cost so he passed on the deal. Flagler ran his railway just west of the Celestial line bypassing Juno altogether. During the eight months before Flagler's railroad was completed, the Celestial Line earned an estimated sixty-eight thousand dollars; by June of 1896, the railroad was sold on the auctioneer's block. The Celestial Railroad was now but a dream.

Two fascinating facts are agreed upon by most sources: Engineer Blus Rice entertained riders with his rendition of "Dixie" intoned on the steam whistle while the passengers sang along. Rice secondly, had a well-trained hunting dog that rode with him along the route. Often the Engineer would rent out the dog to passengers, dropping them off to hunt on his journey south and picking them up again on the return trip.

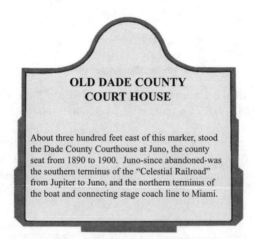

**OLD DADE COUNTY
COURT HOUSE**

About three hundred feet east of this marker, stood the Dade County Courthouse at Juno, the county seat from 1890 to 1900. Juno-since abandoned-was the southern terminus of the "Celestial Railroad" from Jupiter to Juno, and the northern terminus of the boat and connecting stage coach line to Miami.

**US 1 and Oakbrook Square Courtyard Shops, North Palm Beach
PB7 ~ GPS Coordinates: 26.846550, -80.060283**

When Dade County was founded, the area sprawled over an amazing seventy-two hundred square miles. The tiny village of Juno named for a Roman goddess, was listed as the county seat. Cradled between the Atlantic Ocean and the Intracoastal Waterway, the remote little town claimed only a handful of residents. For ten years, from 1890 until 1900, Juno was the center of county government and the location of the county courthouse.

Juno gained prominence as the southern most stop of the legendary Celestial Railroad, named for its inter-planetary route from Jupiter to Juno with stops at Venus and Mars. Henry Flagler offered to buy the railroad but owners placed an unrealistic price on the railway and Flagler declined. Flagler built a small railway bypassing Juno completely. The town was virtually abandoned for a time until Henry Flagler fulfilled his promise to extend the Florida East Coast Railway. Juno was resurrected as a tourist mecca, resort and seaside community.

The Juno rebirth came with a new christening, the community would now be called Juno Beach, a small but distinctive change. The revitalization was geographical as well. In 1898, the Intracoastal Waterway was dredged along Lake Worth Creek to Lake Worth creating the perfect locale for the Town of Juno Beach, strategically placed between the Atlantic Ocean's scenic beauty and the tranquil serenity of the Intracoastal.

In 1929, millionaire E. F. Hutton[5] saw development potential in his winter retreat and began construction on the Seminole Golf Club. The facility would become one of the premiere golf clubs in Florida. The Seminole Golf Club claimed a membership list, which read like the social register.

Bessemer Properties astutely purchased a lot neighboring the golf club to establish a subdivision in 1946. Bessemer made improvements to the pond on the property and created a five hundred-foot fishing pier at the base of Mercury Way[6]. Juno Beach was incorporated in 1953. In the late sixties the community began sprouting condominiums, residential developments and a flourishing population. Year round Juno Beach boasts a compliment of approximately twenty-two hundred residents. During the winter when northern snowbirds take flight and lands sunny Juno Beach the population swells to three times its normal numbers.

Juno Beach has everything one expects of a seaside resort. The little village spans a mere one-point six miles of splendor; sports, shopping and culture all contained in a tiny village with the heart as big as the celestial sky.

BLUE STAR MEMORIAL HIGHWAY

A tribute to the Armed Forces that have defended the United States of America.

Palm Beach Country Club, US 1 Median, Palm Beach
PB8 ~ GPS Coordinates: 26.828000, -80.060850

Commander David McCampbell died in Florida after a lengthy illness on June 30, 1996. His Medal of Honor was officially accredited to West Palm Beach, Florida. Commander McCampbell's full story is told in Brevard County. The following is Commander David McCampbell's Medal of Honor Citation:

DAVID MCCAMPBELL
Commander, United States Navy
Commanding Air Group 15, USS ESSEX
First and Second Battles of the Philippine Sea
19 June and 24 October 1944
Officially Accredited to the State of Florida
(City: West Palm Beach, Florida)

CITATION: "For conspicuous gallantry and intrepidity at the risk of his life above and beyond the call of duty as Commander, Air Group 15, during combat against enemy Japanese aerial forces in the First and Second Battles of the Philippine Sea. An inspiring leader, fighting boldly in the face of terrific odds, Comdr. McCampbell led his fighter planes against a force of 80 Japanese carrier-based aircraft bearing down on our fleet on 19 June 1944. Striking fiercely in valiant defense of our surface force, he personally destroyed 7 hostile planes during this single engagement in which the outnumbering attack force was utterly routed and virtually annihilated. During a major fleet engagement with the enemy on 24 October, Comdr. McCampbell, assisted by but 1 plane, intercepted and daringly attacked a formation of 60 hostile land-based craft approaching our forces. Fighting desperately but with superb skill against such overwhelming airpower, he shot down 9 Japanese planes and, completely disorganizing the enemy group, forced the remainder to abandon the attack before a single aircraft could reach the fleet. His great personal valor and indomitable spirit of aggression under extremely perilous combat conditions reflect the highest credit upon Comdr. McCampbell and the US Naval Service."

The medal was officially presented 10 January 1945.

BLUE STAR MEMORIAL
HIGHWAY MARKER

LAKE PARK
TOWN HALL

Boston entrepreneur Harry S. Kelsey founded Kelsey City in 1921. He envisioned his town as a resort mecca and winter retreat for wealthy northerners. The Town Hall was designed by architect Bruce Kitchell in 1927 and was built by the Arnold Construction Company. Constructed of stuccoed brick and clay tile, this Mediterranean Revival jewel has stylistic features reflective of the late Italian Renaissance, including a rusticated frontispiece, decorative window surrounds and a water table supported by brackets. The Town Hall originally housed the Police and Fire Departments, Town Administration, Library, and Municipal Courtroom. The land boom collapsed in the 1920s and the hurricane of 1928, in which the Town Hall served as a shelter for residents, nearly devastated the city. Service organizations provided diversions for those who remained. The Fire Department sponsored dances here in the Mirror Ballroom on the second floor. The Ballroom was used for many other social events, such as theatrical performances by the Palm Beach Junior College, which occupied the Town Hall in the 1950s. In 1939 the town changed its name to the Town of Lake Park. Lake Park Town Hall was listed in the National Register of Historic Places in 1981.

535 Park Avenue, Lake Park
PB9 ~ GPS Coordinates: 26.798483, -80.063533

Businessman Harry Kelsey took a sabbatical in 1919 to recover from the debilitation of pneumonia. He chose to leave the cold of Boston and wander south toward the sunshine. As president of the Waldorf Systems[7], Kelsey was well versed in the social celebrity of Palm Beach and after spending a little time there clearly saw potential. Kelsey purchased a good deal of property. His instincts proved correct and soon Florida was in the midst of a real estate boom. Harry Kelsey saw an opportunity to develop a playground for northern winter escapees.

Kelsey hired world known designers, the Olmsted Brothers, to create his new city, which he humbly named "Kelsey City." The Olmsted name came to prominence in the mid 1800s when their father's design was selected for New York's Central Park. Dr. John Nolen of Boston worked with the Olmsted Brothers to create the first landscaped city ever established and the second to be pre-planned and graphed; Washington, D. C. was the first. The only guidelines given to the trio of designers was that there were to be three distinct sections of town; residential, retail and manufacturing. A large arch crossed Gateway Road, greeting visitors with, "Welcome to Kelsey City, Gateway to the World's Winter Playground."

Landscape architect Samuel J. Blakely of Egypt, Massachusetts that is, was chosen to create a tranquil tropical like atmosphere. Blakely remained in the area and today his grandson Jeff has followed in his grandfather's footsteps as a well-known landscape architect for the State of Florida. Kelsey also hired building architect Bruce Kitchell in 1927 to design Town Hall and Arnold Construction Company as builders.

Blakely's Town Hall employed a Mediterranean Revival design featuring stucco brick and clay tile. The style is a fusion of Spanish and Moorish influences representing a romantic spirit, intricately crafted with special emphasis placed on the entry and window surrounds. The design features a rusticated frontispiece meaning the main entrance shows deeply recessed joints surrounding each stone creating horizontal bands.

Unfortunately the affluence of the early 1920s began to ebb by the end of the decade. Banks were failing throughout the country and a devastating hurricane left the city in ruins. Kelsey City was left with very few buildings intact. Many citizens simply left after the hurricane, abandoned their property and never returned.

On October 29, 1929 Wall Street came crashing down on investors heads plunging the country into the Great Depression. Harry Kelsey was no exception, by 1931 he sadly left his south Florida Shangri La. He was financially and emotionally bankrupt. Another hurricane slammed into Kelsey City in 1933, it seemed as though Harry Kelsey's beautiful dream was destined to fail. Or was it? The remaining steadfast citizen's refused to let the city slip away and in 1939 the local Garden Club took the initiative and renamed the town hoping to change its bad luck path. The new name was to be Lake Park.

Since that time Lake Park has taken a pro-active stance and has succeeded in becoming, "The Jewel of the Palm Beaches." While maintaining their small town atmosphere, Lake Park has encouraged new development. Harry Kelsey's beautiful city refused to fade into history and continues to flourish to this day. Kelsey created the dream and her citizens proudly maintain the reality.

BLUE STAR MEMORIAL HIGHWAY

A tribute to the Armed Forces that have defended the United States of America

US 1, Kelsey Park, Lake Park
PB10 ~ GPS Coordinates: 26.797800, -80.054533

Adam Payne was born free in Florida. His black parents had escaped slavery and were absorbed into the Seminole tribe. Within a short time after his birth the Seminole were relocated, under armed guard, to Oklahoma and Texas. It was at Fort Duncan in Texas where Payne joined the Army as an Indian scout in 1873. Payne was described as an intimidating mountain of man. Reportedly he was six feet tall, well over two hundred pounds and often wore a buffalo-horn headdress.

Under commanding officer Colonel Ranald S. Mackenzie, Payne was sent to Fort Blanco, Texas. While on a scouting mission, Payne with three other scouts came upon a group of Kiowas[8] spoiling for a fight. The four scouts were forced to fight for their lives and in the end it was Payne who was able to get his party back to camp with their scalps intact.

Colonel Mackenzie recommended Payne for the Congressional Medal of Honor for his bravery in battle and saving the lives of his three fellow soldiers. The award was approved and issued on September 26, 1874, the first Medal of Honor ever awarded to a scout. The Medal of Honor citation misspells his name as Paine. He served two Army enlistments as a scout and was honorably discharged on February 19, 1875. Colonel Mackenzie said of Adam Payne,

"(Adam Payne) has more cool daring than any scout I have ever known."

Most stories would end there but not so with Adam Payne. He left the Army and eventually wound up in Brownsville, Texas. While there Payne got into an altercation with a soldier and the man ended up dead under questionable circumstances. Obviously Payne had some guilt in the situation because he went on the run.

By the holiday season of 1876 Payne joined his people, the Mascogos[9], to dance in the New Year. The ceremony was held in a church where upon the midnight hour the Mascogos would come out and shuffle dance around the church, singing of the dead they had lost that year. As the Mascogos exited the church, Payne had no way of knowing an ambush was hiding in woods bent on his capture.

The account that most people agree on is that Adam Payne was dancing when he heard Sheriff Crowell call his name, as he turned to face him Deputy Sheriff Claron Windus fired his double-barreled shot gun. Deputy Windus, a former Seminole scout and Medal of Honor winner as well, was so close to Payne when he was deliberately gunned him down that the shotgun blast set Adam Payne's clothes ablaze. Payne was dead before he hit the ground. Payne's so called accomplice Frank Enoch was shot during the altercation as well.

Judge W. W. Arnett was summoned to scene by Sheriff Crowell to hold an immediate inquest, certainly not standard procedure. Deputy Sheriff Claron Windus was cleared of any charges. Frank Enoch died within a few hours. Adam Payne's body was returned to his family and buried at Bracketsville, Texas. This is the only case in history where one Medal of Honor winner killed another.

**HURRICANE OF 1928
MASS BURIAL SITE**

Early residents of Glades had to survive many harsh elements. Their goal to create a thriving farming community was often tested by storms, insects, and the lack of many comforts. In 1928 the Glades area was devastated by a powerful hurricane that threatened to destroy the entire area. Several thousand residents were killed and hundreds of homes were destroyed. Despite the death and damage, those residents that survived continued to develop the area. The Glades eventually became a major agricultural community because of their desire and vision. This memorial honors those residents who lost their lives in the 1928 hurricane.

**1053 25th Street, Palm Beach
PB11 ~ GPS Coordinates: 26.736401, -80.062054**

September is the month of peril for south Florida. Of the eight deadliest storms in hurricane history, six dealt their devastating blows during the ninth month. The two exceptions, Cleo and Andrew, were both late August tempests only missing the September date by a matter of days.

In September of 1928, south Florida still bore distinctive scars of the Great Miami Hurricane of 1926. South Florida was on the waning years of a massive population and real estate explosion that had brought thousands into the area, tourism had become a major industry. Henry Flagler had well-established Palm Beach as the winter retreat of choice for northern money. Hurricanes are never prejudiced their devastation covers the complete spectrum of people and places not based on economics or race.

Palm Beach is the location of the famed Coconut Row where millionaires built mansions, one more fabulous than the next. West Palm Beach was the locale for the working class who served those on the other side of Lake Worth. Further west were the communities near Lake Okeechobee; Canal Point, Belle Glade, Pahokee, Chosen and South Bay whose majority populations were made up of migrant workers. These migrant farm workers were the uncounted masses, who fell victim to the storm of 1928, most were unidentified dead only missed by loved ones who simply never heard from them again.

Farming was good around Lake Okeechobee. The drained Everglade swamps left rich, muck soil that produced abundant yields. An earthen levee was built around the lake to keep common summer floods at bay, but at only five feet the dam would not withstand hurricane force waters; though the residents that lived near the levee were blissfully unaware of any pending danger.

By the time Sunday, September 16th rolled around, the hurricane was quickly approaching south Florida and it was already a killer. The Virgin Islands suffered casualties numbering over five hundred. The massive category four storm thrashed Puerto Rico on the feast day of San Felipe leaving only death and ruin in its wake. More than three hundred died on September 13, 1928, south Florida had some advance warning of the devastation to come. Over Friday and Saturday, the Bahama Islands suffered the wrath of the storm that left more than six hundred dead. By Sunday Palm Beach County braced for landfall.

The skies began to darken as the tempest stirred the heavens. Gale force winds provoked fury on the water and white capped breakers pounded the shore. The storm would come ashore between Jupiter and Boca Raton, making landfall about 6:15 in the evening. Though the sun had not yet slipped below the horizon, the skies were dark as night and a noticeable plunge in temperature preceded the onslaught.

Jupiter was victim of excessive damage as the eye of hurricane lingered there torturing the small town. A twenty-foot wall of water crashed into Palm Beach as one hundred fifty mile per hour winds splintered and drowned everything in it path. Boats were tossed like toys onto the shore; shops, churches and homes were blown to bits, bursting under the massive pressure; the streets filled with debris, leaving them impassible; and railroad cars were blown off their tracks. More than a third of all the buildings were a total loss, yet the worst was still to come.

Six thousand people lived along southern banks of Lake Okeechobee, before the next day dawned almost half would die. The five-foot levee instantly melted away with the storm surge, the exact time is unknown. At Belle Glade the water crested at seven feet; at Chosen, eleven feet three inches was measured; and at South Bay, the water rose to eleven feet eight inches. The flood was said to have spanned six miles wide and seventy-five miles long to the south of the lake. More than twenty-five hundred people drowned. Floodwaters remained for weeks and the saturated land left the water with no place to go. It was reported that survivors suffering from exposure and shock were found as much as a week after the disaster.

Every able bodied man volunteered to recover the bodies of the dead. Those unable to stomach the awful sight of the victims, built pine boxes for burial until there was no more wood available. The hurricane casualties could not be buried in the saturated earth, so huge masses were piled onto large trucks and taken to higher ground. Within a few days the sun was baking and bodies began to decompose. It was impossible to escape the stench of death. The rotting corpses were determined by the Health Department to be a health hazard to survivors. Cremation was ordered, great piles of rotting bodies were set ablaze. The men given these terrible tasks felt an obligation in respect for the dead to do so and were haunted with the nightmares of this experience for the remainder of their lives.

Sixteen hundred burned bodies were taken to Port Mayaca for burial, though a proper funeral was not possible. The non-white victims were dumped into makeshift graves along roadside ditches from Pahokee to Sebring and six hundred seventy-four others were dumped into a cavernous twenty-foot hole in the Palm Beach pauper's cemetery without so much as a marker noting their death. The body count soared upward toward twenty-five hundred graves yet this number is considerably less than the deaths actually suspected. Many bodies were swallowed by the muck of the Everglades swamp, for years after the storm farmers turning over the soil would encounter human remains of victims never recovered. After several weeks of casualty recovery, the government called off the search due to lack of funds.

Though the hurricane gave no quarter when taking lives, in death the white and non-white were handled with very different standards. Memorial services were held one white and one non-white, on Sunday, September 30, 1928. First reports listed the death toll at one thousand victims, later the number was updated to a final recording issued by the Red Cross of eighteen hundred forty-nine people.

Compare this body count to modern day Hurricane Andrew in 1992, which ended with sixty-one tragedies and twenty-six billion dollars. In September 1928, whole towns were washed away, families were totally abolished and there was not one corner of Palm Beach County that was left untouched by the diabolical storm. Imagine half the population of the western portion of the county ceased to exist. In today's dollars, the hurricane damage was estimated at sixteen billion dollars. However, this storm must be gauged not by the monetary loss but the loss of lives. One thing that we know positively, the death toll number is incorrect.

The storm that befell Palm Beach County on September 16, 1928 is commonly known as the "Forgotten

Storm." Unremembered in the fact that the powers that be during this time minimized the hurricane's severity, to keep tourists coming to the area, an industry that south Florida had begun to rely on heavily. Forgotten because officials refused to document the extent of the damage that was done by the storm. Finally no one knew the total death toll and never will. Forgotten because the vast majority of those who died were black migrant workers, segregated in life and abandoned in death.

The Okeechobee Storm of 1928 alerted the United States Army Corps of Engineers to rebuild the dike to a height of thirty to forty feet named Hoover Dike in reference to the presidential administration. The present levee has yet to be tested by a category four or five hurricane, but as south Florida residents well know, the possibility is there each and every year.

Recently the National Hurricane Center increased the recorded death toll to twenty-five hundred, though this is still known to be a conservative number. So many of the migratory workers were only known by nicknames even to their friends and whole families were completely wiped out so there was no one left to register the deaths. Many victims were carried away by the storm surge into the sawgrass marshes of the Everglades where humans seldom ventured.

Woodlawn Cemetery today has a stone marker erected in memory of sixty-nine victims of the storm. The State of Florida placed a historical marker where six hundred seventy four victims of the storm were buried. During the seventy-fifth anniversary of the storm a re-enactment of the burial procession was held as well as a remembrance service. Finally after so many years, victims of the forgotten storm are remembered.

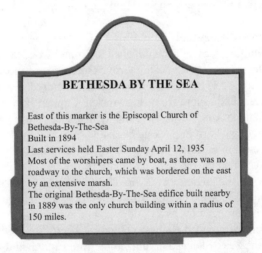

North Lake Trail and S. Woods Road, Palm Beach
PB12 ~ GPS Coordinates: 26.734330, -80.040899

Just over a century ago the area we know today as Palm Beach was then Dade County, which encompassed the span between the St. Lucie River to the north extending down through the Florida Keys. It was there that a community called Lake Worth was formed. The small settlement consisted of a few houses on the eastern shore of the lake and was little more than tropical jungle with an occasional clearing. The small community was named in honor of General William Jenkins Worth whose perseverance and courage managed to bring a peace to the Everglades ending the Florida Seminole Wars.

When the Right Reverend E. Gardner Weed, Bishop of Florida and Archdeacon Carpenter, arrived in Lake Worth during the winter months of 1887-88. There was no organized religion or house of worship within one hundred miles. Reverend Weed determined that this would be an exceptional place to establish a mission. He went to work visiting area residents and calling on guests of the old Cocoanut Grove Hotel to obtain subscriptions in order to purchase a lot for building a proper sanctuary. He also penned an article addressing church papers requesting the services of a clergyman to lead the mission. Reverend Joseph N. Mulford, Rector of Christ Church in Troy, New York answered the call.

Mulford volunteered to come to south Florida without compensation other than traveling expenses. He was quickly approved and in late December of 1888, the Mulford family set out on their journey to Lake Worth. The trip would be adventurous and difficult. The family consisting of Reverend and Mrs. Mulford, William Cluett[10] and Sanford Cluett[11] traveled by train, steamboat, sailboat, horse back and on foot for eight days before reaching their destination on January 2, 1889. During this time there were only four communicants[12], Reverend Mulford immediately began conducting services for the diminutive congregation at the District School House.

With the lot purchased from Mrs. Charles Moore, Reverend Mulford went to work collecting subscriptions for the sanctuary. The parishioners became founding members of Bethesda by the Sea as well as pioneers of Palm Beach. Many of these early settlers' names can still be found on the rolls of Bethesda today. Quite a few of the parishioners were civic leaders, business owners and industrious pioneers of the Lake Worth community.

Most of the homes during this time were built surrounding the lake, necessary for food and transportation. Deer and bear were abundant and supplied major food sources. It is hard to imagine but at this time ocean front property was considered virtually worthless. Homes relied on kerosene for light; wood for cooking and cisterns caught fresh rainwater coming off the roof for drinking. Because depending on the rain for fresh water could lead to extended dry periods most homes had wells. Though strangely enough the wells proved to be somewhat of a hazard, the fresh water attracted bears. Think of it, in the early morning hours going for water only to encounter a dozen or so bears congregating like office personnel around the coffeepot. Coffee would just have to wait as far as I was concerned.

Reverend Mulford designed the new edifice and Mr. G. C. Haight was hired for construction though the Reverend helped considerably. Mulford was an accomplished artist and woodcarver. It was a common sight to see the Reverend every morning walking from the Cocoanut Grove Hotel toward the church site. Their first dilemma was to obtain the lumber for building. The nearest railroad was one hundred fifty miles away so most of the boards were gathered from wood washed ashore from shipwrecks. Captain Porter donated the foundation and heavy wooden doors, not to be outdone Mrs. Porter gave the hymnals and prayer books. Reverend Mulford built the pews, kneeling benches and bookracks from packing boxes he found washed up on shore and others he could beg from guests at the hotel. He custom built the pews ensuring comfort for the parishioners, when someone would pass by Mulford would have them try the seats and mark the pitch of the back most satisfying. Checking his marks he would build the pews at the angle most favored. The church was to seat one hundred parishioners.

Mrs. Mulford was responsible for the church name. Bethesda means house of spiritual and physical healing. The idea was conceived from summer trips as a child with her family to visit the healing waters of Saratoga Springs in New York where the family attended Bethesda Church. Therefore, Bethesda by the Sea translated means The House of Healing by the Sea. She also organized the first Church and County civic society, the Woman's Guild, on January 22, 1889. The society benefited the church and needy families as well as providing fun and fellowship for the community with various activities throughout the year.

By this time there were seven families and seven single members. During the church season, which extended from January through April. Contributions during the first year raised one hundred forty-nine dollars and ninety cents. Reverend Mulford took no salary but the church paid his travel expenses each year totaling two hundred fifty dollars. It was his custom to make an annual trip to New York.

The next church project for the Reverend was the building of a rectory[13]. He wrote to a wealthy and generous patron Mrs. L. H. Boardman, at the suggestion of his wife, explaining the need for a rectory and presenting an accounting of Church funds. Mrs. Boardman responded by donating fifteen hundred dollars for the project. In 1890 Mrs. William Stone Smith traded a lot extending from the lake to the ocean for building a new edifice and rectory in exchange for the old church lot. The Diocese of Florida approved the deal. The rectory was built by Mr. George Lainhart, designed by Mr. R. Newton Breeze with plans furnished by Mr. William Stone Smith. Mrs. Mulford planned a series of musicals and literary affairs to benefit the church building fund, these activities were the forerunners to the Palm Beach Society of the Arts.

It was a momentous time for Lake Worth and Palm Beach when Henry M. Flagler began preparations for creating a winter resort for the wealthy in 1892. As the plans developed suddenly the population increased nearly overnight. Several men in the church with much forethought and vision realized the need for a larger church sanctuary to meet the growing needs of the community. A lot for the new edifice and funds for construction were the first needs to be addressed. Reverend Mulford offered solutions to both problems. He offered to purchase the rectory for two thousand dollars, if the church would agree to move it onto the adjoining lot to the south. The deal was made with consent from the Diocese.

In appreciation of Reverend and Mrs. Mulford the Palm Beach Community as a whole presented them with a twenty-one foot naphtha launch called, *The Gratia*. The community so loved the Mulford's that the gift was given without a single person having been asked to give. Excess funds were used to build a wharf in front of the rectory and operation expenses.

Plans for the new church were obtained from New York architects, Cady Berg & See. Construction began on the new edifice in November 1894 and completed in the spring of 1895. John H. Lee of Troy, New York was the builder. Consecrated on March 18, 1896. Mrs. Mulford described the church as:

"…broad, cloistered porches relieve the glare of the sun, and invite the soft breezes, while the cathedral glass of cool tones of pearl and opal in dormer and chancel windows, induces a feeling of restfulness rarely to be found.
The building is of Moorish style, and seen from the lake on the rising lawn, with its noble cam panile, one might fancy it a bit of architecture transplanted from the sunny slopes of southern Spain. The church also as the architect expressed it, 'has a feeling of the old mission houses of the Pacific Coast.' It harmonizes perfectly with its environment of blue skies, feathery palms and Southern seas.
…The sweet, far sounding tones from the belfry reach up and down the lake almost as far as the tower is seen, and while the clock-faces await the coming of the clock, their hands point always to 'eleven' the hour of Sunday morning service."

For twenty-nine years services were held at this beautiful edifice so aptly described by Mrs. Mulford at the site today known as North Lake Trail. Reverend Mulford retired in 1899 and Reverend L. Fitz James Hindry assumed responsibility of Missionary in Charge. However, the Mulford's remained active in the church. During the coming years as Palm Beach developed as a playground for the rich and winter paradise for those escaping the frigid northern climates. Many distinguished visitors attended services at Bethesda by the Sea, including: Admiral George Dewey, President Theodore Roosevelt, President Grover Cleveland, Alfred G. Vanderbilt, Colonel John Jacob Astor and Mr. Samuel Clemens (Mark Twain) to name a few.

In December of 1903, Reverend Hindry resigned to take another post at Trinity Parish in St. Augustine. Reverend Mulford was asked and agreed to take the pulpit once again with the assistance of Reverend Francis McFetrich. The lot for a new rectory was given by Mrs. George B. Cluett in 1905 as well as an additional lot to the south for a garden. The rectory was built that summer with Reverend Mulford designing the house and again Mr. Charles C. Haight was engaged as builder. Since Mulford's home was already known as the rectory, this house was called the Vicarage. Mulford resigned again in March 1909 and Reverend Charles Temple was appointed in his stead. During Reverend Temple's time the Church of Bethesda by the Sea became an organized parish. Reverend Joseph N. Mulford passed away on June 1, 1920 at the age of eighty-three. During his eulogy Reverend Temple declared, "Bethesda by the Sea is his Memorial." Having built the church with his own hands and heart, he gave it a firm foundation and set it in a direction that other men could continue his great works.

Reverend Temple resigned in 1921 and Reverend Canon James Townsend Russell became Rector. It was during the tenure of Reverend Russell that the new sanctuary and rectory were planned. On Easter Sunday, April 12, 1925, the church at North Lake Trail observed it final service. The grand old church was purchased by Mr. E. Harold Cluett and converted to a private residence. For some thirty-one years the church had hosted services and though this was the end of a chapter, a new beginning was on the horizon.

DUCK'S NEST

Oldest standing house in Palm Beach
Built in 1891 by Henry Maddock for his
home.
Parts of the house were assembled in New
York
and brought by barge to Palm Beach
as this was the only mean of
transportation.

North Lake Trail and S. Woods Road, Palm Beach
PB13 ~ GPS Coordinates: 26.734590, -80.040904

Henry Maddock built Duck's Nest in 1891. Located on what is today North Lake Trail, it was the neighbor to the original Bethesda-by-the-Sea Episcopal Church. The home is said to be the oldest standing residence in Palm Beach. The house was partially constructed in New York then loaded onto a barge and transported down the eastern seaboard. Imagine the sight in 1891 as this unassembled structure came floating down the waterway. When the barge came into view of land crowds would gather to watch it pass. Rumor was that certain tour guides in Palm Beach related to tourists that Al Capone once lived in Duck's Nest. Though the tale is totally false, it was a tantalizing story to repeat to unknowing travelers. Unfortunately stories like these repeated enough times have a strange way of being accepted as fact.

In the early 1970s Palm Beach accepted fifty applications for historical landmarking. Duck's Nest was among the designated structures. Problems arose with the original considerations and the Landmarks Review Commission delayed it decision. Owners were hesitant about accepting the designation based on declining property values and ever increasing real estate values. An Architectural Review Board assembled to study the designated structures finally convinced most property owners to accept the historic distinction.

Much discussion was held concerning the architecture of Addison Mizner. Though looked upon as the father of Mediterranean Revival design, Mizner was a self-taught architect who often got caught up in the details rather than the practicality of structural design. For instance, he once designed a fabulous two-storied mansion and forgot to include a staircase. The Architectural Review Board and preservation became a sore subject for many Palm Beach citizens, many felt that government was best when at the farthest distance. Preservation by legal means was just another bundle of red tape.

Former United States ambassador to Cuba Earl E. T. Smith, serving as chairman, announced the formation of the non-profit Preservation Foundation of Palm Beach. Their purpose involved acquiring, leasing, restoration of and reselling historic locations, though none of the locations involved were ever resold. The organization mirrored that of similar groups from Charleston and Newport. The Preservation Foundation is supported by donations, gifts, contributions and bequeaths from generous estates. The foundation was instrumental in educating youth concerning the beauty found in Palm Beach architecture and the value of preserving the historic structures for future generations. Lessons were taught not only through lectures but also by exceptional example.

The Preservation Foundation felt that with the new landmark ordinances in place that Palm Beach had turned a corner in regard to restoration of historic structures. Unfortunately over the next twenty years a great many historic homes fell victim to the black belching bulldozer. The designation as a historic site involved a house being a minimum of fifty years old. Many of the smaller homes built after elegant mansions were destroyed are slowly qualifying for the distinction, prompting the Landmarks Commission to implement guidelines to maintain the refinement of the area. Palm Beach continues to attract increased populations to the city as well as new construction, unfortunately sometimes this is to the detriment of historic properties.

**FIRST POST OFFICE
IN PALM BEACH**

Just to the east is the site of the first post office between Fort Jupiter and Miami. Originally known as the Lake Worth Post Office, it was succeeded by the Palm Beach Post Office, and the earlier title was later taken by the community to the south, present day Lake Worth. It was in the home of the first postmaster, Valorus O. Spencer, who was appointed in 1880.

North Lake Trail and Country Club Road, Palm Beach
PB14 ~ GPS Coordinates: 26.741537, -80.039624

During an 1867 exploration of the area, a Ft. Dallas[14] resident named Michael Sears and his son, George, discovered an inlet leading to Lake Worth. Nine years later, Michigan families would settle in Palm Beach. In 1880, the first post office was founded for the town called Lake Worth. Most cities were named during this time as the result of completing government paper work to establish a post office. This is as it was for Lake Worth. The post office was located in the home of the first postmaster.

Valorus O. Spencer, a miller and millwright from Richmond, New York, and his wife Jane had come to Florida with their two sons and four daughters. He had come to the Lake Worth area in 1878 and two years later was appointed postmaster. Spencer boarded a rowboat to visit others around the lake with a petition in hand to request the establishment of Lake Worth Post Office, which was approved in 1880. Spencer remained postmaster until his death on September 24, 1895 at the age of eighty-three.

The Lake Worth name proved to be only temporary. E. M. Brelsford started a petition to change the name to Palm City only two years later. His petition was disapproved by the government stating that another city had already claimed that name. Gus Ganford, a prospector from Philadelphia, suggested the name Palm Beach. Again the petition was submitted and in March of 1886, Palm Beach was confirmed as the new name by the United States Post Office.

Two men believed the Lake Worth area to be ideal as a resort location before Henry Flagler arrived on the scene. Robert R. McCormick, a railroad pioneer from Colorado, built a cottage on the east side of Lake Worth. Captain E. N. Dimick established the first hotel in 1884 called the Coconut Grove House by adding rooms to his home. He eventually sold the hotel to C. T. Clark, a millionaire from Pittsburgh. When Henry Flagler arrived in Palm Beach to build his first hotel in 1893, he rented the entire hotel to be used as his headquarters.

West Palm Beach was still untamed wilderness. Flagler was said to have pointed across the lake and stated:

"In a few years there'll be a town over there as big as Jacksonville, and St. Augustine will be a way station for it."

And so it was.

ROYAL POINCIANA HOTEL

The Royal Poinciana Hotel, built by Henry M.
Flagler, was opened February 11, 1894. One of the
largest wooden structures in the world at the time,
the hotel cost over $1 million. Its rooms accommo-
dated 2,000 quests and its dining room seated
1,600. The sprawling six story structure, painted
yellow and white, faced Lake Worth and was surrounded by gardens. The hotel was in use until the
1929-1930 season. It was demolished in 1936.

44 Cocoanut Row, between Towers Hotel and Royal Poinciana Court, Palm Beach
PB15 ~ GPS Coordinates: 26.715833, -80.041600

Newspaper headlines proclaimed in bold lettering, "Flagler Hotel to be called The Royal Poinciana" in an April 1893 issue. Flagler's hotel, like the Ponce de Leon in St. Augustine, would be so much more than just a place for northern guests to lay their head. Henry Flagler intended to create a playground for the rich by building a magnificent structure rivaling the greatest hotels throughout the world.

More than one hundred acres had been amassed for the development of Flagler's sprawling resort. Palm Beach was all abuzz about the hotel and when the groundbreaking ceremony was held on May 1, 1893, nearly the entire town turned out. Unlike his other hotels, The Poinciana would be constructed of wood rather than the stone and stucco previously used. The colonial architecture featured six floors reaching upward into the bright blue Florida sky. Edison's electric lights illuminated the hotel and three Otis lifts sped guests to their floors without the exertion of trudging the sweeping staircase. One hundred and twenty-five private baths were installed in the Poinciana, which could accommodate up to fifteen hundred guests. The elegant ballroom was the backdrop for many society parties.

The landscaping was particularly beautiful. The proximately to the ocean and coconut palms lent a tropical air about the resort. Cabanas, pavilions and bathhouses dotted the beach side while a bandstand and the local yacht club occupied the lake or intracoastal side of the property.

Manager Henry W. Merrill, alongside owner Henry M. Flagler, threw open the doors and welcomed their first guests to The Royal Poinciana on February 11, 1894 in a grand gala affair. By the time the hotel was completed, The Royal Poinciana was the world's largest hotel and the most expensive having a final price tag of two million dollars. This gem of Flagler's resort crown was an instant success and within a years time boasted a larger compliment of guests as compared to any other Florida establishment.

Flagler achieved his aim in making Palm Beach the place to be for the socially prominent. In fact a New York Times society columnist once wrote,

"Everyone who's anyone will be seen this season in Palm Beach. Should you choose not to make the winter pilgrimage, to maintain family dignity close up your home in the city and let everyone believe you've gone."

Unheard of today, the Poinciana only opened for the social season, which began in mid-January and ended by Easter with an exception in 1896. The first run of Flagler's train arrived in March 1896 and onboard were several of the most prominent families in the United States including the Vanderbilt and Rockefellers. Because big business was well represented during the season, three post offices were required to handle all of the correspondence that flooded into Palm Beach during those few short months. Kitchen supplies alone cost a whopping thirty-five hundred dollars per day, many families spent less than that per year on groceries. The electrical power was generated with coal; the resort consumed an exorbitant twenty-five tons every day. Three hundred twenty waiters stood at attention in full livery to meet the needs of the hotel's illustrious clientele.

The highlight of the social season was the Washington's Birthday Ball held in the picturesque ballroom of The Poinciana each February. Although Flagler often went to extremes to entertain his guests, he was staunch on one point: Sunday would be kept at Palm Beach. All casinos and amusements came to a halt on the Sabbath. When asked about the unbending principle, Henry Flagler replied,

"If they do not like it they need not come. I am not asking their opinion in this any more than I consult them about my other affairs. Sunday is to be kept at Palm Beach. Its observance is one of the features of the place."

Guests began each day with a formal breakfast then a trip to the shore. Women would be modestly clad in black swimsuits covering them from neck to ankle adhering to the dress code of the day. By lunchtime the guests would return to the resort for an eight-course luncheon.

Flagler was opposed to the train tracks being right outside the front door of his Whitehall mansion so he had the railroad spur moved north of the hotel. When guests arrived on the train, hotel employees with either a mule-powered car or driving a rickshaw type vehicle would greet them, the fare was a nickel. Obviously Flagler would go to great lengths to entertain his guests. He hired a group black athletes, who played baseball for the Cuban Giants in Havana during the summer, to serve as porters, gardeners and waiters during the working day. But it was not the menial work that attracted Flagler to these men; it was their baseball talents. Flagler staged exhibition games using these players for the entertainment of his guests. The games were spectacular events.

The splendid coconut groves planted along side the hotel provided the perfect atmosphere for formal afternoon teas and evening socials. The festivities would end with enough time for patrons to freshen up and dress for dinner. Formal evening clothes were required for dinner; cocktail dresses of silk, taffeta or lace while men wore black tie and tuxedos. It was such a romantic time; opulence, elegance and refinement was the golden aura surrounding the guests of the Poinciana.

When the Great Depression brought hardship throughout the country, the rich suffered as well. An era came to an end in 1932 when the Royal Poinciana Hotel closed her doors for the last time. Four years later the playground of the rich was laid low when the once beautiful hotel was demolished.

THE ROYAL POINCIANA CHAPEL

This interdenominational Chapel was the earliest church organization in Dade County (of which Palm Beach County was then a part.) The Chapel was formed in 1884 under the auspices of the home missionary society of the congregational church by rev. A. B. Dilley. The first school house in the county was built also to accommodate the sabbath worshippers. The present church building, erected on a site donated by henry m. Flagler and later enlarged, opened in December 1895. Dr. S. M. Lindsay, the minister, calls the Chapel "one of god's service stations on the highway of life."

60 Coconut Row, Palm Beach
PB15 ~ GPS Coordinates: 26.713050, -80.042267

Reverend Alexander B. Dilley initially organized the Lake Worth Congregational Church in 1884. The first meetings were conducted in private homes, the local schoolhouse and later on Commodore Clark's yacht. While Henry Flagler was proceeding with the construction of his magnificent Royal Poinciana Hotel, Reverend Dilley was introduced to him and obviously Flagler was impressed.

Henry Flagler financed the building of a permanent home for Reverend Dilley's congregation to the south of his hotel. His intent was to provide a non-denominational place of worship for his patrons visiting the Royal Poinciana for the season. The Congregational parishioners were highly offended and when Flagler refused to budge on the non-denominational point, the church split. The Congregationalist parishioners relocated to West Palm Beach, where the church is still active today.

Fourteen years after Reverend Dilley had the first Congregationalist services; Flagler completed the four hundred-seat Chapel naming it in compliment to his hotel, the Royal Poinciana Chapel. Dr. Edwin B. Webb was employed as the first minister. He conducted two services every Sunday during the season, that ran from December to March. Dr. Webb passed away two years after taking the Royal Poinciana pulpit, he was eighty years old.

The Chapel's benefactor invited Dr. George Morgan Ward to preside over the services at Royal Poinciana. Dr. Ward declined based on the opinion that he had no wish to minister to the idle rich using worship services as a social occasion. Flagler was stunned; rarely did any one deny his requests. Flagler convinced Ward to meet with him nonetheless.

The meeting was fruitful and the two men agreed on the direction that the Chapel was to take. First, Royal Poinciana would forever remain nondenominational; Dr. Ward would have full control of the pulpit; the messages would be brilliant and energetic; the music ministry was to be superb; and finally, the Chapel would have no debts.

Dr. Ward was tall and handsome with a commanding voice and piercing blue eyes. He was also the youngest man to take the pulpit. Soon Ward and his wife Emma were comfortably ensconced in a room provided by Flagler as part of the preaching salary. As word spread of the dynamic voice at the pulpit of the Royal Poinciana Chapel, the building began to fill capacity as well as the lawn beyond.

Dr. Ward intoned not only inspiring sermons but services became an exciting event. For thirty-one years he stood the pulpit. Dr. George Morgan Ward suffered a massive heart attack while delivering his Palm Sunday service in 1931, by Easter he was dead. In the last days of Dr. Ward, the country was in the grips of the Great Depression. Adam Sarver, simply a member of the congregation with no theological training, maintained the Chapel during those turbulent years. When the new pastor was selected Sarver assisted with the transition. Dr. William Biederwolf, a Princeton graduate and strangely enough a football player, assumed the pulpit. After eight years of leading the Royal Poinciana congregation, Dr. William Biederwolf had a fatal stroke.

Over the next ten years preachers changed often and due to World War II tourist travel was restricted even so Adam Sarver kept the Chapel active. Attendance dwindled, often no more than sixty people would sit for the services. Finally Dr. Samuel M. Lindsay brought continuity back to the Royal Poinciana Chapel and the parishioners returned. Dr. Sam, as he was known, brought personality back to the pulpit after a long dry spell. Dr. Samuel M. Lindsay died at the age of ninety-nine, all the while serving the Chapel.

The Chapel dabbled in a real estate venture, which a number of the congregation disapproved, this caused a rift among the parishioners. Many chose to remove themselves from the Chapel. The Flagler Museum soon purchased the land surrounding it in 1967, including the property on which the Chapel stood. The site was leased to the Chapel for five years at a token one-dollar per year with no option to renew the lease. Obviously the Royal Poinciana would be moving.

The intent was to move the original wooden Chapel to the property that the congregation had purchased. Unfortunately there were some roadblocks to the process, which consumed the entire five-year lease period in order to rectify. The land was zoned residential so a special exception had to be approved to move the Chapel. In the end, the Chapel was reconstructed on the new site at a cost of a quarter million dollars. The Royal Poinciana Chapel was dedicated in a special service held on April 15, 1973.

The Chapel would begin providing services throughout the entire year in 1983. Dr. John U. Miller led the congregation through this transition. Membership began slowly due to the fact that the majority of the Chapel's parishioners were only winter residents of Palm Beach.

Dr. Thomas Kirkman with his wife Ruth took the helm of the Chapel in 1985. Through his tenure the Chapel expanded not only its facilities but also the services available to the congregation. New administrative offices, Sunday School rooms, fellowship hall and the restoration of the original Chapel organ were completed in February 1993 at a cost of two million dollars. The entire bill was paid in full. Dr. Kirkman, after accomplishing so much, retired in October 1995.

The new era began the very next month with Dr. Richard M. Cromie, wife Peggy at his side. The Chapel congregation has steadily blossomed under Dr. Cromie's guiding hand. Ministries are continually evolving to meet the needs of the congregation and community. Throughout the Chapel's history, the house of worship has remained faithful to the original principles on which it was founded. In the words of Dr. Samuel M. Lindsay concerning the Royal Poinciana Chapel,

"The best days of the Chapel are ahead of us, not behind us."

**SEA GULL COTTAGE
PALM BEACH'S OLDEST HOUSE**

Constructed in 1886 by R.R. McCormick, a Denver railroad developer, Sea Gull cottage was purchased by Henry Flagler in 1893 and became Flagler's first winter residence in Palm Beach. The Royal Poinciana, Flagler's first resort hotel in Palm Beach, was located next to Sea Gull. In 1984 Sea Gull was moved and restored by the Preservation Foundation of Palm Beach. It is now the Parish House of the Royal Poinciana Chapel.

**58 Cocoanut Row, beside The Royal Poinciana Chapel, Palm Beach
PB17 ~ GPS Coordinates: 26.713117, -80.042683**

Denver railroad executive Robert R. McCormick joined the well-healed society in Palm Beach during the season. He hired contractors to build a personal retreat in 1886 on the shores of the Intracoastal Waterway. The dark rich interior wood paneling was solid mahogany that had washed ashore most likely due to a shipwreck. McCormick's Sea Gull Cottage is the oldest home in Palm Beach.

Henry Flagler also wintered in Palm Beach and eventually purchased Sea Gull Cottage in 1893 for seventy-five thousand dollars. He began construction of the Royal Poinciana that very same year. In 1890 Henry Flagler employed workers to begin construction on the elaborate marble mansion called Whitehall, a dream come true for his young bride. The cottage was moved from the Intracoastal to a scenic location by the ocean next door to The Breakers hotel.

It was eventually decided that Sea Gull Cottage would be torn down. Earl E. T. Smith, who had many happy memories vacationing at the cottage as a young man, attempted to save the lovely little house through the Preservation Foundation. The cottage was given a reprieve, while governmental red tape was untangled to move the structure once again. The plan was to relocate Sea Gull Cottage to the Royal Poinciana Chapel parking lot. When the Chapel was moved the process had taken five years to obtain the final approval. Smith was determined not to go that route. Smith personally faced the Palm Beach Town Council and within one hour he had permission in hand to move Sea Gull Cottage, with one condition. He was required to fund the transfer, which he did to the tune of six hundred thousand dollars.

The cottage was finally relocated to its permanent home in 1984 and restored. Today the cottage serves as classrooms and administrative offices for the Royal Poinciana Chapel. Worth Builders conducted additional renovations in 2000. Sea Gull Cottage may only be viewed from the outside.

EPISCOPAL CHURCH OF BETHESDA-BY-THE-SEA

The original church constructed in 1889 on the eastern shore of Lake Worth was the first Protestant church building in southeast Florida. The present edifice, erected in 1926 as a monument to international friendship, has served all races, nations, and creeds. This plaque was placed by the Palm Beach County Historical Society to commemorate the 75th anniversary of the church, in recognition of the historic role of Bethesda-by-the- Sea in the life of the community.

A1A and Barton on grounds of church, Palm Beach
PB18 ~ GPS Coordinates: 26.711617, -80.037400

A new era began on March 15, 1925 when the cornerstone was laid for the Church of Bethesda by the Sea at the corner of County Road and Barton Avenue. The church was to be built in a majestic fourteenth century English Gothic style featuring pointed arches, towers, steeply pitched roofs, large pointed stained glass windows and symmetrical design. Amidst a manicured garden of tall palms and tropical flowers the great edifice of Canon Russell's dream became a reality.

Architects Hiss and Weeks of New York and vestryman, James Sheldon collaborated on the church design. The Hageman-Harris Corporation also of New York was hired as builders, constructing the sanctuary of stones cast on the church grounds. Unfortunately Canon Russell was unable to see his dream fulfilled due to the serious illness of his wife; he was forced to resign as Rector.

The first service was held in the new building on November 27, 1927. The church was known as the Spanish Memorial. A unique feature of the church is the placement of the windows allowing the organ music to be piped into either the Nave[15] or the Garth[16]. The grandeur and simplicity of the architecture is grace itself, set in a beautiful tropical garden. During this time special attention was paid toward developing the church school program.

Cluett Gardens were dedicated during the same ceremony in which the third sanctuary of Bethesda by the Sea was consecrated on January 22, 1931. The gardens were donated as a memorial to George and Amanda Cluett by their daughter Nellie. The gothic design of the church was carried over into the garden walls and small structures throughout.

Reverend Tage Teisen was named permanent Rector on February 1, 1939. He was dedicated to Bethesda-by-the-Sea for twenty-two years, the longest rector in church history. Many wondrous changes came to the edifice during this time including the addition of thirty-two magnificent stained glass memorial windows, establishment of a kindergarten program and in 1941, additional classrooms were built on the northern end of the Parish House. Guild Hall was completed in 1956 on the north side of the Garth. The new addition would house eighteen classrooms and a three hundred fifty-seat auditorium. The small kitchen built in 1926 was enlarged and modernized during this phase of construction.

Mrs. Jean Flagler Mook, the granddaughter of Henry Flagler, generously provided funding for new vestry and sacristy rooms[17]. In 1954 the church began to hold year round services. In January of 1956 a Young People's Fellowship for teenagers and the Bethesda Young Churchmen for pre-teens were established. The church school was flourishing with an enrollment of more than three hundred fifty students for the term ending in 1961. The sanctuary would hold six hundred fifty participants and during the winter months it would be filled to capacity, often overflowing into the Garth. It became necessary at this time to hold three Sunday morning services. Reverend Teisen tendered his retirement on January 31, 1961 due to illness and passed away on June 3, 1962.

Over the years many church organization and activities were established at Bethesda-by-the-Sea including the Woman's Guild, the oldest organization; the Altar Guild, who prepared the sanctuary for services; the Woman's Auxiliary, the missionary organization for the parish; St. Mary's Guild, an extension of the Woman's Auxiliary for younger ladies offering aid to the needy in the community; the Festival of Lights marking the Epiphany[18] season and the Massing of the Colors, recognizing members of all branches of the Armed Forces, veterans and their auxiliaries. During the term of 1961-64 the Book Shop was established, the Episcopal Churchmen were organized and a Coffee Hour was held in the Cluett Gardens. The church school was reorganized and a new curriculum introduced.

In 1989, Bethesda-by-the-Sea observed one hundred-years of service. A grand ceremony was held encompassing various celebrations, services and receptions. As the church moves into a new century, Reverend Ralph R. Warren, Jr. offered the following sentiment:

"The world is crying out for the healing message
Of Jesus the Christ, and we here at Bethesda-by-the-Sea,
A 'House of Healing,' have much to do in the name of the
One who brings to our world salvation and wholeness."

BETHESDA-BY-THE-SEA

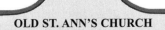

OLD ST. ANN'S CHURCH

Dedicated March 15, 1896, on the southeast corner
of Rosemary and Datura streets. In 1902, it was
moved to this site donated by Henry Flagler, and
served the catholic community until 1913, when
the new church was dedicated. The old church
was then used as the forerunner of St. Ann's
school built in 1926. St. Ann's church is the oldest Catholic Church and parish in the diocese of
Palm Beach. It was developed by the fathers of
the Society of Jesus.

302 Olive Avenue, Palm Beach
PB19 ~ GPS Coordinates: 26.715517, -80.051717

Bishop John Moore dispatched Jesuit Father Conrad M. Widman to Lake Worth in 1892 to establish a diocese in what is known today as Palm Beach. The first Mass was celebrated in the home of John Pucell McKenna
during which McKenna's son was the first child baptized into the Catholic faith. The site of Saint Ann was a gift
of Palm Beach developer Henry Flagler. The parish at Olive Avenue was officially dedicated by Bishop Moore on
March 15, 1896 and has celebrated more than one hundred years in that location.

His Holiness Pope John Paul II directed Bishop Thomas V. Daily to establish the Palm Beach Diocese on
October 24, 1984. Thirty-eight parishes comprised the diocese, which served a congregation of more than one
hundred thousand. By the time the diocese celebrated fifteen years of existence, eleven parishes had been added as
well as four missions and the number of Catholic parishioners had more than doubled. The area extended from the
northern rim at Sebastian to Boca Raton as its southern border. The Palm Beach diocese is one of the youngest
throughout Florida but quite possibly the fastest growing. Mass is offered in eleven languages from English to
Vietnamese including an interpretation in sign language.

Bishop Patrick Barry wrote to his biological sister Adrian Dominican Nun Mother Mary Gerald Barry
issuing an invitation to establish a Dominican school at West Palm Beach in 1923. Sister Barry was well acquainted with the area and needed no convincing to join all three of her brothers in Florida. Two of the brothers were
priests in the Diocese of St. Augustine while the third was a layman in the Catholic Church.

Saint Ann's School was approved with the consecration of Bishop Patrick Barry in May of 1922. Mother
Camilla Madden was contacted to arrange for Dominican Sisters to be sent to the south Florida location. A small
pink house was leased on Second Avenue for Superioress, Rose Dominic Le Blanc, Sisters Alma O'Reilly and
Angela O'Brien. Mother Camilla accompanied the others to assist in establishing the school and was enamored
with the area immediately.

A permanent structure for the school had not yet been built so the sisters taught in the sanctuary, parish
hall and in private homes. The Bishop and Jesuit Fathers diligently tried to procure permanent accommodations for
the sisters. The answer to their prayers came from a very unexpected source. Casino owner Colonel Edward
Bradley donated seven acres on Lake Worth to be used as the location for a girl's academy, today known as
Rosarian Academy. The new school facility welcomed students for the first time on October 12, 1925. Seven sisters, three non-secular teachers and four hundred sixty-three students entered the school at the sound of the bell
early on that fall morning, beginning a wonderful legacy.

School funds were limited; therefore teachers were forced to be creative. Much to the delight of her students Sister Grace de Lellis, who taught biology, rose to the occasion. No laboratory facilities were available to
her students so Sister Grace did the next best thing; she led her class to the ocean reef to study live specimens.
The students made glass bottom pails and studied the sea life they collected. One of the most fascinating of these

discoveries, which alumni remember fondly to this day, was the composure and habits of octopi.

Like most buildings in the area, the devastating hurricane of 1928 dealt a nasty blow to the school and rectory. The roofs were torn from the rafters and many of the glorious stained glass windows of the edifice were reduced to multicolored shards of gravel. The facilities were soon rebuilt but unfortunately like the beautiful stained glass, some things can never be replaced.

St. Ann's Church celebrated one hundred years of service to the parish in 1996. St. Ann's school continues to be one of the premiere facilities throughout the state. A wonderful quote was written in the St. Ann's School Yearbook of 1944, which sums up nicely the value of this church and school to those who have benefited from each:

"Due to your splendid teaching and training in religion and secular knowledge, we graduates leave St. Ann's prepared to do well in this life and the next."

ST. ANN'S CHURCH

FLAGLER PARK

Flagler Park, formerly known as City Park, has been an important public space in West Palm Beach since the founding of the community. The town site for West Palm Beach was laid out in 1893 as a grid pattern of streets running north - south and east - west. The only variation was at the eastern end of Clematis Street, where two angled, short streets branched off to create a triangular, public common area. Over the years, the site has seen a variety of uses. Downtown merchants organized impromptu ball games on the park-like grounds when business was slow. In 1900, a two-story, frame building was donated for use as a reading room and transported across Lake Worth from Palm Beach. It was placed on the southeastern portion of the parcel. The Woman's Christian Temperance Union dedicated a drinking fountain in the Park in 1907. In 1915, a Woman's Club was placed on the parcel. Other amenities were also added to the park, including a shuffleboard court and a bandstand for outdoor concerts. As the City's population expanded during the 1920's, the facilities of the Reading Room were outgrown and a library was built in 1923. It opened in January 1924, as the Memorial Library, named to honor the dead of World War I. It too was outgrown and was replaced by another library in 1962. In 1994, the library was remodeled and the plaza in front of the library was redesigned, incorporating a triangular, in-ground fountain. This forecourt has become the center of downtown activities, continuing the traditional use of this important civic space.

West Palm Beach, Palm Beach
PB20 ~ GPS Coordinates: 26.713802, -80.049249

It was the trend of the day when West Palm Beach was designed to be graphed in a very symmetrical pattern. The first and most famous city grid was Washington D.C. Dr. John Nolen of Boston was the landscape architect responsible for a great number of city designs throughout the country. He was responsible for the D.C. design as well as West Palm Beach in 1893 and Lake Park, to the north. Many cities since have followed the example.

The only exception to this grid pattern throughout the entire vista of the city was a triangular patch at the foot of Clematis Street. Before the turn of the century the green grass lot in the midst of sandy shell scattered streets was known as City Park. Years ago on quiet Wednesday afternoons in the Spring when no patrons darkened the doors of the few shops along Clematis Street, shop owners and clerks would gather together with local boys and play a little baseball at City Park.

The first publicly funded library in the county was founded in 1895, but was simply called a Reading Room. The West Palm Beach Reading Room was the first library to allow patron to "borrow" books and materials throughout southeast Florida. Actually the "Reading Room" was the inspiration of the local Anti-Saloon League to encourage towns people to spend their time reading rather than drinking in the saloons of Banyan Street. The Anti-Saloon League eventually paved the way for the Eighteenth Amendment resulting in prohibition. The Palm Beach Yacht Club lay just beyond City Park, from there citizens watched the first library come floating across Lake Worth. The site must have been spectacular as the great barge lazily drifted past with the two-storied library tied tightly down at all sides. It must have looked like a huge houseboat. The Reading Room remained in the southeastern corner of City Park for eleven years.

John Nolen designed Clematis Street to extend from lake-to-lake with parks at either end, the grandest being City Park. Nearby was the local Women Christian Temperance Union who dedicated a drinking fountain to adorn the park in 1907. Families gathered to play shuffleboard, everyone in the vicinity of the bandstand heard strains of Dixie Land wailed from brass instruments gleaming in the afternoon sun, baseball games played by neighborhood kids of all ages beneath the bright blue summer sky and couples strolled hand in hand. City Park was and is a pleasant place to while away an afternoon.

All of south Florida experienced a population explosion during the 1920s and city facilities including the library had to expand with the numbers. In January of 1924 the new Memorial Library opened it doors. The facilities were dedicated to soldiers who gallantly fought and died during World War I. The library cost a reported thirty thousand dollars to build. The handsome building sported elaborate Spanish style architecture with parapets, decorative railings and carved stonework.

After almost forty years the city chose to construct a new more modern library facility. In 1962 the new City Library was completed using the design of architect Norman Robson. The public was treated to a gala opening but controversy immediately followed. The people were accustomed to the old world charm of the 1924 Memorial Library and the new library was built with an ultra modern appearance, not everyone was pleased.

A new study was done in 1994 on ways to better utilize the City Park area, which was now called Flagler Park. It was noted that this park was the very heart of the city and as such should appeal to everyone. The new design included a picturesque promenade, decorative sculptures as well as an obelisk of the cities' founder and park's namesake, Henry M. Flagler. The beautiful green park remains a wide-open space for various activities throughout the year. Everything from elegant art showings to informative health fairs, the park is the ideal place for people to gather and delight in the heart of West Palm Beach.

West Palm Beach Public Library received an interior facelift in 1999. The design by Peter Robinson leaves a feeling of comfortable surroundings to sit and enjoy the wonders of a good book. The catalog is continually expanding to aptly serve over a half million patrons every year. The library has something for everyone from new computer online resources to children's programs, book clubs to adult enrichment. The library feeds the mind while beautiful Flagler Park fills the soul.

CLEMATIS STREET COMMERCIAL HISTORIC DISTRICT

For over 100 years, Clematis Street (named after the Clematis flower) has been the primary retail street in West Palm Beach. It was a shell-topped road in 1893, when Henry Flagler (1830-1913) began to develop West Palm Beach as the commercial district for his resort community of Palm Beach. The face of Clematis Street was changed in 1904 with paving and the installation of sidewalks and streetlights. The eastern end of Clematis Street developed first, but by 1916, as the population grew, the business district began to expand west. During the real estate boom of the 1920s, new buildings were erected to house a variety of retail establishments in the 500 block of Clematis Street. Among the contributing buildings in the district are the Hotel Clematis and Gruner's Department Store at 512-516 Clematis Street; James Rooming House at 518-20 Clematis Street; Sewell's Hardware at 528-30 Clematis Street; and the Sirkin Building at 533 Clematis Street (designed by local architects Harvey and Clarke) all built between 1920 and 1928. The 500 block of Clematis Street has the highest concentration of historic buildings in the downtown retail area. In 1998 it was place on the National Register of Historic Places.

522 Clematis Street west of Dixie Highway, West Palm Beach
PB21 ~ GPS Coordinates: 26.713270, -80.055958

Clematis Street extends its welcoming length from lake to lake with wonderful respites at beginning and end. The beautifully done avenue is an eclectic mingling of old world charms to modern trendy spots. A full compliment of restaurants, shops, clubs and at the end of it all the fabulous Centennial Park. Along Clematis Street are some very fascinating places.

One of the original businesses on Clematis Street is Sewell Hardware Company. Founded by Worley L. Sewell, Sr. in 1924, the hardware business is still owned and operated by the families' third generation. The building they currently occupy is in fact the second location. The first store was in the old Rhodes Building just west of the Florida East Coast Railroad tracks, unfortunately reduced to rubble in the 1928 hurricane that devastated all of south Florida. The company has flourished to include six stores, a contractor sales division and architectural contracts division. Sewell Hardware Company continues to thrive in the capable hands of a new generation.

A must see sight along the way is Sloan's Ice Cream Parlor at 112 Clematis Street. This ice cream parlor offers much more than thirty-two flavors and sprinkles, though it's not known for the menu items offered. In fact it's the bathrooms that Sloan's are known for. The novel bathrooms feature transparent walls and doors putting users on displaying for the curiosity seekers. But you don't have to be an exhibitionist to use the bathroom here. Once you step inside and close the door the glass fogs up and hides your behind from the viewing public. The double pane glass of the enclosure holds electrically charged liquid crystals. When the door handle is turned and locked the electrical current is broken and the crystals fall out of alignment thus the glass clouds. When the door is opened again the current is restored and the glass clears once again. But don't forget to close the door or your assets, so to speak, will be the featured attraction on Clematis Street. If you have to go badly, consider an alternate location; long waits are common.

As attractive as Sloan's bathrooms are, the most famous part of Clematis Street is Centennial Square. Located at the east end of the street at the front entrance to the city library and named for the hundred year celebration of West Palm Beach. The plaza features benches, picnic tables and a fabulous fountain.

The laughter of children can be heard as the fountain shoots water about here and there in a theatrical dance. The kids bob in and out dodging the spurts of water and having the time of their lives. The fountain is a delightful place to spread out your lunch and take a moment to enjoy the south Florida sunshine. Nearby restaurants offers neatly packed carry out plates so that patrons can take pleasure in the beautiful surroundings. On the particular summer Friday we visited Centennial Square and Clematis Street, a steel drum band played Caribbean sounds lending a tropical feel to the hot summer day. Thursday evenings come alive with "Clematis By Night." Concerts, artists and vendors selling hand made items offer a market place atmosphere, something for everyone.

Clematis Street is one of those little known treasures so wonderful in West Palm Beach. Surprises abound from Sloan's peek-a-boo bathrooms to Centennial Park's magnificent dancing waters. As the sun slips below the horizon, keep your eyes on the acrobatic fountain waters. The spurts shoot high into the air changing colors in rainbow hues and light up the night sky.

SEABOARD AIR LINE STATION

The Seaboard Air Line Railway Station has played an important role in the history of West Palm Beach and Palm Beach County. It is a unique example of early 20th century railroad architecture in the Mediterranean Revival style. The Station opened with the arrival of the Orange Blossom Special on January 25, 1925. It was the flagship station of the entire Seaboard line running from Coleman to Homestead. Harvey & Clarke, the largest architectural firm in Palm Beach County in the 1920s, created this new symbol for the City of West Palm Beach in the prevailing architectural style of the period. The Historic American Buildings Survey documented the station in 1971 and the station was listed on the National Register of Historic Places in 1973. The AMTRAK System began passenger service here in May 1971 and the Tri-County Commuter Rail Organization began passenger service from here to Miami in January 1989. The Seaboard Station was restored with substantial funding by the Florida Department of State and rededicated in April 1991.

Tarmarind Avenue at Datura Street, station courtyard, West Palm Beach
PB22 ~ GPS Coordinates: 26.711950, -80.062250

A flourish of silver medal, the squeal of iron rails and the ringing of her whistle was heard for blocks around as the Orange Blossom Special announced her arrival and the opening of the Seaboard Railroad Station on a brisk January day in 1925. The station with warm orange and creamy whites, bold blues and greens as accent colors dabbed here and there on interior tiles was something to behold, designed by local architect L. Phillips Clarke.

Crowds gathered round the courtyard at Tamarind Avenue and Datura Street while their eyes wandered across the newly constructed station with the two-storied tower on the north end sloping to a single level on the south side, typical of its design. The Mediterranean Revival architectural style brings to life the feel of Spain with arched entries, great Corinthian columns with the strength of Atlas, and elaborate embellishments reminiscent of the matador in all his shining silver glory. Stucco and masonry leave smooth lines and a calming effect, prompting passengers to slow down and notice their opulent surroundings.

The steel rails made their way down the eastern seaboard bringing much more than a huge iron horse spewing steam, they brought progress. More than any other event in Florida's history the railroad changed things. Tourism, today a multi-billion dollar industry, exporting citrus and the ease of transportation allowing for the development of settlements in south Florida; all of these things were the direct result of train transportation.

The Orange Blossom Special was the first train into West Palm Beach, it operated from New York to Florida. In fact, the Special was actually two trains. One line ran to Miami and the other across the state to Tampa and St. Petersburg. The trains split into their respective directions at Washington D.C. The southern train left New York arriving in Washington D.C. after a bumpy five-hour ride. There the train would split in her two directions; the Miami bound line pulling out of the station at 3:05 p.m., arriving Miami with her weary passengers some thirty-one hours later; the Tampa/St. Petersburg riders were only slightly more fortunate, only enduring a little over twenty-eight hours on the train. None-the-less this was far better transportation than any other alternative available. In fact riding the train was a often a social event with drinks in the club car, meals in the dining car, even an observation car allowed a spot to step out and watch the world go by. Sleepers provided a bunk to be lull to sleep while listening to the rhymic chug of the train as it rolled down the track. In 1934, train travel became even more comfortable aboard the Orange Blossom Special with the major addition of air conditioning but then in 1938, diesel fuel replaced coal and steam. Train transportation may have progressed with this innovation but it sure smelled a lot worse. The Orange Blossom Special was retired in 1952 when Silver Star/Meteor trains were put into service, the end of an era had come. But the Orange Blossom Special would live on in the hearts and minds of people all over the world.

In 1939 two young fiddlers, Ervin Rouse and Chubby Wise, took a tour through the train and heard her whistle call. They went straight home with an idea and the song "Orange Blossom Special" was soon born. Rouse and Wise managed to capture the sound of the lonesome whine of the wheels, the rhythm of the train and the wail of the whistle. In 1941, Bluegrass fiddler Bill Monroe had a hit with the song, then in 1965, Country's late great Johnny Cash went to number one with the song as well. Then master musician Roy Clark turned out his rendition several years later to standing ovations around the world.

During the 1960s, the United States entered an era of disposable everything. Tragically, many beautiful historic structures were laid low during this time. Seaboard Railroad Station was saved from destruction and restoration began at the railway station in 1996. Architect Clarke would have been very happy with the results. Great attention to detail left an indiscernible line between the original station and the renovation. The Department of Transportation supplied the funding and the station was expanded to include a complete transit facility on six and a half acres across the railroad tracks.

The new venture included a high-speed rail system, airport and harbor transportation, commuter bus routes, inner-city bus system, taxi pick-up and drop-off points, transportation services for the handicapped and elderly as well as storage for bicyclists making use of the transportation systems. The railway cars seat just over one hundred fifty travelers with the exception of lower capacity cars accommodating handicap facilities, luggage and bicycle racks. The railroad cars are decorative displays of blue skies and clouds with tropical coconut palms in the foreground.

The modernized station has wonderful new characteristics making travel not only simple but fun as well. Elevators and stairs lead to overhead walking bridges for the safety of passengers crossing the tracks. Digital displays throughout keep the traveler informed on train schedules and outside canopies lend protection against the hot sun and rain. Easy accessibility for the handicapped is obviously a priority and careful attention has been given to those with special needs. Automated ticket vending machines, pay phones, snack machine, water fountains and comfortable surroundings are available with the travelers convenience in mind.

Trains run from the early morning hours before dawn to late evening hours. The local zones include Mangonia Park, north of West Palm Beach to the Miami International Airport. Fares are very affordable ranging from two to ten dollars based on the number of zones you travel. Discounts are available for multi-ticket purchases, monthly tickets and weekend travel. Travelers from Seaboard Air Line Station number in excess of ten thousand per day and increasing all the time. For a sense of old world Florida or just to get from here to there economically, take a ride on the rails and listen to a recording of Orange Blossom Special. The sound of the rail and the song are bound to take you back.

PALM BEACH HIGH SCHOOL

This Mediterranean Revival style building housed Palm Beach Junior College, Florida's first public community college, when it was established here in 1933. The college outgrew these facilities after the Second World War and moved in 1948 to Morrison Field, a U.S. Army Air Base, renovated to accommodate the influx of students in peace time. In 1955 the college relocated to its present site in Lake Worth. Among the civic leaders responsible for promoting the concept of the junior college were Palm Beach County Superintendent of Schools Joseph A. Youngblood and Palm Beach High School Principal Howell L. Watkins. The college served as a model for the state-wide system of Junior Colleges. Three students were in the first graduating class of 1936. In 1936 John I. Leonard became the first president of the Palm Beach Junior College. William Manly King (1886-1961), a noted West Palm Beach architect, designed this building in the Mediterranean Revival style so popular in Florida in the 1920's. The design complemented the adjacent Palm Beach High School campus and this building was occupied in 1927. As architect for the Palm Beach County Board of Public Instruction he designed numerous school buildings throughout Palm Beach County. Mr. King also designed hotels in West Palm Beach, the National Guard Armory (1939), the Hibiscus Garden Apartments (1926) and the seal for the City of West Palm Beach. In June, 1991 the building was listed in the National Register of Historic Places. The Mediterranean Revival classroom building continued to serve the needs of the School Board and in November, 1991 it was returned to Palm Beach Community College. The College Foundation undertook the challenge of restoring the building for the continuing education of citizens in our community. This historical marker is dedicated to commemorate the 60th Anniversary of Palm Beach Community College, 1933-1993.

813 Gardenia Street, West Palm Beach
PB23 ~ GPS Coordinates: 26.708700, -80.058900

TODAY'S PALM BEACH COMMUNITY COLLEGE

PALM BEACH
JUNIOR COLLEGE

The earliest junior colleges in Florida were established under private auspices, beginning in 1907 with Palmer College at DeFuniak Springs. The first public junior college was instituted by the Palm Beach County school board during the Depression years to make college opportunities available to those local high school graduates unable to meet the expenses of attending school away from home. Palm Beach Junior College admitted its first students in 1933. Its first goal was to provide two years of acceptable college work. Soon it also offered career or vocational education for persons desiring to work after graduation and adult education programs. In 1939, state legislation provided legal status for the junior college program by authorizing county school boards to organize and maintain such institutions using county school funds. In 1947, Palm Beach Junior College began to receive state assistance under new legislation. Beginning in the 1950's the junior college program in Florida began to expand, aided by the long-term plans of the Community College council created in 1955. The educational goals of Palm Beach Junior College served as a model for Florida's developing community college program.

Congress Ave. (SR 807) at Administration Building, Lake Worth
PB33 ~ GPS Coordinates: 26.612000, -80.086400

Secondary education in Palm Beach County was the concept of County School Superintendent Joe Youngblood and Howell Watkins, principal of Palm Beach High School. Though it might seem absurd to establish a school of higher learning while the country was tightly gripped in the bonds of the Great Depression, these two forward thinking educators realized that so many high school graduates were unable to find work and money was so sparse that going away to college was virtually out of the question. The next step involved coordinating with the University of Florida and Florida State Women's College, later known as Florida State University. If their two-year institution was to be stepping stone for a university education then the curriculum must be easily merged.

The next great obstacle involved, of course, funding. No public subsidies were available, local citizens and civic organizations pleaded with the Palm Beach County Board of Public Instruction to fund the two-year institution. Due to the budget constraints teachers from the local high school volunteered to teach at the college without compensation. Palm Beach Junior College was to be the first and only public two-year higher education facility for fourteen years.

Forty-one students registered for classes; two years later in 1936 three students marched in the graduation processional. Howell Watkins was Palm Beach Junior College's first dean and John I. Leonard, the first president known to his students and colleagues as "Mr. Junior College." During the ensuing years the Junior College blossomed, eventually it became evident that new quarters were required for the ever growing student body.

An ideal location was found and obtained in 1948, Morrison Field. Like so many other stations, the former Air Force Base was abandoned by the military and property returned to the city at the conclusion of World War II. A cavernous airplane hangar became the library and the Officer's Club, where so many young men had caroused in their glory days, aptly became the Student Union. Unfortunately the ideal location was to be short-lived when armed conflict reared its ugly head and young men were shipped out to Korea in 1951[19]. Palm Beach Junior College was on the move once again.

New accommodations were found in Lake Park Town Hall. The facilities were so tiny, much to the chagrin of administration, countless students were denied entrance and enrollment suffered greatly. Chemistry classes were held in the jail, English and Speech met in a nearby church and other teachers met on the lawn, in the hallway just anywhere a vacant space could be found to conduct classes. Ironically, alumni recall these informal sessions lovingly to this day as one of the greatest times in Palm Beach Junior College history. Several alumni went on to become celebrities including Florida's favorite son and world known actor, Burt Reynolds. Reynolds, throughout his career has been a loyal son, always giving back to the state of his birth ten fold. The entertainment he has and continues to provide the world is without equal, as you can probably tell I'm a fan. Others including Monte Markham, who's done everything from Hogan's Heroes so long ago to more recent Baywatch, Melrose Place and Honey I Shrunk the Kids was a student in Lake Park, as well as Terry Garrity, the author of "The Sensuous Woman." The list of distinguished alumni could go on; lawyers, doctors, business executives and people from every walk of life have received the benefits of this worthwhile institution.

The Community College Council was established by the Florida Legislature in 1955. The "master plan" for post secondary education provided educational opportunities for prospective students throughout the state. The success of the Florida program became the standard for community colleges across the nation. The County Commission handsomely rewarded Palm Beach Junior College for their service to the community in 1960. A donation of one hundred fourteen acres in Lake Worth was provided for the construction of a permanent home and the state of Florida conveyed one million dollars for construction costs. Dr. Harold C. Manor led the way into this new chapter of the institutions' history. Under his guidance the college experienced growth like never before as well as expanding student services and course opportunities. The college entered a new era when programs in both technical and vocational fields were introduced, which in turned offered secondary education to those who may never have considered advanced academics.

Palm Beach Junior College faced the Civil Rights era in 1965 with courage and determination. Merging with Roosevelt Junior College, an all black institution, the schools exchanged faculty and began a tenuous period of adjustment. The results were well worth the struggle; two colleges combined to make one strong institution for the benefit of all.

Over the next twenty years satellite centers were built in neighboring communities further expanding the educational opportunities to students. Dr. Edward M. Eissey, college president until 1996, accomplished great feats during his administration including a name change, the first in Palm Beach Junior College history. In 1988, the school became known as Palm Beach Community College. The name was so very appropriate based on the service to the community and her citizens provided by this essential institution. Today, Palm Beach Community College continues to change and grow with the needs of the community. Working with employers, industry, governmental agencies and other schools, the programs offered prepare students to enter the world as productive citizens and assets to not only their college but the city, county, state and nation in which they live.

STUB CANAL TURNING BASIN

The Stub Canal Turning Basin represents an important link between West Palm Beach and the agricultural communities adjacent to Lake Okeechobee. In the late 19th century, Florida began draining the Everglades/Lake Okeechobee basin to provide water transportation routes and to create farmland from swamps. When the Board of Drainage Commissioners authorized the construction of a canal network in 1905, a connection to West Palm Beach was not included. In 1911, local businessman George Currie, on behalf of the Chamber of Commerce, petitioned Governor Albert Waller Gilchrist (1858-1926) for a canal from Lake Okeechobee to Lake Worth. Known as the West Palm Beach Canal, the forty-mile channel was authorized in 1913, and completed in 1917. By 1918, an extension, or stub, was constructed to bring the canal directly into the West Palm Beach business district. The City built shipping facilities and this Turning Basin. The Stub Canal served as a dependable route for passenger travel and for the shipment of produce from, and provisions to, the western agricultural communities until 1925, when improved railroad and highway connections provided other means of transportation.

Howard Park on Parker Avenue, south of Okeechobee Boulevard, West Palm Beach
PB24 ~ GPS Coordinates: 26.703671, -80.061190

Governor Napoleon Bonaparte Broward muscled through an Everglades drainage system plan in 1905, costing the taxpayers a quarter of a million dollars. Opposition to the plan was heavy but Governor Broward was determined to begin the project none-the-less. The initial canal called New River, linked Lake Okeechobee to Fort Lauderdale. George Currie, a West Palm Beach businessman working in conjunction with the Chamber of Commerce, petitioned newly elected Governor Albert Waller Gilchrist to include the city in the canal system. Unfortunately the proposal met with some resistance. In 1912, Florida officials realized that the drainage expenses had become unmanageable. In order to complete the canals bonds would have to be issued.

Within five years a canal reached from Lake Okeechobee to West Palm Beach. Northern newspaperman, William J. Conners, established the Everglades Agricultural Area and amazingly built a toll road to run alongside the Palm Beach Canal. Conners' Toll Road provided a means of travel eventually from Florida's eastern shore to the Gulf of Mexico. West Palm Beach city fathers proposed a means of passenger travel and agricultural shipments via the canals. To this end the city built a dredged harbor and the Turning Basin. The Turning Basin was a tributary off the canal or stub, thus the name Stub Canal Turning Basin. The basin was in use until 1925 when the railroad and modern highway construction made the basin obsolete.

The population and land explosions of the early 1920s came to a sudden but definite halt by 1926. The newly developed property stimulated an increase in citizenry. A series of natural disasters including two devastating hurricanes followed by a severe drought left a need for additional funding. The Okeechobee Flood Control District was formed in response, then bonds were issued. Catastrophe rained down as the Great Depression clutched the country in a strangle hold. Many of the canal projects were left unfinished until the United State Army Corps of Engineers were sent in the complete the systems

Interest in the canal systems came to an abrupt standstill. Over the next several decades the only canal to cross the state from Palatka in northeast Florida to the Gulf of Mexico was aptly named, Cross Florida Barge Canal. President Richard Nixon bent to pressure exerted by Congress in 1971 and brought all canal construction to an end. During the time canals were entrenched, thousands of miles were cut into the Florida landscape. Though construction of canals came to an end, work remained in maintenance and management of the artificial water system.

While doing research for this particular marker I encountered an article, which left me with a different perspective concerning the Everglades. Many years ago during a time when the drive in Florida was frantic building, "Save the Everglades," meant filling in the wetlands to create viable land to build upon. Today when so much of our focus is on conservation, "Save the Everglades" means to leave the land as untouched as possible. Isn't it ironic, how the two prevalent views are direct opposites? For the wilds of the glades, the sake of its creatures and the future of us all, I pray conservation will always prevail.

PIONEER MEMORIAL PARK

The Lakeside Cemetery Association (LCA), formed in 1891, was composed of a group of the earliest pioneer families of what is today Palm Beach County (part of Dade County until 1909). In 1895, the LCA purchased this site to be used as a private cemetery. From 1895 until approximately 1920, the pioneer families buried their dead in this cemetery. Over two hundred of Dade and Palm Beach County's earliest and most prominent citizens were buried here, including many of the earliest public officials, landowners, and business owners. Initially, both African American and white pioneers were buried here, which was very unusual for the time. In 1902, the LCA purchased two acres located two blocks to the south to serve as a separate cemetery for African Americans (today known as Flamingo Park). In 1914, Henry M. Flagler donated to the City of West Palm Beach the land immediately to the west of this site, on which Woodlawn Cemetery was created as West Palm Beach's municipal cemetery. In 1921, the LCA donated this site to the City of West Palm Beach for public park purposes. In 1940, upon the request of the City of West Palm Beach, the LCA released a series of deed restrictions encumbering the property allowing the Norton Gallery and School of Art, provided that this site shall forever be known as "Pioneer Memorial Park." Most of the pioneers buried on this site were exhumed and re-interred in Woodlawn Cemetery. However, as many as forty pioneers were not removed and remain buried on this site today.

US 1 and Jefferson Road, Lake Worth
PB25 ~ GPS Coordinates: 26.701067, -80.053850

The site at what is today the intersection of US 1 and Jefferson Road was purchased by the Lakeside Cemetery Association for use as a private burial place for the founding families of the Palm Beach area. All original families regardless of race, neighbor beside neighbor, utilized the interment acres. The cemetery was active for twenty-five years; however, in 1902 it was decided that the races were to be segregated in death as they were in life. The Association purchased two acres, just two blocks south of the original burial sites and from that point forward all African Americans were interred there. The new burial site was simply known as "colored cemetery" on maps of the day. Today the site is called "Flamingo Park".

Henry Flagler arrived in 1914 and donated a plot of land for use as a municipal cemetery, the burial site would be known as Woodlawn. The Lakeside Cemetery Association donated Woodlawn to the City of West Palm Beach seven years later. The Association released the cemetery on the condition that the property will forever is known as Pioneer Memorial Park. All remaining gravesites were exhumed and reinterred at Woodlawn Cemetery. It is thought that some forty original pioneers were left behind in unknown lots.

In 1940, retired Acme Steel Company head Ralph Hubbard Norton and his wife Elizabeth founded the Norton Gallery and School of Art to house their extensive collection of fine art paintings and sculpture. The

Nortons commissioned acclaimed architect Marion Syms Wyeth to design the museum. The original Art Deco, Neo-Classical edifice opened its doors at South Olive Avenue and South Dixie Highway ceremoniously on February 8, 1941. The site was part of Pioneer Memorial Park and would soon come to be recognized worldwide.

The gallery features more than five thousand works comprised of European, American, Chinese, Modern art and Photography. Claude Monet, Henri Matisse, Pierre-Auguste Renoir and Paul Cézanne are just a few of the European Master represented in four galleries. American artists fill five galleries and include works by Stuart Davis, Edward Hopper, John Marin, Robert Motherwell, Georgia O'Keefe, Andy Warhol, George Bellows and Jackson Pollock. Works on paper and sculpture by Jean Arp, Constantine Brancusi, Pablo Picasso, Alexander Calder, Gaston Lachaise, Jacques Lipchitz and Ossip Zadkine round out the illustrious collection. The gallery is arranged by category of works such as portraits, still lifes, landscapes, abstracts, etc.

Centerbrook Architects and Planners of Connecticut undertook an expansion and renovation project in 1993. Public demand and growth facilitated the undertaking, funded by a collective grassroots fundraising campaign. The galleries required double the initial capacity and the enterprise was finally completed in January 1997. Centerbrook architect Chad Floyd designed the latest augmentation named for benefactors Gail and Melvin Nessel. A gala opening was held on March 8, 2003 highlighting cultured visitor amenities. The forty-five thousand square foot expansion includes a cantilevered spiral staircase, an impressively breathtaking three storied atrium and a glass ceiling by acclaimed modern artist Dale Chihuly. The new aesthetic surroundings accentuate the works housed within. The Nessel Wing adds fourteen galleries, an elegant interior courtyard and spacious facilities for educational and social occasions.

Throughout each year various thematic and special exhibitions are presented representing the ever-expanding spectrum of art. The Norton Gallery records more than one hundred eighty thousand visitors each year. A moderate admission is charged and annual memberships are available. The museum is open seven days per week.

GRANDVIEW HEIGHTS HISTORIC DISTRICT

In response to the heavy influx of new residents into South Florida at the turn of the century and the introduction of the automobile, local developers and real estate agents purchased the less expensive land outside of the West Palm Beach downtown area and developed the first speculative suburbs. Platted in the 1910-1920s as three subdivisions, Grandview Heights is one of the earliest attempts at southwestern expansion of the city. Because of its relatively steep topography for south Florida, it was considered a desirable place to live because it was less than a mile from downtown, within close proximity to the City Terminals, West Palm Beach Canal, the Turning Basin, and had a view of the Everglades. Built for working and middle class residents, the quickly constructed homes were well made but affordable. The neighborhood consists of primarily Bungalow type homes that reflect mainly the Craftsman and Mission styles, both widely popular during the 1920s Florida Land Boom Era.

Palm Street and Florida Avenue, West Palm Beach
PB28 ~ GPS Coordinates: 26.696452, -80.058337

Historical Grandview Heights is the elder of the Palm Beach neighborhoods, having begun construction of moderate homes in 1910. Local builders and craftsmen were largely responsible for the construction of the dwellings in Grandview Heights. The subdivision spanned an area encompassing Alabama and Florida Avenue in the east to Lake Avenue west and N Street south to Park Place's northern boundary.

Most of the residents were people of modest means; shop keepers, ministers and blue-collar workers who labored endlessly to make a living for their families. Housing designs were taken from a variety of sources, but most contractors built early craftsman bungalows distinctive of the south Florida area. It has been said that Grandview Height was the best collection of early craftsman style dwellings throughout the state. A bit of the Spanish influence crept into the mix as a few homes reflected the tropically inspired Mediterranean Revival architecture are found here and there in the neighborhood.

The Craftsman Bungalow style in Grandview Height is an Americanized version of a style first found in Bengal, India's native housing called bangala. The British were the first to adopt this style often utilized for country summer homes. However the British altered the floor design situating the dining room, bedrooms, kitchen and indoor bathing rooms around a central living area. This was the design that American builders adopted chiefly due to the efficiency of the plans.

The features of Craftsman Bungalow architecture are distinctive and simplistic. The dwellings were typically single storied dwellings, having a low-pitched roof extending to wide eaves leaving roof rafters exposed to view. A wide porch extended across the front of the dwelling with square unadorned columns supporting the overhang. Numerous built in conveniences including cabinets, shelving, window seats and benches distinguished the interior. A stone or shell-encrusted chimney reached toward the sky from the roof of each dwelling and gabled dormer embraced windows.

Another common architectural design found in Grandview Heights was the Colonial Revival style. This design was often used for commercial buildings, churches and grand suburban homes. It seems that the builders who chose to use Colonial Revival plans were more apt to build larger business structures rather than the smaller less ornate houses of the common man. Many times the design would be distinctive in that certain elements were exceptionally large or out of proportion in comparison with the remainder of the house.

The front of the home often displayed twin porches of equal size both having an entryway embellished with sidelights as well as a chandelier style fixture above the main entrance. Exceptional pillars rather ornately capped would support the large entry porches. The gabled roof more often than not with dormer windows would have either slate or wooden shingles reminiscent of typically thatched roofs. The exterior would be made of painted clapboard, usually white or fashioned of red brick. A widow's walk was often found above the front porches. Bay windows were predominately embraced by double-hung louvered shutters or hurricane shutters as they were called in south Florida. The interior would feature a grand staircase, sometimes freestanding with no visible means of support. Fireplaces were ornate with a fan decoration above the firebox opening etched in marble underneath an ornate mantle piece. Much of the historic neighborhood was lost in 1989 due to the blight of urban sprawl. Newer structures of metal and glass rose to the heavens in the form of condominiums and business offices blocking the beauty of the landscape. Yet enough of Grandview Heights remains to be named in 1995 as one of West Palm Beaches' historic districts. Grandview Heights was named to the National Register of Historic Places in 1999.

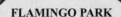

FLAMINGO PARK

This site originally was the southeast corner of an eighty-acre parcel purchased by George L. Marsteller of Charleston, South Carolina, in 1884 for $100. Two blocks to the north between South Dixie Highway and South Olive Avenue the Lakeside Cemetery Association had platted the Lakeside Cemetery in 1895. It operated as a racially integrated facility, unusual for the times. In 1902, the Association purchased these two acres from West Palm Beach to serve as a separate cemetery for African Americans. The Association platter190 lots and interred approximately100 people by 1913. The cemetery never had an official name; maps of the era simply called it "Colored Cemetery." The City's efforts to repossess and resell the cemetery in 1916 were blocked by the Florida Supreme Court. By 1921, unable to maintain the cemetery, the Association donated it to the City without restrictions. No further burials took place. The City converted the cemetery to a public park known as Dixie Playground and later renamed Flamingo Park. Citizens' protests in 1966 and 1991 thwarted subsequent attempts to sell the park for commercial development.

US 1 at Park Place, West Palm Beach
PB26 ~ GPS Coordinates: 26.699609, -80.057175

This shaded little park located on US 1 between Park and Palm Streets is a plat of land with an immense history. Dating back to 1884, the first recorded owner was Charleston born George Marsteller. It is said he owned this little two-acre site as well as seventy-two additional acres. Imagine eighty acres purchased for one hundred dollars, well that was the price in 1884. Though no one really knows an abundance about the history of this little park other than what the historical marker reveals to us, Marsteller probably farmed the property and sold it during the population explosion in the 1920s. In 1895 Lakeside Cemetery was located between South Dixie Highway and South Olive Avenue. It is at this point history takes a turn, oddly enough Lakeside was a racially mixed cemetery, which for this period in United States history was virtually unheard of particularly in the southern states. By 1902 the Lakeside Cemetery Association bent to public pressure and purchased the two-acre park to serve as a separate cemetery for African Americans. It is said the cemetery had no official name but was simply identified as the "Colored Cemetery" on most maps of the day. Records show that the Association platted one hundred ninety burial sites possible for the two acres and by 1913, approximately one hundred persons were buried there.

The city was determined buy the cemetery and vigorously pursued the plan in 1916. The purpose of the sell or what the land was to be used for was not stated. Regardless the Florida Supreme Court blocked the sale. But by 1921, the city managed to obtain the property when the Association claimed to no longer be able to maintain it. The city was deeded the property with no restrictions concerning the use. Evidence shows that no further burials took place in the cemetery after this date.

The city converted the cemetery to a public park known as Dixie Playground. No mention is made on the documentation what became of the one hundred known burial sites. It is assumed they were removed. In both 1966 and 1991 the city attempted to sell the park for business developments, today this side of US 1 is a businesses district. The citizens rose up in protest again and the city backed down. So as the traffic whizzes by on US 1, the quiet little park sits there in the midst of urban sprawl.

Reports say strange lights and little orbs float through the park at night and an elderly black man has been seen sitting by tree there but with the turn of a head or a spoken word he simply vanishes into the night air. Perhaps it's the musing of an anxious ghost hunter or reflections seen from passing cars in the night. Or perhaps some of the graves still remain in the little park and sometimes the residents rise up to watch the traffic go by.

Traffic circle at the intersection of Georgia Avenue and Flamingo Drive, West Palm Beach
PB27 ~ GPS Coordinates: 26.697933, -80.054300

Eighteen years before Palm Beach County was founded, the Florida Pineapple Company purchased some one hundred twenty acres of land on the southeastern shores of the state. The transaction was completed on December 21, 1891 with the company paying approximately twenty dollars an acre for the unimproved land. Over the next thirty years the company valiantly attempted to grow pineapple on the property. It became increasingly evident the crop would not prosper here.

Losing money on the agricultural venture every year spurred the Florida Pineapple Company to consider other alternatives. In 1909, the acreage became part of Palm Beach County and Henry Flagler began creating his wonderland for the prosperous. The company realized a need for moderately priced housing for those of median income. The Flamingo Park subdivision was platted on May 17, 1921 for residential housing. The lots sold slowly at first but eventually the population boom resulted in all of the property being sought after, typically by northern investors. Within five years the subdivision spanned from the Florida East Coast Railway tracks to the east to what is known today as Parker Avenue as its western boundary and extending from Park Place in the north to Belvedere Road, south. Palm Beach businessman, M. E. Gruber was largely responsible for the blossoming district's success.

The landscape featured gently rolling hills leading to the highest coastal ridge north of Miami. As families moved in schools were established, stores opened and public facilities were made available. The traffic circle at the intersection of Georgia Avenue and Flamingo Drive, West Palm Beach was created to serve the community. Soon the population explosion resulted in ever expanding businesses along the Dixie Highway including a movie house, pharmacy, mercantile, furniture store and automobile dealership. To accommodate area vehicular traffic the roads were improved including concrete sidewalks and new fangled roadway lighting.

Most popular in the day were one and two storied Mission Revival architecturally styled single family dwellings. Distinctive in design by wooden frame or clay tile most construction was finished with a stucco veneer. Some of the homes were capped with gabled roofs while others featured the flat roof, giving an air of Spanish flare. Red barrel tiles were largely used as shingling, many structures included a parapet. The Mission style was unique in that it displayed very little in outward ornamentation but was distinguished in the use of architrave or arches surrounding the doors and windows. To further embrace the Spanish influence heavy wooden doors were used having weighty black wrought iron hardware.

Along the height of the ridge, largely consuming the seven hundred blocks, the Mediterranean Revival architecture was prominent. The stature of these residences allowed occupants a breath-taking view of the ocean beyond. This was in the days before lofty condominiums and sky scraping business offices crowded the beautiful scenic shores. Having some similarities to the Mission edifices, the Mediterranean influence differed with wrought iron balconies, towers and turrets enhancing the scenic aqua blue waters in the distance. Many combined the elements used in construction for example a flat roof embraced by a gabled parapet.

Also represented in the Flamingo subdivision were Monterey and American Foursquare architectural styles. The Monterey style was generally two storied with wide porches facing the streets while American Foursquare featured singled leveled homes with wide overhanging eaves and an enclosed foyer, approaches extended across the front of the home. The wooden framed cottages were constructed of durable Florida pine, said to be virtually hurricane resistant. Of course it is common to believe this was based on the strength of the particular hurricane as past history has proven. Local contractors were hired to build the majority of the Flamingo subdivision. Of the more than five hundred structures only two were commissioned by professional architects. Local architects Harvey and Clarke designed the Alfred Comeau House in 1924 and the National Guard Armory, today known as Armory Art Center, which is attributed to William Manly King. King chose to aptly use the Art Moderne style of architecture for the 1939 facility.

In the early days the subdivision extended efforts to preserve the natural flora, unfortunately construction both residential and roadways left little of the native plant life salvageable. Tropical coconut palms, mahogany and black olive trees would eventually border the paved streets. The trees gave the feeling of a Mediterranean ambiance to the neighborhood. As the years passed renovations to the historical homes has of course been necessary to maintain the homes. Few changes have been made ensuring that the over all picture of Flamingo Park neighborhood appears much as it did in the 1920s and 30s.

Urban sprawl brought criminal activity, property values declined, the neighborhood was littered and structures deteriorated somewhat. Homeowners who were intent on taking back and maintaining the historic subdivision founded the Flamingo Park Neighborhood Association in 1986. First, a Neighborhood Watch program was established and crime decreased. Improvements were made to the landscaping and attention paid to needed renovations, putting a fresh face on the structures. Great strives were extended to obtain the historical designation the neighborhood so richly deserved. In the effort historical distinction was noted and street names were placed on the characteristic blue banners befitting a historical district. A House of the Month program was established as well as financial contributions solicited to aid in the struggle to implement programs to improve the quality of life.

Because of the tremendous work of the Flamingo Neighborhood Association, property values have increased and the scenery of the area has made an incredible positive turn. After speaking with the President of the Flamingo Park Neighborhood Association it became obvious why families began moving back to the subdivision, thus Flamingo Park becoming a sought after address. The Association is dedicated to the preservation of this wonderful corner of Palm Beach County and its history but also the push to come together as a community, supporting one another and caring for each neighbor is vastly evident. The community hosts neighborhood clean-up days, a garden tour in the spring, monthly socials, a Halloween Party, Historic Holiday Tour of Homes and Christmas lighting contests during the season.

After a rigorous procedure involving all of the property owners, the neighborhood became Flamingo Park Historic District. The process involved three years of dedication to achieve the momentous milestone. In January of 1994, the district was added to the West Palm Beach Register of Historic Places. Finally and most prestigious, Flamingo Park was named to the National Register of Historic Places on July 14, 2000. The distinction was a well-deserved honor and aptly bestowed on the Flamingo Park Historic District, thanks largely to the determination and care of the Flamingo Park Neighborhood Association. A job well done.

EL CID NEIGHBORHOOD

In 1876, Benjamin Lanehart homesteaded land that is now the north end of El Cid. Soon afterward, Elizabeth Wilder Moore settled on the shores of Lake Worth, just south of Lanehart. Lanehart started the first commercial pineapple operation in the area, and this fruit soon dominated the local agriculture. But by the turn of the century, competition and plant diseases ruined the pineapple business. However, the population of West Palm Beach continued to grow. The El Cid Neighborhood was a product of the 1920's Florida Land Boom era. Pittsburgh socialite John Phipps (1874-1958), the son of Andrew Carnegie's partner in U.S. Steel, assembled these old pineapple fields to develop the district. Beginning in 1921, independent builders sold expensive Mediterranean Revival and Mission-style homes on most of the available lots. Its proximity to downtown and the shore of Lake Worth attracted affluent business, political, and social leaders who dominated the city's development in the 1920's and 1930's. Phipps named his development El Cid after the celebrated medieval Spanish hero, Rodrigo Diaz de Vivar. His Moorish enemies called him Cid, an Arabic word meaning lord. The El Cid District is listed on the National Register of Historic Places.

Intersection of Pershing and Flagler Drive, Palm Beach
PB29 ~ GPS Coordinates: 26.690568, -80.050012

South Florida in the 1920s was experienced a huge population explosion. Flagler's railroad led the way for waves of people, development, industry and money. Palm Beach had become the place to be for northern society during their winter sabbaticals. Affluent neighborhood developments were sprouting all over. El Cid was one of these.

The area, once a commercial pineapple field, produced the major portion of the pineapples shipped north. Benjamin Lanehart owned a great deal of this property with Elizabeth Wilder Moore, his neighbor to the south. Unfortunately as other areas of the state developed, pineapple fields became a common sight. By the turn of century competition put a squeeze on the Palm Beach operation. Then came disaster with the pineapple blight affecting almost the entire harvests. The era of pineapple production at Palm Beach came to an abrupt end around 1930.

A wealthy man from Pittsburgh known as John Phipps arrived on the scene with the influx of people rushing to stake a claim in the Palm Beach real estate market. He developed the area today bordering Flagler Drive adjacent to the Intracoastal Waterway traveling west to South Dixie Highway, the northern border being Flamingo Drive and Dyer Road to the south. Phipps would give his development the exotic name of El Cid.

Phipps grandfather arrived on the shore in Philadelphia from his English homeland, soon moving to Pittsburgh. Grandfather Phipps was a cobbler[20] by trade and found success in making stylish ladies high-top button shoes. The ladies shoes were all the rage and Phipps handiwork became well known. He was successful enough for when it came time for son Henry to enter college, he had his choice of schools. Henry chose Yale University majoring in what is known today as business administration.

Henry met and established a close friendship with one of his classmates, Andrew Carnegie. After graduation Henry was invited to become an accountant at Carnegie Steel. Pittsburgh charcoal man Henry Clay Frick also joined the firm, which prospered producing high quality carbon steel. Unfortunately, Frick and Carnegie were often at odds with very different views on how the business should be conducted. The disagreements became so heated that on several occasions, Phipps had to step in before the arguments came to blows. With their fortunes well in hand the partners decided to sell Carnegie Steel and divide the profits. J. P. Morgan purchased the company, which he in turned named U.S. Steel. Frick and Carnegie went on to become well known philanthropists supporting the arts, using their fortunes to support libraries and museums across the country. Henry Phipps, on the other hand, invested his fortune in moderately priced housing to improve the lives of the working class. Phipp's son John, called Jay, established the El Cid neighborhood in Palm Beach. In the 1920s, El Cid was not exactly a working class development.

The name El Cid came from the battle stories of a Spanish hero named Rodrigo Diaz de Vivar. Enemies knew him as Cid, the Arabic word for lord. Rodrigo Diaz was born 1043 at Vivar, Spain, raised in the court of King Ferdinand I and eventually married into the royal family. He valiantly fought for the Spanish crown throughout his life and in the end was banished. Rodrigo Diaz de Vivar "El Cid" died in 1099, a hero after taking the city of Valencia, Spain.

The majority of the homes throughout El Cid were constructed during the 1920s. A predominate theme is featured in the Mediterranean and mission revival styles of architecture, the influence perhaps in keeping with the Spanish surname. Chief architects were Belford Shoumate, Maurice Fatio and the team of Henry Stephen Harvey and Louis Phillips Clarke. Reportedly, Christian Kirk, who worked as a carpenter for Henry Flagler, built the oldest standing home in El Cid. The three-storied shingle-style home, located at 200 Pershing Way, was built in 1909 and is still today a private residence.

Single family homes in the El Cid neighborhood range in price from two hundred seventy five thousand to one million dollars. Prices vary based on location and condition. Just south of El Cid is Prospect Park reaching from Monceaux Road to Monroe Drive. The area was modeled after Prospect Park in Brooklyn, New York. El Cid was recognized by the city of West Palm Beach in 1993 with a historic designation and added to the National Register of Historic Places two years later. An active Neighborhood Association today lovingly cares for the El Cid historic area.

CONNORS' TOLL HIGHWAY

Prior to 1923, travel into or out of the Lake Okeechobee Area was accomplished only by boat or canoe. In the early 1920's, W. J. Conners, a New York winter visitor bought 4000 acres of undeveloped muck land near this site. Development required that this property be accessible by land. Being a man with financial and executive ability, he was not long in achieving his desire. After obtaining approval from both houses of the State Legislature in the record time of 2 hours and 20 minutes, he set about building the W.J. Conners Toll Road. Although the terrain was unknown, Conners and his engineer, R.Y. Patterson, constructed the road using dredges. A temporary railroad installed on the roadbed hastened construction. First work began on October 16, 1924 and the highway was completed on June 25, 1925, 8 months later. The final cost of the 52 mile road was $1,800,000. The road was hailed as an engineering marvel of the time and contributed greatly to the growth of this area. Although the toll was only $.03 a mile, the average daily toll gathered was $2000. After Conners' death on October 5, 1929, the road ultimately was sold to the State of Florida for $660,000. This memorial is in tribute to his accomplishments.

12790 US 441, Canal Point
PB30 ~ GPS Coordinates: 26.866133, -80.629700

One self-made man can and did make a difference in south Florida. That sentence or something like it seems to always precede a piece on Henry Flagler. But this wasn't Flagler nor was he anything like the devout Presbyterian; in fact, William J. "Fingy" Conners swore like a longshoremen, fought like a prize fighter, threw dice, tended bar, ran the docks and virtually no one recognizes his name or his tremendous contribution to the state of Florida. Conners was a force of nature and a moving force at that.

As a thirteen-year-old boy, Conners set out to make his fortune as an entrepreneur ferrying dockworkers across the Ohio Canal for pennies. Soon his life changed drastically when his boyhood home burned to the ground. Conners, his mother, father, sister and her baby, all escaped the house but the sister dashed back inside to retrieve her sewing machine. It was a tragic mistake. The roof collapsed killing her instantly, a few weeks later his mother died of grief and one year after that the elderly senior Conners passed away as well. Fingy was the one surviving member, with the exception of the infant niece. He was beneficiary of the life insurance policies, collected the fire insurance on their home, inherited his father's saloon and had money in bank.

Conners became involved with dozens of various enterprises some legal and some well, were questionable. By the age of twenty he was well on his way to becoming a millionaire, by thirty the million was his. Conners became well known as a New York newspaperman. He bought "The Enquirer", "The Courier" and "The Express" then merged them into the "Courier-Express", which is no longer in publication. But his fortune was made with the Great Lakes Transit Corporation, running three passenger steamers and twenty-one cargo freighters.

Fingy Conners wintered in Palm Beach like the rest of the northern money. While attending a party for the opening of the Palm Beach Canal in 1917, he heard rumor of land opportunities in the Everglades. Conners soon purchased forty thousand acres of sawgrass swamp and envisioned the largest farm in Florida.

The farm was an utter failure, so Fingy bought the Southern States Land Company's experimental farm, calling it Connersville. He decided to raise cattle. The cows could not digest the sawgrass and died; so Conners bought hogs, floods came and the hogs ran loose through the glades. According to reports Conners still had some money he hadn't spent so Fingy bought more land, twelve thousand acres of lakeshore. He had spent over a million dollars and had not cleared a dime in return. Then Conners had an epiphany. He'd build a road, not just any road but one to bring people into the Everglades where no one had access before.

The fifty-two miles of road built atop soft muck[21], with the foundation and drainage buried in the unknown. Conners had no patience for delays and spent over a million dollars just to get the road underway. Still making no progress, Conners met engineer R. Y. Patterson who agreed to take on the project. Patterson seemed to make Conners' ideas come to life and quickly. The partnership was a success and the men worked together the rest of their lives. The road was built on a twenty-four foot embankment and came to be a sixteen-foot, two-lane road. Seven and half inches of crushed rock was first laid on October 16, 1923 then treated with oil. The rock was allowed to settle then another three inches of gravel was placed and finished with asphalt tar. Road crews worked around the clock for eight months finishing the road on June 23, 1924. Two days later the road was opened to traffic.

Conners hired an airplane to drop thirty thousand leaflets over Palm Beach County. The flyers invited the public to join him in a motorcade to ride the length of his new highway, called "Conners Toll Road". The procession left Palm Beach at three in the morning on July 4th, led by Conners in the first Tin Lizzie automobile in the county. The toll was a hefty one dollar fifty cents for the car and driver, then fifty cents for each additional passenger. The Jacksonville Times Union reported that an amazing fifteen thousand people joined the motorcade, which ended with a barbecue at Conners home near the tollbooth. The large house, embraced by porches all around was the site of many a party hosted by the fun loving Conners.

Conners' folly, as it was referred to by many, was a great success largely due to his wide scale advertising. The last portion of the road was completed in 1925, bringing the total length to two hundred twenty-one miles ending at Sebring. The final tab for the highway was one million eight hundred thousand dollars! Conners printed maps declaring the advantages of traveling his highway and people came in droves. Tolls eventually reached an amazing two thousand dollars per day.

After highway construction was completed, R. Y. Patterson went to work promoting the sale of property along Conners' Toll Road. Reportedly the sale of small tracts along the highway was bringing in up to a million dollars a month. Conners finally had a return on his investment. One wealthy family purchased six thousand acres at Port Mayaca.

William J. Conners passed away on October 5, 1929 at the age of seventy-two, having led a full and fascinating life. Six months after his death, Palm Beach County residents petitioned county commissioners to purchase the highway and bring the tolls to an end. The Conners' estate offered to sell the highway for six hundred sixty thousand dollars. On June 10, 1930, the last toll was collected on Conners' Toll Road. Palm Beach County defaulted on the land payments and the state of Florida foreclosed.

**BLUE STAR
MEMORIAL HIGHWAY**

A tribute to the Armed
Forces that have defend-
ed the United States of
America

**US 441 Canal Point, Palm Beach County Community Building
PB31 ~ GPS Coordinates: 26.867100, -80.628933**

More than six million people pass through Palm Beach International Airport each year, which hosted its first commercial flights in 1936 as Morrison Field. The site was named for Miss Grace K. Morrison whose hard work went into the planning and establishment of Palm Beach Counties' first airport.

**BLUE STAR
MEMORIAL
HIGHWAY
MARKER
AT
REMOTE
CANAL POINT,
FLORIDA**

Eastern Airlines made the first flight out of Morrison Field bound for New York. The flight initiated in Miami then on to Morrison Field and eleven other cities for lay overs arriving just over thirteen hours later in New York. On December 19, 1936 Morrison Field was officially opened with a special dedication ceremony. The site consisted of one landing strip and a tiny administrative building. Within a month another small building was completed by the Palm Beach Aero Corporation for use as a hangar site and called Eastern Airlines Terminal. But things were about to change.

The United States had cautiously began a massive military expansion as World War II raged through Europe. In October of 1940 the United States Army Air Corps notified Palm Beach County that Morrison Field would be converted for military use. Within a month the process began and Morrison Field was activated. All commercial services and private aircraft were sent to the new Lantana Airport.

The surprise attack on Pearl Harbor plunged the United States into World War II. By January of 1942, allied forces prepared to invade France and Morrison Field handled six thousand two hundred airplanes and just over forty-five thousand personnel. Many of these fliers took off from Morrison Field for the D-Day invasion of Normandy on June 6, 1944.

Three years after D-Day, Morrison Field was deactivated. Palm Beach County assumed responsibility of the site in September 947 and the two-storied Air Force operations building was used as the passenger terminal. The County Commissioners voted on August 11, 1948 to change the name of the facility and Palm Beach International Airport was born. Changes were on the horizon once again.

In 1951 the Korean War necessitated the reactivation of Morrison Air Force Base, this time as a training facility. The military were back in force. Twenty-three thousand pilots trained at the facility for the duration of the conflict. At the war's conclusion the United States government was slow to deactivate Morrison Air Force Base and pushed to make it a permanent facility. The proposal met with considerable resistance and in 1959, Palm Beach County assumed control of the airport once again. Palm Beach International Airport experienced a rebirth.

A gala dedication ceremony was held on October 23, 1988 presenting the David McCampbell Terminal. David McCampbell was a Palm Beach resident and Medal of Honor winner. At a cost of one hundred fifty million dollars in revenue bonds, the current facility has twenty-five gates with almost double the expansion capacity. The terminal, in addition to two passenger concourses and a commuter concourse, included seven restaurants, three lounges and a business center. Today, Palm Beach International Airport is home to sixteen commercial and commuter airlines. Morrison Field is only a memory in the minds of veterans who proudly served.

414 Lake Avenue, Lake Worth
PB32 ~ GPS Coordinates: 26.615911, -80.052533

As the population swelled the need for organized education became apparent. The first school was completed and ready for instruction in the fall of 1912. The one room school was twenty-four by thirty-six feet constructed of nearly indestructible Florida pine. The schoolyard faced M Street embraced by Lake and Lucerne Avenues. Amanda Snyder was to be the first teacher dividing her time and attention between each grade level.

Four years later the small school building exceeded capacity. Classes were then moved to the impressive Moorish influenced Mission Revival style structure known today as the Lake Worth City Hall Annex. The building has served the community as a fire station, library, jail, auditorium and then, a school. The year was 1916 and Lake Worth was flourishing.

Today the Lake Worth community supports three elementary schools. Barton Elementary at 1700 Barton Road opened its door in 1956 and is responsible for a student body numbering more than seven hundred fifty eager young minds. Highland Elementary, whose motto is "Highland Has Heart", is dedicated to educational excellence and preparing its students for the rocky road of development. North Grade Elementary boasts the newest facilities, completed in 2000, but is in fact the oldest organized elementary school in the district. Both North Grade and South Grade Elementary schools were dedicated in 1926. South Grade eventually evolved to become the Lake Worth High School. North Grade remains focused on turning out responsible, literate and self-assured young people.

The Lake Worth Community Middle School located at 1300 Barnett Drive is attended by grades six through eight. Where strict attention is paid to developing a close working relationship between the students, parents and teachers in order to achieve the highest quality education. The ultimate goals include providing a safe environment for each student, including the most modern educational tactics in order to constantly challenge each scholastic class as well as assisting with the emotional needs of the youth navigating the difficult path of adolescence. Lake Worth Community Middle School is responsible for the education and extra curricular activities of nearly sixteen hundred students each year.

Lake Worth High School was first dedicated in 1922, holding classes at the prestigious Lake Worth City Hall building that had served the community in so many capacities. The first term resulted in seven female students earning their diplomas in 1923. As the population grew the school realized the necessity of a new facility. At 1701 Lake Worth Road, students in grades nine through twelve received a quality secondary education.

Today approximately three thousand pupils traverse the halls of Lake Worth High School. The contemporary program includes many advanced specialized fields including Junior Air Force Reserve Officers Training Corps, Aerospace Science, Pre-Law and Criminal Justice as well as Pre-Medicine and Allied Health Magnet programs. Illustrious Lake Worth High alumni includes famed soap opera star Deidre Hall who has acted in the popular "Days of Our Lives" program for many years. The school has grown considerably since its founding and first diplomas were issued to a class of seven ladies. The most recent graduating class numbered more than four hundred seniors.

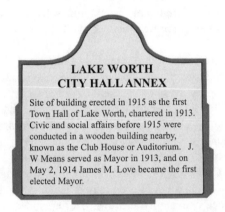

LAKE WORTH CITY HALL ANNEX

Site of building erected in 1915 as the first Town Hall of Lake Worth, chartered in 1913. Civic and social affairs before 1915 were conducted in a wooden building nearby, known as the Club House or Auditorium. J. W Means served as Mayor in 1913, and on May 2, 1914 James M. Love became the first elected Mayor.

7 North Dixie Highway, Lake Worth
PB32 ~ GPS Coordinates: 26.615911, -80.052533

Samuel and Fannie James were former slaves freed by the Emancipation Proclamation later proudly exercising their right to own property. They purchased a sizable plot of land located in what we know today as Palm Beach County. When Samuel passed away, Fannie sold a portion of their property to Palm Beach Farms Company. The company, under the leadership of Harold Bryant and William Greenwood, created a city on the banks of the Intercoastal Waterway. The city was christened with the name Jewel.

Soon the name of the settlement was changed to Lucerne and as homesteaders began to increase a mercantile and restaurant were opened. A fresh water pump was established at the town center where residents gathered to draw water and share news of the day. Mrs. Lockwood was the first white woman to settle in Lucerne and to introduce herself to the neighbors; she threw a party. The idea became a town custom so each time a new building was completed Mrs. Lockwood organized a dance. The first party was hosted in a home known today as the Greater Lake Worth Chamber of Commerce.

During the hottest days of summer short but mighty thunderstorms are common in south Florida during the afternoon hours. One summer afternoon in 1912 a storm was on the horizon, which proved to be anything but ordinary. The storm raged until floodwaters coursed through Lucerne's streets. The downpour flooded homes, dousing everything in its path. Homesteaders fought to protect what they could, neighboring communities dropped their heads in despair believing all was lost. But Lucerne refused to die. Citizens prevailed, losing the battle but winning the war. Palm Beach Farms realized that the city had become an entity of its own and deeded the property to the city of Lucerne including one and a half miles into the riparian[22].

F. H. Billups was appointed the first postmaster and while registering with the state to establish a post office it was discovered that another city had already claimed the name Lucerne. The citizens had to decide on another name and Lake Worth was chosen. In August of 1912, the city of Lake Worth was marked on the map and the post office opened its doors for the first time under her new name.

Lake Worth's first civic organization was established in 1912 called the Social Club. The association is still active today, known as the Pioneers of the City of Lake Worth. The Board of Trade was also founded in 1912, however today the business club is recorded as the Greater Lake Worth Chamber of Commerce. The two associations met in a building simply called the Clubhouse. Construction began on the Clubhouse in 1914 and was completed the following year. Palm Beach architectural firm King, Floyd and Mizner designed the Moorish influenced Mission Revival style structure at Number 7 North Dixie Highway. Eventually the building became the second city school, later the fire station, library and even the jail occupied this edifice. Finally it was known as the Auditorium.

As vehicular traffic increased the need for street lighting was apparent. Because electric service was still several years in the future, Kerosene lamps were used in 1913 to light the way from the North Dixie Highway railroad tracks to the lakefront in 1913. Upon arriving at the lakefront a ferry was established to traverse the Intracoastal Waterway to the sandy shores of the Atlantic Ocean. Those bound for the beach paid the ferry toll of a shiny dime round trip.

On May 18, 1914, the kerosene lamps lighting the way along Lake Worth streets became relics of the past. When the clock struck 6:00 p.m. a switch was thrown and like magic streetlights came to life casting an illuminating glow along the avenues. Progress was constant and by July of 1919, the first wooden bridge crossed the Intracoastal. The span proved to be the longest toll free bridge in the nation.

Education beyond an elementary level became a priority, Lake Worth High School welcomed students for the first time in 1922. The first graduating class in May of 1923 consisted of seven female students. Today graduating seniors number more than four hundred from Lake Worth High School.

Disaster struck Palm Beach County in 1928 more severe than any tragedy ever known in the area. A massive hurricane lay waste to the entire southeastern Florida region, leaving death and desolation in its path. Miraculously Lake Worth only recorded one fatality, however the remainder of the area will never really know for sure exactly the final death toll left by this killing storm. The Auditorium received a great deal of damage resulting in the need for restoration. Due to the massive wreckage throughout the region, repairs to the Auditorium went uncompleted until 1934. Restored to its grand style, the Auditorium was rededicated as the Lake Worth City Hall.

The historic wooden bridge crossing the Intracoastal was reduced to a splintered heap during the hurricane. The second bridge was a massive concrete span completed in 1937. The Lake Worth Pier was constructed in 1954. Known far and wide as the longest municipal pier along Florida's Atlantic coastline, the pier reached nine hundred sixty feet into the ocean. The Lake Worth Pier's claim to fame states that this path into the Atlantic is the closest one can come to the Gulf Stream without the use of a boat. Electric lighting spaced along the walkway allowed fishermen access to the pier twenty-four hours a day.

Lake Worth City Hall became known as the Old City Hall Annex. Organized in 1982, the Museum of the City of Lake Worth was instituted with Helen Greene chosen to be its first curator. The second floor museum tells the stories of Lake Worth history, its pioneers and the cities' development. Exhibits emphasize in amazing detail more than one hundred years of growth and change. The museum is open Monday through Friday from 10:00 a.m. until 3:00 p.m., private and group tours may be arranged by appointment.

BLUE STAR MEMORIAL HIGHWAY

A tribute to the Armed Forces that have defended the United States of America

US 1 at North Boynton Beach City Limits, Boynton Beach
PB34 ~ GPS Coordinates: 26.540650, -80.057467

Blue Star Memorial Highway markers are the projects of Garden Clubs within each county. The program is exceptional, as is the commitment of each club to the communities that they call home. Palm Beach County is superbly represented with numerous garden clubs.

The Boca Raton Garden Club whose motto, "The Telling of our Roots," recently celebrated fifty years as an organization. Mrs. Florance Machle founded the club in her home on June 2, 1953. Thirty-four women gathered that first day and soon the Boca Raton Garden Club was one of the fastest growing clubs in Florida. The club built their meeting house in 1964 and expand it in 1972 to include an auditorium. Proudly the garden club made short work of the mortgage and the paper was burned in only three years. The Boca Raton Garden Club hosts Standard Flower Shows, awards scholarships, supports Junior Garden Clubs and works in the community with continuing civic beautification projects. The Boca Raton Garden Club remains active today.

Known as "A Garden Club that really gets into the dirt!" is how the Lake Park Club is described. The club meets in the historical Evergreen House located in Kelsey Park. The house was built by the founder of Lake Park, Harry Kelsey. Kelsey Park was named in honor of him in the 1920s. Lake Park Garden Club maintains each of the city parks, keeping them blooming and beautiful. The several median areas, the Town Hall and a wonderful Butterfly Garden have been established by the organization adding to the beauty of the landscaping. Children of the community have the opportunity to learn from gardening mentors with the Youth Garden Club.

The West Palm Beach Garden Club meets each month at 4800 Dreher Trail North and consists of six circles. They are Allamanda, Amaryllis, Azalea, Bird of Paradise, Ixora and Oleander. The Delray Beach Garden Clubs consists of Hibiscus, Poinciana, Orchid, and the Seagrape Garden Clubs. Additional Palm Beach County Garden Clubs include the Belle Glade Club, Boynton Beach, Jupiter/Tequesta, Lake Worth, Ocean Ridge, Palm Springs and Wellington.

Obvious by the beauty throughout the county, the local garden clubs are exceptional. Nothing is more important than the education of our youth and the recognition of those that protect us; the garden clubs have excelled in both accomplishments. Each club is to be commended, their reward blossoms around each corner in Palm Beach County.

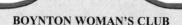

BOYNTON WOMAN'S CLUB

The Boynton Woman's Club was designed in the
Mediterranean Revival style by the famous Palm Beach
architect Addison C. Mizner. The Woman's Club is significant for both its architectural merit and contributions to the
cultural development of Boynton Beach. The Club was
built in 1925 as a memorial to the founder of the town,
Major Nathan S. Boynton. Along with providing a social
and civic center for the community, it served as the town's
first public library and the first meeting place for several
local churches and service organizations. The second floor
features a grand ballroom and stage. The building was listed in the National Register of Historic Places in 1979.

1010 US 1 in parking area, Boynton Beach
PB35 ~ GPS Coordinates: 26.518983, -80.058250

The Boynton Woman's Club is a time-honored institution in Boynton Beach. Founded in 1909, the organization remains dedicated to bettering their community through faithful service. Addison Mizner, the famed architect, was employed to build the Boynton Woman's Clubhouse in 1925. The Mediterranean style building at 1010
South Federal Highway stood two stories high of masonry construction coated with painted stucco. The tile roof
and three-sided loggia give the feel of a distinctive Spanish influence.

Addison Mizner rose to prominence with what came to be known as "Florida Renaissance" architectural
style. Amazingly Mizner was completely self-taught with no formal architectural training and never could draw a
blueprint. Regardless of instituted education, Mizner's talents were widely recognized as the standard in
Mediterranean architecture. Addison Mizner died at the age of sixty-one of a massive heart attack. Unfortunately
at the time of his death, the popular architect was bankrupt.

The Boynton Woman's Club cornerstone was placed in 1932. During a formal ceremony the clubhouse
and property were dedicated to Boynton Beach founder, Major Nathan Smith Boynton. A donation of thirty-five
thousand dollars had been made in memory of the celebrated Boynton Beach namesake.

Nathan Boynton, born at Port Huron, Michigan, had very deep roots seated in American history. His family came to this country just eighteen years after the Mayflower landed on the Massachusetts shore. After completing his education Boynton worked as a mercantile clerk and buggy-whip producer until earning enough money to
establish a grocery of his own. Boynton was successful and invested his money in Michigan pine unfortunately he
was left bankrupt by the Panic of 1857.

For the next several years Boynton moved frequently and found work in various vocations. He married
and became father to a brood, which would eventually number six children. His first son, Charles Lincoln, was
named in honor of the newly elected president who Boynton had great respect for based on his staunch anti-slavery
views. Boynton left his wife and child to join the 8th Michigan Calvary of the Union Army as a private. He rose
to the rank of major and was to the right of Sherman when he marched into Atlanta. After the war, Major Boynton
returned to Michigan becoming the editor and publisher of the "Port Huron Press".

Distinguishing himself in his home state, Major Nathan Boynton was elected mayor of Port Huron three
times then turned to the State Legislature. Obviously something of a Renaissance man, Boynton invented a fire
escape, hook and ladder firetruck and a system of trusses used for fire ladders. Suffering from ill health in 1883,
he and friend William S. Linton wintered in Florida. While touring the Florida East Coast Canal, the parties
aboard Fred C. Voss' boat, *Victor*, took a moment at what is today known as Ocean Avenue. Nathan Boynton sim-

ply stated, "I'll take this." And so it was. The rest they say, is history. Major Nathan Boynton died at Port Huron on May 27, 1911 uttering the final words; "I am tired. I am ready to go."

From shortly after the presentation of the Boynton Woman's clubhouse, the first city library was established in the facility where it remained until 1961. The building received recognition from the Colonial Dames of America and was added to the National Register of Historic Places in America in 1979. The Boynton Woman's Club came to be a makeshift studio for muralist, Bernard P. Thomas. The receipient of the Florieda League of Cities "Great Floridian" award for a muralist, Thomas taught classes in art at the club and students there created the backdrop for the elaborate ballroom stage. Thomas' work was noted throughout the United States for his primarily western themes.

Bernard Preston Thomas was born one of nine children, in Wyoming to Sam and Nellie Mumma Thomas. From a very young age it was apparent that the lad had artistic talents. Imagine knowing from the age of ten the vocation you would pursue in life. Bernard Thomas not only knew but also began to study under famed cowboy artist, Bill Gollings. By the time he graduated high school in 1937, Thomas had a significant portfolio.

He joined the Army and was shipped off the Europe during World War II as a sergeant participating in the Battle of the Bulge. While serving his country, Thomas earned national recognition for his painting "For Thou Art With Me," for the Chaplain Division. However, it was Thomas' sketchbook that fatefully came to the attention of General George Patton who saw that young Thomas was sent to Ecole de Beaux Arts to study under Paris master artist Jon Dupas.

Artist Bernard Thomas returned home to Sheridan in 1946. He became a partner in the Sheridan Sign Company and married a local teacher. Bernard and Betty moved to Boynton Beach in 1953, where their children were later born. He continued to paint and Betty worked in the school system eventually retiring as an elementary school principal after an amazing forty-seven year career. Bernard once stated that his most difficult project had been a mural for the Department of the Interior's Everglades National Park visitors' center depicting the elements of nature. Unfortunately Hurricane Andrew damaged the mural to such an extent that it was later torn down. Thomas created many beautiful works all serving as a monument to his incredible talent. Bernard Preston Thomas passed away at Boynton Beach in 1994.

The Boynton Woman's Club continues to contribute to the community today. Boynton high school graduates are eligible to apply for scholarships awarded by the club. Worthy causes benefiting women, children, peace officers, veterans and the handicapped are all recipients of the Woman's Club caring hands. The clubhouse was treated to a considerable restoration in 1987. The project, under the direction of the Mizner Foundation, took two years to complete. Today the Boynton Woman's Club is as active as ever, a tribute to the community that they have cared for so well.

BOYNTON WOMAN'S CLUB

CITY OF DELRAY BEACH

In recognition of these organizations' contributions to the cultural development of Delray Beach, the city commission designated these locations as historic sites on April 11, 1989.

SCHOOL NO. 4 DELRAY COLORED
        Located this site
GREATER MT. OLIVE MISSIONARY BAPTIST CHURCH
        40 Northwest Fourth Avenue
ST. PAUL AFRICAN METHODIST EPISCOPAL CHURCH
        119 Northwest Fifth Avenue
1899 FREE AND ACCEPTED MASONS, LODGE 275
        89 Northwest Fifth Avenue
ST. MATTHEW EPISCOPAL CHURCH
        404 Southwest Third Street

Late in the 19th century, a group of black settlers establishes a community in this area that became part of the Town of Linton and later the City of Delray Beach. These hardy pioneers established the cultural organizations necessary to foster education, fellowship, and spiritual needs, despite difficult environmental conditions and isolation.

Next door to 53 NW 5th Avenue, Delray Beach
PB36 ~ GPS Coordinates: 26.463017, -80.078150

The year was 1894; Michigan men William Linton and David Swinton arrived to escape the brutal northern winter. They founded a small community dubbed Linton along the Intracoastal Waterway. The little village lived off of the bounty of the land and sea. They grew a variety of fruits and vegetables also taking fish and crustaceans from the Atlantic Ocean. For more than one hundred years the city continued to grow and prosper.

William Linton, a postmaster from Saginaw, Michigan, traveling with friend Nathan Boynton toured the Florida Canal System. During this expedition each man chose a portion of land. Linton invested in one hundred sixty acres with David Swinton. To build the community Linton advertised five-acre tracts for sale in his hometown Michigan newspaper.

Henry Flagler's railroad from West Palm Beach to Miami brought visitors in droves, many of them electing to remain in the growing community. Residents chose to change the cities' name in 1901 to Delray. Taken from a Detroit suburb, the moniker Delray is recognized as a Spanish derivation defined as "of the king." The Chamber of Commerce was founded in 1925. City industries expanded to tourism in addition to produce.

As the 1900s rolled around the area experienced an insurgence of Japanese farmers. The people came to Delray with the intention of raising pineapple. Their farm was called the Yamato Colony, which is today the Boca Raton Airport. The Yamato Colony is today reconstructed as it was in the early 1900s on a two hundred-acre tract known as Morikami Museum and Japanese Gardens. Each year a festival is held at the Gardens celebrating the unique Japanese culture. Called the O-Bon festival, during ceremonies the Asian Gods and ancestral spirits are welcomed with traditional delicacies. More than one hundred fifty thousand people stroll through the gardens each year.

Over the years Delray has continued to thrive. The beautiful architecture gained notice and soon artists, writers and creative personalities were drawn like magnetics to the area. Many winter creative retreats were held in Delray. Historic preservation has taken a front seat during the last several years. The Delray Beach Cultural Loop was established to showcase the importance of history in the city. Galleries, museums, shops and historic churches are featured along the loop. The Old School Square has been reformed into the Cultural Arts Center. A museum, theatre and outdoor pavilion occupy the former Delray Elementary and High School buildings. The nearby square has become an artists' haven nicknamed Pineapple Grove. From a historic village to the glamour of modern art, Delray Beach is an eclectic mix of yesterday's Florida charm with today's modern tastes.

FLORIDA EAST COAST RAILWAY STATION

This 40' freight section is all that remains of the old railroad station constructed in 1896 by the Florida East Coast Railway Company. The station originally stood on the east side of the tracks, one block south of Atlantic Avenue. The original 100' long Stick style building contained ground level waiting rooms and a raised freight area. The station was expanded by 96 feet in the 1920s, and another addition was constructed in the 1940s. Passenger service was discontinued in the 1960s, and the station was scheduled for demolition. The passenger area was razed but public outcry to save the station stopped total destruction of the building. In 1968 the remaining freight section was split into two sections and moved. The 1920s portion was destroyed by fire in 1984, but the original 40' area of the 1896 station was moved and used for several years as an office and for storage at a nursery west of town. In 1994, this surviving section of the historic station was purchased by the Delray Beach Historical Society, which had the building moved to its present location and rehabilitated.

200 Railroad Avenue, Delray Beach
PB37 ~ GPS Coordinates: 26.462883, -80.070233

Just after William S. Linton and David Swinton claimed the land to be called Linton in 1894, on their heels were settlers from the Florida panhandle. Several African American families built homesteads just to the west of Linton and established farms. Matter of fact by the time William S. Linton convinced other Michigan settlers to purchase property, the panhandle farmers were already successful.

Within two years the black families had harvested a winter vegetable crop and convinced the powers that be to provide schooling for their children. The white families were suitably impressed by the farming example and set about creating homesteads of their own. And in the distance the sound of progress could be heard steaming down the steel tracks.

Settlers followed the railway south in 1896 and the population continued to grow. Crops flourished and the railway steamed in profits as a larger yield could be easily delivered to northern markets. Initially the Florida East Coast Railway Company built a large forty foot station in 1896 to the east of the steel tracks. Soon a stick style building with indoor waiting rooms and a wagon level loading dock extended to one hundred foot. Locals were suitably impressed with their thoroughly modern station.

William Linton lost everything in 1898 and settlers who chose to remain in the area had to buy back their land from the bank. To revitalize the area, residents decided that changing the city's name might change its luck, therefore Linton soon became Delray. In addition to the railway station, a post office, schools and churches were soon built; it seemed the Delray name brought growth even if luck was elusive. The black community established civic organizations and soon the city began an exciting resurgence. Within the next decade the Chapman Inn was established and several mercantile stores were founded. John Sunday became the first mayor and during his administration telephone lines were run and two years later the lights went on and water came inside with the city electric and water plants.

During the 1920s all of Florida experienced a population explosion and Delray was no exception. In 1927 the Mediterranean Revival railway station, designed by architects Harvey and Clarke, was expanded by ninety-six feet. The single storied building featured a masonry construction dressed with stucco and Spanish inspired barrel tile roof. To the eventual detriment of the railroad the highway system had its initial beginnings. Slowly railway travel declined until passenger service came to an end in the 1960s. The Florida East Coast Railway Station at 1525 West Atlantic Avenue was scheduled for demolition. The passenger area was leveled but the public voice was finally heard in uprising and the remainder of the building was saved. Tragically in 1984, the 1920s expansion was completely engulfed in flames and within moments reduced to ash and rubble. Amazingly the 1896 section still survives. Used for a time as storage and an office building, it was purchased in 1994 by the Delray Beach Historical Society.

The station has been treated to a complete restoration and located at 200 Railroad Avenue. Today all of the surrounding buildings have joined the railroad theme including the handsome water tower standing along side the station.

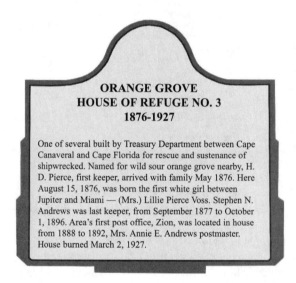

ORANGE GROVE
HOUSE OF REFUGE NO. 3
1876-1927

One of several built by Treasury Department between Cape Canaveral and Cape Florida for rescue and sustenance of shipwrecked. Named for wild sour orange grove nearby, H. D. Pierce, first keeper, arrived with family May 1876. Here August 15, 1876, was born the first white girl between Jupiter and Miami — (Mrs.) Lillie Pierce Voss. Stephen N. Andrews was last keeper, from September 1877 to October 1, 1896. Area's first post office, Zion, was located in house from 1888 to 1892, Mrs. Annie E. Andrews postmaster. House burned March 2, 1927.

300 S Ocean Blvd near Anchor Park, A1A, Delray Beach
PB38 ~ GPS Coordinates: 26.464600, -80.057967

During the mid 1800s the area that is today known as Delray Beach was wild Florida wilderness. It is hard to imagine the coast of never ending condos undeveloped, but the only predominant inhabitants during this time were sand gnats, mosquitoes, panthers, black bear and alligators as well as various other wildlife. Yes, this was long before the Florida Everglades were drained eliminating natural habitats and before men trophy hunted without regard for the declining species.

Once settlers arrived they found a deserted grove of sour oranges, leading people to believe that humans had once touched this land. No one really knows for sure how the grove came to be but there are numerous theories. The first idea suggests that Native Americans scattered the seeds, however, the tribes inhabiting the land at this time were not farmers but gathers. A second theory offers that the seeds perhaps washed ashore from a wrecked schooner. Perhaps this may be true but the trees did not grow directly on the shore. The next suggestion claims the Spanish settlers planted the seeds. This is really not plausible considering the Spanish did not have a settlement here; therefore, why plant food? And finally, it could have been Minorcans escaping the tyranny of New Smyrna in 1763, again possible, but not probable. The Minorcans banded together and most traveled to St. Augustine, remaining there. The only conclusion can be, that each individual must decide for himself which story to accept.

Regardless of the story each of us chooses to believe, when the Orange Grove House of Refuge #3 was built, a sour orange grove did exist. The refuge was the first building to occupy the site to become known as Linton, then Delray Beach. The United States Lifesaving Service planned five refuge houses from Cape Canaveral to Miami in 1874. The houses were meant for rescue, as well as providing safety and shelter to those unfortunate souls shipwrecked on the tumultuous seas.

Construction of the two-storied house was completed in April 1876. Four rooms graced the downstairs while an open dormitory was on the second floor.

Captain Hannibel Dillingham Pierce of Fayette, Maine assumed the position as first keeper on October 7th. Less than a year later his daughter Lily was the first white child born to the area. Pierce left the house in 1877, shortly after Lily's birth. British bachelor, Stephen N. Andrews was the second of only two keepers who ever served the house. After rescuing survivors, it was the keeper's gruesome task to recover the bodies of sailors, when possible and return the remains to their families.

Andrews married a lady called Annie and brought her to the refuge. Annie Andrews served as the first postmistress, her station was called Zion. The post was handled for four years out of the refuge. After twenty years of dedicated service, the Orange Grove House of Refuge was closed for the final time in 1896.

The first Linton settlers were guests in the house for a short time, they often sought shelter there when Mother Nature was angered and stirred up a tempest. Ed Hamilton, one of the barefoot mailmen, was said to have spent the last night before his disappearance in the safety of the refuge. The Orange Grove House of Refuge burned to the ground on March 2, 1927.

**SITE OF THE ORANGE GROVE
HOUSE OF REFUGE NO. 3**

DELRAY WRECK

The old shipwreck known as the Delray Wreck rests at the bottom of the ocean in 25 feet of water about 150 yards offshore the south end of Delray's municipal beach. The wreck is broken and scattered into five sections and has long been one of the most popular diving spots in South Florida. The S.S. INCHULVA was grounded and wrecked by a fierce hurricane on September 11, 1903. Under the command of Captain G.W. Davis, the 386 foot steelhulled British steamship was bound for Newport New, Virginia from Galveston, Texas carrying wheat, cotton, lumber and a crew of 28 men. The storm struck about 5 p.m., tossing the ship and causing the cargo to shift. Steering became impossible, so Captain Davis put out both anchors, but to no avail. The anchors parted and the INCHULVA grounded and was ripped apart. Nine crew members were lost. Dawn revealed to the battered crew that land and a town were just a short distance away. By noon, all the men except Captain Davis and two mates had landed on shore in a small hastily-built raft. They found hot food and coffee at the Chapman House, a local hotel, where many of Delray's residents had taken shelter during the storm. The nine seamen who lost their lives were buried on the ridge overlooking the ocean where the ship had gone down. The surviving crew members were treated, paid and sent to New York. Before leaving for their homes, each crew member signed the guest register of the Chapman House. Under their names they wrote, "Shipwrecked in the S.S. INCHULVA, September 11, 1903, landed on a raft September 12th and received every kindness and attention at the hands of Mrs. Chapman." Captain Davis, his Chief Officer, a 2nd Officer and a seaman from the ship were brought before the Naval Court held at the British Vice Consulate at Jacksonville on September 19th. The Court exonerated the Captain and the crew from all blame.

City's municipal beach, A1A, Delray Beach
PB39 ~ GPS Coordinates: 26.454633, -80.059200

On July 26, 1903, the *SS Inchulva* left Barry, Wales bound for Galveston, Texas. Once the ship docked it was to remain for three weeks while the cargo was assembled and loaded. The payload consisted of seven thousand tons of wheat, one hundred fifty tons of lumber, one hundred eighty bales of cotton, nine hundred sixty-three sacks of grain, one thousand eight hundred forty sacks of cottonseed and one hundred fifty bales of istle[23]. As the ship readied a final inventory was taken and the crew was mustered exposing the desertion of ten crewmembers.

The ill-fated journey began on September 6th. According to mariners legend changing the name of a ship guaranteed bad luck would befall the vessel. Originally built in 1892, the ship was christened the *Alberta*, six years later the ship was sold and renamed *SS Inchulva*. Old salts would say the ships' fate was sealed. Five days later as the ship rounded the Florida horn, the sky grew dark and suddenly the temperature dropped. The sea churned, the wind whipped violently and the crew silently prayed.

Ship's Captain G. W. Davis noted that the *Inchulva* would no longer steer and ordered the two anchors set. The tempest was said to be a minimal hurricane with sustained winds at eighty-five miles per hour. The anchors failed to take hold before the ship shuddered forcefully as it crashed to the ocean floor. A sickening sound reverberated through the ship as the hull splintered under the force of the blow.

Davis and eleven of his men huddled clinging to ropes at the bow as the storm tossed the doomed vessel. A massive wall of water crashed over the stern and nine men vanished beneath the waves destined for Davy Jones locker. The survivors had no idea how far from shore they were and under the cover of darkness it would be daylight before any rescue might be possible. The night passed slowly but as dawn broke on September 12th the relieved men realized that they were only two hundred yards from the beach and safety.

The weary men collapsed on the shore, suffering from the ill affects of exposure to the elements and the corrosive salt water. The *SS Inchulva* survivors were taken to the Chapman House hotel where they were ministered to, fed and bedded down. Eight bloated bodies washed ashore and were buried in a mass grave on a rise overlooking what is today A1A and Casuarina Road. The current carried the ninth casualty north to Boynton Beach where he was buried in the local cemetery. After remaining at the hotel for just over a week, each man who signed the guest book was given money and put on a ship destined for New York then home.

For years the pile of rubble about two hundred yards off the shore was simple known as "the Delray wreck." After curious sport divers researched the wreck, it was identified as the *SS Inchulva*. Only the boiler and three hundred feet of scattered remains rest on the ocean floor covered in sand. Winter storms often reveal more of the wreck, therefore local dive operators suggest spring as the optimum time to dive this site. In only twenty feet of water, the site attracts abundant marine life including large tarpon.

THE BAREFOOT MAILMAN

Along this beach in the 1880's and early 1890's walked United States mailmen on their sixty-six mile journey between Palm Beach and Miami. The trip required three days each way and they passed this spot the second day. They walked barefoot at the wet surf line, the hardest surface, with their mail bags and shoes slung over their shoulders. One of them, James E. Hamilton, drowned trying to cross Hillsborough Inlet.

Spanish River Park, at the south beach tunnel inside park, A1A, Boca Raton
PB40 ~ GPS Coordinates: 26.378917, -80.067950

Dozens of books, a movie, countless newspaper and magazine articles as well as several historical markers and memorials have all told the story of the legendary "Barefoot Mailmen." These men walked on hard packed sand eighty miles in a weeks' time. They must have been men of steel to endure the arduous route with all of its natural perils.

The population between today's Lake Worth and Biscayne Bay had increased enough in the early 1880s to have the United State Postal Service approve mail delivery. The route would run from Palm City known today as Palm Beach to Lemon City, today's Miami, well in a round about fashion.

Let's trace a letter through the route in 1883: the journey began at the lighthouse in Jupiter delivered by sailboat the twenty-two miles north; from here an Indian River steamboat would carry the letter to Titusville; the letter would then travel by rail to New York's port where it would be transferred to a steamer bound for Havana; finally put aboard a schooner in Cuba for delivery in Miami. The route encompassed some three thousand miles and took six to eight weeks. In 1885, when the Postal Service implemented the Star or Barefoot route, it was welcomed with open arms.

The postal contract was put out for bid. Edward Ruthven Bradley, a retired Chicago newsman who had recently settled in Lantana, was awarded the first Barefoot route. The contract totaled seven hundred dollars per year, payable in quarterly installments of one hundred seventy-five dollars. Bradley and his son Louie alternated walking the demanding route.

The route began before daylight on Monday morning at Palm City where the canvas mailbag would be retrieved. The Postal Service made an exception, allowing the Barefoot Mailmen to carry the lighter canvas bag versus the standard heavy cowhide. Taking a small skiff, Bradley would sail down to Lake Worth to what is known today as Boynton Inlet, this is where the walking began. Shoes slung over his shoulder, his shirt tuck neatly inside the bag and sometimes his pants would be placed there as well. Who was to know that the Barefoot Mailman was treading down the beach in only his skivies? Five long miles down the beach he would walk on the hard packed sand. His first night of rest would come at the Orange Grove House of Refuge located at what we know today as Delray Beach. Before the sun rose he was off again walking a twenty-five mile stretch to a rowboat waiting his crossing at Hillsboro Inlet. By the end of the day he would reach the New River House of Refuge at Fort Lauderdale and again pass the night there. The following day would find him rowing four miles to New River then taking to the sand again for a ten mile walk on the beach reaching Baker's Haulover at the headwaters of Biscayne Bay. Twelve miles down the bay a rowboat brought him to his final destination at the Lemon City post office. After a night's rest, the return trip to Palm City began reaching the final stop by Saturday afternoon. The round trip encompassed one hundred thirty-six miles, eighty by beach and fifty-six aboard a series of small skiffs hidden in the bushes awaiting his arrival. After only one day of rest on Sunday, the journey began all over again. Often for the company and to subsidize their income, the Barefoot Mailmen allowed travelers to come along for a fee of five dollars. The charge was justified because the mailman was forced to slow his pace and offer passage across the various inlets.

After two years the exhausted Bradley father and son gave up the grueling route. Edward R. Bradley would go on to become the Dade County School Superintendent. Brothers Frederick and Otto Matthaus took the route, walking it together. They soon discovered that the task was much more than they anticipated and subcontracted others to take stretches of the route.

James E. "Ed" Hamilton, a native of Trigg County, Kentucky moved to Hypoluxo Island, anxious to start the job. He had quickly tired of farming and thought the "Barefoot Mailman" route would be much more fun. Heavy rains in September and October of 1887 had left the low lands along the route under water making the trek all the more difficult. Ed arrived on October 10th with the mail at Hypoluxo on schedule though he claimed to be feeling ill. He refused to postpone his trip; the mail must get through and set out on his way. When Saturday afternoon came and went, Ed failed to return. An investigation began into Ed Hamilton's disappearance.

Charles Coman, the keeper of the New River House of Refuge, had encountered a stranger traveling south along the beach. He questioned the man concerning how he'd crossed the inlet. The stranger stated that hunters had ferried him across, but Coman believed it to be a lie. During those days removing another man's boat was akin to the old West's horse thievery and punishable by law.

Louie Bradley and Charles Pierce retraced the route in search of their friend. Upon arriving at Hillsboro Inlet they discovered Hamilton's boat was no where to be found. His mail pouch, trousers and shirt were hanging on the limb of a tree and near the edge of the water were his skivies. Obviously Ed Hamilton had attempted to swim the inlet to retrieve his boat from the other side. To those that knew him drowning was quickly discounted, Hamilton was known to be an excellent swimmer. Sharks were often seen in the inlet but none were spotted this time of year. However, the inlet was infested with alligators. Large, potential man-eaters and their tracks around the inlet were abundant. Even an exceptional swimmer could not have escaped.

Coman identified the stranger suspected of removing Hamilton's boat. The man was charged with tampering with government property and brought to trial in Federal Court at Jacksonville. Due to the lack of an eyewitness and conclusive evidence, the suspect was acquitted. His name was never listed in the court records. Rumor was that approximately one week later the individual was gravely injured in an "accident," there were no witnesses.

The Barefoot Mailmen under contract to the United States Postal Service were:

Edward R. Bradley (1st contract)
Louie Bradley (under the same contract, father and son took turns)
Andrew Garnett, Garnett later became Dade County Treasurer, school board member
    Hypoluxo Postmaster
George Sears
Frederick Matthaus & Otto Matthaus, (brothers, sharing a contract)
Charles Pierce

Bob Douthit
Dan McCarley
George Charter
Ed Hamilton (killed - probably by alligators)
H. J. Burkhardt (last mailman under contract and probably the fastest)

Barefoot Mailman not under contract (used during last two years):

Edward "Ned" Peat
Stafford (complete name)
Dan Kelley

The highway system began in 1892 when a shell road was completed from Lantana to Lemon City. The Postal Service failed to renew the contract for the Barefoot Mailmen and the Bay Biscayne Stage Line assumed the route. Henry John Burkhardt was the last official Barefoot Mailman. He settled at Hillsboro Inlet. Today a reenactment is held annually, known as the Boy Scout Barefoot Mailman hike along the beach.

BOCA RATON TOWN HALL

Designed in the Mediterranean Revival style by the architect Addison C. Mizner and completed by the architect William E. Alysmeyer, the Boca Raton Town Hall opened in April 1927 as the city's first municipal building, fire station and police department. The Cramer & Cramer Construction Company developed architectural plans with an elaborate front entrance, a gilded dome atop the bell tower and interior finishes with products of the Mizner Industries. The Woman's Club opened Boca Raton's first public library here in 1927 and the second floor served as a private residence of the fire chief for a number of years. In the early years, the Council Chamber/Court Room was the only public meeting room in Boca Raton and was used by numerous social groups, as well as providing a polling place for city voters. In 1975, the city declared that the building should become a museum and in 1976 the Boca Raton Historical Society located its office here. In recognition of its historic and architectural significance, the Boca Raton Town Hall was listed in the National Register of Historic Places as "Old City Hall" in 1980. Several municipal offices occupied the building until 1983 and the Town Hall was restored to its original architectural design by the Boca Raton Historical Society in 1984 for use as a local history museum and archives.

71 North Federal Highway, Boca Raton Historical Society, Boca Raton
PB41 ~ GPS Coordinates: 26.351300, -80.086550

Boca Raton was assumed to come from the Spanish derivation meaning Rat's Mouth, however, that was not the case. The spelling has over time changed from Boca Ratones, when translated means "Thieves Inlet" eventually the "es" was dropped but the pronunciation remained "Rah-tone." This was how the village was noted on eighteenth century maps.

Tequesta Native Americans were the earliest settlers of the land but by the time the Florida East Coast Canal was founded and the railway system came steaming down the coast in the 1890s, pioneers began to make their home here. Pineapple cultivation began with Joseph Sakai and a group of Japanese immigrants as well as an active African American community from the panhandle implementing winter garden crops. Boca Raton was indeed the melting pot, which America became known for.

While all of Florida experienced the great population boom, Boca Raton incorporated and city fathers had visions of their small village as a resort community. Architect Addison Mizner was chosen to make the dream a reality. The first step came with the construction of the Cloister Inn[24]. The exclusive hotel would feature one hundred rooms when it ceremoniously opened the ornate doors in early 1926. The hotel cost an exorbitant one point twenty-five million dollars to build.

The Spanish Mediterranean style so identified with Mizner's work was carried through to the interior, which was designed with rare pieces obtained from ancient churches and universities in Spain. Unfortunately as the first patrons signed the guest register, the hotel was already bankrupt. Mizner was financially ruined but his distinctive Mediterranean style prevailed and became the standard throughout south Florida. The unique color that Mizner called "Boca Pink" became his signature for the remainder of his career. Addison Mizner once stated that the color was inspired by a breathtaking sunset witnessed on the ocean's horizon. The Cloister was painted Boca Pink and the Boca Raton Resort & Club sports the same color to this day. By the end of the decade Boca Raton was one of Florida's most popular cities.

Addison Mizner added the Boca Raton Town Hall to his portfolio in 1927. William Alsmeyer, also an architect, completed the project. Located at 71 North Federal Highway, the building still bears the distinctive stamps of a Mizner design. The Spanish influenced ironwork, tiling and ornately carved woodwork were all supplied by Mizner Industries.

The next decade brought green beans to the forefront as the predominant winter crop in high demand in northern markets. The Army Air Corps flew in to develop a radar training school during the World War II years beginning in 1942. More than thirty thousand servicemen, their families and contract workers flooded Boca Raton, which began the decade with a population of seven hundred twenty-three. Of course, when World War II was over the base was abandoned. The majority of the military population moved on to the next duty station and Boca Raton was back to "normal."

The 1950s brought entertainment attractions to Boca Raton with the establishment of Africa USA, today's Camino Gardens; Ancient America, which was the site of ancient Indian middens are today known as the Sanctuary neighborhood; as well as the Winter Bible Conference Grounds known as Bibletown, utilizing the buildings of the World War II Air Field. The 1960s brought another population explosion, within the decade the census soared to almost thirty thousand residents once again. This time the population was not temporary military but permanent citizens. The increased land usage pushed the bounds of the Everglades further west and former farmland was used as housing developments. Industry began to move in with the anchor being IBM computer facilities in 1967. Remarkably in 1981, it was at this IBM facility that the first personal computer was developed, completely changing the way we communicate, conduct business and influencing our everyday lives.

Restoration became the city focus during the next two decades. Projects included the Town Hall and Florida East Coast Railway Station. The facilities were eventually opened for public tour. The Boca Raton Town Hall is today home to the Boca Raton Historical Society.

**BLUE STAR
MEMORIAL HIGHWAY**

A tribute to the Armed
Forces that have defended
the United States of
America

**Across from Boca Raton Historical Society, Boca Raton
PB42 ~ GPS Coordinates: 26.351000, -80.086317**

As World War II raged in Europe, the United States quietly prepared to enter the fray. But by the time Pearl Harbor was hit on December 7, 1941, America was left with no choice but to defend our home shores and join the allies in the fight. Airport facilities around the country were appropriated into government service.

The Boca Raton Airport was overrun with thirty-five hundred construction workers and more than eleven million dollars was infused into the facility. The airport was to become the only radar training station in the United States. The facility, known as Boca Raton Army Air Field, was commissioned in October 1942. Training of airborne radar operators, mechanics and electronics officers would be conducted at the new Air Field.

The Boca Raton Air Field spanned an area of more than fifty-eight hundred acres. Radar operation was a new technology, therefore every aspect of the war benefited from the training conducted at Boca Raton. The airmen aboard the *Enola Gay* on the historic bombing of Hiroshima in 1945 were trained radar operators at the Boca Air Field. As the war drew to a close, radar training was moved to Biloxi, Mississippi. The Boca Raton Air Field was a ghost town of tall weeds, where only the sweeping breeze caressed abandoned landing strips once alive with the constant arrival and departure of B-17s and B-29 bombers.

Boca Raton gained control of the deserted Air Field from the War Assets Administration in December 1948. It took seven years and the diligent work of Boca Raton's Tom Fleming to convince the Florida Legislature to approve the conversion of the base into a new university. Finally the proposal was sent to Washington D.C. where the Civil Aeronautics Administration had the final word. The land restrictions were lifted, one thousand acres were approved for use as a university reserving two hundred acres for the airport.

The Boca Raton Municipal Airport was then established. Florida Atlantic University was founded on July 15, 1961. The university opened in September 1964. The airport went through numerous agencies before finally being taken over by the Boca Raton Airport Authority. The best of the Air Force years remained; a municipal airport serving the public as well as a university providing advanced education for Florida's youth.

F.E.C. RAILWAY DEPOT
BOCA RATON

The rails of Henry Flagler's Florida East Coast Railway first reached Boca Raton in 1895 providing an essential link in the extension of the railroad system south to Miami and the Florida Keys, and fostering the tourism and agricultural development around which the community of Boca Raton was founded and grew to prosper. The 1930 railway depot on this site was not the first station in Boca Raton. While the F.E.C. was crucial to the opening of the area, it was during the era of the 1920s and 1930s that Boca Raton received its unique architectural character, due largely to the influence of the architect and developer Addison Mizner. In 1928, following the collapse of the explosive Boom Era in southeast Florida, Mizner lost his extensive hold-ings in Boca Raton. Clarence A. Geist, a self-made man who began his career as a brakeman in New Jersey and rose to become a utilities magnate in Philadelphia, bought the bankrupt development. Geist, too, had vision, and set out to build on Mizner's achievements. His plans included the construction of a passenger depot on the F.E.C. line to provide service for guests of the exclusive Boca Raton Club, the crown jewel of Mizner's plans for Boca, and to provide a gracious entrance to the showplace community. In order to ensure the station would be designed in a style to complement the Club, Geist donated the necessary land and rights to the F.E.C. and is reputed to have made a considerable investment in the railway at the time. Built in 1930, the station was designed by F.E.C. architect Chester G. Henninger in the Mediterranean Revival style of architecture with a gently pitched gable roof, stuccoed walls and arched loggias with delicate spiral columns. This distinctive style, generally associated with the work of Mizner, contributed richly to the unique physical character of Boca Raton which remains visible today. The F.E.C. Railway Passenger Station in Boca Raton was operated until 1968 when passenger service along the line was discontinued. A living testament to the Boom Era in Florida history, the station was listed on the National Register of Historic Places in 1980, and was restored in 1989 by the Boca Raton Historical Society with the generous assistance of the Count and Countess de Hoernle and the widespread support of the community.

747 South Dixie Highway, Count deHoernle Pavilion, Boca Raton
PB43 ~ GPS Coordinates: 26.343100, -80.088917

Located at 747 South Dixie Highway at the Count deHoernle Pavilion in Boca Raton, the Boca Express Train Museum is an interesting and educational look at railway transportation in the 1930s and 40s. Open only on Friday afternoons from October through April, planning is required to see the exhibits.

Displays feature the Florida East Coast Railway Passenger Station, Seaboard Airline Dining and Lounge Cars. The Passenger Station was built in the Mediterranean Style made famous by Addison Mizner. A two-story tower and a five bay loggia on the eastern side bordered the single story Passenger Station. The structure was built for Clarence Geist who purchased Mizner's holdings when the population explosion came to an end. Unfortunately he went bankrupt. Chester G. Henninger was the architect and was greatly influenced by Mizner's popular Spanish architectural style.

The Seaboard Airline Dining and Lounge Cars are very similar. Both cars were built in 1947 and were typical of the modern streamline cars having pure curves and sleek lines. The cars were utilized on the New York to Florida route. Though these cars were not used on the Florida East Coast line, the railway museum provides an apt setting for their retirement.

Originally from Germany, Count and Countess Adolph deHoernle moved to Florida in 1981. The couple donated money, time and expertise to a wide variety of community programs. Children's charities, medical pro-grams, senior citizens assistance and educational support received the benefit of the deHoernle's generosity. Many venues bear their name in appreciation for all the philanthropic couple has given to the city of Boca Raton. After Count deHoernle passed away in 1998, the deHoernle Pavilion was dedicated to his memory. Countess Henrietta deHoernle, though elderly, continues to serve the community with wonderful enthusiasm.

The museum is administered by the Boca Raton Historical Society. The society has implemented an educational program targeted toward children in grades three through five called "Ticket To Ride." The curriculum allows the children to experience train travel as it was back in the day. Reservations are required by instructors to participate, but be forewarned the schedule is often full a year in advance. The program is free of charge for the students. Boca Express Train Museum is listed on the National Register of Historic Places. A small admission is charged for adults, children under the age of twelve are admitted free. The day I visited, unfortunately was not one of the few that the museum was open. However, we wandered around the railway cars and watched several young kids delight in the train and ringing the bell.

End Notes

[1] A boat, which travels to and from America with correspondence of the State or Government, sometimes to the homeport and other times to a squadron at sea.

[2] Pronounced "yay-ga"

[3] Pernicious anemia is caused by an inability to absorb vitamin B12 (cobalamin) that is naturally found in certain foods.

[4] according to which source you choose to follow

[5] When he spoke everyone listened or so his advertising campaign said.

[6] Streets were named by the Juno Garden Club in honor of the "celestial" legend bearing the names of Greek Gods and Goddesses

[7] Waldorf Hotel Chain fame

[8] Native American Tribe

[9] A Seminole and black mixed race people.

[10] Mrs. Mulford's father

[11] Mrs. Mulford's fifteen year old nephew

[12] People entitled to receive Holy Communion.

[13] The official residence of the Reverend and his family provided by the Church.

[14] Miami

[15] The central sanctuary

[16] The garden

[17] Rooms where sacred vessels or vestments are kept and various meetings are held.

[18] The twelve days after Christmas, celebrating the visit of the three wise men to Baby Jesus.

[19] The Morrison Field/Palm Beach Junior College later became Palm Beach International Airport.

[20] Shoe maker

[21] The soil left over after a swamp is drained, composed mostly of rotted plant matter.

[22] On the banks of or into a waterway.

[23] A plant used to make paper.

[24] Today the Boca Raton Resort & Club.

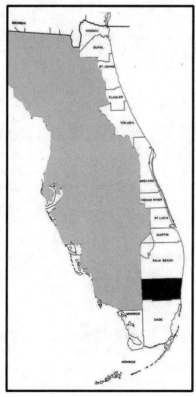

Broward County

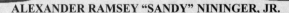

ALEXANDER RAMSEY "SANDY" NININGER, JR.

Graduated from Fort Lauderdale High School 1937 and from United States Military Academy at West Point with Honors 1941.
Awarded Posthumously the First Congressional Medal of Honor of World War II by President Franklin D. Roosevelt on January 29, 1942.

CITATION BY ACT OF CONGRESS OF THE UNITED STATES

"Alexander R. Nininger, Jr., Second Lieutenant, Fifty Seventh Infantry (Philippine Scouts), United States Army. For conspicuous gallantry and intrepidity above and beyond the call of duty in action with the enemy near Abucay, Bataan, Philippine islands, on January 12, 1942. This officer, although assigned to another Company not then engaged in combat, voluntarily attached himself to Company K same Regiment, while that unit was being attacked by enemy forces superior in fire power.

"Enemy snipers in trees and fox holes had stopped counter-attack to regain part of position. In hard-to-hand fighting which followed, Lieutenant Nininger repeatedly forced his way to and into the hostile position. Though exposed to heavy enemy fire, he continued to attack with rifle and hand grenades and succeeded in destroying several enemy groups in fox holes and enemy snipers.

"Although wounded three times, he continued his attacks until he was killed after pushing alone far within the enemy position. When his body was found after recapture of the position one enemy officer and two enemy soldiers lay dead around him."

800 Sandy Nininger, War Memorial Auditorium, Fort Lauderdale
BO1 ~ GPS Coordinates: 26.133533, -80.135117

Alexander Ramsey Nininger, Jr., known playfully as Sandy to his wide circle of loving family and friends, was a typical boy. He was raised along the banks of New River and graduated from Fort Lauderdale High School in 1937. Sandy was fortunate enough to be accepted into the United States Military Academy at West Point. Obvious by his future actions his parents, family, community and the Academy produced a remarkable young man. Second Lieutenant Nininger graduated from West Point in May 1941. In November Nininger was assigned to the 57th Infantry Regiment, Philippine Scouts Division.

The Philippine Scouts performance during World War II was nothing less than exemplary. The division's actions while engaged in combat against the Japanese from December 1941 until the Philippines fell in May 1942 was simply heroic. The conditions these men lived in from day to day were formidable. Food and medicine was in short supply; exposure to tropical diseases left the men weak and feverish; the weapons for use in defending themselves and subduing the enemy were inadequate and even so they had very little ammunition; and finally they had no hope of support from the United States.

Lieutenant Nininger's Company was not engaged in combat, according to his award, so he gallantly volunteered to join Company K who was under Japanese attack. The enemy hid in trees and foxholes until hand to hand fighting followed, Nininger rushed their position repeatedly with rifle and hand grenades. He was wounded three times but continued his assault alone until a mortal projectile ended his life. When finally the division recaptured the position Lieutenant Nininger's body was found, lying at his feet were an enemy officer and two soldiers who he had taken before being killed. He died in action during the Battle of Bataan near Abucay on January 12, 1942. Nininger died a hero. He was twenty-three years old.

Many of the soldiers from the 57th Philippine Scouts were decorated for valor, Lieutenant Alexander Ramsey Nininger, Jr. was the first World War II soldier awarded the Congressional Medal of Honor. President Franklin D. Roosevelt awarded the medal posthumously on January 29, 1942.

Lieutenant Nininger embodied the ideals taught at West Point including Duty, Honor and Country; living and dying as an example that future Army Officers would do well to emulate. Many tributes commemorating this outstanding individual's heroism and life exist today including: the First Division of Cadets Barracks, which was dedicated in his memory; a statue of Lieutenant Nininger stands in his hometown of Ft. Lauderdale; and the Alexander "Sandy" Nininger State Veterans' Nursing Home, which was also named for this brave soldier. Last but certainly not least, Lieutenant Alexander Ramsey "Sandy" Nininger, Jr., is fondly remembered by everyone whose lives he touched during his lifetime so tragically cut short.

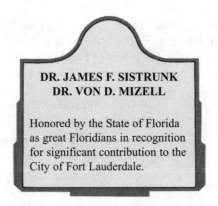

DR. JAMES F. SISTRUNK
DR. VON D. MIZELL

Honored by the State of Florida as great Floridians in recognition for significant contribution to the City of Fort Lauderdale.

1409 NW Sixth St, Mizell Center Lobby, Fort Lauderdale
BO2 ~ GPS Coordinates: 26.129468, -80.160388

In a community called Midway near the Florida's State capital, James Franklin Sistrunk was born in 1891. He realized a life long dream upon graduation as a medical doctor from Meharry Medical College at Nashville in 1919. It was one of few black colleges allowing students the opportunity to enter the medical field. During World War I, Sistrunk served his country as a medic and stretcher barer. After the war he moved to a small village named Dunnellon near Ocala to practice medicine.

Dr. Sistrunk relocated south to Fort Lauderdale in April 1922. Unfortunately not only did the hospital there deny medical attention to blacks but their doors were also closed to a qualified and experienced surgeon, who just happened to be African American. For the next sixteen years Dr. James F. Sistrunk ran a small clinic for patients regardless of race or ability to pay and made house calls for those homebound. He took fees in the form of eggs or oranges, very few could afford medical care. It was said that Dr. Sistrunk brought more than five thousand children into the world during his forty-four year career.

Von Delaney Mizell was born at Dania just south of Ft. Lauderdale in 1910. Mizell attended Morehouse College in Atlanta and finished his medical degree at Meharry Medical School graduating in 1938. He then returned home to care for people denied treatment by white hospitals and doctors.

Drs. Sistrunk and Mizell joined with Mrs. Leona Collins in founding the Provident Hospital for Blacks. Their facility began in a dilapidated building near Dr. Sistrunk's office. The trio worked tirelessly to raise funds for the clinic located at Northwest Sixth Street and Fourteenth Terrace. The community soon joined in the fund raising and soon Provident was a top notch facility.

Listed as a non-profit general hospital in accordance with the standards set forth by the American Hospital Association, Provident was the only hospital in Florida owned and operated by a black staff caring for racially mixed patients. As a fully qualified surgeon, Dr. Sistrunk offered a full service facility and going above and beyond his medical practice, the doctor was known to assist those in financial need. Dr. Mizell was listed as the hospital director and as such he implemented an intern-training program for black physicians. Dr. R. L. Brown and Dr. Calvin H. Shirley were eventually added to the Provident staff. While working tirelessly to break down racial barriers, the staff continued to manage office visits, hospital care and house calls.

The city of Fort Lauderdale eventually assumed responsibility of the hospital until desegregation in the dawning days of the 1960s. When Broward General Hospital began admitting all people regardless of race, Provident became obsolete and faded into history. Dr. James Franklin Sistrunk pass away on March 20, 1966. His legacy remains in the generations of children Dr. Sistrunk delivered during his meaningful career. Several memorials stand to recognize Dr. Sistrunk and his gifts to Fort Lauderdale including Sistrunk Boulevard, Dr. James F. Sistrunk bridge as well as the Sistrunk Historical Festival all named in his honor.

Dr. Von D. Mizell continued the struggle for racial equality by founding the first NAACP chapter in Fort Lauderdale. Suitably the headquarters were located on Sistrunk Boulevard. Dr. Mizell lead the 1942 summer boycott of Fort Lauderdale's "Colored School," today known as Walker Elementary. Historically black students were to attend a six-month school term from July through December in order to work the fields during winter and spring harvest seasons; whereas, white student reported to school in September for a nine-month term. Dr. Mizell fought the educational system with the support of many black parents. By order of the federal court, the 1943-44 school term would be the same for black as well as white students.

Dr. Von Delaney Mizell passed away in 1973. The Provident Hospital facility was reopened as the Von D. Mizell Cultural Center and Library in his honor. The edifice eventually became too small to house the ever-growing center. In 2002 a grand new facility was dedicated as the African American Research Library & Cultural Center, open daily at 1409 Sistrunk Boulevard. Today the Von D. Mizell Center is a hub of civic activity for the community.

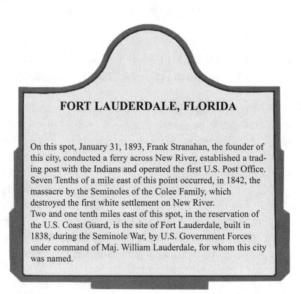

Brickell Drive and SE 1ˢᵗ Street, Fort Lauderdale
BO3 ~ GPS Coordinates: 26.118650, -80.137400

Before white man ever landed on what was to be American soil, the Tequesta Indians were in south Florida. Known as the "Glades Culture," pottery has been found dating their existence around 2000 BC, which precedes any other inhabitants throughout the United States by more than eight hundred years. The Tequesta lived off the bounty of the land and sea; though never farmers, the people hunted, fished and gathered indigenous vegetation to survive. Seldom roaming further north than today's Palm Beach or further south than Miami, the

Tequesta were peaceful and joyous before the white man brought "civilization" that would drive them to near extinction. By the mid-1700s, the Tequesta as well as Ais Native tribes had virtually disappeared. Some historians and sociologists believe that the few surviving members of each tribe who remained despite starvation, disease, being driven from their homes as well as deplorable treatment and slavery were simply absorbed into the Seminole nation. The Seminole were first noted in southern Florida during the early 1800s along with a few white planters who dared to brave the inland swamps and untamed wilderness.

New River, now known as Fort Lauderdale, was the destination of Major William Lauderdale in 1838 leading his Tennessee Volunteers. The Second Seminole War was raging. Lauderdale's orders were to seize Seminole lands then capture or annihilate any warriors encountered. Major Lauderdale had his men clear the site and build a wooden blockhouse to be called New River Fort. The Tennessee Volunteers were involved in a minor skirmish, then abandoned the fort on the march to their Tennessee home. The Seminole Wars would continue until 1858, unfortunately by that time only some three hundred Seminole remained in Florida most hidden deep in the Everglade swamps.

The fort later became a safe house for runaway slaves and military deserters because of its remote location. In all, Fort Lauderdale served as the site for three separate military fortifications. The sole purpose of these forts involved defending settlers from the Seminoles who were forced to safe guard their way of life. The forts were located at first the fork of New River; the second built at Tarpon Bend; and finally the largest, on the site of what we know today as Bahia Mar.

As the Seminole Wars came to an end in 1858, the tribe was splintered and severely weakened. The United States Life Saving Service, which eventually became the Coast Guard, constructed a House of Refuge on the former site of Fort Lauderdale. The facility provided rescuers to pluck shipwreck victims from the perils of the deep as well as a safe haven to allow the sailors to recover from the unfortunate incidents.

By 1892, Frank Stranahan financed a rock road from Lantana to Lemon City[1], eventually opening an Indian Trading Post, post office, bank and ferry crossing New River. Stranahan established a settlement where only a military fortification existed though at first the only other inhabitants were Seminole. Much of what is known as Fort Lauderdale today was little more than swampland until Charles Green Rhodes developed a plan to form canals. Utilizing the same rationale employed in Venice, canals were created with long land masses called finger islands, between each waterway. Fort Lauderdale picked up the nickname "Venice of America."

Henry Flagler extended the Florida East Coast Railway into the city in 1896 bringing reliable, fast paced transportation to southeastern Florida. The steel lines of the railway brought a swelling population and by 1911, Fort Lauderdale was incorporated. William H. Marshall was chosen as the first mayor and the Florida Board of Trade passed legislation demanding an accessible port. The Fort Lauderdale Harbor Company was formed by leading citizens Marshall and Stranahan opening the port to ships exporting south Florida produce, certainly a boost to farmers. The harbor became known as Port Everglades, which is deceptive in that it is not a part of the Everglade system at all. The deep-water harbor would eventually bring substantial income to the area when large cruise companies chose Port Everglades as their base of operations.

Broward County was excised from parts of Dade and Palm Beach counties four years later. The first bridge, at today's Las Olas Boulevard, connected the mainland to the outlying island and the alluring white sand beaches beyond in 1917. Settlers relied chiefly on agriculture, cattle and citrus; eventually Fort Lauderdale's popularity made tourism an important industry of its own. Within five short years the population boom waned and a series of hurricanes in 1926 and 28, devastated the city.

Fort Lauderdale might have been down but she refused to fade, the city came back from disaster bigger and better than ever. The first olympic-sized swimming pool complex was built at the Casino Hotel and quietly Fort Lauderdale began her assent. The Collegiate Aquatic Forum, a unique winter attraction, was opened in 1935. By the end of World War II, Fort Lauderdale's population experienced another resurgence.

During the late 1950s, Fort Lauderdale became world renown as the Spring Break Shangri-La for college students escaping the doldrums of school for the sand, surf and round the clock party waiting for them there. The trend spawned several forgettable movies, a Connie Francis song and numerous police records for kids who abandoned their inhibitions at the Broward County line.

Eventually the city tired of the Spring Break invasion and began to discourage student from the annual migration south. Fort Lauderdale concentrated their tourism efforts toward a more mature visitor. In doing so cultural endeavors were focused upon including world recognized restaurants, championship golfing, galleries, theater, shopping and of course, preserving their natural attributes of glorious beaches as well as the rich history of the area.

The Fort Lauderdale Museum of History offers a wealth of interesting displays and sites for those interested in learning more about this fascinating city. Open Tuesday through Sunday, the Museum provides a guided tour for a small admission fee and should be placed on your vacation list of things not to be missed.

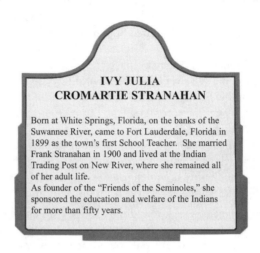

**IVY JULIA
CROMARTIE STRANAHAN**

Born at White Springs, Florida, on the banks of the Suwannee River, came to Fort Lauderdale, Florida in 1899 as the town's first School Teacher. She married Frank Stranahan in 1900 and lived at the Indian Trading Post on New River, where she remained all of her adult life.
As founder of the "Friends of the Seminoles," she sponsored the education and welfare of the Indians for more than fifty years.

**335 SE 6th Street, Fort Lauderdale
BO3 ~ GPS Coordinates: 26.118650, -80.137400**

The Cromartie family lived along the banks of the Suwannee River in a settlement called White Springs. On February 24, 1881, the family welcomed a baby daughter that they named Ivy Julia. In 1899, the Cromartie family moved to Broward County where Ivy graduated from Lemon City High School the very same year. She passed the teacher's exam at eighteen years of age, becoming the first teacher in Fort Lauderdale and the youngest in all of Florida.

Frank Stranahan left his birthplace in Vienna, Ohio for Florida in 1890. He was twenty-six years old and full of ambition. Stranahan first came to Melbourne but after three years moved to the wilderness of New River in 1893. He managed the Lantana-Lemon City stage line stop over and mail route. He was the first white man to become a permanent resident of the Fort Lauderdale area. When straight-laced Frank noticed the fiery Ivy Julia Cromartie, he was smitten at first glance. Society demanded that Mrs. Stranahan give up her salaried teacher's position, however the determined young lady refused to give up teaching completely.

The couple resided at the Indian trading post and post office Frank had built, which happens to be the oldest existing structure in Broward County. The lady of the house voluntarily taught Seminole children to read and write the English language for more than fifteen years. Frank Stranahan operated the trading post, the bank and the ferry. He put up the money for the first road to be built from the New River to Miami. He was by far the largest landowner but by the time of his death he had given vast portions of the property for public use as a hospital and park, which was named in his honor. So it is reasonably said he was in fact a founder of Fort Lauderdale. Frank Stranahan controlled supplies, money and transportation in the city, which made him quite powerful.

Stranahan's business acumen was well known throughout Fort Lauderdale, he was civic minded and set on developing the settlement into a city of reckoning. When Fort Lauderdale was incorporated in 1911, Stranahan shocked the entire population by failing to throw his hat into the political arena. Some felt Stranahan was standoffish and unfriendly, yet to those that really knew him they realized that he was instead a very private individual who valued his anonymity more than anything else.

However, when Stranahan felt he'd been wronged, the culprit best stay out of his way. He could be vicious in his attack. Eventually Frank Stranahan did enter city politics. Though in the 1926 city election he lost the race, his response was far from kind:

> "(I) believe that only Jesus Christ and his 12 apostles could straighten out the people of Fort
> Lauderdale and get them on the road to prosperity".

In addition to teaching the Seminole children, Ivy Stranahan established "Friends of the Seminoles." She assisted in persuading them to relocate to the reservation at Dania and once there rather than desert them to their own devices, Ivy Stranahan helped these people learn to deal with the government, racism and the backlash directed toward them as a result of the Seminole Indian Wars. Strongly supporting the rights of all women, not just white women, Stranahan taught the Seminole women a means for supporting themselves financially by giving them sewing machines and teaching them to use them.

Ivy Stranahan was an advocate for women's rights and was elected president of the Florida Suffrage League in 1917. She often traveled to Tallahassee in support of legislation giving women the right to vote. She also volunteered with the Audubon Society as well as the establishment of Everglades National Park in order to preserve some of Florida's disappearing wilderness and conservation of natural resources. Ivy Julia Cromartie Stranahan lived the remainder of her life at the Indian Trading Post on New River built by her husband in 1910. She would live to see the small settlement develop into a major metropolitan city.

Frank Stranahan was not immune to the hard times, which befell south Florida businessmen in the late 1920s. The population and land explosion was dwindling fast and then disaster struck with the devastating Miami hurricane of 1926. Stranahan was eventually hospitalized; the diagnosis was a nervous breakdown. It is believed that he was also in great pain, possibly dying of cancer. Frank Stranahan crept quietly onto the porch railing of his home, tied a heavy grate to his leg and jumped into the New River on June 23, 1929.

Mrs. Stranahan suffered none of her husband's mental disturbance. Ivy outlived him by forty years and recouped most of their family fortune in the process. Still active throughout her life, Ivy became state leader to the Florida Federation of Woman's Clubs and the Florida Equal Suffrage Association. She fought for the Seminole's right to receive federal benefits in the 1950s and for the rest of her life protected the memory of her husband's good name. After the first ugly headlines announcing his suicide, the term was never seen in print again. It seems Mrs. Stranahan wielded some power of her own. She continued to be a driving force in Fort Lauderdale and throughout the state until Ivy Julia Cromartie Stranahan passed away on August 30, 1971, she was ninety.

Several stories have circulated about Mr. and Mrs. Stranahan, one suggests that it was common knowledge that the couple was teetotalers wasn't exactly accurate. Ivy Stranahan was vehemently opposed to alcohol and her husband refused to sell liquor to the Native Americans but it seems Frank Stranahan did imbibe from time to time.   The manager of Pioneer House, which was the restaurant ran out of the Stranahan home for forty years, stated that often Ivy would be entertaining her allies in the temperance league in the front room while Frank staggered up the back staircase to his room quite inebriated. To support the allegations, when the attic was cleaned in January of 1980, a small stash of liquor was found, obviously hidden from the lady of the house. It seems Ivy Stranahan was a force to be dealt with even after her death. A reporter for the Miami Herald once stated that while researching a story on Broward County, he requested information on the Stranahan's from the local historical society. When the lady returned with an envelope containing the article announcing Frank Stranahan's suicide, she said in a hushed tone, "Don't tell anyone where you got this." Obviously Ivy Stranahan's power extended beyond the grave.

Today the Stranahan House is today a historical museum. Over the years the house has been a trading post, residence, restaurant and conference center. The Fort Lauderdale Historical Society with assistance from the Board of Realtors and the community restored the Stranahan House in a way that would make Ivy proud. The home was beautifully restored in 1984. The docents at the Stranahan House Museum are extremely knowledgeable and take exceptional care of their charge. A small fee is charged for an interesting and informative tour of the home.

Over the years it has been said that the Stranahan's have refused to leave their home in spirit at least. From time to time voices in conversation are heard when no one occupies the room, the smell of cigar smoke permeates the air when no one is allowed to smoke inside and at times one gets the feeling of being observed even though you're all alone. Vagrants offer a stern warning among themselves to seek shelter in the night anywhere else rather than the seemingly deserted Stranahan House; you see Ivy has been known to chase away those trespassing on her porch during the night. Ivy Julia Cromartie Stranahan was inducted in the Florida Women's Hall of Fame in 1996. A distinction that she certainly deserved.

THE STRANAHAN HOUSE
SIDE VIEW

FLORIDA'S FIRST
POST OFFICE

THE STRANAHAN HOUSE

FORT LAUDERDALE
HISTORICAL MARKER

TUNNEL PIONEERS
An Exceptional Job – Well Done

This tablet is dedicated in recognition of the splendid services rendered the community by the tunnel pioneers, a group of local residents who so unselfishly gave of their time, talents and finances, to bring the much needed New River Tunnel into being.

335 SE 6th Avenue, Fort Lauderdale
BO3 ~ GPS Coordinates: 26.118650, -80.137400

A span was built fording New River and dedicated on August 26, 1926 as the Federal Aid Highway Bridge. The name was derived from the fact that federal funding enabled the construction to be completed. Eventually the name was shortened to simply Federal Highway.

The route was difficult and time consuming at best for travelers crossing New River. The wooden drawbridge was very slow to open and cumbersome to close. The wooden structure creaked and moaned as the chains drew open to allow ships safe passage. From start to finish the process consumed the greater part of an hours time. When the community was faced with the replacement of the old trestle, the people were equally divided. One sect preferred the construction of another drawbridge whereas the opposition favored a new unique idea, that of a tunnel.

Henry E. Kinney led the pro-tunnel sect while the bridge received support from a loftier position, that of Governor LeRoy Collins. Kinney was editor of the Broward edition published by the Miami Herald. Many felt that Kinney abused his position with the newspaper to garner votes in favor of the tunnel. The Governor loudly claimed that a tunnel of this sort would result in the "worst traffic jam in Florida".

The vote was taken in November 1956. After a vigorous campaign no clear leaning was evident either in favor of the bridge or the tunnel. Imagine the scene where tempers flared over this simple issue and in fact the opposing side were extremely vehement in their convictions. When the final tally was read there were seven thousand eight votes for the tunnel and six thousand, four hundred one votes for the bridge. The majority vote carried and the tunnel was approved.

The Florida Department of Transportation began construction of the tunnel in August of 1958. The process was slow going but finally the tunnel was completed as 1960 came to an end. A ceremonious dedication was staged on December 9, 1960. It was the tunnel's chief opposition who officially opened the site. Governor LeRoy Collins gallantly cut the red ribbon and the New River Tunnel was opened for Fort Lauderdale travelers.

Primary tunnel supporter, Miami Herald Broward Bureau Chief Henry E. Kinney passed away in July 1985. The Florida Legislature voted unanimously in 1986 to rename the tunnel in his honor. The Henry E. Kinney Tunnel is the only one of its kind throughout the entire state of Florida. The Florida Department of Transportation continues to this day to maintain the tunnel.

Some say in the early morning hours when travelers enter the portal beneath the waters of New River a single male figure wearing a sedate brown suit will often bolt in front of vehicles and disappear into the mist. Many believe this to be the spirit of Henry Kinney continuing his hold on to the tunnel he so passionately supported. Others tend to feel the ghostly figure is perhaps a traveler who lost his life in the depth of the tunnel. The spirit is destined to dwell eternally in place where death finally claimed him. Whoever the spirit once was remember as you enter the murky underground of the Henry E. Kinney Tunnel, you are never alone.

COOLEY MASSACRE

This monument marks the site of the earliest white settlement on New River that of the Lewis Family in the 18th century and that of the Cooley Massacre of Jan. 6, 1836 when members of William Cooley's family were murdered in a surprise attack by the Indians at the onset of the Second Seminole War.

Brickell Drive and SE 15th Avenue, Fort Lauderdale
BO4 ~ GPS Coordinates: 26.117617, -80.128567

Along the banks of New River near the spot known as Sailboat Bend is a patch of blood soaked earth covered by one hundred seventy-five years time. It is said in the early days of January as the red sun slips below the horizon that muffled screams can still be heard at the site of the Cooley homestead. The tortured souls of a murdered family doomed to wander the ethereal plain searching for eternal rest.

William Cooley, a Maryland native, arrived at New River in 1824. He built a large coonte[2] mill on what was formerly the Lewis property. In addition to his lucrative starch enterprise, Cooley was also involved in local politics as Justice of the Peace and temporary light keeper at the Biscayne Bay Lighthouse.

Cooley was well known to the Seminole. He lived as their neighbor, could converse in their tongue and showed them kindness. Cooley's relationship with the Seminole was such that he named two of his sons after their chiefs. Therefore even though the Seminole had attacked settlers in the past, Cooley felt at ease leaving his family alone.

The United States government resolved that the answer to avoiding the Seminole uprisings was to displace the entire tribe. Western territory, today the state of Oklahoma, had been set aside as an exile called a reservation for Native Americans. Nearly four thousand Seminole were herded west by 1834, others refused to be pushed from their homes and revolted.

Alibama, a chief in the Creek nation, was brutally murdered by white settlers. The men were identified and William Cooley as justice of the peace saw that they were arrested. The suspects were sent to Key West for trial and from there released supposedly for lack of evidence. Most believed that because the victim was an Indian very little effort was placed in convicting the men. The Seminole blamed Cooley when no one was held accountable for Chief Alibama's murder.

Osceola attacked and killed Indian agent Wiley Thompson on December 28, 1935. That very same day Major Francis Dade and his men were ambushed leaving one hundred eight men dead, only three survived to tell the tale of the brutal onslaught. The Second Seminole War began with a vengeance and by the time the third war was finished the Seminole would be nearly wiped from the face of the earth.

William Cooley left his home to salvage a wrecked ship at Hillsboro Beach. A band of Seminole watched and waited for William Cooley to leave his home. A short time later Mrs. Cooley smelled smoke as her home was set ablaze. She bolted from the house with her baby held tightly against her heart, her son and daughter in tow along with their tutor. As Mrs. Cooley ran screaming as a bullet tore through her body and into the babe in her arms. Both fell to the hard ground as their life's blood spread a crimson blanket on the earth. The Cooley's eleven-year-old daughter was shot repeatedly until her lifeless body lay in a heap. A Seminole warrior with death in his eyes brandish a club until the mangled body of the Cooley's nine year old son breathed his last ragged breath and died. The slightly built tutor tried to defend himself to no avail. The warriors surrounded him then taunted and tortured him. Lying half-dead, his scalp was torn from his body and when death finally came it was a welcome relief from the pain. The house was left a smoldering ruin just beyond the murdered bodies of the Cooley family. William Cooley's coonte mill was left untouched.

When Cooley returned home, the gruesome sight was enough to turn a grown man's stomach. Doubts raced through his mind, had he been home would this massacre have happened? Would he have died as well, he certainly wished for death now? Cooley and sixty other settlers quickly fled the area sailing for the Cape Florida Lighthouse and safety. Many of the settlers sought refuge at Indian Key and others did not stop until they reached Key West. Most carried nothing with them save the clothes on their backs.

Once the settlers reached safety, a distraught William Cooley returned home to bury his family. Cooley returned to the Cape Florida Lighthouse for a time but it was obvious his heart was crushed. The Seminoles moved inland and things were quiet for five months. It would take a full fifty years for the county to recover and rebuild their numbers after the brutal massacre.

SLIP F 18

Bahia Mar marina
Dedicated to the "Busted Flush" Home
of Travis McGee
Fictional Hero & Salvage Consultant
Created by John D. MacDonald,
Author
1916-1986

Bahia-Mar Yachting Center, 801 Seabreeze Blvd, Fort Lauderdale
BO5 ~ GPS Coordinates: 26.114583, -80.108217

Born in Sharon, Pennsylvania, John Dann MacDonald received his Bachelor of Science Degree from Syracuse University in 1938 then went on to earn a Masters in Business Administration from Harvard the next year. He married Dorothy Mary Prentiss in 1937, the couple had one son.

MacDonald served as a Lieutenant Colonel during World War II with the Office of Strategic Services, which eventually become the CIA. During his tour in Europe, MacDonald wrote a short story and sent it to his wife describing the conditions he was forced to face during the war. This was the only way his letters could reach his wife without extreme censorship. Once Dorothy MacDonald received the missive she submitted it to a magazine for consideration. The article was accepted and MacDonald was paid twenty-five dollars for the short story and his writing career began.

Once his tour of duty in military service was completed, MacDonald chose to be a full time author. He spent four months writing in every waking hour. He submitted as many as fifty articles at a time for publication and unfortunately met with considerable resistance. MacDonald was quickly becoming destitute, however with the support of his wife continued to write. In 1945, his work began to receive the recognition it truly deserved.

MacDonald moved his small family to south Florida in 1949. After having written some forty books and well over one hundred articles and short stories, his publisher pushed him to create a character that would endure the test of time through a series of books. MacDonald's work all wove an underlying theme throughout dealing with moral and social issues such as the ecology, racism, political corruption, real estate fraud, marital infidelity as well as illegal narcotics.

John MacDonald developed a series involving mysteries solved by a central character named Travis McGee. Initially the hero was to be called Dallas McGee, however when President Kennedy was assassinated in the city MacDonald changed the name out of respect for our fallen leader. The name Travis was chosen in reference to a United States Air Force base. McGee was described as a Korean War veteran and former football player; a two hundred pound society reject sporting sandy hair and ice blue eyes. The author goes on to say that his character drove an antique Rolls Royce and resided on a houseboat called *The Busted Flush*.

MacDonald wrote that McGee's home was moored at the Bahia-Mar Yachting Center, Slip F18. The named was derived from a poker hand in which the houseboat was collateral. The Travis McGee books standard premise involved the hero resolving some tragic problem of a friend or relative.

The Travis McGee books, twenty-one in all, were filled with drama as well as laughter; the author revealed his depth of feeling for his adopted state of Florida. However it was the realistic everyday glimpse into life and well defined plots that resulted in John MacDonald's recognition as one of the country's most admired mystery writers. Rights to several of the Travis McGee books have been sold to Fox Pictures. By the time John Dann McGee passed away on December 31, 1986, he had written more than five hundred articles and sixty-six novels. The widely recognized author has sold more than seventy million books worldwide.

INDIAN HAULOVER

Bahia Mar is the site of a haulover where Indians took their canoes from New River Sound into the Atlantic Ocean. A Second Seminole War fort named for Major William Lauderdale was built near here in 1838. It was active until the War ended in 1842. House of Refuge Number Four, originally built about two miles to the north in 1876, was moved to this site in 1892. Barefoot mailmen walked their weekly route from Hypoluxo to Miami along these beaches. The Coast Guard began using the House of Refuge in 1915. It was made permanent as Coast Guard Base Six in 1926. Base Six saw considerable action against rum runners during Prohibition. It remained in active service until after World War II. The City of Fort Lauderdale purchased the property for use as a public yacht basin and park in 1947.

S. R. A1A at entrance to Bahia Mar Hotel & Resort, Fort Lauderdale
BO6 ~ GPS Coordinates: 26.113150, -80.105983

On this site, many years before the white man set foot on Florida soil, Native Americans utilized this moderate crossing from New River Sound to the Atlantic Ocean. Artifacts found during excavation confirmed the fact that grand feasts were held here. The Seminole bill of fare included all manner of bounty provided by the Atlantic Ocean. Surprisingly this tells us that little has changed with the exceptions of landscaping and ethnicity through the generations. The Native Americans came to feast and enjoy the good things in life, likewise today visitors from all over the world flock to Fort Lauderdale to absorb the wide array of festivity in the resort community often called, the "Venice of America."

New River was actually the site of three Fort Lauderdales, four if you include the modern day city. However, three of the four were actual fortifications. It seems every time war was declared against the Seminole a new fortification was built. The second wooden fort became House of Refuge Number Four in 1875. The house provided shelter for those unlucky souls who found themselves shipwrecked in tumultuous waters. When Prohibition began the Coast Guard assumed command of the house and it became known as Coast Guard Base Six. From this vantage point rumrunners from the Bahamas were chased and brought to justice. The base was eventually expanded to include a huge houseboat called the *Moccasin*. Brought in from Miami, the boat served as the headquarters for the Coast Guard until a massive hurricane in 1926 blew the *Moccasin* to the opposite side of the Intracoastal Waterway.

A rumrunner, James Horace "Jimmy" Alderman was captured by the Coast Guard with one hundred sixty cases of rum from the Bahamas. But Jimmy Alderman didn't come quietly. He and his accomplice Robert Weech fought like demons to avoid arrest. During the shoot out Boatswain Sidney C. Sanderlin was killed instantly; Secret Service Agent Robert K. Webster was also shot and killed; Motor Machinist Mate First Class Victor A. Lamby was gravely paralyzed with a bullet lodged near his spine, he died within days; and Seaman Second Class Jodie L. Hollingsworth, lived but lost his right eye and the majority of the right side of his face. Alderman was stabbed six times with an ice pick and was beaten within an inch of his life, Weech was also bruised and covered in the blood of their victims.

The Coast Guard ship looked as though it were bathed in the life essence of law men just doing their jobs apprehending rum runners Alderman and Weech who refused to be taken without a fight. The patrol boat aimlessly drifted until their distress flag waving SOS from the masthead was finally seen. The bootlegger pirates turned murderers were found handcuffed and bound on the deck, Alderman was barely conscious.

Alderman was taken to Miami to stand trial in Federal Court. The process was swift, the verdict was guilty and the sentence was death by hanging. Federal law required that the sentence be carried out in the county that the crime occurred. Alderman would be the first and last criminal executed in Broward County, this was also the last judicial hanging in United States history. The Broward County commissioners tried to avoid the sentence for as long as possible by refusing the gather a quorum. But finally the council had no choice but to carry out the federal judge's orders.

The next hurdle to overcome was that no one in the county knew how to go about hanging this man. Finally the only person with any experience in the area was found, the one-legged sheriff of Palm Beach County. It was determined that the only site out of the public eye to carry out the sentence was a metal seaplane hangar at Bahia Mar. Alderman requested a red rose to signify his religious rebirth and burial in white clothes to represent the church. It is amazing how quickly a death sentence leads a criminal to God.

James Horace "Jimmy" Alderman was taken under heavy guard to the hangar at Bahia Mar. At 6:04 a.m. the sentence was carried out. The execution did not go smoothly, Alderman kicked and choked for twelve minutes before finally being pronounced dead by the physician standing by. Per the judges' orders the sentence was carried out in private, even so several reporters managed to sneak their way in to view the execution. Due to the graphic nature of the execution, none of their editors would allow the stories to run.

The base remained active until the final days of World War II then Coast Guard Base Six faded into history. The property was purchased by the city of Fort Lauderdale with plans to build an extensive yachting center.

The plans were approved and accepted on Friday the 13th in the midst of a hurricane with hopes that this wasn't a sign of things to come. Finally, often deterred by Mother Natures' wrath, the four hundred-slip marina was completed. It was the largest marina in the world.

Patricia Murphy of New York opened her wonderfully successful Candlelight Restaurant in the 1950s, a magnificent resort complex was built and Bahia Mar South opened its luxurious doors offering one hundred fifteen rooms in 1966. A pedestrian walkway along the beach was soon completed as was the fifteen story Bahia North tower hotel. After more than thirty years the Candlelight Restaurant was torn down and renovations were completed on Bahia North and South as well as the marina. Patricia Murphy is remembered fondly with gardens dedicated to the beauty she brought to Fort Lauderdale.

Local resident author John MacDonald created a character based out of Bahia Mar called Travis McGee. The first book begins with a vivid description of the Bahia Mar marina. On February 21, 1987, a Literary Landmark plaque was placed at Slip F18 where the character kept his boat called the *Busted Flush*. Supposedly the boat was won in a poker game, the winning hand being of course, a busted flush.

Now owned by the Radisson franchise, the Bahia Mar Beach Resort and Bahia Mar Yachting Center were treated to an eight and a half million-dollar renovation. The resort features several fine dining options, beautifully decorated rooms, a landscaped pool area and state of the art fitness center for the convenience of their guests. The conference center facilities will meet the needs of any organization or group. Space is available for every occasion from a small business meeting to an extensive corporate conference. The marina offers all the amenities a boater could ask for from shipbuilders to a marina store.

The Indian Haulover sight has most definitely changed over the years, but the spirit of joy and pleasure lives on at Bahia Mar. Sit quietly and listen to the ocean's surf, feel the warm sea breeze gently caress your skin and watch the sun as it slowly dips beneath the horizon. Paradise, it seems, has been here all along.

US 1 & Southeast 24th Street, Fort Lauderdale
BO7 ~ GPS Coordinates: 26.093009, -80.136840

Like so many of its kind, the Merle Fogg Airport at Fort Lauderdale was conscripted by the United States Navy during the World War II years. The facility was to be used as a naval aviation flight training school in support of Navy aircrew as well as ground maintenance personnel.

Many of the instructors had just completed aviation training at Pensacola, most had very little flight experience and none of them had any experience at flight combat. Training was rigorous and complicated. A number dropped out unable to sustain the strenuous pace and absorb the difficult material. In 1943, a young Ensign named George Herbert Walker Bush was assigned to NAS Fort Lauderdale for pilot training. This young man would go on to be the United States' forty-first President.

NAS Fort Lauderdale lost ninety-four brave service members during the war. The number includes fourteen men who disappeared under mysterious circumstances on United States Navy Flight 19. While on a navigation training mission over the Atlantic, five Avenger aircraft vanished. Only speculation remains concerning the fate of these men and their aircraft.

As the war drew to a close the Navy no longer required the use of NAS Fort Lauderdale. In keeping with the standard, the property was returned to Broward County. The county then returned the land to its original use as an airport. Still there were some minor changes, most apparent was the name. Today Fort Lauderdale-Hollywood International Airport is one of the finest commercial airline terminals in the country.

Only two NAS buildings remained, the #15 Junior Officers Bachelor Officers Quarters, which housed our forty-first President and the Link Trainer building. Former President Bush returned to the NAS site to sign a mural done by Bob Jenny entitled "The Final Approach." Sadly Broward County has planned to demolish the Officers Quarters building for airport expansion but the Link Trainer building is to remain. The NAS Fort Lauderdale Historical Association was founded in order to preserve all of the World War II facilities located in the Fort Lauderdale area. This admirable association is collecting all manner of documentation and memorabilia connected with the facilities in hopes of creating a museum to pass along this valuable glimpse into history. The goal of this organization involves educating the young and informing adults. Our obligation is to honor these proud men and women who gave of themselves, sometimes giving all.

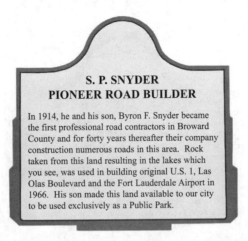

S. P. Snyder Park, 3299 SW 4th Avenue, Fort Lauderdale
BO8 ~ GPS Coordinates: 26.083217, -80.151317

Work on the Dixie Highway through Broward County was completed 1915. Through the years many of the roads we travel today were first Snyder Road Contractors projects including U.S. 1, Las Olas Boulevard and the runways of the Fort Lauderdale-Hollywood International Airport. These roads were made of rock quarried from what is today S. P. Snyder Park. The expansive reservoirs left after the rock was removed soon filled with ground water from the underground aquifer and became the beautiful lakes in the park today. Byron F. Snyder offered the ninety-three acre park to the city of Fort Lauderdale with the stipulation that it be used as a public park.

The agreement with Byron Snyder has been observed. Though I wonder if he'd get a chuckle out of some of the usage. For the past four years, Snyder Park has had a park within a park. That may sound confusing, well let me explain. Four year ago, Ronnie Lakatos founded something called Bark Park. What, you might ask, is that? The facility is a two-acre, fenced grass expanse tucked away into the corner of Snyder Park. But Bark Park only caters to our four legged canine friends.

The park features two plastic agility courses, one for big pooches and another for the little tykes. The plastic is used for cleanliness, wood tends to absorb those messes and odors we'd like to be rid of while plastic on the other hand can be easily hosed down and sanitized. Their courses were specially designed to challenge the bowwows a bit. Different shaped hurdles are used as well as ramps, podiums, specially designed hills and jumping blocks.

Strict attention is paid to flea and tick infestation so that all the dogs can enjoy the park in comfort. Two turtle shaped sandboxes provide lots of fun rolling in the dirt. On those days when the temperature soars or after a tough workout on the agility course, the doggie fountains supply a cool drink to soothe a parched throat. The fountains have ground levers that activate when the dogs' paws step on them, shooting up a cool spout of water. There is a five-acre lake just across the street where the canines can take a little aquatic exercise or just doggy paddle around the edge a bit. The park allows the dogs to romp and run without worry of busy streets, they can be much better pets at home if they have been allowed the time to vent that energy.

Thanks to sponsors such as Purina, weekly clinics ranging from fly ball competitions to the basics of care and grooming are offered. Many other programs are available throughout the year including an annual dog walk for children's cancer charity and even Christmas picture day for your pet! A portion of the park may be rented for special occasions.

Fort Lauderdale with Bark Park was ranked second throughout the United States as an Animal Friendly City by Animal Wellness magazine. A small fee is charge for admission, annual passes are also available. Byron Snyder would get a chuckle out of Bark Park and I'm sure he would approve.

MACKEY AIRLINES, INC.

Founded in 1946 by Colonel Joseph Mackey, Mackey Airlines became (August 5, 1952) the first certified carrier in Broward authorized to engage in scheduled foreign transportation. Operations began January 2, 1952 between Fort Lauderdale, West Palm Beach and Nassau, N. P. Bahamas. Increased certification later allowed service to all Bahama Islands from Fort Lauderdale-Hollywood, Miami, West Palm Beach, St. Petersburg, Tampa and Jacksonville. Mackey operated without mail pay or subsidy. Passengers increased from 15,000 to 150,000 annually, Mackey and Eastern Airlines merged January 1, 1961.

Fort Lauderdale International Airport, Near Parking Garage B, Fort Lauderdale
BO9 ~ GPS Coordinates: 26.071967, -80.143033

Eastern Airlines was first organized way back in 1927 when its parent company, Pitcairn Aviation began. The company soon changed its name to Eastern Air Transport. Eastern Air dominated the American skies, by 1932 flights were being made from Miami to New York all in one day! Then Eastern expanded again, this time going international to Toronto and Bermuda.

The airlines' future was dependent on getting a government contract to deliver airmail. The Post Office consolidated in the late 1920s, giving Eastern complete control of the entire Eastern seaboard. Unfortunately in 1934, Congress found that the post office was not authorized to issue the contracts and banned the airline involved from carrying mail, Eastern Air Transport was one of them. So they simply changed their name to Eastern Airlines. Colonel Joseph Mackey founded Mackey Airlines in 1946 in Broward County. Nearly six years later on August 5, 1952 the first international flights out of Broward County took place. Beginning with Fort Lauderdale, West Palm Beach to Nassau, Bahamas then adding St. Petersburg, Tampa and Jacksonville into the mix. Mackey stayed afloat without the subsidy provided by mail freight. Soon fifteen thousand passengers a year swelled to one hundred fifty thousand, leading to a merger between Mackey and Eastern Airlines on the first day of January 1961.

Eastern introduced a new service during the late 1950s, Air Shuttles. Basically a commuter service during a time when air travel wasn't a common practice. The shuttle took off on hourly hops between New York, Washington D.C. and Boston. No reservations, no meals and no waiting; Eastern promised that if all their regular flights were full, they would send out another. The shuttle service was extremely successful spurring the addition of jets in 1967.

Unfortunately by 1978, airline deregulation caused a flat spin no pilot could pull out of. Small cut-rate airlines popped up everywhere offering flights at rock bottom fares. Eastern could not compete and began losing money. They began a costly advertising campaign hawking their service quality and experienced pilots; the flying public wanted only cheap fares. Eastern Airlines was virtually bankrupt and in 1986 sold to Frank Lorenzo. Labor disputes and mismanagement were Lorenzo's downfall, Eastern continued to spiral downward. In 1989, Lorenzo sold Eastern's shuttle service to Donald Trump. Frank Lorenzo filed for bankruptcy relief in 1991; all Eastern Airlines flight operations were shut down.

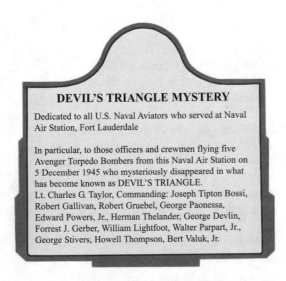

DEVIL'S TRIANGLE MYSTERY

Dedicated to all U.S. Naval Aviators who served at Naval
Air Station, Fort Lauderdale

In particular, to those officers and crewmen flying five
Avenger Torpedo Bombers from this Naval Air Station on
5 December 1945 who mysteriously disappeared in what
has become known as DEVIL'S TRIANGLE.
Lt. Charles G. Taylor, Commanding: Joseph Tipton Bossi,
Robert Gallivan, Robert Gruebel, George Paonessa,
Edward Powers, Jr., Herman Thelander, George Devlin,
Forrest J. Gerber, William Lightfoot, Walter Parpart, Jr.,
George Stivers, Howell Thompson, Bert Valuk, Jr.

Dead end of Lee Wagner Blvd, Ft. Lauderdale
BO10 ~ GPS Coordinates: 26.070600, -80.155400

Theories abound concerning the mysteries of the Devil's Triangle or Bermuda Triangle, whichever you prefer. There is no label on navigational charts that records the triangular space reaching from Bermuda to Miami then San Juan connecting again to make the perfect shape. Explanations span the full range from human error, purely scientific, voodoo as well as aliens to a government conspiracy. Whatever tact you chose to take, it is simply personal prerogative. People have spent a lifetime searching for the true explanation and died still wondering: What secret does the Devil's Triangle hold?

The facts are:

It was a rainy afternoon on December 5, 1945 at exactly 1410[3] when a squadron of five TBM Avenger Torpedo Bombers making up United States Naval Flight 19 departed from NAS[4] Fort Lauderdale. There were fourteen men aboard. Flight 19 flew into the cloud filled sky for advanced overwater navigational training and were never seen again. The apparent trouble began around 1600[5] with a garbled missive indicating the squadron was off course and experiencing malfunctions with their directional gauges. Then the radio went completely silent as if the Atlantic swallowed the men and planes without a trace.

A rescue plane with thirteen crewmen was immediately dispatched in search of the lost squadron. The pilot radioed in ten minutes into the flight and they too were never heard from again. Numerous searches were conducted; no wreckage, no bodies and no indications of any foul play were ever found.

A senior flight instructor led the squadron and the remainder were all qualified pilots. Scattered rain blanketed the area but visibility remained six to eight miles in the showers and above twenty-five hundred feet the sky was clear, visibility ranging from ten to twelve miles. Winds gusted to thirty-one knots and seas rolled at six to eight feet, which is considered moderate to rough. The weather conditions were determined to be average for the day's training exercises.

Officials know for certain that the Flight 19 planes would exhaust their fuel by 2000[6] and that the rough seas were not conducive for a water landing. Many believed that the planes made a forced landing and simply sank committing the crew to a watery grave. The rescue or recovery operation continued for a full fives days when the weather turned ugly making it impossible for the search to continue. As for the first rescue plan and her crew was also lost, a merchant ship just off the Fort Lauderdale shore sighted an incredible burst of flame and later passed through an oil slick. It is presumed that the rescue aircraft exploded with her entire crew lost. Even though the site of the explosion was known, no sign of the plane or crew was ever found.

Neither the United States Coast Guard nor the Board of Geographic Names do not recognize the Bermuda Triangle officially. Noted only is the unexplained disappearances within the unofficial zone including large vessels, small boats and aircraft as well as the lives that have been lost there.

Unofficially the government claims rare environmental manifestations have resulted in the disappearance and further that the brutally swift Gulf Stream can quickly erase all evidence of disaster. Another consideration is that in this area a magnetic compass will not register true north, only magnetic north. This variance could result in as much as twenty degrees off course, if this variance is not taken into consideration the crew and craft could be in grave danger.

THE BERMUDA TRIANGLE MEMORIAL

Though the NAS Fort Lauderdale Historical Association takes no official stance regarding the Devil's Triangle, the explanation of choice seems to be pilot error. The USCG[7] records the losses as unexplained accidents due to possible pilot error. Imagine how many incompetent pilots, captains and crews would have existed based on this premise. Obviously that should say something for their training and licensing. Whatever explanation you choose to take concerning Devil's Triangle, the planes and crew are gone never to return. The answer to this riddle will probably never be found.

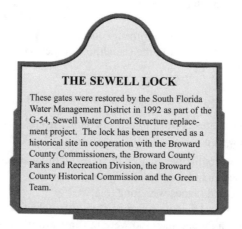

THE SEWELL LOCK

These gates were restored by the South Florida Water Management District in 1992 as part of the G-54, Sewell Water Control Structure replacement project. The lock has been preserved as a historical site in cooperation with the Broward County Commissioners, the Broward County Parks and Recreation Division, the Broward County Historical Commission and the Green Team.

6521 West SR84, Fort Lauderdale
BO11 ~ GPS Coordinates: 26.094600, -80.229300

Naturally occurring conditions such as drought, flood and tropical storms in addition to the blossoming population of the south Florida frontier pushed the United States Congress to pursue legislation that ultimately established the Central and Southern Florida Flood Control Project in 1948. The initial program was a forerunner for today's South Florida Water Management District developed and administered under the watchful eye of the United States Army Corps of Engineers.

The Florida Water Resources Act was approved in 1972, allowing the state to create districts in order to manage water as a natural resource. Responsibilities were divided into five districts each managing regional water resources and handling environmental protection. Natural drainage sites as well as key landmarks determined a boundary for each district. Florida voters went to the polls in 1976 approving a constitutional amendment allowing taxes to be levied to fund water resource projects.

Sewell Lock was replaced by Structure G-54, which is simply a gated spillway that can be opened and closed as the need arises. Located on the North New River Canal, the structure drains a total area of approximately thirty miles. This structure was added as a part of the South Florida Water Management District in 1992 to manage the particular Water Conservation Area.

The Fort Lauderdale Station handles eighteen hundred miles of canals and levees, regulating the flow and water level for each of twenty-four districts within Broward County. There are twenty-five pumping stations with more than two thousand various sized water control structures or locks. Today the focus of responsibility continues to be flood control, water supply and most importantly water quality.

WILD IGUANA SUNNING AT SEWELL LOCK

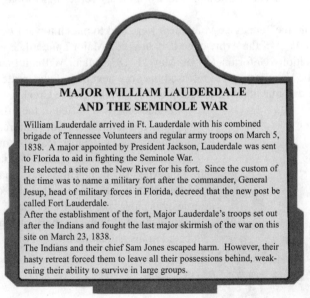

**MAJOR WILLIAM LAUDERDALE
AND THE SEMINOLE WAR**

William Lauderdale arrived in Ft. Lauderdale with his combined brigade of Tennessee Volunteers and regular army troops on March 5, 1838. A major appointed by President Jackson, Lauderdale was sent to Florida to aid in fighting the Seminole War.

He selected a site on the New River for his fort. Since the custom of the time was to name a military fort after the commander, General Jesup, head of military forces in Florida, decreed that the new post be called Fort Lauderdale.

After the establishment of the fort, Major Lauderdale's troops set out after the Indians and fought the last major skirmish of the war on this site on March 23, 1838.

The Indians and their chief Sam Jones escaped harm. However, their hasty retreat forced them to leave all their possessions behind, weakening their ability to survive in large groups.

**Forest Ridge Blvd, dead end off Pine Island, Fort Lauderdale
BO12 ~ GPS Coordinates: 26.080216, -80.268535**

"Maitland" was the original family name of the south Florida namesake until his ancestor the Laird of Maitland was made Earl of Lauderdale. The accolade was bestowed as a result of his exemplary military service to Scotland. William Lauderdale's lineage can be traced by marriage to Robert Bruce, King of Scotland as well as Sir William Wallace, who was later depicted in the bio-fictional movie "Braveheart."

Generations of Lauderdales have lived quiet unassuming lives as farmers, military officers and professional men. William Lauderdale was born in Virginia around 1780 in Virginia. He grew up in a wealthy family in Sumner County, Tennessee becoming a prominent planter. When the command to battle sounded in 1812 William Lauderdale answered the call. Like his forefathers, he rushed to the front to face the enemy head on and served honorably on the battlefield.

Andrew Jackson called up the Tennessee Volunteers to New Orleans where the War of 1812 blazed. William Lauderdale was made a lieutenant and although the Volunteers never saw combat in New Orleans, Lauderdale became a Jackson confidant. Lauderdale returned to his Goose Creek Plantation in Hartsville, Tennessee. Andrew Jackson summoned him once again for the Battle of New Orleans in 1815. He was made Jackson's Chief Quartermaster. James Lauderdale, William's brother, was the highest-ranking Tennessee officer killed.

It seemed wherever Jackson led, now Major William Lauderdale was sure to follow. By the 1830s the United States Army was embroiled with decimating the Seminole people. The government was relatively successful, but it would take three bitter wars and millions of dollars before the task was complete. Unlike the Ais and Tequesta natives in south Florida, the Seminole refused to be quietly annihilated. Still today descendants of the proud tribe remain in Florida.

Major William Lauderdale would carry the United States ensign further into Indian Territory than any other white man. Again at Jackson's command Lauderdale led his Tennessee Volunteers serving as mounted spies into Seminole territory. The battalions' order involved using whatever force necessary to remove the Seminole from their home. The Second Seminole War raged and proved to be the bloodiest as well as the most costly of the Seminole Wars. The Tennessee Volunteers arrived at the mouth of New River and constructed a wooden fortification. At the suggestion of General Thomas Jesup, leader of military forces in Florida, the site was named Fort Lauderdale.

In the spring of 1838, the Tennessee Volunteers were told to march toward Baton Rouge, Louisianna. The Volunteers would be mustered out of the Army once they arrived. Major Lauderdale was eagerly anticipating his return to his Tennessee plantation. Unfortunately on May 11, 1838 Major William Lauderdale suffered a pulmonary disorder and died, the Volunteers were released the very next day. Lauderdale would never see his home again, even in death he would not be allowed to return to his beloved Goose Creek.

Lauderdale was buried in the officers' cemetery with all of the pomp due an officer of his stature. Unfortunately over time his gravesite has been lost, experts continue the search even today. Continuing the family tradition, William Lauderdale's son fell during the Mexican War. The site of what was once a meager wooden fortification has grown to become one of America's grandest cities, his namesake Fort Lauderdale. It is said that the only monument dedicated to the memory of Major William Lauderdale is located in his namesake city at Forest Ridge Park.

STATUE HONORING MAJOR WILLIAM LAUDERDALE

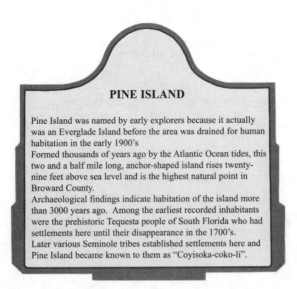

PINE ISLAND

Pine Island was named by early explorers because it actually
was an Everglade Island before the area was drained for human
habitation in the early 1900's
Formed thousands of years ago by the Atlantic Ocean tides, this
two and a half mile long, anchor-shaped island rises twenty-
nine feet above sea level and is the highest natural point in
Broward County.
Archaeological findings indicate habitation of the island more
than 3000 years ago. Among the earliest recorded inhabitants
were the prehistoric Tequesta people of South Florida who had
settlements here until their disappearance in the 1700's.
Later various Seminole tribes established settlements here and
Pine Island became known to them as "Coyisoka-coko-li".

Forest Ridge Blvd, dead end off Pine Island, Fort Lauderdale
BO12 ~ GPS Coordinates: 26.080216, -80.268535

Before the arrival of Europeans, a small, peaceful Native American tribe inhabited south Florida known as the Tequesta. They built settlements near what is today Biscayne Bay and on the barrier islands. The chief of the tribe would live in the main village located at the mouth of the Miami River.

The tribe lived off the bounty of the land and sea. Men hunted and fished for food, while the women gathered food from the forest and collected the sea offering in the shallow waters. The sea cow or manatee was considered a delicacy and only served to the elders of the tribe. Food sources were hard to come by and the tribe never became large or powerful. The people used shells and sharks' teeth as tools. They made hammers, chisels, fishhooks, cups and spears from these implements. Can you imagine the size of a shark whose teeth were used to carve out a canoe?

The Europeans befriended the Tequesta bringing brightly colored cloth, steel knives and rum. The Native Americans were apprehensive about these new pale faced people. The new arrivals brought much more than trinkets and alcohol, they also brought disease for which the Tequesta had no immunities. The Indians were badly used as slaves and when their small numbers attacked the entire tribe was virtually wiped out. The few remaining proud, peaceful Tequesta were absorbed into other tribes.

One of Florida's Native Americans most powerful spiritual leaders and medicine men was a Mikasuki named Abiaka or by his English name, Sam Jones. He was a little known member of the Lower Creek band of Seminoles. Sam Jones and his followers lived near Pine Island. Even though quite elderly, Jones fought in many battles of the Second Seminole War. Other times he prepared warriors for battle. During the Battle of Okeechobee, Sam Jones played an integral part in the defensive planning against Colonel Zachary Taylor. Surrender was not ever an option for Jones.

He participated in all three Seminole Wars. A bounty was put up for Sam Jones to be captured dead or alive using whatever means necessary. He was never apprehended. Sam Jones died somewhere in Big Cypress Swamp in 1866. It was said by some that he was ninety-two years old, others said he was one hundred fourteen. Abiaka or as we know him, Sam Jones is chiefly the reason that any Seminoles remained in Florida and continue to dwell there today. Broward County has established Pine Island as a protected park. Ironically a statue of Major William Lauderdale on horseback stands near the entrance. Lauderdale was sent to subdue the Seminoles in 1838 and establish a post, thus Fort Lauderdale was born.

End Notes

[1] Miami

[2] Plant used in making arrowroot starch.

[3] 2:10 pm

[4] Naval Air Station

[5] 4:00 pm

[6] 8:00 pm

[7] United States Coast Guard

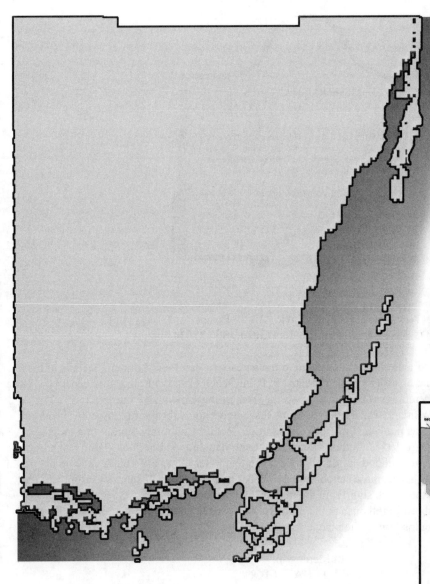

Dade County

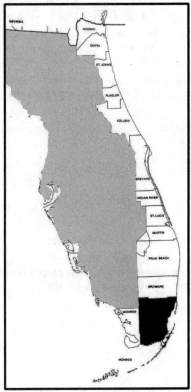

BAREFOOT MAILMAN

In the 1800s, mail was often carried between the coastal communities of South Florida by barefoot mailmen. These carriers walked most of the route barefoot on the firm sand near the water's edge. In the 1880s, the U.S. government established regular mail service from the Palm Beach area to Miami. The usual route was from Hypoluxo Island, passed the Orange Grove and Ft. Lauderdale Houses of Refuge and Baker's Haulover, then to Miami by small boat, and back again, a distance of over 120 miles which the barefoot mailmen covered in six days. In the 1890s, a new county road to Lemon City ended the barefoot route.

Northeast Haulover Park, Miami Beach
MD1 ~ GPS Coordinates: 25.913010, -80.121824

There are several state historical markers dedicated to the legendary Barefoot Mailmen. Details of these men and their service are related in a historical marker located in Palm Beach County. Rather than repeat the same information, we will relate to you here a few of the memorials the lives of these men have inspired.

The moniker "Barefoot Mailman" was used to describe these brave souls for the first time in Theodore Pratt's book using that title, which was published in 1943. In addition, Robert Cummings starred in a movie immortalizing the Barefoot Mailmen in 1951. Author Margaret Garnett, daughter of Barefoot Mailman Andrew Garnett, wrote a work describing her childhood entitled Pioneer Daughter. Her father eventually gave up his postal position to become the Dade County Treasurer, a school board member and Hypoluxo Postmaster. Annually the local Boy Scout Troop hikes along the beach signifying the trek of the Barefoot Mailman.

In the shadow of the Hillsboro Lighthouse at the northern side is a memorial to the infamous Barefoot Mailman, the only one to die during his term. The plaque reads:

In Memory of
JAMES E. HAMILTON
United States Mail Carrier
Who Lost His Life Here In The Line of Duty

In addition a beautifully done stone statue sculpted by Frank Varga of Varga Studios in Delray Beach was placed at the site of the Hillsboro Lighthouse. A restaurant in Hillsboro Beach was named for the famed postmen and out of respect a monument was placed on the beach just beyond. Unfortunately, the restaurant was destroyed by fire in 1988 but the monument still remains. It reads:

In Memory of
THE BAREFOOT MAILMEN
WHO TRAVERSED THESE SANDS
FROM PALM BEACH TO MIAMI
IN THE LATE 1880s

Former Lantana City Manager and an advocate for historic preservation, Michael Bornstein set out to reenact the famous Barefoot Mailman trek. The journey began on February 28, 2003 and entailed traveling on foot and by boat from Hypoluxo to the Miami River. Bornstein strove to make the trip as authentic as possible including clothing, hat and bag similar to what was used during the era. He made his first stop at the Hillsboro Lighthouse to attend a ceremony honoring James Edward "Ed" Hamilton who lost his life during his journey.

Bornstein made the trip in days beginning when he boarded a boat bound for Boynton Inlet where the journey traditionally began. Michael Bornstein is in hopes that the trek reenactment will become an annual event and others will eventually join the tribute.

ARCH CREEK

Until 1973, when it collapsed, the forty foot natural bridge of oolitic limestone that spanned Arch Creek was one of South Florida's earliest landmarks. Prehistoric Indians occupied this site hundreds of years before European exploration. In the early 1800s, Seminole Indians lived in the area until forced out by United States soldiers during the Second (1836-42) Seminole War. During the Third (1855-59) Seminole War a military trail connecting Ft. Dallas and Ft. Lauderdale passed over the bridge. In 1892 the first county road to South Florida crossed here, as did the Dixie Highway, which opened in 1915. In the past, this natural bridge has attracted both tourists and settlers. A community known as Arch Creek grew up around the Arch Creek station of the Florida East Coast Railroad. By 1903, there were sufficient settlers to warrant the opening of the Arch Creek Post Office, which later became the North Miami Post Office.

1855 NE 135th Street, North Miami
MD2 ~ GPS Coordinates: 25.900583, -80.162400

In the days before the ancient tribes of Tequesta Native Americans were banished from the earth, prior to the formation of the brave Seminoles, an age-old Indian settlement was built around the Arch Creek Natural Bridge. The unique naturally created limestone formation was an ideal location providing everything a village needed to survive. The Native Americans built an eight-foot wide trail that crossed the natural bridge, which was to become Dade County's first roadway.

By the late nineteenth century white settlers began building homesteads at Arch Creek. The Seminole Indians had been vanquished to the west and only a handful remained silently hiding in the Everglades, a ghost like people. In 1891, a man by the name of Ihle was first to establish a small palmetto frond hut and begin farming the area. He had purchased eighty acres from the state at one dollar an acre. Today the site can be placed at North East 116th Street and Biscayne Boulevard. At the time his closest neighbor was said to be in Fort Lauderdale. Over the next thirty years Mr. Ihle grew shallots, squash, bananas, sugar cane, Puerto Rican pineapples, lemons, guavas, limes, rose apples, Jamaican apples and tomatoes.

For a number of years the only public transportation available overland through Arch Creek was a mule-driven stagecoach traveling from Lantana to Miami. In 1896, Henry Flagler brought steel rails putting the stage out of business. That same year a train depot was built at the town site, which would eventually take the traveler to Miami. About this same time settlers from Elmira, New York came to the area, pitched a tent camp and planted groves of grapefruit. Within five years, a permanent community had developed with the train depot at its center.

A post office was established at Arch Creek and a school was built all located in the vicinity of what is today 125th Street and the Florida East Coast railway tracks.

The small farming community thrived. Additional housing was built as settlers and farm workers moved into the area, a church, mercantile, blacksmith and tomato packaging houses all huddled near the railway. By the mid 1920s, all of Florida experienced an incredible population explosion. The Biscayne Canal was built but an unfortunate consequence was that it also drained the land of moisture ultimately ending most of the farming ventures. However, people moved in anyway and the now dry land became housing developments. Arch Creek officially became the Town of Miami Shores on February 5, 1926. Streets, sidewalks, town hall, waterworks and fire protection brought the tiny village into a modern day city. Tragedy struck in September 1926 when a hurricane ripped into Miami Shores dousing the population explosion. People began to lose their property to the tax assessors' gavel on the City Hall steps. The city floundered, but managed to survive. The original Arch Creek settlement was in danger of becoming a used car lot. In 1973, disaster struck again when the natural bridge collapsed.

By the late 70s there was a drive by local citizens to preserve the Arch Creek area. Archaeological digs revealed an ancient burial site as well as a Tequesta garbage mound which told the story of a vanquished people. Eventually the location became a park to safeguard what remained of the extinct Tequesta and the artifacts left to tell of their plight.

Strange things began to be noticed around the park, everything from dramatic temperature changes and eerie senses to sightings of figures that should not or could not possibly be present. Eric King, a naturalist who manages the park, tells of many unexplained appearances and events, which have convinced him over the years that the Arch Creek Park is a haven to spirits of another realm.

Tales include a meeting with a toothless man who said to King that he believed spirits were all about them, then the man simply disappeared into the mist and has not been seen again. William Milliken, who died at the hands of marauding Seminole Indians, was buried on the grounds of what is today the park; however, the grave which was well marked has mysteriously disappeared. After turning off the lights one dark night in April 2000, King swears he saw the specter of longtime park manager Wesley Wilson. Upon seeing the figure, the doors slammed shut and the phone began to ring. When King answered the phone, the line was silent. Wilson was seen again in June of 2003, looking at a particularly unnerving Tequesta Indian display. Perhaps Wesley Wilson is simply still on the job, from the other side, making sure his park continues to be cared for. Bronzed shirtless figures are often seen running through the trees as if stalking game. And finally the presence of park activist Alice Cohen is often felt along the path where her ashes were spread in her beloved park in 1986.

Arch Creek Park is open from sunrise to sunset each day with picnic tables, nature trails and facilities. Special programs such as Ghost tours and Historic Natures Walks are offered at a nominal fee on Saturdays by reservation only. Many special programs are held throughout the year. Though Arch Creek Park is small the historic impact and wonderful natural appeal makes it a place not to be missed. Ghost hunters will delight in this unique park.

BLUE STAR

A tribute to the Armed Forces
that have defended the United
States of America.

US 1, Miami
MD3 ~ GPS Coordinates: 25.893119, -80.164127

The following is a memorandum distributed by the National Garden Clubs, Incorporated Chairman describing the origins of the Blue Star program:

The National Garden Clubs, Inc. have ha a program in place to honor service men and women since 1945. It's the Blue Star Memorial Program, and it began with the planting of 8,000 Dogwood trees by the New Jersey Council of Garden Clubs in 1944 as a living memorial to veterans of World War II. The following year the National Council of State Garden Clubs, as it was called at the time, adopted the program and began a Blue Star Highway system, which cover thousands of miles across the Continental United States, Alaska and Hawaii. A large metal Blue Star Memorial Highway Marker was placed at appropriate location along the way.

The program was expanded to include all men and women who had served, were serving or would serve in the armed services of the United States. Memorial Markers and By-Way markers were added to the Highway Markers, to be used at locations such as National cemeteries, parks, veteran's facilities and gardens.

The Blue Star became an icon in World War II and was seen on flags and banners in homes for sons and daughters away at war, as well as in churches and businesses.

This program has been active all through the years to the present, a fitting tribute always and especially now. Many states and regions have been very dedicated, but there is room for growth in some areas. A "Guidelines" booklet can be ordered from Member Services for $5.00, which explains all procedures, including awards available to clubs. I would be happy to be of assistance at any time.

ALL TO SEE, LEST WE FORGET
THOSE WHO HELP TO KEEP US FREE

Maria Nahom,
National Garden Clubs, Inc.,
National Blue Star Memorial Chairman

CAN YOU FIND THE MARKER IN THIS PICTURE?

453

At the park on bay, N.E. 96th Street, Miami Shores
MD4 ~ GPS Coordinates: 25.863983, -80.171017

The area that came to be called Biscayne was first surveyed in 1845. The Florida Surveyor General divided the area into two lots and filed this with the Land Department of Washington DC calling it section nineteen. Each of the lots contained approximately one hundred sixty-five acres. Thirty years later another survey was conducted, section nineteen was then divided into seven lots totaling three hundred thirty-eight acres. Strangely enough, section nineteen never changed but somehow the land mass doubled.

William H. Gleason began homesteading at Biscayne on June 24, 1878 alongside William H. Hunt. Gleason claimed a land patent on section nineteen, which according to the 1875 survey totaled some three hundred thirty-eight acres. Edward L. White filed suit in the seventh judicial circuit court of Florida declaring the error in land surveys and contending that Gleason was aware of the discrepancy. The case was tried and in the absence of a jury, the judge decided the case in Gleason's favor. Florida's Supreme Court upheld the decision. In order to claim the homestead patent, Gleason would have had to live on the property for five years. It is doubtful that he was unaware of the acreage discrepancy. Notable in the political arena, Gleason rose to the office of Lieutenant Governor. Though his dealings in the world of civic leadership were not always without a scandal, William H. Gleason did much to better the state of Florida.

Gleason's partner, William H. Hunt leased the United States property at St. Lucie Rocks. The Secretary of the Treasury signed a contract on March 19, 1875 with Hunt for a term of twenty years for property to be used as a rescue station. The facility was called Gilbert's Bar and from there many a sea drenched sailor was plucked from a certain watery grave.

Like every other corner of Florida the 1920s brought a drove of people into the area. The destructive hurricane of 1926 brought an end to the population explosion and expansion prospects for the Biscayne community. The causeway linking both areas of town was scrapped. The Atlantic beachside community instituted a lawsuit to separate and become a town on its own. In 1931, Florida's Supreme Court granted the

THE ACTUAL MARKER OVERLOOKING BEAUTIFUL BISCAYNE BAY

majority landowner Shoreland Company the ability to separate and become the Town of North Miami.

Retired veterans and their families began flocking to the area after World War II. The Town of North Miami flourished ~ homes, roads, stores and various businesses began to expand and continued to grow. Within ten years the area was noted as the fastest growing town in the United States. On May 27, 1953, the town officially became the City of North Miami and is ever growing.

BLUE STAR

A tribute to the Armed Forces that have defended the United States of America.

US 1, Miami
MD5 ~ GPS Coordinates: 25.843640, -80.184377

Located in North Miami at 13170 Northeast Eighth Avenue in the midst of a glade is a simple memorial to the men and women who gave all in the name of our country during World War II, Korea and Vietnam. Rising in a heavenward apex of thirty feet are two concrete piers supporting three walls of copper. Embossed on the gleaming sheets are the names of those fallen military heroes to whom we owe a debt of gratitude for the freedoms we celebrate today.

The monument was first dedicated on Memorial Day of 1965. At that time only those who died while serving the United States in World War II and Korea were represented, after the Vietnam conflict a third side was added to the monument. Neighboring the memorial is the Army and National Guard armory where today soldiers fighting terrorism in operation Enduring Freedom train.

The City of North Miami takes great strides to recognize and remember those who have valiantly served the United States. Those soldiers who stand the wall so that we can sleep soundly, knowing we are safe; the city places particular importance on influencing the youth of today to respect the principals of freedom, patriotism and country. Exposing children to the heroism of our fallen soldiers instills a sense of pride in the United States and brings to their awareness the price of freedom.

Traditionally each Memorial and Veterans Day special ceremonies are conducted at the monument. The programs begin promptly at 10:00 a.m. with the presentation of colors regally proffered by an official color guard troop from the National Guard Armory, the North Miami Police Honor Guard delivers a rifle salute and a local choir sings a medley of flag-waving tunes. The formal ceremony is followed by a simple lunch for the audience.

During the remainder of the year, individuals make pilgrimages to the memorial to honor lost family members and friends. They often take pencil and paper to trace the name of a loved one on the wall. Mementos, flowers, letters, dog tags and medals are left in remembrance of those who paid the ultimate price. The memorial honors the dead and lifts up the living in recognition of valor.

GRACE METHODIST CHURCH

Oldest church in continuous service in Dade County. This sanctuary, built in 1959, is the third. The second was built in 1905 at 6311 N.E. 2nd Ave. after a hurricane destroyed the first. Original church was built in 1893 where an Indian trail (N.E. 61st St.) crossed military trail (N.E. 5th Ave.) in Lemon City. The church was named Lemon City Methodist by its founders who had met for several years in Pierce's sponge warehouse on Biscayne Bay. This pioneer church was renamed Grace in 1934, nine years after Lemon City became a part of Miami.

6501 North Miami Avenue, Miami
MD6 ~ GPS Coordinates: 25.835767, -80.196183

The Methodist community at what was once Lemon City met in a smelly sponge warehouse on Biscayne Bay until the funds to build a proper sanctuary were raised. The edifice became a reality in 1893, called Lemon City Methodist Church. The lot was at the crossing of an Indian trail and one forged by the military. Today the intersection is North East 61st Street and North East 5th Avenue. This Methodist Church is the oldest uninterrupted congregation in Miami-Dade County. Just over ten years later the forces of a tremendous hurricane would reduce the little wooden church to shattered remains.

The second edifice was completed in 1905. The location is known today as 6311 North East 2nd Avenue. Bethany Baptist Mission occupies the sanctuary today, they celebrate its one hundredth year in 2005. As the church grew so did the bayside neighborhood surrounding it.

Candy baron James Nunnally largely owned the Morningside district. Nunnally employed the acclaimed architect firm of Kiehnel and Elliot to plot the neighborhood in the early 1920s. The architectural firm earned their credentials by designing the Carlyle Hotel and Coral Gables Elementary School following the infamous Addison Mizner Mediterranean revival architectural style.

The Morningside community was progressive with modern conveniences such as running water, gas lighted streets, sewage system and underground gas lines. Grace Methodist Church built a house in 1924 on quiet shaded 2nd Avenue. The two storied Spanish Mediterranean revival home features a classic red barrel tile roof with soft pastel façade. Arched wooden framed windows close with brass locks and the interior has distinctive Moroccan arches.

Lemon City was incorporated into Miami in 1934 and the congregation renamed their edifice Grace United Methodist Church. As the membership grew, a larger facility was required. The sanctuary at 6501 North Miami Avenue was completed in 1959. The Morningside neighborhood evolved into a four hundred sixty-four house gated community on Biscayne Bay.

The Trujillo family purchased the house in Morningside the first day it was placed on the real estate market. The Trujillo's were enamored with the classical old world feel of the home and immediately undertook an extensive renovation. The project would take two and a half years to complete including the addition of a swimming pool and family room. Famed designer Luna Bella created a wonderful ambience using distinctive furnishings and lighting. The Trujillo's added several of their own designs including an elaborate black iron gate at the garage and ornate door lamps. Other examples of their work can be seen at the estate of the late Gianni Versace mansion at Miami Beach.

Morningside became Miami's first historic district in 1984 and in 1992 the neighborhood was listed on the National Register of Historic Places. Today the church is known as Grace United Haitian Methodist Church catering to the large population of Haitian people living in Miami. Services at Grace and Bethany Baptist Mission, occupying the 2nd Avenue edifice site, are conducted in Creole.

**MIAMI WOMAN'S CLUB
AND FLAGLER MEMORIAL LIBRARY**

The Miami Woman's Club was founded in 1900, four years after the City of Miami was incorporated, as the Married Ladies' Afternoon Club. It was affiliated with the Florida Federation of Women's Clubs in 1903, the General Federation of Women's Clubs 1905, and the Dade County Federation of Women's Clubs in 1916. Henry M. Flagler was the Club's benefactor. The Miami Woman's Club is credited with the founding of the Public Library System of Miami-Dade County. The Club's history parallels that of the City of Miami. The members exemplify the motto, "Not for Ourselves alone". This "Spanish Renaissance" structure was dedicated as "The Miami Woman's Club and Flagler Memorial Library" in 1926 and was listed in the National Register of Historic Places in 1974.

**1737 N. Bayshore Drive, Miami
MD7 ~ GPS Coordinates: 25.791620, -80.186991**

The county library system of Dade County got its start in 1894 with the establishment of facilities in Coconut Grove and Lemon City. The Married Ladies' Afternoon Club was first organized in 1900. The club was to become one of the city's most distinguished social and cultural diversified groups in the city of Miami. One of the first goals of the organization was to further the growth of the public library system, which was non-existent in Miami.

Antoinette Elizabeth Gazzam Frederick was a charter member of the club and named as one of the first twenty-one club pioneers in their Yearbook of Founding Members. The pioneers began to purchase books from various places and collecting books from private libraries to incorporate into the first library. Antoinette was elected President of the club for the 1903 term. She was to remain at the post for six years.

The Coconut Grove Library Association established a formal library building of its own in 1902 and later that same year the Lemon City Library and Improvement Association built a home for its library. The Married Ladies Afternoon Club listed one of its main objectives as, "reading and the discussion of literature." The club was unique because few women were formally educated during this time whereas these predominantly wealthy ladies had that opportunity and were afforded the opportunity to read various important authors, holding intelligent conversations pertaining to these works. The Miami ladies established a reading room for the collection of books they amassed but had no particular home. In fact the collection was moved six times during 1905.

On July 4, 1906 the club evolved to become the Women's Club of Miami. Antoinette was elected President of the Florida Federation of Women's Clubs in 1910, bringing the Miami Club to state recognition. She also served as President of the Housekeepers Club, today formally known as the Coconut Grove Women's Club and is listed as a charter member of the Trinity Episcopal Church.

After her presidency was over Antoinette became official Librarian for the Women's Club. Tragedy struck in 1910 when her husband John succumbed to pleurisy, he was exposed to during a survey trip in the

Everglades. Mourning but determined to go on, Antoinette put all of her energies into the aim of the Women's Club library.

Henry Flagler donated property in 1913 for the Miami Women's Club. Located at Avenue B and Twelfth Street, today Southeast Second Avenue and Flagler Street, the simple building would be their first permanent home. Flagler included a provision to his generous gift of property in that a public reading room always is maintained in the building. The club continued to struggle financially until in 1915 the City Commission of Miami came to the rescue. The Commission earmarked fifty dollars each month in support of the Women's Club library project. Flagler's building bequeath was eventually sold once the organization had amassed enough money to build a new facility.

Construction began in 1925 under the direction of architects and builders August C. Geiger and F. H. Foster. Built in an elaborate Mediterranean Revival design, the edifice embraces a lovely courtyard garden. The new address was 1737 North Bayshore Drive and the building would be christened the Flagler Memorial Library. Construction was completed in 1926 and the Miami Women's Club had a permanent home of their own, gained under their own strengths for the first time.

The Junior League of Miami sponsored a children's museum established in 1950 in a building at Biscayne Boulevard and Twenty-sixth Street. The site was immediately too small to accommodate the exhibits to enhance the children's experience. In 1952, the Women's Club invited the Junior League to utilize a section of their facility at Bayshore Drive. The Flagler Library eventually became known as the Museum of Science and Natural History. Over the next year the Guild of the Museum of Science was established. Their purpose would be to provide a fully voluntary staff for administration of the Museum Store, docents to lead tours and various programs directed toward the youth learning experiences throughout the museum.

In 1974, the Miami Women's Club was added to the rolls of the National Register of Historic Places. Today the organization continues to uphold the standards that the original pioneers intended. Though times have drastically changed, the club has managed to evolve with societies' expectations. The Miami Women's Club today supports it members to achieve personal goals as well as improve the community in which they live.

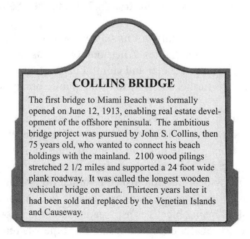

COLLINS BRIDGE

The first bridge to Miami Beach was formally opened on June 12, 1913, enabling real estate development of the offshore peninsula. The ambitious bridge project was pursued by John S. Collins, then 75 years old, who wanted to connect his beach holdings with the mainland. 2100 wood pilings stretched 2 1/2 miles and supported a 24 foot wide plank roadway. It was called the longest wooden vehicular bridge on earth. Thirteen years later it had been sold and replaced by the Venetian Islands and Causeway.

East End of Venetian Causeway, Miami Beach
MD8 ~ GPS Coordinates: 25.789833, -80.178450

Imagine a time when Miami Beach did not have a solid wall of high rise hotels and condos; a time when there were no blaring horns; never ending concrete and asphalt, barely a patch of grass or palm tree swaying in the breeze. The Atlantic shore was wild, white sand beaches gave way to thick masses of mangrove trees and roots growing from muck and mire of inland swamp. There were no inhabitants. The land was unforgiving and would be hard to tame.

John Collins was a successful businessman used to an easy life in New Jersey. He was seventy-five years old when he left it all to join other capitalists intent on growing coconuts. Their endeavor failed, undaunted Collins bought out his partner's shares making him the lone landowner of what was then known as Ocean Beach. A Quaker filled with faith, Collins believed fruit could be grown and planted avocados. Realizing some protection from the harsh sea breeze was necessary, he planted a windbreak of Australian pines. The trees continue to survive on their name sake avenue, Pine Tree Drive today.

Arthur Collins and Thomas Pancoast, John's son and son-in-law had other ideas concerning the property at Ocean Beach. They envisioned selling waterfront lots to wealthy northerners and building a retreat for those escaping harsh icy winters. The men formed the Miami Beach Improvement Company borrowing as much money as they could, buying up five hundred eighty acres along the southern tip of Miami Beach.

The only way to traverse the waterway to Miami Beach from Miami was via a ferryboat. John Collins decided that a bridge from the mainland was necessary unfortunately he went broke before the task could be completed. Collins borrowed fifty thousand dollars to complete his bridge. He realized that a powerful, strong and enduring work force was needed to complete the difficult chore ahead. Using amazing ingenuity, John Collins used elephants as beasts of burden alongside workmen to clear the land. The work was perilous, disease carrying mosquitoes, poisonous snakes and biting horseflies slowed the work progress. Roads were carved out of the mangrove forests and the first houses were constructed of locally quarried coral rock.

Famous showman Doc Dammers was employed in February 1913 to host an event to auction off some of the beachfront property. Entertainment included hot air balloons, parachute drops as well as gifts of silver and china. The function lasted for three days and sixty-six thousand dollars worth of acreage was sold. Four months later on June 12, 1913, a convoy of cars crossed the two and a half-mile long wooden Collins Bridge. It had taken twenty-one hundred wooden pilings to support the twenty-four foot wide plank trestle. Collins Bridge was touted as the longest in the world.

The Miami Beach Corporation, Ocean Beach and Alton Beach merged creating Miami Beach, incorporated in 1915. The city only claimed just over six hundred residents, the founding fathers realized an advertising campaign was needed to bring in permanent inhabitants. Carl Fisher, automobile parts mogul, loaned Collins the money to complete construction of the bridge. Fisher purchased an illuminated billboard declaring "It's June in Miami" located in the midst of Times Square. Advertisements featured white sand beaches, crystal blue water, balmy tropical weather and beautiful bathing suit clad ladies. Of course, like every other corner of Florida, Miami Beach experienced a population boom in the mid 1920s. More than six million dollars in prime real estate was sold.

The population explosion fizzled and much of the property had to be sold to pay off debts as the depression hit in earnest. In 1926 a devastating hurricane swept through south Florida. Miraculously the bridge was spared despite the wreckage left in the wake of the deadly storm. It was ten years of rebuilding and recovery before Miami Beach regained her previous radiance. The majority of the restoration projects reflected an Art Deco style of architecture, bright colors and modern appearance was the theme throughout Miami Beach. By the end of the 1930s the Collins Bridge was sold and eventually replaced by the Venetian Causeway as it is today.

BLUE STAR

A tribute to the Armed Forces that have defend-ed the United States of America.

US 1, MIAMI
MD9 ~ GPS Coordinates: 25.775151, -80.135199

Imagine the fear of a young Army enlistee about to leave home for the first time, first to training and then to the front lines of World War II. Imagine the same enlistee on the bus to boot camp, leaving his northern home while ice and snow still clung to the frozen ground and stepping off into eighty degree sunshine. Staying in an elaborate hotel better than the home he left, this young man is seeing his last glimpse of heaven before being shipped off to war.

Miami Beach formerly a winter retreat for frost bitten northerners, warm climate for retired arthritic bones and a gleaming white sand box for vacationers from all over the United States. For three years beginning in 1942 Miami Beach was known by another name that of Army Air Force Technical Training Command. More than a half a million soldiers trained here as well as ladies of the WACs[1].

The Army Corps of Engineers were housed in the Sterling Building, officers took shelter at the Firestone mansion and beautiful Haulover Beach heard the distinctive peal of gun shots as the recreation area was turned into a firing range. During idle hours soldiers enjoyed their time on Biscayne Street's Servicemen's Pier. Even Clark Gable of "Gone With the Wind" fame did a stint at Miami Beach.

While many began their Army career on these white sand beaches others came to an end through the Army Redistribution Station. Imagine their elation as war weary veterans were flown in from battle to a tropical playground where their wives waited, debriefings were held as well as rest and relaxation well earned before being released or reassigned. Even as new recruits trained, others waited for orders or retirement paperwork; the war would bear its ugly head when enemy submarines fired killing torpedoes aimed for unarmed merchant ships all within sight of the white sandy beaches of Miami.

Many of the young men met Miami girls and vowed to return to them after the war, some did not wait for the wars end and left young brides when they were given their first assignments. It was a common saying "once you got Miami sand in your shoes you would always return". After the war some vets loaded their families into cars, enrolled at the University of Miami using the GI Bill and purchased homes. Still others became snowbirds returning for a winter respite from the icy north, while others vacationed on the crowded sun bathed beaches under the tropical summer sun. Others came back in their elder years wearing black socks and sandals to play golf on the lush green grass where they once paraded, marching in perfect rows.

Today a great number of Camp Miami Beach utilized buildings are still in use. Most sites have been meticulously preserved and appear as they did when the young Army enlistees stepped off the bus. The area bus-tles with activity today. Restaurants, hotels, bright neon lights and modern buildings standing side by side with history as eclectic as the personalities of this vivacious community. Still the history is there, lovingly preserved by a concerned citizenship, a tribute to all who dwell there. A simple tribute reads:

In memory of those Who gave their lives for their country,
In gratitude to all who served, and To the City of Miami Beach for serving them,
This plaque is dedicated by World War II Veterans in Reunion.
December 7, 1999

TUTTLE HOME

On this site stood the home of Miami pioneer, Mrs. Julia D. Tuttle. Mrs. Tuttle came to Miami in 1890 and was responsible for much of the city's early development. She encouraged the Florida East Coast Railway to extend its line to Miami. Her home was a two-story stone building, originally officers' quarters for old Fort Dallas, constructed in 1849 for use against the Indians. The building also served as Dade County's first courthouse.

401 NW 3rd Street in Lummus Park, Miami
MD10 ~ GPS Coordinates: 25.771904, -80.131938

Born in 1840 near Cleveland, Julia Deforest Sturtevant was to become an important part of south Florida history. She married Frederick Leonard Tuttle on January 22, 1867 and the couple made their home in Ohio. Julia first saw south Florida in 1875 on a visit to her father who had homesteaded at Biscayne Bay. She was twenty-six years old and was immediately taken with the area. Ephraim Sturtevant had traveled south with a friend by the name of Brickell, unfortunately a falling out between the men ended their association.

Frederick Tuttle died in 1886. Julia was left with her children, Harry and Fanny. In the interest of her children's delicate health, Julia Tuttle decided to move south. Probably the decision was made more to appease her own interest, but the children provided a wonderful excuse. She purchased six hundred forty acres of land on the northern banks of the Miami River, including what had once been Fort Dallas in 1891. Just across the way was the Brickell property. Other than the river, the only transportation available was by stagecoach. The stage line ran from Lantana to Lake Worth then on to Lemon City at Biscayne Bay. Julia Tuttle looked at this wilderness and saw only potential. She immediately realized that the rocky bluff, white sand beaches and maritime forest could eventually blossom into a fabulous city.

Julia owned a large dilapidated house, which had once been part of Fort Dallas during the Seminole Indian Wars. She restored the home into a grand show place over looking the Miami River. A wide sweeping porch completely surrounding the second story of the house provided one of the most magnificent views of Biscayne Bay anywhere. Practical to a fault, Julia Tuttle realized that to grow the area would have to be accessible by rail. She set out to convince Henry Flagler to extend the Florida East Coast Railroad to Biscayne Bay.

Julia Tuttle had first met James Ingraham, president of the Florida Railroad, at a dinner party in her home in Cleveland before she moved south. She had pitched the idea of continuing his rail line from Fort Myers on the Gulf Coast across the Everglades to Miami. Ingraham was vague in his answer but in April of 1892, he led an expedition along the route. When he arrived at Tuttle's home after crossing the brutal swampland of the Everglades he was spent and half starved. After exploring the area hosted by Julia, he was convinced but the railway board of directors declined the proposal. Within six months Ingraham went to work for Henry Flagler.

In February of 1895, Florida experienced a killing freeze destroying the orange groves. James Ingraham told the following story of how the railroad finally made it to Miami:

"I found at Lauderdale, at Lemon City, Buena Vista, Miami, Coconut Grove and at Cutler orange trees, lemon trees and lime trees blooming or about to bloom without a leaf hurt, vegetables growing in a small way untouched. There had been no frost there. I gathered up a lot of blooms from these various trees, put them in damp cotton, and after an interview with Mrs. Tuttle and Mr. and Mrs. Brickell of Miami, I hurried to St. Augustine, where I called on Mr. Flagler and showed him the orange blossoms, telling him that I believed that these orange blossoms were from the only part of Florida, except possibly a small area on the extreme southerly part of the western coast, which had escaped the freeze; that here was a body of land more than 40 miles long, between the Everglades and the Atlantic Ocean, perhaps very much longer than that, absolutely untouched, and that I believed that it would be the home of the citrus industry in the future, because it was absolutely immune from devastating freezes. I said: 'I have also here writ ten proposals from Mrs. Tuttle and Mr. and Mrs. Brickell, inviting you to extend your railroad from Palm Beach to Miami and offering to share with you their holdings at Miami for a town site.'

"Mr. Flagler looked at me for some minutes in perfect silence, then he said: 'How soon can you arrange for me to go to Miami?'"

On April 15, 1896, the whole of Miami cheered as the Florida East Coast Railway steamed into town. Julia had achieved her objective and because of this is known as the only woman to have founded a major United States city. Julia Sturtevant Tuttle passed away on September 14, 1898, she was fifty-eight years old. Less than twenty years later, Miami boasted more than ten thousand residents. Today, a Hyatt hotel occupies the site that was once Julia Tuttle's home.

HAULOVER BEACH
SPORT FISHING DOCKS

The originally known Lighthouse Dock, once at this site, marked the beginnings of this area's fame as a sportsman's paradise. Folklore and history relate that a man named Baker (c. 1810) "hauled over" fishing boats from the bay to the ocean. In 1926, Captain Henry Jones (1883-1968) built the first dock with a permit from the War Department. By 1937-1939, the Lighthouse Restaurant and the Ocean Bay Trailer Park shared this property. These early docks served as the foundation of an international sport fishing tourist industry as charter boat fisherman searched for marlin, sailfish and other big-game fish in Miami's abundant Gulf Stream waters. Adjacent to these docks was an official weighing station of the Metropolitan Miami Fishing Tournament, the oldest and largest fishing contest in the world. Many record catches were certified here. Captains navigated their charters beneath the hazardous Haulover Bridge with its treacherous currents. They also contended with the threat of enemy submarines, just outside the Inlet, from 1942 to 1943. Some captains assumed duties as sub-spotters. A Coast Guard vessel was moored here during World War II to ensure civilian safety, making this a strategic military site at that time. In 1944 the Lighthouse Dock became part of the Haulover Beach Park. The Dade County Parks Department assumed management and changed the name to Haulover Beach Docks. In 1951-1952 the docks were replaced by a marina, built farther to the north. Calling these docks home were the captains, their boats, and the only women working as mates for their husbands. The earliest pioneer captains at these docks were: Henry Jones, Henrietta; George Hamway, Popeye; Joe Reese, Ethel Lee; Slim Caraway (Marjorie) Lady Luck; John Sacon (nee Saconchik), Martha Mary; George Helker, Gremlin; Ralph Nemire (Iris), Seacomber; Harry Stone, Oke Doke; Ira Gregory, Lucky Strike; Elsworth Stone, Anhow; W.D. Murphy, Pat; Charles Smith (Mary), Interim; Harold Alford (Jeannette) Privateer; Otto Reichert, Restless; Robert Paterson, Huskee; Frank Kurek, Sportsman; Ernie Luebbers, Mystery; B.C. Millard, Surf King; and Paul Goerner, Vee Gee. Other individuals contributing to the success of the Haulover fishing fleet: Official Dock Photographer, Doris Barnes; Dock/Weigh Masters, Norton/Waggoner; and Taxidermist, Al Pflueger. They recorded the feats of tourists and such celebrities as Hollywood superstar Robert Mitchum and TV host Arthur Godfrey.

Haulover Beach Park Marina, 10800 Collins Ave, Miami
MD11 ~ GPS Coordinates: 25.768689, -80.132781

The site today on Collins Avenue was once called Lighthouse Dock, which gained notoriety as a fisherman's haven. The name Haulover is said to have gotten its origins from an early 19th century fellow named Baker who hired out his services to "haul over" fishing boats from the Intracoastal to the ocean. The first dock was constructed at the site in 1926 by permit of the War Department commissioned by Captain Henry Jones.

The Miami-Dade Parks Division began developing parks in 1929. Commodore Matheson donated the property for the first county park named in his honor, Matheson Hammock Park. In the years preceding World War II, the Lighthouse Restaurant was established as well as the Ocean Bay Trailer Park. Docks were built to accommodate the sportsmen who flocked to the area. Eventually the Metropolitan Miami Fishing Tournament was established with a weigh station adjacent to the docks near Haulover Bridge. The tournament has become the oldest and largest fishing contest in the world.

During the years of World War II the beach at Lighthouse Dock was used as a firing range for training Army boot camp recruits. The Coast Guard ported at the dock there and local captains were enlisted to serve as submarine spotters. Lighthouse Dock became Haulover Beach Park in 1944. The docks evolved to become a marina in 1951 just north of the original site. Local captains, the only working women there were their wives employed as mates, called the marina home in the 1950s.

The county today maintains more than twelve thousand acres divided into two hundred eighty parks.

Amazingly more than twenty-five million tourists and locals utilize the parks resulting in Miami-Dade Parks being touted the United States' largest and most utilized facilities. The parks division has been awarded for excellence on a national level numerous times and recognized as an exceptionally well administered system.

Haulover Beach Park is embraced between the Atlantic Ocean and the Intracoastal Waterway. The park encompasses one hundred eighty acres with exceptional amenities. An underground tunnel beneath the busy highway leads patrons to Haulover Beach. A restaurant, ice cream shop, tourist memorabilia, bicycle and kite rentals, picnic tables, a short golf course and tennis courts add to the amenities of this fabulous beach.

The Haulover Marina is a full service facility. Boats ranging from the largest ninety-foot yachts to the merest sixteen-foot skiffs can find a slip here. Boat rentals, bait, charters, fuel, supplies and facilities; full service leaves little to be desired.

Just down the beach things drastically change or rather disappear. Warning signs greet visitors to waylay shock when further investigation reveals it all. Bare bottoms and bodies without tan lines walk proudly down the beach, sun bathe in the nude and romp in the surf without encumbrance. This is one of only two beaches in Florida where it is legal to bare it all. The beachgoers are a diverse crowd from every walk of life, gender, age, nationality and life experience. Haulover Beach Park truly has something for everyone and bringing new meaning to the words "full service".

FREEDOM HOUSE
(Casa De La Libertad)

On December 1, 1965, planes began bringing refugees to the U.S. from Cuba, fulfilling President Lyndon B. Johnson's promise that "those who seek refuge here in America will find it." Old Army barracks near Miami International Airport were converted into "La Casa de la Libertad" (Freedom House), where over 260,000 refugees were processed prior to joining relatives in Miami or resettling in other cities. The last of 3,048 Freedom Flights arrived in Miami on April 6, 1973.

Miami International Airport, Miami
MD12 ~ GPS Coordinates: 25.795033, -80.278267

Miami was known to Cuban refugees as the "magic city." Why magic one might ask? The enchantment was not with the magnificent city herself but with an ideal, something most Americans take for granted, freedom. Imagine an oppressed people knowing that freedom is only an hour away.

Their journey would begin approximately eighty-five miles east of Havana at Varadero and end at Miami International Airport. Imagine the feeling the newly freed people must have had as the big silver bird touched down at that enormous airport and they stepped onto American soil for the first time. Of course, they were met by the United States Immigration Department and welcomed to freedom. Actually the first family ever to register at the Cuban Refugee Center came almost five years prior to President Johnson's promise of asylum. Felix Antonio Gutierrez arrived with his wife and two children on February 27, 1961. The family settled in Milwaukee. The very first person to step from plane arriving from Cuba was Mrs. Virginia Olazabal Delgado. She went to live with other family member in the Bronx, New York. Mrs. Delgado was seventy-five years old.

Twice daily freedom flights brought an average of thirty-six hundred Cubans per month into Miami. Where did they go? What did they do? Approximately a third of the refugees remained in the city, changing the dynamics completely and forever. Fortunately, the city was tolerant and accepting of the vast changes.

Language is the greatest barrier and most frequent concession one sees all about Miami. From the Florida Turnpike "Espera Luz Verde," meaning wait for the green light to Chinese restaurant menu option Chicken Chow Mein, Fried Rice & Egg Roll reading "Chow Mein de Pollo, Arroz Frito, Egg Roll;" the Spanish language is everywhere. There are areas of Miami where Spanish is the first language, recently I saw a sign at a convenience store addressed to its employees reading, "Speak English on duty."

Another distinguishing factor is food. "Mariquitas," are small flakes of toasted banana that have become a popular snack food and black beans, which have become a popular item on most menus and staple ingredient for home cooks. Black beans are most often found atop a bed of white rice garnished with chopped onion and dashed with oil and vinegar. The corner drugstore looks All-American except for the sign that reads "farmacia Navarro-medicinas a Cuba, precios de discount." The shelves do not appear unusual except all of the magazines are written in Spanish and are stocked with telltale items such as guava paste and marmalade.

When asked about their first thoughts of America, the reply came: "Magnifico, Liberty!" Yet today many still long for the freedom of our shores. In one month recently eighty-six Cubans cast off in twelve small home-made boats bound for American shores, thirty-three lost their lives in the attempt. Sometimes the price of freedom is extremely high.

BLUE STAR

A tribute to the Armed Forces that have defended the United States of America.

US 441, Miami
MD13 ~ GPS Coordinates: 25.781661, -80.207773

The following are memories shared by U.S. military officers, recruits, WACs and civilians during the time that the most sought vacation destination became "Camp Miami Beach" during World War II.

Many spoke of seeing coconuts for the first time ever and then being treated to a taste of the sweet nectar within. A coconut grove behind the Colony Theater on Lincoln Road supplied the fruit where a local hacked them open and showed you how to drink the coconut milk.

The little photo shop on Washington Avenue where the guys had their pictures made to send home.

A gambling casino located in the Colonial Inn on Collins Avenue.

Attending dances on Saturday nights beneath the stars, unless of course you had watch, at the Versailles Hotel.

Fan Dancer Sally Rand often lost her fan "accidentally" revealing her attributes then responding "Don't you look you nasty men?"

Grabbing a sandwich at Joe's Broadway Delicatessen on Washington Avenue and the food poisoning panic when everyone became deathly ill from eating contaminated pickles.

The excitement of spotting Al Capone on his yacht touring Biscayne Bay.

Average recruits marched beside celebrities such as Clark Gable, Tony Martin or Robert Preston.

Local girls watching the young soldiers march even though it was bad girls who chased the guys. Many of these young girls became war brides before the young men went off to war.

The only soda pop came from twenty gallon barrels and was often flat half way through.

Northerners were shocked to find separate facilities for blacks and whites even though they fought side by side. The Woolworth store cafeteria had two drinking fountains one marked "White" the other "Black".

Forgetting for a moment that the war looms large and you are at boot camp on off duty Sundays on the tropical sugar sand beach as girls in bathing suits sunned on the beach and the warm waters of the Atlantic welcomed you for a refreshing dip.

Eating dinner cafeteria style at the famed Caribbean Club and being expected to take KP duty afterwards.

Marching on the municipal golf course converted to a drilling field just behind the Lincoln Theater.

Letters from home soggy with sweat from the tropical heat exceeding 100 degrees, of course the letters were read so many times that the high humidity made the ink run and blur.

Being assigned midnight guard duty and being given a table leg for a weapon. Then jumping at every noise after the local newspaper announced a serial killer on the loose.

Sleeping on wobbly emergency cots while palmetto bugs and cockroaches called your boots home.

The blares of an ambulance as pneumonia victims are sped to medical help. Pneumonia was a side affect from the shots reacting with the tropical heat.

Soldiers were restricted from the Charles Hotel further than the front veranda so they'd bribe local kids to go in and buy the best ice cream in the city covered with Betsy Ross fruit salad at fifteen cents per bowl.

Just a few memories of excited young soldiers who were treated to paradise before being sent to the hell of war. Many of these young soldiers gave their lives, never to return to American soil. Others returned and came back to Camp Miami Beach to live out the rest of their lives, some returned each year and still more would spend the last years of their lives in the tropical wonderland. Camp Miami Beach was said to have hosted more than a half million military personnel from 1945 until 1949.

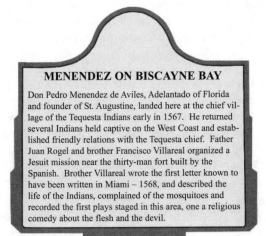

MENENDEZ ON BISCAYNE BAY

Don Pedro Menendez de Aviles, Adelantado of Florida and founder of St. Augustine, landed here at the chief village of the Tequesta Indians early in 1567. He returned several Indians held captive on the West Coast and established friendly relations with the Tequesta chief. Father Juan Rogel and brother Francisco Villareal organized a Jesuit mission near the thirty-man fort built by the Spanish. Brother Villareal wrote the first letter known to have been written in Miami – 1568, and described the life of the Indians, complained of the mosquitoes and recorded the first plays staged in this area, one a religious comedy about the flesh and the devil.

Bayfront Park, the marker was being housed in a warehouse at the park due to vandalism, Miami Beach MD14 ~ GPS Coordinates: 25.776650, -80.185217

Spain dispatched Pedro Menendez de Aviles to settle their La Florida holdings. He was to be governor or as the Spanish called him, Adelantado of the peninsula. Menendez set sail with soldiers and religious leaders to establish civilization out of the Florida wilderness including the intent to Christianize the Native American people. Once there Menendez realized the paltry sums given by the Spanish King would not begin to cover what was needed, he personally financed the struggling village at St. Augustine to keep the community afloat.

The first order of business was to defeat the French encroaching on Spanish held territory and in doing so found it necessary to befriend the bronzed Native Americans. Winning over the Indians was a difficult process due to the long history of Spanish Conquistadors mistreatment of the tribal people. During the winter of 1566, Pedro Menendez de Aviles set out to tour the peninsula with two intents; first, his son had been lost to treacherous seas somewhere along the Gulf Coast, unfortunately he was never found and secondly, Menendez intended to sign the first trade treaty with the Calusa people. The treaty was a success for a short time, trading Spanish gold for cloth and mercantile goods.

Numerous Spanish forts were constructed along the Atlantic coastline including a wooden watchtower at Biscayne Bay. The mission of these fortifications involved recovery of treasure ships and keeping a keen eye out for pirate vessels intent on attack. These forts maintained protection for the Spanish gold fleets and a determent to coastal raiders.

Within two years Father Juan Rogel, a Jesuit priest serving Menendez, reported that five of the fortifications had fallen to Native American attack and pirate invasion. Rogel blamed the situation on the inattention of the Spanish soldiers distracted by their lust for the Native American women. One solution offered was that the tribal chief provided at the Spanish soldiers disposal Native American slave women kept as prostitutes. The promiscuous problem would continue to plague the progress of the Spanish conquest for two centuries.

Menendez impression of the Native Americans was sent to King Phillip II as follows:

"The Floridas are entirely peopled by savages, without faith and law, unenlightened by the law of Our Lord Jesus Christ, his Majesty was in duty bound for the conquest and settlement of the land."

Father Juan Rogel felt the Native Americans could be taught and molded, his observations to the crown were:

"They (Indians) are rational animals well prepared for saving themselves. Keeping them in hand, they are a harvest so ripe that one can swing the sickle on whatever side one chooses, as they see I, the minister one who is looking out for their spiritual and temporal welfare and who preaches life and doctrine to them."

Menendez came to Miami in order to set up a Jesuit mission with Brother Francisco Villareal as its spiritual leader to the Tequesta. Thirty Spanish soldiers were stationed at the mission and within the walls twenty-eight crude houses and a chapel was built. Hostilities broke out with the Natives and when the smoke cleared only Brother Villareal and eighteen soldiers remained. The Spanish detachment escaped with nothing but their lives, returning to St. Augustine. The trouble eventually settled with the assistance of a Christianized Tequesta Chief but the peace did not last, within a few years the mission was abandoned completely. Another attempt to Christianize the Native Americans during the 18th century resulted in the same outcome, finally the Spaniards simply vanquished the entire tribe into extinction.

Father Rogel followed Diego de Landa to the Mexican jungles to bring religious teachings to the Mayan people at a settlement called Hacienda Tabi. The native people had no desire to abandon their teachings and be converted to Christianity and eventually brutally murdered Father Juan Rogel. Hacienda Tabi began to experience continuous unexplained tragedies. Paranormal specialists determined that Rogel's angry spirit remained at Tabi and ironically for a religious leader is considered the most evil, vengeful spirit there.

A discovery was made in the late 1990s near the mouth of the Miami River just east of the Brickell Avenue Bridge and adjacent to the Sheraton Biscayne Bay Hotel. There amidst modern metropolitan sprawl was an ancient ceremonial structure dubbed the "Miami Circle". The circular stone carvings and postholes are believed to be the work of an ancient people as an heavenly observatory or temple. The discovery was approximately four feet below the surface and covered an amazing two-acre site.

Some believed the Miami Circle to be the work of a Central American Mayan people who dwelled for a time in south Florida more than two thousand years past. To support this theory several primitively formed axes, known to be produced by the Mayan or related people, have been found near the site. Others feel that this formation is the work of the extinct Tequesta who inhabited the area more than five hundred years ago. The one fact that is positively known, nothing else similar to the Miami Circle has ever been found in Florida.

The site of the formation will soon be the location of twin tower apartments, various businesses and shops to be called Brickell Pointe. State law only provides historic protection when human remains are found at the archaeological site. No skeletal remains have been found at the Miami Circle. The developer, Brickell Pointe Limited, have been sensitive as well as generous with their time and money. If parts of the formation can be moved to an alternate site to preserve it, Brickell has indicated a willingness to fund the project. However, other historic preservationists believe the site should be protected and left whole in place. Further details concerning the fate of the Miami Circle can be found in the article entitled, Tequesta.

Many people get the feeling of treading on sacred ground at this site. Testing continues to this day to further identify the Miami Circle, its creators and carbon dating to determine during what period of time the formation was completed. Whatever the answers are, it is certain we have much to learn about the ancient people who dwelled here before white men destroyed their civilization.

TEQUESTA

Indians lived at the mouth of the Miami River (200 yards southwest of this spot) for more than 15 centuries before White men came. The principal town of the Tequesta Indians, including six mounds used for dwelling, burial, and religious rites, was discovered here by the Spaniards. They built in it the earliest White settlement in S.E. Florida, a fort and Jesuit mission, in 1567. When the British obtained Florida in 1763, most of the Tequesta departed with the Spaniards to Havana and thereafter vanished as a tribe.

In Bayfront Park, this marker is housed in a warehouse at the park due to repeated vandalism, Miami Beach
MD14 ~ GPS Coordinates: 25.776650, -80.185217

Before Europeans landed on Florida's sandy shores the Tequesta called this peninsula home. When Juan Ponce de Leon arrived in 1513, the Tequesta were there and wary of the strange looking little people attempting to claim lands that had always been their home. A prime site at the mouth of the Miami River was home to tribal chiefs whereas the remaining people would dwell in villages along the river and coastal islands.

Living off the bounty of the land and particularly the sea, the Tequesta were hunters and gathers. While the men fished or hunted for larger game such as sharks, sea cows or manatees, porpoises, bear, wild boar or deer; the women, children and elders gathered clams, conch, oysters, turtle eggs, palmetto berries, coco plums, sea grapes and palm nuts. The women would grind certain roots to make flour. The manatee was considered a delicacy that was only served to the chief or tribal leaders.

Food supplies were not always plentiful and the Tequesta's diet suffered. They did not grow to be large, powerful men like the tribes to the west. Yet the Tequesta were larger than the Spaniards invading their lands. They were intelligent enough to fashion shells and sharks teeth into tools. Of course, the Tequesta made their own canoes for transportation and implements such as hammers, chisels and spears.

When Europeans arrived they brought with them colored cloth, steel knives and rum, which fascinated the Native Americans; they also brought fierce battles, slavery and devastating disease. When the Spanish arrived the Tequesta numbered about eight hundred individuals, within three generations the tribe had very few remaining members and these people were absorbed into other indigenous tribes.

To continue the discussion of the Miami Circle from Menendez on Biscayne Bay and its significance to the Tequesta people: Miami citizens, the state of Florida and several political leaders banded together to preserve this wonderful example of Native American artifacts. The historical importance of this site was clearly recognized and using a combination of county and state funds the property was purchased and preserved for future generations.

Studies began to determine the importance of the Miami Circle as a historical archeological site. In order to protect, preserve and present the site to the public a drive began to include the area as a National Historic Landmark in conjunction with Biscayne National Park. Seven Tequesta sites were already a part of the park and with the addition of the Miami Circle many more opportunities for the park could be made possible.

President Bush recently signed legislation for the National Park Service to study the feasibility of the Miami Circle becoming part of Biscayne National Park. The addition of this wonderful relic will add to the allure of the national park. Because the park spans across the bay, to coastal islands and including the offshore waters, visitors have not had access to all parts of Biscayne. The additional attraction will possibly allow the inclusion of a ferry service across the Miami River to the nearby islands. Close to one million visitors each year flock to the park to enjoy the natural wonders of south Florida and to learn about tribal people such as the Tequesta who first lived there. Sites such as the Miami Circle and artifacts from the Tequesta must be preserved for the generations to come. To understand the future we must have a full understanding of the past.

MIAMI SENIOR HIGH SCHOOL

Miami High School — Dade County's first – opened in 1902 with fifteen students occupying a two-room wooden structure behind the elementary school at 301 N.E. First Avenue. From 1911 to 1915 the high school shared the new Central School with the elementary grades before getting its own building at 201 N.W. Third Avenue. The present complex was completed on this site in 1928 at a cost of $1,500,000 and was designed by the well-known architectural firm of Kiehnel and Elliott in the popular Mediterranean style with Norman-Sicilian features. Courtyards, arcades, and open corridors link the library, classrooms, auditorium, cafeteria, offices and workshops. The auditorium served as a community cultural center with operas, concerts, and plays. From its beginning Miami Senior High School has promoted high standards of scholarship and produced outstanding teachers, athletes, and business and civic leaders.

2450 SW 1st Street, Miami
MD15 ~ GPS Coordinates: 25.771433, -80.235800

The first formal county school was established in 1902 in a two room wooden structure located on Northeast First Avenue. Fifteen students were enrolled, which held classes directly behind the elementary school at 301 Northeast First Avenue. Within one year's time the student body increased to an amazing two hundred sixty four pupils and classrooms had to be shared with the lower grades.

In 1911, a three storied masonry structure was built for the new Central School. Meant to serve the elementary students because of their immense numbers the high school was forced to share the building. The high school moved to a new building in 1915 at 275 Northwest Second Avenue.

Construction began on the current facilities on March 18, 1927. Designed by architects Kiehnel and Elliott, the structure was meant to embody the Spanish Colonial Revival style, however most describe the impressive structure as a much more elaborate French Romanesque inspiration. Built at 2450 Southwest First Street, the first senior high school covers an amazing nineteen acres. Two million feet of Florida pine lumber was used in the construction in addition to six hundred forty-two tons of steel, twelve box carloads of interior tile, twenty thousand barrels of cement, sand and rock and seventy-nine marble and slate blackboards.

A very celebrated Valentines Day 1928 had students cross the threshold for the first time. Just beyond the front of the building lay Colombia Park and leading to the doorway are twelve stately royal palms representing each year of formal education. Unfortunately much of the park was paved over to add additional parking. The students fought losing the majority of the park in 1968 but lost to the opposition. Still the motto "Non verbis sed operis," translated to mean "Not by words, but deeds," is embodied by the faculty, staff and students of Miami Senior High School.

The roof features flat tar and gravel topped with red barrel clay tile, created by the Miami Tile Company utilizing materials imported from Cuba. The main entrance features three sets of imposing doors. The portals are heavy paneled, massive wooden double doors accented with thick iron straps as well as oversized hinges and studs. The grand entrances are embraced by French Romanesque arches emitting a feeling of entering a castle or cathedral.

The imposing lobby has three orbital arches supported at each side by stately columns. In fact legend has it that one of these columns contains a time capsule but there is no record to substantiate the claim. The main foyer features the Gold Star Honor Roll, memorializing the alumni who died in the service of their country throughout World War II. Oddly enough a ticket window is in place and still in use today flanked by Italian palace inspired lanterns. Three Denman Fink murals bedeck the room, representative of science and technology, history and civics as well as government and the arts.

The floor covering is terra cotta tile used throughout, much of it original to the building. Four inner courtyards often called patios lead to hidden gardens amidst academia. A small secret room exists between the Home Economics classrooms. Cozy with a fireplace, the room was built as a meeting room for the Superintendent of Schools. The facility has a built in air conditioning system. The room is designed with high ceilings and transoms, which allow a gentle breeze to cool the building.

The school theatre, please do not refer to it as an auditorium, rivals any glamorous concert hall. The facility has perfect acoustics gained by wooden slats covering cork paneling. Stage performances may be done without amplification or microphone enhancement due to the impeccable design of the facility. The building is three stories with a gabled roof and vaulted ceilings. The rooms are finished with an orchestra pit and flight system used during elaborate stage productions. The theatre will accommodate one thousand thirty-one patrons including ten balcony sections.

Four one-half metric ton chandeliers illuminate the building. Miami Senior High School alumni designed the beautiful works of art, which were made in Tampa. The fixtures are suspended by iron chains, which may be lowered in order to change lights and be cleaned. Two of the four chandeliers have at one time come crashing down to the floor below. Fortunately on both occasions the theatre was unoccupied most probably saving someone from grave injury or death. Gargoyles and griffins embellish the clock area of the main theatre floor symbolizing ancient literary prose. The center arch features a tree of knowledge flanked by the griffin and dragon figures as well.

Strangely enough the theatre has had its share of unusual visitors. During the 1970s an unwelcome family made a home beneath the stage. It was common to see startling shining eyes peering back at the students ~ in fact the family was a of the fox variety. And at the opposite end of the spectrum, in the rafters of the theatre for a time was home to the only colony of bats in Dade County.

Because the Miami Senior High School boasts a more than one hundred-year history it is natural to expect a spirit or two about the campus. Stories are told of a young freshman girl entering the restroom and encountering the specter of a girl with rivers of blood streaming down her face and the hilt of a knife protruding from her right shoulder. The freshman student screamed in terror as the apparition disappeared before her eyes. The young lady was so unnerved she required a sedative. Another story involves a security camera capturing the image of a young

man bedecked in graduation robes walking through the theatre as if at commencement at precisely 10:43. When the security guard hurried to investigate, he heard a wailing scream and found only a darkened spot on the floor where the image had stood. The spot still remains.

The Miami High School is dedicated to the academic excellence and extra curricular advantages in

MIAMI SENIOR HIGH SCHOOL

order to graduate a well-rounded individual. Maintaining the same standards of education for more than one hundred years has been the goal of this enduring facility. The Miami High School was added to the National Register of Historic Sites in 1990.

BLUE STAR

A tribute to the Armed Forces that have defended the United States of America.

US 1, North Miami Beach
MD16 ~ GPS Coordinates: 25.763692, -80.191609

During the course of World War II, Germany held the vast majority of Western Europe. The United States and her allies began capturing a large number of German and Italian soldiers even though the fight was tough. The difficulties were where to hold the captives. Britain was unable to take the POWs[2] because of the vast numbers; therefore it is a little known fact that many of the captives were shipped to the United States.

Strict rules imposed by the 1929 Geneva Convention detailed how POWs were to be kept. In fact the housing was to be equal to that of any American soldier. These guidelines were followed to the extent that one camp forced its guards to live in tents because the barracks housing the prisoners was still under construction. The food supplied the prisoners was to equal that of the soldiers as well. This circumstance did not please Americans living near the camps who were subjected to food rationing.

Florida took in more than ten thousand prisoners. The primary camps were at Camp Blanding and Camp George Johnston. In Dade County, Kendall's Civilian Conservation Corps was converted to a German POW camp as well as another camp at Homestead. These facilities held between two hundred fifty and four hundred prisoners.

The majority of the captives were taken in North Africa although some were fished from the waters of the Atlantic just off Americas East Coast. German submarines would lay in wait as American merchant ships came close to the coast then fire their killing torpedoes into the unsuspecting ships. Many of these ships were sunk within sight of the Miami beaches. Miami refused to enforce the blackout order by the United States Army in order to maintain as much of the tourist trade as possible. The bright city lights aided U-boat captains when targeting ships along the coast.

German and Italian prisoners were assigned to clean Miami streets, work in military garages, as well as aid grove farmers short laborers due to the war. Non-commissioned Officers were given supervisory positions while Commissioned Officers were not forced to work. The prisoners were usually housed in separate camps with private homes given to high-ranking officers. Like most other POWs throughout the U.S. they were paid around one dollar a day for their work, which they could spend at camp exchanges.

Life was easy for the prisoners compared to the treatment received by American soldiers at the hands of the Germans, Italians and Japanese. In fact German and Italian soldiers were allowed to use local white only beaches that their black soldier guards were restricted from. POWs were allowed time for recreation, worship with a German speaking minister as well as voluntary classes in democracy and the American way of life.

Certainly prisoners attempted escape although with conditions and treatment was overwhelmingly good, the number of escape attempts was very small. Several problems existed with escape including the fact that they were thousands of miles and an ocean away from their homeland. After VE Day on May 8, 1945, the United States repatriated the POWs. Twenty-five prisoners out of Florida's six hundred fifty could not be accounted for. It is believed that these men chose to remain in the United States using whatever means necessary.

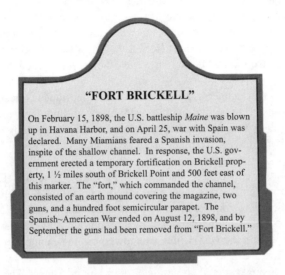

"FORT BRICKELL"

On February 15, 1898, the U.S. battleship *Maine* was blown up in Havana Harbor, and on April 25, war with Spain was declared. Many Miamians feared a Spanish invasion, inspite of the shallow channel. In response, the U.S. government erected a temporary fortification on Brickell property, 1 ½ miles south of Brickell Point and 500 feet east of this marker. The "fort," which commanded the channel, consisted of an earth mound covering the magazine, two guns, and a hundred foot semicircular parapet. The Spanish~American War ended on August 12, 1898, and by September the guns had been removed from "Fort Brickell."

Brickell Avenue and 18th Road overlooking Biscayne Bay, Miami
MD17 ~ GPS Coordinates: 25.756017, -80.195150

The second class United States battleship, the *USS Maine* was built strictly for the United States Navy. Congress approved the construction on August 3, 1886, however, the ship took nearly nine years before it was finally completed. Three years were spent just waiting for the armor plating to be installed.

The ship faced a great many firsts including: the first ship to be made purely the product of an American design; secondly, the ship was built completely at a United States Naval Yard; and finally, she was the largest vessel to be built at a Naval Yard. There was some obvious design problems concerning the *USS Maine,* most importantly the configuration of her gun turret. The arms were not counterbalanced, therefore if set in the same direction, the ship would keel over. Firing across the ship's deck through the superstructure was possible and in fact intended. This was a massive design flaw in that when the shell was fired it created a vacuum that could damage the deck and superstructure. Any slight timing mistake and a shell fired before the gun was properly aimed, the *USS Maine* could actually sink herself.

It seems the *USS Maine* was more attraction then practical battle ready ship. She was displayed for several ceremonial events including the 1897 New Orleans Mardi Gras. On December 15, 1897 the *USS Maine* began her final voyage to points south toward Florida and her ultimate doom. The impressive show boat arrived in the Havana Harbor on January 24, 1898. Captain Charles Sigsbee was ordered to conduct a purely ceremonious visit. Of course now we understand that the United States government had misinterpreted the situation in Spanish held Cuba and the United States Cuban Consul Fitzhugh Lee was oblivious to the insurgence surrounding him. The *USS Maine* sailed unknowingly to her death.

In the dark of a tropical winter night as the *USS Maine's* crew settled for the evening a thunderous explosion ripped through the hull. It was 9:30 PM, February 15, 1898 and within scant minutes the popular ship sank to the floor of the Havana Harbor. Ammunition explosions continued to boil the water for hours after the *USS Maine's* final death knoll. Two hundred fifty-two men lost their lives that fateful night.

United States media was quick to determine that Spain was at fault, the Navy concluded that a mine igniting the forward magazine resulted in the explosion. President McKinley, who had valiantly tried to avoid war with Spain, was forced to order military troops into Cuba. American citizens demanded retribution for the loss *USS Maine* and favored war with Spain. The battle cry sounded, "Remember the *Maine*" as United States forces prepared for war.

South Florida, due to their close proximity to Cuba, was gripped with fear. The United States Army was ordered to erect coastal defenses. An earthen mound of forty-five feet wide, twenty feet high was built and two guns were aimed directly at Biscayne Bay. The site is known today as the intersection of Brickell Avenue and Eighteenth Road. The military site was dubbed Fort Robert W. Davis for a Florida State Representative who pushed for the construction in protection of Miami. However, the citizens called the earthen mound Fort Brickell and the name stuck.

Miami was never in any real danger. The city was of no importance concerning the Spanish-American war and the waters beyond the city were so shallow that war ships could not have gotten close enough to fire on the city had they wanted to attack by sea. Regardless, two hundred Miami citizens formed the Miami Minutemen and established of a volunteer home guard. The unit drilled with guns at the Royal Palm Hotel owned by Henry Flagler.

The Spanish-American war ended three and a half months after it began. The *USS Maine* remained in her watery grave of the Havana Harbor until 1911. That year divers patched the hull enough to float the ship and inspect the damage done. Studies were conducted and a court of inquiry determined that the *USS Maine* sunk as the result of a design flaw. A coal bunker fire exploded the ammunition magazine and not a Spanish mine as originally determined. After the inspection the *USS Maine* was towed out to sea and sunk at its final resting-place some thirty-six hundred feet beneath the ocean waves.

Pieces of the *USS Maine* are scattered about the eastern United States. The mainmast stands at Arlington National Cemetery; her foremast was placed near the seawall at the Naval Academy in Annapolis, Maryland; one of her bow anchors lay at Pennsylvania's City Park; the *USS Maine* capstan rests at the Battery in Charleston, South Carolina; and her bow scroll is in Bangor, Maine. Small mementos were fashioned from parts of the ship into ashtrays, plaques, models and various other trinkets.

Fort Robert W. Davis, alias Fort Brickell, was left unfinished by the end of the Spanish-American war. The fortification was never completed nor utilized again.

CAPE FLORIDA
LIGHTHOUSE

Cape Florida, the southern tip of Key Biscayne, was discovered by John Cabot in 1497, less than five years after Columbus first landed in the West Indies. Cabot continued his voyage into the Gulf of Mexico, but returned to Key Biscayne the following spring, and named it "The Cape of the End of April." Juan Ponce de Leon landed on the key in 1513, and christened it "Santa Marta." Its present name "Biscayne" is derived from the Indian word "Bischiyano" which meant "the favorite path of the rising moons." After the United States received Florida from Spain in 1821, and at the urging of the Navy, plans were drawn for a lighthouse on the tip of the Cape. The tower was completed December 17, 1825, and is one of the oldest structures in South Florida. In July of 1836, shortly after the beginning of the Second Seminole War, the lighthouse was attacked by Indians. John W.B. Thompson, the lighthouse keeper, was injured, and his Negro helper Tom was killed, before the arrival of a rescue ship. A temporary army post, Fort Bankhead, was established on the Cape in 1838, and became the headquarters of the 2nd Dragoons, commanded by Colonel William S. Harney, the "old Indian Fighter." At the same time, the key was a main base of the Navy's "Florida Squadron," under Lieutenant Commander John T. McLaughlin. The lighthouse was raised to its present height of 95 feet in 1855, but the light was wrecked by southern sympathizers in 1861, and was dark for the duration of the Civil War. It was restored in 1867, and guided ships through the dangerous reef waters until 1878, when it was extinguished for the final time. Larger ships needed a light further out at sea, and the new Fowey Rock light took its place.

Cape Florida State Recreation Area, Key Biscayne
MD18 ~ GPS Coordinates: 25.666217, -80.156450

Many explorers and adventurers made brief stops at Cape Florida during the early years before Spain's King Phillip II chose Menendez to establish a post on the la Florida peninsula. Cabot and Ponce de Leon both claimed what was to become Biscayne at one time. The first Spanish land grant approved in south Florida was for Key Biscayne in 1790.

Three acres of land were sold to the United States government at the Navy's insistence for a lighthouse at the southern end of the cape. The initial beacon was completed on December 17, 1825. In addition a keepers' cottage was also constructed to accommodate the lighthouse keeper and his family in this extremely remote location.

When the Seminole massacred Major Dade and his men in December of 1835, the Second Seminole War commenced. Within months Cape Florida Lighthouse keeper William Cooley received word that his wife, children and their tutor had been brutally murdered during a Seminole raid. The massacre was a surprise attack on his home. He immediately left the lighthouse service, never to return.

John W. B. Thompson took over the duties as lighthouse keeper. On July 23, 1836 Thompson and his assistant, a free man of color named Tom, came under attack by Seminole rifle fire. John and Tom held off the marauding band until nightfall when the Seminole finally managed to reach the base of the lighthouse. They set fire to the only way out for the keeper and his assistant, oilcans fed the fire and soon the entire tower was in flames. The iron tower floor branded their feet and soon they were resigned to burning to death. In an effort to speed the process John Thompson threw a keg of gunpowder, knowing the ensuing explosion would end their lives. Witnessing the explosion, the Seminole burned the keepers' cottage and made an escape in Thompson's small boat.

The explosion had in fact doused the flames. Unfortunately, Tom lay dead and John Thompson was severely wounded. His feet were burned nearly to the bone and Thompson had several minor gun shot wounds. He lay for twelve hours in the blazing Florida sun with mosquitoes feasting on his naked flesh. John Thompson was at the mercy of the elements as fever overtook his senses.

A passing naval vessel noticed smoke streaming from the smoldering ruin of the cottage and gutted lighthouse. Making their way toward the lighthouse, the sailors found Thompson on the tower but were unable to get to him. In order to enact the rescue, an expert marksman fired a musket ball with a line attached until it snagged the railing for John Thompson to tie off. The critically injured man used what remained of his waning strength to tie a knot in the rope then he collapsed in a heap. Two crewmen scaled the tower walls using the rope and gently lowered Thompson to the ground on a small wooden litter. John Thompson did recover from his injuries, though his feet were forever crippled.

The 2nd Army Dragoons set up their headquarters at Cape Florida in 1838 under the command of Colonel William S. Harney, they dubbed the post Fort Bankhead. Lieutenant Commander John T. McLaughlin led the Navy's Florida Squadron as they patrolled the Atlantic shore of Biscayne Bay. In addition to the fortification, a hospital was also established. When the hostilities with the Seminole came to an end Fort Bankhead was abandoned and the Dragoons galloped away.

The Cape Florida Lighthouse was rebuilt in 1855, construction would take two years and by the time of its completion the tower would extend sixty-five additional feet from its original height making the finished beacon ninety-five feet tall. By this time the Seminole had been vanquished, the only remaining Native Americans were hidden concealed within the Everglades swamps. Occasionally the Seminole would venture out to trade with the lighthouse keeper. The wife of one keeper wrote a story of one particular Indian who arrived late in the evening; rather than wake the household, he simply slipped into bed beside one of their children where he was found the next morning.

During the first days of the Civil War a Confederate raiding party disabled the beacon at the Cape Florida Lighthouse. The guiding light remained dark for the remainder of the war. The light burned bright again in 1867 and continued to guide ships along the treacherous water for eleven years when the lamp was doused for the final time as a safety beam. Fowey Rock light, which was more powerful and placed out at sea, was activated in 1878.

A one and a half million-dollar restoration project was completed in July 1996 in time for the Miami Centennial celebration. The tower was renovated and a replica of the lighthouse keepers' cottage like it appeared in 1825 was erected. The grand opening was staged February 28, 1998.

Today the lighthouse and keepers cottage is part of Bill Baggs State Park and Recreation Area. The four hundred six-acre tropical park features not only the lighthouse but beautiful beaches and breathtaking aqua blue seas. Park rangers conduct twice daily tours of the lighthouse, the modernized cottage and the cookhouse, which has been turned into a small theater showing an introduction to the history of the Cape Florida Lighthouse and Key Biscayne. The view atop the one hundred nine steps is quite possibly the best in south Florida. From that vantage point you can watch dolphin leap in the clear blue water, graceful sails as they navigate the reef and on the horizon you might see a huge white cruise ship bound for sun-kissed Caribbean ports. Cape Florida Lighthouse remains the longest standing structure in south Florida and a sight not to be missed. Walk the path shaded by swaying coconut palms into living history.

CAPE FLORIDA LIGHTHOUSE

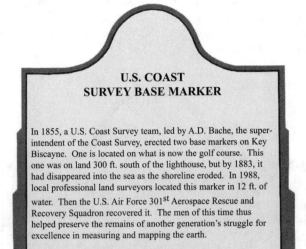

**U.S. COAST
SURVEY BASE MARKER**

In 1855, a U.S. Coast Survey team, led by A.D. Bache, the superintendent of the Coast Survey, erected two base markers on Key Biscayne. One is located on what is now the golf course. This one was on land 300 ft. south of the lighthouse, but by 1883, it had disappeared into the sea as the shoreline eroded. In 1988, local professional land surveyors located this marker in 12 ft. of water. Then the U.S. Air Force 301st Aerospace Rescue and Recovery Squadron recovered it. The men of this time thus helped preserve the remains of another generation's struggle for excellence in measuring and mapping the earth.

Lighthouse on Key Biscayne, Key Biscayne
MD18 ~ GPS Coordinates: 25.666217, -80.156450

Key Biscayne has two granite markers placed by the United States Coast Surveyors on what were once the northern and southern points of the island. These markers were placed in 1855 and used to establish navigational charts and maps. A. D. Bache was the Superintendent of the United States Survey office and it is his name that appears on the one marker still within view on the golf course. The remaining marker has disappeared from view due to beach erosion and is today in twelve feet of water.

Alexander Dallas Bache was an important scientific figure during the early nineteenth century. His work in the scientific community brought America into a modern era equal to that of Europe. Educational institutions of the time owe a debt of gratitude to Bache for his scientific advancements and leadership.

Born on July 19, 1806, Bache was born to a prominent Philadelphia family. His lineage was like a who's who of the American political arena in the late eighteenth and early nineteenth centuries. He was a great grandson of Benjamin Franklin; nephew of George Dallas, Vice President under James K. Polk; and grandson of Alexander James Dallas, Secretary of the Treasury under President James Madison.

At the age of fifteen, Bache went to the United States Military Academy graduating first in his class four years later. He accepted a position to teach math and natural history at the academy where Bache remained for two years. At the end of his tenure, he served as a lieutenant in the Army Corps of Engineers.

In 1828, at the age of twenty-two, Bache left the Army to teach natural philosophy and chemistry at the University of Pennsylvania. He established a magnetic observatory to conduct research in terrestrial magnetism. A. D. Bache was now recognized as an American authority in the scientific field. He was an active member of both the American Philosophical Society and the Franklin Institute, raising the scientific standards of the institutions to height thus far unknown to the American academic community.

After spending two years in Europe, A. D. Bache returned to America to fill the position of Superintendent of the United States Coast Survey Office upon the death of his predecessor Ferdinand Hassler. The Coast Survey office, thanks to Bache's influence, supported more scientists than any other institution in America and elevated the status of the agency to one of the premiere organizations in the world. A. D. Bache was much more than an administrator for the Coast Survey, he involved himself personally in the field work as well, hence his name engraved in the granite of the survey marker at Biscayne Bay.

Bache was a primary member of the Lighthouse Board, Superintendent of the Office of Weights and

Measures as well as regent for the prestigious Smithsonian Institute. During the Civil War, Bache focused the Coast Survey in support of the war effort. He consulted with the Union Army and Navy on battle plans, worked with Philadelphia defense plans and with the Navy in evaluating new advanced weaponry. Alexander Dallas Bache died in Newport, Rhode Island on February 17, 1867.

WOMEN TAKE ACTION IN CORAL GABLES
The Roxcy O'Neal Bolton House 1965-1988

Built in 1933, this Mediterranean Revival house is a contributing structure in the Coral Gables Plantation Historic District, one of the earliest developments in the city planned by George Merrick. Throughout the late 1960s and the 1970s, this house became a meeting place for those who campaigned for equal rights for women. Resident and pioneer feminist Roxcy O'Neal Bolton opened her home as headquarters to organize numerous rallies and marches and founded the Miami Dade Chapter of the National Organization for Women. In an effort to bring public attention to the special needs of women, organizational meetings were held in this house to establish Women in Distress, the first women's rescue shelter in Florida and the Rape Treatment Center at Jackson Memorial Hospital. Community meetings were also held here to create the Citizen's Crime Watch of Dade County, one of the first of its kind in the country. Under Roxcy Bolton's leadership, the perseverance of all those who volunteered their time here created a forceful voice for justice for those who would otherwise not be heard.

At Alhambra Circle and Madrid, Coral Gables
MD19 ~ GPS Coordinates: 25.753800, -80.282083

Roxcy O'Neal was born in Mississippi in 1926, though her inauspicious birth held no clues to the impact she would have on all women across the United States. Her forward thinking and specific concerns involved areas of equality, abuse and crime against women never before publicly addressed by any individual or organization. The inroads Roxcy made continue to influence the lives of every woman in America, who owe her a debt of gratitude for the rights, laws and services available to us today.

She led a very traditional life, married United States Navy Commander David Bolton and with him had three children. Roxcy kept her home and raised her children, but that is where the tradition ended. She dedicated her life to the plight of equality for women not only in the workplace but also in society; Roxcy opened her home to the abused and fought for the rights of rape victims.

The Florida National Organization for Women was founded under the direction of Roxcy Bolton who served as the Miami Chapter President and National organization Vice President in 1969. She took this association very seriously and as an example challenged the Jordan Marsh Department store dining room. The restaurant would expeditiously seat the male diners while women were required to stand in line cafeteria style. Roxcy entered the facility and observed numerous empty seats in the men's section while the women stood in a long line, she ceremoniously sauntered to men's section and announced, "Men and women sleep together; why can't they eat together?" then sat herself down. The results were as expected and policy slowly changed.

In 1970, Roxcy Bolton tackled the Equal Employment Opportunities Commission. Men did not only direct the federal agency founded to provide equality in the workplace and eliminate discrimination but all of its investigators were male as well. Roxcy's protest brought changes to the commission that should have been in place from the very beginning. The process took a woman of courage willing to fight the good fight to forcing organizations meant to support the rights of women to adhere to its own mandate.

Roxcy was very aware of the distressing problem of domestic abuse, she began sheltering women and children in her home. When it became evident that some other arrangements had to be made, Roxcy founded Women in Distress. The non-profit service provided a place for victims of domestic abuse to find a safe haven, rescue services for women and children in distress and other means of assistance to alleviate situations of personal crisis. Unfortunately this was a time when domestic situations were virtually ignored by police and governmental agencies. Finally a house was secured and Roxcy kept not only her own home but that of the shelter as well. She cooked, cleaned, counseled, and cared for all those who were in need and sought help at the Women in Distress shelter. She asked for donations of food, clothing, bedding and every means of support for the women and children in trouble. This shelter was the first of its kind in the state of Florida. Another first for Florida came when Roxcy founded the first Crime Watch group, holding meetings to help curb violent crimes against women.

In the early 1970s, Roxcy campaigned for another cause ~ rape. Most women refused to report the crime because the police often treated them with disdain and it wasn't something that was spoken about in polite company. Roxcy refused to be silenced, in fact not only did she speak on the subject but also she led a march against rape down Flagler Street. She badgered public officials until they were finally convinced to do something about it. In 1974, Roxcy's hope became a reality when the first Rape Treatment Center in Florida was created at Jackson Memorial Hospital in Miami as well as staffed with a full time doctor and several nurses. The Rape Treatment Center was renamed in honor of Roxcy Bolton in 1993.

Roxcy Bolton enlisted the aid of numerous Florida female civic, political and society leaders in order to realize a long thought out dream of a park and historical gallery museum dedicated to women of Miami-Dade County who had made a difference in their communities. This would be the first park of its kind in the United States, it was dedicated in 1992. Three years later the park received a fifty thousand-dollar anonymous donation in order to build the park's first picnic pavilion.

A groundbreaking ceremony was held on March 7, 1999 for the Roxcy O'Neal Bolton Women's History Gallery. Two hundred people attended the event for the six thousand square foot facility. Coral Gables architect Ana Alleguez led a committee of architectural firms owned by women. The design featured an octagonal exhibit hall, elaborate terraces, keystone veneer wall and an antique 1800s era cast iron bell. The facility would be available for meetings, cultural events and exhibits honoring the achievements of women in Florida's history. The Safe Neighborhood Parks Bond and Quality Neighborhood Improvement programs provided one million dollars in grants to complete the gallery. The gallery is opened to the public daily and admission is free. Special programs are frequently scheduled. This wonderful informative and interesting museum as well as the beautifully designed park should not be missed.

At the entrance to the park is a coral rock monument marks the spot of a time capsule. Miami artist Frieda Tschumy designed the bronze cylinder buried beneath the coral monument, which contains priceless mementos from many famous women important in Florida's history. The contents of the capsule include writings of environmental activist and author Marjory Stoneman Douglas, author Zora Neale Hurston and Cuban anthropologist Lydia Cabrera. The capsule will be opened on August 26, 2020, the one-hundredth anniversary of the Women's Suffrage Amendment.

Roxcy O'Neal Bolton remains a woman whose ideas and actions created a great impact on her city, state and country. Women everywhere owe her a tremendous debt of gratitude in her fight for equal rights. It has been said of her:

> "She 'Roxcy Bolton' is a remarkable woman…a formidable adversary, a persistent advocate, a woman of courage and conviction who is not afraid to go it alone if need be…and she is a loyal and staunch friend. Florida is a much better place for women…and men…because Roxcy Bolton widened the gate to equality."

She has received numerous awards and honors in regard to the work in which she so staunchly believed.

Hers is certainly a name that will be forever remembered as shaping the history of Florida. Roxcy O'Neal Bolton was inducted into the Florida Women's Hall of Fame in 1984, an honor she so richly deserved.

ALHAMBRA WATER TOWER

The "lighthouse" which has never seen the sea, serves as a testament to founder George Merrick's vision for the City of Coral Gables, and a time when everyday things could be turned into works of art. The water tower was built in 1924 and consists of two separate structures. The inner steel tank, purely utilitarian in looks and purpose, was enclosed in a reinforced concrete and wood frame structure designed to resemble a lighthouse. This concealed the less attractive water tank inside with an aesthetically pleasing and architecturally playful façade. Purchased by Consumers Water Company in 1926, the Alhambra Water Tower was part of the City's domestic water supply system until 1931 when it was disconnected from the system and abandoned after the utility company started buying water from the City of Miami. In response to citizen outcry to save the tower from demolition, the City purchased it for a token sum in 1958, thus avoiding the destruction of this unique landmark. In 1993 the tower was extensively restored based upon 1924 photographs. The Alhambra Water Tower was listed in the Coral Gables Register of Historic Places in 1988.

In traffic triangle at 2000 block of Alhambra Circle, Coral Gables
MD20 ~ GPS Coordinates: 25.752500, -80.284950

ALAHAMBRA WATERTOWER

George Merrick founded Coral Gables in the 1920s, envisioning the Spanish-Moorish architecturally influenced community in evidence today. Two Coral Gables water towers were built each resembling a lighthouse though the ocean is nowhere in sight. The first called the Alhambra Water Tower and the second standing on Indian Mound Trail. The Indian Mound tower was damaged beyond repair during the devastating 1926 hurricane and never rebuilt.

The Alhambra tower was constructed in 1924 with an inner steel tank sealed in concrete and encased in a wooden frame shaped to resemble a lighthouse of Moorish design. On the exterior about fifty feet up the side of the "lighthouse" frame was a sundial approximately four feet in diameter on the southern side. Two years later the Consumers Water Company purchased the water tower and utilized it for five years providing water for the Coral Gables community. The system was disconnected in 1931 and the faux lighthouse was abandoned. Water from that point forward was purchased from the city of Miami.

During the 1950s water began to be pumped in to Coral Gables from wells in the Everglades. For twenty years the Alhambra tower stood neglected, Mother Nature slowly wrecking havoc on the wooden structure. As the unique edifice fell into disrepair, the utility company decided to demolish the tower. Coral Gables citizens rose up in protest, urging the city to take action. The tower was purchased for a token sum in 1958 and the Alhambra Water tower was saved.

The wooden structure was restored though no one knew how to repair the sundial. The gnomon[3] was twisted out of alignment. The numbers on the dial required repainting as well. Simple repairs were made but the sundial was no longer functional.

In 1988, the Alhambra Water Tower was named to the Coral Gables Register of Historic Places and the well-known landmark was slated for a complete restoration. The refurbishment was completed in 1993 including a copper dome roof and amazing fresco paintings. The outer shell was plastered and received a bright coat of paint. Unfortunately in 1997 part of the plaster broke away including the section adhering the sundial. When repairs were made the sundial was finally restored to accuracy.

Today the area surrounding the Alhambra Water Tower is a residential neighborhood with the "lighthouse" at the heart of a pretty little park. Coral Gables continues to support the Moorish architecture George Merrick was so proud of and is a neighboring community independent of Miami. The sights and historical significance of Coral Gables is not to be missed especially that of the exceptional Alhambra Water Tower.

CORAL GABLES HOUSE

In 1899, Dr. Solomon Merrick, a Massachusetts Congregational minister, purchased a 160-acre tract of land located near Miami. Rev. Merrick and his son, George, settled in a log cabin already standing on the property and planted grapefruit and vegetables on their land. The rest of the Merrick family soon came to live on the Florida property, which they called "Guavonia" after the fruit that grew there. They lived in a newly constructed frame house which was incorporated into the larger home, completed in 1906. Called "Coral Gables", this house was built of native limestone rock quarried from a nearby site, now Venetian Pool. As Merrick's crops prospered, more land was acquired, bringing the plantation to about 1,600 acres where George Merrick envisioned and later developed a new, Mediterranean-style community. It was named "Coral Gables", after the home. In 1966, W.L. Philbrick purchased the house, which had become known as Merrick Manor, and created the Merrick Manor Foundation to maintain the building as a historic site. In 1976, the Foundation donated this home to the people of Coral Gables. Merrick Manor, now known as Coral Gables House, is listed on the National Register of Historic Places.

907 Coral Way, Coral Gables
MD21 ~ GPS Coordinates: 25.748983, -80.273100

The Merrick family was a well-respected and connected part of the Duxbury, Massachusetts community of academia. Solomon Merrick, the patriarch of the family, was a graduate of Yale University School of Divinity, dedicating his being to the needs of the congregational church. Althea Merrick, his wife, was a noted professor of art history. As the Merrick's aged the harshness of northern winters had them longing for a more pleasing climate in which to retire. Hearing the beauty and availability of Florida lands, the couple determined to move south to establish a family home and retirement community for other clergy. This fateful decision would have a profound impact of south Florida forever.

Dr. Merrick purchased one hundred sixty acres approximately five miles southwest of Miami, which at the time was known as a frontier town for its remote location. Solomon and his young son, George Edgar, moved into a small log cabin already standing on the property when they arrived in the Florida wilderness. While preparing for the remainder of the family to arrive, father and son planted grapefruit, oranges, guava and vegetables. The two would make a weekly four hour trip to Palm Beach selling produce from the back of a mule drawn cart to the affluent clientele of Henry Flagler's Royal Palm Hotel in Palm Beach.

Finally the rest of the family arrived at the south Florida humble home that they called Guavonia, for the guava fruit grown there. Construction began on the plantation house, which would take six years to complete, in 1900. The frame house would be built from native materials of oolitic[4] limestone and pine. The coral rock quarried for construction left a quite large chasm, which was used to create the Venetian Pool in 1924. Althea Merrick designed the home based on the architectural styles found in their Massachusetts home as well as incorporating amenities suitable for the subtropical climate. The Ludovici tiled gabled roof was taken from the summer home of former President Grover Cleveland's "Grey Gables" estate in Buzzard's Bay, Massachusetts. Lush gardens, grotto, waterfalls and small pools embellished the elaborate landscaping creating an amazing oasis in the midst of Florida's yet untamed backwoods.

The address is today known as 907 Coral Way. The location was during this period only accessible by primitive trails barely accommodating a small wagon. Merrick developed a roadway making travel to Miami a much easier endeavor. The crops prospered and Merrick purchased more land increasing his acreage ten fold. The plantation was now called Coral Gables representative of the construction materials and elaborate gabled roof. George Merrick would go on to create a Mediterranean architectural designed community surrounding the Coral Gables estate of the same name.

Wyndham Llewellyn Philbrick, called Phil, purchased what had come to be known as Merrick Manor in 1966. He created the Merrick Manor Foundation and committed to maintaining the estate as a historic site. Like Merrick, Philbrick had an amazing impact on Coral Gables.

Philbrick was born at Tallahassee on October 5, 1900 but moved to Jacksonville at the age of six where he was raised. He moved to Dade County at the age of nineteen and within three years opened the Philbrick Mortuary. Philbrick became associated with a number of Miami firsts: he operated the first ambulance hearse service; first handicap ramp; first dial-a-prayer; and the first air conditioned funeral parlor in the south. The killing hurricane of 1926 was an exceptionally busy and burdensome time for Philbrick. The W. L. Philbrick Funeral Parlor came to nationwide attention when he embalmed one of his most infamous patients, Al Capone.

As a civic leader, Philbrick served as a Coral Gables City Commissioner. His was a vocal and emphatic voice in support of the city citizens. Stories are told of Philbrick dumping garbage in front of his fellow commissioners in protest of a garbage rate hike; he rode his bicycle up and down the City Hall corridors in support of city bike paths; and once was taken by police from the commission chambers when he refused to stop speaking.

The Merrick Manor Foundation donated the Coral Gables house to the public in 1976 for use as a historic museum and park. Today the one and a half acre site is open during daylight hours, representatives conduct tours through the house on Wednesdays and Sundays. The Coral Gables house has been restored as it might have appeared in the mid 1920s, furnishing of the period adorn the home. A small admission fee is charged to continue to support the care and maintenance of this valuable historic site.

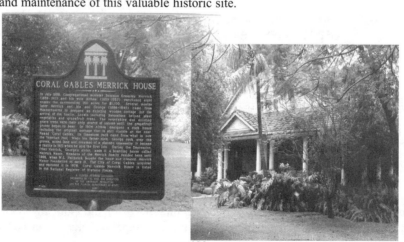

MERRICK HOUSE HISTORIC MARKER

CORAL GABLES HOUSE

VENETIAN POOL

This pool was originally a quarry from which limestone was taken for the construction of early Coral Gables homes. In 1924, Denman Fink, artist-architect and uncle of Coral Gables founder George Merrick, transformed it into a unique pool resembling a natural lagoon in a Venetian setting. His design included bridges, towers, a casino and lush landscaping.

In the 1920s, the pool was used to promote Coral Gables and to highlight the city's distinctive architecture. William Jennings Bryan lectured here on the merits of living in Coral Gables, Jan Garber, Paul Whiteman, and their orchestras played for social functions. Annette Kellerman and Jackie Ott, "the aqua tot," were among the famous visiting swimmers. The pool was drained in 1926 for a performance in the basin by the Miami Grand Opera Company.

George Merrick's Coral Gables Corporation sold Venetian Pool to the City of Coral Gables in 1927.

2701 DeSoto Boulevard, Coral Gables
MD22 ~ GPS Coordinates: 25.746067, -80.273433

The Venetian Casino was the brainchild of Coral Gables founder George Merrick. He took advantage of the chasm left by harvesting the limestone from the site to turn it into a beautiful and eventually famous attraction. Merrick employed the talents of his artist-uncle Denman Fink and architect Phineas Paist to transform the scarred landscape into the dream Merrick had in his minds' eye. Construction was completed in 1924 and the facilities were opened to visitors.

Inspired by the canals of Venice, the featured pool is fed by underground artesian wells. The red terra cotta roof tiles enhance buildings lending a Spanish flavor. Lush tropical landscaped gardens, cascading waterfalls, a hidden mystical grotto and a magnificent solid rock diving platform high above the aqua blue waters below complete a picture of opulence. Swooning couples enjoyed the Venice experience in gondolas that once silently navigated beneath the romantic stone bridge leading across the man-made waterway to an island shaded with large palms swaying in the semi-tropical breeze of south Florida.

The Venetian Pool has attracted many celebrities and dignitaries over the years including famed bathing beauty movie actress Esther Williams and Johnny Weismuller of Tarzan fame. The pool was actually drained in 1926 to accommodate a command performance by the Miami Grand Opera Company in the basin, while the orchestras of notables Paul Whitman and Jan Garber entertained poolside for dancers as they swirled beneath the star filled sky on the outdoor terrazzo dance floor. Celebrities also include noted synchronized swimmer and creator of the modern one-piece bathing suit, Annette Killerman. Child star Jackie Ott, coming to popularity as the aqua tot, performed exciting eighty-five foot dives at the Venetian Pool. William Jennings Bryan would often conduct campaign speeches during his three runs as the Democratic Presidential nominee.

The Venetian Pool, as it is called today, remains the enchanting spectacle of George Merrick's dreams. In 1927, the facilities were sold to the City of Coral Gables. Even now the attraction is a one of a kind experience, offering splendor to more than one hundred thousand visitors last year.

For many years the pool was drained nightly during the active summer months allowing the artesian spring to refill eight hundred thousand gallons of water as the night passed. Due to the ever-multiplying area population the aquifer was affected, therefore it became necessary to find a modernized method of water purification.

In 1988 a natural underground filtration system was developed in order to recycle the water, allowing the water to be changed daily without affecting the natural resources.

A full historical restoration was completed throughout the complex in 1989. Today the site is as beautiful and alluring as the day it opened in 1924. The facilities are opened seven days per week during the summer months and Tuesday through Sunday for the remainder of the year. A modest admission fee is charged. The facilities are available for private parties and they continuously offer special events, classes and programs. The Venetian Pool is perhaps the only facility of its kind to be listed on the National Register of Historic Places. It is truly a sight to be seen the beauty of George Merrick's Venetian Pool will take your breath away!

**THE BEAUTIFUL
VENETIAN POOL**

GEORGE EDGAR MERRICK
1886-1942

Dreamer, writer, poet, philosopher, lover of the beautiful – He made his dream become a reality in the creation of Coral Gables, City Beautiful. Dade County Commissioner from 1914 to 1916, he advocated and promoted good highways and transportation.

He founded the University of Miami and gave land and money to establish it.

He was a founder of the Historical Association of Southern Florida and was its first President. He was a Director of Fairchild Tropical Garden and a Trustee of Plymouth Congregational Church. He was Miami Postmaster from 1940 until his death.

dream city of Coral Gables, whose first streets were laid in 1921, is a monument to him.

**Front of City Hall in Merrick Circle, 405 Biltmore Way, Coral Gables
MD23 ~ GPS Coordinates: 25.748850, -80.263167**

George Edgar, son of Reverend Solomon and Althea Merrick, came to Coral Gables at the age of eleven.

First with his father, the young man sold produce from the back of a mule drawn wagon to the wealthy patrons of Henry Flagler's Royal Palm Hotel in Palm Beach. Educated at home by his professor mother, George was enamored with poetry, writing, romantic castles of Spain, Mediterranean architecture as well as great European master artists. He spent time apprenticing with two uncles studying illustration and architectural design. His father felt the boy needed a much more practical vocation so when George came to age he was sent off to law school. While he was away at school south Florida began to grow rapidly, especially Miami.

Solomon Merrick passed away in 1911 and George was called home to handle the family business. He had an adept business sense, therefore under his care the Coral Gables plantation flourished. As his notoriety in the community grew, so did George's vision for a city designed with a Mediterranean architectural flare filled with plazas, esplanades and fountains. In 1914, George Merrick was elected a Dade County Commissioner where he advocated the building of highways and transportation conveyances.

George began buying large quantities of property in an effort to realize his dream city. He married the daughter of Coconut Grove hotel owners Charles and Isabella Peacock. Eunice and George settled in a coral rock home designed by his uncle, H. George Fink. By 1921 George had accumulated approximately three thousand acres of land. Things were falling in place for the development of his envisioned community, which unlike Flagler was meant for people of simple means and middle income rather than an elaborate playground for the rich.

The first lots of Merrick's "American Riviera" were sold in 1921 and the first streets were mapped out. Wonderful designs for the opulent civic buildings, both grand and modest residences, schools and churches were planned and built. The Mediterranean aura began to take shape and on November 14, 1921 the first real estate advertisement appeared stating:

" ... the building of Coral Gables... a monument to the achievement of worthwhile perseverance
in the creation of beauty and the bringing true of dreams."

A Venice-like system of canals was dredged throughout the city lending a bayside view to all residents. Magnificent city gates declaring "Coral Gables: Miami's Riviera" welcomed residents and guests. Merrick hired William Jennings Bryan, United States Secretary of State and three time democratic presidential candidate, at the rate of one hundred thousand dollars per year to sell Coral Gables real estate.

Attention to detail down to city lampposts and decorative signs made George Merrick's dream a beautiful reality. In 1925, the city was incorporated having more than six hundred homes, sixty-five miles of paved streets and eighty miles of concrete sidewalks. Over the brief span of four years, seven million dollars worth of real estate was sold thus gestation had ended and the city of Coral Gables was born.

The city has architecture representing more than forty-five countries with consulates and foreign offices for each. International traders and banks from around the world continue to operate in the small bedroom community. Merrick's love for exotic cultures are evident along the roadways, in the structures and at the city gates. Italian style graceful gondolas slipped along the bay with fully costumed gondoliers at the pole. A sugar sand beach with palm thatched gazebos left a tropical feel of Fiji or Tahiti.

The mid 1920s brought the biggest population boom in Florida's history. People flocked to the semi-tropical warmth of south Florida where even the coolest days were balmy to the northern travelers. Answering the need for pleasing accommodations, the Biltmore Hotel was constructed. Following Merrick's lead, Leonard Schultze and S. Fullerton Weaver designed features of the hotel to emulate the Giralda tower of the Cathedral of Seville, Spain. The four hundred-room resort was built in an amazing ten months opening with a flare in January 1926. Wondrously the Biltmore appears today much the same as it did the day those opulent double doors were thrown open for visitors the very first time.

George Merrick also established the University of Miami at Coral Gables in an attempt to provide higher education for the middle income families living in the city of dreams. The concept was embraced by many wealthy individuals as well as the academic community, establishing a healthy endowment and building fund. As building plans were made and the first corner stone placed with great ceremony. Great trouble also loomed ominously on the horizon.

Merrick was very prominent in the Coral Gables community and as its founder he created the Historical Association of Southern Florida and served as the first president of the organization. His love of beauty blossomed as the Director of the famed Fairchild Tropical Garden. Following his father's lead, George maintained ecclesiastical ties as a Trustee of Plymouth Congregational Church.

By 1926 sales of real estate in Coral Gables began to wane, therefore Merrick had to come up with an inventive project to revive the loss in commerce. He conceived of a seventy-five million-dollar housing development, the largest in Florida history, creating fourteen villages representing various international countries. He joined with the American Building Company and former Ohio Governor Myers Cooper to attract property buyers. The project was ill fated from the beginning.

The killing hurricane of 1928 brought devastation across south Florida including the beautiful city of Coral Gables. Like a boxer's one-two punch, the great American depression felled the final blow to the population growth, real estate markets and prosperity. George Merrick sunk heavily in debt and was disgracefully forced out of the Coral Gables City Commission. He silently faded away to Matecumbe Key to property left to his wife, Eunice, by her parents. He was reduced to managing a resort.

Within five years George rebuilt his real estate business to become one of the largest firms in the state. He was never able to reach the pinnacle he had once held or recover his wealth, but eventually returned home to his beloved city. In 1940, he was appointed postmaster for Dade County. George Edgar Merrick passed away in 1942.

Coral Gables is a living monument to the life and dreams of George Merrick. The city is as beautiful today as the image George envisioned and built. Ordinances are in place to preserve the historical significance of the city and maintain the exotic Mediterranean feel of its original intent. Eunice Merrick was interviewed in 1962 and said the following of her husband's glorious Coral Gables:

"His original plan for the Gables was to be a botanical garden with flowering trees at all times."

These plans were truly realized, Coral Gables blooms bright year round.

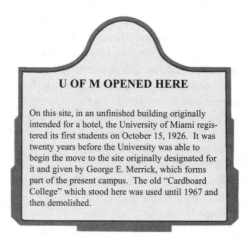

U OF M OPENED HERE

On this site, in an unfinished building originally intended for a hotel, the University of Miami registered its first students on October 15, 1926. It was twenty years before the University was able to begin the move to the site originally designated for it and given by George E. Merrick, which forms part of the present campus. The old "Cardboard College" which stood here was used until 1967 and then demolished.

University Court & University Drive, at Baseball field of Youth Center, Coral Gables
MD24 ~ GPS Coordinates: 25.740583, -80.264900

First created in 1925, the University of Miami was founded and supported by George Edgar Merrick as well as others who felt the need for an institution of higher learning in south Florida. During the population explosion funds were easily obtained, however the American depression and the deadly hurricane of 1926 virtually brought the process to a halt but the University fought to survive.

Five hundred sixty students matriculated the fall of 1926 regardless of the hardships the institution experienced. Primarily the school offered classes in Liberal Arts, a School of Music and general evening studies. Over the next decade and a half the University barely managed to keep its head above water. It was the perseverance and vision of the University of Miami's first president, Dr. Bowman F. Ashe who managed to maintain the facility in spite of the hardships. Dr. Ashe instituted Schools of Law, Business Administration, Education, Graduate Studies, Engineering and Medicine as well as the Marine Laboratory, today known as the Rosenstiel School of Marine and Atmospheric Science.

Under the leadership of second university President Dr. Jay F. W. Pearson enrollment exploded to over ten thousand students and half again that number by the end of his tenure. In order to stay in step with the expanding student body additional facilities, faculty and programs were added to the already state of the art institution. Research was the administration emphasis for third President Dr. Henry King Stanford. The Center for Advanced International Studies, Institute of Molecular and Cellular Evolution, the Center for Theoretical Studies and the Institute for the Study of Aging were all created during Dr. Stanford's term of office. Fourth President Edward T. Foote II created three new schools including Architecture, Communication and the Graduate School of International Studies. During this time dormitories were renovated to incorporate a system of residential colleges.

Today Donna E. Shalala administers the university as its fifth president. Shalala brings a wealth of experience and vision to the challenging position. She served as the first woman Chancellor of a Big Ten University at the University of Wisconsin, then leading Hunter College, The City University of New York. President Shalala went on to be selected as Secretary of Health and Human Services, holding the position longer than anyone in United States history. She worked with President Bill Clinton during his administration managing a budget of more than six hundred billion dollars. The University of Miami is certainly fortunate to benefit from the vast wisdom brought by Donna E. Shalala.

THE ACTUAL MARKER

The first football team in 1927 was in search of a name, that much we know for sure, how the name Hurricanes actually came to be is a subject of some mysteries. There are two schools of thought involving the name: the first, it is believed that the team was named for the killing hurricane of September 16, 1926 in hopes that the players would blow away the competition in much the same way of the storm; the second story involved Miami News columnist Jack Bell who asked player Porter Norris in 1926 what the team was to be called. Norris replied that university staff intended to name the team for a local flower, Jack Bell responded that the players would never stand for a sweet smelling name and suggested the use of "Hurricanes" in deference to a storm which delayed the play of the first school game.

Colors for the University of Miami were chosen from a likely source, the Florida orange tree. Orange, of course, represents the juicy citrus, green for the foliage and white for the fragrant white flowers. Certainly fitting color selections based on the fruit that is representative of the state. Another meaningful object of the University of Miami is the War Canoe Trophy. The canoe was carved from a two hundred-year-old Everglade cypress tree taken down by a burst of lightning. The Seminole Indians decorated the canoe and donated the vessel to the city of Hollywood for use during the annual grudge match between the Hurricanes and the Gators.

Today the University of Miami remains privately supported and has in excess of fifteen thousand students having one hundred fifty undergraduate degrees, one hundred thirty masters programs, sixty doctoral specialties and two professional areas of study. Classes are a mix of domestic students from each and every state in the union as well as one hundred ten foreign countries. The school Alma Mater seems to sum up the feeling for south Florida as well as the honor and pride so evident for the University of Miami:

Alma Mater
Southern suns and sky blue water,
Smile upon you Alma mater;
Mistress of this fruitful land,
With all knowledge at your hand,
Always just to honor true,
All our love we pledge to you.
Alma Mater, stand forever
On Biscayne's wondrous shore.

DINNER KEY

Picnickers in sailboat days gave the key its name. In World War I, it was a Naval air base. In 1930, Pan American World Airways here inaugurated flying boat service to Latin America, erecting huge hangars and a terminal. The U.S. Government dredged first channel in history especially for aircraft. Over 100,000 visitors a month came to see the giant Flying Clippers. Coast Guard established seaplane base in 1932. In World War II, Navy and Pan American operated flying boats here until Latin American airports built for hemispheric defense enabled use of more economical land-planes. City of Miami purchased key in 1946.

3500 Pan American Drive, In front of City Hall, Dinner Key, Coconut Grove
MD25 ~ GPS Coordinates: 25.728017, -80.234183

In the midst of Biscayne Bay is a small island that was bridged to the mainland during the United States involvement in World War I. The Navy utilized the island as a training base. The landing field continued to be used for non-scheduled commercial flights after the war's end. The devastating hurricane of 1926 completely destroyed the airstrip.

A newly founded airline called Pan American Airways purchased the New York to Rio to Buenos Aires Airline in 1930 and began flying twin engine Commodore planes known as flying boats from Miami to Buenos Aires and return. Pan American also purchased the former naval base at Biscayne Bay and it was from there on December 1, 1930 that their first flight was initiated. Famed aviator Charles Lindbergh was a technical advisor for Pan American and it was these "flying boats," which established an essential connection from North to South America.

Pan American purchased a Cuban houseboat for use as its first passenger terminal. Anchored to pilings and barges, the houseboat seaplane base was the first of its kind. The first plane hangar was built and opened in 1931. Additional facilities were added including filler brought in to expand the land space as well as approval by the Congressional Rivers and Harbors Committee to dredge a deeper channel in order to accommodate larger sea going aircraft. Families began to gather along the banks of Biscayne Bay bringing with them little picnics as they watched seaplanes arrive and depart. From this time on the island was dubbed Dinner Key.

During this grand time of expansion a two storied terminal building was constructed. The stark white stucco structure was rectangular with single story "wings" on either side. The building features decorative moldings surrounding the crest of the building having winged globes, rising suns and adorned with magnificent eagles at each corner. Inside, in addition to the normal waiting areas, restaurant, lounge, customs and ticket counters, was an immigration office, international post office and office of public health. The corridor featured a massive three and a half-ton revolving world sphere. The magnificent globe attracted throngs of tourists and travelers to view the sight.

During World War II, the United States Navy bringing with it the Coast Guard returned to Dinner Key. Pan American continued to serve the needs of international travelers from the Biscayne Bay sight. As landing strips began to be established in Latin America, the call for seaplanes diminished. Again at the end of World War II, the Navy and Coast Guard abandoned the Key. The final flight arrived at Biscayne Bay's Dinner Key on August 9, 1945.

The City of Miami purchased the abandoned Dinner Key in 1946, however it was almost ten years before the sight was put to use. In 1954 the former Pan American terminal was renovated to become the Miami City Hall. During more recent remodeling artistic scenes of the zodiac were completed as murals throughout the facility as well as the Da Vinci's history of flight along the cornice depicted in terms of the seaplanes used during the days of Pan American at Dinner Key.

HOUSEKEEPERS CLUB

On Thursday afternoon, February 19, 1891, Flora McFarlane and five other pioneer women of Dade County founded the Housekeepers Club, the first organized women's club in South Florida. The purpose was to bring the housekeepers of the area together for companionship. The club's first project was to raise money for a new Sunday school building. Miss McFarlane was elected president and dues were set at 40 cents a year.

The Housekeepers Club met in the schoolhouse and later at Union Chapel before 1897. In that year the group built its own wooden clubhouse on property donated by Ralph M. Munroe. The present building of pine, masonry and native rock was constructed in 1921. At each location the club maintained its active involvement in the civic, social and cultural aspect of the community. On March 17, 1957, the Housekeepers Club became the Woman's Club of Coconut Grove. Chartered by the State of Florida in 1970, the club is federated with the General, Florida, and Dade County Federations of Women's Clubs.

South Bayshore Drive & McFarlane Road, Coconut Grove
MD26 ~ GPS Coordinates: 25.726683, -80.239867

Together with five others, Flora McFarlane founded the first club for women in south Florida on February 19, 1891, known as the Housekeepers Club. The club existed to serve civic, social and cultural needs of the ever-growing Miami bedroom community. Because of the meticulous minutes of this club, the history of it as well as the Coconut Grove community is miraculously complete. McFarlane was selected as the organizations first president and it was decided that the first project would involve building a new Sunday School facility for the Union Chapel. Dues were set at forty cents annually and fund raising began.

Originally meeting in the local schoolhouse, by 1897 meetings were held at Union Chapel until their own clubhouse could be completed. Ralph M. Munroe donated the sight for a clubhouse. The address is known today as 2985 South Bayshore Drive where the Housekeepers Clubhouse was built. Architect Walter C. DeGarmo designed the pine, masonry oolitic limestone structure completed in 1921. A twelve-foot porch on three sides embraced the lovely clubhouse from which a magnificent view of Biscayne Bay could be enjoyed.

The largest annual fund raising event for the Housekeepers Club each year involved the historical pageantry staged beneath the stars to entertain the community. Prosperous Coconut Grove citizens were enlisted to act in various plays depicting the early days of Florida's founding fathers. Later other performances of "A Tour of the Orient" and "A Trip Around the World," were offered. Audiences were forced to imagine curtain drops, set changes and the portable stage. However, the setting beneath the clear starry skies across the ebony heavens lending an air of romance for bundled couples in the audiences.

Noted politicians and real estate salesmen working with George Merrick enthusiastically supported the Housekeepers Club pageantry. Largely due to Merrick's participation many civic, fraternal organizations and clubs joined the productions in various capacities from acting to building sets as well as other behind the scenes motivation and donating funds to ensure the continued success of the Housekeeper's Club mission.

The pageants gained such a following that the Coconut Grove mayor proclaimed a local holiday to be held each year when the play was first released. This proclamation allowed everyone from the local grocer to schoolchildren to attend the performances.

The Housekeepers Club evolved into the Woman's Club of Coconut Grove on March 17, 1957. The State of Florida bestowed a charter on the new Woman's Club in the 1970s and with that honor came national recognition as the Dade County Federation of Women's Clubs.

The lovely 1921 clubhouse still stands as the headquarters for Florida's oldest women's clubs. In 1975 the building was listed on the National Register of Historic Places. Walking about the property is in itself a beautiful stroll, take a moment and soak in the feeling of history all about you.

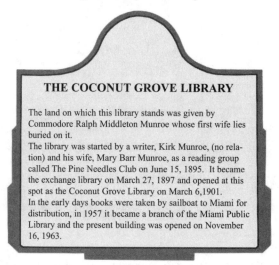

THE COCONUT GROVE LIBRARY

The land on which this library stands was given by Commodore Ralph Middleton Munroe whose first wife lies buried on it.

The library was started by a writer, Kirk Munroe, (no relation) and his wife, Mary Barr Munroe, as a reading group called The Pine Needles Club on June 15, 1895. It became the exchange library on March 27, 1897 and opened at this spot as the Coconut Grove Library on March 6, 1901.

In the early days books were taken by sailboat to Miami for distribution, in 1957 it became a branch of the Miami Public Library and the present building was opened on November 16, 1963.

2875 McFarlane Road, Coconut Grove
MD27 ~ GPS Coordinates: 25.726750, -80.240550

Commodore Ralph Middleton Munroe built his home called the Barnacle just south of what is today Miami in 1891. The city of Miami was then known as Fort Dallas from which the Commodore worked as a wrecker. A bit of a pirates' vocation, Munroe profited from the misery of others as he salvaged goods from ships broken apart along the coral reefs from Key Biscayne to Key Largo.

When his first wife Amelia passed away on April 2, 1882, she was buried on the northern banks of the Miami River. Munroe generously donated property in her honor to become the first Coconut Grove library with the stipulation that a grave site for Amelia always be maintained there. Amelia Munroe was moved to lie near the library.

Ironically the library was created by a couple of the same name, though of no relation of the Commodore, Kirk and Mary Barr Munroe. The concept began with a reading group the couple founded called the Pine Needles Club on June 15, 1895. Both individuals, especially Mary, were instrumental in founding the Coconut Grove Library.

Kirk Munroe was born at Prairie du Chien, Wisconsin in 1850 and grew up to be an adventurer and author. Munroe wrote of his adventures in books directed toward children. He traveled across the western United States writing railroad adventures and eventually moved to Florida where he described the mysteries of the Everglades and wildlife living there.

Mary Barr and Kirk Munroe were married on September 15, 1883. The couple honeymooned on a three-month cruise from St. Augustine to Lake Worth, their first exposure to south Florida. While on one of his adventures just a few years later, the couple traveled along Florida's coral reef ending at Biscayne Bay where they felt that they had come home. The Munroe's bought property at Coconut Grove and built their home called Scrububs.

Mary Barr Munroe embraced Florida as if she had lived there her entire life. She aggressively fought to save the plume birds being poached for their beautiful feathers used as couture adornment. She founded the Southern Tropical Audubon Society and as a member of the Florida Federation of Women's Clubs, she actively participated in the creation of Royal Palm Park today known as Everglades National Park. Mary was a regular at the Coconut Grove Library where she taught children to read. The library became a part of the book exchange program on March 27, 1897 and officially opened as an independent library on March 6, 1901.

Mary believed that women could make a difference in the world, she certainly did. In an article published by The Tropic Magazine of Miami appearing in 1915, she came out strongly berating those who poached, wore or sold plumes from the egrets of the Everglades, stating:

"It seems incredible that to-day there should be in the United States any person able to read who is not aware of the fact that the 'aigrette' is the nuptial plume worn by the egret and snowy heron at the nesting time of the year, by both parents, and that to procure them it is necessary to shoot the birds, which means that the young are left to slowly die of starvation. After a few more years of such reckless slaughter during the breeding season the egret and snowy heron will be classed among the extinct birds of the country."

Lucy Worthington Blackman described Mary Munroe's diatribe when she encountered women wearing the feathers of the slain birds:

"Wheresoe'er Mrs. Munroe's keen eye saw an aigrette waving, there she followed, and cornering the wearer — be it on the street, in the crowded hotel lobby, on the beach, at church or entertainment or party — there compelled her (the lady) to listen to the story of cruelty and murder of which her vanity was the contributing cause."

Mary Barr Munroe passed away in 1922 and was buried at Woodlawn Park Cemetery in Miami. Eight years later her husband, Kirk Munroe, was laid by her side.

Books were first delivered by sailboat from Miami to Coconut Grove and in 1957 it became a branch of the Miami Public Library system. A new facility was built there, dedicated on November 16, 1963. At 2875 McFarlane Road, the Coconut Grove Library celebrated its centennial anniversary. The facility has a magnificent view of Biscayne Bay including a wing replicating the original library constructed in 1901. On permanent display is a memorial to Midshipman Julian Bishop, Class of 1912, United States Naval Academy. The display depicts a unique depiction of Sea Life. The Coconut Grove Library is opened Monday through Saturday with the exception of Friday.

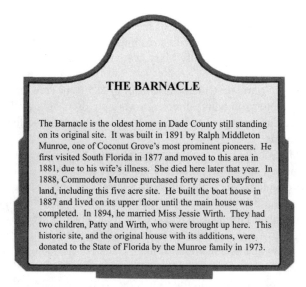

THE BARNACLE

The Barnacle is the oldest home in Dade County still standing on its original site. It was built in 1891 by Ralph Middleton Munroe, one of Coconut Grove's most prominent pioneers. He first visited South Florida in 1877 and moved to this area in 1881, due to his wife's illness. She died here later that year. In 1888, Commodore Munroe purchased forty acres of bayfront land, including this five acre site. He built the boat house in 1887 and lived on its upper floor until the main house was completed. In 1894, he married Miss Jessie Wirth. They had two children, Patty and Wirth, who were brought up here. This historic site, and the original house with its additions, were donated to the State of Florida by the Munroe family in 1973.

3485 Main Highway, in front of the Barnacle State Park, Coconut Grove
MD28 ~ GPS Coordinates: 25.726567, -80.243850

Ralph Middleton Munroe got his first taste of sunny south Florida in 1877 while escaping the cold of his New York home. Several years later a grim diagnosis would bring Munroe back to Florida though this trip was heartbreaking. Amelia Munroe, his wife, and her sister Adeline were given a death sentence unless they moved away from the frigid winters of the north. Munroe immediately thought of Biscayne Bay.

Unfortunately it was too late for Amelia, she passed away of tuberculosis before they arrived at Biscayne Bay. He buried her along the northern banks of the Miami River and later moved her to property he had donated for the construction of the first Coconut Grove Library. Her sister also died during the trip. Once Munroe arrived back in New York he was given the sad news that his baby daughter had also passed away

In 1882 having nothing left to keep him in New York, Munroe returned to Biscayne Bay in order to assist the Peacock family in opening their Bay View Villas. Later the hotel was renamed the Peacock Inn, unfortunately the stately hotel eventually burned. He purchased forty acres of bayfront property and built a boathouse, which was completed within a year. Munroe lived on the upper floor and he housed his sailboat, the *Kingfish*, below. He eventually closed in the lower floor, moved the sailboat to a dock and completed construction on his main house. The main room was built in an octagonal shape, Munroe dubbed the manor "Barnacle." It remained a small living space until his second marriage and subsequent children required additional footage. The entire structure was lifted and new first floor was insert below. Renovation was completed in 1908. Fortunately neither the deadly hurricane of 1926 nor ferocious hurricane Andrew in 1992 had a major impact on the Barnacle.

Ralph Munroe's passion in life was designing magnificent yachts and in 1887, he along with others in the community founded the Biscayne Bay Yacht Company conveying on him the title Commodore, which followed him for the remainder of his life. Over his life span, Munroe was very proud of the fifty-six yachts he created.

Only one replica of Munroe's life's work remains the *Egret*, the last of the original designs to withstand rough seas, fierce storms and even one of the deadliest hurricanes in history that of 1928. However, hurricane Andrew left the one hundred one-year-old *Micco* in a heap of hardwood splinters.

Ralph began a new life in 1894 when he met and married Jessie Wirth. The couple had two children, Patty and Wirth. The family spent much of their free time sailing the waters of Biscayne Bay. The children were avid sailors at a very young age. Ralph Munroe took to wrecking, as if a pirate collecting booty though it was said that his endeavors were always honorable. He often contracted with insurance underwriters and/or owners to recover lost goods, taking the going rate as his fee.

Today the tropical hardwood hammock is much like it was found by Ralph Munroe in the 1920s. He was determined to preserve as much of the local flora and fauna as possible, Munroe only allowed one road barely wide enough to take a horse drawn buggy. Commodore Ralph Middleton Munroe was a historian, naturalist and avid photographer bent on keeping Florida or at least his little corner of it, as natural as possible.

Today Commodore Munroe's home is the Barnacle Historic State Park. The park is open year round. Scheduled guided tours are conducted Friday through Monday and by reservation the remainder of the week. A modest admission fee is charged, which also covers the tour. Special events are held throughout the year and numerous activities are available including camping, swimming, scuba diving, fishing, boating, boat tours and picnicking. Trails wind around the park for nature observation, bicycling and horseback riding. Of course, don't miss the beautiful beach. Commodore Ralph Middleton Munroe would be proud of the park that has been created from his wonderful home, the Barnacle.

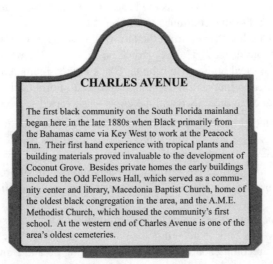

CHARLES AVENUE

The first black community on the South Florida mainland began here in the late 1880s when Black primarily from the Bahamas came via Key West to work at the Peacock Inn. Their first hand experience with tropical plants and building materials proved invaluable to the development of Coconut Grove. Besides private homes the early buildings included the Odd Fellows Hall, which served as a community center and library, Macedonia Baptist Church, home of the oldest black congregation in the area, and the A.M.E. Methodist Church, which housed the community's first school. At the western end of Charles Avenue is one of the area's oldest cemeteries.

Main Highway and Charles Avenue, Coconut Grove
MD29 ~ GPS Coordinates: 25.725750, -80.245250

Like the rest of America, a thick ugly line called segregation divided Cocoanut Grove[5]. One side of town was known as "Colored Town" and the other "White Town". Each was a community of its own catering to their own people, as prejudice demanded. Markets, restaurants, churches and all the services that make up a town were represented mirrored on each side of that heinous barrier of discrimination.

A great number of the inhabitants of "Colored Town" were immigrants from the Bahamas who settled in Coconut Grove. These people worked as cooks, housekeepers, bellhops and gardeners as well as other service positions at the nearby Peacock Inn. As time passed they opened businesses such as the Wallace family, serving the best barbecue in town; the Dew Drop Inn, a soda shop where the youth gathered to socialize; the Cash family store, which was the town's first mini-mall a poolroom on one side, a grocery store and sewing shop on the other end. The Cash family lived in a small apartment above their business.

Times changed and "Colored Town" became West Coconut Grove. The neighborhood became a concrete jungle with wall to wall multi-storied apartment buildings, each appearing the same as the next. The high-rises were owned by far away investors and ran by managers who could do little to improve conditions, as the buildings needed repairs or refurbishment. Those black families whose circumstances prospered moved to other neighborhoods to escape the decline of West Coconut Grove. As time passed the disgraceful blight of crime and drugs crept into the once proud suburb.

Segregation of the races has long since been abolished but still there is an invisible line of separation between the haves and have-nots. Nearly half of those that reside in West Coconut Grove live below what is considered the poverty level. Vacant buildings become a haven for the down trodden of society and overgrown lots littered with the refuse of the ambivalent scar the landscaping. But things they are a-changing.

A program called Initiative for Urban and Social Ecology (INUSE) has been developed by the University of Miami in an attempt to improve the living conditions and quality of life in West Coconut Grove. Every department of the university is involved in the project. Individual programs involve everything from design and refurbishment of dilapidated buildings, improvement of health care, child development, legal aid and assistance in starting and maintaining business within the community. The ultimate goal is to not only to improve the community but the encourage residents to fight against the forces that would drag down the society. The drive is to have citizens remain in the community, what was once flourishing suburbia is now becoming again a shining example of a culture that can be saved when the residents band together for one incredible goal.

A number of buildings that have over time shaped the history of Coconut Grove can be found like a time line along Charles Avenue. It was this area that was the heart of the black community. Through tragedy and triumph, growth and decline, Coconut Grove continues to survive.

The hub of society on Charles Avenue from the late 1800s was Odd Fellows Hall. People gathered there in fellowship for town meetings and dances. Tragedy struck on July 15, 1917 when a group of white supremacists used explosives to reduce the historical building to rubble. Black citizens gathered in justified anger ready to stage a mass riot that could have resulted in innocent lives being sacrificed. Fortunately the cooler head of both black and white clergymen managed to calm the crowd and the crisis was averted.

Union Chapel[6] was founded in 1891, but due to a difference of opinion involving the style of worship, the church split in 1895. Reverend S. A. Sampson and fifty-six other members began ecclesiastical meetings in the parlor of Mrs. Edith Albury's home. The congregation called themselves the Fifty-six Baptist Church in reference to the founding membership. Count Jean D'Hedouille graciously gave a gift of property to the congregation for the construction of a sanctuary on Thomas Avenue. When construction of the edifice was completed, it was celebrated as St. Agnes.

The Thomas Avenue location of St. Agnes Church gradually became too small as the congregation flourished. In 1903, a new sanctuary was built to accommodate the ever growing church. The name was changed once again on May 25, 1922 upon the recommendation of Deacons Washington and Bumey to the designate used today, Macedonia Missionary Baptist Church. Finally in June of 1948 the congregation moved to the site where it can be found today, the intersection of Main Highway and Charles Avenue, twenty-eight years later the church was incorporated as a non-profit organization. Unfortunately hurricane Andrew left the sanctuary with a great deal of damage, however, like the phoenix risen from the ashes, Macedonia rebuilt to its original glorious splendor. Macedonia Missionary Baptist Church holds the distinction of being the first church founded by blacks in all of south Florida.

Coconut Grove pioneer Ebenezer Woodrow Franklin Stirrup purchased property that comprises most of the city today. He also owned Charlotte Jane Memorial Park cemetery. Stirrup built a home directly across the way from what would later be the address of Macedonia Missionary Baptist Church in 1897. E. W. F. Stirrup, as he was commonly known, secured his families' future by stipulating in his will that his home must never be sold, but be available to any member of the family that needed a place to live. His granddaughter, Dazelle Dean Simpson, obviously received much more than a place to grow up but also inherited his pioneering spirit. Dr. Simpson was Florida's first board certified black pediatrician, not to mention that she was also a woman, which was an amazing feat in and of itself.

Constructed in 1890 of virgin pine hard wood, the Mariah Brown house was built at 3298 Charles Avenue. Mariah and Ernest Brown left Eleuthera, Bahamas bound for Coconut Grove. The home was the first erected in Coconut Grove but unfortunately time and the elements took their toll and the home was torn down in 1999. The house has been replicated as it appeared in 1890 at its original Charles Avenue site. Charles Avenue continues to benefit from the University of Miami's INUSE program, blossoming into a new revitalized community. The citizens have fought the good fight to retake their society from forces that would drag it down. Coconut Grove has now become a pleasant place to visit and for those that live there a safe and comfortable atmosphere to call home.

Ransom School

In 1896 Paul C. Ransom first brought students from an eastern preparatory school to this site, which he named Pine Knot Camp for a winter term of study and outdoor life. In 1903 it became the Adirondack-Florida School with the Fall and Spring terms in the Adirondacks and the Winter term in Coconut Grove. Closed in 1942 because of the war it was reopened in 1947, in 1949 the Trustees located the school here permanently and named it Ransom for the founder.

The "Pagoda," the first major building was completed in 1902 designed by Green and Wicks Architects of Buffalo, N.Y. The large two-story building of durable Dade County pine remains unchanged except for minor interior alterations. It continues as an integral part of the campus and includes a museum in which the story of the school is on exhibit. The historical importance of the "Pagoda" won for it a place on the National Register of Historic Places in 1973.

Ransom-Everglades School, Coconut Grove
MD30 ~ GPS Coordinates: 25.724283, -80.245583

Paul C. Ransom established the first all-male migratory boarding school in 1896. During the spring and fall months classes were held at Meenagha Lodge in the Adirondack Mountains of New York then while the brutal winter covered the northern state with ice and snow, classes migrated south to the Pine Knot Camp in Florida. Paul Ransom's background as an attorney and lawyer served him well, the preparatory school was very successful.

Noted Buffalo, New York architects, Green and Wicks designed the first educational building of the Coconut Grove campus in 1902. Called the Pagoda, the two story native pine frame, board and batten sided building had a distinctive Chinese influence. The year was 1903, the school was an oasis in the wilderness of live oaks and mahogany hammocks where native panthers still roamed the forest.

As World War II loomed heavily on the horizon the school closed but reopened in 1949 as the war came to an end. The school trustees made a fateful decision to close the northern branch of the school and renamed the southern branch in honor of its founder, Ransom. The Ransom School remained a strictly male college preparatory school dedicated to providing each young man with the skills, academics, study habits and price to succeed in the university of his choice. However this is not where the education of these young men ends, they are also taught social skills, sportsmanship, responsibility and the gentlemanly conduct required to be valuable members of society.

Students are expected to participate in the governing processes of school policy. This provides experience in representative government, which may lend a basis for future endeavors of leadership. Classes are small for individualized education but concentration is also placed on outside activities as well. Ransom endeavors to graduate a well-rounded young man prepared for advanced education and taking his place as a vital member of his community, state and nation.

In 1955, Mr. and Mrs. Edward F. Swenson, Jr. founded the Everglades School for Girls. Established to be the "sister" school of the Ransom School. Everglades served young ladies in grades seven through twelve. Mrs. Swenson served as president of the Trustees and under her leadership the school proved its merit and academic standards above those normally found in public school facilities. Miss Gertrude Pierce was named Headmistress; it was through her guidance with the assistance of her outstanding faculty and staff that the students were held to the highest standards of education, deportment and grace.

During a time when women were fighting for equality in the world, the Everglades School for Girls taught not only academic excellence but also concentrated on individual achievement. Over the nineteen years of the girls schools existence honors were recognized in academics, fine arts, music and drama. The original Ransom "Pagoda" school was placed on the National Register of Historic Places in 1973. The Ransom and Everglades schools merged in 1974, combining two exemplary boarding schools to become one co-educational day school serving grades seven through twelve. Individualized education was still the emphasis, where each teacher was responsible for only eight students.

Through time each school had achieved a reputation as a superlative college preparatory school. Together they continued the excellence in education while still addressing each student's strength of character before embarking on the realities of society. Grade six was added in 1991 and a reorganization process began. Ransom Everglades Middle School was founded to address grades six through eight on the former Everglades campus. The Upper School attending grades nine through twelve was located at the former Ransom School campus.

In 2003, Ransom Everglades Schools celebrated its one hundredth anniversary. Today the schools continue to strive for academic excellence and a well rounded student body that its forerunners initiated including: The Adirondack-Florida School, founded in 1903; Ransom School for Boys, founded in 1946; and Everglades School for Girls, founded in 1955.

The Paul Ransom Cottage as well as the original two-storied educational building still stands on the Ransom Everglades campus. The cottage is only one of few remaining buildings left from the turn of the century era. Over the years it has served as the infirmary, headmasters' residence, meeting hall, housing for faculty and students, an art studio and band room. The cottage has now been completely renovated and opened for use in October 2001. Today student groups, alumni, parent associations and the Board of Trustees meet in the Paul Ransom Cottage.

The two-storied original educational building made of durable Florida pine remains much the same as the date it was built with only minor improvements of modernization. Today it houses a museum that provides a time-line of Ransom Everglades School's illustrious history. The school continues to prepare its students for collegiate education as well as life in society as upstanding members of their community.

```
COCOANUT GROVE
PUBLIC UTILITIES COMPANY

The Cocoanut Grove Public Utilities Company was established
in 1916 by William Matheson and his son Hugh to provide
local residents with telephone and water services. A ground
level storage tank, tilled from wells on the site by two diesel
engines, furnished water to the Grove until 1925 when a new
plant was built at 3575 S. LeJeune Road. The telephone fran-
chise, which began with only six customers, was serving near-
ly 300 subscribers in 1925 when it was purchased by Southern
Bell. The building adjacent to the storage tank housed the
telephone exchange and was occupied by the company super-
intendent from 1921 until 1935.
```

Hibiscus Street and Devon Road, Coconut Grove
MD31 ~ GPS Coordinates: 25.723400, -80.248733

Hugh Matheson was sent away to a boarding school at Pine Knot Camp[7], which was a migratory school that spent the cold winter months at Coconut Grove. His parent William J. and Harriet were vacationing at Henry Flagler's exclusive Ormond Beach Hotel to the north at Daytona Beach, when Hugh convinced his father to take the trip south for a visit to his eldest son. To ensure his father would make the trip Hugh sent a sailboat with the invitation south. Instead his father weighed anchor and sailed his yacht the *Laverock* to see Hugh.

William Matheson was enamored with the entire Key Biscayne and Coconut Grove area from the beginning. He returned less than a year later and began to purchase property, like so many of his peers, to build a home to escape the northern winters. His mansion was said to be the southern most estate in the United States, fifteen miles south of the Coconut Grove post office. The house was described as being perched on a rocky ridge with an expansive patio beyond a wide veranda supported by perfectly spaced columns. The view swept across an emerald green lawn adorned with coconut palms swaying in the light breeze from the bay just beyond. A wooden boat dock reached into the beautiful blue water as the sun added sparkles to the bay.

Miami's 1930 Social Register listed three homes for William J. Matheson; the summer address, a prestigious 540 Park Avenue, New York City overlooking the magnificent Central Park; his country residence of Fort Hill, Lloyd Neck of Long Island, New York where he went to retreat from the hustle and bustle of the city; and then there was 3645 Ingraham Highway, Coconut Grove, Florida where Matheson escaped the brutal northern winters. Oddly enough the Coconut Grove house was dubbed the Swastika Estate, which was the symbol in India for the sun. When World War II began the swastika came to symbolize the German Army, Hitler, murder, war and all the vile things associated with it, the name was no longer used for the Coconut Grove mansion. After his death, Matheson would bequeath the house to his youngest son Malcolm. The house, like Hitler's regime, was eventually demolished.

Matheson's contemporaries were like reading a who's who of American business and society. The ensuing years saw a gradual increase in wealthy northerners making the southern pilgrimage each year. The roll included Henry Flagler, who became the father of southern Florida's development through transportation and elegance, opened his Royal Palm Hotel in 1897 while planning to bring his railroad to the sea; David Fairchild of the famed Fairchild gardens first visited in 1898 and returned to realize his dream fourteen years later; James Deering, president and owner of International Harvester Company began building his magnificent "Viscaya" in 1914 and his brother Charles purchased the property that was to become the community of Cutler in 1915. Other winter retreat visitors and part-time residents included Carl Fisher, president of the Prest-o-Lite Company; Marshall Field, Chicago retail magnate; Andrew Carnegie, the world renown steel manufacturer; Arthur Curtis James dealing in copper and railroads; Charles Armour, president of Armour Meats; and Glenn Curtiss, famed aircraft builder.

Hugh, the eldest Matheson son, graduated from Yale University and immediately went to work for one his father's chemical companies. Meanwhile back at the south Florida estate his father began buying portions of the island Key Biscayne. The island was undeveloped with the exception of the old Cape Florida Lighthouse that was no longer in use. The only way to reach the island was by boat and of course there were no modern utilities.

William J. Matheson began clearing the island for planting limes, mangoes and avocados. Unfortunately, the salt mist rising from the Atlantic prohibited the trees from developing property and they never bore enough fruit to be commercially successful. Matheson spent much of his time in New York tending to his various businesses and never lived in Coconut Grove full time.

It is obvious that although William J. Matheson had a horrifying experience on an ocean voyage as a young man that he maintained an attraction to the ocean throughout his life. In 1912 he became the commodore of the Biscayne Bay Yacht Club and maintained the position until 1923. His tenure was the longest in club history with the exception of its founder Ralph Middleton Munroe. Matheson's close friend Arthur Curtis James, the second richest man in the world, was a frequent guest at the club with his infamous yacht the *Aloha*. During his time as Commodore all of the yachts were wind powered, comparatively today only five members have wind powered ships.

The chemical plant proved to be disastrous to Hugh Matheson. He was diagnosed with a potentially deadly disease referred to as Mad Hatters Disease, commonly known as lead poisoning. It was not uncommon for workers exposed to these conditions to succumb to this illness. Most of the workers were poor, had little or no access to medical treatment and died without ever knowing the cause. His physician prescribed fresh air and a warm, sunny climate. Coconut Grove filled the bill to a tee. Eventually the lead would systematically be eliminated from his body.

Two wonderful events would come from Hugh's move to south Florida. First, he would fall in love and marry his private nurse, Ligouri Hardy; secondly, his father would turn over management of all his Florida holdings to Hugh. In fact his father would do all the planning and foot the bill, but Hugh made everything happen. William purchased most of Key Biscayne and Hugh drained, filled, cut roads, created a yacht basin, planted groves, built cottages for workers and planted coconut palms by the thousands. Hugh created eighteen miles of unpaved roads on the island.

In 1909, William contracted the building of a Moorish style mansion as a weekend getaway home that he used primarily for entertaining. The house was called "Mashta" meaning home or resting spot by the sea. The palatial estate featured a huge ballroom and high domed ceilings, made especially for elegant parties.

During World War I, William J. Matheson turned his General Chemical company over in the service of the United States government. Matheson's chemical background, knowledge of patent law, industrial success and business sense made him a prime asset to the government against the enemy forces in Germany. When the war finally came to an end, Matheson's company was producing more than fifty tons of mustard gas every day in addition to tear gas and other deterrent chemicals.

William Matheson created, with the assistance of son Hugh, the Coconut Grove Public Utilities Company. A water storage tank filled by wells and pumped by two diesel engines provided water for the city until 1925 when a new water treatment plant was built. Telephone lines served six homes initially but by 1925 when Southern Bell purchased the communication business nearly three hundred had the telephone installed their homes.

In 1926, Miami and parts of Coconut Grove were devastated by a killer hurricane. The exact number will never be known for sure but more than one hundred seventeen Dade County citizens lost their lives to the atrocious storm. Key Biscayne was spared to a point. Thousands of coconut palms were mowed down and the lower level of Matheson's Mashta House was completely flooded. Restoration for Key Biscayne and Mashta was left to Hugh.

The American Institute of Park Executives approached William J. Matheson in September of 1929 with the prospect of purchasing what was called Matheson Hammock. William J. Matheson replied to the request by saying,

"I have been waiting for someone to ask for it – it ought to be public property."

He donated eighty acres to Dade County for use as the first county park.

On May 15, 1930, while returning from a trip to the Bahamas aboard his yacht the *Seaforth*, William J. Matheson suffered a fatal heart attack. He left a wife, Harriet, daughter, Anna Woods and sons, Hugh and Malcolm. His estate was estimated at approximately a quarter of a billion dollars. The Matheson children donated the northern portion of Key Biscayne, six hundred eighty acres, to Dade County for use as a park in exchange for assurances that a causeway bridge would be built from the mainland. Dade County Commissioner Charles H. Crandon negotiated the donation and it was readily agreed upon. Unfortunately World War II interfered with the construction until November 1947. The causeway was named for infamous United States aviator Edward Rickenbacker. The Rickenbacker Causeway would allow the public access to what is known today as Crandon Park, named for the Dade County Commissioner who approved the original deal.

The park has attractions for visitors from tot to senior. The beautiful gleaming white beach spans a length of two glorious miles and is named as one to the top ten beaches in the United States. Millions flock to the shore each year to enjoy the lovely sea side allure. Crystal clear calm water, a wooden esplanade through the wild sea oats swaying in a gentle salt air breeze, concession stands selling cold drinks and snacks, picnic tables and grills for pleasant outings by the shore. Cabanas are available for rent for those that require or desire more than SPF protection from the sun. Just offshore is a sandbar, which protects swimmers from crashing waves and the dangerous undertow. The sandbar, which changes from time to time due to storms and currents, remains to protect one of the most famous beaches in the world.

CORAL GABLES WATERWAY

When developer George Merrick (1886-1942) and the Coral Gables Corporation conceived the master plan for Coral Gables in the 1920s, the city's boundaries encompassed waterfront acreage allowing access to waterways. The original city boundaries went from Key Biscayne, south to Soldier Key and then back to the coastal wetlands called Chapman Field Park. Merrick's promotional brochures advertised his new city as "Forty Miles of Waterfront" offering a ride in a gondola (narrow boat with curved ends used on the canals in Venice) from the Biltmore Hotel to Tahiti Beach (now part of the Cocoplum neighborhood). Though his grand vision was not realized due to the 1926 land bust, the Coral Gables Waterway has endured. The eight-mile-long waterway cuts west from Biscayne Bay to the intersection at Cartagena Plaza, then curves north, paralleling Riviera Drive on its way to the Biltmore Golf Course. It also connects the waterway's western loop through the University of Miami campus and the Mahi Waterway. The Coral Gables Waterway today has rugged limestone that rises up to 20 feet or more to the crossing beneath the LeJeune Road bridge.

4200 Granada Boulevard, Coral Gables
MD32 ~ GPS Coordinates: 25.705733, -80.260633

Coral Gables was the dream of George Merrick who planned the Mediterranean inspired community and by 1925 had it become a reality. Merrick's plans involved offering every possible convenience to the public as well as creating a center for international business. This was quite a feat to develop a world known business center within an intimate cozy community. Even today the city continues to focus on nature, the thematic cityscape and host of the international community.

Historical preservation became a priority in Coral Gables. It was the first city in Florida to create a Historical Resources Ordinance and Board to protect and preserve their valuable historical legacy. The city is rich in historical significance and is intent on maintaining those sites in the tradition and care entrusted by George Merrick eighty years before.

In addition to the historical importance, close attention to culture is an integral part of Coral Gables society. The economy is strengthened with twenty-six consulates, more than thirty fine art galleries, exquisite fine dining restaurants and many community supported live theater groups. Because of the high concentration of retail and service industries it has been unnecessary to elevate property taxes. Though while the business section of Coral Gable prospers, residential areas have been strictly protected from encroachment.

Coral Gables continues to be recognized throughout the United States. The city is the only place in Florida and only one of two cities throughout the nation to have a Class One Fire Department, a fully-accredited Police Department and an award winning Building and Zoning Department. Having all three nationally recognized service organizations is a credit to leadership, staff, personnel and voters of Coral Gables.

The future for Coral Gables is bright. While continuing to grow and develop with advancing technology, the city is intent on protecting and preserving its historical integrity. Maintaining the superlative public services and continually revitalizing the commercial districts in keeping with always changing trends. Preserving the unique face of Coral Gables as well as the spirit of community continues to be of utmost importance. It is easy to imagine the look of pride George Merrick must have worn every time he gazed upon his dream become reality. In 1926, George Merrick said this of his creation:

"The Building of Coral Gables has not been a thing of the moment, but a wonderful monument that will as solidly endure as does the everlasting coral upon which it is founded."

US 1, Miami Beach
MD33 ~ GPS Coordinates: 25.705849, -80.288278

In June of 2003, the Fallen Hero Scholarship program was founded. The program provides scholarships for the children and spouses of soldiers from Florida who have lost their lives in service of our country. Since the creation of the scholarship as of December 2004, forty children of nineteen fallen soldiers have been awarded scholarships by the program.

Florida Governor Jeb Bush has stated,

"Florida is committed to creating a supportive environment for our servicemen and women and their families. These scholarships ensure that the children of our fallen heroes have the opportunity to continue their education without the worry of any further financial burden being placed on their families."

The children and spouses are to receive a full four years university tuition, local and dormitory fees good at any of Florida's public universities, community colleges or the value of the fund may be transferred to private colleges in Florida, select technical schools and most out of state colleges. The actual value of the scholarship depends on when the child will enter college and the cost of education at that time. Today the scholarship is valued at approximately fifty thousand dollars.

THE PERRINE LAND GRANT

In 1838, the United States Congress granted a township of land in the southern extremity of Florida to noted horticulturist Dr. Henry Perrine and his associates. This land was to be used in experiments aimed at introducing foreign tropical plants and seeds into Florida. Although Dr. Perrine did not select a township before his death in 1840, he indicated the area he preferred, and his family later selected the land which came to be called the Perrine Land Grant. Born in 1797, Henry Perrine was trained as a physician. During a visit to Cuba in 1826, he became interested in tropical plants which might be successfully introduced into the southern United States. As American consul in Campeche, Mexico (1827-1838), Dr. Perrine began to send Mexican plants to a friend on Indian Key in Florida and to seek government support for future agricultural experiments. Eager to find a way to utilize the tropical soils of the south, the leaders of Territorial Florida gave their support to Dr. Perrine in the efforts to obtain land for his project, which culminated in the grant of 1838. Events of the Second Seminole War made it impossible for Dr. Perrine to settle on the Florida Mainland in 1838. He took his family to Indian Key to care for his plants and await the war's end. On August 7, 1840, Indians attacked the Key, killing Dr. Perrine and six others; his family escaped uninjured. Dr. Perrine deserves recognition as a pioneer whose efforts stimulated interest in tropical agriculture in Florida.

U.S. 1 at 16165 S. Dixie Highway, Perrine
MD34 ~ GPS Coordinates: 25.618200, -80.345700

Born of French Huguenot[8] genealogy and originally hailing from Cranbury, New Jersey, Henry Edward Perrine was born on April 5, 1797. He began teaching school at a young age in nearby Rockyhill, New Jersey. He then concentrated on his eventual vocation as doctor. While attending the medical needs of Bond County, Illinois, he married Ann Fuller Townsend.

A tragic accident in his twenties nearly ended his life. An assistant used a beaker, by accident, which Perrine had been using to dose himself with a natural Peruvian bark guarding against malaria. The assistant had measured out a draught of arsenic in the beaker. Before the doctor realized the change, he had sipped the poison. He narrowly escaped a dreadful end. Dr. Perrine would never quite recover his health after the incident. He retired to a much milder climate in Natchez, Mississippi to recover his vigor. Perrine was, three years later, appointed Ambassador to the Yucatan.

Edward Perrine remained in Mexico for ten years and during his tenure there he developed an interest in growing tropical fruits and vegetables. He began sending seeds to south Florida friends to establish a farm there to be in progress once he left Mexico, one of the such friends was Charles Howe at Indian Key.

The Perrine family grew to include three children Sarah, Hester and Henry Jr. Perrine was offered property outside of New Orleans but his heart was set on south Florida. In order to obtain property Perrine was forced to travel to Washington and request a land grant. The process involved in obtaining this property is unclear at best, several different stories were told to explain the acquisition. But in the end, Perrine received the grant of more than twenty-three thousand acres in south Florida in July 1838. In order for the grant to be approved Perrine joined Judge James Webb of Key West and his old friend Charles Howe, who was the postmaster of Indian Key to form the Tropical Plant Company.

Aware that the Seminoles were warring, Dr. Perrine moved his family to Indian Key in December 1838. Some twenty miles south of Cape Sable, Indian Key became home to about twelve families who developed a settlement there. Believing the Indians would not venture far from their Everglades hideout; the families built homes, one store and three warehouses. Dr. Perrine's dwelling was the largest of the houses on the Key having three stories, surrounded by wide porches with arched walkways. Water surrounded the house on three sides and from one entryway a short pier extended into the wharf for unloading supplies brought in by ship. Beneath the pier were holding pens for sea turtles used as a primary food source, the pens filled and emptied with seawater based on the tides. Another cellar was built beneath the house provided an indoor bathing facility for the family, of course it too was supplied with salt water and had a dressing room above for privacy.

In the early hours of August 7, 1840, Dr. Perrine was startled by gun shots and breaking glass. He was sitting up with their eldest daughter who was ill with a fever when he heard the shrieks of Indians. He gathered his family about him, all of them in only their nightclothes, his daughter held closely in his arms. Noticing Henry Jr. was not with them the doctor hid the rest of the family in the dressing room downstairs and went for his son. After securing the family, Dr. Perrine returned upstairs to retrieve his firearms. Much to his dismay, he discovered that he had no percussion caps therefore the guns were useless. Peering out a window he found the house virtually surrounded by Indians, their means of escape was limited. He bade the family to descend into the bathing room and then into the turtle pens until he came for them. Mrs. Perrine, the two daughters and one son followed his directions and were soon immersed chest deep in cold salt water hidden by the darkness. Afraid and alone the family waited for the husband and father who was destined never to return to them.

The Seminole were attempting the force their way into the house when Dr. Perrine called from upstairs in perfect Spanish that he was a "medicine man." All became quiet below, believing it was safe, the doctor descended the stairs. First he carefully concealed the trap door leading to his family, this act saved their lives. He knew that the Seminole were friendly to the Spaniards, therefore he realized his only hope was to assume the role of a Spanish doctor, confident the Indians would spare him and his family.

The Seminole were intent on destroying everything they saw. The house was completely sacked then they ascended the stairs to find Dr. Perrine. Below the family heard screams of pain as heavy blows met bone then a single gunshot and all was quiet. Footsteps and dragging trunks reverberated through the wooden house as the Indians plundered. No hope of rescue was forthcoming, as all of the soldiers fit for duty had recently been sent on a naval expedition. After the carnage was over the Perrine family was informed that several soldiers had left their hospital beds to come to their aid but in their haste to get to the family the men loaded two four pound canon on a small boat. Unfortunately they had mistakenly brought six-pound cartridges and when they were fired the guns recoiled so hard that the canon shot overboard. The unarmed soldiers were forced to retreat or chance capture. The Indians killed one of the soldiers as they attempted to escape.

The acrid smell of smoke began to drift down to the hiding place of the surviving Perrine family. As the chamber filled with the dark thick soot, they were forced to lie on their bellies in the inches of water left by the ebb tide to avoid death by suffocation. As orange flames began to consume the wood above their heads they tore scraps from their clothes to wrap about their faces as a filter. The terrified family made their way through the narrow confines beneath the house to the turtle crawl but found their way blocked. The burning timbers above them began to creak and moan finally showering red-hot coals down on the family below, their eyes watering and lungs burning from the acrid smoke. Henry Jr. panicked and broke free from the rest, clawing his way to the outside.

He would rather die at the hands of the Indians than to be burned to death. Once young Henry reached the sunlight and clear air, he was certain the remainder of his family was doomed but was elated when his Mother carrying the eldest daughter and his sister made their way out of the turtle crawl to safety.

One party of Indians had left in a boat filled with stolen goods while others were left to sack the store and while there discovered rum, proceeding to become inebriated. The exhausted family crept to another waiting boat partially filled with stolen goods. Young Henry tied his shirt to a pole to signify distress and poled out to open ocean. In the distance the survivors could see two Indians in pursuit, however, when another boat appeared on the horizon. The Indians retreated.

The homeless and destitute Perrines were taken aboard the schooner *Medium* where they were swaddled in sheets to cover their nakedness left from their shredded garments. Their burns from the falling coals were treated and they were given a place to collapse in exhaustion. The following day two soldiers were dispatched to retrieve what was left of Dr. Perrine's body for burial, unfortunately the fire had destroyed his remains and only a few bones were recovered. The family was transferred to a man-of-war, *Flirt* until passage could be arranged on the steamer *Santos* taking them to safety at St. Augustine.

Mrs. Perrine moved with her children to Palmyra, New York where she continuously beseeched Congress to transfer the land rights south of Miami to the Perrine family. The girls married and Henry Jr. studied law, passing the bar in 1848. He went on to join his uncle in California to establish sawmills. Old family friend, Charles Howe assisted Mrs. Perrine to prove the land grant belonged to family. They were told that to establish rights to the thirty-six square mile grant, each acre must be settled and cultivated by at least one family each. Howe employed thirty-six Bahamian families to live on the land and plant a crop of their choice. The grant was eventually approved. Henry Jr. gave up life in California and moved to the family grant in 1876 bringing enough supplies to maintain the family for some months.

Being a northern lawyer, Henry was not adept at living off the land. The wilderness defeated him within eight months. Ants invaded his food supplies, the rocky land was not readily adaptable to planting and money ran out before he was able to build a wharf. He was determined to build a tribute to his father called Perrineville. Unfortunately what the land didn't reject, a hurricane soon destroyed.

Homesteaders began arriving in response to the promise of one hundred sixty acres free to those who would work the land. Still Congress protected the Perrine's grant. The Florida Central and Peninsular Railroad and Flagler's Florida East Coast Railway put in with the Perrine family and after a Senate investigation a decision was made on January 28, 1897. The settlers received two thousand acres each, the Perrine heirs ten thousand acres and the railroad companies five thousand acres each. Charles Howe's heirs demanded that half of the Perrine grant should be deeded to them for the families' early work on the property. After a number of years fighting this out in court the Florida Supreme Court decided the property was dismissed, yet ownership of the land continued to be questioned. By the time the court settled the case only Henry Perrine Jr. was still alive.

Eventually a settlement in Dade County was named in honor of Dr. Perrine in 1903. The community was developed to house those men and their families working to extend the Florida East Coast Railroad to Homestead. Many plants researched by Dr. Perrine now grow throughout Perrine as well as the state including sisal hemp and Citrus Limonum or better known as the Key Lime.

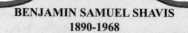

BENJAMIN SAMUEL SHAVIS
1890-1968

Ben Shavis was a man who made life a littler nicer for the residents of the black community of West Perrine. He staged clean up campaigns, worked with community youth, encouraged people to purchase their homes and served as a Sunday school superintendent. Officially he was chairman of the Perrine Negro Council and rallied his neighbors to register and vote. In November of 1948, when Perrine was an incorporated city, Shavis was the only black among the fifteen candidates running for seven city commission seats. His election seemed secure until racial tensions forced his withdrawal from the race. In 1978 the community of West Perrine dedicated this park in honor of Ben Shavis.

Ben Shavis Park, SW 179th Street and 104th Avenue, Perrine
MD35 ~ GPS Coordinates: 25.603400, -80.360817

Benjamin Shavis was a man who Dr. Perrine would have admired. He struggled endlessly to improve the lot of the black community in Perrine. Working with the pure essence of any community, the youth; assisted residents in buying their homes and served as a leader in his church. Shavis, as chairman of the Perrine Negro Council, staged a door to door campaign to register the community to vote. In an attempt to officially better his community, Ben Shavis ran as the first and only black man to qualify as a candidate for city commission. Unfortunately he was forced to withdraw from the race under the strain of racial uprisings. Benjamin Shavis meant so much to the community of Perrine; a park was dedicated as a memorial to him in 1978.

NAVAL AIR STATION
RICHMOND
WWII L.T.A. Facility

At this site, on 15 September 1942, the United States Navy established a 2,000 acre (810 hectare) lighter-than-air facility. The Navy constructed 3 huge hangars, each 17 stories (175 fee/54 meters) high, 297 feet (110.5 meters) wide, and 1,088 feet (404.8 meters) in length. Among the largest wooden structures in the world, each covered about 7 acres (2.8 hectares). This base was home to Fleet Airship Wing 2 and Airship Patrol Squadron ZP-21, consisting of 25 "K" class blimps. Airships from NAS Richmond searched for German submarines over the Atlantic Ocean, Gulf of Mexico, and the Caribbean Sea. Other station activities included training homing pigeons, helium equipment operators, and night torpedo bomber crews. Exactly 3 years to the date of the commissioning of NAS Richmond, a severe hurricane and resulting fire destroyed all 3 hangars containing 368 military and civilian aircraft, 100 automobiles and 25 airships. Winds of 170 mph/272 kmh to 196 mph/309 kmh were recorded at nearby Homestead Air Base. The facility was never rebuilt. In this area of the base you can see the remaining concrete supports for the 51 wooden truss arches of hangar number 1 and the sole remaining massive main door support.

SITE OF
NAS RICHMOND

12400 SW 152nd Street, Railroad Museum, Miami
MD36 ~ GPS Coordinates: 25.616833, -80.400033

World War II was very prevalent in Miami throughout the duration. As the United States involvement in the war accelerated several military facilities were established in the southern Florida city. NAS[9] Richmond was created in 1942 about twenty miles south of Miami on twenty-five hundred acres of Florida wilderness. The facility was not commonly known and if asked most would assume the LTA[10] airship station to be located erroneously in Virginia. The name was taken from the Richmond Lumber Company, which harvested the durable and nearly indestructible Dade County pine.

NAS Richmond was first comprised of three extremely large airship hangars and support buildings constructed of native pine and millions of board feet of Pacific Northwest lumber. When Dade County pine was dried it tended to be insect resistant and so hard that metal working tools were required build with it.

The base was ceremoniously commissioned on September 15, 1942. The wooden airship hangars were the largest known facilities on earth. The amazing airship or blimps, as they were more commonly known, were ported here for testing and deployment. Their mission involved defense of the Panama Canal and as submarine spotters in the blue waters of the Atlantic. The Nazis surrendered in May and Japan, September 2, 1945.

Ironically, three years to the day of NAS Richmond's commissioning and thirteen days after the end of World War II, the facility would lay in ruins. The facility was the victim of a tremendous hurricane that reduced the massive hangars to basic piles of ash and embers. These were the days when a listing of names each year didn't identify hurricanes and even though this particular storm had no official name, no one would ever forget the devastation left in its wake. The thing so difficult to understand is that NAS Richmond was built to withstand wind forces of one hundred twenty miles per hour, it was constructed to endure and survive a hurricane of massive force. The Navy dispatched large numbers of aircraft as well as civilian planes, automobiles and trucks. The massive doors were slid shut and as the wind began to blow. Everything was tucked carefully within the confines of the safe haven. Unfortunately over a span of eight hours this particular storm left little that could be identified.

The first signs of the incoming storm began around noon on September 15, 1945. As the winds increased, everything was secured and finally the hangar doors slid into place. The hurricane made land around mid afternoon with NAS Richmond directly in its line of travel. The winds were measured at ninety-four miles per hour by five o'clock. The skies were dark as midnight, the pressure was building and the hangars were bound up tight. This situation could lead to a vacuum causing an explosion. By five-thirty the fire alarm was blaring and everyone available searched for the source of the flames. Six minutes later the power went dead and hangar one sprout bright orange flames.

By this time the rain had completely ceased, which was unusual at this point in a massive storm such as this. Winds now roared to their peak of one hundred twenty six miles per hour. The winds actually fed and spread the flames. Sailors who sought the safety of the hangars from the storm were now trapped in an inferno. The contents of each hangar eventually caught flame aircraft, blimps, vehicles, canvas, paint and various petroleum products. The people inside sought the safety of the concrete inner stairwells. Outside firefighters did what they could but few could get to the blaze because of fallen debris everywhere and others were occupied with blazes all over town resulting from the storm. It was said that the blaze at NAS Richmond could be seen from twenty miles away.

The sailors fought the fire hard alongside civilian employees. Twenty-six were wounded and one man lost his life to the blaze. NAS Fire Chief Harry Shulze was a retired Chicago fireman and civilian employee at the base. Shulze led the firemen into hangar one but everything went wrong and the roof collapsed killing him instantly. The inferno burned through the night until it was spent. At daybreak all that remained was the smoldering ruins of what was NAS Richmond. The damage was the greatest loss of federal property in the shortest span of time ever recorded with approximately thirty million dollars in damages and lost property.

The property that was NAS Richmond was leased to the University of Miami for use as a remote campus for soldiers returning from the war going to school on the GI Bill and as a botanical research facility. University Business Administration student and railroad fan William J. Godfrey realized that the school's South Campus had miles of vacated railroad tracks and determined in August of 1956 that the property could possibly be utilized as a railway museum. But just as the Gold Coast Railroad Museum started advertising train rides on various Sundays through the month, the plan hit a snag. It would be the first of many bumps in the track that the museum was forced to hurdle.

The snag happened to be the Cuban Missile Crisis and the government decided they needed the property once again. The government determined to utilize the property as a CIA listening post for spying on the Cubans. The museum was forced to find other accommodations. The result was both a blessing and a curse; the museum was moved to Fort Lauderdale but in doing so the University transferred all ownership of the locomotives, cars and memorabilia to the Gold Coast Railroad Museum. On November 13, 1966 the museum steamed away from the South Campus.

For seventeen years the museum remained at their Fort Lauderdale location until fate once more intervened. The Florida Department of Transportation issued a notification that the proposed Interstate 595 was routed directly through the museum facilities. The notice was in fact their eviction and the museum was put on the track to a new location once again.

The National Park Service planned a National Monument to be located at Biscayne Bay and the federal prison near the newly opened Metro Zoo had some spare property. With the assistance of United States Representative Dante Facell, a swap was made and the Gold Coast Railroad Museum once again had a home. Oddly enough the property was the site of the former NAS Richmond. The museum had finally come home again. Flatcars, boxcars, gondolas, it took all of these and more to move the museum once again. The modern Seaboard Coast Line diesel electric locomotive pulled the Gold Coast Special back home. Just when the museum was coming together, disaster struck again.

On August 24, 1992, hurricane Andrew came onshore at one hundred seventy miles per hour. The site of the Gold Coast Railroad Museum was again in the path of a tremendous storm. The museum was devastated.

Many supporters were just unable to take this final straw and left the project for good. In fact this could have been the final death knell of the museum were it not for FEMA[11].

FEMA vowed that all non-profit facilities would be rebuilt first unfortunately the museum was a massive undertaking and would take eight very long and arduous years to complete. Most of the supporters simply gave up under the strain but a small group remained devoted come hell or high water. The museum endured though it was not the facility that it deserved to be. The initial entry and museum store was set up in a house trailer where patrons viewed the assorted displays in the hot tropical sun or sudden summer rains. The exposure to torturous elements was taking its toll on the displays as well.

Today the Gold Coast Railroad Museum, Inc. is one of the finest in the country. A wonderful display is in place detailing former NAS Richmond and the volunteers there are exceptional. Visitors can expect to be treated to a fantastic display with enthusiastic docents. The museum is open seven days per week with a small admission fee charged.

**GOLD COAST
RAILROAD MUSEUM**

Little remains of NAS Richmond. Huge concrete piers stand tall marking the doorway of one of the largest wooden hangars in the world. Yet it is said that the spirit of NAS Fire Chief Harry Shulze still keeps a vigil on his former duty station. He has been seen by various people silently keeping watch. As for the museum, like a phoenix rising from the ashes, it endures bigger and better than ever.

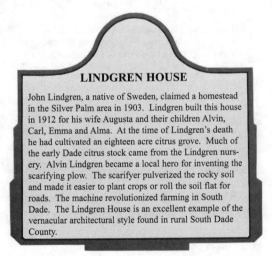

LINDGREN HOUSE

John Lindgren, a native of Sweden, claimed a homestead in the Silver Palm area in 1903. Lindgren built this house in 1912 for his wife Augusta and their children Alvin, Carl, Emma and Alma. At the time of Lindgren's death he had cultivated an eighteen acre citrus grove. Much of the early Dade citrus stock came from the Lindgren nursery. Alvin Lindgren became a local hero for inventing the scarifying plow. The scarifer pulverized the rocky soil and made it easier to plant crops or roll the soil flat for roads. The machine revolutionized farming in South Dade. The Lindgren House is an excellent example of the vernacular architectural style found in rural South Dade County.

**Redland
MD37 ~ GPS Coordinates: 25.587147, -80.413473**

Located at the heart of what is known as the Redland District is the Lindgren House, built in 1912. John Lindgren arrived in the United States from Sweden some nine years before with his wife and their four children. He homesteaded and established a moderately sized citrus grove of eighteen acres. His citrus is said to have supplied much of the rootstock for Dade County.

Lindgren passed along his fruit growing interests to his eldest son. Alvin Lindgren revolutionized the southeastern Florida citrus industry by inventing a unique instrument and technique for preparing the rocky soil for planting. His scarifying plow made it possible to work with the Dade County calcareous[12] soil resulting from the native limestone rock.

Because the soil of the Redland district was distinctly bedrock until reaching the water table, it was extremely hard to grow anything in the area. That coupled with the intense tropical weather, growing crops was a challenge. However, Alvin's invention allowed the topsoil to produce beautifully and evolve the Redland District into a virtually ideal farming community.

Astonishingly after the land had been cleared of hardwood trees, farmers actually used small dynamite charges to break through the limestone. The scarifying plow would crush the oolitic limestone usually to depth of six to eight inches allowing enough room for tender roots to spread. However for planting trees ten to twenty inches were required for large root balls, therefore soil filled trenches were created. The trees were planted in neat rows perfectly spaced. The most prevalent groves were limes, avocado, mangoes and the less common lychees. A lychee is a rounded fruit with bumpy skin, which is red in color. The fruit inside is slightly pink appearing much like a grape but distinctly sweeter and somewhat acidic.

Alvin Lindgren's invention of the scarifying plow made the abundant crops and bounty of the land possible in the Redland District. In fact southeastern Florida is the only place in the United States where tomatoes can grow year round. The Lindgren's contribution to the area in which they chose to live made a difference in the lives of many.

COOPER RESIDENCE

George H. Cooper, Sr. and his wife Virginia purchased this land in 1933. The Coopers moved this house, originally a much smaller wood frame structure, to this location. They hired a stone mason, Jack Herndon, who began and completed all of the exterior and interior stone work. The home has been added onto over the years and is architecturally significant for its oolitic limestone construction. More commonly known as coral rock, oolitic limestone is a masonry material native to South Florida. The home was purchased by the Cooper's daughter Barbara Hanck and husband in 1961. It was lovingly cared for by the Hancks and was sold to the Helman family in 1995.

SW 248 St. & SW 142 Avenue, Redland
MD38 ~ GPS Coordinates: 25.536821, -80.421224

Though the white man was late in settling the wilds of south Florida, there is evidence of man having lived in the area more than ten thousand years ago. Imbedded in the ancient oolite or native limestone is the evidence of the ancient Tequesta. Unlike the Tequesta who were eradicated in the early 1800s by the white man's disease, settlement battles and slavery, there is still a throw back around from those ancient days: the mosquito.

Redland was developed in anticipation of Henry Flagler's railroad. The settlement was established in the early 1900s, as principally an agricultural community southwest of Miami, but the promise of the railroad never came to be. The name was derived from the potholes of red clay found atop the typical oolite limestone rock common to the area. The clay was an

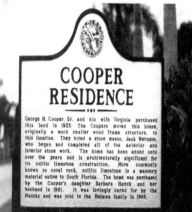

COOPER RESIDENCE MARKER

508

anomaly rare to south Florida and of great interest to many of world's great botanical experts.

After the community was founded George and Virginia Cooper purchased property in 1933. The couple had a small wooden frame house built and hired a local mason to complete the building with the more durable native rock. Obviously the stone is long lasting, the structure still stands after more than seventy years as a private residence, although with great modifications.

Literature concerning Redland speaks of stepping back in time to the early days of south Florida settlement. Well it is certainly true and in evidence just viewing the Cooper home. What was surrounded by clapboard homes, a field of local produce, native stone houses, barns and fencing is still present today. Metropolitan Miami is only minutes to the northeast however it is as if crossing that divide is covering a time warp.

One story is told of hurricane Andrew's devastation in the area that exemplifies the pioneering spirit of those who live in Redland. The owner of a residence called Cocoplavis had just finished a major remodeling project utilizing parts and particles of original settler Maude Brickell's home on Brickell Avenue. After the hurricane had finally passed leaving little but piles of debris where there were once homes and businesses, the owner was asked about her damages; the response:

"Oh, the wind came and knocked everything down. I just picked everything back up again."

Today such places as the Fruit and Spice Park, Burr's Berry Farm and countless u-pick'em stands along the way serve up a bit of what Redland has stood for all these years. Burr's is a family business left to the generations and specializing in succulent Florida strawberries with what is said to be the best homemade milk shakes around. Then there is the unique Knaus Berry Farm whose German Baptist owners dress in traditional costumes and serve fresh baked goods, produce and is known for their homemade cinnamon rolls. Most of the stands open around Thanksgiving and close by the beginning of May, that's the season, the season of Redland.

Today the little known village so reminiscent of yesterday feels like it is under attack. Developers want to come in and build condos, strip malls, modernize the community but Redland old-timers and new arrivals with that pioneering spirit are fighting back. The Redlands Citizens Association tells anyone who will listen how important it is to keep the agricultural way of life without change. Today the region has been described as magical, lush and bountiful; a definition that certainly applies but for how long will it continue to be the land that the pioneers still recognize?

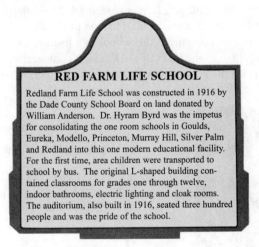

RED FARM LIFE SCHOOL

Redland Farm Life School was constructed in 1916 by the Dade County School Board on land donated by William Anderson. Dr. Hyram Byrd was the impetus for consolidating the one room schools in Goulds, Eureka, Modello, Princeton, Murray Hill, Silver Palm and Redland into this one modern educational facility. For the first time, area children were transported to school by bus. The original L-shaped building contained classrooms for grades one through twelve, indoor bathrooms, electric lighting and cloak rooms. The auditorium, also built in 1916, seated three hundred people and was the pride of the school.

SW 248th St. & SW 162 Avenue, Redland
MD39 ~ GPS Coordinates: 25.536451, -80.437412

William Anderson donated land to the Dade County School Board for a school specializing in the agricultural life surrounding this area. The facility opened in 1916 and with sixteen thousand square feet it was known as the second largest rural school in the United States. Architecturally designed in a U shape, having one hundred forty-four windows allowed for a steady breezeway assisting in keeping a moderate temperature throughout the building. Wide eaves shadowed the bright tropical sunlight, beautiful landscaping and a red shingled roof toping off the structure.

Under the guidance of Dr. Hyram Byrd numerous county schools were consolidated to make up the Red Farm Life School's modern facility. This was a time in history when one-room schoolhouses especially in rural communities were common, however here each grade had a classroom. The facility featured indoor bathrooms when many homes still utilized outhouses as well as electrical lighting. Though in later years the original curriculum was modernized, the Farm Life School continued to operate until 1992. The school eventually served only the elementary grades.

The school was unable to continue the 1992-93 school year after the devastation of hurricane Andrew on August 24, 1992. The terrible storm ripped away part of the red shingled roof and flooded a good bit of the school. The remains are tucked neatly between Redland Elementary and Redland Middle School; the school was left in shreds. Bared to the elements the paint has begun to peel and stubborn weeds push their way through the wooden floorboards.

The Dade County School System was determined to repair the historic school, however five years later they abandoned the idea. Instead of saving this piece of history the school system decided it was in their best interest to just tear it down. When word was passed of these intentions former students and the community banded together, circling the wagons with the sole purpose of saving this enduring center of their region. After years of diligence the school system deeded the property to the Dade County who in turn leased the property to the committee formed to save the school.

The Pioneer Museum of Florida City offered their help in the grant application processes and the committee managed to acquire eight hundred eighty thousand dollars in funds for the project. Most of the funding was received from the Florida Department of Historic Preservation and the Dade County Preservation Fund. The project is indeed a grand undertaking and because of financial constraints preserving the entire facility as a museum is unrealistic. The intent is to restore one of the front classrooms, as it would have appeared in 1916, as a museum and lease the remainder of the facility to other schools who have expressed an interest in the property.

A member of the recovery committee and former student of the Redland Farm School in 1928, George Grunwell wrote an especially good history of the school. His text made it possible for the site to be listed as a historical site. The state of Florida has also recognized the school as a historic site; national designation is being pursued. It has been said that this facility was the heart of the Redland community where agriculture was and is the primary source of income. That is simply reason enough to save the Redland Farm Life School.

THE ACTUAL MARKER

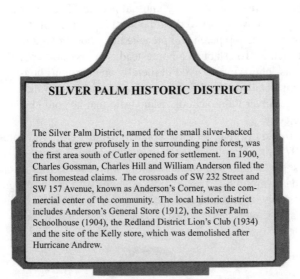

SILVER PALM HISTORIC DISTRICT

The Silver Palm District, named for the small silver-backed fronds that grew profusely in the surrounding pine forest, was the first area south of Cutler opened for settlement. In 1900, Charles Gossman, Charles Hill and William Anderson filed the first homestead claims. The crossroads of SW 232 Street and SW 157 Avenue, known as Anderson's Corner, was the commercial center of the community. The local historic district includes Anderson's General Store (1912), the Silver Palm Schoolhouse (1904), the Redland District Lion's Club (1934) and the site of the Kelly store, which was demolished after Hurricane Andrew.

Southwest 232ⁿᵈ Street and Southwest 157ᵗʰ Avenue, Redland
MD40 ~ GPS Coordinates: 25.551209, -80.445656

Although Flagler's railroad never reached Redland and the Silver Palm District, it did arrive at Goulds only nine miles to the north in 1903. The stop made it much easier for William Cauley to ship his tomatoes to markets in the north. Cauley made a fortune developing storage facilities, business offices, a tavern, eatery and single family homes, all tightly woven on a ten-acre tract along the railroad. Many of the tiny wooden residences built from durable Florida pine still stand today after more than one hundred years.

The early 1900s saw the population of Dade County explode to quadruple its original numbers. Much of the low lands were drained off to make room for ever sprawling housing developments and the need for additional farm lands to support the increase in human consumption.

Charles Grossman was the first to claim a homestead in the Silver Palm area. Soon his friend and hunting partner Will Anderson joined him from Indiana. Anderson established his homestead and began working for the Drake Lumber Company bringing in dry goods and groceries to the scattered remote lumber camps. He established the William Anderson General Merchandise store in 1911, the first of its kind in the far removed wilderness of southeast Florida. The mercantile had a prime location at the intersection of the only main road through the area and just across from the Silver Palm Schoolhouse. Anderson lived in rooms above the store, which continued to operate for more than twenty years before the building was converted to apartments.

The Redland District Lions Club was first established on June 9, 1925. The club was originally chartered with twenty-nine members from the small farming communities of Redland, Homestead and Florida City. It was reported that the club sent locally grown citrus on the Norcross Bartlett Northeastern Greenland Expedition across one-mile thick ice. The fruit was largely responsible for keeping the adventurers in good health.

On July 28, 1934 the membership broke ground on a new clubhouse. The gala opening was observed on March 26 of the next year. The structure was built of native coral, hardwood maple flooring and a massive four hundred-year old Spanish door brought from Cuba by member R. L. Short. The clubhouse has been superbly maintained and is still very much in use today.

The Redland Lions aided the community by working with various other civic organizations to connect Silver Palm Drive, known as Southwest 232nd Street, US 1[13]. In addition the Club worked to make the roads of Redland safer and improve the hurricane warning system in the region. The club further improved the community by establishing the County Health Unit, still active today as the Homestead Health Clinic.

Southern Dade County was made up of many unusual people. There was a Preacher Tems said to have lived in a tree, no one really knows how he survived but he must have lived off the land for he had no other means of support. He held court from his tree top perch and preached to whoever would listen or to no one at all but always in a sing song style in rhyme. To establish a homestead, settlers had to remain on the plot of land for a period of time. A man known as John Wingate lived in literally an enormous hogshead. When a moderate hurricane blew it away, Wingate simply rolled it back in place once again. J. R. Walker was a lay Methodist minister who plied his chosen trade at the Silver Palm School. Many said that he could be heard for miles, singing hymns as he walked to the school each day.

Anderson's Corner fell into disrepair and was condemned in 1975. The public protested to save the building from demolition and by 1977, the school was listed on the National Registry of Historic Places. Finally eight years later the William Anderson's General Merchandise Store was renovated to its original condition. William Cauley's railroad village is today a grouping of small antique shops with crafts, art galleries and small specialty restaurants. Cauley Square hosts live bands and carriage rides each weekend. The little market area provides a wonderful setting to while away a slow paced day just browsing from shop to shop.

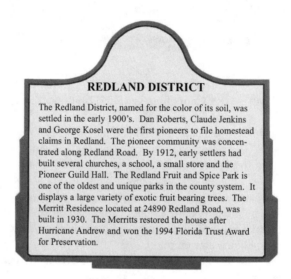

REDLAND DISTRICT

The Redland District, named for the color of its soil, was settled in the early 1900's. Dan Roberts, Claude Jenkins and George Kosel were the first pioneers to file homestead claims in Redland. The pioneer community was concentrated along Redland Road. By 1912, early settlers had built several churches, a school, a small store and the Pioneer Guild Hall. The Redland Fruit and Spice Park is one of the oldest and unique parks in the county system. It displays a large variety of exotic fruit bearing trees. The Merritt Residence located at 24890 Redland Road, was built in 1930. The Merritts restored the house after Hurricane Andrew and won the 1994 Florida Trust Award for Preservation.

Redland
MD41 ~ GPS Coordinates: 25.535519, -80.494143

Arriving in Redland is as if crossing over some imaginary dateline into yesteryear. Time slows to a crawl and life's natural pace calms to a relaxed state of being. The virtual Garden of Eden grows despite red hard packed clay and the nearly impervious shell of limestone rock concealing an aquifer of pure fresh water. The allure of Redland drew such names as illustrator, naturalist John James Audobon and noted horticulturist David Fairchild.

Hidden away in virtual oblivion at 24801 Southwest 187th Avenue in the Redland district is a one of a kind tropical paradise known as the Fruit & Spice Park. No where else in the United States is a botanical haven of this kind. The thirty-acre garden features more than one hundred varieties of citrus fruits, sixty-five diverse banana trees, forty assorted grapes, sixty bamboo medleys as well as more fruits, vegetables, herbs, spices and nuts than imaginable.

Visitors may spend an hour or whole days tasting their way through the vast tropical wonderland. The park is opened seven days per week with the exception of major holidays and for a small admission fee guided tours are offered every weekend. Amidst the lush garden are picnic facilities where guests may sit and enjoy the bounty of the Fruit & Spice Park.

Special "fruit safaris" are available under the expert direction of the Park Manager. The facilities practice a unique exchange program across the globe to share and develop various plant specimens some never before introduced to the world. Through the efforts of the Fruit & Spice Park fresh produce is being introduced to local markets, gourmands and chefs seeking menu-enhancing edibles. The park is another example of stepping into a world of its own and enjoying the diverse banquet that life in Redland has to offer.

KOSEL HOMESTEAD

George Kosel, a native of New York, filed a claim for a 160 acre homestead in 1902. He planted a grove, Kosel's Jungle Grove, which produced strawberries, oranges, mangos, grapefruit, and a large variety of avocados. George married Maria Gazzam who also had a homestead claim in Redland. The couple had two children, George Kosel, Jr. and Bodil Kosel Lowe. Bodil still lives on the homestead of her grandmother, Bodil Olsen Kosel. Built of Dade County pine by George in 1905, this house has been added onto over the years but the original structure still remains. Bodil still maintains the avocado grove.

18725 SW 256th Street, Redland
MD42 ~ GPS Coordinates: 25.528463, -80.494876

The Kosel family of New York claimed a one hundred sixty-acre homestead in 1902. They established an farm called Kosel's Jungle Grove. The family still maintains the grove to this day. The matriarch of the family Bodil Kosel kept a homestead between Redland and Plummer. She often told a story of what became the Florida legend of the Ox Woman. This woman was known by various names Sarah Smith McLain was her given name but to some she was the Widow McLain, to the children she was Aunt Sarah and many only knew her as the Ox Woman. She came to Dade County around 1907 it is said, driving a team of oxen with only her dogs and a shotgun at her side. Few knew Sarah's entire tale and she didn't speak of it but her story was one of intrigue, strength, humor and history.

Sarah Smith was born to a father who was known as the biggest man in the tiny south Georgia town of Racepond. She was one of four giant sisters, Hannah or Big Six, Mrs. Lydia Smith Crews and Nancy Smith or Big Nancy. These four never had children but they did have three normal sized sisters who lived to raise families in Georgia. Sarah Smith married a man by the name of David McLain but it seems the marriage did not last. David McLain was hung in Folkston, Georgia for killing a man. Annie Mayhew Fitzpatrick knew the Ox Woman as a young girl and wrote this stanza introducing her:

"Yes, I be the Widow McLain.
My man by a posse was slain.
Neither witty nor pretty
I'm asking no pity
I'm off to my homestead again.
I'm off to my home on Long Key
My pigs and my cow avail me.
In the open I cook Wash my clothes in a brook
I'm the Widow McLain, yes I be."

Bodil Kosel's home was one of Sarah McLain's favorite places to stop on her trips around Dade County. She'd often spend the night, get a good meal, a bath, feed for her dogs and oxen. When she would stop in Sarah would sing sad songs, read the Bible and tell stories of how the eradicated Seminoles were actually one of the lost tribes of Israel.

Annie Mayhew Fitzpatrick remembered the Ox Woman would travel to central Florida about twice a year and bring back a beef cow. She would cut it up, covering it with pine branches to preserve the meat and people would gather from miles around to buy the fresh beef. Annie was standing in line one day for a portion and when it was her turn she asked for steak, the Widow McLain responded "It's neck I'm cutting, honey," realizing it was neck or nothing she paid for her portion. The Ox Woman charged the same price whether it was neck or sirloin because fresh beef was so uncommon in the area.

One of the Kosel boys once told of a man who was hunting near the widow's shack. He decided it might be a fine place to while away the winter and the widow agreed she could use a hand around the place. The very next day the man turned up at the Kosel homestead with his story. The widow forced him to chop wood for his morning coffee and before he could eat he was required to swim across Taylor's Creek with huge pieces of sheet iron. To beat it all the mosquitoes in the glades were so bad, the poor fellow was blotched from head to toe with big red welts.

The Widow McLain showed up at the Brewer homestead one evening during a torrential downpour, soaked to the skin. Of course, the Brewer's took her in and when Sarah explained she had no dry clothes Mrs. Brewer found the largest gown she owned for her to wear until her clothes dried. The sight was something to observe. The gown barely touched her knees and her arms hung at least a foot beyond the lacy sleeves. Imagine that weather beaten face against a girlie gown of lace and ribbon.

Many said due to her enormous size that Sarah was in fact a man. This was completely untrue. Though she was six foot four inches tall, it was said that she was soft and white beneath her clothing with the obvious figure of a woman. Blond hair, which she always wore in a bun, and blue eyed, Sarah always conducted herself politely, was kind and helpful to all who passed her way and was always grateful for kindness extended to her. She was never known to use her great strength to harm.

The widow Sarah Smith McLain suffered a stroke in 1919, her sister arrived from Georgia to fetch her home but Sarah was having none of it. The Ox Woman died shortly after her sister departed and she was buried at Fort Denaud Cemetery near Fort Myers. Her grave is unmarked but the location is known.

PIONEER GUILD HALL

In 1907 the women of Redland formed the Pioneer Guild. Their motto was "to do the most good in the most places for social, church and civic purposes". The land was donated by John Bauer. He also donated the land for the Episcopal Church and built a general store at this crossroad. Redland pioneers hosted teas, barbecues and parties to raise funds to build the Pioneer Guild Hall. Constructed in 1912, the building contained a stage, dance floor, and soon became the community's center for social activity. During the summer, volunteers taught children art, dancing and etiquette. Pioneer Guild Hall is the last remaining building found at the important historic crossroad.

26400 Redland Road (SW 187th Avenue), Redland
MD43 ~ GPS Coordinates: 25.520853, -80.494284

The ladies of the Redland Community in an effort to establish civic associations and events formed the Pioneer Guild in 1907. The organization was to meet the various needs of the community. The first order of business was to raise money for a community center. The benevolence of John Bauer resulted in his donation of property for the center as well as lots for the Episcopal Church and a mercantile. The Redland ladies hosted various social occasions in order to erect the building. After a host of afternoon teas, Saturday barbecues and elegant parties, the funds were finally available for the construction of the Pioneer Guild Hall.

Located at 26400 Southwest 187th Avenue, the large wooden structure was completed in 1912. The interior featured a raised stage and hardwood dance floor. Soon regularly scheduled community activities were planned. When the children were out of school for the summer volunteers conducted art, dance and etiquette classes. Today, the Pioneer Guild Hall still stands as a lasting reminder of Redland's history. The facility continues to support the community as a meeting hall.

Redland is but a bedroom community of Homestead, which is a suburb of the vast mother city of Miami. Homestead has risen in population to exceed thirty thousand residences. The numbers do fluctuate as northern snowbirds arrive and depart as well as the various migrant workers who move in for a time to harvest citrus, other fruits and vegetables.

Homestead Air Force Base was converted to a lesser-used reserve base in 1994 in the aftermath of hurricane Andrew. The city is known as the gateway to the Everglades and likewise the gateway to the Florida Keys. Local points of interest include amazing tropical gardens bringing splashes of color against the deep green foliage.

A pioneer museum details the early days of the community beginning with the ancient Ais Indians and continuing through their decimation as well as the Spanish occupation, British holdings and the Spaniards once again until Florida finally became a part of the United States. Visitors and locals alike enjoy the tropical gardens, pioneer museum, stock car racetrack and the amazing Coral Castle. Tragedy struck in 1992 with the onslaught of brutal Hurricane Andrew. The devastation left little untouched but in true pioneer spirit; Redland, Homestead and the glades picked up straightened out and made repairs ready to face the next obstacle or celebrate a new triumph.

WALTON HOUSE

W. K. Walton built this home circa 1919. Walton planted four acres of avocados and eventually established one of the first commercial avocado nurseries in south Dade. This wood frame, stucco covered residence is designed in the style of an English cottage and is not typical of other houses built during the same period in rural south Dade. Its most outstanding feature is the large gable roof, which imitates the thatch roof typical of English cottages. The Blanco family purchased the home in 1985 and are responsible for its restoration and rare plant garden. Hurricane Andrew did very little damage to the structure.

28501 SW 187th Ave., Redland
MD44 ~ GPS Coordinates: 25.501571, -80.493837

A quaint English cottage complete with towering gable and thatched roof finished in stucco over its wooden frame located in the midst of tropical Florida was strangely out of place. The odd dwelling was designed and built by W. K. Walton in 1919. Surrounding his country estate Walton planted four acres of avocados that was to be one of the first commercial groves in Florida.

In fact avocados were first introduced to the United States in Florida around 1833, twenty-three years before California began growing what was then exotic fruit. By the time Florida became a part of the United States owned, avocado grew wild throughout the hardwood forest in Miami. The seeds were brought in from Cuba by the Spaniards years before and became an important food source in the wilds of unsettled Florida. During the dark days of the Great Depression Florida supplied approximately sixty percent of the world's avocados.

Avocados thrived in the well-drained sandy soil of Florida, with proper care and the correct fertilization the crops prospered. Florida avocados were known to have a better flavor, higher butter fat content and the plants proved to be more impervious to cooler temperatures. The plants can attain a height of up to sixty-five feet, remaining green year round. Oddly enough the fruit is considered a berry with a singular seed at the center of the creamy meat, the consistency of cream cheese. The fruit could well be the ordinary green or less known black, purple or red based on the variety.

Unlike most fruit, Avocados are not edible straight off the tree. Once the fruit is harvested, gauged by the size and time span, it will ripen gradually off the tree. The season ranges from June to the height of the season usually early fall until the end of each year. The fruit favors moderate temperatures of sixty to seventy-five degrees. When temperatures vary, remaining warm into the late fall the fruit will ripen at odd times of the year or fail to mature.

The avocado is a very healthy food source, high in both Vitamin A and potassium. The fruit is meant to be eaten raw, it is not appetizing to cook. It is best-utilized cubed in salads, mashed into a dip, sliced thin as an appetizer or on sandwiches. Guacamole is a particularly popular dish.

The Blanco family purchased the Walton house and avocado groves in 1985. The family restored the pretty English cottage to its original lovely vision. The groves became an impressive rare plant garden. Luckily the devastation of Hurricane Andrew left the cottage virtually untouched. The English dwelling has stood the test of time and remains a private residence today.

US 1, Homestead
MD45 ~ GPS Coordinates: 25.468379, -80.473256

Area garden clubs sponsor Blue Star Memorial Highway markers in honor of those who have fought and died in the military service. The Miami-Dade County area has a vast array of gardening organizations. Including the East Everglades Orchid Society, the South Florida Orchid Society, Tropical Fern and Exotic Plant Society as well as the Miami Medical Center's Nursing Home Garden Club to name a few. Dade County is also home to one of the most acclaimed gardens throughout the United States, Fairchild Tropical Botanic Garden.

The East Everglades Orchid Society was formed as an organization serving those with a common interest. The society provides education, exhibits, competitions, social opportunities and a number of programs of interest to its membership. They host three orchid shows each year.

The South Florida Orchid Society was organized in 1945 as a branch of the American Orchid Society. This organization hosts the world's most renowned event in orchid circles, the Miami International Orchid Show.

More than two hundred growers represent their unique rare and exotic blossoms. Each March more than five hundred thousand plants are displayed at the Coconut Grove Convention Center.

One of the most unique clubs is the Miami Medical Center Nursing Home group. They practice a particularly interesting Horticultural Therapy Program utilizing plants and gardening to improve the mental and physical acuity of the patients participating. The therapy is known to improve motor functions, alertness, problem solving skills, socialization and self-esteem. Additionally the program gives residents a sense of being needed and control often lost when forced to depend on others for one's care. It is an extremely impressive means of therapy with proven positive results.

The Tropical Fern and Exotic Plant Society is a group chiefly interested in plants native to south Florida and tropical locales. Begonias, bromeliads, heliconias and hibiscus as well as many other tropical plants are represented. The group enjoys lectures, presentations, demonstrations and various projects through the community. The society meets at Fairchild Tropical Botanic Garden the fourth Monday of each month with the exception of July and August.

Located at 10901 Old Cutler Road in Coral Gables, Fairchild Tropical Botanic Garden has been a Dade County mainstay since 1938. Colonel Robert H. Montgomery founded the botanical garden and named it for his friend David Fairchild. Dr. Fairchild retired to Miami after traveling the world introducing various plants including mangos, alfalfa, nectarines, dates, horseradish, bamboo and flowering cherries to the United States. He developed the Section of Foreign Seed and Plants for the Department of Agriculture at the age of twenty-two. Many of the plants Dr. Fairchild planted are still growing in the garden including a giant African baobab tree at the entrance. Dr. David Fairchild passed away in 1954.

The gardens are open every day with the exception of Christmas. The first Wednesday of the month is Contribution Day when visitors are allowed to set their own admission fee, otherwise a modest ticket price is charged. A narrated tram tour is offered hourly and included in admission is the Conservatory and Whitman Tropical Fruit Pavilion. The Garden Café is open daily offering light lunches or a refreshing drink for those hot tropical days.

End Notes

[1] Women's Army Corps

[2] Prisoner's of War

[3] the arm whose shadow indicates the time

[4] A variety of limestone, consisting of small round grains, resembling the roe of a fish.

[5] The spelling of the name eventually changed to Coconut Grove that we see today.

[6] Also known as Plymouth Church

[7] Known today as the Ransom School.

[8] Protestant

[9] Naval Air Station

[10] Lighter Than Air

[11] Federal Emergency Management Administration

[12] A soil that consists of or contains calcium carbonate

[13] South Federal Highway

Monroe County

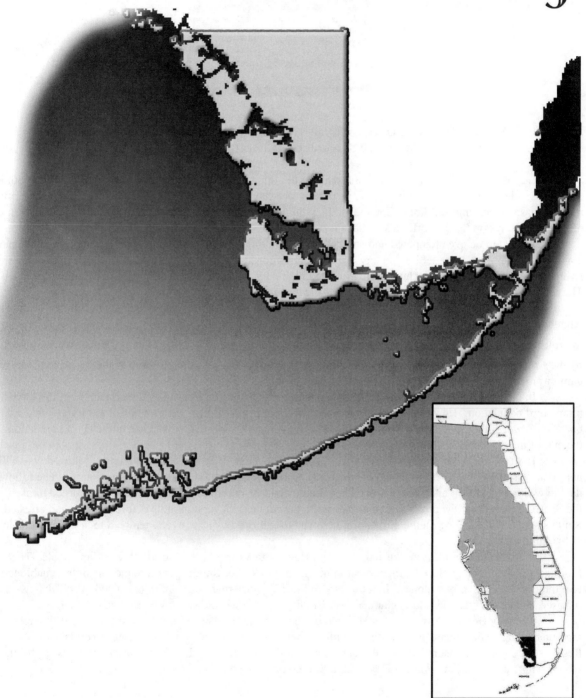

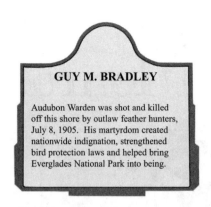

GUY M. BRADLEY

Audubon Warden was shot and killed off this shore by outlaw feather hunters, July 8, 1905. His martyrdom created nationwide indignation, strengthened bird protection laws and helped bring Everglades National Park into being.

Flamingo Visitors Center, Everglades National Park, Main Park Road, Flamingo
MO1 ~ GPS Coordinates: 25.141083, -80.924033

Guy Bradley was born 1870 and raised along the Intracoastal Waterway of Florida's east coast. Both his father and older brother were part of the distinguished few that were known as the Barefoot Mailmen delivering mail to coastal communities. For a time the Bradley family assumed responsibility for the Fort Lauderdale House of Refuge, always on hand to offer a safe haven to victims of shipwreck.

Known to be even tempered and somewhat shy, Guy taught himself to play the fiddle and tried his hand at a number of odd jobs never settling on any one occupation for long. Ironically, he spent much of his time in the Everglades guiding backcountry hunts for egrets and plume birds. He eventually married and had two children. The family attended the small Union Church near their home.

By the turn of the twentieth century, plume birds were being hunted at a rate of five million a year. The Audubon Society watched in horror as many of these birds crept ever closer to extinction. The organization vowed to protect the few remaining rookeries[1]. Guy Bradley was working as a Monroe County Deputy when approached by the American Ornithologists[2] Union, at the urging of the Audubon Society, to serve as the first Everglades game warden.

In November of 1902, Guy accepted the position and dedicated himself to the protection of the dwindling plume bird population. He was known to travel thousands of miles through the swamps of the Everglades in his boat, *Audubon*, willing to face any hardship bravely. Guy happily reported an increase in the egret population at the end of his second year of service.

Bradley went into the Everglades after a man by the name of Walter Smith whom he believed was killing heron on Oyster Key. He set out in *Audubon* on July 8, 1905 after Smith and never returned home. The following day he was found, still in his boat. Warden Guy Bradley had been shot to death. Walter Smith turned himself in to the Sheriff at Key West the next day and confessed to the murder. Several months before Bradley had arrested Smith's son Tom for killing plume birds. Smith vowed to kill Bradley if he ever attempted to arrest any member of his family again.

Warden Guy Bradley was buried on a shell ridge with a view of the Florida Bay at Cape Sable. The Florida Audubon Society placed a monument in his memory. Walter Smith spent five months in jail unable to raise five thousand dollars in bail money. In a travesty to justice, a jury ruled that Smith had acted in self-defense and released him. The Everglades later claimed Guy Bradley's grave when a storm washed away the site.

The Guy Bradley Award was established by the National Fish and Wildlife Foundation in 1988, recognizing outstanding achievements in wildlife law enforcement. The National Audubon Society Everglades Ecosystem Restoration Campaign honors individuals each year with the Guy Bradley Lifetime Conservation Award for those who promote conservation. Warden Guy Bradley's memory lives on.

BLUE STAR MEMORIAL HIGHWAY

A tribute to the Armed Forces that have defended the United States of America.

US 1 and Atlantic Blvd, Key Largo
MO2 ~ GPS Coordinates: 25.093050, -80.441467

Located at mile marker 81.5 in Islamorada is the Florida Keys Memorial. Every year millions of tourists pass the engraved stone tribute without ever realizing the sacrifice of many World War I veterans who died while building a bridge to paradise. As travelers make the trek along US 1 each pass an eerie sight in the beautiful green blue waters. Coffin-like rectangles rise dark from the gulf side waters just south of Lower Matecumbe Key. These make shift monuments represent piers of a planned bridge never completed. The gray pyres of concrete stand in memory of veterans prepared to die for their country in battle but gave their lives instead to a storm while attempting to survive Americas' Great Depression. Eight bridge anchors and an island are all that remain of the veterans efforts after the devastating hurricane of September 2, 1935.

The Florida Federal Emergency Relief Association created eleven Veteran's Camps, three of which were located in the Keys. Working alongside the veterans was the Civilian Conservation Camp employees. These men, in an ironic twist, as civilian workers were required to wear uniforms, take a physical examination and work within a military structure. Each veteran's camp had a superintendent, whereas the civilian camp had a commander or captain.

The World War I veterans sent to work in these federal camps were a mixed cross section of Americans. Represented were educated men, professional athletes, tradesmen and career soldiers. Many bore the scars of war from poison gas, shell shock or shrapnel wounds, others had no injuries at all. Many of the men kept their families near in whatever hovel their meager pay would support. When the hurricane tore through it did not distinguish between veteran, man, woman or child; all were subjected to the danger and many paid dearly.

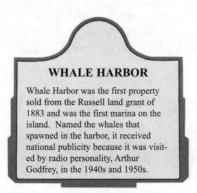

WHALE HARBOR

Whale Harbor was the first property sold from the Russell land grant of 1883 and was the first marina on the island. Named the whales that spawned in the harbor, it received national publicity because it was visited by radio personality, Arthur Godfrey, in the 1940s and 1950s.

US 1, MM 84, Islamorada
MO3 ~ GPS Coordinates: 24.935571, -80.614378

Whale Harbor Inn was in its hey day in 1927. The Inn was built for ten thousand dollars and eventually ran by a man named Al Luckey. Fresh water had to be brought in from Homestead. A fish camp just north of the Whale Harbor bridge was called Starck's Fish Camp named for owners Ruth and Captain Buck.

The fish camp hosted charters for recognizable names such as Vanderbilt, R. J. Reynolds, Anita Bryant, Jane Mansfield and the Firestone family. Captain Buck often recalled Ms. Mansfield was "very healthy," obviously he had an eye for the ladies. President and Mrs. Truman were once guests with Edward R. Murrow tagging along for the story.

Arthur Godfrey enjoyed the hospitality of Whale Harbor Inn saying, "For a while, I had it all to myself." Once the celebrities arrived, people flocked to the Inn and business was booming. The tiki hut overlooking the glorious blue waters of the Atlantic bore a sign advertising Whale Burgers on the menu.

Today Starck's Fish Camp is part of Chesapeake and Whale Harbor Inns. The tiki hut and docks are a parking lot.

ISLAMORADA RAILWAY

The Islamorada Post Office stands today where the railway station was located before it was destroyed by the 1935 hurricane.

US 1, MM 84, Islamorada
MO4 ~ GPS Coordinates: 24.928605, -80.622203

Native Americans first called the Florida Keys home before European explorers ever stepped foot on the island shores. Families who came to be known as Conches settled Key West. Small farms and fishing communities popped up here and there along the chain of islands. The Russell family homesteaded at what was then known as Umbrella Key, today known as Windley Key. Florida East Coast Railway purchased the Russell family homestead in 1908 for eight hundred fifty-two dollars, eighty cents.

Henry Flagler was determined to extend his railroad to Key West even though almost unanimously people thought it was impossible. Flagler spent years working out the details of the route, paying particular attention to the areas of open water the rails would have to ford. The price tag was estimated at approximately fifty million dollars and required five years of intensive labor. At one time more than twenty five hundred men were employed in the construction of the enormous project.

Employment with Flagler's railroad was a very good venture. Wages were one dollar, twenty-five cents per day and included housing, meals and hospitalization insurance. All food, water, clothing, supplies and housing had to be brought in on barges. Building materials and tools also had to be brought in by boat. Working conditions were dismal. Temperatures soared, mosquitoes and sand flies were relentless and the only thing plentiful was salt water.

Henry Flagler anxiously awaited the completion of his dream, for his health was failing and he realized that his time on earth was growing short. Ever supportive the construction crews worked twenty-four hours a day to bring Flagler's dream to reality. On January 22, 1912 Henry Flagler boarded his private railcar called *Rambler* to ride the rails to its final destination, Key West. With his dream realized Henry Morrison Flagler passed away in May of 1913.

For twenty-three years the Florida East Coast Railway chugged along. By 1935 more than fifty million passengers had made the one hundred fifty six-mile journey from Miami to Key West. A round trip ticket cost four dollars, seventy-five cents. The railroad brought with it other benefits as well. Post Offices were able to get daily deliveries, supplies and fresh water from the mainland was easily obtained as well as transportation access became a much simpler prospect.

Along the tracks polished keystone was quarried and the railroad made delivery of the sought after building material virtually effortless. In fact the stone was used for numerous buildings throughout the United States including the St. Louis Post Office as well as the New York City Chapel. The quarries remained active until the mid 1960s and are today a protected historical site.

An urgent alarm was sounded throughout the Florida Keys on September 2, 1935. The impending hurricane spurred the Florida East Coast Railway engineer to assemble the locomotive and a few baggage cars for a race against time and the brutal storm. At Homestead he determined to move the locomotive to the rear of the train to enact a faster retreat. Unfortunately waves were already crashing over the track as the train roared into Islamorada. When the train squealed to a stop, families hurriedly boarded but tragically the time spent in Homestead was the death knell for the train and its passengers. A huge eighteen-foot swell plunged over the train, homes and businesses. Everything in its path was dragged out to sea and what was not drowned was demolished by two hundred mile per hour winds. All that remained was rubble. The hurricane was said to be the most powerful storm ever to pommel the area. More than five hundred bodies were recovered, the exact number of lives lost will never be known.

The Florida East Coast Railway was completely destroyed, never to recover. A monument to those who lost their lives to the Labor Day hurricane, September 2, 1935 is located at Islamorada from locally quarried stone. The hurricane tragedy will never be forgotten for it touched the lives of every person living, working or visiting the Keys on that fateful day.

ORIGINAL ISLAMORADA
RAILROAD BUILDING

ISLAMORADA
CHAMBER OF COMMERCE

ISLAMORADA POST OFFICE

The third Islamorada post office was built in 1934. This building also contained a restaurant and a filing station, and was destroyed in the 1935 hurricane. Members of the Russell family held the postmaster position for 59 years.

US 1, MM 83, Islamorada
MO5 ~ GPS Coordinates: 24.928052, -80.623391

The Florida East Coast Railway brought the first reliable mail service to the Upper Keys in 1908. It was that year that John H. Russell built the first post office after Elsie M. Rue filed the initial application. John H. Russell served as the first postmaster to a population of just over one hundred fifty residents. Rue was appointed postmaster on October 21 followed by John A. Russell, the following year. Thus began the long Russell dynasty in the postal service.

A wooden clapboard post office was built in 1909 and remained until its replacement was built of coral rock in 1926. The facility became somewhat of a mini-mall when additions included a mercantile, eatery and full service filling station. All that remains of this facility today is the old concrete foundation located at mile marker 82.8 overlooking the brilliant blue green waters of the Atlantic.

The devastating hurricane of 1935 had an effect on every aspect of the Keys and the post office wasn't to be spared. A new facility was built from durable Florida pine by John A. Russell on a lot provided by the Red Cross for his home. James Clifton Russell assumed the postmaster position when his brother retired in 1937.

A new concrete facility was built on an oceanside lot at mile marker 83.2. Later Marty's TV Store was to occupy the building and the older wooden building was moved to its current location where the facility became the Keys Shell Shop. Clifton Russell served as the Islamorada postmaster until 1967 when he retired ending the fifty-nine year reign of the Russell family to the postal service.

Jenevieve Stout was appointed the subsequent postmaster upon Clifton's retirement. Three years later the present post office was dedicated. Today the present post office stands only a few feet north of where the postal service began at Islamorada in 1909.

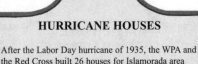

HURRICANE HOUSES

After the Labor Day hurricane of 1935, the WPA and the Red Cross built 26 houses for Islamorada area families whose home had been demolished. Seven houses still stand in the vicinity of the monument. They are constructed of poured concrete and steel with foundations 18 inches thick and 6 to 8 foot cisterns beneath the floors. The walls are 12 inches thick. The cisterns hold enough water to sustain a family of four through the dry season. They were built to be "hurricane proof."

US 1, MM 82, Islamorada
MO6 ~ GPS Coordinates: 24.918369, -80.634645

The Red Cross, Works Progress Administration and Federal Emergency Relief Administration banded together after the desolation left from the Labor Day 1935 hurricane to provide shelter for those who were left homeless from the torrential flooding, tidal surges and destroying winds. The homes built were known as Red Cross houses, strong enough to withstand hurricane force winds and rain.

Twenty-nine houses were built. The foundations were eighteen inches thick, walls were a massive twelve inches thick and water cisterns beneath the structure ranged from six to eight feet deep. Twenty-three of the Red Cross houses were massive concrete structure but six others were built from durable Florida pine. Many of the residents were desperate for shelter so rather than wait in turn, they were given the funds to purchase materials and build their own dwellings.

Homes were built having one to four bedrooms. They were identical only differing in the length dependent on how many bedrooms the house featured. The interiors varied only slightly. The lower section of the house held a side by side cistern, each compartment was independent so that each side could be cleaned. The walls, floors and roofs were all reinforced concrete mixed with seawater and smoothed to harden. Steel rods were driven into place to reinforce the stability of the walls.

A conveyor belt delivered the concrete for pouring into the wooden forms used to create the massive walls. Once the concrete dried the forms were removed and the wall stood strong and tall. The saltwater caused rusting to the steel reinforced bars but were very easily reparable. Today very few of the Red Cross Houses still stand. Left in disarray over the years many of the structures have been torn down.

**HELEN WADLEY
BRANCH LIRBARY**

The public library building was constructed originally by the Red Cross and the Works Progress Administration (WPA) three years after the "Great Hurricane" of 1935, to serve as a community hurricane shelter. Prior to that time no protective buildings existed in Islamorada, consequently, hundreds of veterans and local citizens died with little or no protection from high winds and water. The poured concrete and steel walls of the shelter are 18 inches thick at the base. Additionally, it served as the local school, replacing the previous school destroyed by the storm. Later it functioned as a church and a U.S. Coast Guard facility before becoming a library in 1966. A library addition was built onto the rear of the original structure in 1983.

**US 1, MM 81.5, Islamorada
MO7 ~ GPS Coordinates: 24.918188, -80.635987**

The Red Cross building at mile marker 81.5 has known many uses since its construction in 1935. The Islamorada School was destroyed so the building first served as a school for area children until a facility could be built. Once the school was in place, the building was utilized by the local Baptist congregation, once the new sanctuary was built just across what was to be US 1, the United States Coast Guard was housed there. Eventually the concrete and steel facility became a hurricane shelter.

In 1966, the Red Cross building was officially opened in its current capacity as the Islamorada branch of the Monroe County Library System. The facility was named for Helen Wadley, who passed away in 1995. Helen was president of the Friends of the Library for many years and it was through her dedication and community service that the library was expanded and upgraded to the computer age.

The Helen Wadley Library is a welcoming facility. The furniture is meant to offer comfort while one enjoys reading from the vast collection. A special Florida Room features materials ranging from the earliest days of Native American and Spanish occupation to the modern tourism of the Florida Keys. The library is open Monday through Saturday, ready to meet the public's needs. Various special programs are offered throughout the year bringing culture, education and entertainment to all patrons that pass through the library doors.

HURRICANE MONUMENT

The Florida Keys Memorial, known locally as the "Hurricane Monument," was built to honor hundreds of American veterans and local citizens who perished in the "Great Hurricane" on Labor Day, September 2, 1935. Islamorada sustained winds of 200 miles per hour and a barometer reading of 26.35 inches for many hours on that fateful holiday. Most local buildings and the Florida East Coast Railway were destroyed by what remains the most savage hurricane on record. Hundreds of World War I veterans who had been camped in the Matecumbe area while working on the construction of U.S. Highway One for the Works Progress Administration (WPA) were killed. In 1937 the cremated remains of approximately 300 people were placed within the tiled crypt in front of the monument. The monument is composed of native keystone, and its striking frieze depicts coconut palm trees bending before the force of hurricane winds while the waters from an angry sea lap at the bottom of their trunks. Monument construction was funded by the WPA and regional veterans' associations. Over the years the Hurricane Monument has been cared for by local veterans, hurricane survivors, and descendants of the victims.

MM 81.5, Old State Road 4A, Upper Matecumbe Key
MO8 ~ GPS Coordinates: 24.916867, -80.636283

Hundreds of World War I veterans were housed at three work camps as they constructed US 1 for the Works Progress Administration and some two hundred seventy people lived at Islamorada; countless others were visiting along the beautiful Florida Keys. It was the summer's last hurrah, Labor Day weekend before the kids returned to school when tragedy struck.

September 2, 1935 will be remembered as the day two hundred-mile per hour winds tore through the Florida Keys as an eighteen-foot wall of water drowned what the wind left behind. By morning homes and businesses were reduced to rubble, families were torn apart and the death toll rose by the hour. Though the exact number of dead will never be known, more than five hundred people were brutally murdered by the killer storm. Of the two hundred seventy citizens living in Islamorada, one hundred sixty-seven were listed as dead or missing.

Two years later the Harvey Seeds Post of the American Legion in Miami raised over three thousand dollars in order to build a memorial for those lost the 1935 hurricane. The final cost would be approximately twelve thousand dollars, the design came from the Florida Division of the Federal Art Project and construction was handled by the Works Progress Administration. The plot was donated by the Monroe County School Board and construction sponsored by the Monroe County Commissioners. Forty men worked to complete the sixty-five by twenty foot monument with broad coral slab steps quarried from nearby Windley Key and Key Largo leading to an elevated flooring area. Later a crushed coral bed, flagpole and concrete sidewalk were added. Eventually landscaping added to the beauty of the simple monument.

A crypt built into the upper level cradles the bones and ashes of many who perished on that fateful

September day. Ceramist Adela Gisbet created a twenty-two foot map of the Keys representing Key Largo to Marathon inland into the crypt cover. The monument rises eighteen feet heavenward with a carving of a tidal wave and coconut palm bending to the force of the mighty winds. The design was created by Harold Lawson and developed by Lambert Bemlemans; other artists contributing to the memorial were William Shaw, Allie Mae Kitchens and Emigdio Reyes. The memorial has a bronze plaque created by John Klinkenberg reading:

HURRICANE MEMORIAL

"Dedicated to the memory of the civilians and war veterans whose lives were lost in the hurricane of September 2, 1935."

More than four thousand people gathered from all over the United States for the dedication ceremony of the sad memorial. Initially scheduled for Armistice Day, November 11, which happened to be a Thursday; the date was changed to accommodate those wishing to pay their respects to Sunday, November 14, 1937.

The service began at 12:30 with a presentation of the flag as the Work Progress Administration Symphony played Verde's "Aida". Reverend J. Yancy of the Matecumbe Methodist Church offered the invocation and Mrs. Charles Moon of Coral Gables led the singing of "America". O. A. Sandquist introduced the speaker Colonel P. J. O'Shaughnessy. President of the University of Florida, Dr. John Tigert presented a telegram from President Franklin Delano Roosevelt reading:

"I join in the dedication of the monument to those who met death in the awful visitation that swept the Florida Keys on Labor Day, 1935. The disaster, which made desolate the heart of so many of our people brought a personal sorrow to me because some years ago, I knew many residents of the Keys. I tender to all whose hearts were torn by the loss of loved ones an assurance of heart-felt sympathy."

Nine-year-old hurricane survivor Fay Marie Parker pulled the cord to unveil the memorial. The Russell family laid a wreath in memory of fifty members their family lost to the storm. A closing prayer was offered and the audience sang the National Anthem.

By the late 1990s the monument began displaying some signs of aging. The Matecumbe Historical Trust eventually restored the memorial to its original glory. On March 16, 1995, the United States Department of Interior placed the 1935 Hurricane Memorial on the National Register of Historic Places. Millions pass the Florida Keys Memorial each and every year, though few take the time to stop and pay their respects. The beautiful monument continues to stand reaching heavenward as a reminder of the power of natures' storms and in memory of those who lost their lives to the September 2, 1935 killer hurricane.

PIONEER CEMETERY

This cemetery memorializes the determination and vision of over 50 pioneer Anglo-Bahamian Conchs who labored to settle and organize the first community on Matecumbe Key. Descendants of three Islamorada pioneer families, the Russells who homesteaded in 1854, the Pinders in 1873, and the Parkers in 1898, are buried on this land. Deeded to Richard Pinder on January 20, 1883 by President Chester A. Arthur, the land now is the property of the Matecumbe United Methodist Church. North and adjacent to the cemetery lay the first church on the key, built in 1884 and transported to this site by raft ca. 1890. Next to it the first two-room frame school-house was built ca. 1900,
and later replaced by a coral-rock building.
A raging hurricane struck Islamorada on Labor Day in 1935, killing 50 members of the Russell family alone. The storm also destroyed the church, the schoolhouse and the "Millionaires' Row" of beachfront homes adjacent to this property. The survivors' descendants rebuilt their homes, a new church and a school west of this site and east of Henry Flagler's Overseas Railway, now US 1.

MM 82 on the beach at Cheeca Lodge, Islamorada
MO9 ~ GPS Coordinates: 24.914528, -80.635274

The oldest church of Islamorada was built in 1884 out of hardy Florida pine. When the pioneering Parker family relocated to the southern portion of Upper Matecumbe Key around 1894, the church was moved with them.

It must have been quite a sight watching the wooden church building afloat between two sailboats like the biblical stories of Noah's Ark. The church finally came to rest near what is today Cheeca Lodge beside the clear blue waters of the Atlantic.

Eventually William Matheson made a generous donation of property for the construction of the Islamorada School, Methodist Church and

THE PIONEER CEMETERY HISTORICAL MARKER

cemetery. Etta Dolores Pinder was the name appearing on the first headstone at the new cemetery. A member of Upper Matecumbe's first homesteader family, the Russells, was interred in a garden of the dead just north of the new cemetery site.

Marking the cemetery at Cheeca Lodge is an angel who has stood a silent vigil for more than seventy years. It was said that more than fifty

graves were known to be interred at this site, but over time many of the Conch pioneers' final resting-places were lost. When the killer

**PIONEER CEMETERY
ANGEL
SURVIVED THE 1938
HURRICANE**

hurricane of 1935 was unleashed on the indefensible Keys, the mighty wind lifted up the Angel of Pioneer Cemetery in flight. The beautiful symbol of death was driven into the pavement of Old Highway 4. She was later returned to her soundless sentry, a broken wing the scar of that awful day.

Owner of Washington DC's Olney Inn, Clara Mae Downey expanded her holding when she built the Islamorada Olney Inn in 1946. Eventually the Inn was sold; the new owners were heirs of the A & P grocery store chain, Carl and Cynthia "Che-Che" Twitchell. A complete renovation was enacted and with it came a new name. Cheeca Lodge was the result of a combination of the two owners' names. Carl Navarre, a Coca-Cola bottler, purchased the property in the 1970s. The Navarre family still owns a home on the property to this day. Cheeca Lodge & Spa is owned by Cheeca Holdings and managed by Vail Resorts of Vail, Colorado. The resort continues to embrace the beautifully maintained Pioneer Cemetery, safely held within a white picket fence and obviously respectfully cared for.

**ISLAMORADA
BAPTIST CHURCH**

During the "Great Hurricane of 1935, the Matecumbe Methodist Church was destroyed. It was originally located near the beach on the Atlantic side of the Upper Matecumbe Key. In 1937, the congregation built a new wooden church adjacent to the Hurricane Monument north of here. The building was moved to this site in 1958 and became the home of the local Baptist congregation.

**US 1, MM 82, Islamorada
MO10 ~ GPS Coordinates: 24.911712, -80.642129**

The first ministers to offer services in the Keys were Methodists Sonelian and Giddens based out of Key West and traveling to the Upper Keys. Reverend J. M. Sweat was assigned by the Florida Methodist Conference to serve various congregations in the Upper Keys in 1887. Travel was at best difficult during this time, roads were hardly more than foot paths between farms and boats were required to ferry between the islands.

Henry Flagler's Florida East Coast Railway route down the Keys played an important part in the development of the church. Ministers could easily travel from one church to another and volunteers would fill the pulpit in the interim. The Florida Times Union newspaper gave a glowing report of the Methodist church on August 20, 1908 while covering the story of the railroad's route to Key West.

Islamorada settler Richard Pinder financed the construction of a one room Florida pine Methodist church in 1894. His son Preston supervised the construction and remained a dedicated member for more than fifty years. Located on the Upper Matecumbe Key, the church served the pioneering families of Russell and Pinder. Other attendants arrived from Umbrella and Long Island Keys to the north. Reverend John Watkins, known by parishioners as Uncle Johnny, was the very first permanent pastor of the Methodist congregation.

Reynolds Cothron and his son Alonzo arrived in the Keys as railroad workers and soon Alonzo met Florence Pinder and fell in love. The couple wanted to marry on the Upper Matecumbe Key and the Reverend Munro was summoned from Key West to perform the ceremony. Theirs was the first marriage performed at the little pine church built by the Pinder family on June 9, 1926.

The railroad brought a population boom to the Florida Keys. The Methodist congregation swelled to over one hundred parishioners, but the death knell was about to sound throughout the Keys. On Labor Day, September 2, 1935, a killing hurricane swept through the Keys destroying everything in its path. The Upper Matecumbe Key Methodist Church was reduced to a heap of shattered splinters. The parsonage was extensively damaged but could be rebuilt.

The church bell was found; the congregation refusing to be beaten hung it from a tree branch and rang the call to worship. The parsonage served as a makeshift meeting house while Preston Pinder built another edifice at mile marker 81.5. Tragically Reverend and Mrs. Carlson who had assumed the congregation at Matecumbe were both killed by the storm.

The Methodist Church continued strong in the Upper Keys until January 4, 1954 when the First Baptist Church of Islamorada began observing services at what is today the Helen Wadley Branch Library. Reverend John Whitt led the services. The Methodist church continued to dominate religion in the Upper Keys until the 1950s. On January 4, 1954, the First Baptist Church of Islamorada was in its infancy when the Reverend John Whitt of Homestead began holding services in the present Islamorada library building. This was largely due to the efforts of Doris Albury and Elnora Woods who had organized a Sunday School in 1953.

Reverend Whitt resigned and Dr. Lacy took the pulpit in his place. The Baptist Keys Mission was officially organized in the spring of 1954. The Key Largo Baptist congregation met at the newly established Key Largo Civic Club until the Matecumbe Methodists generously donated their sanctuary and all furnishings in 1958. The Baptists at Homestead provided alms for moving expenses. The first service in the new Baptist Church was held on May 11, 1958. Additions were made the next year and the following year a parsonage was constructed.

September 10, 1960, Hurricane Donna swept through the Florida Keys with one hundred thirty-five gusting to one hundred seventy-five mile per hour winds. The Baptist Church suffered some damage but miraculously no one was killed. Several weeks passed with the congregation gathering in the hot tropical sun for services. A new sanctuary was completed in 1969 and is still in use today.

TEA TABLE KEY

Just west of the bridge from Upper Matecumbe, this small island was a Navy base called Fort Paulding in the 1830s.

US 1, MM 79, Islamorada
MO11 ~ GPS Coordinates: 24.896445, -80.662246

Tea Table Key's history seems to have begun with the Second Seminole War in 1835 lasting until 1842. The war began with the massacre of Major Francis Dade and his troops in December of 1835. The troops were marching home from Tampa when they were overcome by the warring Seminole. Dade County was named for this dedicated military hero whose life was brutally ended by the Seminole insurrection. Within two weeks of Major Dade's ambush, the slaughter of William Cooley's family near Fort Lauderdale shocked approximately two hundred settlers so badly that they abandoned their homes for the safety of fortifications at Indian Key and Key West.

In July of 1836 the Seminole attacked the Cape Florida Lighthouse killing the assistant keeper, leaving keeper John W. B. Thompson for dead amidst the inferno of the burning lighthouse tower. Captain John Whalton, the lightship keeper at Carysfort Reef and one of his crewmen were victims of the third major battle of the Seminole War. Captain Jacob Housman organized the Florida Militia on Indian Key under orders to put down the

Indian revolution. Under the leadership of Commanding General Zachary Taylor two naval ships, the *Madison* and *Campbell* were deployed to monitor the waters off the Florida Keys in June 1838.

Commander of the ship *Campbell*, Lieutenant Coste reported to Secretary of the Navy James Paulding that a fortification at Tea Table Key was named in his honor. Of course the distinction would have been a disappointment had Secretary Paulding knew that the entire command spanned only three and a half acres of mangrove with two thatched roof huts. Few settlers identified the small maritime-forested area as Fort Paulding referring to it as merely Tea Table Key. Another type battle soon ensued when settler Lemuel Otis, who farmed parts of Tea Table Key, claimed the property was his homestead and brought legal action against the government.

Apparently additional structures were built on Tea Table Key during this period because charges were levied against Lieutenant Coste for utilizing military troops to build his private residence. Coste was supported by his First Lieutenant John Faunce in a post to the Office of the Revenue Cutters dispelling the accusations made. In fact Faunce reported that Lieutenant Coste specifically instructed that no military personnel were to be allowed to assist in the building of his personal quarters. Personnel were used to build two structures where provisions and boats awaiting repair were stored. Other letters of support were issued by Key West civilians offering evidence that Lieutenant Coste purchased materials and paid builders from his private account for the construction of his home.

On August 7, 1840 the Seminole attacked Indian Key soldiers. Midshipman Francis Key Murray reported

**SOMETIMES THE HUNT FOR MARKERS
CAN BE A CHALLENGE!**

that he and twelve other servicemen attempted to put down the insurrection. Unfortunately seven of his men were either sick or injured and their only artillery was one malfunctioning four-pound canon. The fight was virtually one sided, twelve soldiers against approximately sixty Indians.

It was thought that after the attack Tea Table Key was abandoned. However, reports from Lieutenant Commander J. T. McLaughlin dispelled this notion. On November 17, 1841 McLaughlin wrote to his superiors that soldiers with small arms were drilling at Fort Paulding. It may be that only the drill field and flagstaff remained on Tea Table Key when the Second Seminole War finally came to an end in 1842. The Seminole would rise one final time before being vanquished from Florida. Only a sparse few Native Americans remained, hiding deep in the Everglades. The Seminole were now a ghostlike people, seldom seen except as fleeting shadows dissolving into the haze of the swamp.

INDIAN KEY

Indians lived on this island over 1000 years ago. In 1722, it was known as Boys Island. In Dec. 1838, Lt. Coste established a Naval base here and named it Ft. Paulding. This was the base for the West Indian Squadron, used to blockade the coast to keep the Indians from receiving supplies from the Bahamas or Cuba. The Navy's first steamship, "The Sea Gull" was based here.

While the Navy was looking for the Indians in the Everglades, the Indians attacked nearby Indian Key on Aug. 7, 1840 destroying the village and county seat of Dade County.

US 1, MM 78, Islamorada
MO12 ~ GPS Coordinates: 24.893467, -80.668204

Scientists have revealed that Native Americans dwelt on the islands of the Keys for thousands of years before Europeans "discovered" them. Ponce de Leon was given credit in 1513 for his exploration of a new route for the Spanish Treasure Fleet sailing home from Mexican shores via the Straits of Florida. Unfortunately his route was known as waters with great peril. The sharp coral reefs laid waste to many a Spanish vessel as well as tremendous hurricanes that sentenced the huge sailing ships to a watery grave.

The Calusa tribe was the first named people of the Florida Keys. They collected riches from Spanish ships sunk in the clear waters off their shores. Soon European diseases and battles vanquished the Calusa who had virtually disappeared by the time of the English occupation in 1763. Fishermen from the Bahamas saw a vast opportunity and took up wrecking as a means of survival. Pirates of the Atlantic and Caribbean waters soon arrived showing no prejudice; they robbed everyone to cross their path.

Once Florida became an American territory in 1821, piracy was banished. Americans took over the wrecking trade and drove the Bahamians back to their little islands to the southeast. Key West was the ideal wrecking station and many Americans became wealthy off the trade. A young man from Staten Island, New York named Jacob Housman arrived in a ship stolen from his father to find his fortune in wrecking at Key West. He was very successful until the standing government accused him of shady business deals. To avoid further investigation, Housman moved his operation to Indian Key.

The island was an ideal location for Housman with fresh water to the north and dangerous reefs nearby that left a buffet for the wrecking business. He purchased Indian Key in 1831 and built his own empire from the coral ground up. Housman developed the island into a busy port village with fifty residents, most relying on him for their very existence. Indian Key made Jacob Housman a wealthy man and soon Key West accused him once again of illegal activities. He ignored the allegations largely because Indian Key was his territory and on it he was king. Welding his considerable power, Housman had the Florida Legislative Council create Dade County in 1836 and name Indian Key the center for county government making it independent of Key West.

Jacob Housman advertised his hotel on Indian Key as a therapeutic resort for those suffering from tuberculosis vowing that the warm tropical climate and clean salt air breeze would improve the affliction. To make the grounds more appealing he brought in topsoil by barge to aid in elaborate tropical landscaping. By the mid 1830s, Indian Key boasted a permanent population of over one hundred residents. Despite his successes, numerous court battles with the Key West government left Housman virtually bankrupt. When the Second Seminole War was waged in 1835, the Native American trade was lost. Finally to cut his losses Housman was forced to mortgage the island.

Dr. Henry Perrine moved his family to what he thought was safety at Indian Key in 1838 to wait out the Second Seminole War. Dr. Perrine spent his time in self-imposed exile to start a tropical plant nursery. He experimented with agave to harvest hemp for rope making, as well as tea, coffee, bananas and mangos. Jacob Housman realized Indian Key was a prime target due to their surplus of goods warehoused there. In a change of tune, Housman begged for government protection. A small detachment was stationed at Tea Table Key, however they proved to be ineffective with only five able men.

A band of one hundred Seminole attacked Indian Key on August 7, 1840. Many of the inhabitants managed to escape including Housman and his wife but Dr. Perrine was not so lucky. The doctor managed to get his family to safety but while trying to negotiate with the Seminole, Dr. Henry Perrine was brutally murdered, his body left to the flame of a funeral pyre that was once his home. Every standing building with the exception of one was burned leaving only soot blackened stone foundations.

A few of the inhabitants returned to Indian Key but Housman vowed never to return. He sold the island and sought work with a wrecking crew at Key West. Less than a year later while salvaging in rough seas, Jacob Housman was crushed between two ships. Indian Key was eventually abandoned completely. Dr. Perrine's plants soon grew wild consuming the ruins of the island.

Today the only way to reach Indian Key is by boat. By far the winter months are the most pleasant times to visit Indian Key. The breath-taking voyage across the clear blue green waters offers many amazing sights. Often dolphins are seen jumping in the surf following the boat along its trek and from time to time the added treat of a surfacing green sea turtle can be spotted as they rise for a breath of air. The Florida Park Service continually strives to maintain the historical ruins of the island. Visitors from all over the world make the trip each year to the unspoiled Florida State Park, open year round from 8:00 AM until the sun slides below the horizon each evening.

FLORIDA EAST COAST RAILROAD
OVERSEAS EXTENSION
"THE RAILROAD THAT WENT TO SEA"

Oil magnate Henry M. Flagler first visited Florida in 1878. Realizing Florida's potential for growth, he developed railroads and hotels which transformed the eastern seaboard. The Florida East Coast Railroad reached Miami in 1896 and soon was completed to the Homestead area. Years of planning were devoted to determining the feasibility of extending the F.E.C. Railroad to Key West which was labeled "Flagler's Folly." Construction was begun in 1904 under the supervision of Joseph C. Meredith. After Meredith's death in 1909, William J. Krome guided the project. Viaducts, trestles, and bridges were constructed under harrowing conditions. Thousands of workers battled against insects, hurricanes, and intense heat as well as food and water shortages. On January 21, 1912, the Overseas Extension of the Florida East Coast Railroad was completed. The next day, Henry Flagler's special train arrived in Key West. Flagler died in 1913, but his Overseas Extension continued to carry visitors to Key West until 1935, when the Labor Day hurricane damaged the line beyond repair. A portion of the Overseas Extension near Tea Table Key was among the surviving remnants of this great engineering project which helped to open the Florida Keys to tourism.

MM 78 U.S. 1 between Upper and Lower Matecumbe Keys, Florida Keys
MO13 ~ GPS Coordinates: 24.889833, -80.676033

No one really knows what possessed Henry Morrison Flagler to extend his already successful Florida East Coast Railway the one hundred fifty-six treacherous miles to Key West. The decision did not come easily but once made Flagler was determined that nothing would stand in his way. Therefore, "the overseas railroad" dubbed as the railroad that went to the sea began with the planning stages in 1901.

Flagler spent two very long years contemplating the route that the rails were to take. The first consideration involved traveling through the Everglades swamp to Cape Sable then taking a south-westerly track to Key West. This option required a very lengthy span over open sea, this notion was soon abandoned. Finally it was decided that the track would move south from Miami to Homestead then hop from island to island until the ultimate destination at Key West was achieved.

The first phase of construction began in 1904 at Homestead. Excavators cut canals so that shallow draught barges could work from each side of the tracks using the fill dirt to create a high roadbed. Laborers cut through the dense undergrowth of the maritime forest along the length of Key Largo until they arrived at the first of many complications. The crew came to the banks of a lake not previously identified on any of the surveys and unfortunately the bottom was a muck of peat too unstable to drive supports for a bridge. So there was nothing else to do but detour.

Engineers had initially planned to connect all solid embankments of each island, however the federal government had other ideas. Fearing that these solid wall embankments would change the tidal flow, the government insisted bridges be installed. Local Conchs knew the power of hurricanes that often thrashed the keys and insisted the long unstable bridges would not stand up to the immense winds and tidal surges. So the first of the huge viaducts were built having one hundred eighty-six arches. Special concrete was imported from Germany, which was guaranteed to harden under water. As if to prove a point the first of several hurricanes came roaring through in 1906 leaving the partially finished viaduct mutilated but repairs were quickly made and construction continued to completion in 1907.

The first section from Homestead to Knights Key was officially opened on January 22, 1908 but there was still a long way to go. A special train carried Flagler the length of the finished rails ending just west of Marathon, one hundred six miles from Miami. Passenger service began two weeks later on February 5. The first Pullman service for the rail line left New York City at 2:10 PM and arrived at Knights Key 7:30 AM three days later. Waiting at the Knights Key dock was a steamer waiting for passengers to board for the six-hour trip to Havana.

The second phase of construction began in 1908 with the biggest challenge yet, the infamous Seven Mile Bridge. All combined the structure was nine miles long having four viaducts. Another hurricane hit in 1909 with greater force than its predecessor did three years before. Five of the bridge spans had not been bolted into place and were blown into the sea, embankments were washed away but miraculously the viaducts of German concrete held tight.

It took two years to recover from the damages, which delayed the project considerably. Flagler was already anxious about the completion date, now a sense of dread engulfed him. Henry Flagler feared he would never see the Florida East Coast Railway reach Key West. As the workers approached the much deeper Bahia Honda channel in September of 1910 yet another hurricane plowed through the line. The Lower Keys were targeted, much of the track bed was washed away and the center span crossing Bahia Honda was moved.

Flagler's health was failing and in response the crews began by working in twelve-hour shifts both day and through the night with the aid of electric lights. The worker's dedication succeeded, on January 21, 1912 the railroad to the sea was completed. Early the next morning Flagler boarded his personal railroad car along with government officials and Latin America diplomats to make the trip to Key West where a three day fiesta was ready and waiting their arrival. The first northbound trip left Havana on August 2, 1912 around 10:30 AM, docking at Key West at 6:30 that very afternoon departing after a one hour lay over for Jacksonville slated for arrival about 2:00 the following afternoon. The train would pull into its destination, Pennsylvania Station in New York City at 8:00 PM of the third day.

The train ran two passenger trains each day from Key West to Miami, which were slated as four hour trips but realistically was more like six or seven hours. The train traveled a maximum of forty-five miles per hour, slowing to fifteen miles per hour across the bridges. When the Key West Extension was completed only passenger steamers docked at the Key West pier. Flagler envisioned twelve piers at Key West carrying both passengers and freight. Unfortunately this dream was never realized, only three freight ferries were ever put into service.

The Florida East Coast Railway never saw a profit, in fact its receipts barely covered operating expenses. Once Flagler died, the railway went into a tailspin and never recovered. Automobiles were coming into vogue and soon they were bumping along across the wooden ties eventually traveling all the way to Key West. By 1931 only one train traveled the tracks and the line went into receivership. Roadwork had already begun running alongside the railroad tracks. Then the Great Depression gripped America, tragically followed by the Labor Day hurricane of 1935.

The damage from this murderous storm was extensive. A special rescue and evacuation train was dispatched from Miami but could travel no further than Islamorada. At some points the tracks were twisted and bent and at others they had simply been washed away completely. Key West was spared by this particular storm and one of the Florida East Coast trains was trapped there unable to move north. Finally the train was loaded onto a barge and floated north spurring a newspaper headline, "FEC's Havana Special Arrives from Key West Months Late."

It is claimed that Flagler had left several million dollars as a contingency fund to cope with this type of disaster, but this was of little interest to the FEC, who now had a good excuse to rid themselves of this white elephant. The line had cost over twenty-seven million dollars to build and could have been repaired for approximately one and a half million dollars, but the remains were sold for a mere six hundred forty thousand. Henry Flagler was surely turning over in his crypt. These men had no heart for Henry Flagler's dream, he would have been severely disappointed.

The remains of Flagler's railroad were used to construct US Highway 1 to Key West. There are points along the route where small reminders of the railway to the sea still remain. Many of the viaducts have been designated as National Historical Monuments, while others have been removed to allow ships an ease of passage. Today a tourist train is run between Knights and Pigeon Keys at the midst of Seven-Mile Bridge.

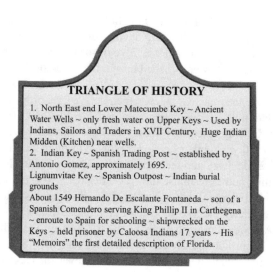

TRIANGLE OF HISTORY

1. North East end Lower Matecumbe Key ~ Ancient Water Wells ~ only fresh water on Upper Keys ~ Used by Indians, Sailors and Traders in XVII Century. Huge Indian Midden (Kitchen) near wells.
2. Indian Key ~ Spanish Trading Post ~ established by Antonio Gomez, approximately 1695.
Lignumvitae Key ~ Spanish Outpost ~ Indian burial grounds
About 1549 Hernando De Escalante Fontaneda ~ son of a Spanish Comendero serving King Phillip II in Carthegena ~ enroute to Spain for schooling ~ shipwrecked on the Keys ~ held prisoner by Caloosa Indians 17 years ~ His "Memoirs" the first detailed description of Florida.

MM 78 US 1, Indian Key
MO14 ~ GPS Coordinates: 24.889400, -80.677067

The first indigenous people of Florida roamed the land some twelve thousand years past. They followed the food source about the territory, most big game animals that they depended on for survival. These natives were not farmers but hunters tracking animals such as mastodons, camels, mammoths, bison and wild horses. Much of the peninsula was grassland then, the sea levels were much lower than we know them today and rainfall was scarce.

Overtime the big game began to disappear from over hunting and varying climatic conditions; the natives had to adapt. Food sources changed to small mammals and the bounty of the sea. Populations increased and many of the Native Americans moved inland to live off the land. Crops such as corn, beans and squash were grown to sustain the people. Pottery has been used to identify the various tribes. Many of the groups would bury their dead with pottery in the vast middens. Today the only evidence that many of the Native American tribes even existed are the middens left behind.

The Florida Territory was home to more than one hundred thousand Native Americans in 1500 AD. Various tribes were represented including Appalachee, Calusa, Timucuans, Tequesta and other tribes. By the seventeen hundreds European diseases, the blight of slavery and various battles had begun to annihilate the indigenous people. Spanish Florida became an appealing place for other Native Americans to settle.

The Lower Creeks moved into north Florida from Georgia in the 1700s. The Timucuans, Tequesta and Appalachee that remained were absorbed into the Creek tribes and eventually there was a single people called Seminole. By 1815 there were only five thousand natives.

The name Seminole was derived from the Spanish word cimarrones meaning, "wild people". Even though the people were all lumped together under one name, two distinct languages were spoken. The Lower Creeks spoke the Mikasuki language and the Upper Creek spoke Muskogee.

Americans and Seminole began fighting over Florida land. These altercations led to the President Monroe's War Department order on January 11, 1818 directing Major General Andrew Jackson to attack. President Monroe described the Seminoles as:

"a tribe which has long violated our rights, and insulted our national character."

General Jackson traveled down the Apalachicola River to Spanish Florida where he burned every Seminole village he came to, destroyed their crops, seized cattle and horses. Though the Seminole tried to fight back they were outnumbered ten to one. When the Indians gave out of ammunition they reverted to bows and arrows, which were no match against the American Army's rifles.

Congress passed the Indian Removal Act in 1830 in order to relocate the Seminole people to Oklahoma. Osceola was not a Seminole leader but he assumed a chief's position and was accepted as such by the tribe. Many of the older leaders wanted to give in but Osceola would not hear of it. It was said that Osceola once became so angered concerning a treaty offer that he violently stabbed the offending paper with his knife.

Five years later the Seminole still had not agreed to move to Oklahoma. In retaliation they massacred Major Dade and one hundred eight of his men beginning the Second Seminole War. Osceola led the Seminole at the Battle of Withlacoochee and several other major altercations of the war. Major General Thomas Jesup was the third commander of the Seminole war and it was he who devised a plan to bring Osceola in under a flag of truce in October of 1837. The plan backfired and rather than putting an end to the fighting it spurred five more years of war.

The three Seminole Wars lasted nearly fifty years at a cost to the United States of forty million dollars. Just over three thousand Seminole were relocated to Oklahoma and nearly fifteen hundred were killed. It was said that approximately three hundred Seminole escaped into the Everglades. The territory was so harsh that American Soldiers refused to follow the Native American into the vastness of the swamp. Even the great power of the United States military in the end could not vanquish the Seminole people. In the end the no treaty was signed, no peace was made and no surrender enacted. The Seminole War was simply over.

Congress passed the Wheeler-Howard Act in 1934 recognizing Indian tribes. The Seminoles tried to organize in the 1930s and 40s but too many of its members were still untrusting of the Federal Government. By 1954 six tribes had lost federal support and it appeared that the Seminoles would follow suit. The Seminole leaders drafted a constitution and charter for the tribe, which was approved by the Secretary of the Interior. The Seminole Tribe of Florida was established on August 21, 1957 by a majority vote. A sect of the Seminole broke away from the main group and in 1962 they chose to become the Miccosukee Tribe of Indians of Florida.

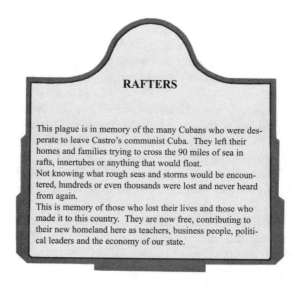

RAFTERS

This plague is in memory of the many Cubans who were desperate to leave Castro's communist Cuba. They left their homes and families trying to cross the 90 miles of sea in rafts, innertubes or anything that would float.
Not knowing what rough seas and storms would be encountered, hundreds or even thousands were lost and never heard from again.
This is memory of those who lost their lives and those who made it to this country. They are now free, contributing to their new homeland here as teachers, business people, political leaders and the economy of our state.

US 1, MM 77, Islamorada
MO15 ~ GPS Coordinates: 24.885053, -80.686309

It is difficult to imagine the dangers that exist when you gaze out over the crystal clear blue green waters of the Atlantic when you are standing safely on the shore. It is difficult to imagine just ninety miles from the laid back Keys where paradise is just beyond the door that people live in oppression, virtual slaves of a Communist regime. Those are the realties left behind in exchange for Freedom. Freedom is something that those beyond our boarders dream of and we as Americans take for granted every day.

It is those realities that wash up on Florida shores many times each year. Rafts fashioned from whatever materials available, which are carefully assembled in hopes that they will float just long enough to reach American shores. The Cubans push off from their native soil knowing that the fates are stacked against them but willing to accept the risks for the possibility of freedom. These people are willing to risk their very lives, the lives of their families, the lives of their children not for the promise of freedom but merely the possibility.

Reports are filed virtually daily by the Coast Guard or Immigration Office of families a mother, father and child who leave Communist Cuba with others seeking freedom. Unfortunately after many days of exposure to the burning tropical sun, frigid nights on the water with little food or water, floating on a makeshift raft constructed out of whatever pieces of garbage lashed together then entering water more than three thousand feet deep; the dangers were obvious. The journey demanded its toll. This time the family was lucky, they survived. Not so for their fellow travelers who were lost along the way; six bodies resigned to the briny deep, a burial at sea. Many times the rafts are found empty while others cradle the lifeless bodies; freedom was their very last thought.

Prisoners write from Havana's Combinado del Este prison of the twelve Cubans every day who are imprisoned charged with "illegal exit." Many of these people will never know life outside their cold concrete cell again, the dream of freedom fading as each year passes without hope. The risk of prison for these would be refugees was obviously worth the promise of freedom. It is freedom, which they will never know again even the limited freedom allowed by their own country.

The United States Immigration and Naturalization Service report that only one in three of every Cuban refugee makes it to American shores. Current United States policy, though it could change at any time, states that refugees intercepted at sea are subject to return to their native country unless they can prove that in doing so their lives would be in danger. However, the other side of the coin states that if refugees make it to dry land they are allowed to merge into American society. To many the policy seems to be a taunting game called "wet foot, dry foot." In order to win players must make it to shore without being caught while avoiding the perils of nature, lack of provisions, substandard vessels and later day slavers waiting to snatch up illegal immigrants for their sweat shops, prostitution rings and other illegal trades. Those are the dark realities and this is no game.

Ironically, Castro uses the refugee's ambition for freedom to relieve economic hardships in his country. During times of economic downturns, Castro's guards turn a blind eye to Cuban rafters. At times it is said that Cuban ships, for a price, will load a strange human freight unleashing them very near the United States shore. Released to escape without harm. The Coast Guard has noted that some of these crafts would not be safe in a swimming pool much less the open ocean. Nothing illustrates the escapes like the personal stories, here are a few of the hundreds just like these that occur every year:

Cuban medical student William Domingo Albelo dreamt of practicing medicine in a free society, so in 1972 he boarded a wood and rubber raft with eight others having freedom dreams of their own. Among the passengers was an elderly woman with her small dog, the only companion she had and refused to leave behind. Two weeks into the journey Albelo helplessly watched as the raft broke apart from the power of the mighty sea. One after another his fellow travelers drowned including the small dog. Today Albelo is a doctor but his dreams have turned to nightmares as he can not erase from his memory the price others paid for freedom.

Walter Mas Gomez visited the shrine of San Lazaro near Havana to pray for safe passage before setting out on the ninety miles voyage; Gomez vowed to shave his head for five years should he make it to Florida. Aida Lina Rodriguez with her baby, Jesus, traveled on the make shift raft as well. Their raft was comprised of six two hundred-pound inner tubes and one nine hundred pound tube, oars were fashioned from wooden fish boxes. It had taken months to prepare the raft as they slipped the vessel into storm tossed waters, too late to turn back now. As the storm intensified Aida and her son were lashed to the center of the raft, should it capsize the pair would surely drown. Two days later a yacht caught sight of a red flag waving in the wind and notified the Coast Guard, as they approached the beacon was identified as an emaciated refugee waving the young boy's red shirt. They were fortunate to make land without fatalities, Immigration allowed them to stay and Gomez has kept a shinny bald pate; an easy debt to pay.

In the early morning hours of mid August several would be refugees met on the rocky beach near Havana. As if enjoying a day in the sun, by the time other beachgoers reached the shore the party was already set up for a day of picnicking and swimming alongside the ever present iguanas enjoying the warmth of the sun and sand. By mid afternoon, two by two the escapees wandered away into the near by woods where their raft was hidden amidst the undergrowth. With the assistance of a hard to come by compass they entered the water and set sail.

Soon the common late afternoon storm washed the band very close to the Cuban shore, six hours and no progress was made. Soon the party was discouraged thoughts of desperation filled their brains. Rolando Leon Herandez refused to succumb to the negative thoughts, refusing to admit defeat. Within hours a second storm hit driving the small raft off course once again, but this time the fates were with them steering the exhausted band toward Florida. They took turns rowing through the night, with aching shoulders and blistered hands they continued through the pain. With first light came a snowy white seagull fluttering from one shoulder to the next, surely a sign of hope. The baby traveling with them silencing his cries and vomiting from dehydration, watching the bird on its solitary flight. Five days later land was spotted and salvation was within their grasp. A Massachusetts yacht responded to their prayers, on August 21 the emaciated band of refugees stepped on the free soil of the Florida Keys for the very first time.

Some thirty-five years ago Cuban born Lorenzo Calas fashioned a raft made from metal drums welded together and covertly delivered it to the cove of Manati, an eastern province on Cuba. During the attempted escape he was apprehended by the police and sentenced to six and a half years in a Cuban jail. After his release, his community fearing that an association with him would implicate his neighbors ostracized Calas. Despite the perils,

Calas never let go of the dream. He built a second raft this time attaching a small water pump motor to it and again delivered it to the cove where he was arrested many years before. Calas, four of his sons and a nephew set sail leaving his wife and two younger sons behind for fear they would not be strong enough to make the journey.

The trip was hazardous from the beginning; a sudden storm took their supplies, the motor failed and soon the refugees were adrift with no direction to roast under the blazing sun, starve without food and water or drown in the waters of an angry sea. A week after they set sail that fateful day, a passing freighter plucked them from the sea. Two and a half years later Lorenzo Calas sits in his comfortable West Palm Beach home, driving his used Cavalier to work each day at the Osceola Sugar Mill where he earns thirteen dollars and eighty cents per hour. He comes home to his wife and sons each day, who eventually joined him in America. Today he sends evidence of his happy life back to Cuba, pictures of the house, car, their Disney World vacation and the smiles of his children who have experienced the bounds of communism and know that freedom has its price.

Two Havana restaurant workers Angel Morell and Luis Enrique Urdaneta made plans to leave Cuba for America more than twenty years ago. They silently crept to the well-guarded beach. The only light was the brilliant red tip of a guard's cigarette. The boys hid in the shadows until they could make a break for the water. Mumbling a quick prayer and crossing their heart the two young men slipped into the sea. After six days without food or water the boys were facing a certain death. Urdaneta no longer able to stand the agony slipped into the water and drowned. Morell was too weak to save his friend and collapsed into oblivion. For three additional days Angel Morell baked under the tropical sun, suffering alternately between fevers and chills. The young man contemplated death but the survivor in him refused to give in. Soon a merchant ship happened along and brought the semi-conscience young man aboard. After four day in Jackson Memorial Hospital suffering from terrible burns, Angel Morell was released.

Today he lives in a small apartment overlooking the Orange Bowl in Miami. Asthma has kept him from working over the last several years but he survives. His body and soul still bares the scars of the journey so long ago, still he doesn't like to speak of Cuba. The pain forces him to remember the burns he suffered so long ago still ache but it is the pain in his heart that refuses to be medicated. You see Morell vowed to bring eventually bring his young wife and son to America, unfortunately their freedom was the price he paid for his own.

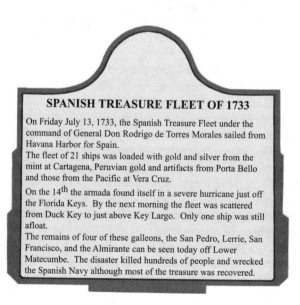

SPANISH TREASURE FLEET OF 1733

On Friday July 13, 1733, the Spanish Treasure Fleet under the command of General Don Rodrigo de Torres Morales sailed from Havana Harbor for Spain.

The fleet of 21 ships was loaded with gold and silver from the mint at Cartagena, Peruvian gold and artifacts from Porta Bello and those from the Pacific at Vera Cruz.

On the 14th the armada found itself in a severe hurricane just off the Florida Keys. By the next morning the fleet was scattered from Duck Key to just above Key Largo. Only one ship was still afloat.

The remains of four of these galleons, the San Pedro, Lerrie, San Francisco, and the Almirante can be seen today off Lower Matecumbe. The disaster killed hundreds of people and wrecked the Spanish Navy although most of the treasure was recovered.

US 1, MM 77, Islamorada
MO15 ~ GPS Coordinates: 24.885053, -80.686309

The sandy ocean bottom off the Florida Keys is littered with the skeletons of ships that met their end generally by the wicked forces of mother's nature's magnificent storms. These Spanish treasure ships stored safely in their holds Incan gold, Mayan and Aztec treasures and oriental porcelains.

It was said that eighteen vast ships were lost in 1733 but as many as four times that number traveled the seas. Ten of these ships were banished to the watery depths on September 15, 1733 between Tavernier Creek and Long Key. A great many of the wreckage sites are popular scuba diving locations today, in fact, this author has dove most of them.

The *San Jose* is an impressive galleon lying in approximately thirty-five feet of water near Tavernier Creek. The site produced thirty thousand dollars in gold and silver on the first day of salvage. The galleon was originally armed with forty canon, before the last hurricane season the ribs and keel were exposed but the forces of nature tends to change these things. The San Jose was the subject of one of the first court cases involving discovered undersea treasure, the state of Florida versus Tom Gurr. Dr. Mendel Peterson working for the Smithsonian Institute assisted Mr. Gurr in recovering more than two thousand artifacts, which were in turn donated to the Washington D.C. museum.

El Capitana el Rubi Segundo known today as *El Capitan* for obvious reasons. She rests at a relatively shallow depth of twenty feet on the reef called Hen and Chicks. The galleon was Don Rodriga de Torres' flagship, she led the flotilla to their ultimate demise on the ocean floor. Reggie Roberts discovered the wreck of *El Capitan* while fishing, sharing his find with friend Art McKee. After diving on the site Art found a 1721 coin and began guiding tourists out to the wreck, which gave up more treasure. Art McKee opened what was to be the first treasure museum, today called Treasure Village. The finding was not without cost, Art McKee lost his boat

THE SPANISH TREASURE FLEET

the *Rosalee* as the sea enacted her toll. The *Rosalee* lies near *El Capitan* today. El Capitan is little more than several huge piles of ballast stones but the occasional relic can still be found at the site.

Just south of the entrance to Snake Creek, off of Windley Key is a small Spanish ship listed as the *Carmen*. The wreck site is called *Chaves* for the ship's captain. The ship lies in only ten feet of water on a bed of white sand rather than the common beds of turtle grass usually found on the seabed. The only remains of this wreck is a small heap of ballast stones, yet occasionally an ancient relic is found by a lucky diver.

Two and half miles south of the Snake Creek Bridge is the galleon *Herrera*, known to the Spaniards as *Nuestra Senora de Belen y San Antonio de Padua*. Lying in eighteen feet of crystal clear blue water the English built ship has given up a number of interesting artifacts over the years. Clay figures of fish, animals and human likenesses have been found in addition to animal hides, jugs and most common, olive jars. And just beyond the *Herrera* is the *Tres Puentes*. This ballast pile has yielded a great number of silver ingots and still to this day produces the occasional coin.

The *San Pedro* is approximately one and a quarter miles south of Indian Key. Many coins have been retrieved from this site. Many of the ballast and a canon were moved from this site to create an artificial wreck site as a snorkel site at John Pennekamp State Park. The site has limited visibility due to the sandy bottom constantly being stirred up by the crowds there, however, a make shift ballast site has attracted a great number of colorful fish. For those unable to scuba dive this is a lovely site that gives much of the feeling of diving on an underwater site.

Sunk in twenty feet of water, approximately three quarters of a mile off Lower Matecumbe Key, the galleon *Lerri* sometimes referred to as *Terri* is a massive one hundred fifty foot ballast pile. Oddly enough for the treasure fleet, *Lerri* has produced little in the way of artifacts. However, the site is very popular for the photographic opportunities available of her on the relatively shallow dive with lots of beautiful fish.

The area has also claimed many ships in addition to those of the 1733 Spanish Treasure Fleet. One interesting wreck is that of the *USS Alligator,* located between the coral heads on the ocean side of Alligator Light. The ship was part of the West Indian squadron under the command of Commodore David Porter who took command of the Man of War when her commander, Lieutenant W. H. Allen was critically wounded in a battle with pirates at Matanzas, Cuba on November 9, 1822. Ten days later the ship was sailing along the Florida Keys when it was overtaken by a massive storm. The *USS Alligator* was driven onto the reef where she lies today on the reef, which bears her name.

During the building of Henry M. Flaglers' Railroad to the Sea a number of hurricanes hampered the construction. The storms of 1906, 1909 and finally the death knell storm of 1935 littered the ocean floor with workboats, train cars, rails and various buildings. Many have slowly rusted away but signs of this wreckage can be found beneath the Lignum Vitae Bridge as well as the Niles Channel Bridge.

In Key West is a shrine to the most profitable and quite possibly the most valuable treasure finds of the Florida Keys, the Mel Fisher Maritime Museum. The facility houses more than twenty million dollars in treasure and historical artifacts from the ship *Atocha*. The exhibits include gold and silver bars, some four thousand silver coins, a gold chalice[3], a six inch gold cross, certainly the most beautiful and possible the finest collection of emeralds in the world, swords, guns, pottery and personal items from the 1622 Spanish Fleet.

The Mel Fisher Maritime Museum, sponsored by visitor donations, was founded in 1982. Nearly a half million tourists walk through the heavy double doors at 200 Greene Street, Key West every year. The Museum is opened year round and charges a modest admission. The artifacts there are an amazing example of the findings from the Spanish Treasure Fleet.

ROAD & FERRY

In April, 1926, Monroe County began construction of a road on the east end of Upper Matecumbe to connect with other islands. It eventually made it possible to drive to Key West by using a ferry. The first car drove to Key West on Jan. 25, 1928 by boarding a ferry here at todays Boy Scout Sea Base and crossing 40 miles of water to No Name Key.
Later the ferry docked at Grassy Key, traveling by road to the west end of todays Marathon. From there a ferry crossed to No Name Key.
It was on the Morning of March 29, 1938 that the daughter of the Cuban Council cut the ribbon opening the road without the ferry by using the widened railway bridge.
A toll booth was erected here to collect $1 for car and driver and 25 cents for each additional passenger. The toll was removed in 1954.

US 1, MM 73, Islamorada
MO16 ~ GPS Coordinates: 24.847393, -80.743936

Most assume the history of US Highway 1 began with the murderous hurricane of 1935. Well, that would be only part of the story. In all actuality the highway actually got its start in 1917 only five years after the railroad was completed. Of course the massive damage of the hurricane did have its affects; the destruction forced the completion of the roadway to be pushed forward.

As more families were able to afford automobiles and the railroad opened the Florida Keys to the tourist trade, Monroe County realized the need for a road was pressing. A permanent roadway would do more than link the Keys with the mainland without being dependent of the schedule of the rails. A one hundred thousand-dollar bond issue was floated in order to construct roads from Key Largo to Big Pine Key and build a bridge from Key West to Stock Island. By the 1920s all of Florida was experiencing a population explosion and Florida was gradually becoming the vacation capital of the world. It was also during this time that the first of the snowbirds began their winter migrations to sunny Florida.

There was some controversy concerning which route the highway would take and in the end it was decided that the road would wind through Card Sound as suggested by the real estate and tourism industries. Dade County was responsible for building eleven miles of roadway from Florida City to Card Sound and Monroe County would take over from there. Monroe County built a drawbridge to connect the two county sections.

A moderate hurricane in 1926 damaged both the roadway and the bridge. Construction was finally finished on the bridge two years later and when done the height was increased from five to nine feet. Transportation to the Upper Keys was complete but the Lower Keys were still dependent on ferries to cross the waters so sparkling blue that when the sun hits the water it hurts your eyes.

Three ferries were put into use to travel the distance to Key West. One traveled south, the other north and the third was a spare in case one of the other two broke down. When fire destroyed one of the two functioning boats, no spare was available. The ferry trip consumed four hours of travel time and each barge only transported twenty cars. Each vehicle and driver was charged a toll of three dollars fifty cents under fourteen feet, those over sixteen feet were charged six fifty, extra passengers were charged one dollar each.

The ferry service had definite problems. Transportation was slow, had limited space and was very costly when you consider that the average family income in 1925 was approximately eight thousand dollars a year. The ferries continually ran aground and were forced to await the high tide to float again. Since the majority of the Keys population was concentrated in Key West, residents were not exactly happy with the situation.

Washington DC was under the attack of the World War I veterans who had no work, no prospects and were desperate for the "army bonus" promised to them. True to his word President Roosevelt used these same vets to complete the railroad in the Florida Keys. Thus killing two birds with one stone; the veterans had employment and the Florida Keys was getting the transportation it so desperately needed. Then the unthinkable happened. The violent hurricane of 1935 struck without mercy. The train was stalled at Islamorada and could go no further, the veterans and their families in small makeshift houses not strong enough for protection, no one was prepared for the intensity of this storm and by the time they realized the danger, it was too late to run. The final body count will never be known but estimates are that more than five hundred people lost their lives that fateful day.

The hurricane could not have come at a worse time. The country was in the midst of the great depression and Monroe County, like so many others, was virtually bankrupt. After several failed attempts the FERA[4] was organized by President Roosevelt in an effort to rebuild after the damage of the hurricane. Negotiations ensued over whether to repair the railroad or complete the highway. Florida East Coast Railway had little interest since the death of Henry Flagler in maintaining the railway therefore the highway became the first priority. During this time ferry service was restored and Pan American flew into Key West for the very first time.

The state purchased the railway easement for six hundred forty thousand dollars, taking a loss of more than half a million dollars. Henry Flagler would spin in his grave. The Toll and Bridge District issued revenue bonds to pay for road construction with tolls collected. Contractors were hired, steel beams were used to widen the roadway and the steel was covered with reinforced concrete making a twenty-foot roadway.

The Bahia Honda Bridge was sixty-five feet tall and posed quite a problem reinforcing it with the concrete slab. Finally the roadway was completed and opened for the first automobiles on March 29, 1938. President Roosevelt traveled the road in a caravan one year later.

World War II brought a military presence to Key West. By 1942, a fresh water and electricity was available throughout the Keys. After the modifications, the new route was dedicated with a ribbon cutting ceremony in 1944. Rather than take the Card Sound loop the military preferred a more direct route and the highway renamed

US 1 was routed straight through. Today US 1 stretches the eastern seaboard from Key West mile marker 1 to Maine, which is the route that this "Get Off the Interstate" series will follow.

Card Sound Bridge had fallen victim to several fires and the wooden bridge was in severe disrepair. The center section was removed and from that time forward the bridge was utilized as a fishing pier. Pigeon Key was the headquarters for the Toll and Bridge Commission. The toll was one dollar for each vehicle and a quarter for each passenger. Reports were filed for misuse of toll funds in 1953 and to resolve the issue Monroe County residents were given a free pass identified by a numbered windshield decal. The action did not dispel the rumors and finally the county put an end to the tolls. Initially the highway was called "The Florida Freeway," a play on words and a jab at the local government concerning the abuse of toll funds. The local residents preferred the name US 1, when all was said and done, that was the name used.

The Card Sound Bridge was rebuilt once again in 1969 and during a five-year period between 1978 and 1983 all of the Florida Keys bridges were replaced with modern spans. The old bridges remain but were modified so that they could not be crossed; the old spans are popular fishing spots. Seven-Mile Bridge was a definite challenge, construction took three years and forty-five million dollars, an additional five million dollars were needed to convert the old span into a fishing pier. Today the sites of Bahia Honda, Seven Mile and Long Key bridges are listed on the National Register of Historic Places in recognition of their time as Florida East Coast Railway bridges.

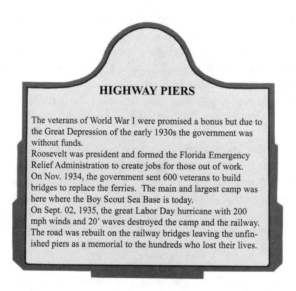

HIGHWAY PIERS

The veterans of World War I were promised a bonus but due to the Great Depression of the early 1930s the government was without funds.
Roosevelt was president and formed the Florida Emergency Relief Administration to create jobs for those out of work.
On Nov. 1934, the government sent 600 veterans to build bridges to replace the ferries. The main and largest camp was here where the Boy Scout Sea Base is today.
On Sept. 02, 1935, the great Labor Day hurricane with 200 mph winds and 20' waves destroyed the camp and the railway. The road was rebuilt on the railway bridges leaving the unfinished piers as a memorial to the hundreds who lost their lives.

US 1, MM 72, Islamorada
MO17 ~ GPS Coordinates: 24.839206, -80.758607

Henry Flagler did what no one believed possible, he believed when everyone had doubt and he proved that one man could make a difference. The trek to Key West was a long and arduous journey, in order to begin the trip Flagler hired convicts for two dollars and fifty cents per month. The Keys were truly wilderness territories with no fresh water, electricity and primitive transportation. The locals stored rainwater in cisterns but with the additional workmen that supply would never last. Flagler had water delivered by boat from Miami.

Outsiders described the Keys as worthless heaps of coral reef, the leavings after the God created the Florida peninsula. After a brief conversation with his General Manager Joseph Parrott, Flagler said "on to Key West". The rails were complete to Florida City so there was one hundred twenty-eight miles to Key West, fifty miles across open water. The government objected, believing that filling in the island gaps would change the natural tidal flow so Flagler adapted. Viaducts were built with concrete arches rivaling Roman structures of biblical days.

Still additional laborers were needed and in order to get quality workers he raised the going rate from one dollar a day to one dollar fifty cents. Most of the workers hired were New York hobos who rode the rails as far as Miami and disappeared into the night. Flagler hired black men, then Cubans and Islanders, anyone willing to work. Grecian sponge divers were hired to do the underwater work.

The majority of the workers lived in tents, cooked their meals over open fires and they would stay aboard double decked quarter boats[5] luxurious because they had window screens against the biting mosquitoes, sand gnats and flies. Work days were ten to twelve hours allowing a one hour break for lunch. Supervisors who treated their men cruelly were immediately fired, the camps were clean, the food was good, fresh water was plentiful and liquor was not allowed in the camps or near the men. The most vocal complaint of the workers was the ban on alcohol and the lack of feminine companionship. Sunday was their only day off, many of the men would travel to Miami for booze and women, but if they returned to camp inebriated they were paid and asked to leave immediately. Flagler was a strict taskmaster and everyone had to tow the line.

Flagler wanted a major supply depot approximately halfway down the Keys, that village became Marathon. Built out of mangrove swamps and marshland, the only vehicles able to ford this wilderness were mule driven carts. A reporter doing a story for the Miami newspaper wrote that Flagler's biggest obstacle was persuading workers not to run away, however, after spending a night under the conditions the laborers were exposed to he understood the compulsion completely. The men wore full coats, gloves, long sleeved shirts and still the mosquitoes bit and flies swarmed. While the men tried to sleep at night the mosquitoes would sting through the canvas of their cots from underneath. Flagler placed great importance on medical care for his men and because of this they remained free of the ravages of malaria and yellow fever.

Everything seemed to be going well when the crew encountered a shallow lake never found on any of the land surveys. Again Flagler's plan had to be modified but this too was taken in stride and the work continued. Because of the unexpected complications it was decided to work straight through hurricane season which spanned from mid summer to late fall.

It was mid-October 1906, when the warning went out that a hurricane had hit Havana and was headed toward the Keys. The warning was too little, too late. As the seas grew angry and the winds picked up, the quarter boat housing the workers snapped the line from its mooring, the mighty winds blowing the floundering vessel out to open sea. The houseboat was tossed, no longer able to withstand the strain to the threatening storm. The men dropped to their knees and prayed for salvation, knowing that death was near. Fearing death by drowning the men broke into the first aid kits, consuming lethal doses of opiates. Survivors were thrown into the dark waters of sea holding dearly to any debris that passed their way. As the winds abated seventy men were rescued but more than one hundred men died in the storm. Most of the deaths had come to those on the quarter boat. The fatal storm had the managing supervisor exclaim:

"No man has any business connected with this work who can't stand grief."

Although Flagler was disturbed by the loss of life, he refused to be defeated. From his St. Augustine estate he sent a message simply saying, "Go ahead." The storm damage had to be repaired before further construction was completed. Just another delay, the men took it in stride and continued on. When asked about the construction, Flagler described it as perfectly simple. The work was anything but simple. The Long Key Viaduct consisted of two hundred fifteen concrete arches all perfectly matched. By 1908, fifty miles lay between Henry Flagler's dream and Key West.

In order to attract investors, Flagler built one of his magnificent hotels on Long Key and began offering a vacation package with through service by rail from New York to Knights Key. The most daunting challenge yet was to be called the Seven-Mile Bridge spanning the vast distance between Knights Key and Little Duck Key, but this task too was met.

Henry reached the age of eight-two in 1912 and three weeks later found himself aboard his private rail car enroute to Key West. Unfortunately by this time Flagler's eyesight was failing, so he was unable to see the beautiful crystal clear blue green water as the train chugged down the track. However he knew the sight well, for once you've had this vision it is one you never forget. In an emotional speech Flagler declared, "Now I can die happy, My dream is fulfilled."

Another hurricane slammed into the Keys in October of 1909. This time the workers were ready, management stated,

> "We have found it more economical to sink our floating equipment in the most protected waters
> and raise it and repair it when the storm has passed."

Fourteen men lost their lives but more than three thousand others survived the storm in shelters built near Marathon. The bridges and arches withstood the ravages of the storm in good shape but more than forty miles of roadbeds and track was washed out to open sea.

Mother Nature was hardly done, the very next year another hurricane bashed the Keys. Ever resilient the residents battened down their hatches and waited out the storm. One man gave his life to this storm and the massive wall of water dislodged one of the main supports of the Bahia Honda Bridge. Improvements came as a result of every storm and this one involved the installation of wind gauges to every bridge; warning lights would flare when winds threatened to fifty miles per hour.

Flagler's dream was realized but the price was dear. Two hundred men had given their lives and although most were the results of hurricane as many as twenty-one were lost to accidents with dynamite and at least twelve more were maimed for life. Death benefits were paid to each family and those left injured received disability payments for the remainder of their days. The cost in labor and materials totaled just over twenty-seven million dollars or approximately two hundred thousand dollars per mile.

The railroad never earned a profit and barely took in enough money for maintenance on the line. After Flagler's death very little interest remained in the railroad, he was the heart and soul after his death the railroad's days were marked. The trains continued to operate for twenty-five years though Key West was slow to become a major port. Most felt the island was too small, the wharves and warehouses needed were never built. Yet Key West was about to experience growth in a way never expected.

As America suffered through Prohibition, Key West openly ignored the law. People flocked to the little island, which earned its reputation as the ultimate party town, a distinction still held to this day. Soon the Great Depression and repeal of Prohibition cut into the tourist trade of Key West. It was during this time that US 1 was being improved and developed threatening the very existence of Flagler's railroad.

Hurricanes constantly hampered the construction of the railway as if Mother Nature was determined bring it down no matter what the cost. Mother Nature finally won with her display of power on September 2, 1935. Unable to vanquish the actual railroad construction, Mother Nature managed to slay the spirit. When the hurricane warnings first sprang to life an official in Islamorada telephoned Jacksonville requesting a train to evacuate to veteran workers. J. J. Haycraft took the helm of a locomotive and headed south into the storm. A reliable oil fired engine was used vice the coal burning locomotive due to the faster acceleration speed. Haycraft set out late that afternoon and made his first stop at Windley Key to pick up the first of the refugees. The train was stalled there for a time snarled in heavy steel cable that took more than an hour to unfurl.

Islamorada was still twenty miles in the distance. The sky was darkening, the seas were rising and the waves were swelling to white capped curls of destruction. The dark night was lit sporadically by streams of white lightning crossing the sky. The storm had taken the electricity darkening every corner, residents clustered in the only shelter from the stinging rain. Haycraft feared the tracks below him would collapse under the power of the storm but it was the only vehicle available destined for safety. Before the safe haven could be attained the salty seawater of the Atlantic swept the locomotive paralyzing it in defeat. Many of the train car lay on their sides useless.

Nearly three hundred of the veteran workers were left dead after the storm. Many of these men drowned while others were found impaled by flying debris. Ernest Hemingway traveled north to join the rescue and recovery. Sadly he identified two girls who ran the sandwich shop near the ferry stop. The locomotive was recovered and set upright once again.

Florida East Coast Railway petitioned the federal court for permission to abandon the line, the request was approved. The line was sold for six hundred forty thousand dollars. The state of Florida used the existing track route as the basis for the highway system to Key West. The original road opened in 1938 and remains the route to Mile Marker 1 today. The bridges were finally replaced by 1983.

Henry Flagler accomplished what no man before him would even attempt. By opening the transportation avenue to the public, Flagler created south Florida and made it the tourist meca it is today. It is he that is responsible for the economic stability brought by the tourist trade. Even though Key West developed slowly beginning as a jumping off place for tourists traveling to Cuba. Today the city is a twenty-four hour a day party beginning with the beautiful sunrise and coming to a zenith with the most amazing sunset. The entire community stops for that brief moment to watch the magnificent orb slide beyond the horizon and then carries on with non-stop parties.

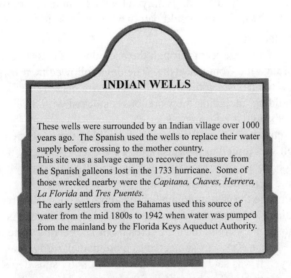

INDIAN WELLS

These wells were surrounded by an Indian village over 1000 years ago. The Spanish used the wells to replace their water supply before crossing to the mother country.
This site was a salvage camp to recover the treasure from the Spanish galleons lost in the 1733 hurricane. Some of those wrecked nearby were the *Capitana, Chaves, Herrera, La Florida* and *Tres Puentes*.
The early settlers from the Bahamas used this source of water from the mid 1800s to 1942 when water was pumped from the mainland by the Florida Keys Aqueduct Authority.

US 1, MM 70, Islamorada
MO18 ~ GPS Coordinates: 24.839645, -80.791894

Spanish explorers dubbed the island known as Islamorada translated to mean "Purple Isle." No one really knows how the island inherited this unusual distinction. Islamorada was a popular stopping off locale because it was known to have fresh water wells so important to travelers. Native Americans established villages around the wells that lured Spanish explorers. Because of the Spanish influence the Indians began adopting aspects of their language derived from the Cuban fisherman who frequently visited the area. Their proximity to the sea resulted in the Indians developing excellent diving skills and collecting treasure from vessels floundering on the reef. The Indians were known to take European slaves from the wrecked ships. Conditions of survival in the Upper Keys were difficult at best, but circumstances were about to change.

During the decade of 1820 to 1830 while the Native American flourished on Indian Key, a lack luster sailor arrived on Indian Key. John Jacob Housman's seamanship skills were not the best, however he did have a ruthless sense of business. After wrecking his ship off shore of the Florida Keys he determined that the genus of his fortune could be made in the salvage business. He practiced in Key West until Housman was accused of unscrupulous activity. Various owners of lost vessels took their stories to the courts and challenged the wrecker's percentage of their goods. The courts supported the wreckers, while this seemed unfair to the vessel owners keeping a portion of their goods was better than sacrificing it all.

In order to make life more pleasing Housman left Key West for Indian Key, where he could operate without the courts' supervision. He purchased Indian Key on his 30th birthday. Housman then established the first mercantile on Indian Key and began salvaging once again. John Jacob Housman amassed four wrecking vessels, built wharves, warehouses to store goods and thirty rental cottages. Most of the construction was completed through the labor of twelve African slaves, he purchased off slavers passing through. To attract residents Housman improved the area with paved streets, a landscaped town square and built the Tropical Hotel. The first Florida Keys resort attracted many well-known names as guests such as James Audubon.

Housman was known to be unethical in business often forgiving debts in exchange for illegal favors. In order to maintain his monopoly at Indian Key without government restrictions, he convinced the territorial legislative representative who owed Housman a favor to establish Dade County to include Indian Key and make Housman's town the center of county government. This action made him completely independent of Key West.

His wealth grew, as did his reputation in the community. However in 1838, his illegal embezzlement was traced back to Housman and his wrecker's license was revoked. The Seminole War decreased his hold over the Native Americans and Housman's wealth suffered. Betrayed by the Seminole, Housman proposed to the government that for every Indian caught or killed they would pay two hundred dollars. The Seminole discovered the plan and on August 7th, 1840, they attacked.

John Jacob Housman and his wife leapt through the back door of their home down the pier and into the water, as the Seminole burst through the front entryway. The dogs followed their owners out barking after them and in an effort not to be discovered Housman drowned the dogs with his bare hands. The Housman's survived but the Indians burned every building, including the warehouses stocked with his ill-gotten gains to the ground. By morning nothing was left but smoldering ruins.

The Housman family retreated to Key West where everything that remained of their holdings was auctioned off and Housman himself was forced to seek work on a wrecker. Less than a year later John Jacob Housman was crushed to death between two ships he was salvaging. He was forty-two at the time of his death. In the end his evil ways came home to roost.

During that August rampage the Seminole massacred another Indian Key resident Dr. Henry Perrine. The Perrine family had come to Indian Key as a safe haven from the Seminole Wars. As his family escaped through the turtle crawl beneath their home, they could hear the screams of Dr. Perrine as he died.

In September of 1935, Indian Key was subjected to more damage from that violent hurricane than any other area along the Florida Keys. It was said that when the winds finally subsided and the dead could be accounted for many could not even be identified. The brutality of the storm had ripped the faces away leaving little but bloodied bones. Other victims were dragged out to sea, the bodies never seen again.

President Roosevelt proposed that since many of the dead were veterans that they be buried at Arlington National Cemetery. Unfortunately because there was no way to preserve the bodies, transportation to Virginia was out of the question. Finally to avoid disease from the decaying corpses, four funeral pyres were lit and the bodies cremated. The ashes were placed in a massive urn at the Florida Keys Memorial of Islamorada. For years skeletons could be found on small islands of the Florida Bay, many still remain.

Ernest Hemingway, hearing of the devastation, boarded his boat the *Pilar* to offer any help he could. Along with him were his wife and two sons. In the end Hemingway published an article accusing the government of sentencing the veterans to an untimely death. The article was entitled, "Who Murdered the Vets?" published in a magazine called The New Masses. His major point involved accusations that the government sent World War I veterans to work on Florida Keys bridges without protection from massive storms and no opportunity to evacuate.

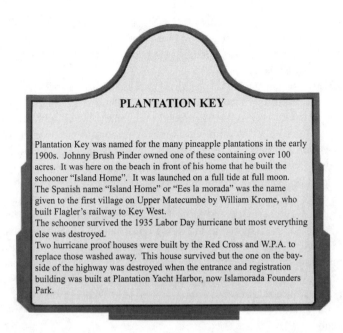

PLANTATION KEY

Plantation Key was named for the many pineapple plantations in the early 1900s. Johnny Brush Pinder owned one of these containing over 100 acres. It was here on the beach in front of his home that he built the schooner "Island Home". It was launched on a full tide at full moon.
The Spanish name "Island Home" or "Ees la morada" was the name given to the first village on Upper Matecumbe by William Krome, who built Flagler's railway to Key West.
The schooner survived the 1935 Labor Day hurricane but most everything else was destroyed.
Two hurricane proof houses were built by the Red Cross and W.P.A. to replace those washed away. This house survived but the one on the bay-side of the highway was destroyed when the entrance and registration building was built at Plantation Yacht Harbor, now Islamorada Founders Park.

US 1, MM 69.5, Islamorada
MO19 ~ GPS Coordinates: 24.838229, -80.797866

Plantation Key has a long but simple history. Its first residents of course were Native Americans proven by the fact that a large midden was discovered dating to approximately thirteen to fifteen hundred years ago. Artifacts taken from the mound date to that period but unfortunately little is known of the first residents because years ago residents had little interest in the historical value of these ancient people. The mound was leveled in 1858 for construction.

Over the years the area has been identified by many names including Bull Island, Long Island, Snake Creek Key, Vermont Key and a seafarers legendary name, Pearl City. Plantation Key is the name that seems to have stuck, derived from the various pineapple plantations throughout the area. Harper's Monthly Magazine described Plantation Key in February of 1871 as having good soil, many seventy to eighty foot tall tress, large plantations of cocoa-nut palms and pineapples which have been extremely successful.

As the population grew two schools were established in 1891 in Key Largo and Plantation Key. A new Plantation Key business was established in 1903 with the building on the property of Key pioneer Johnny "Brush" Pinder. The forty-five ton, sixty-foot schooner called *Island Home* was constructed to transport produce and passengers north and south to Miami and Key West. The ship was a consolidated effort; designed by Key Wester John Watkins, expert workmanship by Bahamian carpenter "Old Whiskers" Haskell and Johnny "Brush" Pinder provided the financing and building facilities.

The *Island Home* featured a small trunk cabin aft accommodating four passengers, the covered hatch protected cargo from the elements and the ship held a full complement of sails. Atop the cabin was the perfect sightseeing platform for passengers to watch the world go by; enjoy lunch as they sailed the beautiful blue green waters and an ideal locale to sit with a glass of wine enjoying the highlight of the day as the sun slowly slipped below the horizon. Larger sailing vessel continued to be built through the years, later Willie Roberts of Key West joined Pinder's crew and together they built Roberts' *Back Country Skiff*.

At the turn of the century Florida East Coast Railroad was in the midst of building Flagler's railroad to the sea. Three lakes were noted on the surveys and as the railroad tracks were laid one by one the lakes were filled and erased from existence. The survey maps also indicated the extensive agricultural fields growing winter crops such as tomatoes, pineapple, alligator pears[6], cocoanuts, limes, sugar apples[7] and oranges. At least half of the Key was set aside as farmland. Plantation Key never grew into a popular settlement like the neighboring settlements of Tavernier, Rock Harbor and Islamorada. By 1905 the village had a grand total of six homesteads and five years later the school graduated eight students.

The Volstead Act, which began the era of prohibition, resulted in the shallow waters of Plantation Key becoming a popular haven for Rum Runners from the Bahamas. The railroad bought agricultural land used for the production of pineapple thus the industry was vastly affected, the *Island Home* schooner was sold to a Miami businessman in 1923 but its legend lives on today with her likeness carved into the door of San Pedro Catholic Church.

On December 5, 1933 prohibition was repealed and the hidden creeks were no longer needed. In 1935 the population increased once again with the arrival of World War I veterans hired as railway workers. The veteran's families warranted the construction of a new school at Islamorada but the Labor Day hurricane of 1935 destroyed it all.

A legendary Plantation Key character arrived on Plantation Key in 1941 by the name of Arthur McKee, Jr. McKee was employed as a Navy Diver assigned to aid in the construction of the fresh water pipeline. McKee gained notoriety as one of the world's first treasure divers with his 1948 discovery of the 1733 Spanish Treasure Fleet. The find was authenticated when McKee brought up silver coins dated 1732. His discovery produced so many silver bars he became known as "Silver Bar McKee." McKee established Plantation Key's first treasure museum in 1949 called Treasure Harbor, three years later he opened "Treasure Fortress," which is still in business as a mini-mall called Treasure Village. McKee inspired another well-known Florida Keys character by the name of Mel Fisher many years later.

About that time another Plantation Key landmark was established called Plantation Yacht Harbor. Rumor was that Mafia gangster Meyer Lansky who had retired to Miami after getting out of prison for tax evasion financed the establishment. To support the theory Buddy Lansky, Meyer's son, was manager of the facility for some time. Plantation Yacht Harbor was to be the south's premiere gambling mecca but it never came to be and Meyer Lansky died of a heart attack at his Miami home in 1983.

Coral Shores High School opened at the Upper Keys in 1951 and two years later graduated its first class of thirteen students on June 10, 1953. A sheriff's substation was established in 1958 but officers still had to travel almost seventy miles to Key West hauling prisoners to jail. Dr. Cohn established the first medical practice as well as the first hospital, Venetian Shores Medical Center. In 1962 the hospital was replaced with more modern facilities at the Overseas and Mariners Hospitals.

Vacation Village post office was established in 1962 and five years later Plantation Key became the county seat for Monroe County. A small courthouse was built as facilities for the Justice of the Peace. In January 1981 at the first trial, under the direction of Judge Julio Gomez, the first jury was chosen from Plantation Key citizens.

LONG KEY FISHING CLUB

Henry M. Flagler began construction on the Key West Extension of the Florida East Coast Railroad southward from Homestead in 1905. Despite destructive hurricanes in 1906, 1909, and 1910, the Key West Extension was completed in January 1912 at a cost of $49 million. With completion of Long Key Viaduct, the first bridge built on the line and the trademark of the East Coast Railroad, Flagler's East Coast Hotel Company established the Long Key Fishing Club in 1906. This "Garden of Eden" soon became the mecca for the world's greatest saltwater anglers Zane Grey, writer and pioneer of Florida Keys fishing, was president of the exclusive Long Key Fishing Club which consisted of the Lodge, decorated with matchless displays of mounted Florida game fish, guest cottages and storehouses. The accommodations and service were of the highest quality. One of the principal aims of the Club was the cessation of wholesale destruction of game fish species. Because of his leadership and contributions to the development of Long Key, the crystal clear stream running in from the Atlantic to the boundaries of this park was named Zane Grey Creek. On September 2, 1935, a hurricane swept the Florida Keys destroying the Long Key Fishing Club and ending operation of the Key West Extension.

U.S. 1 at Long Key
MO20 ~ GPS Coordinates: 24.804200, -80.847183

The Spaniard called it Cayo Vivora or Bivora translating meaning Viper Key, maps of 1864 dubbed it Long Island, today we know the island as Long Key. For nearly forty years the United States War Department claimed the island and after the island lost its appeal to them it was sold to the Hines brothers and Samuel Filer. The men established huge groves of coconut trees, whose fibrous husk were used to make rope. Sailing vessels depended on the durable husks chiefly for their ability to stretch for considerable lengths before breaking.

As the Florida East Coast Railway was making its way to Key West, one of many devastating hurricanes struck Long Key. It was a late season storm, which tend to be more intense, on October 17th , 1906. Construction had just begun on the Long Key viaduct. The men took shelter in their makeshift homes on two huge quarter boats. The vessels were much like the large flat boats floating down the Mississippi but with houses sitting mid deck. The house rose some twelve feet from the waterline and area beneath the decks was used as galleys and dining rooms.

The two boats broke from the moorings with a massive wave. One boat was driven hard to the shore, land locked and the other dragged by the current toward the Gulf Stream. Once caught in the wind and current, the great force of the torrent hauled the large boat out to sea. The wood creaked and split, soon breaking apart; the men desperately clung to anything that would float but in the end sixty-seven were consigned to the murky deep.

Local newspapers noted by mid November huge quantities of lumber were shipped in to the Keys. The houseboats were discarded in favor of buildings built of durable Florida pine. The quarter boats were still used for construction crews working on the bridges but when the winds began to howl and flooding rains began to fall, the boats were abandoned. The first Florida East Coast engine passed over the Long Key viaduct on January 20, 1908.

By the fall of 1908 buildings were being constructed on Long Key including a mercantile, two storied hotel and a line of neat little cottages. During this time the Long Key Fishing Camp got its start. Mackerel, king and sailfish were plentiful and the tourists flocked south to take advantage of what was being boasted as the

"Fishing Capital of the United States." Also during this time northerners began making those yearly migrations south to escape the dread of winter snowfalls and in time they became known as "snowbirds". In the January 20, 1910 issue of Leslie's Weekly this was reported concerning these winter treks:

> "The winter vacation is now the thing. Every physician advises it. Every man and woman who can afford it takes it." So stated Leslie's Weekly, January 20, 1910, in regard to the Long Key Fishing Camp.

Long Key Fishing Camp came to national attention when a dentist turned cowboy who then evolved into an outstanding writer became a regular resident. The avid king fisherman was Zane Grey. Year after year Grey returned to fish the waters of the Florida Keys just for sport. Long Key has a waterway named in his honor called Zane Grey Creek.

Guests arrived by boat or train. By December 28, 1908 the Long Key Post Office was opened with camp manager Louis P. Schutt as postmaster. Boats were docked on the Gulf. The guest list was quite impressive bearing the names Herbert Hoover, Franklin Delano Roosevelt, Andrew Mellon, William Hearst, Charles Kettering and many other well-known people of the day.

In March of 1917 the Long Key Fishing Club was officially founded with Zane Grey as its first president. The club advocated fishing as a sport, a catch and release program and education to the novice fisherman as well as the pursuit of good times in the process. The first organized fishing tournaments began when Zane Grey issued annual bronze, silver and gold awards in various categories. The season ran during the winter months from mid December to mid April and was active for only eighteen years; it died along with most everything else that fateful Labor Day when the fiercest hurricane to date came calling. The post office was destroyed and mail began to arrive though Craig, Florida.

After the historical hurricane the land was totally decimated and many survivors left never to return. Mary and Del Layton, Miami grocery storeowners, purchased a plat on Grassy Key but Long Key was the area they had set their sites on. Eventually the couple bought forty acres on Long Key. Ironically another hurricane called Donna in 1960 resulted in the post office being returned to Long Key.

The Layton's so loved the beautiful Key that they spent the majority of their time there until finally becoming full time residents. The township of Layton was incorporated on September 18, 1963. Del Layton revived the Long Key Fishing Club on July 22, 1969. On October 1, 1969, the Long Key State Park was dedicated preserving one thousand acres. Layton has tried many times to have the post office name changed in their favor, however to this day Long Key remains.

**BLUE STAR
MEMORIAL HIGHWAY**

A tribute to the Armed
Forces that have defended
the United States of
America..

**122nd Street and US 1, in median, Marathon
MO21 ~ GPS Coordinates: 24.730933, -81.026700**

Located some seventy miles west of Key West, the Dry Tortugas are a group of islands surrounded by small cluster reefs. History tells us that Juan Ponce de Leon was the first to step foot on the islands, June 13, 1513. De Leon named the islands Las Tortugas for the abundance of turtles. The connotation "Dry" was added to maps years later indicating to sea going vessels that the island had no fresh water. The Dry Tortugas, as we know them today, consists of seven islands, they are Loggerhead Key, Bush Key, Garden Key, Middle Key, Hospital Key, Long Key and East Key.

For many years the islands remained completed desolate. The only inhabitants were pirates using the islands as hideouts or bases for attacking merchant ships attempting to sail north to the Gulf of Mexico. Spain negotiated in 1819 to surrender Florida to the United States, however the actual conversion did not take place until two years later. The United States first order of business was to conduct a survey of the Florida coast. Commander Matthew C. Perry was charged with the task and recommended the construction of lighthouses at Cape Florida, Key Largo, Sand Key and the Dry Tortugas. Later Commodore Perry opened trade agreements with Japan in 1853 on behalf of the United States Government.

Garden Key was chosen as the site to build the Dry Tortugas Lighthouse in 1824. From that vantage point all of the surrounding islands could be illuminated. Disaster struck when the ship carrying the supplies and materials to build the lighthouse was lost at sea. The loss delayed construction for more than a year. The tower rose sixty-five feet heavenward and was completed in March of 1826. Keeper John R. Flaherty arrived with his family several months later. Trouble began immediately when the United States Revenue Cutter transporting the family could not accommodate all of their belongings. The Garden Key Light having fifteen lamps with metal reflectors was first lit on July 4, 1826.

From the beginning Flaherty's wife Rebecca was extremely dissatisfied with her situation. She hated the heat, boredom, mosquitoes and isolation. She penned her complaints to first lady Louisa Adams, wife of President John Quincy Adams. Keeper Flaherty was said to be lazy and incompetent. Mariners made countless complaints because ships were endangered by the reef due to the thick buildup of soot on the lantern glass. The beam was virtually obliterated and Flaherty seemed to be unconcerned. Eventually he swapped duties with the keeper at Sand Key Lighthouse near Key West bringing his wife back to civilization but his bad habits followed.

Mariners continued to complain concerning the light, it seems the beam was not strong enough and many ships found themselves aground before seeing the light. Eight additional lamps were added but this did little to resolve the problem. The Garden Key Lighthouse was essential for vessels entering the Gulf of Mexico to transport goods to the Mississippi River beyond. However by this time the United States Government had other plans for the Dry Tortugas.

The United States military determined that control of the Dry Tortugas meant also having power over navigation in the Gulf of Mexico. Without control of this significant waterway foreign foes could attack from the south then into the Mississippi River into the heart of the nation. In order to protect this vulnerable body of water a fortification was proposed on Garden Key. Construction began on the "Gibraltar of the Gulf" in 1846. The six-sided fort would stand an amazing forty-five feet with walls eight feet thick. It would cover most of the sixteen-acre key and consist of sixteen million handmade red clay bricks. The fort was built to provide coastal defenses with four hundred fifty canon and fifteen hundred soldiers, unfortunately with the use of the rifled canon Fort Jefferson was obsolete shortly after construction began.

Planned to be the greatest fort in the United States, the facility must carry a distinguished name. Fort Jefferson, in honor of our third President Thomas Jefferson, was officially selected in 1850. The original light-house was located in the angle of Bastion C and renamed Tortugas Harbor Lighthouse. That same year officers' quarters were completed and the island became a military reservation. In support of the military a new one hundred fifty-foot lighthouse was built on Loggerhead Key in three miles to the west of Fort Jefferson, the Tortuga light was downgraded to a fourth order harbor light.

For thirty arduous years work continued on the fort and it was never fully completed. No active warfare was ever involved at Fort Jefferson, its major value came during the Civil War as a prison. In 1864, nine hundred men were imprisoned there and over the ten-year period more than twenty-two hundred were incarcerated at Fort Jefferson.

The most notorious of the Fort Jefferson prisoners were the group convicted of conspiracy to assassinate President Abraham Lincoln and Dr. Samuel Mudd. Dr. Mudd was found guilty of conspiracy and harboring assassin John Wilkes Booth by setting his broken leg after leaping from the State Box while the President lay dying.

Prisoners Samuel Arnold and Michael O'Laughlen were sentenced to life for conspiracy to kidnap President Lincoln and Edman "Ned" Spangler was convicted for aiding John Wilkes Booth in his escape from Ford Theater. The prisoners arrived in 1865.

A yellow fever epidemic laid low the prison in 1867. Among the dead were Michael O'Laughlen and the fort's physician. Without malice, Dr. Mudd stepped in and even though he had also contracted the disease, he expertly cared for the sick and dying. His professionalism and tenderness for his patients, both inmates and prison staff, resulted in the noncommissioned officers and soldiers circulating a petition in support of Dr. Mudd sent to the President.

Dr. Mudd's wife was steadfast in support of her husband. She continually wrote to the President declaring her husband's innocence and begging for his release. On February 8, 1869, President Andrew Johnson pardoned Dr. Samuel Mudd. He returned home and resumed his medical practice. After going out in the freezing rain tending his patients, Dr. Mudd contracted pneumonia. With a soaring fever, he passed away on January 10, 1883. Dr. Samuel Mudd was forty-nine years old.

President Johnson pardoned Samuel Arnold and Ned Spangler on March 1, 1883. Arnold wrote in detail his part in the conspiracy to kidnap President Lincoln; the work was published as Samuel Bland Arnold: Memoirs of a Lincoln Conspirator by Michael W. Kauffman. Arnold died of tuberculosis at the age of seventy-two on September 21, 1906. Ned Spangler accepted five acres of farmland given to him by Dr. Mudd, near his own home in Maryland. Spangler died in 1875.

In October of 1873 a horrendous hurricane tore through the Dry Tortugas. Leaving devastation in its wake, the Tortuga Harbor Light was so badly damaged that even after repairs, lighthouse inspectors recommended the tower be torn down. Congress approved five thousand dollars in 1974 for the construction of an iron beacon. Completed in April of 1875, the three-story boilerplate iron tower was angled on top of Bastion C.

During the Spanish American War in 1898, Fort Jefferson became a naval facility. The fort required some refurbishment after being abandoned for thirteen years. From 1888 through 1900, the remote location made the ideal quarantine station.

Eight years later the Dry Tortugas was transferred from the Department of Defense to the United States Agricultural Department. Because the attraction of the Tortugas to multitudes of seabird colonies, the islands were designated as a fowl preserve. In 1912, a fire destroyed the lighthouse keeper's cottage. Instead of rebuilding the keeper's home, the Lighthouse Service automated the beacon. The light was extinguished for the last time in 1921. A light was replaced on the tower but was for decorative purposes only.

When World War I was declared, Fort Jefferson was put into use again as a military facility. The grounds were used as a seaplane port. President Franklin Delano Roosevelt issued a mandate on January 4, 1935 naming Fort Jefferson as a National Monument. The fort was the first marine sanctuary to be designated in this fashion. The military arrived once again during World War II, establishing an observation post on the remote island chain.

President George Bush made the site a National Park in a bill signed on October 26, 1992. Today the National Park has thousands of visitors each year. Primitive camping, tours of Fort Jefferson, pristine beaches and the most beautiful unspoiled reef can be found at the park. The bountiful sea life that can be seen is absolutely amazing. The only way to reach the Tortugas is by boat or seaplane but there is a multitude of hosts available to make the trip. It can be quite expensive to make the trip but is guaranteed to be well worth the cost. Fort Jefferson and the Dry Tortugas are truly sights that would never be forgotten. Nature, history and a remote tropical paradise, what more could anyone want?

Bahia Honda State Recreation Area, near the facilities inside the park, Bahia Honda Key
MO22 ~ GPS Coordinates: 24.655767, -81.278650

The island we know today as Bahia Honda has been recorded on maps of various explorers by many names. The very first writings detailing the island was noted Vaya Honda on the Spanish Derrotero[8]. Spanish Priest Father Alana charted the island chain noted as Baia Onda, twenty years later explorer William Roberts identifies the island as Bahia Honda in his book "First Discovery and Natural History of Florida." Juan Elixio de la Puente's charts of 1765 annotates the island as Cayo de Bayahonda, the DeBrahm chart in 1772 called the landmass Rice Island and the Gauld maps of 1775 describe the isle as Cabbage Island.

Yet the evolution was still incomplete. The United States Revenue Cutter *Marion* logged the island in 1832 as Key of Honda. The book "Piloting Directions for the Gulf of Florida, the Bahama Banks & Islands" written by J. W. Norie described the island as,

"a large island on the east side, a mile long, with a sandy beach, remarkable for a number of tall palmetto cabbage-trees, the first of the kind you fall in with coming from the westward this island is therefore called Cabbage-Tree Island."

The name stuck until finally in 1849 Author F. W. Gerdes in his work "Reconnaissance of the Florida Reefs and All The Keys" christens the island with the name it still is known by today, Bahia Honda Key.

Bahia Honda is an appropriate name for in Spanish it simply means, deep bay and in fact the island has one of the deepest natural channels in the Florida Keys. The island is also unique in that it has several natural white sugar sand beaches that are quite beautiful. Because of the reef surrounding most islands the sand is kept from the shore prohibiting sand beaches thus making Bahia Honda a very special place indeed. Another particularity is deep waters dropping off very close to the shore, from the majority of the chain of Keys islands one can walk for quite a distance in shallow waters.

During the construction of the Florida East Coast Railway to the sea two large two storied dormitories were built to house the veteran workers at the Bahia Honda Bridge in 1908. Located on the beautiful blue-green oceanside at mile marker thirty-seven, which literally mean you are thirty-seven scenic miles from the very end of US Highway 1 at Key West

Today Bahia Honda is a noted State Recreational Area offering wonderful opportunities for birding, boating, camping, fishing, picnicking, snorkeling and swimming among other possibilities. Guided tours are available throughout the year, with extra opportunities offered during the more populous times of the year.

Snorkeling tours travel to Looe Key Reef National Marine Sanctuary for some of the best and most scenic views in the Florida Keys. Each trip encompasses approximately one and half-hours with an abundance of time to observe the natural splendor of the amazing coral reef. Ocean Kayaks are available for rent by the day or half-day. This is a lovely way to see the wonders of Looe Key in a relaxed and easy pace. The Marine Sanctuary provides the best natural white sand beaches in the Florida Keys.

Swimming is open from both the Atlantic and the Florida Bay in the crystal clear, warm tropical waters abundant with a rainbow of aquatic life. Charter boats and guides are available with various packages offered for some of the best tarpon fishing throughout the south. Bahia Honda is truly an angler's paradise.

Special programs are offered throughout the park concerning a wide range of subjects for individuals or groups. The "How to Snorkel" is one of the most frequently requested programs. A safety vest, instruction and transportation are offered, though you can rent mask, snorkel and fins or bring your own. Wetsuits are recommended when the warm waters dip below seventy-eight degrees in only the most extreme winter months; for the majority of the year a swim suit is all that is necessary to enjoy the beauty of the reef. You will want to bring a bathing suit, towel, sunscreen and a dry change of clothing as well as most importantly basic swimming skills.

The park is open daily. Reservations for camping, special programs and tours are recommended especially during the summer months and holidays. Visitors will pay a nominal entrance fee but once inside the park, all facilities are available for use with the exception of rental equipment. The receipt you are given upon entry is good for the entire day, meaning you may leave and return at your leisure. Bahia Honda State Recreational Area is certainly a must see in the Florida Keys.

A one of a kind facility can be seen some twenty miles to the south of Bahia Honda on Sugarloaf Key at mile marker seventeen. Known to virtually only the locals, the Bat Tower is a most unique attraction. Richter C. Perky created the edifice in 1929 as a fishing camp. In order to control the pesky mosquito problem, he had an epiphany. Bringing in bats known to be mosquito eaters was a very natural solution. Perky amassed an enormous collection of the small flying mammals and placed them in a specially constructed habitat like tower.

Unfortunately Perky's bats flew away as soon as he placed them in the tower. Throughout his lifetime Richter C. Perky never gave up on his concept, leaving food to attract the flying furry creatures. The bats never returned to Perky's tower.

**BLUE STAR
MEMORIAL HIGHWAY**

A tribute to the Armed Forces
that have defended the United
States of America.

**College Road and US 1 in median near Hyatt Beach House Resort, Key West
MO23 ~ GPS Coordinates: 24.571133, -81.748267**

The entire island of Key West is smaller than most Florida cities. The island is a mere four miles in length and a span of two miles wide. Of course, the city is known world wide as the southern most city, located at the end of US Highway 1, one hundred sixty miles southwest of Miami. The name Key West was loosely translated from Cayo Hueso, which literally means Bone Island. Key West is the county seat of Monroe County with a permanent population of nearly twenty-seven thousand residents. The city swells during its year round tourist season to one and a half million. Bordered by the Atlantic Ocean to the east and the Gulf of Mexico to the west. Not to be missed is the nightly festival held each evening at Mallory Square celebrating the mystic beauty of the setting sun. Street performers delight the crowd juggling, walking the tightrope, escape artists, painters, the list could go on and on; all the while the southern most bagpipers moan their eerie tune. In a city known for their round the clock party atmosphere, it is a common phenomenon each day as the sun slips slowly beyond the horizon and everything comes to a standstill. No drinks are served; all conversations cease, the slow easy life of the Keys comes to a quiet halt while all eyes turn toward the setting sun. Then the party starts all over again.

The weather rarely varies more than ten degrees from coolest winter day to the hot, humid summer. Frost, ice, sleet or snow has never touched Key West soil and easterly trade winds keep tropical days at a comfortable temperature. The seasons are different here divided only by two rather than the usual four, the dry season marks the days of December to April while May through October can be a little soggy.

However, the absence of snow and ice are by far overshadowed by the horrendous power of hurricane season from June 1 through November 30; late storms are historically the most intense. Key West has been marked by the National Weather Service as the most likely locale for hurricane strikes throughout the United States, though I believe the residents of South Carolina might argue the distinction. The Florida State Emergency Management Agency has issued a mandate that all residents required to evacuate must be notified thirty-six hours in advance. The mandate is based on the fact that there is one way onto the Florida Keys and likewise one way out.

From May through October the Florida Bay is known to put on a magnificent display as seen no where else in the world. Resulting from high temperatures, humidity and calm winds, waterspouts occur fifty to five hundred times during that short six month span.

As you reach the final pearl in the Florida Keys strand, Key West sits amid verdant green waters observed while passing over some forty-two bridges on the trek from Miami. Imagine the tropical waters dotted with billowing white sails of Spanish explorers; a black ensign snapping in the breeze identifying the scourge of the sea in black-hearted pirates; and crystal clear waters magnifying the skeletons of long dead ship wrecks and salvage vessels lost to Poseidon's mighty wrath. Along the route Presidents, tourists and locals alike pass cigar factories, sponge divers selling their finds as well as fishing boats and shrimping fleets bobbing at docks.

Key West has sustained a Navy presence since 1823. The Naval Air Station on Boca Chica Key is a mere five miles east, northeast of the city. The modern facilities feature three asphalt runways with overruns of seven hundred to one thousand feet and many tenant commands.

The premier pilot, radar specialist and enlisted maintenance personnel training facility offers flight training and operations of the F-14A and A-Plus Tomcat fighters of Squadron One Zero One. The Joint Interagency Task Force provides detection, monitoring and deterrence against drug smuggling operations attempting to bring contraband into the United States. The Caribbean Regional Operating Center aids navigation, issues radar advisories and handles communications for air traffic controllers protecting the Atlantic seaboard. The Naval Atlantic Meteorology and Oceanography Detachment offers twenty-four hour weather forecasts, watches and warnings as well as setting conditions of hurricane readiness. Finally, the Marine Corrosion Test Facility on Fleming Key tests the effects of seawater and environmental conditions on equipment and materials. At Sigsbee Park is the Navy Exchange and Commissary as well as base housing and a visitors RV park for Naval personnel visiting the area.

Unfortunately during recent years the United States government has seen fit to downgrade the military numbers in our country. One of the first Key West facilities affected was the Naval Station at Fort Taylor known to locals as the Little White House or the Truman Annex. Only the northern area of the Truman Annex is in use as a berthing pier for large naval vessels. Formerly a submarine and repair pier the basin is used for smaller craft.

During the early 1980s this area was overrun by impounded craft from the Cuban refugee incidents. The NAS[9] Key West was realigned effective September 1, 2001 placing responsibility of the Joint Interagency Task Force South from Howard Air Force Base, Panama. Recent terrorist activities resulting from the September 11th tragedies and the implementation of Enduring Freedom has managed to increase the numbers of military personnel and revive Naval Air Station Key West. Heroes in paradise.

SOUTHERN TERMINUS OF OVERSEAS RAILWAY

On January 22, 1912, the "Flagler Special," the first passenger train ever to arrive in Key West and Henry M. Flagler, Florida's empire builder, were tumultuously welcomed by the largest outpouring of citizens in the City's history. The train's arrival just a few blocks from here marked the completion of one of the world's most remarkable railroads. For twenty-three years ~ from 1912 to 1935 ~ passenger trains were operated on a daily schedules between Key West and New York and automobile and train car ferries were operated between Key West and Havana. In 1938 the railroad was converted to the overseas highway.

Entrance U.S. 1 and Holiday Inn, 3841 North Roosevelt Blvd, Key West
MO24 ~ GPS Coordinates: 24.571617, -81.753350

Henry Morrison Flagler boarded his private railroad car "Rambler" at 10:43 on the morning of January 22, 1912. Eighty-two year old Flagler had lived to see a dream come true and now he would ride the train to its ultimate destination at the very tip of the United States, Key West. Several dignitaries accompanied the now blind old man to enjoy the ride in the comfort of his elaborate car with magnificent views along the route.

Major J. N. Fogarty of Key West received thundering applause from the waiting crowd as he slowly stepped off the train. As Flagler stood on the platform tears glistened with the sun shining on his cheeks. The miracle train brought modern technology in the form of telegraph, telephone and mail service in its wake. The society created by Flagler now connected to the rest of the United States would blossom into a tourist mecca and tropical paradise.

The Key West steamship terminal for ships carrying freight and passengers to Havana was not yet complete. It would still be several years before this task was realized. Modernization continued on the railway including new innovations over the years of use. Henry Flagler retired to his seaside cottage, Nautilus in Palm Beach and quietly slipped away on May 20, 1913. He was laid to rest in his beloved St. Augustine beside his first wife Mary Harkness and their daughter Jennie Louise with her baby forever sleeping in her arms. The Flagler Mausoleum was built alongside the extraordinary Flagler Memorial Presbyterian Church that was built when Jennie Louise died in childbirth.

Henry Flagler's vision was largely responsible for developing the eastern Atlantic coast of Florida. His magnificent hotels welcomed more than forty thousand visitors each night. The Florida East Coast Railroad made the state accessible to tourism by improving the transportation.

Henry Flagler had a very strained relationship with his son, Harry who he had supported for numerous years. Henry's will indicated Harry would only receive a token bequeath of five thousand shares of Standard Oil stock, each of his three granddaughters received eight thousand shares. Harry refused to continue working in his father's business. After only two years of involvement he quit in favor of a career in music. In fact, after his graduation from Columbia University in 1897 Harry Flagler worked with the New York Art's Committee in creating the New York City Philharmonic Society in 1903. Harry never met his father's widow, Mary Lily.

Jean Flagler Mathews, Harry's daughter, acquired her grandfather's West Palm Beach mansion Whitehall. Harry Flagler died of a heart attack in 1952. Jean restored Whitehall to its original magnificence and opened it as a museum memorial to Henry Morrison Flagler on February 6, 1960.

Henry's widow Mary Lily married ne'er do well Robert Bingham on November 16, 1916. Following the advice of her attorneys Mary Lily had Bingham sign a prenuptial agreement excluding him from his bride's estate. Shortly after their first anniversary Mary Lily added a handwritten codicil to her will leaving Bingham five million dollars. Mary Lily was acting very odd during this time and several family members believed Bingham had forced her to add the change to her will. Their fears were realized when Mary Lily died very suddenly only one month after having changed her will. The cause of death was listed as "acute heart disturbance," which in laymen's terms simply means her heart stopped. Because the family felt her death was suspicious, they had Mary Lily exhumed but the results of the subsequent autopsy were never released.

Robert Bingham was awarded the five million dollars but Mary Lily left the lion's share of her estate to her brother William and sisters, Jessie and Sarah. Her niece Louise Wise was also remembered extremely well including the houses. The Florida East Coast Railway went to the brother and sister who maintained ownership until they were forced into bankruptcy in the 1930s. Ed Ball slowly bought shares until he owned a controlling interest in the railway.

Henry Flagler's second wife, Ida Alice remained in New York's Central Valley, a private sanitarium, until her death in 1930. Though she suffered from delusions and severe mental disabilities, Ida Alice remained in good physical health through the years. True to his word, Henry made sure she was well provided for her entire life. When Ida Alice Flagler passed away her estate was worth thirteen million dollars.

Records show that Flagler spent in excess of six hundred forty million dollars, in early 1900s dollars, on the railroad to the sea. The railroad was definitely a wonderful investment for the Florida Keys, however once Flagler had passed away the passion and dedication for the railroad died as well. The Labor Day hurricane of 1935 was the death knell for the railroad.

Early morning of September 2, 1935 World War I veterans working in three camps to build bridges across the Keys waterways were preparing for evacuation in fear of an oncoming hurricane. Locomotive 447 was at full steam heading toward the Keys to rescue the stranded workers. After several delays the train arrived at Islamorada. Hundreds of workers rushed to the safety of ten cars meant to take them to safety. At 8:20 P.M. a seventeen-foot tidal surge devoured the train.

When the water receded only the locomotive and oil tender were left standing. The vast majority of the workers were lost that fateful day and forty miles of railroad were washed out to sea. Many of the bodies were never found and others were so damaged that identification was impossible. Most of the bodies were cremated and the ashes placed in the Islamorada Hurricane Memorial.

Amazingly the concrete and steel bridges remained steadfast. Unfortunately the railroad was bankrupt. Flagler's dream was buried along with the bodies of the dead. The railroad property was sold to the state for six hundred forty thousand dollars, a fraction of the construction cost, for the building of US 1; the Overseas Highway completed in 1938.

Today the several bridges still stand as fishing piers. The bridges stand strong to this day. The Long Key, Knight's Key or Seven Mile, and Bahia Honda Bridges are all listed in the National Register of Historic Places. Henry Morrison Flagler once summed up the philosophy of his life. He said in part,

**FLAGLER
STATION**

'To help my fellow man to help themselves and to see if a plain American could succeed there where the Spanish, French and English had not.'

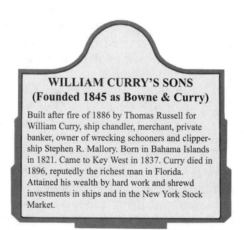

**WILLIAM CURRY'S SONS
(Founded 1845 as Bowne & Curry)**

Built after fire of 1886 by Thomas Russell for William Curry, ship chandler, merchant, private banker, owner of wrecking schooners and clipper-ship Stephen R. Mallory. Born in Bahama Islands in 1821. Came to Key West in 1837. Curry died in 1896, reputedly the richest man in Florida. Attained his wealth by hard work and shrewd investments in ships and in the New York Stock Market.

**E. Martello Tower inside Museum at Faraldo Circle, Key West
MO25 ~ GPS Coordinates: 24.552167, -81.754800**

William Curry arrived in 1837 on the island of Key West from the Bahamas as a poor immigrant bent on finding a fortune in the United States. Imagine what it was like in those days, pirates abounded, most wreckers, including Curry, made their living off the ill fortune of others. In less than twenty years Curry was Key West's first millionaire.

Curry began construction of a home for his family in 1855. The architecture and furnishings would be a mix of many styles taken from allover the world because of the vast array of things taken from various shipwrecks. The widow's walk was common in New England homes, ornate trellises and balustrades from New Orleans as well as columns and colonnades were usual in the southern states. Amazingly it would take more than forty years to complete the lavish dwelling.

Milton Curry, his son, had the mansion completed in 1899. He chose one hundred-year-old antique furnishings and Victorian pieces to adorn the beautiful home. The elaborate vestibule was designed in bird's eye maple wood with hand made spindles as well as famous Tiffany stained glass sliding doors. The family set the formal dining room with Haviland china and today replicas of original solid gold Tiffany flatware are used. Renowned author Henry James' 1853 Chickering piano is featured in the music room.

Key West merchants felt threatened as a new breed of Jewish peddlers moved into their territory. To fight the competition, the Merchants' Protective Association was established. The Jewish peddlers, ever creative, responded by opening mercantiles of their own from the money earned peddling. Ironically some of those Jewish mercantiles still remain open to this day, whereas only one of the Association members descendants was able to maintain their businesses. Poetic justice maybe.

Just next door to the Curry Mansion built in 1899 is a majestic house that today is called the Curry Mansion Inn. Voted the Best Bed and Breakfast in Key West, quite a distinction compared to the number there, the Inn offers twenty-eight beautiful rooms that leaves visitors feeling as if they were a guest of the Curry Family. The Mansion is utilized today as a museum listed on the National Register of Historic Places. A wonderful pool and cool tropical garden add to the ambiance of a wonderful place to spend your limited time in Key West. I say limited time because anything less than a lifetime is just too short a time spent in this tropical playground.

As you enter the thick stone walls of the East Martello Tower the first thing that strikes you further is that it is at least ten degrees cooler inside than in the hot tropical sun just outside the door. Called the bastion of Florida Keys history the museum is definitely a hodge-podge of all the amazing characteristics that make Key West one of the most amazing cities in the United States. It takes all kinds to make a community and Key West has a representation of all classes, races, ethinicies, sexes and ages. As matter of fact, it is this combination that makes the city the fascinating place it is today.

The museum is designed to resemble the impregnable Martello watchtowers of Italy. The likeness is incredible. The tower was never completely finished but never saw hostile actions to warrant completion. Featured are eight-foot thick granite walls resembling the Castillo San Marco in St. Augustine. Climb to the top of the central tower where the most incredible panorama view of the Atlantic Ocean is revealed. In the courtyard is an eighty-year-old playhouse that gives today's child a sense of how children spent their day to day hours in historic Key West in the early 1900s. The museum is said to be the best-preserved example of military architecture in the country, I agree.

The museum includes everything from the wrecker's influence, Cubans, military and even the voodoo doll Robert line the corridors. The first thing I recall when thinking of it is the large, black, ornate funeral car or hearse. Fine Art is represented in works of local artists Mario Sanchez and Stanley Papio. Sanchez's work in painted woodcarvings and drawings portrays the life of Key West in the early 1900s with street scenes depicting daily life. Papio was known as a dynamic junkman. He was a former wanderer, classic in Key West, who collected refuse all over the island and created art. The saying "one man's trash is another man's treasure," was probably written for him. His welded sculptures represent animals, people or objects mostly displayed in his yard in the upper Keys. Sanchez has both signed and unsigned lithographic prints in the small museum store. Both Sanchez and Papio are recognized as renowned folk artists all over the world.

The Fort East Martello Museum and Gardens located at 3501 South Roosevelt Boulevard in Key West is open everyday with the exception of Christmas. For a small admission fee, the wonders of old Key West are yours to be viewed. The facilities and grounds are available for rent as an incredible setting for that special occasion.

Mr. and Mrs. Thomas Otto lived in Key West around 1898 and though pillar of the community, they were known as horrible taskmasters toward their servants. The couple had a young son by the name of Robert Eugene, called Gene by his few friends. The family had one serving girl who was determined to curse the family through their most favored possession, which of course was their son. The girl was known to have studied a vague blend of religion combining Catholicism and Voodoo. She made a three-foot replica of Robert Eugene complete with little sailor suit and favored toy, giving it to young Gene whom fell in love instantly. The doll was quickly named Robert. Maybe the doll had special powers and maybe they were imagined but none the less Robert was involved with many curious happening over the last hundred years or so.

Like an alter ego, Gene blamed the stuffed Robert for any of his sins or bad luck that might occur. Often Gene's parents heard him converse with the straw doll and like any parent, they imagined "well, as long as the imaginary friend doesn't talk back." Gene's doll not only talked but had a sinister giggle, which would send chills down your spine. Strange misfortunes soon began to befall the family and Gene would always blame Robert. While most could believe the sins of the child had come home to roost, the family blamed Robert. It became the family joke. But neighbors soon came to believe as well when Robert was noticed running up the steps and staring out from the turret room giving them the evil eye.

Most children often outgrow these obsessions but into his teens, Genes never did. In response, his parents relegated Robert to a trunk in the attic. Upon his parent's death, Gene retrieved his cherished dolly. Gene married, which wasn't exactly happy. Soon his wife realized she had married one man and a doll. She insisted Gene return the doll to its trunk but he refused, when she did Gene threatened divorce. He insisted that as their child Robert should have his own room overlooking the street. It wasn't long before all of Key West questioned Gene's sanity, which is saying something when you speak of Key West society.

When the public began to complain of the strange happenings concerning Robert, Gene relented and put the doll back into the attic. Robert watched people, mimicking their every movement, he was heard giggling demonically when people stared back in horror. Gene swore Robert was in the attic but strangely he'd be found in a rocking chair beside the window in his room the very next morning. Repeatedly this happened and no one could explain why.

Robert Eugene Otto died in 1972 and many thought the curse of Robert would die with him. When the doll was forcibly removed from the house Anne, Gene Otto's wife, assumed his place in the turret room rocking chair to guard against Robert's return, but he was patient. Anne died and still Robert waited. When a new family bought the house their little girl found the straw doll in an attic trunk and called him her own. Imagine what happened next? Today more than five decades later, as an elderly woman, she still bares the scars of his torture mentally and physically.

Though Robert's evil has diminished somewhat he is still a menacing presence. He is known to often walk about the museum and taps on the glass when he sees a pretty girl. His fingerprints have been recorded by the Key West police and found on the glass. Don't be disappointed if when visiting museum that pictures to remember the demonic doll don't develop, Robert refuses to be photographed. Photography would take away his soul and he'd never live again. But be assured he lives. Each year he makes the trek to the Customs House, a few blocks away, where candy left for him disappears through the night. Peppermints tend to keep him from misbehaving.

Visitors of the Artist House, also a Bed and Breakfast, report unsettling sounds, pacing and stares from an unseen apparition. It appears Anne is still protecting the house and keeping watch for Robert and his ugly deeds. Anne is benevolent and has never harmed anyone. However, there is only one way to know for sure and this is your invitation.

EAST MARTELLO MUSEUM

AFRICAN CEMETERY
AT HIGGS BEACH

Near this site lie the remains of 294 African men, women and children who died in Key in 1860. In the summer of that year the U.S. Navy rescued 1,432 Africans from three American-owned ships engaged in the illegal slave trade. Ships bound for Cuba were intercepted by the U.S. Navy, who brought the freed Africans to Key West where they were provided with clothing, shelter and medical treatment. They had spent weeks in unsanitary and inhumane conditions aboard the slave ships. The U.S. steamships *Mohawk*, *Wyandott* and *Crusader* rescued: the *William*, where 513 were rescued: and the *Bogota*, where 417 survived, in all, 294 Africans succumbed at Key West to various diseases caused by conditions of their confinement. They were buried in unmarked graves on the present day Higgs Beach where West Martello Tower now stands. By August, more than 1,000 survivors left for Liberia, West Africa, a country founded for former American slaves, where the U.S. government supported them for a time. Hundreds died on the ships before reaching Liberia. Thus, the survivors were returned to their native land, Africa, but not to their original homes on the continent.

West Martello Tower, Key West
MO26 ~ GPS Coordinates: 24.547567, -81.785983

The overseas crossing from Africa was often fatal on the slavers' ships. No care was taken to provide for the human cargo, to care for their sickness, to feed their want, to quench their thirst or mourn their numerous losses. On this particular slaver voyage, a virtual fleet of human suffering, the United States Marshal officers managed to rescue two hundred and ninety five Africans. The officers attempted to minister to the sick and feed the hungry but some were beyond their help and in the hands of their God.

Daniel Davis, a local carpenter, was charged with construction of barracoons[10] and burials. He was paid five dollars and fifty cents per burial. A sandy ridge along the southern shore overlooking the ocean was chosen as the site. According to a 1912 work by Jefferson Browne described the typical African funeral:

"The first burial was of a child six weeks old, whose young mother was barely in her teens. Her devotion to her offspring made her an object of much sympathy to the visitors to the camp, and, upon the death of the child, our people provided a handsome coffin to bury it in. The interment took place some distance from the barracoon, and the Africans were allowed to be present at the services, where they performed their native ceremony. Weird chants were sung, mingled with loud wails of grief and mournful moans from a hundred throats, until the coffin was lowered into the grave, when at once the chanting stopped and perfect silence reigned, and the Africans marched back to the barracoon with out a sound."

The site was chosen because in 1860 this area was not only remote but rarely did anyone visit this area of the island as most of the dwelling and businesses were centered on the opposite side of the island much as it is today. When the Civil War began the Army decided to fortify this site because of the direct link to the Atlantic Ocean. At this time East and West Martellos were known as Fort Taylor Towers No. 1 and No. 2 and constructed in January 1862. During the ground breaking the graves were discovered along with the skeletons and stench of decaying bodies. The workers were appalled but under orders to removed the corpses and inter them in another location. Construction was eventually halted and the towers were left uncompleted.

It was believed that Tower No. 1 simply collapsed, but this could not be further from the truth. These building were constructed to remain for more than one hundred years; many have lasted from the 1500s during the time of the Spaniards. Some say the building was used as target practice for Fort Taylor, others report that bricks were removed to build other structure in town. The only people who know for sure are long dead, not that it matters except to historians at this point. The site has been used as a cattle stockade, Army barracks, apartments, etc. In 1898, the Army returned for the Spanish American War occupation. During World War II the site became an anti-aircraft battery. Monroe County assumed responsibility of the towers after the Army left for the final time.

A record was kept of the cemetery, however, few saw the maps of 1861 until the United States Army Corps of Engineers went searching for them. Simply marked "African Cemetery" with nine X's to represent the graves various locations. The map was transposed to modern maps to garner the exact location of the burial sites. Not wanting to disturb the sanctity of the site, new technology was used.

Ground-Penetrating Radar or GPR was the best resolution to this dilemma. In effect it works by reflection of pulses of energy transmitted into the ground. The energy bounces off the buried features and is detected with a receiving antenna. The density of the soil is reflected in different ways sending detectable signals to the user. This instrumentation allows the user to see beneath the surface without disturbing the site.

The cemetery was discovered very much where expected, however much of it due to modern construction had been desecrated over the years. The area on the beach was virtually untouched. Nine graves were extremely clear and six others were vague. The details matched exactly with known gravesites.

Two hundred ninety-five graves were dug at Higgs Beach, today fifteen remain. What happened to two hundred eighty bodies? To answer the question with certainty archeological excavation had to be done. I witnessed the team of archaeologists dig on June 14, 15 and 16 of 2002 and was amazed at the care that was taken with this sacred ground. It is a credit to all involved the way this exploration was conducted. The question was answered and the ground was again consecrated on September 16, 2002. It was further remembered with this historical marker.

The West Martello Tower has been and is today the home of the Key West Garden Club. As it should be, flowers are left in honor of the dead. No fee is charged for viewing the beautiful tropical paradise, walk quietly here and observe the solitude of those gone before us. Those who never knew our freedom except in death. Leaving a suitable donation should be your privilege rather than your obligation.

CONVENT OF MARY IMMACULATE
(1878)

Built by the Sisters of the Holy Names of Jesus and Mary, a Canadian Order which first established a school here in 1868. Designed by William Kerr of Ireland, of Romanesque style, with dormered, mansard roofs and central tower. In the Spanish- American war the Sisters offered their services as nurses and the Convent to the Navy as a hospital and rendered devoted service to the wounded and yellow fever victims.

St. Mary's Star of the Sea is the oldest diocese in southern Florida, having been established sometime prior to 1850. From the beginning, there were black families among the congregation - some free and some slaves. They were assigned a separate part of the church, but most other churches on the island had separate churches for black and white congregations.

After an arson fire in September 1901 destroyed the parish church, which at that time was southwest of Duval between Eaton and Fleming, the church purchased this lot and the new church was dedicated in 1905. They are preparing to celebrate their hundredth anniversary next year.

Truman Avenue between Simonton and Margaret Street, Key West
MD27 ~ GPS Coordinates: 24.552800, -81.796433

St. Mary, Star of the Sea is the eldest catholic parish in all of south Florida. Father John F. Kirby had the first Catholic Church built in Key West at what is today the corner of Duval and Eaton Streets, in 1851 though it was not dedicated until February 26, 1852. The name was derived from her boarders of the Atlantic Ocean and Gulf of Mexico. Of some two thousand residents at that time some three hundred were catholic and this was a mixed congregation of blacks and whites, slaves and freemen. This was extremely unique for the time. When Father Joseph N. Brogard arrived in November 1852 a tower bell was erected on the church grounds, people of all denominations took pleasure in the peel of Angelus, rung three times a day.

At the conclusion of the Civil War, Bishop Verot of Havana was given the tasks of supplying the church spiritually, financially and materially. To enact a spiritual reconstruction his plan had two parts, to educate the blacks in the community and introduce parish missions. In 1868 Bishop Verot requested Sisters from a convent in Montreal, Canada be sent to establish the first Catholic school in south Florida. Sister Superior Mary Euphrasie, Sisters Mary Octavie, Mary Angelique, Mary Pierre and Mary Monique all boarded the merchant ship *Sedwidge* ultimately bound for Texas with a stop at Key West for supplies to make their journey.

The Convent of Mary Immaculate is the oldest educational institution in south Florida, housed in the beginning in the government building, which during the Civil War was used as a goat shed. Wasting no time the Sisters formed a school for white girls on November 9, 1868 with twenty-six young ladies in attendance. A layman, Mr. Chappik, taught the school for boys, established by Father Allard, during the same period. Within a year's time the St. Francis School for all black children and a school for Cuban girls were also organized. I find it somewhat amazing that white males and females were placed in different schools while all black children were massed together, this is just a curiosity.

Construction on the Convent of Mary Immaculate began on January 14, 1875 at a cost of thirty-five thousand dollars. Ever frugal the sisters would work the construction site themselves during their few spare hours of the day in order to save on building expenses. William Kerr, an Irishman, was chosen as the architect for the convent. Originally arriving in Key West in order to build military fortifications, Kerr designed the convent after a building in France. The walls were built of native coral rock and was built on eight and a half acres facing what was then known as Rocky Road. The road eventually came to be known as Division Street but is today called Truman Avenue. The property was purchased from the Baldwin family for one thousand dollars. The building was completed in 1876 and there were three hundred students enrolled. The Cuban chapel, Nuestra Senora de la Caridad del Cobre, Our Lady of Charity of Ed Cobre, was established in 1879 on Duval Street but there was always trouble finding a priest to staff it. In 1898 the chapel was closed but moved to its present location on Windsor Lane. The chapel is directly behind St. Mary, on the rectory grounds and was eventually converted into a parish hall. Today it is known as St. Ann's Hall and contains the parish gift shop.

The Convent Sisters opened the St. Joseph College for white males in 1881 replacing the original boy's parochial school. The first graduation exercises were held on the night of February 15, 1898 for the students of the Convent of Mary Immaculate. It was during this ceremony that word reached Key West, Spanish forces in Havana harbor had sunk the battleship *Maine*. This ignited the Spanish-American War lasting for four bloody months and bringing an end to Spanish rule in Cuba.

For two weeks victims from the *Maine*, injured and dead, were brought to Key West. The small Navy-Marine Hospital and Barracks Hospital at the Army Post were filled to overflowing. Mother Mary Florentine, Mother Superior of the convent, approached Commander James M. Forsyth offering all convent buildings and grounds, as well as the personal services of the Sisters as nurses for the Navy's use. Eventually it would be called the Key West Convent Hospital. Commander Forsyth forwarded the generous offer to his commander-in-chief. This was the reply he received from the United States Flagship *New York* on April 7, 1898:

"SIR-

I. Acknowledging your letter of the 5th instant, stating that the Lady Superior in charge of the schools of the 'Sisters of the Holy Names, Convent of Mary Immaculate,' at Key West, has called on you, and offered, in case of war, to place the convent and two school buildings of the order at the disposition of the naval authorities for hospital purposes, and that the Sisters tender their personal services as nurses.

2. 1 cordially agree with your opinion expressed, that this is a most generous and patriotic tender, and beg that you will make known to the Lady Superior, and to the Sisters, my appreciation of their offer, and acceptance in case it becomes necessary.

Very respectfully,
W. T. SAMPSON,
Captain U. S. N., Commander-in-Chief
U. S. Naval Forces. North Atlantic Station."

Major W. R. Hall, a doctor in the United State Navy, arrived on April 21st for the conversion of convent to hospital, which was completed very quickly. The parlor was now a drug store; classrooms served as wards for the wounded and the upstairs offices became operating rooms. Lieutenant John B. Bernadou of the *Winslow*, a torpedo boat was the first patient treated. Nine doctors were assigned to the medical facility with Major Hall in command.

Tragedy struck when the church erected under the direction of Father Kirby was intentionally set a flame on September 20, 1901. The arson was easily detected when it was discovered that the heart of the fire began at the center of the organ. Mass was said in the convent music hall, which was built by the United States Government during the Spanish-American War. Immediately work began to clean up the site and begin construction on another edifice. The church purchased property adjacent to the convent and schools.

The overall design of the church is High Victorian Gothic sometimes called Ruskinian featuring arches and pointed windows frequently borrowed from the look of medieval cathedrals. Architecturally the construction character is known as Ugden steel, which is today no longer practiced. It is the work of Father Friend who not only financed the construction but who prodded it along with his unique energy and creative abilities. Native coral stone was dug from the site of construction and cut into blocks. This is in fact the first Catholic Church in south Florida not built of wood. Massive doors stood along the east and west sides of the building replacing the usual windows. The interior features the Byzantine style with massive domes having square bases, rounded arches, spires, minarets[11] and many mosaics. An organ, shipped from Massachusetts, accompanies the choir in a magnificent loft. Just beyond the altar is a glorious stained glass window of Our Lady, Star of the Sea. The church was dedicated on August 20, 1905 in services conducted by the Right Reverend W. J. Kenny, Bishop of St. Augustine.

The Sisters of the Holy Names of Jesus and Mary expanded the convent to double its size in 1904. An artistic steeple added balance and the convent school is said to be the most beautiful educational facility in Florida. Sister Louis Gabriel came to the Key West convent on August 25, 1897; she is responsible for designing the beautiful grotto on the grounds containing statues of Our Lady of Lourdes and Bernadette. She served valiantly for more than fifty years at Key West and had born witness to many hard times including three major hurricanes leaving behind death and destruction each time. Sister Louis was heard to say that as long as the grotto stood Our Blessed Mother Mary would protect their small island home from taking the brunt of another hurricane. Most can attest to that since the dedication of the grotto on May 25, 1922, no major storm has devastated Key West. Sister Louis Gabriel died at peace on September 13, 1948 and was buried with her fellow nuns on the convent grounds.

St. Mary Star of the Sea parish celebrated one hundred years of service to the community on February 26, 1952. A weeklong celebration followed. The Convent of Mary Immaculate became Mary Immaculate High School that very same year and four years later graduated it first co-educational class. In August of 1956 St. Mary's was restored replacing the termite-infested floors, replacing the terrazzo tiles and adding new pews increasing the seating capacity to six hundred parishioners. The rectory was replaced with a more modern structure in April 1959.

Sadly after more than one hundred years of servitude the Sisters of the Holy Names of Jesus and Mary in Key West ended with the death of the last nun, Sister Dolores Wehle. Unfortunately staffing problems made the closure of the mission necessary. The Archdiocese elected to close the High School in 1986; again it was a sad day for the island.

The nun's cemetery was moved in 1989. Father Quinlan had the eighteen nuns moved to a beautiful location near the grotto. The grave markers were all cleaned and refurbished to show their dates spanning for one hundred years. The first sister's death dates to 1869 and the last 1969. The Father also took great interest in restoring much of the church property. It was through his dedication that St. Mary's was recognized as a National and State Historical Site.

The convent chapel was completely renovated in 1995 and renamed as the Chapel of Divine Mercy. The Blessed Sacrament in the Divine Mercy Chapel was opened for prayer and reflection twenty-four hours per day just one month later. The church continues its service to the community with ministries to the Sick, Special Ministries to Aids patients, Prison Ministries, Family and Home Life Ministries, the Eucharistic Ministry, as Lectors, Senior Acolytes, Volunteers to the Homeless, Christian Education of Children, RCIA Team and support team for Education of Adults, Bible Study and Adult Education Classes. St. Mary's will celebrate her one-hundredth anniversary of consecration on August 20, 2005.

SOUTH FLORIDA'S
FIRST PUBLIC LIBRARY

On April 8, 1892, a group of citizens organized the Key West Library Association. The first public library was open in the old Masonic Temple September 15, 1892. After 1896, the operation was assumed by other civic groups, including the Key West Woman's Club, which for 44 years provided library service. Through the group's efforts, funds were raised to build the Monroe County Public Library, which opened in November 1959.

700 Fleming Street - Monroe County Public Library, Key West
MO28 ~ GPS Coordinates: 24.557733, -81.800033

The first building of the Key West Masons was constructed in 1869 on the northeast side of Simonton Street. The second floor was used for Masonic purposes while the first floor was utilized for entertainment and eventually the first public school in Key West. The building went down in a blaze in 1886 and a larger three-storied brick building took its place. This building was completed in 1889.

It was in the 1889 Masonic Lodge that a group of citizens gathered to form the first Key West Library Association. With books donated from extensive private collections and many bequeathed in estates the first public library was established. The library opened on September 15, 1892. Though one had to prove at this time that they were trust worthy enough to borrow a book, the library was quite popular. It remained at this location for twenty-three years.

Over time various civic organizations took responsibility of the library but it was in 1915 that the library moved to a second location. The brick residence was the home of Captain Martin L. Hellings who managed the International Ocean Telegraph Company. His wife, Eleanor Hellings, was quite an individual in her own right. Mrs. Hellings founded the Christian Science Church in Key West. Eventually the Key West Woman's Club came to occupy the house at 319 Duval Street. It was there that the second public library of Key West was established in 1915. The Key West Woman's Club maintained the library for some forty-four years. Through the efforts of this organization and several others, funds were raised to build the Monroe County Public Library.

The May Hill Russell Branch Library opened its doors in November 1959. Located at 700 Fleming Street in Key West, the library is open Monday through Saturday. Having been founded in 1892, it is the oldest library in south Florida and the southernmost public library in the continental United States.

The library offers a expansive enrichment program involving lecture series, author presentations, art shows, music, an International Film Festival, Thursday Morning Book Club, Preschool Story Time, Toddler Playtime and a Mothers' Support Group, to name a few. The library also has an extensive Florida and Florida History section, has proven to be quite helpful to me during the writing of this book. Fact hunters are available to help out when trying to find that elusive topic. Historical information of local interest including pictures, legal documents and records, maps of Monroe County as well as the remainder of the state are at your disposal to assist in whatever your project might be.

The staff can help when meeting rooms are needed for group meetings or presentations. As an added bonus, if the library doesn't have the work you need, let the librarian know and she may be able to locate it through the inter-library loan service. Visit your local library today, a wealth of information awaits you there.

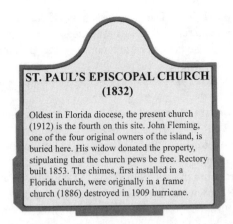

**ST. PAUL'S EPISCOPAL CHURCH
(1832)**

Oldest in Florida diocese, the present church (1912) is the fourth on this site. John Fleming, one of the four original owners of the island, is buried here. His widow donated the property, stipulating that the church pews be free. Rectory built 1853. The chimes, first installed in a Florida church, were originally in a frame church (1886) destroyed in 1909 hurricane.

**Corner of Eaton and Duval Streets, Key West
MO29 ~ GPS Coordinates: 24.556967, -81.803417**

The first organized religion established in Key West was the Episcopal. Many who had not known this religion in the past flocked to the Protestant Episcopal Church, united as one to form a congregation. A Young novice by the name of Reverend Sanson K. Brunot of Pennsylvania arrived on December 23, 1832. He came highly recommended even though his years in the ministry were so few. His health was definitely an issue, Brunot suffered from consumption as had many of his family; he felt the sultry weather would help to relieve the symptoms of his disease.

The first Sunday school was organized November 1832 and in January 1833, there were between fifty and sixty children in attendance. The first service was held on Christmas Day 1832. By spring wardens and vestrymen were elected but sadly by this time Reverend Brunot's health began to decline. He felt his time on earth was quickly coming to an end and wanted to die at home in the arms of his family. Reverend Sanson K. Brunot left Key West in May of 1833 and died amidst his family in Pittsburgh. He advised the vestrymen to apply to the Missionary Society of New York for funds. By July they took his advice and the Missionary Society appointed Reverend Alva Bennett of Troy, New York, contributing two hundred dollars per year toward his salary. The congregation promised an addition five hundred dollars per year. The new Reverend arrived in October 1835 and remained for only six months. The first Holy Communion and services were held at the courthouse. It was obvious that what this congregation required was a church.

Reverend Robert Dyce next took the pulpit and immediately took it upon himself to have a sanctuary built. He managed to convince Mrs. John William Charles Fleemon to donate a lot in Key West including furnishings. Construction planning began on July 10th, 1938 and it was decided to erect the edifice of native coral rock having thirty-six pews and a gallery at one end. By March of the following year the church was coming along and the pews were sold at auction. The church cost a total of sixty-five hundred dollars.

Several laymen served the pulpit over the next few years until Reverend J. H. Hanson took the reins. Under his direction the Church was very nearly completed. Reverend C. C. Adams could be called the savior of the Church, although he would supremely dislike the insinuation. He came to St. Paul's in October 1946. Adams did so with reluctance for he had just learned that the Church was blown away in a hurricane that very month. By suggestion of the Georgia Episcopal Church in Savannah, he started out toward Key West to check the danger and sail across the sea to beg and pled for money to rebuild. He had the congregation agree that the vestry be forever free of charge and the point was agreed upon.

He returned in December having collected over three thousand dollars, which was a huge amount of money, by the standards of the day. The first service held in the wooden framed Church was July 30, 1848. The Church was consecrated on January 4, 1861.

Both blacks and white attended the service, both slave and freedman. Four rows in the back were reserved for the blacks and disruptive children. The practice remained enforce until the blacks built a sanctuary of their own, also named St. Peters'. The Church still stands today, catering to the black population. Some of the older black congregation failed to accept the new trend and continued to worship in the only way they knew how, with chants, song and dance. By January 5, 1859, the parish was able to retire their debt and become self-supporting – in effect retiring their connection with the Missionary Society as well. Reverend Adams resigned on April 1, 1855.

E. O. Herrick had been previously connected with Key West when as a United States Army Chaplain, he was stationed for several years at Fort Monroe. He accepted the appointment to Key West in December of 1856 and died in Watertown, New York on October 1, 1907. More than eight thousand dollars worth of improvements to the pastorate and church were completed.

From 1873 until 1880 several church leaders were sent to conduct services at Key West. Unfortunately many succumbed to Yellow Fever. Reverend Gilbert Higgs left Key West in June of 1903. He served for thirteen years and when he passed away in retirement at Atlanta, Georgia, he was returned to Key West for burial. Services were held in the parish school, September 11, 1911. Gilbert Higgs, of St. George, Bermuda, was not only a fine clergyman dedicated to his flock but a man of great energy and an eye for fine art. It was through his backbreaking work that the tropical garden was established at Higgs Beach. The beach was obviously named in his honor.

Over the years numerous pastors held the pulpit of the Episcopal Church in Key West. The stone Church, built in 1847, was destroyed by fire in 1886. But later the same year another sanctuary was constructed with a full compliment of chimes. During this period they were the first set of chimes in Florida. The Ladies' Missionary Society was organized in 1851. Patrons of the chimes were William Curry and Horatio Crain.

The first official parish meeting was planned for March 5, 1911. Bent on finding a way to rebuild St. Paul's, an alms plate was passed to raise money for the construction of a new edifice. In 1912, St. Paul's population soared to seven hundred baptised parishioners and three hundred communicants. It has only improved from there.

Duval & Caroline Streets, Key West
MO30 ~ GPS Coordinates: 24.557950, -81.804483

Joseph Yates Porter was born at Key West on October 21, 1847, two weeks after the death of his young thirty-year-old father. In honor of the man he would never meet, the infant would bear his name proudly, but fate and tragedy were not through with him. To test his metal, God certainly gave him much more than any child should bear, but Joseph Yates Porter was up to the task; his dear mother passed away when he was but a boy of twelve. Unfortunately he was in those unstable developing years and he became the ward of his paternal grandfather, William L. Porter of Boston, living in Charleston, South Carolina.

His maternal grandfather had also succumbed to the tragedy of yellow fever at the early age of thirty-seven. Captain Thomas Mann Randolph, a Virginian, was commander of the United States revenue cutter *Washington*. Yellow fever had become a theme that marred young Joseph's life.

Young Porter graduated from the Jefferson Medical College in Philadelphia in 1870. He married Miss Louise Curry, daughter of well known Key West wrecker and millionaire William Curry, on June 1, 1870. The couple bore four children. William R, named for the grandfather who raised his father, grew to be an insurance agent. Mary Louise, who married the Honorable W. Hunt Harris a state senator of Monroe County; Roberta, wife of W. W. Mountjoy of New York City; and Joseph Yates, Jr., who followed in his father's footsteps at the College of Physicians and Surgeons in New York City.

Dr. Joseph Yates Porter joined the United States Army as acting Assistant-Surgeon at Fort Jefferson. He spent three and a half very long and lonely years in the remote post. It was while he was there that he valiantly fought an epidemic of his old nemesis yellow fever in 1873. He was tested by the state of New York and eventually appointed First Lieutenant Assistant-Surgeon of the United States Navy in June 1875. Five years later he was promoted to Captain and served as a Naval Officer for nineteen years. During his career Dr. Porter served at the Tortugas, Key West, Tampa, Miami and Texas.

His last years in the Navy were terribly tiresome and physically draining. In 1887, he fought the scourge of yellow fever at Key West and Tampa. He had no sooner quieted the worst of evil in south and west Florida when Dr. Porter was summoned to Jacksonville in 1888. Yellow fever was spreading and threatening to take the lives of two-thirds of the Florida population.

When one thinks of retirement at Key West, the imagination wanders to tropical breezes with the smell of the sea and jasmine wafting through the air. Warm salt water to soothe what ails you and life's slow movement that means one has now set their watch to Key West time. But this was not to be when Dr. Porter retired in 1889.

In 1889, the State Board of Health created a position entitled State Health Officer to fight and concur the deadly disease that had so affected Dr. Joseph Yates Porter's life. In 1899, the final yellow fever epidemic gripped the state. The Florida Legislature of Monroe County elected Porter the State Health Officer officially in 1900. The following is a statement written in the Miami Herald in March 1927:

President of the Florida State Board of Health, R. P. Daniels, M.D. wrote in May 1890:

"In making this selection, the Board realized that it was not only giving expression to its own preference, but was voicing the almost unanimous sentiment of the people of the state - that Dr. Porter was the one man best fitted, by the qualifications of capacity, experience and popularity, to fill the office."

Imagine in a sea of immigrants Dr. Porter was born, lived and died in the same home. He lived his life as a man full of grace and good intentions, the efforts he put forth in Florida were above and beyond what any man could have been expected. The generations of Florida pay homage to this great man, well deserved for he delivered them from the death grips of yellow fever. At eighty years old, Dr. Joseph Yates Porter breathed his last and permanently inked his name in the annals of Monroe County, Florida and America. A man well deserving and humble enough to simply say, "Thank You."

AUDUBON HOUSE

Captain John H. Geiger, skilled pilot and master wrecker, built this house in 1830. It is typical of the era when, in 1832, the famed naturalist John James Audubon, visited Key West to study and sketch the birds of the Florida Keys. On March 18, 1960, Mitchell Wolfson, native son of Key West, and Mrs. Wolfson, also a native Floridian, dedicated the house as a public museum to be named Audubon House, commemorating the artist's visit to Key West. Furnished with antiques of the period, the museum proudly exhibits numerous original Audubon engravings. This restoration sparked the preservation and restoration movement in Key West.

205 Whitehead Street, Key West
MO31 ~ GPS Coordinates: 24.558267, -81.806167

The story of the Audubon House is conflicting and curious in its detail. What is known for sure is that today the Audubon House & Tropical Gardens is a beautiful vision of old Key West as it might have appeared in the years of Audubon and earlier still Captain John H. Geiger. We know the house was slated for destruction in 1958 but for the care and concern of the Mitchell Wolfson Family Foundation it was saved from the wrecking ball. The foundation is a not for profit organization and in saving the Audubon House they set the bar for historical restoration throughout the Keys and most especially Key West.

It has been said that harbor pilot and master wrecker, Captain John H. Geiger, built the home for himself, his wife and nine children. What is known is that the Captain lived in Key West during the height of wreckers, pirates, yellow fever, slavers and Seminole Wars. We know that Audubon either knew or knew of Captain Geiger because Key West records show that George Lehman, Audubon's assistant, painted the cordia tree with the white-crowned pigeon sitting in the tree known in history today as the Geiger tree. We know that John James Audubon spent time in the home, whereas we also have evidence that (unlike the old joke saying, "Washington slept here") Audubon probably didn't.

Visiting the museum that is the Audubon House & Tropical Gardens is a stroll through the brain of John James Audubon. His beautiful works can be enjoyed from every angle and as many as twenty-eight first edition works haunt the home. Mitchell Wolfson purchased the Birds of America folio in 1960 from Duncan H. Read of Virginia. The folio was displayed at the Audubon House for a time until it was in fact stolen. Though recovered, it became apparent that the work deserved far more protection than was afforded at the Audubon House. The Historical Museum of Southern Florida in Miami arranged to acquire the work. Mr. Wolfson made this move possible.

Audubon came to the Keys and Dry Tortugas in 1832, then after having documented and drawn eighteen new bird species for his folio he left. Many of these birds were said to been found in the front or back yard, it depends on whose telling the tale like it really matters which side of the fence he viewed the creature from, at the Geiger home.

Because of letters to and from Audubon and his wife we determine that for fear of "night fever", or yellow fever as we know it today, the Mrs. Audubon begged her husband to sleep aboard the revenue cutter, *Marion*. Audubon never mentions having met Geiger at all or of sleeping in the house. However, he does state in his writings that while visiting Indian Key he slept in a "hammock under the eaves" of Mr. Egan's home.

None the less the house has been superbly decorated with antiques from estate sales and auctions in

Europe. The furnishings are an eclectic hodge-podge, common to a wrecker's home during this time. Antiques would have been retrieved from ships importing goods from all over the world, thus the collections.

A stroll through the garden is a tour through a tropical paradise only found in the ambiance of Key West. The colors, scents, and flavors one drinks in can only quench a thirst found in Key West. The native geckos, a wandering Hemingway six-toed cat, orchids in a menagerie of colors, the brilliant herb garden flavors the air and bromeliads, then the common hibiscus splashing color at every turn. The museum gift shop offers everything from Audubon prints, books, educational toys and the variety of museum items found only in those exclusive shops carefully chosen for those of exquisite taste.

A call to the gardens will enable you to rent a special backdrop for that date you'll always want to remember. The Audubon House is also open for private tours arranged for selective guests. An evening under the stars in a tropical paradise, what more could any brides ask for?

Recent Research leads us to believe that in fact the Geiger house was not built until after the 1846 hurricane that devastated Key West, probably in 1850. Perhaps it was rebuilt or perhaps the numbers are transposed or perhaps the research is very accurate. If it is true Audubon could not have visited here. Different recordings show Geiger came to Key West in the late 1820s. That he married a Bahamian, Lucretia Sanders and the couple bore twelve children. Regardless of what is and is not true, we choose to believe that at 205 Whitehead Street, John James Audubon spent time drawing birds and left us a legacy we will never forget. We also choose to believe that this was Captain John H. Geiger's home at one time, he raised a family beneath that very roof and beyond in the garden where they played amidst a Garden of Eden. Let us have the wonderland and believe.

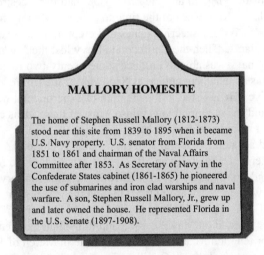

MALLORY HOMESITE

The home of Stephen Russell Mallory (1812-1873) stood near this site from 1839 to 1895 when it became U.S. Navy property. U.S. senator from Florida from 1851 to 1861 and chairman of the Naval Affairs Committee after 1853. As Secretary of Navy in the Confederate States cabinet (1861-1865) he pioneered the use of submarines and iron clad warships and naval warfare. A son, Stephen Russell Mallory, Jr., grew up and later owned the house. He represented Florida in the U.S. Senate (1897-1908).

Clinton Place intersection of Whitehead and Front Streets, Key West
MO32 ~ GPS Coordinates: 24.558550, -81.806483

Stephen Russell Mallory was born in Trinidad, West Indies in 1813; the second son of Reading, Connecticut, Civil Engineer Charles Mallory. When he was but a year old his parents moved the family to Havana where Stephen's father passed away. In 1820, Mrs. Mallory settled her family in Key West. To survive she opened a boardinghouse.

Mallory was educated at the Jesuit College at Springhill, Mobile and Nazareth, Pennsylvania. At the young age of nineteen President Jackson appointed Mallory Inspector of the Customs at Key West. While tending his post, he read the law with Judge William Marvin of the United States district court at Key West. At twenty-seven, Stephen Russell Mallory was admitted to the Florida Bar Association.

He soon gained a grand reputation as an attorney, becoming a judge for Monroe County, Judge of Probate and in 1845, Collector of Customs. Stephen Mallory married the daughter of a wealthy Pensacola family soon thereafter.

During the Second Seminole War he volunteered and served for many years in active warfare. In 1850, Mallory was elected as a delegate for the Nashville Commercial Convention, a distinction he declined. Stephen Mallory's sights were set just a bit higher. In 1851 he was elected to the United States Senate for six years. His opponent, David L. Yulee, contested the election but the seat was awarded unanimously to Mallory. He was re-elected at the next term and remained in place until Florida seceded from the Union. Mallory resigned to support the southern states.

Jefferson Davis was selected as President of the Confederacy on February 18, 1861. With experience as Chairman of the Senate Committee on Naval Affairs, Stephen Russell Mallory was named Secretary of the Confederate Navy on February 21st. Unfortunately Mallory's job was daunting from the beginning. He found himself head of a Naval Department with virtually no ships on the eve of the greatest war ever fought in the waters of the United States as well as the newly formed Confederacy. His first steps were to organize and administer, then begin building ships and boats provided he could obtain ordnance and machinery. His ports were rapidly becoming blockaded and time was wasting. Materials were still in their crudest states; timber still stood in the forest, iron in the mines and there were neither furnaces for smelting or welding nor workshops; hemp for rope had to be planted, grown and harvested, then dried and braided. There were no rope walks, no rolling mills to create iron plate or workshops to build marine engines. To a lessor man the task might seem hopeless, but for Mallory this was only a challenge.

Mallory first approached England and France to purchase ironclad warships but there were none to be had and the most outstanding ironclads the *Virginia* and the *Mississippi* had to be destroyed to prevent them falling into the waiting hands of the Union Navy. Now was not the time to give up, Mallory formed plans based on his ingenuity. Perhaps some of his father's Civil Engineering genes had crept into the mix. The Southern industrial plants in no way compared to Northern plants. Then the Confederate Navy lost the *Nashville*, *New Orleans*, *Memphis* and *Norfolk* early in the war. The navy was able to produce some twenty-two ironclads during the war.

In all aspects Mallory was an excellent choice as Secretary of the Confederate Navy, he had amazing ideas and was extremely innovative. He assisted in the creation of experimental weaponry and tactics, which included torpedoes, submarines and secret amphibious raids. Most of these ideas came to fruition and were improved upon to be integral parts of today's modern Navy.

General Robert E. Lee evacuated Petersburg, Virginia losing Richmond. Mallory was forced to take flight with the remainder of the Confederate Cabinet. Even after defeat was certain, he fought in guerrilla warfare in the last days of the war. When the end finally came in April of 1865, Stephen Mallory escaped with Jefferson Davis some say they were disguised as women. At Washington, Georgia the group went their separate ways but a local informant alerted Union troops of their flight. Mallory headed toward LaGrange, Troup County, Georgia where his family was waiting. Mallory was arrested on May 20, 1865 and immediately taken to Fort Lafayette in the New York harbor. He was confined for ten months and released on parole in March of 1866.

Mallory returned to Pensacola in July 1866, still under parole but permitted to resume his law practice. Quietly he continued to oppose using military force during the South's Reconstruction and opposing black rights.

Stephen Russell Mallory died November 9, 1873 in Pensacola, Florida. He was interred in St. Michael's Cemetery. Many of his Confederate contemporaries continued to blame him for the loss of the Civil War, because he constantly solicited funds in favor of the Navy when land based troops badly needed food, clothing and ammunition. Even so others look at Mallory for who he was and at all he accomplished as a man of vision. Even though aligned with the losing side he fought to the end and risked death for a cause in which he believed. Right or wrong, Stephen Mallory was a hero.

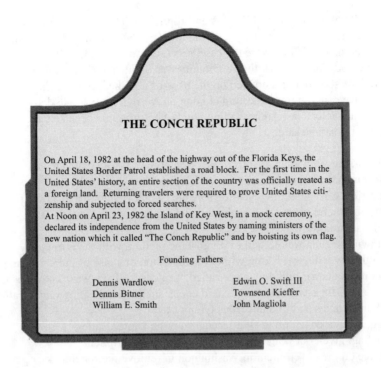

THE CONCH REPUBLIC

On April 18, 1982 at the head of the highway out of the Florida Keys, the United States Border Patrol established a road block. For the first time in the United States' history, an entire section of the country was officially treated as a foreign land. Returning travelers were required to prove United States citizenship and subjected to forced searches.

At Noon on April 23, 1982 the Island of Key West, in a mock ceremony, declared its independence from the United States by naming ministers of the new nation which it called "The Conch Republic" and by hoisting its own flag.

Founding Fathers

Dennis Wardlow   Edwin O. Swift III
Dennis Bitner   Townsend Kieffer
William E. Smith   John Magliola

Visitors Center, 402 Wall Street, Key West
MO33 ~ GPS Coordinates: 24.559350, -81.806783

On April 23, 1982 the United States Border patrol in a bonehead act put up a roadblock at the Last Chance Saloon in Florida City. The traffic jam backed up traffic for some seventeen miles. Skeeter Davis, owner of the Last Chance, immediately picked up the phone and called Key West Mayor Dennis Wardlow to report the goings on. Well Mayor Dennis Wardlow was none to happy, as you can imagine.

Of course with any "Civil" War no matter how tongue in cheek it might be the media jumped on this like bees to honey. As stories of the traffic jams went out on the presses, over the radio and on the television for all to see; reservations were canceled all over the Keys. The hotels began to empty, deliveries were delayed, spoiled or stopped completely. Everyone involved in the tourist industry suffered and all at the hands of the United States Government. You know, "we're from the government, we're here to help."

Community leaders huddled down around the Mayor; Ok, boss what now? Well cooler heads prevailed and true to our justice system, they'd take it to court. Dave Horan filed an injunction in Federal Court in Miami. Mayor Wardlow and Ed Swift jumped into Dave's airplane and to Miami they went. Surprise, Surprise, the court supported the Border Patrol; OK, boss what now?

The Court essentially ordained the United States treating the Keys as if they were a foreign country. On the steps of the Courthouse the press had to know, "What are you going to do, Mr. Mayor?" With some prompting in a voice much stronger than he felt Wardlow said, "We are going to go home and secede".

The news reached the Keys far ahead of the returning leaders and what met them was a mixed crowd. Some supported the state secession and other believed Wardlow had lost his ever-loving mind. Rumors flew, the American banner would be lowered and in its place the Conch Republic flag would wave in the tropical breeze. Uh-oh or that's probably what the mayor said when the calls started coming in. So obviously a compromise had to be reached. It was, the American flag would stay and the Conch flag would fly beneath it. Some thought this was a kick in face to the Conchs but the mayor knew best.

Then the law came to town. Feds in blue blazers with James Bond cuff microphones and flesh colored earphones against Margaritaville shirts, cut off khakis and flip flops. The Feds certainly blended in well. They were intimidating. Were arrests soon to be made? Would the Keys be placed under martial law? Would they declare prohibition all over again? If that were the case, secession would be lots less fun.

All giggles aside, the fear was real, the community was divided and something had to be done. Mayor Dennis Wardlow squared his shoulder and hopped on the back of a flatbed truck in Clinton Square in front of the Old Customs Building to have an old town meeting at noon on April 23, 1982. He delivered one of the best speeches I've ever heard, no Gettysburg Address mind you but befitting the occasion and obviously deeply heart felt. Wardlow cleared his throat and said:

> We the people of Key West are called Conchs...Sometimes we are called Conchs with affection, sometimes with humor and sometimes with derision.
> I proclaim that Key West shall now be known as the Conch Republic and as the flag of our new republic is raised, I thereby state to Washington and the rest of the United States, and the world that the Conchs are and were.
> When Jamestown, Virginia was settled by Englishmen fed up with the arrogance, the derision, the abuse of rights by a despot, a king without compassion or sense of humanity another group was settling in the Bahamas and they were called "Conchs". They were known as Conchs because they hoisted flags with the tough, hard conch shellfish indicating they'd rather eat conch than pay the King's taxes and live under his tyranny.
> That's our flag, it has a conch on it. We secede from the United States.
> We raised our flag, given our notice, and named our new government.
> We served notice on the government in Washington to remove the roadblock or get ready to put up a permanent border to a new foreign land.
> We as a people may have suffered in the past but we have no intention of suffering in the future at the hands of fools and bureaucrats.
> We're not going to beg and beseech the nation of the United States for help. We're not going to ask for something we should naturally have as citizens – simple equality.
> If we are not equal, we'll get out. It's as simple as that.
> The first step was, like Mariel, up to Washington. This step is up to us.
> We call upon the people of the Florida Keys to join us or not, as they see fit.
> We are not a fearful people. We are not a group to cringe and whimper, when Washington cracks the whip with contempt and unconcern. We're conchs and We've had enough.
> We're happy to secede today with some humor. But there is some anger, too.
> Big trouble has started in much smaller places than this.
> I am calling on all my fellow citizen here in the Conch Republic to stand together – lest we fall apart – fall from fear, from a lack of courage, intimidation by an uncaring government whose actions show it has grown too big to care for people on a small island."

> Signed,
> Dennis Wardlow, Prime Minister

Just after the Proclamation, the newly self proclaimed Prime Minister declared war on the United States and a member of his staff promptly attacked a Sailor with a loaf of stale Cuban bread. Sixty seconds later the Prime Minister surrendered to the Admiral in charge of Naval Air Station Key West and the Union Forces then demanded one billion dollars in foreign aid and War Relief to rebuild the nation after the long Federal siege! Of course, the Conch Republic believes, "the check is in the mail."

That's the story of how the Conch Republic was born. But what has happened since? The United States has never acknowledged the Republic at all; not a letter saying your full of ...well you know or even that this is not legal so get your act together. The Conchs reacted in the way only the Conchs would, they turned it into a party.

Each year they began celebrating Conch Independence. Flags are flown, passports were issued and traveled on, visas were issued to visitors and the government functioned as a nation. Still the United States said nothing. The excitement of the event seemed to dwindle and finally the tourism industry decided "Conch Republic Days" would be no more, not enough tourists or 'heads on beds' as they say. Visitors just didn't support the event and the time was between snowbirds and sun worshipers, not quite Spring Break so what was a party town to do?

Well avid supporters took of the cause. Rear Admiral Finbar of the Conch Navy as well as Paul and Evalena Worthington of the Schooner Wharf Bar refused to let the party die. The Conch Republic Independence Celebration was on again!

It began as a three-day event themed, "Last Tango on Tank Island," and has expanded with time to become a week long fun filled event. Citizens are indeed Conchs and Americans weather the rest of the world recognizes it or not. By an act of Congress they hold a dual citizenship and will fight for the right to be both.

The Honorable Secretary General of the Conch Republic has an "Official Conch Republic Diplomatic Passport" which has been accepted in thirteen Caribbean Nations as well as Germany, Sweden, Havana, Mexico, France, Spain, Ireland and Russia. I've never known anyone to visit the Keys for even a short time without leaving with the fever. The sun shine, tropical breezes, ice cold beer, scuba, snorkel, sailing, bone fishing or even Tortuga Rum Cake, it just gets under your skin and the moment you cross the seven mile bridge or turn the curve toward Florida City you are planning your next trip to paradise. There is nothing like riding down US 1, top down, hair blowing in the wind, those sparkling blue waters and the warm Florida sun on your face. From Skeeter's at Florida City to Mile Marker 1 and the Sunset Celebration closing the day, it's a way of life, a frame of mind, it's the Florida Keys.

End Notes

[1] Breeding colonies

[2] Study of birds

[3] Known as a poison cup.

[4] Federal Emergency Relief Administration

[5] houseboats

[6] Today known as avocados.

[7] Sweet pulpy tropical fruit with thick scaly rind and shiny black seeds.

[8] Mapping document

[9] Naval Air Station

[10] Temporary housing

[11] slender tower with balconies

KEY WEST LIGHTHOUSE

NEXT IN THE SERIES

Having completed both coastal Georgia then the Atlantic coast of Florida our next stop will be eastern South Carolina. "Get Off the Interstate: The True Stories of Eastern South Carolina's Historical Markers" is our next project in the works. We have already begun the first preliminary work in South Carolina in the days since we have completed the Florida book and will be getting into the state in earnest in the coming months. I say "we" because the writing these books require the efforts of numerous people.

The next book in the "Get Off the Interstate" series will differ somewhat in that Interstate 95, the "Interstate" we're getting off of, travels a considerable distance inland. We will be covering approximately one third of South Carolina from I-95 to the coast. Unfortunately we can not include full states in one book. It would take a life time in itself to complete a project of that magnitude and would consist of numerous volumes as well as several years of research. Therefore we continue the march northward up the eastern seaboard from the southern tip of the United States at Key West to the northern boarder ending at Houlton, Maine; one state along the Eastern Seaboard at a time.

It has been thrilling to travel through the backroads of Georgia and Florida. We definitely have the greatest job in the world. We have learned so much, met so many marvelous people and saw some of the most beautiful sights in the world. We look forward with anxious anticipation getting to know South Carolina and her history. We will be covering eighteen South Carolina counties and hope to have the third edition out in the Spring of 2006. Come travel with us through South Carolina as we continue our journey and "Get Off the Interstate". We certainly hope you are as anxious as we are to discover "The True Stories of Eastern South Carolina's Historical Markers".

INDEX

TRAVEL NOTES

TRAVEL NOTES